Capital Budgeting and Finance: A Guide for Local Governments

Capital Budgeting and Finance: A Guide for Local Governments

by A. John Vogt

International
City/County
ICMA
Management
Association
icma.org

INSTITUTE *of* GOVERNMENT
The University of North Carolina at Chapel Hill

International
City/County
ICMA
Management
Association
icma.org

ICMA is the professional and educational organization for chief appointed management executives in local government. The purposes of ICMA are to strengthen the quality of local government through professional management and to develop and disseminate new approaches to management through training programs, information services, and publications.

For further information about the publications or services for local governments offered by ICMA, write to Publications Department, ICMA, 777 North Capitol St., N.E., Suite 500, Washington, D.C. 20002. To order publications, call 800/745-8780 (outside the United States, call 770/442-8631, ext. 377) or visit the ICMA Bookstore online at http://bookstore.icma.org.

INSTITUTE *of* GOVERNMENT
The University of North Carolina at Chapel Hill

Established in 1931, the Institute of Government provides training, advisory, and research services to public officials and others interested in the operation of state and local government in North Carolina. The Institute and the university's Master of Public Administration Program are the core activities of the School of Government at The University of North Carolina at Chapel Hill.

Each year approximately 14,000 public officials and others attend one or more of the more than 200 classes, seminars, and conferences offered by the Institute. Faculty members annually publish up to fifty books, bulletins, and other reference works related to state and local government. Each day that the General Assembly is in session, the Institute's *Daily Bulletin*, available in print and electronic format, reports on the day's activities for members of the legislature and others who need to follow the course of legislation. An extensive Web site (www.sog.unc.edu) provides access to publications and faculty research, course listings, program and service information, and links to other useful sites related to government.

Operating support for the School of Government's programs and activities comes from many sources, including state appropriations, local government membership dues, private contributions, publications sales, course fees, and service contracts. For more information about the School, the Institute, and the MPA program, visit the Web site or call 919/966-5381.

Library of Congress Cataloging-in-Publication Data

Vogt, A. John.
    Capital budgeting and finance : a guide for local governments / by A. John Vogt.
        p. cm.
Includes bibliographical references.
        ISBN 0-87326-137-2 (pbk.)
    1. Capital budget—United States—States.   2. Local finance—United States—States.
    I. Title.
    HJ9147.V64 2004
    352.4'8—dc22

                                                                        2003027452

Printed in the United States of America.
08 07 06 05 04
5 4 3 2 1

Design: Will Kemp
03-154

Contents

Note to the Reader

Capital Budgeting and Finance: A Guide for Local Governments provides the reader with a full range of material on capital budgeting, including a comprehensive glossary and a bibliography. The text includes descriptions of practices in specific local governments, as well as examples of working documents in current use in local governments across the United States. Other tables and charts are more general. The book has been designed to help the reader distinguish case examples and sample documents from more general other information. See the following key.

Text features

- **Boldface type in the text**   Terms defined in the glossary. A great number of additional terms are defined in the glossary as well.
- **Sections of text with a vertical bar at the left margin**   Specific local government examples of the topic under discussion. Names of the jurisdictions are set in boldface. These sections often include examples from more than one jurisdiction. Sometimes tables and other illustrative material from the local governments are included; if so, the vertical bar at the margin extends to include this material.
- **Text surrounded by a box (sidebars)**   Additional information on a specific topic under discussion.

Illustrations

- **Exhibits**   Material that is either a direct reproduction or a shortened version of material in use by a specific local government. Every exhibit is numbered and is introduced in the text.
- **Figures**   Charts, graphs, diagrams. Every figure is numbered and introduced in the text.
- **Tables**   Tabular material. Every table is numbered and introduced in the text.

Foreword

This volume is an important new resource for local government management and financial professionals. Produced in partnership with the Institute of Government, School of Government, at The University of North Carolina at Chapel Hill, *Capital Budgeting and Finance: A Guide for Local Governments* fills a need for a comprehensive text on capital budgeting in an era when many local governments risk disaster unless they make wise decisions regarding infrastructure. ICMA and the Institute of Government intend this book to take its place beside the classics of local government finance, on the manager's bookshelf as well as in the classrooms of MPA programs and budgeting seminars.

For many local government managers, one of the most visible measures of their accomplishment is the built environment they leave behind—the new civic center, the connector road, the waste treatment facility. Helping a community plan, build, and pay for traditional brick-and-mortar projects and communication networks is an important aspect of the manager's job, yet until now this activity has been addressed only piecemeal by ICMA's Municipal Management Series. With *Capital Budgeting and Finance*, managers, professors, and students at last have a text focused on capital projects.

Capital planning and budgeting is central to economic development, transportation, communication, delivery of other essential services, and environmental management and quality of life. Much of what is accomplished by local governments depends on a sound long-term investment in infrastructure and equipment. Almost every instance of business attraction and retention is affected by capital planning and implementation of capital plans. This volume lays out all the steps in providing the physical structure of local government, from selecting capital projects to planning how to pay for those projects to structuring and selling debt.

Following the work of the National Advisory Council on State and Local Government Budgeting, local governments everywhere have the benefit of an accepted body of policies and practices for public budgeting. *Capital Budgeting and Finance* brings alive the policies and practices that address capital budgeting, with careful explanations of planning and implementation issues, clear and practical identification of choices to be made, and dozens of detailed illustrations drawn from towns, cities, and counties.

A. John Vogt, the author, is well known to local government managers. As a member of the faculty of the Institute of Government of the University of North Carolina at Chapel Hill, Jack has trained generations of public finance managers. His workshop, "Capital Budgeting for Smaller Cities and Counties," is a staple of the ICMA University, regularly drawing rave reviews. In 2003, Jack received the S. Kenneth Howard Career Achievement Award, given by the Association for Budgeting and Financial Management. In his own words, "Teaching, public service, and working with and writing for local government officials and MPA students have defined my work life over the last thirty years." ICMA is proud to bring his expertise to a larger audience.

ICMA staff members who contributed to this project include Christine Ulrich, editorial director; Mary Marik, copy editor; Will Kemp, graphic designer; and Dawn Leland, director of publications production. ICMA is grateful to the Institute of Government for its partnership on this project. We are most deeply indebted to Jack Vogt for his devotion to the cause of improving local government financial management, and the thousands of hours he has spent writing and polishing this remarkable book.

Robert J. O'Neill, Jr.
Executive Director
International City/County Management Association

Acknowledgments

Many people have contributed in many ways to the preparation of this book. First and foremost have been the ICMA editors: Christine Ulrich, Barbara de Boinville, Mary Marik, and Nedra James. Christine Ulrich, editorial director at ICMA, helped define the book's objectives and advised throughout the writing.

Faculty and staff at the Institute of Government, School of Government, at The University of North Carolina at Chapel Hill (UNC-CH) provided encouragement and valuable help. Michael Smith, dean of the School of Government, allowed me to devote the time needed to write the book. Thomas Thornburg, associate dean, made sure day-to-day support was available for the project. David Ammons, director of the school's master of public administration program, and Deil S. Wright, professor of public administration at UNC-CH, encouraged me time and time again to finish the book. Colleagues David Lawrence and Fleming Bell provided advice on legal issues and Gregory Allison on accounting questions. Alex Hess, Marsha Lobacz, and Edie Hughes, librarians at the School of Government, provided invaluable assistance. Other School of Government staff helped also: Charlene Brummitt, Kay Spivey, JoAnn Brewer, Patricia Connor, Linda McVey, Susan Dunn, and Carrie Holbert. Matthew Dutton, research associate, helped prepare graphs. Donald Hayman and Warren "Jake" Wicker (deceased in June 2003), honorary members of ICMA and former School of Government faculty, instilled in me the desire to tap into the wisdom and experience of a variety of city and county managers and other local officials.

Numerous state and local government officials generously shared advice and information. Notable are staff of the North Carolina Local Government Commission, Department of State Treasurer. The commission approves and sells nearly all North Carolina local government debt. These staff members include Bob High, former secretary to the commission and deputy state treasurer who now works as a financial adviser for Davenport & Company; Janice Burke, current secretary to the commission and deputy state treasurer; and Vance Holloman, Bob Newman, Martha Lasater, Tim Romocki, and Benny Bowers.

Local officials provided much insight and a practical outlook. These officials include Ellen Liston, assistant manager, Coral Springs, Florida; Paul Spruill, county manager in Beaufort County, North Carolina, and formerly assistant manager and budget director, Chatham County, North Carolina; Wally Hill, former county administrator, Yuma County, Arizona, and current county administrator, San Bernardino County, California; Sonya Smith, policy analyst, Office of the Texas Comptroller of Public Accounts; Lee Madden, debt manager, and Carey Odom, treasurer, Charlotte, North Carolina; Isabel Rogers, director of administration, Conyers, Georgia; Judy Ikerd, budget administrator, Catawba County, North Carolina; Lezlie Philp, budget manager, Greeley, Colorado; Joe Bartel, director of budget and management, Forsyth County, North Carolina; Michael Abeln, director, capital and debt management, Minneapolis, Minnesota; Eric Peterson, town manager, Hillsborough, North Carolina; David Vehaun, finance director, Rock Hill, South Carolina; James Greene, assistant manager, Concord, North Carolina; Dan Faust, director of finance, Maplewood, Minnesota; Jeff Causey, assistant manager and finance officer, Alamance County, North Carolina; Arthur Rullo, budget director, Scottsdale, Arizona; Eric Williams, city manager, and Traig Neal, director of finance, Henderson, North Carolina; John Hartman, budget officer, Loveland, Colorado; Lithia Brooks, finance officer, Brunswick County, North Carolina; Loris Colclough, former chief financial officer, Winston-Salem, North Carolina; Clinton Gridley, city administrator, Cedarburg, Wisconsin; Gayela Emory, senior management analyst, Reno, Nevada; Scott Fogleman, budget director, Cary, North Carolina; Allison Hart, city manager, and David Tungate, budget officer, Irvine, California; Rick Hester, manager, and John Massey, finance officer, Johnston County, North Carolina; and W. Patrick Pate, assistant city manager, High Point, North Carolina and immediate past president of the Government Finance Officers Association of the United States and Canada.

Professionals in the municipal bond industry supplied important information and advice. Rating agency officials were especially helpful. They include Richard Marino, Robin Prunty, and Geoffrey Buwick of Standard & Poor's Corporation; Rebecca Blackmon Joyner of Moody's Investors Service; and Amy Laskey and David Becker of Fitch Ratings. Investment bankers Richard Marvin and Ryan Maher of Legg Mason Wood and Walker provided answers to questions about selling debt. Alison Peeler and Blair Bennett of Ferris, Baker Watts provided information on debt refunding; and Gundar Aperans, a bond counsel with Robinson Bradshaw, provided advice on legal questions. Meredith Fraley and Kim Anderson of Bingham Arbitrage Rebate Services provided information on federal arbitrage rebate requirements and regulations. K. Lee Carter, of the North Carolina Capital Management Trust, a mutual fund for local government investments, helped with investment and financing questions. Bob Ehlers, retired from a successful financial advisory career and author of one of the best books on municipal debt, *Ehlers on Public Finance*, furnished both inspiration and specific information.

Finally, Mary Radcliffe Vogt, wife and good friend for so many years, has contributed much to this project. She, our three children, and our eight grandchildren are the next project. While many have contributed to this book, the author is responsible for its contents.

1 Capital budgeting: rationale, scope, and policy framework

This chapter introduces **capital budgeting** in local government. Capital budgeting might consist of special procedures that take place mainly within the **operating or annual budget,** or it might consist of procedures that make up an altogether separate process that nevertheless connects to the operating budget. This chapter:

- Examines the reasons why a local government should have a separate capital budget process to plan, budget, and finance expenditures for capital projects and acquisitions
- Defines a capital expenditure and identifies and discusses those capital expenditures that are suitable for inclusion in the **capital budget** as well as the cost items that are properly charged to a capital project or acquisition
- Explains the policy framework for local government capital budgeting.

Reasons for capital budgeting

Why should a local government have a specific process for planning, budgeting, and financing expenditures for capital projects and acquisitions? Six reasons for capital budgeting, illustrated by examples from local governments, are presented here.

Stakes are high

The capital **infrastructure,** facilities, and equipment built or acquired by local governments are often large and very expensive, requiring considerable amounts of money to be raised and spent to bring the projects and acquisitions to fruition. Special planning, financing, and management procedures are called for to ensure that the projects and acquisitions are needed, well designed, and efficiently implemented—that is to say, to ensure that the money invested in them is well spent. A project does not have to be huge, however, to justify its inclusion in a separate capital budget.

Cary, North Carolina, a fast-growing city in the Research Triangle area, is planning to spend $144.6 million for a wastewater treatment plant.[1] This project is more than five times the size of Cary's 2001–2002 water-sewer operating budget and about 33 percent larger than the city's combined water-sewer and **general-fund** oper-

ating budgets for that year.[2] The project will be financed with bonds, development fees, and other sources. To ensure that this enormous investment achieves its intended purposes, the city included the project in its 2001–2002 capital budget and its 2003–2012 capital improvement program (CIP) and budget rather than in its annual budget. Most spending for the project will occur in the years 2005 through 2009.

Grafton, Wisconsin, is allocating $511,000 for stormwater management ponds and $628,010 for a library renovation. While these projects are not that large, their combined costs equal about 20 percent of Grafton's general-fund spending for 2000, and special nonrecurring financing is needed for them.[3] As a result, these projects have been included in Grafton's one-year 2000 capital improvement fund rather than in the city's general fund.[4]

Decisions extend for years

By definition, capital assets (also known as fixed assets) have useful lives that extend beyond one year. Much of the equipment acquired and used by local governments has a useful life of anywhere from a few years to as many as twenty years, and infrastructure and most buildings generally last for decades. Thus, because the citizens and employees who will use these capital assets must live for many years with the results of the decisions to build or acquire them, those decisions need to be based on careful planning. Only then will the resulting projects and acquisitions suit the needs they are supposed to serve.

For example, an aerial ladder fire truck that costs $700,000 and can be configured in different ways to meet specific firefighting and rescue needs will be used in a first-line capacity for about twenty years. If it is not properly configured, the local government may have to live with an inadequately designed truck for a long time. Perhaps it could modify the truck, sell it, or trade it in and acquire a new truck that is properly configured. These alternatives would cost additional money, however. Instead, the local government needs to plan very carefully to make sure that it acquires the right truck in the first place. This is more likely to occur in a multiyear capital planning and budget process than in a one-year operating budget.

The annual or operating budget is designed primarily to fund services of benefit for just one or two years. Therefore, it makes sense economically to put expenditures with long-term benefits into a capital budget, which takes a multiyear perspective.

Spending varies from year to year

Capital assets are long lived, so the need to replace them typically recurs infrequently. Moreover, growth and development often occur in spurts, requiring local government spending on infrastructure to be concentrated in some years and limited in others. These factors create problems for the operating budget, in which resources generally change incrementally in any year, and most new resources are needed for service enhancements or expansion. If that budget also has to cover major capital projects and acquisitions, it will have to stretch or contract greatly from year to year, creating planning and revenue-raising challenges and potential political repercussions as taxes and user fees are adjusted to meet annually changing requirements. Again, planning and budgeting for such projects and acquisitions require a long time frame and special financing sources, both of which are difficult to incorporate in the operating budget.

Implementation takes time

Depending on their size, complexity, environmental risk, and other factors, undertaking and completing most infrastructure and capital facility projects take anywhere from several years to as long as a decade. This includes time to define the project, secure approval, finish the design, acquire and prepare land, schedule the project, and construct it. Even the acquisition of sophisticated and expensive equipment can take several years from identification of need through approval, preparation of specifications, order, delivery, installation or preparation for operation, and acceptance. Local operating budgets generally provide spending authority that lasts for only one year. Although unspent appropriations for capital projects or acquisitions that are obligated by contracts are encumbered, state and local laws usually require the reappropriation of such encumbered funds in the next year's budget, and local governing boards sometimes have trouble understanding why they must reappropriate such funds. These issues can be avoided by budgeting capital projects and acquisitions in project ordinances or capital expenditure ordinances that provide spending authority that remains in force for the project duration or acquisition. The use of these project ordinances is more likely to occur when there are identifiable procedures or an altogether separate process for capital budgeting.

North Carolina cities, counties, and public authorities are authorized to use such project ordinances to budget for bond- or debt-financed capital projects or for the acquisition of any capital assets,[5] and many local units in the state use such ordinances. The city of **Cary, North Carolina,** for example, uses project ordinances to authorize and appropriate funds for projects and acquisitions in its capital budget and multiyear CIP.[6]

Debt financing is often used

While some local governments, especially small ones, follow a strictly or predominantly pay-as-go approach to capital finance, many finance large capital projects and acquisitions by issuing bonds or another form of debt. The bonds and debt are then repaid, with interest, in installments in future years. For major facilities and debt issues, the repayment term can extend for twenty years or more. For intermediate-size projects or equipment acquisitions, the repayment terms range from several years to fifteen years or so. Repayment terms should not exceed the estimated useful lives of the assets financed with the debt. When local officials or citizens (through a voter referendum) approve and issue debt to finance a project, they are in effect requiring officials and citizens in future years to pay for their decision. Debt ties up revenues in future annual budgets. Because of these long-term consequences, officials should make sure that debt-financed projects are well planned, designed, and carried out. This is more likely to occur in a multiyear capital budget than in an annual budget.

Capital projects differ from year to year

Changes that occur in the operating budget from year to year are generally small or modest. Most expenditures recur, and officials can draw on budget experiences in recent years when formulating next year's budget. However, the capital projects or acquisitions requested in one year are often very different from the ones requested or approved the year before or over the past several years. This is because, as has already been explained, many capital assets have long, useful lives, with the need for them recurring infrequently. To compensate for this lack of relevant experience in recent years, local officials should exercise special care in budgeting for major capital projects and acquisitions.

Identification and classification of capital expenditures

This section defines capital expenditure. It then identifies the types of capital expenditures, projects, or acquisitions that belong in the capital budget and considers the particular cost items that are properly charged to a capital project or acquisition.

What is a capital expenditure?

Broadly conceived, a **capital expenditure** is an outlay of significant value that results in the acquisition of or addition to a **capital asset** (or a **fixed asset**),[7] in other words, property that is held or used for more than one year and usually for many years. ("Fixed" does not mean "immobile"; an automobile is typically a fixed asset.)

Fixed assets include many types of property that a local government owns and uses in its operations:

- Land or rights to land
- Buildings
- Additions to or renovations of buildings that exceed a specified cost (for example, $5,000) and add value to the building, improve it, or extend its useful life
- Improvements to land other than buildings that exceed a specified cost (for example, $5,000) and add value to the land or improve its utility (such as drainage systems, parking lots, landscaping, and similar construction on land)
- Equipment, vehicles, and furnishings that have useful lives longer than one year and exceed a specified cost (for example, $5,000), as well as additions to or refurbishings of capital equipment that exceed a specified cost (for example, $1,000).

Expenditures that are used to add to or renovate buildings; improve land; or acquire or refurbish equipment, vehicles, and furnishing should exceed a specified dollar amount in order to be classified as capital expenditures. The specified dollar amount—that is, the significant value—is usually determined locally. For example, it may be recommended by the finance officer and approved by the manager or the governing board on the basis of accounting and property control needs for these types of fixed assets. The range for significant value for most cities and counties is currently around $500 to $10,000. Small entities use a dollar amount toward the lower end, and large entities use one toward the upper end of this range. Significant value is not an issue with regard to expenditures for land or buildings because the specified dollar amount that defines significant value is typically well below the costs of acquiring land or constructing buildings.

Because infrastructure is costly, local government spending for such assets is also almost always classified as capital spending. However, the resulting assets (such as streets, roads, bridges, storm drainage facilities, water and sewer lines, parks and open space) are usually immobile and have value only to the local government that builds them and the community that uses or benefits from them. For this reason, accounting principles, which traditionally have required the recording and reporting of **enterprise fund infrastructure** (such as water and sewer) as fixed assets in the accounting records of a public entity, traditionally have not required **general-purpose infrastructure** (such as streets) to be recorded. This practice changed, however, with Statement No. 34 of the **Governmental Accounting Standards Board (GASB).**[8] Statement No. 34, ratified in 1999, requires local governments and other public entities to record and report all capital spending on infrastructure assets, whether for enterprises or general government needs (see sidebar below).

In governmental budgeting and accounting, only expenditures to acquire tangible assets or property have usually been considered to be capital expenditures and have been recorded as fixed assets.[9] Expenditures to acquire **intangible assets,** such as a patent or a license for a specific technology, have seldom been recorded as fixed assets. However, a growing number of local governments are recording expenditures for computer software and certain other intangible property as fixed or capital assets.[10] If the software is an operating system and the computer cannot function without it, or if the software comes in a package with the hardware, the software is capitalized as part of the computer's costs. If the software is an application program and has value of its own, the software is capitalized separately from the hardware.

Which capital expenditures belong in the capital budget?

Not all capital expenditures, projects, and acquisitions have to be included in the capital budget. Inexpensive capital expenditures and those for fixed assets that recur yearly or frequently may be reviewed in the annual or operating budget process, approved in the operating budget resolution or ordinance, and accounted for in the general fund or another operating fund.

The meaning of inexpensive varies with the size of the local government. A small city or county might exclude from the capital budget any projects costing between $1,000 and $25,000, for example. These capital assets would be handled in the jurisdiction's operating budget process. However, more costly capital projects and acquisitions would be included in the capital budget, which would involve multiyear planning, special budgetary review, inclusion in a **capital projects fund** or **special revenue fund,** and, if legally available,

---

Major changes caused by GASB Statement No. 34

- Governments report the results of government-wide operations in two new reports: the Statement of Net Assets and the Statement of Activities
- Infrastructure is quantified and reported in the Statement of Net Assets
- Infrastructure, fixed assets, and long-term liabilities are brought into the calculation of net assets (a long-term concept similar to fund balance)
- Governments depreciate infrastructure or use a valuation method that produces estimates closer to current values
- Operating results are reported for the general fund and newly defined major funds
- Reporting on the operations of major programs is highlighted
- Management discussion of two-year trends, major achievements or challenges, and significant changes are required in the Management Discussion and Analysis.

Hyman C. Grossman, LaVerne Thomas, and Diane P. Brosen, "GASB 34: What Implementation Means to the Rating Process," in *GASB 34: What It Means for You,* IQ Report (Washington, D.C.: ICMA, December 2000), 5. (ICMA item nos. 42626 and E-43020).

approval via a project ordinance rather than the operating budget ordinance. A medium- or large-size city or county would use a higher cutoff—around $25,000 to $100,000—and handle in its capital budget only capital projects and acquisitions that cost more than this amount.

The useful life of the capital asset can also help determinate whether a capital project or acquisition goes into the capital budget. For example, a medium-size city might reserve its capital budget only for capital assets that cost more than $30,000 and have an estimated useful life of five years or more.

Table 1–1 shows the minimum-dollar and useful-life cutoffs applied by several medium- and small-size cities and counties to determine which capital projects and acquisitions to include in a CIP. Because the CIP is a multi-year plan for major capital assets, inclusion in the CIP typically means that

Table 1–1

Criteria for including capital projects and acquisitions in the CIP, by selected cities and counties

City	2000 population[a]	Minimum-dollar cutoff[b]	Useful-life cutoff[c]	Applies to
Hillsborough, North Carolina	5,446	$10,000	N.A.	2000–2002
Conyers, Georgia	10,689	$5,000	5 years	1996–2000
Mauldin, South Carolina	15,224	$1,000	N.A.	2000–2004
Gainesville, Georgia	25,578	$20,000	N.A.	2001–2005
Campbell, California	38,138	$25,000	N.A.	2000–2006
Fayetteville, Arkansas	58,047	$10,000	N.A.	2002–2006
Largo, Florida	69,371	$25,000	N.A.	2001–2005
Greeley, Colorado	76,930	Projects—$50,000, equipment—$100,000	N.A.	1999–2003
Athens–Clarke County, Georgia	101,489	$20,000	3 years	2001–2005
Winston-Salem, North Carolina	185,776	Projects—$50,000, equipment—$150,000	10 years	2002–2006
Glendale, Arizona	218,812	$50,000	N.A.	2003–2012
Greensboro, North Carolina	223,891	$100,000	10 years	2001–2007
Buncombe County, North Carolina	206,330	$250,000	5 years	2002–2008

[a]Data from the 2000 U.S. census.
[b]The minimum-dollar and useful-life cutoffs are taken from the jurisdiction's budget or CIP documents.
[c]N.A.: Not applicable.

the project or acquisition is also treated as a capital item in other phases or parts of the capital budget process.

Not all local governments use specific minimum-dollar or useful-life cutoffs for determining which capital projects and acquisitions to include in the CIP and to treat differently for capital budget purposes. Not applying these cutoffs can give a local government flexibility in using the capital budget to meet particular needs. However, it can lead to uncertainty among requesting agencies and decision makers about which projects and acquisitions will be given the planning and special review that occurs in the capital budget process.

In its 1997–2002 CIP, **Junction City, Kansas,** includes land acquisitions, infrastructure projects (roads, bridges, intersections, drainage systems, and sewer systems), new construction or additions to public facilities, remodeling projects, park and golf course improvements, and civil defense projects.[11] This CIP does not refer to any minimum-dollar or useful-life cutoffs for these projects; apparently these types of projects are all included in the CIP.

Equipment and vehicles   A local government may include large-equipment acquisitions in the CIP, either as part of a larger capital improvement project or on their own. A few local governments exclude all stand-alone equipment from the CIP, instead planning and budgeting for such equipment entirely within the operating or annual budget. Most local governments use a high minimum-dollar cutoff to distinguish between major items of stand-alone equipment that are included and planned for in the CIP and other stand-alone equipment that is reviewed and included in the operating budget.

A local government that excludes equipment from its CIP may nonetheless use a special fund and have special planning and budgeting for some or all of its equipment needs. Many medium- and small-size cities with equipment or capital replacement funds include such funds—as well as major construction projects—in the CIP.

The list of eligible CIP projects in **Junction City, Kansas,** excludes equipment, suggesting that the city handles equipment acquisitions in the annual budget process and in the general fund or other operating funds. Similarly, the list of eligible projects for the 2003–2007 **Sedgwick County, Kansas,** CIP does not include equipment acquisitions.[12] Some equipment may be part of a larger capital improvement project that is included in the CIP; however, equipment acquisitions or replacements that stand on their own are not included in the CIP or the capital budget but are instead planned and budgeted entirely or primarily in the annual or operating budget. **Rockville, Maryland,** recently changed its policy on equipment: its 1999–2004 CIP does not list equipment among eligible projects, but its 2001–2005 CIP includes "significant one-time investments in tangible goods," suggesting that equipment is included.[13]

Greeley, Colorado, and **Winston-Salem, North Carolina,** include very expensive equipment in the CIP and capital budget (see Table 1-1). Only equipment that costs $100,000 or more is included in the Greeley CIP, while capital projects need cost just $50,000 to be included. The Winston-Salem CIP uses a $150,000 cutoff for equipment and a $50,000 cutoff for construction projects, land acquisitions, and landscaping projects.[14]

Chandler, Arizona, divides capital expenditures into three general categories. The first consists of major CIP projects (street construction, park improvements, and building construction, for example). These projects cost more than $50,000, are usually financed on a long-term basis, and are usually budgeted in special capital cost centers. The second category consists of operating capital equipment items (such as communications equipment, certain vehicles, and office furniture) that cost more than $5,000, have a useful life of more than one year, and are included in departmental operating budget accounts. The third category is for replacement of vehicles, computers, and other operating capital equipment items. These expenditures are planned and budgeted in a capital/computer replacement fund that raises revenues from annual charges to operating departments using the vehicles and equipment. This enables Chandler to replace its vehicles and equipment on schedule and to spread out the cost of doing so over periods ranging from three to ten years, depending on their useful life.[15] In effect, capital budgeting in Chandler is a two-part process, one focused on construction projects in the CIP and the other focused on vehicle and equipment acquisition with the operating budget and the special fund contributing to that purpose.

Fayetteville, Arkansas, has a "shop fund" for financing vehicle and equipment replacements and acquisitions in its CIP and budget.[16]

Information and communications technology The capital budgets and CIPs of some local governments have given special attention in recent years to spending for information and communications technology.

"Information technology" is a special category in the **Alexandria, Virginia,** FY 2002–FY 2007 Proposed Capital Improvement Program.[17] That CIP projects that Alexandria's information technology spending for the 2002–2007 period will be $18.5 million of the city's total capital spending from its own sources of $197.3 million for this period. In **Chatham County, North Carolina,** six of the twenty-nine projects in the county's 1999–2004 CIP are for technology: accounting/payroll software ($240,350), upgrade of the county's computer system ($414,501), new central permitting hardware and software ($107,250), upgrade of the emergency public safety communications system ($1,972,150), e-911 communications ($44,659), and a geographic information system (GIS) ($479,244). Spending on information and communications technology accounts for about 15 percent of Chatham County's total estimated capital spending in the 1999–2004 period.[18]

Streets and schools Road and street improvements dominate the capital budgets and CIPs of many cities, and school projects in some states are a major portion of county capital budgets and plans.

The capital improvement program included in the **Madison Heights, Michigan,** 2002–2003 budget allocates 45.2 percent of projected funding and appropriations for road improvements and another 38.3 percent for neighborhood projects, most of which are for residential street repair and reconstruction. The road improvements include thoroughfare projects and rehabilitation, traffic signal upgrades, improvements to industrial subdivision streets, some street maintenance, and related vehicle replacements.[19]

The 2000–2010 CIP for **Orange County, North Carolina,** a fast-growing county in the Research Triangle area, puts total project spending at $224.8 million; $153.6 million, almost 70 percent, is for school buildings or capital projects.[20]

Deferred or capital maintenance Expenditures for ordinary maintenance are operating outlays under **generally accepted accounting principles (GAAP)** and are suitable for the annual budget; seldom are they appropriately included in the capital budget or plan. However, deferred or capital maintenance rehabilitates infrastructure and buildings, extends or restores their useful lives by many years, and may be included in a capital budget or plan. For example, the 2001–2005 CIP for Kansas City, Missouri, identifies a backlog of $325 million in deferred maintenance needs for streets, traffic signals and signs, bridges, boulevards, parks, recreational facilities, and buildings.[21] This is a huge amount, even for a large jurisdiction such as Kansas City, and it constitutes an important portion of its CIP.

Large, nonrecurring operating expenditures In general, ordinary maintenance projects, such as painting an elevated water storage tank, are accounted for as current rather than capital expenditures and are included in the operating budget. However, if these projects are very expensive relative to the ongoing operating budget of a local government, and if they recur infrequently, they may be usefully included in the local capital budget and plan. A capital budget or plan might include other large, nonrecurring operating expenditures—for example, a major study of organization and management needs or the preparation of a long-term needs assessment for local services.

Placing large, nonrecurring operating expenditures in the capital budget and plan puts them in competition with requested capital projects for available financing, particularly if there is significant pay-as-go financing of capital needs. Therefore, ordinary maintenance projects and other nonrecurring operating expenditures that are included in the capital plan or budget should be clearly labeled or included in a special section of that plan or budget. Whether included in the operating budget or the capital budget and plan, such expenditures should not be capitalized in the fixed-asset accounting records.

The 2002–2003 "Projects Budget Guide" of **Sunnyvale, California,** notes that this budget includes not only major additions, improvements, or replacements of public facilities and infrastructure, but also "one-time projects designed to address a significant community need or problem; for example, a feasibility study on the need for higher capacity at the Water Pollution Control Plant."[22]

Debt service, lease-purchase, and installment-purchase payments GAAP defines periodic **debt service** on bonds or other debt issued for capital projects or payments on lease-purchase or installment-purchase contracts for such projects as operating expenditures, not capital expenditures. Nonetheless, some local governments include such debt service and lease-purchase and installment-purchase payments in the capital budget and CIP.

Capital budgets and CIPs are designed primarily to show capital expenditures for capital projects and acquisitions. They should also show the impact of capital projects and acquisitions on future operating budgets. Debt-financed projects and projects funded through lease-purchase or installment-purchase contracts result in debt service or lease or installment payments that must be paid years ahead out of operating budgets or special revenue or reserve funds. Most capital budgets and plans show this impact by presenting separate annual debt service and lease payment schedules in the CIP and the capital budget.[23]

Yet other budgets and plans, such as Asheville, North Carolina's (see page 10), combine debt service, lease payments, installment payments, and capital project and acquisition spending in the same schedules or funds. This practice runs the risk of confusing capital spending with subsequent operating spending for debt service and lease payments that result from past or recent capital budget decisions. A local government that combines debt service, lease-purchase, and installment-purchase payments with direct pay-as-go capital spending in one schedule or fund must also show one or more revenue sources to cover the fund's outlays.

It helps in these situations if the revenue sources are earmarked by law or local policy to fund the debt service, lease payment, and capital spending purposes. The advantage of combining these types of spending in one schedule or fund is that it shows in summary fashion how much of total future annual resources a local government will be allocating for capital purposes as well as the balance between debt and pay-as-go financing.

The 2000–2005 CIP of **Asheville, North Carolina,** has two capital reserve funds that include annual debt service and lease-purchase or installment-purchase payments as well as direct, pay-as-go financing for capital projects and acquisitions.[24] One is a general capital reserve fund and the other is a street-and-sidewalk fund. Both are financed predominantly with locally earmarked contributions from the city's general fund. These contributions range from $4.6 million to $4.9 million annually over the five-year CIP in the general capital reserve fund, and from $2.5 million to $2.8 million annually over this period for the street-and-sidewalk fund. The CIP shows about one-third of the general capital reserve fund's annual revenues going for debt service on bonds and certificates of participation (property-secured debt) and for recurring lease-purchase and installment-purchase payments for capital assets, and about two-thirds going for pay-as-go capital project and acquisition financing. In the street-and-sidewalk fund, these proportions are reversed, with two-thirds of the annual revenues going for debt service and lease or installment payments and one-third for direct or pay-as-go capital financing.

What specific cost items are chargeable to a capital project?

A capital project or acquisition should include all expenditures or items that are needed to put the capital asset being built or acquired into operating condition.

Cost items for construction projects   Cost items for construction projects include

- Construction labor and materials
- Planning as well as architectural and engineering design
- Legal services related to the project
- Acquisition of land or other property for the project, including brokerage fees
- Preparation of land for construction and landscaping during or after construction
- Easements related to the project
- Equipment and furnishings that are affixed to the project
- Initial inventory of movable furnishings and equipment
- Interest and other financing charges during construction
- Construction management and contract monitoring costs.

A number of issues can arise in charging costs to a construction project:

Preliminary planning and design   Preliminary planning and design for a project typically occurs before the project is approved; the cost for this work is charged to the general fund, another operating fund, or sometimes a special fund or account. If the project is approved, the preliminary planning and design costs for it can be charged to the project, with the project budget reimbursing the fund or account to which the work was originally charged. Although an initial step, preliminary planning and design are necessary for completion of a project and therefore constitute a legitimate project expense. However, the accounting required to allocate the costs for this work to the approved projects prompts many local governments to instead carry such costs permanently in the accounts or funds to which they were originally charged. Any reimbursement made to those accounts or funds charged for the cost is most likely to occur when the preliminary planning and design are contracted out and when bond or debt financing is involved in the project. Of course, if a project is not approved, the costs of any preliminary planning and design for it are absorbed permanently by the account or fund originally charged.

Planning and engineering carried out by in-house staff   In medium- and large-size local governments, in-house engineering and planning staff may do the planning and design for a project—both the preliminary work, if there is any, and the preparation of blueprints and specifications for construction. Whether done in-house or contracted, such work is essential to completion of the project, and its cost is therefore appropriately charged to the project. However, in-house planning and design on projects are often not charged to the projects because (1) the general fund or another operating fund already includes the salaries and support expenses of the engineering and planning staff doing the work and (2) extra or special accounting is necessary to allocate the costs of such work to specific projects.

Construction work done by a unit's own employees   A local government's own construction crews may complete certain parts of a construction project (for example, landscaping) or, on a relatively small project, most or all of the construction.[25] Although the costs can be charged to the project, this often does not happen because the cost of using the local government's workforce is already budgeted in the general fund or another operating fund and because of the special accounting required to allocate the workforce's time to particular projects.

Initial inventory of movable equipment and furnishings for a project   To become operational, a project will typically require not only equipment and furnishings that are affixed to the building or facility being constructed or renovated (for example, fixtures) but also movable furnishings and equipment (for example, desks and chairs). To the extent that existing or old furnishings and equipment will not or cannot be used, new furnishings and equipment will be needed. The initial inventory of movable furnishings and equipment needed for such a building or facility can and should be budgeted among the project's costs. However, any new movable furnishings and equipment associated with the construction or renovation of a building or facility are appropriately recorded separately from the building or facility on the local government's fixed-asset records because such furnishings and equipment may eventually be moved from the premises.

Exclusion of certain project-related costs   Legal restrictions may prevent expenditures for certain items associated with a capital asset from being charged as a capital cost of the asset. Instead, they must be budgeted and accounted as operating expenditures. For example, although expenditures to buy land for a landfill and ready it for use are properly charged as capital costs to the landfill, expenditures for closure and postclosure outlays for a landfill—which are expensive and may be capitalized under accounting principles—are nonetheless considered operating expenditures according to interpretations of statutes authorizing bonds in some states.[26] Consequently, these latter outlays—at least in these jurisdictions—may not be financed with bonds or considered part of the landfill's fixed or capital costs.

Cost items for equipment acquisitions   For equipment acquisitions, the capital costs include not only the purchase price of the equipment, but also any separate transportation charges to move the equipment to its place of intended use and costs, if any, for installation and testing before the local government accepts the equipment.

If new equipment is acquired to replace old equipment, the old equipment may be traded in or sold by auction or other means. In either case, the value of the old equipment traded in or the amount realized by selling it is accounted for as the sale of an asset and thus as a revenue. The new equipment should be recorded on the books at its total or gross purchase price. However, the capital plan or budget can and should show not only the total or gross purchase price of the new equipment, but also the value of the trade-in or proceeds of the sale of the old equipment. Because the capital plan or budget projects the amounts associated with the transaction, the trade-in value or sale proceeds of the old equipment would be estimated amounts. Such trade-in value or sale proceeds may be considered "associated revenue" of the transaction.

To acquire and be able to use certain major equipment, a local government may need to modify or renovate the office space or building where the equipment will be housed. If this is necessary and the renovation costs are significant, the capital budget should show both the equipment acquisition costs and the remodeling or renovation costs, preferably as part of the same project. However, on the local unit's fixed-asset records, the renovation costs need to be capitalized or recorded separately from the equipment acquisition costs.

Policy framework for capital budgeting

Many local governments have policies to guide the capital budget process. While subject to review and periodic updating, such policies define the process, identify roles and responsibilities, establish limits, and give the process legitimacy and continuity. In so doing, they can shape not only capital budgeting practices, but also the costs incurred over time for capital projects and acquisitions. These policies can even shape decisions regarding which projects are approved and funded.

Some policies for capital budgeting are based on state statutes or regulations or on local charter requirements. Most are strictly local policies adopted by resolution or other action of the local governing board. Yet other policies formulated and used by management and staff are not formally approved by the governing board. These policies may be included in the document presenting the annual budget or CIP to the governing board, and therefore board review or acceptance of the document may be viewed as tacit approval of the policies. Legally based policies or policies formally approved by the governing board provide a firmer foundation for capital budgeting.

Cities and counties generally use three types of policies to guide capital budgeting. The first type relates to capital planning. These policies typically require the preparation and approval of a CIP and may also call for an accompanying multiyear financial forecast. Second are financial policies, which identify the different sources of capital finance that are legally available to and used by a local government. These policies usually give special emphasis to debt, placing limits on the amount of different kinds of debt that may be incurred for capital purposes and setting requirements for the repayment of the debt. Third are substantive policies and goals that influence the kinds of specific projects and acquisitions that are given priority for approval and funding in capital budget decisions. The remainder of this section illustrates these different types of capital budgeting policies.

Capital planning

Policies that require a local government to do capital planning are sometimes based on legal stipulations.

The charters of both **Largo, Florida,** and **Chandler, Arizona,** require a multiyear CIP. Largo's city charter calls for the city manager to submit a five-year CIP to the city commission (governing board) by March 1 of each year and requires the commission to adopt the CIP on or before May 1.[27] Similarly, the Chandler city charter says that a five-year CIP must be prepared annually and submitted to the city council for its review and approval. The CIP must include project cost estimates, recommend financing and timing, and estimate the operating budget impact of projects.[28]

Alexandria, Virginia, has a more defined legal requirement for capital improvement programming.[29] According to the city's code, the city manager must submit to the council capital improvement projects for the ensuing fiscal year and for the five years thereafter, with recommendations as to how the projects for the ensuing fiscal year will be financed. This code makes clear that the council may approve, reject, or amend the capital projects and the recommended means of financing, and that the council does not authorize capital projects or make appropriations for them unless such projects are included in the capital budget adopted by the council. The language of the city code about project financing and approval helps to clarify that the CIP is principally a planning tool and that council action for both the projects and financing is needed to implement the plan.

The capital improvement policies of **Greensboro, North Carolina,** are based on a resolution adopted by the city council. The council approved these policies initially with its adoption of the 1995–2001 CIP. In a separate action, the council approved financial policies that Greensboro uses to guide annual budgeting, financial management, and debt issuance.[30] Greensboro's policies for capital planning require the city to

- Develop a six-year CIP annually, to be adopted in conjunction with the annual budget

- Include in the CIP capital projects and acquisitions that cost at least $100,000 and have a useful life of at least ten years

- Appropriate funds for capital projects with project ordinances pursuant to state statute

- Estimate operating expenses for all CIP projects and include such estimates in the CIP

- Set annually, by city council action, levels-of-service standards for the quantity and quality of capital facilities and criteria for the evaluation of capital project requests; for example, a service standard might refer to the capacity of a facility in relation to volume of use, and if volume of use significantly exceeded capacity it could trigger a request for facility expansion

- Include in the CIP an inventory of existing capital facilities and document any maintenance or replacement plans for these facilities

- Follow debt policies and ratios adopted by the city for any CIP projects financed with debt

- Coordinate city debt financing with the "overlapping" capital needs of Guilford County, North Carolina, in which Greensboro is located.

Glendale, Arizona, uses somewhat more specific management, financial, and planning policies to help staff with the development of the CIP.[31] Those policies stipulate that the CIP should

- Support council goals and objectives

- Address all city and state legal and financial limitations

- Maintain the city's favorable investment rating and financial integrity

- Ensure that all geographic areas of the city have comparable quality and types of services.

Financial policies

Many local governments have capital financing and debt policies that the local government board management approves to guide the jurisdiction.[32] Such policies usually appear in the CIP and/or the operating or annual budget.

Junction City, Kansas, has a debt management and fiscal policy, adopted initially by resolution of the city commission (governing board) in 1991 to guide capital budgeting and other financial operations.[33] Among other things, this policy

- Requires a financial plan to accompany the city's CIP

- Establishes a capital improvement fund for major facilities, financed with tax levies that provide increasing pay-as-go revenues as debt service on existing bonds declines over time

- Establishes fire equipment and motor pool reserves to finance replacement of such assets

- Limits city debt by reference to specific ratios—for example, debt per capita for general obligation (GO), revenue, warrant, and lease-purchase debt; GO debt outstanding in relation to the statutory debt limit; annual debt service for GO debt as a percentage of governmental expenditures; and annual debt service on revenue debt as a percentage of proprietary fund expenditures

- Sets guidelines for **benefit district debt**

- Establishes debt repayment schedules that are related to the useful lives of the debt-financed facilities and that protect the city's capacity to borrow in the future.

Asheville, North Carolina, has had governing board–approved financial policies to guide its financial operations, including capital budgeting, for many years.[34] The policies most relevant to capital budgeting and finance require the city to

- Prepare a five-year operating budget to forecast operating revenues, expenditures, and debt service

- Establish a capital reserve fund to finance general capital assets with a value of $7,500 or more, and earmark annual revenue equal to 7¢ per $100 on the property tax rate and certain sales tax revenue to fund it; the fund covers both pay-as-go capital spending and debt service on bonds or debt issued for general capital improvements

- Establish a street-and-sidewalk reserve fund and earmark annual revenue equal to 4¢ per $100 of the property tax rate and state-shared gasoline tax revenue to fund it; the fund covers pay-as-go financing and debt service on bonds for street and sidewalk projects

- Update and readopt annually a six-year CIP that shows project costs, funding sources, and the impact of projects on the operating budget and that is tied to the city's comprehensive, long-range growth plan

- Require that debt issued for any capital project not exceed the project's useful life

- Limit outstanding GO debt to 8 percent of assessed or taxable valuation, and limit total debt service on tax-supported debt to no more than 15 percent of total general government operating revenues

- Maintain a minimum bond rating of AA.

The 1999–2004 CIP of **Cedar Falls, Iowa,** includes a financial guidelines and analysis section that emphasizes debt policies.[35] The overall purpose of this section is to produce a CIP that Cedar Falls can afford and that has a minimum impact on property tax rates and other revenues. The guidelines on debt call for Cedar Falls to

- Maintain level tax rates devoted to debt service

- Maintain a balance between debt service and current operating expenditures

- Reduce the use of debt capacity for certain projects— for example, construction of the Interstate Substitution project

- Maximize intergovernmental grants-in-aid to offset local debt and costs

- Issue new GO bonds at no more than replacement levels so that GO debt does not increase

- Minimize the property tax impact of debt by limiting debt and balancing debt repayment schedules.

Like Cedar Falls, **Deerfield, Illinois,** attempts to keep an even debt service levy, allowing debt capacity to increase as tax valuation grows and new capital needs arise.[36]

Substantive goals

Some local governments have policies or goals for CIPs and capital budgets that give priority to capital projects and acquisitions in certain service or program areas. Policies establishing such priorities usually are approved at the outset of the CIP or the capital budget process, before requests are made and reviewed. Sometimes these policies are established in a long-term service or capital needs assessment or a comprehensive planning effort that takes place apart from the CIP process. Service or program polices and goals channel the specific capital project or acquisition requests that are made as well as decisions toward the end of the process to approve and fund certain projects.

A policy in **Glendale, Arizona's** 2003–2012 CIP sets forth a general program or service priority for projects by stating that they should encourage or sustain economic development.[37]

One of the policies of **Madison Heights, Michigan,** states that the city's CIP will give priority to projects that support development efforts in areas with a majority of low- to moderate-income households.[38]

Evanston, Illinois, goes farther in specifying programmatic priorities among service areas to guide capital project selection. Its CIP has policies for the following service areas: economic development ("develop and implement programs to upgrade and maintain streetscapes in the downtown"), the environment ("participate in development of areawide solutions to the problem of solid waste disposal and promote local recycling and waste reduction efforts to minimize solid waste disposal requirements and conserve resources"), parks and recreation ("undertake improvements to enhance and protect the lakefront park system"), public buildings ("undertake the rehabilitation of the police/fire headquarters"), and transportation projects ("continue the city's program for maintaining curbs, gutters, and sidewalks").[39]

Conclusion

This chapter has provided an overview of the reasons for capital budgeting, defined a capital expenditure, and discussed the kinds of capital projects and acquisitions that are suitable for review and approval in the capital budget. It has also explained the policy framework for capital budgeting. The next chapter provides a model of the local capital budgeting approach and compares the model with three different stages of capital budgeting in actual practice.

Notes

1 Town of Cary, North Carolina, Capital Improvements Budget, Fiscal Year 2001–2002, 123. The 2003–2012 CIP is part of this document.

2 Town of Cary, North Carolina, Annual Operating Budget, Fiscal Year 2001–2002, 21.

3 Village of Grafton, Wisconsin, 2000 Annual Program Budget, 33.

4 Ibid., 172–173.

5 General Statutes of North Carolina, Chapter 159, Section 13.2.

6 Town of Cary, North Carolina, Capital Improvements Budget, Fiscal Year 2001–2002, 9–10, especially section 8 of the "Utility Capital Improvements Budget Ordinance, Fiscal Year 2002."

7 This definition appears in Government Finance Officers Association (GFOA), *Governmental Accounting, Auditing, and Financial Reporting* (Chicago: GFOA, 1994), 318, 330. The same definition, albeit referring to "capital asset," appears in the 2001 edition. See *Governmental Accounting, Auditing, and Financial Reporting* (Chicago: GFOA, 2001), 619.

8 Governmental Accounting Standards Board (GASB), *Statement No. 34: Basic Financial Statements—and Management's Discussion and Analysis—for State and Local Governments* (Norwalk, Conn.: GASB, 1999), paragraphs 18–29.

9 For example, the policies manual of the North Carolina Department of State Treasurer refers to fixed assets as "tangible in nature." See "Policies Manual— Fixed Assets," 3, www.treasurer.state.nc.us.

10 *Governmental Accounting, Auditing, and Financial Reporting*, 223–224, recognizes the appropriateness of including certain intangible property among general fixed

assets. Accounting for public enterprises follows commercial accounting principles, which provide for the inclusion of intangible as well as tangible property among fixed assets.

11 City of Junction City, Kansas, 1999 Budget, 76.

12 Sedgwick County 2003 Adopted Budget, 537, www.sedgwick.ks.us. The 2003–2007 CIP is presented in the county's 2003 budget.

13 FY Adopted Operating Budget and Capital Improvement Program, City of Rockville, Maryland, 179; and Operating Budget & Capital Improvement Program Adopted FY 2001, City of Rockville, Maryland, 181.

14 City of Greeley, Colorado, Operations and Capital Improvement Plan, Annual Budget, January 1, 1999–December 31, 2001, 314. The CIP presented in the 1999 budget is for 1999–2003. Capital Improvement Program Instruction Manual, FY 2002–2006, City of Winston-Salem, North Carolina, 3.

15 2002–2003 Annual Budget, Chandler, Arizona, 331, www.chandleraz.org.

16 City of Fayetteville, Arkansas, Proposed 2003 Annual Budget and Work Program, 37 and 184, www.accessfayetteville.org.

17 Proposed Capital Improvement Program, FY 2002–2007, City of Alexandria, Virginia, 29.

18 Chatham County Fiscal Year 1999–2000 Budget, 199–256.

19 City of Madison Heights, Michigan, Adopted Budget for Fiscal Year 2002–2003, 227, www.ci.madison-heights.mi.us.

20 Orange County, North Carolina, Manager's Recommended 2000–2010 Capital Improvement Plan, 1.

21 Budget (and) Five-Year Capital Improvements Plan, City of Kansas City, Missouri, 2000–2001/2004–2005, 8.

22 City of Sunnyvale, California, Adopted Fiscal Year 2002/2003 Budget and Resource Allocation Plan, Volume III, "Projects Budget Guide," www.sunnyvale.ca.us.

23 For instance, the Alamance County [North Carolina] Capital Improvement Plan FY 2003–2007, 8-5 through 8-11, www.alamance-nc.com, shows capital project expenditures separately from debt service and other operating

budget or cash flow impacts of the projects.

24 City of Asheville, Adopted Annual Operating Budget, Fiscal Year 1999–2000, 145–159, www.ci.asheville.nc.us. The 2000–2005 CIP is included in the city's 1999–2000 operating budget. Asheville's 2003–2008 CIP appears to separate project expenditures and resulting debt service or lease payments into separate schedules.

25 State statutes and the complexities of construction limit a local government's use of its own workforce on construction projects. See, for example, the General Statutes of North Carolina, chapter 143, section 129. This statue requires the contracting of construction or repair work if the work costs $100,000 or more.

26 See, for example, General Statutes of North Carolina, chapter 159, section 48(b)(18).

27 Largo, Florida, Annual Budget, Fiscal Year 2001, CIP-1.

28 Capital Improvement Program, 2002–2003, Chandler, Arizona, 3, www.chandleraz.org. The Chandler CIP is for 2002–2007.

29 Alexandria, Virginia, FY 2000–2005 Approved Budget—Capital Improvement Program, 10.

30 Capital Improvements Program, City of Greensboro, 1997–2003. Essentially, the same policies continue to guide the Greensboro CIP process. See Greensboro, North Carolina, Adopted Budget, 2001–2002, Projected Budget, 2002–2003, 10–11. Except where otherwise indicated, the policies for Greensboro and other local governments cited here are paraphrased rather than quoted. A concerted effort has been made to maintain the meaning of the full text of the cited policies.

31 Glendale, Arizona, 2002–2003 Budget, "Introduction" to the 2003–2012 Capital Improvement Plan," www.glendale.az.us.

32 Guidelines for the development of a local government debt policy are set forth in Patricia Tigue, *A Guide for Preparing a Debt Policy* (Chicago: GFOA, 1996).

33 City of Junction City, Kansas, 1999 Budget, 41–46.

34 Asheville's "financial policies" were originally approved in the late 1980s. The policies presented here were in effect in for 2001–2002. See City of Asheville, North

Carolina, Adopted Annual Budget, 2001–2002, 13–15.

35 July 1, 1999–June 30, 2002, Financial Plan, City of Cedar Falls, Iowa, 7.1–7.2.

36 Annual Budget, Fiscal Year 2001–2002, Village of Deerfield, Illinois, 17.

37 Glendale Arizona, 2002–2003 Budget, page 5 of the section presenting the city's

2003–2012 Capital Improvement Plan. www.glendale.az.us.

38 City of Madison Heights, Michigan, Adopted Budget for Fiscal Year 2002–03, 47, www.madison-heights.mi.us.

39 City of Evanston, 1999–2000 Budget, which appears in the 1999–2004 Long-Range Capital Improvement Plan, 6–9.

2 Capital budgeting process: model and practice

This chapter presents a comprehensive model of the local government capital budgeting process. The model reflects some of the more sophisticated capital budgeting practices in cities and counties, as well as local capital budgeting practices that have been discussed in public administration and related literature in recent years.[1]

Not all local governments follow all the steps outlined in the model. Indeed, relatively few medium- and smaller-size cities and counties do so. Nor do many need to follow all the steps. Therefore, the chapter also presents—and illustrates with specific examples—three different levels of capital budgeting actually practiced by medium- and small-size jurisdictions. These levels of practice are compared with the model.

A model of capital budgeting

The comprehensive model of the capital budgeting process for medium- and smaller-size cities and counties consists of ten steps (see the list on page 20).

Decide which types of capital projects and acquisitions to include in the CIP and capital budget

Local governments must decide which types of capital projects and acquisitions to include in their **capital improvement program (CIP)** and approve in the capital budget. Chapter 1 discussed how to decide whether particular expenditures are in fact capital expenditures, whether they belong in the CIP and capital budget or in the annual or operating budget, and what specific expenditure items are properly charged to a capital project or acquisition.

Organize the capital budgeting process

Local governments also must decide how comprehensive the capital budgeting process will be, who will be involved, and how it will be organized. Some of these organizational requirements will be covered in depth in subsequent chapters.

- **Assign responsibility for coordinating the process** One or more local officials should be chosen to develop capital budgeting polices and procedures and make sure specific steps are taken and work performed. The most likely choices for this coordination role are an assistant city or county manager, another top-level official in the manager's or chief executive's office, the budget director, the finance director, the planning

---

Comprehensive model of capital budgeting process for local governments

- Decide which types of capital projects and acquisitions to include in the CIP and capital budget

- Organize the capital budgeting process

- Prepare and approve a multiyear CIP

- Evaluate and prioritize requested capital projects and acquisitions

- Assess the financial condition of the jurisdiction and forecast its capital financing capacity

- Identify capital financing options and select appropriate financing for specific projects and acquisitions

- Develop and follow a capital financing strategy

- Prepare and recommend a capital budget

- Authorize capital projects and acquisitions and appropriate money to fund them

- Implement the capital budget.

In actual practice in local governments, some of these steps are often combined or taken in different sequence.

---

director, or another department head (for example, the engineer) familiar with capital budget concepts and techniques. Managerial staff or the budget director would have an overview of needs and resources. The finance director would be in a position to identify financing options and integrate financial limits with needs. The planning director would be able to incorporate strong planning into the process. In a small local government, however, the manager or chief executive officer may have to take responsibility for coordinating the process rather than delegate this role to someone else.

- **Determine the involvement of local officials** Local governments must decide who will participate in the capital budgeting process and what roles they will play. The city or county manager or chief executive officer provides general direction and recommends the CIP and capital budget to the governing board. The requesting agencies identify capital needs. The local governing board can establish goals, policies, and decision criteria or ranking criteria at the start of the process, and it reviews and approves the CIP and the capital budget. The finance director forecasts financial resources and identifies financing options. The planning director and staff integrate long-term needs assessments into the CIP and capital budget. Other officials may be involved as well.

- **Determine forms of public participation** Decisions must be made concerning the part that citizen advisory or regulatory boards, neighborhood associations, community organizations, and the general public will play in the capital budgeting process. Will neighborhood associations and community organizations be asked to submit capital project and acquisition requests? Will a citizens' advisory committee or regulatory body—for example, the planning board—be asked to review and comment on requests and offer recommendations? Will citizens be surveyed to ascertain their views about capital needs and priorities? These important questions must be addressed.

- **Identify relevant legislation and norms**   Federal and state laws, regulations, and policies, as well as professional requirements and norms, can influence the prioritization of needs or requests for local capital projects and acquisitions. They also can influence capital financing. It is important for local officials to establish links with federal, state, and professional agencies that can affect capital budgeting decisions, or that might offer **grants** or other resources that could be tapped to finance particular projects.

- **Identify necessary steps and make a timetable**   Choose the specific steps that must be taken in the local capital budgeting process; set up a calendar for preparing and approving any capital plan, the one-year capital budget, and any specific capital projects and acquisitions. Although in a general sense this step should come first, final determination of the stages of the process and the specific calendar will necessarily depend on decisions about how broad the participation in the process will be and the extent of participation by different participants.

- **Design capital budgeting request forms and instructions**   The format to use and the information to include in the capital plan, budget, and recommendations for projects must be decided. Particular local officials (for example, the engineer, purchasing director, or one or more outside consultants) can be designated to help requesting agencies with the more technical parts of their requests, such as construction or major equipment cost estimates.

- **Recognize points of contact between the capital budget and the operating budget**   The same set of community and program needs drives both capital and operating budget requests, and the two budgets affect each other. Projects and spending approved in the capital budget influence future operating budgets. For example, capital budget decisions can result in new staff and operating expenditures for new facilities, savings in operating costs, increases or decreases in recurring operating revenues, and debt service and lease payments on bonds or lease contracts issued to finance capital projects. Decisions made in the operating budget to improve or expand services can necessitate future expansion of capital facilities or the acquisition of major new pieces of equipment.

- **Determine governing board authorization procedures**   The governing board will use certain procedures to authorize and appropriate revenue or financing for capital projects and acquisitions.

- **Set up the means for implementing capital projects**   For example, the criteria for selecting architects and engineers to design major projects must be identified. A project or construction management capacity also must be put in place.

Prepare and approve a multiyear CIP

A capital improvement program typically covers five or six years. For that period it identifies capital project and acquisition needs; calculates cost or expenditure estimates for those needs; identifies probable sources of financing; evaluates, prioritizes, and schedules projects and acquisitions; and forecasts the likely impact of projects and acquisitions on the operating budget.

Major capital needs can be identified in long-term comprehensive or community plans, in multiyear needs assessments for specific programs or services, in accounting records or other records of existing facilities and other fixed assets, in renovation or replacement schedules for existing capital assets, and in other sources.

Chapter 3 covers the formats used and the steps involved in CIP preparation and approval. It also discusses approaches for long-term capital needs assessment that some local governments use in developing their CIPs.

Evaluate and prioritize requested capital projects and acquisitions

Capital needs compete with each other for limited resources and, through annual debt service or lease payments and pay-as-go capital spending, with ongoing and new service needs in the operating budget. Accordingly, capital project and acquisition requests have to be evaluated and prioritized. Evaluation and ranking occur in the CIP process. Projects and acquisitions scheduled for funding in the first few years of the CIP forecast period generally have a higher priority than those placed in the later years; however, the allocation of some projects and acquisitions to particular CIP years may reflect scheduling considerations more than they do relative merit and priority.

There are different approaches to evaluation and priority setting or ranking, ranging from judgments by decision makers about whether particular capital needs or requests are high, medium, or low in priority, to more complicated approaches that refer to specific criteria to establish priorities. Some ranking systems are quantitatively based assessments of project benefits and costs, and they consider the time value of money associated with project revenues and costs that occur over many years.

Evaluation and ranking in the context of the CIP process may be sufficient for some capital projects and acquisitions. For others, the evaluation and ranking must be revisited because of what a unit's financial forecast shows (for example, resources more limited than expected), what in-depth or engineering-based project evaluations turn up, or simply what new developments arise after a project is placed in the CIP.

For large construction projects or major equipment acquisitions, in-depth or engineering-based project evaluation is typically needed to determine the scope of the project, estimate or address project benefits, calculate costs, prepare plans and specifications or provide the basis for doing so, and determine project feasibility. Such an evaluation gives the governing board and other local officials a basis for deciding whether to go ahead with a planned project or acquisition and commit funding to it. In-depth or engineering-based project evaluation is likely to be contracted to an architectural or engineering consulting firm with recognized expertise in evaluating and planning for the type of project or system being evaluated.

Chapter 4 addresses evaluation and ranking systems that local governments use to help prioritize needs for capital projects and acquisitions.

Assess financial condition and forecast capital financing capacity

Any assessment and forecast to determine a local government's capacity to finance capital needs now and in the future must consider all revenues, reserves, and spending over the forecast period—not just capital financing sources. The sources of financing for capital as well as operating needs are taxes and other revenues that are raised from year to year. After operating requirements and reserves are funded, the annual revenues that remain are the source for both pay-as-go capital financing and recurring debt service and lease payments on bonds and other debt issued for capital projects and acquisitions.

Assessment of the current financial condition involves an examination of the adequacy of annual revenues in relation to service needs and spending, operating **fund balances,** capital reserves, revenues earmarked for capital purposes, fee and grant revenue available for capital projects, outstanding debt in relation to legal debt limits and rating agency criteria for borrowing, and the percentage of annual spending that goes to debt service or payments on capital leases.

A financial forecast must consider all of these variables and also forecast revenues, spending, reserves, and debt; it must evaluate local economic prospects for the community and make assumptions about how growth will affect local government revenues and spending. The financial forecast typically covers the same future period as the multiyear CIP and supports both that program and planning for the operating or annual budget.

Chapter 12 explains how a jurisdiction can assess its financial condition and forecast its capital financing capacity.

Identify capital financing options and select appropriate financing

The specific capital financing options available to a local government are usually prescribed by state law. Familiarity with traditional financing practices and the limited experiences of some local officials with nontraditional financing options can further narrow the choices for a city or county. Efforts by local officials to become familiar with new or emerging capital financing sources, grants that are available to fund capital projects, or possible interlocal or public–private sector financing can significantly expand the capital financing options of a city or county.

Capital financing sources fall into two broad categories: **pay-as-go financing** sources and **debt financing** sources. Pay-as-go sources are comparable to equity financing of capital needs in the private sector. Such financing is raised through stock offerings or other contributions of capital by owners, partners, or stockholders. Pay-as-go financing for local and other governmental entities comes from taxes and other revenues or capital contributed directly by the taxpayers or citizens. Pay-as-go or equity finance stands in contrast to debt financing, where the local government or private firm borrows capital and incurs debt to finance capital projects and acquisitions. Local government pay-as-go sources include

- Annual, general-purpose revenues that are applied to capital projects and acquisitions
- Annual revenues that are earmarked (by state law or local policy) for capital projects and acquisitions
- Operating fund balances that are not needed to support operations
- Capital reserves
- Equipment or vehicle replacement revolving funds, or infrastructure and facility rehabilitation revolving funds (forms of capital reserve fund except they are set up specifically to replace equipment or renovate infrastructure and facilities, and recurring annual revenues are channeled into the funds each year to meet the intended needs)
- Special assessments, capital recovery charges, and impact fees
- State and federal grants
- Cooperative arrangements with other local governments
- Public sector–private sector partnerships or privatization.

These pay-as-go sources are not necessarily mutually exclusive. For instance, a special revenue can be earmarked to rehabilitate streets and be channeled through an infrastructure rehabilitation fund, or a certain number of mils or cents on the general tax rate may be earmarked to help fund a joint public-private project.

Debt sources of capital finance may be classified by the collateral that is pledged to secure the debt. Using this criterion, local government debt sources can include

- **General obligation (GO) bonds** secured by unlimited taxing power
- **Revenue bonds** secured by the net revenues or earnings of a self-supporting enterprise
- **Special or limited obligation bonds or debt** secured by one or more sources of nontax revenue or by a tax limited as to rate or amount
- Lease- or installment-purchase debt, including **certificates of participation** and obligation, which are usually secured by the property being financed with the debt. These leases are actually purchases or sales with payments occurring over time. The lessee is considered to be the owner of the leased property at the outset of the transaction under rules and regulations of the Internal Revenue Service (IRS). These leases are considered to be capital leases under generally accepted accounting principles.[2]
- **Long-term true leasing arrangements** other than lease- or installment-purchase debt. The lessor remains the owner of the leased property under a true lease pursuant to IRS rules and regulations. Despite this, if such a lease covers a major portion of the property's useful life or meets other criteria, it can be classified as a capital lease under generally accepted accounting principles.
- **State loans** for particular purposes (for example, local water or wastewater treatment projects). Many states have set up revolving loan programs from which local governments can borrow to help finance certain local infrastructure. The programs are sometimes financed with federal grant funds as well as state borrowing or appropriations, and they generally provide loans to qualifying local governments at below-market interest rates.

Chapter 6 examines the use of pay-as-go or equity sources of capital financing by medium- and small-size local governments; and Chapter 7 addresses debt financing.

Develop and follow a capital financing strategy

A capital financing strategy for a local government starts with a community's economic condition and prospects. For example, local governments in a fast-growing region may have to rely heavily on debt and certain pay-as-go sources, such as impact or development fees, to finance the infrastructure needed to accommodate growth. On the other hand, local governments in areas where growth is limited or nonexistent are less likely to rely on debt and more likely to rely on certain other pay-as-go sources such as annual revenues earmarked for capital purposes, capital reserves, and state grants and loans.

A local government's capital financing strategy should take into account the capital needs facing the jurisdiction and, of course, the legal and practical availability of different sources of capital financing. Embodied in financing policies approved by the local governing board, the strategy provides a framework to help local officials choose appropriate financing for particular projects and limit debt to that which the jurisdiction has a capacity to service. Specifically, the strategy can help a local government

- Use a variety of financing sources to support the CIP and finance capital projects
- Achieve a reasonable balance between pay-as-go sources and debt sources—enabling the jurisdiction to meet priority capital needs in a timely way through debt issuance while preserving flexibility in future operating budgets by relying on pay-as-go financing for certain capital needs
- Plan and structure **debt issuance** with an eye toward local capital financing capacity, current versus future needs, and the useful lives of the projects financed by debt
- Protect and improve a local government's bond rating
- Effectively use the advice and assistance of financial professionals in choosing among capital financing options and issuing debt.

Chapter 5 explores the capital financing strategies of local governments.

Prepare and recommend a capital budget

For a local government with a CIP, the recommended capital budget flows from that program and is represented by the capital projects and spending in the first year of the program. Many local governments without a CIP use a one-year capital budget that is prepared with the annual or operating budget and is usually presented as a separate section of that operating budget. Such a capital budget typically includes major projects that are budgeted and accounted for in capital project funds, and sometimes equipment replacement and acquisition and infrastructure rehabilitation spending that is budgeted and accounted for in special revolving funds.

Authorize capital projects and acquisitions and appropriate money to fund them

The local governing board authorizes and appropriates money for capital projects and acquisitions. The board bases its decisions on whatever preceding steps are taken in the capital budget process—that is, whatever policies the board has established for capital budgeting, capital improvement programming, project evaluation and ranking, financial forecasting, selection among financing options, use of a capital financing strategy, and capital budget or specific project recommendations from the city or county manager and staff.

In some medium-size local governments, the governing board may authorize the manager to approve very small capital projects or acquisitions or, more commonly, to approve modest changes in the scope or cost of projects previously approved by the board.

Board authorization and appropriation of money for projects often occur simultaneously, with authorization in effect taking place with one or more appropriations for the project. Board authorization and appropriation for other projects, usually the large or bond-financed projects, may occur in separate governing board actions or at different times. Appropriations can be for a fiscal year or by project. Annual appropriations usually lapse at the end of a fiscal year; in the case of multiyear capital projects, the governing board would need to reappropriate previously appropriated but lapsed funding with the start of the new fiscal year. Project appropriations or ordinances, on the other hand, typically have a project life and do not lapse at the end of a fiscal year.

Implement the capital budget

The last step in the capital budget process is implementation. Failure here can sink all the plans, budgets, and financial strategies made earlier in the process. Key facets of capital budget and project implementation are obtaining and managing the funds available for projects or acquisitions; purchasing equipment; designing, contracting for, and managing the construction of buildings and other improvements; and accounting for capital construction or acquisitions. The new requirements for accounting for and reporting investments in infrastructure, or for alternatives to such accounting and reporting, are presented in Statement No. 34 of the Governmental Accounting Standards Board and have become an essential part of project implementation.[3]

While the steps for capital budgeting outlined here are arranged in the general order in which they might occur, this sequence is not set. Some local governments, for good reasons, might order them differently. For example, for some proposed projects, the evaluation of project feasibility takes place before the projects are put into the CIP, or the identification and selection of financing for a project may occur before the project's priority is established.

Moreover, many of the steps in the process overlap or take place simultaneously. For example, ranking among projects typically occurs within the CIP. It is set out as a separate step in the capital budget model to underscore its importance. Evaluating and prioritizing requests for capital projects should occur, not only in the CIP, but throughout the budgeting process as projects are juggled with one another in relation to the available financing. Although local governments should devise a capital financing strategy before selecting financing for particular projects, knowledge of the available financing options partly determines the strategy.

In summary, each step in capital budgeting influences every other step. Rigid adherence to a particular sequence of steps is not recommended.

Capital budgeting in practice

The comprehensive approach to capital budgeting outlined in this model presumes the existence of many needs for major capital projects and acquisitions; the realization that jurisdiction-wide, multiyear capital planning can match those needs with available resources; and the presence of administrative and professional staff who are familiar with capital budget concepts and techniques. These conditions do not exist in all jurisdictions, however, and not all local governments need to take a comprehensive approach. Many use just a few of the steps in the model.

This section will discuss three levels of capital budgeting practices for medium- and small-size local governments. These levels are distinguished in terms of

- Whether there is multiyear capital planning and financial forecasting for the jurisdiction
- Whether special capital budgeting procedures and formats—often called the capital budget or the capital improvement budget—are used within the annual budget to review and present major capital asset needs

- Whether and to what degree capital project funds or other special accounting funds are used for capital spending
- To what extent different capital financing sources are available and used
- Whether appropriations for major capital projects and acquisitions are made in the operating or annual budget resolution or in separate multiyear or project ordinances.

Each of the levels of capital budgeting is described and illustrated by practices in specific local governments (see the sidebar below).

Level 1

The first level of capital budgeting is found in numerous cities, towns, villages, townships, and counties throughout the United States, where recurring capital needs are modest, and major capital projects arise infrequently— that is, once every several years at most. This scenario could describe a medium- or small-size city, town, or county in a region that is experiencing little or no growth or perhaps even decline. It also could characterize a very small town or village with a population of not more than five thousand. In such a town, administrative staff is limited: there may be a manager or administrator who is also the finance director, and a town clerk; no manager or administrator, but a finance director and a town clerk who share administrative duties; or a town clerk, who is also the finance director, and elected town commissioners who attend to administrative duties.

Capital budgeting at Level 1 takes place mainly or entirely within the annual budget process and has the following characteristics:

Capital budgeting as practiced by local governments

- **Level 1** At this basic level, any multiyear capital planning that occurs is specific to the project. Capital financing comes mainly or entirely from annual revenues and operating fund balances. The occasional large project is financed from these sources and from grants and state loans. Procedures and formats used for budgeting for capital assets are the same as used for budgeting current outlays within the operating or annual budget process.

- **Level 2** Multiyear planning occurs for some types of capital spending (for example, equipment replacement, projects in particular functional areas such as utilities, or for specific projects). There is usually no jurisdiction-wide capital planning or financial forecasting. Capital financing comes from operating revenues and balances, earmarked revenues or reserves, and basic debt instruments. Special procedures and formats are used for budgeting for major capital projects or certain types of capital projects and acquisitions, but they take place within the general context of the operating or annual budget process.

- **Level 3** Capital budgeting practices reflect or approach the comprehensive model presented in this chapter. Multiyear and jurisdiction-wide capital planning and financial forecasting occur. Capital financing comes from a wide variety of pay-as-go sources and debt sources. Special budgeting procedures and formats are used for capital projects in a separate capital authorization and budget process.

- There is no multiyear capital planning and forecasting for the jurisdiction. If there is a large project, planning for it is project specific and done by a consulting engineer or architect.

- There is no separate capital budget or capital budgeting process. The procedures and formats used in the operating or annual budget for making and reviewing equipment and other capital asset requests are essentially the same as those for making and reviewing position, salary, and other operating items. When the jurisdiction must undertake and finance a major project, the consulting architect or engineer works with local officials to prepare the budget for it.

- Most spending for capital assets is budgeted and accounted for in the general fund or another operating fund. When a major capital project is undertaken, a separate capital project fund is created for it.

- Financing to meet most capital needs comes from the general fund and other operating fund revenues and balances. For the occasional major project, financing may come from grants or from debt issued through—and secured and subsidized by—a state bond bank, a revolving loan program, or a similar program that many states have created to finance infrastructure needs in small communities. A few local governments operating at this first level issue GO bonds or other basic debt to finance the occasional major project.

- Appropriations for capital spending are usually made in the annual or operating budget ordinance. Capital project ordinances that provide multiyear or project spending authority either are not legally available or, if they are available, are used for only the occasional major project.

Capital budgeting in **Sawmills, North Carolina,** closely approximates the Level 1 characteristics. Sawmills has no formal multiyear capital plan or financial forecast. The town's annual budget for 1999–2000 has a separate "FY99 Capital Improvement Expenditure Summary," but this summary is used for presentation purposes only and is not part of a separate capital budget.[4] There are no separate capital project or special revenue funds for capital spending; the capital expenditures listed in the summary are budgeted within the general fund or the utility fund. Projected capital spending for both funds totals $829,025 for 1999–2000: $74,300 for general fund capital spending and the rest for water-sewer capital projects and spending. Financing for all of these expenditures comes from annual revenues and from the accumulated balances of the two funds. Sawmills has no outstanding bonds or debt. Appropriations for capital spending are made in the town's 1999–2000 annual budget ordinance.[5]

Level 2

Capital budgeting practices at Level 2 are significantly more developed than they are at Level 1. Level 2 jurisdictions experience significant growth or have considerable infrastructure and fixed assets that must be replaced or maintained. Thus they face major needs for new capital projects and equipment as well as recurring requirements related to the replacement of equipment and the renovation of facilities and infrastructure. Level 2 jurisdictions may have a city or county manager or chief executive officer, a separate and professionally trained finance director, and planning staff. Some may have an in-house engineering capacity. Many of these local governments, however, do not have a separate budget officer or budget staff. Planning and budgeting fall to the manager and the finance director, both of whom have limited time for capital planning.

Level 2 capital budgeting tends to have the following characteristics:

- Some multiyear capital planning occurs, but it is usually for a specific function or service area—often utilities—or related to schedules for replacing equipment or renovating specific infrastructure (such as streets). There is no formal jurisdiction-wide, multiyear capital plan and financial forecast. Or, if such planning and forecasting do take place, the results are not included in the budget document that is presented to the governing board for review and approval.

- Special formats and procedures for requesting and reviewing major capital projects and acquisitions are used within the context of the operating or annual budget process. The operating or annual budget document is likely to have a special section that presents major capital projects and acquisitions that are up for approval and funding that year.

- Recurring capital expenditures to replace equipment or to replace or rehabilitate facilities and infrastructure may be budgeted and accounted for in the general fund, other operating funds, or one or more special revolving funds established specifically for such purposes. Expenditures for major capital projects—for example, the construction of a new law enforcement building—are budgeted and accounted for in one or more capital project funds.

- Financing for equipment replacement and other recurring capital needs comes from general fund or other operating fund revenues or balances, special revenues earmarked for this type of capital spending, or charges to departments that use the capital equipment and assets. Major capital projects or acquisitions are financed from operating fund balances, if available; grants; basic debt instruments, such as GO bonds for general government projects and revenue bonds for enterprise projects; general and special capital reserve funds; and lease- or installment-purchase agreements for equipment.

- Authorization and appropriation for recurring capital spending occur in the operating or annual budget ordinance. Appropriation of funds for major projects takes place in one or more project ordinances if legal authority exists to use such ordinances; otherwise, it takes place in the annual or operating budget ordinance or resolution.

Capital budgeting in **Grants Pass, Oregon,** resembles Level 2, according to the Adopted Operating/Capital Budget, Fiscal Year 1996–97.[6] This budget document includes no formal, multiyear CIP or financial forecast, neither does it indicate that such programming and forecasting occur. It presents a one-year capital budget. The general fund part of the capital budget specifies $2,513,465 for street projects and $2,288,106 for general land and building projects. Financing for these projects comes from a variety of sources, including special assessments, transfers from the general fund and the gas tax fund, state street grants, and fund balances.

The enterprise fund portions of the capital budget include $799,122 for water projects and $3,342,325 for wastewater projects. These projects are included in water and wastewater construction funds and are financed mostly with transfers from the water and wastewater operating funds. The capital budget also authorizes $4 million in new bonds for a major expansion of the city's wastewater treatment plant. Grants Pass has an equipment replacement fund from which it finances expensive equipment replacement; less expensive equipment replacement is financed from departmental capital outlay accounts in the general fund and the enterprise fund. Spending for the equipment replacement fund, operating capital outlay accounts, and one-year capital budget is appropriated in the annual budget.

Level 3

Level 3 capital budgeting, which resembles the comprehensive model presented earlier in the chapter, is found in jurisdictions that are experiencing substantial growth or have major replacement and rehabilitation needs for existing infrastructure, facilities, and equipment. They are likely to be large- or medium-size local governments that have the same administrative and professional staff resources as Level 2 entities with the addition of professional budget staff who prepare not only the operating budget but also the multiyear CIP and financial forecast. The planning capacity is stronger than in a Level 2 jurisdiction. The finance director or an analyst in the finance department has significant expertise in capital and debt financing and is able to use a variety of financing sources and to tailor financing to specific projects.

Level 3 capital budgeting tends to have the following characteristics:

- There is a jurisdiction-wide, multiyear CIP and usually an accompanying multiyear financial forecast. In small local governments, these multiyear plans may extend only three years or so into the future. In most medium-size jurisdictions, they extend five or six years, and some extend ten years. The multiyear plans are formal; they are included in the operating budget or in a separate document that is presented to the government board, which reviews and typically approves these plans. Besides the jurisdiction-wide CIP, there are often other long-term assessments of needs for particular services or types of projects, multiyear schedules for replacing equipment and rehabilitating facilities and infrastructure, and feasibility studies by consulting engineers or architects with significant contributions by staff planners and engineers for major projects. These other long-term planning activities typically feed into the jurisdiction-wide, multiyear CIP and financial forecast.

- The recommended capital budget for any year flows out of the CIP and is represented by the first year of the CIP. If the capital budget is based only on the CIP, it is likely to emphasize the larger, infrequently recurring capital projects and acquisitions. Some Level 3 capital budgets include not only such projects but also capital replacement and rehabilitation funds and even expensive departmental operating capital.

- Recurring capital expenditures for replacement equipment and the rehabilitation or renovation of facilities and infrastructure are usually budgeted and accounted for in the same types of funds that are used for such capital spending in Level 2 jurisdictions. Similarly, capital expenditures for major projects are typically budgeted and accounted for in capital project funds as in the Level 2 entities.

- A diversified set of capital financing sources is used in accordance with a capital financing strategy. Pay-as-go sources include not only operating fund revenues and balances and capital reserves, but also impact fees or capital recovery charges to new development, interlocal financing, and public sector–private sector partnerships. Debt sources include not only basic debt instruments, such as GO and revenue bonds, but also certificates of participation or obligation, special obligation debt for particular types of projects, and sometimes tax increment or economic development bonds.

- The authorization of projects and the appropriation of money for them are likely to take place in project ordinances that provide multiyear or project spending authority. Rather than use a single project ordinance for each project, a local government may use one or two comprehensive capital project ordinances that flow from the CIP and the recommended capital budget for any year. Such an ordinance appropriates money for multiple projects or acquisitions that are up for authorization and funding in a year.

San Clemente, California, uses a Level 3 capital budget process.[7] The Annual Budget & Capital Improvement Program, Fiscal Year 2000–2001 includes a CIP for 2001–2005 and an accompanying financial forecast for the same period. The city also has established various long-term master plans, which the city updates, to guide maintenance and development of infrastructure and facilities. Projects and acquisitions in the first year of the CIP become the recommended capital improvement budget for that year, and the larger projects and acquisitions are budgeted and accounted for in six capital project funds. Financing for the projects is derived mainly from impact fees, including charges to new development for major road projects, beach parking, public safety facilities and equipment, and a civic center. Capital financing also comes from water, sewer, and golf depreciation reserves; other special enterprise funds; and fleet and capital equipment replacement reserves. Although the city makes limited use of bonds or other debt financing, its reliance on a wide variety of pay-as-go sources is consistent with Level 3 capital budgeting. Appropriations for capital projects occur when the city council adopts a resolution approving the first year of the CIP.

Hickory, North Carolina, has a capital budgeting process that closely matches Level 3 capital budgeting and the comprehensive model for it.[8] Hickory has a five-year CIP and a five-year financial forecast that supports both the CIP and the annual budget. Many of the projects in the CIP come forward from the city's long-range master and functional plans. The functional plans include a ten-year library plan, a five-year water/sewer extension plan, a comprehensive downtown development plan, a business/industrial master plan, a drainage policy and master plan, a twenty-year sidewalk master plan, and a ten-year parks and recreation plan. The capital projects and acquisitions in the first year of the CIP become the city's recommended capital budget for the year. The major projects or acquisitions are budgeted and accounted for in capital project funds. Various capital financing sources are used, including GO bonds for street and water-sewer projects; state revolving loans for water projects; installment-purchase financing for public safety facilities, library buildings, and police, fire, sanitation, streets, and water-sewer equipment; intergovernmental agreements for street and road projects; and capital reserves for parking facilities and right-of-way acquisitions. Finally, Hickory appropriates money for major capital projects and acquisitions in capital project ordinances.

Concluding note on capital budgeting levels

The analysis here has clustered certain planning, budgeting, accounting, and financing procedures to form each level of capital budgeting practiced by local governments. Each level also reflects capital needs and the availability of staff resources to plan and budget for those needs. Categorizing capital budgeting in three levels is useful because it underscores that practices vary in complexity and sophistication among different local governments and that not all jurisdictions use the comprehensive model of capital budgeting presented in the chapter. Indeed, probably only a small portion of medium- and small-size cities and counties in the nation use the comprehensive model.

Many jurisdictions mix formats and practices from two of the levels of capital budgeting described here. For instance, a small local government that faces limited capital needs and that follows a capital budgeting process similar to Level 2 may have a multiyear CIP. Also, a local government may use most but not all of the practices represented by a particular level of capital budgeting. A medium-size city such as San Clemente, California, may have a CIP (a Level 3 characteristic) but choose to appropriate money for projects in its annual or operating budget (a characteristic of Levels 2 and 3) rather than use project ordinances.

Notes

1 Robert L. Bland and Irene S. Rubin, *Budgeting: A Guide for Local Governments* (Washington, D.C.: ICMA, 1997), chapter 7; Patricia Tigue, *Capital Improvement Programming: A Guide for Smaller Governments* (Chicago: GFOA, 1996); and A. John Vogt, "Budgeting for Capital Outlays and Improvements," in *Budgeting: Formulation and Execution,* ed. Jack Rabin, W. Bartley Hildreth, and J. Miller (Athens, Ga.: Carl Vinson Institute of Government, University of Georgia, 1996), 276–291. This third item is an adaptation of an earlier publication by the author. GFOA is publishing a series of monographs entitled *Putting Recommended Budget Practices into Action.* These monographs address aspects of capital budgeting: *Priority Setting Models for Public Budgeting* (Chicago: GFOA, 2001), and *Benchmarking and Measuring Debt Capacity* (Chicago: GFOA, 2000).

2 IRS criteria for distinguishing between "conditional sales" (installment purchase) and "true" leases are set forth in Rev. Rule 55-540, 1955-2 C.B. 39, 1955 WL 10043 1955. Despite its age, it is still in effect, except to the extent that it has been modified by 2 Revenue Procedure 2001-19 I.R.B. 1156, 2001 WL 471300 (IRS RPR, May 7, 2001). Accounting principles for distinguishing between "capital" (installment purchase) leases and "operating" leases are set forth in GASB, *Statement No. 13* (1990); and National Council on Governmental Accounting, *Statement No. 5* (1982). Summaries of the principles presented in these statements appear in Governmental Accounting Standards Board, Original Pronouncements, *Governmental Accounting and Financial Reporting Standards: Statement 34 Edition* (Norwalk, Conn.: GASB, 2001), 99–105 and 551–560.

3 GASB, *Statement 34: Basic Financial Statements—and Management's Discussion and Analysis—for State and Local Governments* (Norwalk, Conn.: GASB, 1999), paragraphs 18–29.

4 Town of Sawmills, North Carolina, Annual Budget, Fiscal Year, 1999–2000, various pages. Sawmills has a town manager and another official who is finance director. The town's annual budget document has earned the GFOA's Distinguished Budget Presentation Award.

5 Sawmills, like all other North Carolina cities and counties, is authorized by state law to use capital project ordinances to appropriate money for capital projects or assets. See General Statute 159-13.2.

6 Adopted Operating/Capital Budget, Fiscal Year, 1996–1997, City of Grants Pass, Oregon, xiv–xv, and schedules for capital improvement projects, water projects, wastewater projects, and equipment replacement.

7 City of San Clemente, California, Annual Budget & Capital Improvement Program, Fiscal Year 2000–2001, 47-91, 93-98, 99-100, 251-258, 261-292, and 315-382.

8 Hickory, North Carolina, Annual Budget 2001-2002, Recommended Budget, sections on "City Council Goals and Financial Policies," "Capital Improvement/Grants Projects," "Capital Reserve Fund," and "Five-Year Financial Forecast".

3 Capital improvement programming

A capital improvement program (CIP) is the primary tool that local governments use to plan for major capital projects and acquisitions. It identifies major capital needs over a multiyear forecast period. This chapter

- Defines a CIP, using two forms that illustrate its basic structure and references to local government practices
- Presents examples of CIP forms and supporting information that medium- and small-size local governments incorporate in their CIP documents
- Discusses the purposes served by a CIP
- Examines issues in CIP preparation and approval, including coordination of the process, step-by-step implementation, involvement, the relation of the CIP to other long-term planning, and other issues
- Presents CIP to the local governing board and community.

The capital improvement program

A CIP is a forecast over a period, most commonly five or six years, of needs for major capital projects and acquisitions; appropriations or expenditures to be incurred for the projects and acquisitions; sources of financing for the projects and acquisitions; and the impact of the projects and acquisitions on future operating or annual budgets.

A CIP is essentially a long-term plan. Projects and acquisitions in the first year of the CIP forecast period become the capital budget for that year. The CIP planning process is usually repeated annually. Most capital project or acquisition requests initially enter the CIP in one of the later planning years (that is, the fifth or sixth year) of the forecast period.

Two prototype formats for presenting a CIP

Local governments use two basic forms to present capital project and acquisition needs in the CIP.

- **Jurisdiction-wide summary form**   This form (Exhibit 3–1) shows capital project and acquisition costs for various years by function, financing sources, and impact on the operating or annual budget. The "Prior years" and "Current year" columns are for projects in process. Such projects were approved in a prior year's CIP, and costs for them were incurred in past years or are being incurred in the current year. Additional costs are budgeted for or planned during the forecast period, which covers the upcoming budget year and five planning years. These years include costs for projects in process and projects getting under way sometime during the forecast period. The column "Years beyond year 6" is for projects that get under way in the CIP forecast period, probably in one of the later planning years, but for which costs will continue beyond year 6. Some CIP summary forms do not have prior years or current year columns; they show only projects that will be undertaken or costs that will be incurred in the budget year or one or more of the planning years.

Besides project spending by function, the CIP summary form shows the financing sources used to support the spending. The amount of financing for any year should equal spending for the year. The impact, if any, of capital projects and acquisitions on the operating budget will begin as they are completed and then continue.

There are, of course, other types of jurisdiction-wide CIP summary forms besides the one shown in Exhibit 3–1. In addition to financing sources and impact on the operating budget, a summary form can show capital spending by fund, by project, by fund and project, or in some way other than by function.[1] Many small local governments use a jurisdiction-wide CIP summary that lists all projects and shows spending for each one[2] (Exhibit 3–4 on page 44 is arranged this way). Some CIP summary forms do not show the impact of capital projects on the operating budget but instead present such data on a separate schedule or summarize the impact in narrative form.

- **Project detail form**   This form (Exhibit 3–2) can be used to present spending, financing, operating budget impact, and other relevant information for a specific project. It includes

  Identifying information such as project title, account number, requesting agency, fund, and type

  Spending broken down by line-item category for the years covered by the CIP

  Applicable financing sources and operating budget impact by year

  Project description

  Project priority

  Project's relationship to other projects

  Comments on the financing source(s) and operating budget impact

  Stage of implementation.

For a large project, this form may extend to two pages, with identifying and financial data provided on the first page and narrative information on the second. While the form in Exhibit 3–1 summarizes the CIP for the entire jurisdiction, the form in Exhibit 3–2 is used to summarize relevant facts

Exhibit 3–1
CIP Summary Form:
A Prototype

Item	Prior years	Current year	Year 1 budget	Forecast period Year 2 plan	Year 3 plan	Year 4 plan	Year 5 plan	Year 6 plan	Years beyond year 6	Totals
Project and acquisition expenditures by function										
Public safety										
Street and transportation										
Recreation and culture										
Community development										
Economic development										
Water/wastewater										
Stormwater										
Information technology										
General government										
Total project expenditures										
Financing sources										
Operating revenues: general										
Operating revenues: enterprise										
Special or earmarked revenues										
Capital reserves										
Equipment/vehicle replacement fund										
Lease/ installments purchases										
Bonds proceeds: general obligation										
Bond proceeds: revenue										
Bond proceeds: other										
Certification of participation										
Special assessments										
Development fees/contributions										
Grants/intergovernmental revenue										
Total financing sources										
Impact on operating budget:										
Debt service: bonds & COPs										
Lease/installment purchase payments										
Increased operating costs										
Decreased operating costs										
Additional revenues										
Other										
Total operating impact										

Exhibit 3-2
CIP Project Detail Form:
A Prototype

Project title:	Project acount number:		Requesting agency:	Fund:				Type of project or acquisition: Replacement: Renovation: Expansion: New:		
	Prior years	Current year	Forecast Period							Project totals
			Year 1 budget	Year 2 plan	Year 3 plan	Year 4 plan	Year 5 plan	Year 6 plan	Years beyond year 6	
Project spending by category										
Planning and design										
Land and land preparation										
Construction: contracted										
Construction: local unit workforce										
Equipment/furnishings										
Other (legal, etc.); specify										
Contingency										
Total Project Expenditures										
Financing sources The sources used for the project would be listed here, using financing categories from Exhibit 3-1.										
Total Project Financing										
Impact on operating budget The impact categories applicable to the project from Exhibit 3-1 would be listed here										
Total Operating Impact										

Project description/justification:

Project priority:
Meets legal mandate(s):
Removes/reduces hazard:
Consistent with board goals:
Promotes development:
Improves efficiency:
Financing source(s):

Project implementation:
Feasibility study:
Plans/design:
Land:
Construction:
Equipment:

Operating budget impact:

Relation to other projects:

about a project. Both forms are presented with a jurisdiction's CIP document. In most cases, the requesting agency is likely to include additional information with the project request to explain and justify what it wants.

The defining characteristics of a CIP

A CIP covers several years, focuses on major projects, forecasts appropriations or expenditures, identifies capital financing sources, and shows the impact on future operating budgets. It plans for the forecast period and budgets for the upcoming year, it recurs and is updated annually, and it introduces projects in later years of the forecast period. Most projects show up initially in the CIP as entries in one of the later years of the CIP forecast period.

Covers a multiyear period   The most common forecast period used in local government CIPs is five or six years (the budget year and four or five planning years). This period enables officials to realistically foresee emerging capital needs and estimate project costs, and it allows them enough time to plan projects and arrange financing. A shorter forecast period may not allow enough time for planning and arranging financing for major projects or for identifying and accommodating the relationships between projects. A period much longer than five or six years addresses a distant future that is difficult to predict and thus must involve significant guesswork and generalities.

Although five or six years is the norm, some medium- and small-size local governments find it convenient to work with a three- or four-year CIP. For example, Hillsborough, North Carolina, has an effective three-year CIP.[3] Cities or towns that are preparing a CIP for the first time have found it useful to start with a three- or four-year CIP. On the other hand, some local governments have CIPs with forecast periods that extend beyond five or six years. For example, Campbell, California, has a seven-year CIP,[4] and Raleigh, North Carolina, uses a ten-year CIP forecast period divided into two five-year phases: phase 1 includes detailed cost schedules and phase 2 presents aggregate estimates.[5] Reno, Nevada, uses a twenty-year CIP forecast period! Like Raleigh, Reno divides the full period into five-year phases or blocks. While year-by-year and detailed project and cost data are presented for the first five years, aggregate data are presented for each of the three successive five-year blocks.[6]

Mecklenburg County, North Carolina, takes still another approach. It uses a ten-year capital needs assessment that includes a three-year CIP. The CIP presents detailed project, cost, and financing data and specific project recommendations that are approved by the county commissioners; the needs assessment, as the name suggests, identifies future projects without providing detailed cost and financing data.[7]

Includes major capital projects and acquisitions   Usually the CIP focuses on large and expensive capital projects and acquisitions with long useful lives. Expenditures for these projects occur infrequently, require multiyear planning, and present challenges for the operating or annual budget. The CIPs of many medium- and small-size cities and counties also include recurring expenditures for the rehabilitation or replacement of infrastructure, facilities, and major equipment. Such spending is often financed with annually recurring revenues that are earmarked for this purpose.

Table 1–1 pointed out that local governments may use a dollar cutoff and sometimes a useful-life cutoff to determine which capital projects and acquisitions to include in the CIP. These cutoffs vary depending on the size of the local government. Towns with just a few thousand people may use a dollar cutoff of only $1,000, while cities or counties with 100,000 or more people may use a cutoff of $100,000 or more. Although most local governments include expensive equipment acquisitions as well as infrastructure and facility projects in their CIPs, some large jurisdictions restrict the CIP to infrastructure, land, buildings, and other improvements to real property.

Forecasts appropriations or expenditures Appropriations make revenues or the proceeds of capital financing sources available to spend on projects. They often also authorize or approve projects. Expenditures are payments made pursuant to appropriations. For many CIP projects and acquisitions, appropriations and expenditures occur in the same year. For others, however, the appropriations and expenditures occur in different years of the CIP forecast period. For example, the appropriation for a project may occur in one year, with only a portion of the spending for it occurring in that year and the rest spread over the next two years while construction is completed.

When project appropriation and spending occur in different years, officials must decide whether the CIP should allocate project costs by year according to when the appropriation is made or when the spending occurs. In the example just cited, an appropriation-based allocation for the CIP would show all costs in one year, and an expenditure-based allocation would spread the costs out over three years.

Most CIPs allocate project costs by year according to when spending occurs. For example, the 2001–2005 CIP of Norman, Oklahoma, presents an expenditure schedule for each project.[8] But the CIP of Madison Heights, Michigan, allocates costs by year according to when appropriations are made. The "Planning Overview" for the Madison Heights 2003–2007 CIP refers to "scheduled appropriations by year."[9] Winston-Salem, North Carolina, switched from an expenditure-based to an appropriation-based CIP several years ago to focus officials' attention more on decision making and less on project monitoring.[10]

Forecasts sources of financing **Capital financing** refers to the revenues, debt proceeds, and other financing sources that are raised to pay project costs. (Chapters 6 and 7 address local government capital financing sources in depth.)

The financing sources for the 2001–2005 CIP of **Maplewood, Minnesota**, total $15,476,135 and illustrate the kinds of sources that are available for capital financing purposes in many medium- and small-size local governments:

- Bonds and notes, including five-year capital notes for equipment acquisition (none shown in funding schedule for 2001–2005), general obligation (GO) bonds for projects that are repaid from general revenues ($2,980,000), and special assessment bonds that are repaid from charges to property that benefit from city improvements ($2,840,000)
- Capital improvement projects fund ($2,521,655) from annual property tax levies

- County participation, the county share ($119,240) of city projects such as roads
- State aid ($4,554,240) for street construction projects
- Park development fund ($800,000) from park availability charges levied against new development (revenue from the charges may be used only in the neighborhoods in which the charges are levied)
- Sewer fund ($250,000) for sanitary sewer projects
- Vehicle and equipment replacement fund ($761,000) from depreciation of city vehicles and equipment or rental charges to departments that use city vehicles and equipment
- Fire truck replacement funds ($650,000).[11]

Of course, each local government has its own financing sources for CIP projects, and specific sources vary from state to state and among localities in the same state. Variations depend on legal provisions and restrictions as well as on differing philosophies and customs regarding borrowing and capital financing.

Forecasts operating budget impact   The impact of CIP projects and acquisitions on present and future operating budgets can be significant. Some projects can add recurring expenditures and new positions, possibly creating the need to increase taxes or raise other revenues to offset the new operating expenditures. Others can result in significant savings in future operating budgets.

The impact of capital projects and acquisitions on the operating budget is too often overlooked or underestimated because it occurs several years out and is difficult to estimate. Sometimes officials downplay the impact because highlighting it could work against securing approval and funding for a project.

Despite the difficulties and risks, the CIP should estimate, or at least discuss, the impact of projects and acquisitions on the operating budget. This impact can include one or more of the following:

- **Annual debt service on bonds or other debt issued to finance CIP projects**   Debt service for a large general project can add substantial new costs to the operating budget. If debt service for projects built in the past is declining, debt for new CIP projects may be serviceable without a tax rate increase.

- **Lease- or installment-purchase payments**   Many local governments acquire equipment and other property through capital leases. The resulting annual payments have to be paid from future budgets.

- **New positions and additional program or operating expenses**   These are likely to result from new or enlarged facilities.

- **Savings in maintenance and operating expenditures**   Savings can result from projects to renovate or rehabilitate old, high-maintenance infrastructure and facilities, thereby reducing ongoing maintenance expenditures. Energy-saving, or green, building projects can also produce savings in future operating budgets.

- **Additional annual revenues**   New programs run in new facilities may produce new revenues from user charges. Or new city infrastructure, such as a new street, may result in private sector development that adds to the tax base and property tax revenues.

- **Reduced annual revenues**   A CIP project may be built on a site that was previously owned privately and produced property tax revenue.

If it is difficult to specify the operational budget impact of particular capital projects, the local government can at least acknowledge in the CIP that such projects will probably affect future operating budgets and can perhaps comment on the range of possible effects.

Exhibit 3–3 shows how **Forsyth County, North Carolina,** conveys the operating budget impact of projects in its 2003–2008 CIP.[12] The "additional related operating outlays" in Exhibit 3–3 are mostly lease- and installment-purchase payments. The dollar impact shown in any year is cumulative over the CIP period rather than incremental. That is, the amount for an item in a year includes the amount shown in prior years for the item.

Exhibit 3–3
Impact on future annual operating budgets of the general fund, 2003–2008 CIP, Forsyth County, North Carolina (dollars, in millions)

Item	FY 2003	FY 2004	FY 2005	FY 2006	FY 2007	FY 2008
Additional debt service	0	410,989	2,657,241	2,657,241	3,149,133	2,955,598
Additional current outlays	250,000	475,000	500,000	475,000	500,000	325,000
Additional related operating outlays	0	0	189,000	189,000	189,000	463,560
Offsetting general fund revenues	0	0	236,282	236,282	236,282	373,562
Net CIP impact on general fund	250,000	885,989	3,109,959	3,084,959	3,601,851	3,370,596

The 2002–2006 CIP of **Fayetteville, Arkansas,** does not include a schedule like the one shown for Forsyth County.[13] Instead, it discusses the "minor impact on operational budgets" and says, "Most of the projects planned over the next five years replace high-maintenance water lines, sewer lines, and street segments." Three specific impacts of the operating budget are then identified:

• New acquisitions from the vehicle and equipment replacement fund will add $150,000 annually in monthly replacement and maintenance charges to departmental budgets

• The in-house pavement improvement program will reduce street renovation and maintenance costs by more than $100,000 annually

• The traffic signal replacement program will save the city $42,000 in utility costs annually.

Plans for full forecast period and budgets for upcoming year Many local governments recognize the essential nature of the CIP as a planning tool. Greeley, Colorado, describes its 2001–2005 CIP as "a five year plan for the evaluation of the City's facility and infrastructure needs."[14] A similar statement appears in the 2001–2005 CIP for Largo, Florida: "The CIP neither appropriates funds nor authorizes projects; it is a five year planning document for significant capital projects."[15]

When the concept of a CIP is first explained to them or when they are asked to approve a recommended CIP, some local governing board members may balk at the idea of approving a multiyear capital plan that extends five or six years into the future. They may fear their approval would commit them to all projects and acquisitions shown in the plan. While board approval of the CIP can mean board authorization and funding of capital projects in the first year, projects and acquisitions shown in later years of the CIP forecast period are subject to change and approval later on, in CIPs and capital budgets for subsequent years. Of course, costs for projects approved in the budget year or coming forward from the current year or prior years are likely to be firm figures, and board approval of the CIP implies continued commitment to these projects and costs.

Board approval of the CIP typically occurs with a general resolution that indicates that the board accepts the CIP and recognizes that the CIP represents the general direction the local government plans to take in meeting future capital needs.

In Greensboro, North Carolina, the resolution states:

Now, therefore, be it resolved by the City Council of the City of Greensboro:

That the City Council recognizes the capital improvements programming process as the translation of community goals and objectives into needed physical facilities which are essential to residential, business, and institutional and leisure activities, and

That the City Council does hereby adopt the report entitled "Capital Improvements Program FY 2001–2007."[16]

The resolution then lists CIP spending by general functional area and financing by source. Note that the Greensboro city council adopts the CIP report only; it is not approving any proposed projects or spending in the

CIP itself. Such approval is done separately in project ordinances adopted each year for projects coming out of the CIP.

While the full CIP is essentially a plan, the capital projects, acquisitions, and costs in the first year become the proposed capital budget for that year; then, after governing board review and approval, they become the adopted capital budget for the year.

Recognition of project and acquisition costs in the first year as budgeted amounts and of those costs in subsequent years as planned figures occurs in the 2000–2004 CIP of **Loveland, Colorado:** "All projects included in the first year of the Capital Plan are funded in the 2000 proposed budget. Projects included in the 'out-years' (2001–2004) will be approved by Council in concept only."[17]

Governing board authorization and appropriation of money for capital projects and spending in the first year of the CIP can occur in several different ways. The three most common are (1) transfer of the first-year CIP projects and spending to the operating budget with authorization and appropriation occurring there; (2) authorization and appropriation in one or more separate capital project ordinances approved by the governing board; and (3) inclusion of one or more special provisions authorizing and appropriating money for first-year projects and spending in the resolution used by the board to approve the CIP.

The city council of **Greeley, Colorado,** approves capital projects and spending in the first year of that city's CIP by including them, along with operating budget requirements, in the appropriation ordinance approved by the council for each fiscal year.[18] On the other hand, the city council of **Cary, North Carolina,** approves capital projects and spending in the first year of its combined capital budget and CIP by including them in separate capital project ordinances approved by the city council.[19]

Recurs and is updated annually The CIP is conceived as an annual process, and most local governments repeat the process and update the CIP each year. This provides an opportunity to revise planned projects included in the CIP in a prior year in light of recent developments and to add new projects and spending as needed.

The purposes served by annual repetition of the CIP are apparent in the following statement taken from the 2001–2005 **Greeley, Colorado,** CIP:

While the program serves as a long-range plan, it is reviewed annually and revised based on current circumstances and opportunities. Priorities may be changed due to grant opportunities or circumstances that caused a more rapid deterioration of an asset resulting in a liability issue. Projects may be revised for significant costing variances.[20]

In a few communities, the CIP may be a one-time event. A local government without a CIP may prepare one in anticipation of a proposed bond issue or unusually large capital needs. The CIP gives local officials a basis for taking the proposed bond issue to the voters or for planning an unusually large project; however, because of limited staff resources or limited capital needs, the officials may decide not to prepare a CIP in subsequent years. While a one-time CIP for a bond issue or to meet unusually large capital needs is better than no CIP at all, annual repetition of the CIP process is customary and enables a local unit to take much fuller advantage of the planning opportunities a CIP offers.

Introduces projects in the later years of the forecast period   To take advantage of the multiyear nature of the CIP, local governments should anticipate most new capital project and acquisition requests before the time of need and introduce them initially into the CIP in one of the later planning years (years 4, 5, or 6 in Exhibit 3–1). Then, as the CIP process is repeated annually and the standing requests are reviewed, those that pass muster move up a year or more toward approval and funding, and marginal requests are weeded out. When the requests that survive reach the budget year, they are approved and funding arrangements are made for them. This whole process gives officials several years to look at requests before they must decide to approve them and commit funding.

Of course, not all capital needs can be foreseen years in advance. Some must be approved and funded almost immediately after the need for them becomes apparent. If this happens with too many projects, however, the CIP loses much of its value as a planning tool.

What does it take for local officials to look ahead, forecast needs, and make most of their capital project and acquisition requests in one of the later planning years of the CIP forecast period? Identifying needs down the road requires time and a disposition to take a broad and long view of needs. It also requires—or is greatly facilitated by—a team orientation that encourages officials from different departments to work together. Without a certain level of trust, the fire chief, for example, may be reluctant to put many of the fire department's capital requests into the later planning years for fear that the police chief will place most police department requests in the early planning years, resulting in the funding of many more police requests than fire department requests.

The allocation of projects and costs by year in the CIP forecast period can indicate the extent to which local officials are anticipating future capital needs and taking advantage of the planning opportunities afforded by the CIP. Front loading capital project amounts into the first few years of the CIP period may indicate inadequate forecasting and planning. On the other hand, if project costs are distributed more or less evenly by year or if more costs are found in the later planning years, this could indicate a more prudent, long-term orientation by the jurisdiction. Avon, Connecticut, has a well-balanced distribution of costs by year in its 2001–2005 CIP[21]:

FY 2001	$1,445,380
FY 2002	$4,839,437
FY 2003	$5,852,588
FY 2004	$6,463,887
FY 2005	$1,326,787

Of course, a concentration of capital spending in the first few years of a CIP may not indicate inadequate planning. It may simply reflect the greater capital needs in the earlier years of the forecast period or the availability of a major funding source that will not be available later. The substantial needs in the early years of the current CIP may have initially entered the CIP years ago.

CIP forms used by local governments

This section presents examples of forms and information found in the CIP documents of selected medium- and small-size cities and counties. In some cases, materials are reproduced. In others, abbreviated versions or outlines are used. The forms and materials presented here relate to

- Manager's message
- Introduction
- Summary forms
- CIP budget-year appropriations or spending
- Project detail forms
- Project request information
- Financial analysis and schedules.

Manager's message

The city or county manager, administrative officer, or chair of the committee responsible for preparing the jurisdiction's CIP usually writes a message that provides an overview of the CIP and highlights its important recommendations. The message is typically in the form of a transmittal letter addressed to the governing board. If the manager presents the CIP in a document that is separate from the operating budget, the message usually opens the CIP. If the CIP is presented as a section within the operating budget, the CIP message may open that section or become part of the operating budget message for the year. In either case, the comments about the CIP are likely to emphasize the capital project recommendations for the first year of the CIP forecast period. In some instances where the CIP is presented as a section within the operating budget, there is no identifiable CIP message; rather, major recommendations are incorporated into the introduction to the CIP section.

Two illustrations of the manager's messages or manager's recommendations are presented here. The first is a message introducing the 2003–2007 CIP of Alamance County, North Carolina (Exhibit 3–4).[22] Although this CIP is presented as a section of the county's annual operating budget, it stands on its own and would serve as a good message for a separately presented CIP. The manager's CIP message for Alamance County covers four main areas:

- **Overview of projects and their costs by major area**   School system, community college, county facilities, and economic development
- **Revenues and funding sources**   Federal and state funds, grant funds, county financing or debt proceeds, the public school capital building fund (state bond proceeds available for local school construction), and county funds including capital reserves
- **Impact of the CIP on the county's operating budget**   Includes new debt service and property tax rate increases that could be needed to fund increases in the operating budget resulting from the CIP
- **Project highlights of the CIP.**

Exhibit 3–4

Manager's Message,
Alamance County,
North Carolina

Alamance County
Capital Improvement Plan
FY2003 - 2007

CAPITAL IMPROVEMENT PLAN

May 20, 2002

Board of Commissioners
Alamance County
North Carolina

Gentlemen,

I respectfully submit to you the proposed Capital Improvement Plan (CIP) for Alamance County for fiscal years 2003 through 2007. The CIP includes projects with a total estimated cost of $26,387,488, a decrease of approximately $7.4 million from the current year. The projects are divided into four main groups – Alamance-Burlington School System projects, Alamance Community College projects, County Facilities projects, and Economic Development projects. There are a total of seventeen (17) different projects identified in the CIP, the same as last year. The only two changes in the projects included in the plan is the elimination of the ACC Phase III project as it is now underway, and the addition of the Burlington Animal Shelter Improvement project. This plan should address most of the County's capital improvement needs in the immediate future. The only major capital project pending to be included will involve school facilities. Currently, the County and the school system have appointed a committee, the Joint Facilities Oversight Committee, to develop recommendations for a major capital plan for the school system. The findings of this committee will be available later this year and will be incorporated into next year's capital improvement plan.

As mentioned earlier, the CIP has divided the seventeen projects into four major groupings. The table and chart below show the division of total costs between these major areas.

Table 1 - Project Cost Summary By Major Area

Project Area	Cost of Projects
Alamance-Burlington School System	$ 13,068,467
Alamance Community College	203,021
County Facilities	12,116,000
Economic Development	1,000,000
Total	$ 26,387,488

Exhibit 3–4
(continued)

Project Areas

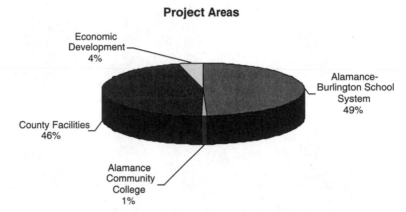

Economic
Development
4%

Alamance-
Burlington School
System
49%

County Facilities
46%

Alamance
Community
College
1%

Revenue and funding sources are varied and are provided from all levels of government – federal, state and local. The table and chart below shows a summary of revenue and funding sources for the CIP projects.

Table 2 - CIP Revenue/Funding Sources Summary

Revenue/Funding Source	Amount
Federal Funds$	800,000
State Funds	617,448
Grant Funds	500,000
Financing Proceeds	10,000,000
Public School Capital Bldg Fund	5,341,555
County Funds	9,128,485
TOTAL$	26,387,488

Exhibit 3–4
(continued)

CIP Funding Sources

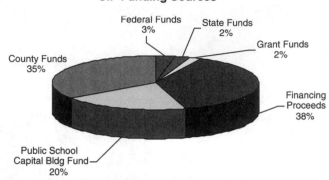

Federal Funds
3%

State Funds
2%

Grant Funds
2%

County Funds
35%

Financing
Proceeds
38%

Public School
Capital Bldg Fund
20%

As you can see, about three-quarters of the funding (73%) for these projects will come from County financing and County funds. The proposed CIP also relies heavily on funds available through the State Public School Building Capital Fund as requested by the Alamance-Burlington Board of Education.

In developing the schedule of financing sources for the CIP, County staff had to analyze the impact on the County's General Fund. Large increases in spending that impact the General Fund will likely translate into property tax increases. The source of increases in spending that impact the General Fund will be in the form of additional debt service requirements. The CIP as presented will add approximately $1.3 million in annual debt service payments during the next five years. Based on current trends, it seems unlikely that the County could assume this much additional debt service without a property tax increase.

Some highlights of the proposed Capital Improvement Plan include:

> Proposed funding for the third year of the Alamance-Burlington School System 5-Year Capital Improvement Plan.

> Plans for a jail expansion are still included in the amount of $9.3 Million. The County has already incurred about $300,000 in design costs and another $210,000 is included as part of the proposed budget. These funds have come from annual appropriations, so the amount to be financed has shrunk to only $9.0 Million based on current estimates.

> The Alamance-Burlington Airport Authority has prepared and submitted to the County a Five-Year Capital Improvement Plan for their facilities. This has been included in the County Facilities portion of the CIP and the amounts reflect the full amount requested by the Airport Authority for local funds. Should the County move forward with funding the requests, it is likely this amount could be reduced through partnerships with other local government agencies.

> The City of Burlington has proposed to embark on a project to increase the size of the animal shelter and create a pet adoption facility within the shelter. They have requested the County participate in the project in the amount of $250,000. The County Board is considering the request, but has taken no position yet.

> Several projects that are part of the County Facilities portion have been delayed at least one year due to projected funding shortfalls for FY2002-2003.

In addition to the above notes and the projects included in the plan, the County is exploring the need for a new EMS Medic Unit Base, the construction of a new cell at the Landfill, and the construction of new library facilities in the Mebane area of the county. Because all of these projects are in very early stages of development, no estimated costs have been developed. Therefore, they are not yet included in the CIP.

Exhibit 3–4
(continued)

The development of the CIP is only one step in the maintenance and development of county facilities and infrastructure. The CIP provides a guide for decision-makers and citizens. The development of a robust CIP permits full examination of alternatives and funding options during a longer time frame. This should lead to better quality decisions and the maximizing of County resources.

Once the plan is prepared or updated (on an annual basis in Alamance County), it is presented to the Commissioners for their approval. After the CIP is approved, staff will attempt to include funding in the appropriate fiscal year to proceed with the project. If funds are appropriated in an annual budget, the Commissioners (usually in the form of approving bids or a major purchase) still must approve the actual projects themselves. Thus, the CIP is only one of many steps toward the completion of a project. The system is designed to have several checkpoints requiring review and approval by top-level decision-makers.

To summarize, the CIP represents a $26 million plan to address the capital improvement needs of Alamance County. At the present time, no projects have received an appropriation that would require a tax increase. However, many projects that are included could cause a tax increase to occur if the Commissioners decide to pursue the project. As users review the tables included in the CIP, they may want to focus on the "Operating Costs" and "Debt Service" lines included in cash flow projections. These two lines will translate into additional annual appropriations and most likely a tax increase. The table below shows some initial projections of tax rate increases that would be needed to fund projects currently in the CIP.

	FY2005	FY2006	FY2007
Operating Costs	$ 1,127,935	$ 1,179,976	$ 1,234,488
Debt Service Payments	1,329,231	1,329,231	1,329,231
Total Estimated Appropriation	$ 2,457,166	$ 2,509,207	$ 2,563,719
Estimated Pennies on the Tax Rate	2.75	2.80	2.85

I believe the CIP as presented is a solid proposal and I recommend its adoption by the Board. As I conclude, I would like to thank the Board members for their support and assistance in developing the CIP. We look forward to continuing to serve the citizens of Alamance County.

Sincerely,

David S. Cheek
County Manager

Jeffrey G. Causey
Assistant County Manager

San Clemente, California, takes another approach. San Clemente's 2001–2005 CIP is set up to be a section within its annual budget document. A general introduction rather than a manager's message opens that section. The city manager's annual budget transmittal letter, which is about twenty pages long, includes a summary of the city's CIP and project spending proposed for the 2000–2001 budget year. A graph is included that shows the city's budget for CIP projects over the past ten years, and capital improvement projects in several city areas are discussed, including downtown revitalization, a business park, a shopping center, and a coastal district.[23]

Introduction

The introduction to a CIP, whether the CIP is presented as a separate document or included in the operating budget, typically explains the purposes served by capital improvement program and provides an overview of the process. As noted, in cases where there is no separate CIP message, the introduction usually summarizes and highlights CIP recommendations.

Greeley, Colorado, presents its CIP within the city's annual budget and opens the CIP section with a four-page introduction addressing the following questions:

- What is a CIP project?
- What is a CIP?
- What are the objectives of a CIP? Ten objectives are listed.
- What are the changes in the CIP development process? Ten changes are identified, including project definition, project cost estimation, and how capital improvements are prioritized in the CIP process.
- How is citizen input incorporated in the CIP development process?

- How does the CIP impact the operating budget? Its general impact is discussed, not specific impacts or projects.
- How is CIP formulated? The calendar for CIP preparation is summarized, and the officials involved in the process are identified.
- What are the funding sources? The main sources are enterprise revenues and a 3 percent sales tax on food.
- What issues must the CIP address in the future? The cost of capital needs far exceeds funding sources; new revenue sources will have to be identified and used.[24]

Summary forms

Exhibit 3–1 presented a prototype summary form that could be included in a CIP document. This section presents three summary forms actually used by local governments. One shows how a small town summarizes its CIP, and the second and third show how local governments summarize particular types of capital spending in their CIPs. These examples illustrate the variation in practice among local governments in CIP summary presentations.

To provide an overview of its 2002–2004 CIP, Hillsborough, North Carolina, used a three-part summary: CIP revenues by source and capital spending by department and fund; budgeted and planned spending by project or item for the general fund; and budgeted and planned spending for the water fund (see Exhibit 3–5).[25]

The CIPs of many medium- and small-size local governments include special CIP summary forms that schedule future acquisitions and replacements of equipment. The summary form included in the 2003–2007 CIP of

**Exhibit 3–5
Summary of CIP;
Hillsborough,
North Carolina**

CIP REVENUES BY SOURCE

	FY02 BUDGET	FY03 PLANNED	FY04 PLANNED	TOTAL REVENUES	% of CIP REVENUES
General Fund - Operating Revenues	399,100	161,000	271,100	831,200	14.4%
General Fund - Lease-Purchase/Bond Financing	0	0	0	0	0.0%
Powell Bill Funds (NC State Street Funds)	102,000	75,000	80,000	257,000	4.4%
Water Fund - Operating Revenues	253,900	389,500	245,000	888,400	15.4%
Water Fund - Lease-Purchase/Bond Financing	1,800,000	0	0	1,800,000	31.2%
Water Fund - Grants	2,000,000	0	0	2,000,000	34.6%
TOTAL	4,555,000	625,500	596,100	5,776,600	100.0%

CIP EXPENSES BY DEPARTMENT/FUND

	FY02 BUDGET	FY03 PLANNED	FY04 PLANNED	TOTAL EXPENSES	% of CIP EXPENSES
General Fund					
Governing Body	0	0	0	0	0.0%
Administration	0	0	0	0	0.0%
Finance	0	0	0	0	0.0%
Planning	0	0	0	0	0.0%
Ruffin-Roulhac	37,000	0	0	37,000	0.6%
Police	60,200	53,600	78,100	191,900	3.3%
Fire Inspections/Code Enforcement	0	0	0	0	0.0%
Fire Protection	20,900	17,400	69,000	107,300	1.9%
Motor Pool	0	0	50,000	50,000	0.9%
Sanitation	0	0	0	0	0.0%
Streets	102,000	93,000	80,000	275,000	4.8%
Cemetery	0	0	0	0	0.0%
Fairview Community Policing Center	213,000	0	0	213,000	3.7%
Tourism	68,000	72,000	74,000	214,000	3.7%
General Fund Total	501,100	236,000	351,100	1,088,200	18.8%
Water Fund					
Engineering	0	0	25,000	25,000	0.4%
Billing & Collection	22,000	10,000	30,000	62,000	1.1%
Water Plant	3,352,900	0	0	3,352,900	58.0%
Water Distribution/Wastewater Collection	152,500	333,500	190,000	676,000	11.7%
Wastewater Treatment	526,500	46,000	0	572,500	9.9%
Water Fund Total	4,053,900	389,500	245,000	4,688,400	81.2%
TOTAL - ALL FUNDS	4,555,000	625,500	596,100	5,776,600	100.0%

Exhibit 3–5
(continued)

DEPARTMENT/FUND	PROJECT/ITEM	FY02	FY03	FY04	TOTAL
General Fund:					
Ruffin Roulhac	Replace Roofs on Buildings	24,000	0	0	24,000
Ruffin Roulhac	Office Rehabilitation	13,000	0	0	13,000
Police	Vehicles	49,200	49,600	26,600	125,400
Police	Equipment	11,000	4,000	51,500	66,500
Fire Protection	Capital - Building Repairs	20,900	17,400	69,000	107,300
Motor Pool	Design for New Motor Pool Facility	0	0	50,000	50,000
Street	Packer/Roller	19,000	0	0	19,000
Street	Guardrail on Hayes Street	12,000	0	0	12,000
Street	Vehicle for Public Works Director	0	18,000	0	18,000
Street	Repaving	71,000	75,000	80,000	226,000
Tourism	Grants	68,000	72,000	74,000	214,000
Fairview Community Policing	Construction of Community Policing Center	213,000	0	0	213,000
General Fund Total		**501,100**	**236,000**	**351,100**	**1,088,200**
Engineering	Vehicle	0	0	25,000	25,000
Billing & Collections	Small Pick-up Truck (Meter Readers)	17,000	0	0	17,000
Billing & Collections	Large Meter Replacement	5,000	10,000	20,000	35,000
Billing & Collections	Test Bench	0	0	10,000	10,000
Water Plant	Equipment	27,900	0	0	27,900
Water Plant	Repair Roof on Operations Building	25,000	0	0	25,000
Water Plant	Plant Upgrade	3,300,000	0	0	3,300,000
Water Distribution	Small Capital	18,000	0	0	18,000
Water Distribution	Replace Small Water Lines	20,000	20,000	30,000	70,000
Water Distribution	Pick-up Truck (Replacement)	0	21,500	0	21,500
Water Distribution	Master Plan	30,000	0	0	30,000
Water Distribution	Generator	0	30,000	0	30,000
Wastewater Collection	Sewer Rehabilitation	30,000	30,000	40,000	100,000
Wastewater Collection	Pick-up Truck (Replacement)	29,000	22,000	0	51,000
Wastewater Collection	Master Plan	0	30,000	0	30,000
Wastewater Collection	Small Equipment	25,500	0	0	25,500
Wastewater Collection	Lakeshore Drive Outfall	0	85,000	0	85,000
Wastewater Collection	TV Sewer/Video System	0	55,000	0	55,000
Wastewater Collection	Generators	0	40,000	40,000	80,000
Wastewater Collection	Brady Road Pump Station Uprgrade	0	0	80,000	80,000
Wastewater Treatment	Aerators	16,000	16,000	0	32,000
Wastewater Treatment	Small Equipment	10,500	30,000	0	40,500
Wastewater Treatment	Plant Upgrades	500,000	0	0	500,000
Water/Sewer Fund Total		**4,053,900**	**389,500**	**245,000**	**4,688,400**

Loveland, Colorado, shows planned equipment replacement from an **internal service fund** (see Exhibit 3–6).[26]

Exhibit 3–7 is a summary of planned street improvements and related projects in the CIP of Cedarburg, Wisconsin, for the 2003–2009 period.[27] Spending for such projects recurs yearly in a range from $395,000 to $903,500. Like Cedarburg, many medium- and small-size local governments plan and finance recurring capital rehabilitation project expenditures in their capital improvement programs.

Exhibit 3–6
Summary form,
Loveland, Colorado

Capital Improvement Plan

Internal Service Fleet Fund

Revenues

Description	2003	2004	2005	2006	2007
Fund Balance - Fleet	3,611,960	2,660,570	2,627,730	3,015,160	2,702,850
Vehicle Replacment Charges	752,080	774,800	798,050	822,000	846,650
Total Revenue	**4,364,040**	**3,435,370**	**3,425,780**	**3,837,160**	**3,549,500**

Appropriations

Description	2003	2004	2005	2006	2007
Fleet Services					
Vehicle Replacement	960,000	666,540	334,070	984,200	335,110
Transfer to Golf	48,870	-	-	-	-
Transfer to Water & Power	298,820	98,940	70,010	84,010	5,850
Transfer to Solid Waste	330,380	-	-	-	-
Transfer to Storm Water	65,400	42,160	6,540	66,100	4,420
Total Fleet Fund	**1,703,470**	**807,640**	**410,620**	**1,134,310**	**345,380**
Ending Balance	**2,660,570**	**2,627,730**	**3,015,160**	**2,702,850**	**3,204,120**

INTERNAL SERVICE FLEET FUND

The Fleet Replacement Fund, managed by the Finance Department, provides for the annual replacement of vehicles when they have outlived their useful life. Funding is provided by an internal service charge to all the departments based on the anticipated replacement cost and remaining life of the vehicles in the fleet. Beginning in 1999, Fleet Management for the utilities was transferred to the Utility Accounting Division and the utilities no longer pay replacement charges into the fund. Vehicle replacement is included in the utilities capital program. Transfers from the fleet fund to the utilities are to return balances paid to the fleet fund prior to the utilities taking over management of their fleet. The Solid Waste Enterprise Fund, and the Golf Enterprise Fund have followed the utilities model and are no longer paying replacement charges into the fund.

Exhibit 3–7
Summary of street improvements, Cedarburg, Wisconsin

REVENUES:	2003	2004	2005	2006	2007	2008	2009
Beginning Balance	37,224	(294,256)	(4,576)	10,424	65,424	40,424	40,424
General Fund transfer							
Property Tax	380,000	405,000	425,000	440,000	450,000	465,000	480,000
State/Federal Grant - Bridge							
State/Federal Grant - Keup Rd.	51,120	289,680					
Village Grafton	115,172						
Special Assessments			10,000	10,000	10,000	10,000	10,000
Debt Proceeds							
Local Road Improvement Program (LRIP)	25,728		20,000		20,000		20,000
Total	**609,244**	**410,424**	**450,424**	**460,424**	**545,424**	**515,424**	**540,424**

EXPENDITURES:	2003	2004	2005	2006	2007	2008	2009
Keup Rd. - Covington Sq. to Highland	603,500						
Spring St. - Hilgen to Park Ln. (S,W)	110,000						
Hawthorne Ave. - Bridge Rd. to end (S)	95,000						
Appletree Ln. - Jefferson to Meadow (S,W)	95,000						
Wilson St. - Madison to Grant (W)		75,000					
Hillcrest Ave. - Jackson to Lincoln (W)		60,000					
Cardinal Ave. - Zeunert to Pioneer (W)		85,000					
Lincoln Blvd. - Washington to Madison (W)		95,000					
Hanover Ave. - Jackson To Lincoln (W)		60,000					
Jackson St. - Hanover to Madison (W)		40,000					
Dorchester Dr., Oxford Ct. & Oxford Dr. (S,W)			180,000				
St. John Ave. - Center to Western (S,W)			70,000				
Fieldcrest St. - Cambridge to Lexington			85,000				
Center St. - Hanover to Madison (S,W,SS)			105,000				
Hamilton Rd. - Hilbert to Park (S,W)				115,000			
Park Ln. - Wilshire to Hamilton (S)				55,000			
Hilbert Ave. - Hamilton to Spring (W,S)				55,000			
Maple St. - all				30,000			
Spring St. - Washington to RR Tracks (S,W)				140,000			
Cleveland St. - Washington to Evergreen (S)					115,000		
Johnson Ave. - Lincoln to Hamilton					110,000		
Kennedy Ave. - Grant to Wilson (W)					80,000		
Grant Ave. - Madison to Grant (W)					100,000		
Van Buren Dr. - all (S)					60,000		
Taft St. - all					40,000		
Westlawn Ave. - Madison to Wilson (SS,W)						95,000	
Jackson St. - Kennedy to Washington (SS,W)						110,000	
Concord St.- Washington to Taunton (S,W)						50,000	
Castle, Regency, Cedar Rdg - Warwick to Regency						110,000	
Taunton Ave.- Pioneer to Concord (S, SS)						40,000	
Hamilton Ave. - Washington to Hilbert (S,W)						70,000	
Riveredge - Tyler to end (S,W)							163,235
Bristol - Lexington to Glenwood (W)							
Glenwood - Arbor to Bristol							117,000
Holly - Lexington to Oriole							
Lexington - Arbor to Fieldcrest							83,000
Doerr Way							100,000
Oriole - Bristol to Holly							44,000
Total	**903,500**	**415,000**	**440,000**	**395,000**	**505,000**	**475,000**	**507,235**

| BALANCE: | | (294,256) | (4,576) | 10,424 | 65,424 | 40,424 | 40,424 | 33,189 |

(S) = Sanitary sewer work.　　(W) = Water main work.　　(SS) = Storm sewer work.

CIP budget-year appropriations or spending

Because the first year of the CIP forecast period is or becomes the capital budget for that year, local officials are faced with immediate decisions on the projects and acquisitions included in that first year. Therefore, most local CIPs give special attention to appropriations or spending for that year. Exhibit 3–8 summarizes project funding and spending for 2001 from the 2001–2005 CIP of Greeley, Colorado. Greeley has a two-year operating budget, and the Greeley CIP emphasizes project funding and spending for the first two years—2002 as well as 2001. The CIP presents the same project funding and spending information for 2002 that Exhibit 3–8 shows for 2001.

Exhibit 3–8
Funding and
spending,
Greeley,
Colorado

2001 CAPITAL IMPROVEMENTS BY FUND

	FUNDED (in millions)
Food Tax	$3.8
Public Improvement	2.1
Development Fees	3.9
Bonds	11.0
Sewer	1.8
Water	12.7
Total	$35.3

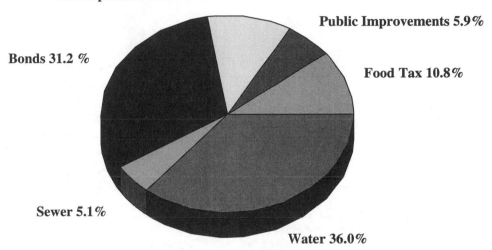

Development Fees 11.0%

Public Improvements 5.9%

Bonds 31.2 %

Food Tax 10.8%

Sewer 5.1%

Water 36.0%

NOTE: Water and Sewer figures are the Sewer Construction Fund, Sewer Capital Replacement Fund, Water Construction Fund, Water Capital Replacement Fund, and Water Rights Acquisition Fund.

2001 CAPITAL IMPROVEMENTS BY PROJECT TYPE

	FUNDED
Streets and Bridges	$7.4
Drainage	1.9
Parks	6.4
Public Buildings	3.7
Other Repair/Maintenance	1.4
Utility Maintenance	2.5
Utility Construction	12.0
Total	$35.3

Exhibit 3–8
(continued)

2002 CAPITAL IMPROVEMENTS BY FUND

	FUNDED (in millions)
Food Tax	$3.8
Public Improvement	0.9
Bonds	1.5
Development Fees	1.9
Sewer	2.2
Water	6.3
Total	$16.6

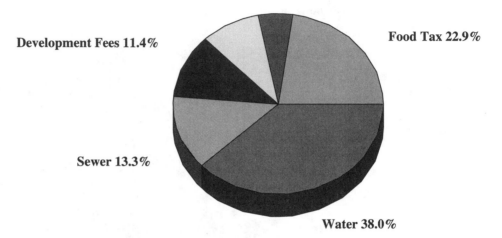

Bonds 9.0%   **Public Improvements 5.4 %**

Development Fees 11.4%   **Food Tax 22.9%**

Sewer 13.3%

Water 38.0%

NOTE: Water and Sewer figures are the Sewer Construction Fund, Sewer Capital Replacement Fund, Water Construction Fund, Water Capital Replacement Fund, and Water Rights Acquisition Fund.

2002 CAPITAL IMPROVEMENTS BY PROJECT TYPE

	FUNDED
Streets and Bridges	$3.1
Drainage	1.4
Parks	1.3
Public Buildings	1.3
Other Repair/Maint	1.0
Utility Maintenance	2.0
Utility Construction	6.3
Total	$16.6

Project detail forms

Exhibit 3–2 showed a prototype of a CIP project detail form for presenting specific information about a CIP project or acquisition. Actual project detail forms used by two local governments are presented here to illustrate how such forms can be used and how their formats may vary.

The form in Exhibit 3–9 is taken from the 2003–2008 CIP of Chatham County, North Carolina.[28] The form shows a project to be undertaken in FY 2004 to expand the county's social services building. Costing $3,518,087, the project will be financed with installment-purchase debt, for which debt service payments are scheduled to begin in FY 2004 at $428,034. These payments decline gradually as the installment-purchase debt is paid down. The form shows that besides debt service there are other decreases and increases in operating costs. The narrative accompanying the form defines and justifies the project and presents other relevant information. The advantage of this kind of form is that it presents year-by-year and detailed data along with supporting information.

The 2001–2005 CIP of Greeley, Colorado, includes four abbreviated project detail forms: one for parkland acquisition and three for sewer system improvements (see Exhibit 3–10).[29] Each form names a project, indicates its costs in 2001 and 2002, identifies the funding source, briefly describes and justifies the project, and comments on its operating budget impact. The advantages of this form are its brevity and easy-to-understand format. The form is used for presentation purposes. Greeley requires any agency to provide fuller and more detailed data about any CIP request it is making.

Some local governments collect and report CIP project request information electronically. For example, Cary, North Carolina, recently computerized its CIP project request procedures and forms. Town departments now submit an electronic project detail form (see Exhibit 3–11) for each CIP request they make.

Project request information

Winston-Salem, North Carolina, has a CIP *Instruction Manual* that is sent to all city agencies and other groups that make CIP requests.[30] The manual includes a project financial form that is very similar to the financial portion (top three sections) of the project detail form shown in Exhibit 3–2. Besides filling out the project financial form, the requesting agency must answer detailed questions for each request:

Status

Is the project being requested for the first time, or was it requested but not included in a previous year's CIP?

Justification

- How will the project improve services to citizens and other clients?
- Is it needed to bring the city into compliance with laws or regulations? Has the city been cited for violation of these laws or regulations or has the city paid a fine?
- Will the project improve the health and safety of citizens or employees?
- How does the project fit with the long-term plans of the city, the county, or the state? Specific plans can be cited here, such as Vision 2005 for

Exhibit 3–9
Project detail form,
Chatham County,
North Carolina

Social Services Building Expansion

Project Description: Construction of an 11,600 sq. ft. expansion of the Social Services building in Pittsboro on land behind the existing building to house Social Services (DSS) and OPC Mental Health, Developmental Disabilities and Substance Abuse (OPC) staff.

Project Definition and Justification

Define problem: DSS and OPC are out of space for staff and filing of records. The County received a letter in late October 2000 from NC Department of Health and Human Services giving a 60-day time period for the County to respond as to how it plans to accommodate the Department of Social Services in the immediate future. Currently, nine DSS positions are occupying rental office space because there is no room in the main DSS building. In addition, both facilities lack sufficient space to store records. Since 1984 DSS staff have increased from 34 to 62. Even with Welfare Reform units like Child Support, Child Protective Services, Medicaid, and Children's Health Services continue to demand attention as the County population grows. A facilities study conducted by Architect Kurt Lent showed that DSS and Mental Health need an additional 2,170 square feet to meet current space needs. Within the next 10 years, an additional 11,600 square feet will be needed to house projected staff and records.

Recommended Solution: Construct an office space immediately that can be added onto at a later time. Because of overlapping client populations and the need to coordinate services, we recommend co-locating DSS and OPC Mental Health.

Alternatives: Rental space is an option, but is limited in Pittsboro. The current situation would find some relief in electronic imaging of files. Staff is gathering information on such an alternative in early 2003. Implementation of imaging technology will not, however, relieve the need for additional office space for workers at the facility nor the workers currently in rental offices.

Stage of Project
Feasibility Study is complete. Project Ordinance has not been adopted.

Relation to Other Projects
The existing Mental Health building could be renovated to accommodate other County (or non-profit) offices.

Description of Land Needs
The 1.25 acres of land owned by the County behind the current building will be used for this project.

Professional Design Work Detail
Professional design services will be required.

Operating Impact
The expense of debt service and increased operating costs in FY 2004 and 2005 will be an estimated $400,000 each year as a result of this project.

Exhibit 3–9
(continued)

Budget Summary

	Prior to FY 2003	FY 2003	FY 2004	FY 2005	FY 2006	FY 2007	FY 2008	Beyond FY 2008	Project Totals
Project Elements									
Planning	0	0	186,480	0	0	0	0	0	186,480
Construction	0	0	2,731,000	0	0	0	0	0	2,731,000
Furnishings	0	0	222,705	0	0	0	0	0	222,705
Equipment	0	0	227,902	0	0	0	0	0	227,902
Contingency	0	0	150,000	0	0	0	0	0	150,000
Total expenditures	0	0	3,518,087	0	0	0	0	0	3,518,087
Funding Sources									
Installment purchase	0	0	3,518,087	0	0	0	0	0	3,518,087
Total funding sources	0	0	3,518,087	0	0	0	0	0	3,518,087
Operating Effect									
Decreased costs	0	0	0	14,400	14,400	14,400	14,400	0	57,600
Increased operating costs	0	0	0	38,246	39,394	40,576	40,576	0	158,792
Debt service	0	0	0	428,034	415,134	402,235	389,335	376,435	2,011,173
Total Operating Effect	0	0	0	451,880	440,128	428,411	415,511	376,435	2,112,365

Exhibit 3–10
Four abbreviated
project detail forms,
Greeley, Colorado

PROJECT NAME:	*Park Land Acquisition*				
FUNDING AMOUNT:	Park Development Fees	2001:	$385,354	2002:	$1,266,000
DESCRIPTION:	This program will be used to designate fund for park land acquisition and development according to the new park development fee ordinance. This ordinance states that the City Council must approve all expenditures of these funds on a project-by-project basis.				
IMPACT ON OPERATING BUDGET:	The operating impact for the City is expected to be very small. There could be some mowing prior to actual construction estimated at $12/hr for no more than 15 hours. Any funds not specifically designated by City Council in a particular year will earn interest and accumulate for future-year projects.				

PROJECT NAME:	*Odor Control at the Wastewater Treatment Plant*		
FUNDING AMOUNT:	Sewer Construction Fund (accumulated reserves for construction)	2001: $350,000	2002:
DESCRIPTION:	This funding will be used to address the perceived odor problem at the wastewater treatment plant on the east side of town. These funds will be used to cover the influent wet well and two biological absorption towers for the scrubbing of effluent air.		
IMPACT ON OPERATING BUDGET:	No additional costs are expected for the operations budget, which already includes the cost of chemicals and monitoring odor levels.		

PROJECT NAME:	*Sewer Main Extensions/Oversizing*		
FUNDING AMOUNT:	Sewer Construction Fund (accumulated reserves for construction)	2001: $250,000	2002: $250,000
DESCRIPTION:	When the line is required by the City to be oversized for serving future growth, the developer is reimbursed for the cost of the oversizing.		
IMPACT ON OPERATING BUDGET:	Negligible (creating capacity for the future to prevent replacement at a higher cost)		

PROJECT NAME:	*Poudre Trunk Extensions*		
FUNDING AMOUNT:	Sewer Construction Fund (accumulated reserves for construction)	2001: $50,000	2002: $832,000
DESCRIPTION:	This is the first phase of a two phase project that will extend the 35 inch sheep draw sewer from F Street, east 59th Avenue to 83rd Avenue. Phase I in 2001 and 2002 follows a path close to #3 Ditch between 59th Avenue and 71st Avenue. Phase II scheduled for 2005 continues the along on the north side of the #3 Ditch and west along the Poudre River Basin to approximately 83rd Avenue. Both projects total approximately 3 miles of sewer line.		
IMPACT ON OPERATING BUDGET:	Negligible, estimate provided of $2,500 for maintenance beginning in 2004.		

Winston-Salem, the consolidated housing and community development plan, the state transportation improvement program, and the New Century Plan for downtown development.

• How would delays in starting the project affect city services? What if the start of the project were delayed five years beyond the planned schedule?

Cost analysis

• Who prepared the cost estimates for the project—the requesting department staff, other city staff, an outside consultant, a potential contractor, or someone else?

Exhibit 3–11
Electronic project detail
form, Cary, North Carolina

Project Title:	Carpenter Fire Station Rd Wide.(NC55 to Green Level to Durham Rd)
Project Category:	TRANSPORTATION
Project Type:	Road Capacity
Priority:	C C=Committed via Developer Agreement or Contract U=Untouchable (Very High) H=High M=Medium L=Low

FY 2004 Capital Costs:	$822,000
FY 2005-2014 Costs:	$5,678,000
Project Manager:	Tim Bailey
Responsible Department:	Engineering

Description

A four-lane road with curb and gutter and sidewalk on both sides. A left turn lane will be added at critical intersections.

Justification (Please mention specific reason for Level of Priority assigned to this project)

To meet the thoroughfare plan and traffic needs for the future. Related to growth associated with 2 large Planned Unit Developments.

Impact if Cancelled or Delayed

Traffic congestion since roadway system capacity will not meet projected demand

Project Drivers and Operating Impacts

Part of Master Plan	✓
Externally Mandated	☐
Better Way	☐
Growth Related	✓
Service Related	☐
Annual Savings in FY04 $:	$0
1st Full Year Personnel Costs in FY04 $:	$0
1st Full Year Oper. Maint. Costs in FY04 $:	$0
Special Code:	0

0=No Special Code Known for this Project
APEX 23%=Apex Pays 23% as Project Relates to Water Plant
D=Developer Funded
H=Homeowner Supported
L=Local Govt Supported
IP-FIRE=Installment Purchase Financing for Fire
IP-GG=Installment Purchase Financing for General Government
PAYG=Pay-as-You-Go Financing (Fund Balance Transfer)

Project Cost Summary

Year of Initial
Appropriation: Post FY 2002

	Appropriated Capital Costs
Appropriated Through FY 2003:	$0
FY 2004 In Last Year's CIP:	$822,000
FY 2004 Being Requested:	$822,000
FY 2005:	$2,000,000
FY 2006:	$3,678,000
FY 2007:	$0
FY 2008:	$0
FY 2009:	$0
FY 2010:	$0
FY 2011:	$0
FY 2012:	$0
FY 2013:	$0
FY 2014:	$0
Project Total:	$6,500,000

Check if Cash Flow Is Same As Appropriations ☐

If not, please fill in Cash Flow Section at Bottom of Form

Transportation Development Zone

NW TDF Zone:	100%
North TDF Zone:	0%
Central TDF Zone:	0%
SE TDF Zone:	0%
Base TDF Zone:	0%
Town-wide Zone:	0%
Total S/B=100%:	100%

Transportation Projects Only

Powell Bill Eligibility:	16.5%
TDF Eligibility:	100.0%
% Not Eligible for PB or TDF:	0.0%

Cash Flow Start Date	Cash Flow End Date	Months Per Quadrant	1st Quad	2nd Quad	3rd Quad	4th Quad	Total Quad S/B=100%
7/1/03	7/1/06	9	10%	30%	30%	30%	100%

Exhibit 3–11
(continued)

Town of Cary	Capital Project Request Report	For FY 2004 Capital Planning Purposes

Project Title: Carpenter Fire Station Rd Wide.(NC55 to Green Level to Durham Rd)	
Project Category: TRANSPORTATION	
Projec Type: Road Capacity	
Priority: C C=Committed U=Untouchable (Very High) H=High M=Medium L=Low	

FY 2004 Capital Costs:	$822,000
FY 2005-2014 Costs:	$5,678,000
Project Manager:	Tim Bailey
Responsible Department:	Engineering

Description

A four-lane road with curb and gutter and sidewalk on both sides. A left turn lane will be added at critical intersections.

Justification

To meet the thoroughfare plan and traffic needs for the future. Related to growth associated with 2 large Planned Unit Developments.

Impact if Cancelled or Delayed

Traffic congestion since roadway system capacity will not meet projected demand

Project Drivers and Operating Impacts		**Project Cost Summary**		**Transportation Development Zone**	
Part of Master Plan:	Yes	**Year of Initial Appropriation:** Post FY 2002		NW TDF Zone:100%	
Externally Mandated:	No		Appropriated / Capital Costs	North TDF Zone:	0%
Better Way:	No	**Through FY 2003:**	$0	Central TDF Zone:	0%
Growth Related:	Yes	FY 2004 In Last Year's CIP:	$822,000	SE TDF Zone:	0%
Service Related:	No	FY 2004 Being Requested:	$822,000	Base TDF Zone:	0%
Annual Savings in FY04 $:	$0	**FY 2005:**	$2,000,000	Town-wide Zone:	0%
1st Full Year Personnel Costs in FY04 $:	$0	**FY 2006:**	$3,678,000		
1st Full Year Oper. Maint. Costs in FY04 $:	$0	Check if Cash Flow Is Same As Appropriations **FY 2007:**	$0	Total S/B=100% 100%	
Special Code:	0	**FY 2008:**	$0	**Transportation Projects Only**	
0=No Special Code Known for this Project		☐ **FY 2009:**	$0	Powell Bill Eligibility:	
APEX 23%=Apex Pays 23% as Project Relates to Water Plant		**FY 2010:**	$0	17%	
D=Developer Funded		If not, please fill in Cash Flow Section at Bottom of Form **FY 2011:**	$0	TDF Eligibility:	
H=Homeowner Supported		**FY 2012:**	$0	100%	
L=Local Govt Supported		**FY 2013:**	$0	% Not Eligible for PB or TDF:	
IP-FIRE=Installment Purchase Financing for Fire		**FY 2014:**	$0	0%	
IP-GG=Installment Purchase Financing for General Government		**Project Total:**	$6,500,000		
PAYG=Pay-as-You-Go Financing (Fund Balance Transfer)					

Cash Flow Start Date	**Cash Flow End Date**	**Months per Quadrant**	**1st Quad**	**2nd Quad**	**3rd Quad**	**4th Quad**	**Total Quad S/B=100%**
7/1/03	7/1/06	9	10%	30%	30%	30%	100%

- Do the cost estimates beyond the upcoming budget year assume inflation in material and service costs above current prices? If so, what inflation factor is used?
- Upon completion, will the project affect the number of positions needed by the requesting agency and its annual operating expenditures? Will there be any savings in operating expenditures because of the project?
- If the project were delayed one year beyond the planned schedule, what would be the total expected cost of the project? What would this cost be if the start of the project were delayed five years?

Financial analysis

- What are the proposed financing sources for the project?
- Are these sources secure, or are they subject to an approval process, adjustment, or cancellation?

Time frame analysis

- What are the forecasted starting and finishing dates for site acquisition, architectural/engineering studies, construction, and equipment purchase?
- What plans must be completed or approvals secured before construction begins?
- What other projects of the requesting department, other city departments, or outside agencies must be started or completed before this project begins? What specifically must take place on these other projects before this one is started or completed?
- What other projects must await the start or completion of this project before they may be started or completed? What stage of completion must this project reach before the other projects can proceed?

Priority
Each requesting agency must rank each of its CIP requests by priority.

Financial analysis and schedules

In addition to the financing sources for projects and their impact on the operating budget, the CIPs of many local governments include other financial analyses and schedules. If the CIP is presented separately from the operating budget, such analyses and schedules usually appear in a special financial section of the CIP document. If the CIP is presented in the operating budget, the financial analyses and schedules may be placed in the CIP section of that document, in the section that addresses outstanding debt and debt service, or in a section that presents an overall financial forecast. The financial analyses and schedules that accompany a CIP usually focus on:

- Revenues earmarked or available for capital financing
- Capital reserves
- Availability of grants and outside sources of revenue
- Outstanding debt and new debt proposed in the CIP
- Debt service schedules on outstanding and proposed new debt

- Debt capacity in relation to legal debt limits, the ability of the jurisdiction to repay debt, and the effect of proposed new debt on the jurisdiction's bond ratings
- The effect of the CIP on tax rates, utility charges, other revenues, and operating fund balances in the future.

Chapter 5 addresses financial strategy issues related to CIP financing.

Purposes served by a CIP

General reasons for capital budgeting were discussed in Chapter 1. In this section additional, specific purposes served by a CIP are explained.

Allows orderly replacement and rehabilitation of existing capital assets

To maintain quality and efficient services, a local government must maintain, repair, and periodically replace or rehabilitate equipment, facilities, and infrastructure. Police patrol vehicles generally need replacement once every two or three years, sanitation vehicles once every five to seven years, construction equipment every ten years or so, and first-line fire trucks approximately every twenty years. Depending on the quality of construction, wear and tear, and ongoing maintenance, buildings can have useful lives that range from twenty to forty years or more. Within that period, however, many buildings undergo major refurbishing to keep them serviceable or to meet changing needs. Infrastructure (such as streets, bridges, drainage systems, and water and sewer lines) typically lasts for decades, but it also requires periodic rehabilitation to keep it in good shape. Sometimes higher service standards and expanding use may necessitate reconstruction or enlargement of infrastructure.

Without planning, capital replacement and rehabilitation are easily overlooked or postponed and then become more costly and rushed when they have to be undertaken. A CIP can help a local government plan for the orderly replacement and rehabilitation of major equipment, facilities, and infrastructure, thereby saving money and ensuring good-quality services over time.

Athens–Clarke County, Georgia, gives special emphasis to "capital maintenance and repair projects" in its 2000–2009 CIP. This category provides for replacement of fire trucks, construction equipment, and other equipment; rehabilitation of parking facilities; repair of bridges and drainage systems; and numerous other capital projects. Both the jurisdiction-wide CIP summary form for years 2000 to 2009 and the proposed capital budget for FY 2000 separately identify capital maintenance and repair projects and distinguish them from capital addition and improvement projects. For instance, the 2000 capital budget, which is the first year of the 2000–2009 CIP, includes $5,042,600 in capital maintenance and repair projects, $4,539,200 in capital addition and improvement projects, and total capital spending of $9,581,800.[31]

Allows time for project design

Planning and design of a construction project center on the preparation of engineering feasibility studies, architectural sketches, blueprints, and specifications. For a small or simple project, this process can take months. For a major project or one that is complex, it can take years. The planning and design time for any project extend for as long as it takes to secure the environmental and other regulatory clearances that are needed before construction may proceed.

More equipment and equipment systems are being designed to meet the specific needs of customers. Planning and design for such equipment can take a year or more. Although planning and design are not involved in most equipment acquisitions, careful research is usually required to make sure that the right type of off-the-shelf equipment is being purchased. Such research can require months.

A CIP enables officials to foresee capital needs before they must decide to fund and implement projects or make acquisitions. Without a CIP, a local government may not see those needs until they have arrived, at which point planning and design must be done in haste with too little time available to consult with those who will use the buildings or facilities. The resulting plans and designs are then likely to have errors. Some of those errors can be corrected during construction, which will add to construction costs; others will be uncorrectable, and officials and citizens will have to live with the building or facility with its design flaws.

The 2001–2006 CIP of Rockville, Maryland, includes a city hall expansion project. The estimated cost is $9,086,000.[32] Payments for planning and design work for this project are spread over two years and come to $711,000, about 8 percent of the project's total cost. Like many expansion and renovation projects, this one is complex. Therefore, the city is taking several years to plan it. The CIP helps to give Rockville the time to do this.

Winston-Salem, North Carolina, is also renovating its city hall.[33] The project's estimated cost is $5.5 million, and the city's 2000–2004 CIP includes $325,000 for planning and design work. This is being spent on an office space utilization plan, detailed construction drawings, and a separate landscaping plan. The need for three different sets of plans for this project underscores its complexity and the importance of having time to complete planning and design work.

Allows time to arrange financing

Although less plentiful than they once were, federal and state grants are still available to local governments for certain types of projects such as water-sewer system improvements. By identifying major capital requirements before they are needed, a CIP can give local officials the time they need to identify grant sources and design projects to meet grant requirements. It can also help demonstrate to grantor agencies that the project merits grant funding and has been coordinated with other capital plans of the requesting jurisdiction.

Elizabethtown, North Carolina, offers an illustration of the valuable part that a CIP can play in helping a very small town obtain grant and subsidized loan funding to help finance major water and sewer system improvements. The town's water-sewer system serves not only city residents but also industries and residents in the surrounding areas. Several years ago, the town manager and his staff prepared a CIP for the water-sewer system that forecast system needs over a twenty-year period, 1999–2000 to 2019–2020. The CIP identified $9.8 million in water and $12.3 million in sewer improvement needs.[34] Town officials used the CIP as well as underlying engineering studies as the basis for applying for state grant funds to help defray the projects' costs. As of 2002, the state had awarded Elizabethtown $2.8 million in grants for these projects.[35]

Local governments are undertaking more projects involving multiple jurisdictions or agencies and public-private sector arrangements. These projects and arrangements enable the participants to take advantage of economies of scale, spread risks, and save money. However, they are usually complex and take time—often years—to put together. A CIP can give local officials the time to explore and, when advantageous, arrange such interlocal or public-private sector projects.

Officials of **Loveland, Colorado**, have used that city's CIP to plan and arrange financing to construct a joint city–county police headquarters and courts facility.[36] The city's share of the project's cost is $11 million, which is being financed through a **sale/leaseback arrangement** with payments extending over a seven-year term. Funds for the lease payments come from a reserve fund established by the city council.

Even when a local government finances a major project entirely on its own without grants or participation from other entities, a year or more may be required to put together an effective financial package. This is especially true when voter-approved debt will be used. Planning and holding a referendum on proposed bonds for a capital project or a set of projects can take up to a year or more. A CIP can be a useful springboard for local officials to plan for a bond referendum, demonstrate to citizens that the projects to be financed with the bonds are needed, and provide the time to search for and obtain other financing sources to leverage the bond proceeds.

Allows time to identify sites and purchase land

A CIP gives officials adequate time to look for suitable land for projects. Furthermore, the advance notice provided by the CIP can put officials in a good bargaining position with the owners of the land. Officials will not be under pressure to acquire the land quickly but will instead have the time to bargain for a reasonable price. If an acceptable price cannot be obtained for a particular site and officials cannot use or choose not to use condemnation, a CIP can provide time to search for an alternative site. Land costs in a community may fluctuate. A CIP that identifies land acquisition requirements before they are needed enables officials to take advantage of these fluctuations and buy land when costs are down.

Parkland and open-space acquisition is becoming a large expenditure item for many local governments, and a CIP can be a useful tool for planning such acquisitions. The CIP included in the Campbell, California, 1999–2000 operating and capital budget identifies $1,412,500 for parkland and open-space acquisition in 1999–2000 and further parkland acquisitions in 2000–2001 and 2002–2003.[37] The 2000–2010 CIP of Orange County, North Carolina, includes $3 million in bonds for the purchase of parkland, and the county manager's CIP message refers to recommendations that, if implemented, could lead to "an aggressive plan to preserve natural resources, cultural resources and farmland in our County."[38]

Coordinates projects and acquisitions

If a capital project planned by one department of a local government goes forward without taking into account the related capital projects of another department or entity serving the community, the result can be unnecessary expense and inconvenience.

In **Greensboro, North Carolina**, a special committee of department heads has recommended to the city's executive team that greater collaboration among departments become a formal and required part of the city's CIP process.[39] The committee's recommendation notes that there are too many instances when one department seeks capital funds or a location for a project without regard to how other departmental needs for space or future growth could be accommodated in a joint project. Joint projects can reduce the need for land, funds, and project management. The presence of a strong CIP process in Greensboro supports officials' efforts to achieve greater interdepartmental coordination in planning and implementing major projects.

Plans for economic development

A CIP is the primary tool that local governments have to plan for the following infrastructure and facilities that support economic growth: streets and water-sewer lines, schools, community colleges, libraries, other cultural venues, and parks and open space. It is not surprising, therefore, that economic and community development projects have become an important part of many local CIPs and that developers and the business community are increasingly active in the local CIP process.

Two examples from local government underscore the importance of CIPs in economic development. **San Clemente, California,** is experiencing significant growth, and its 2001–2005 CIP includes street, water-sewer, drainage, and parks and median projects intended to accommodate this growth. Many of these projects are being financed with developer fees and are directly tied to specific commercial and residential development projects.[40]

Lenoir County, North Carolina, faces a different economic development scenario. It is in a region of North Carolina that is hard-pressed to attract and hold industry and jobs. As a result, the county's 2000–2004 CIP proposes significant spending to address this challenge. The "Economic Development" section of the county's CIP includes $3.6 million—about a quarter of all project spending in the county's CIP—for water-sewer infrastructure, shell buildings, and other incentives or support for industry and business.[41]

Strengthens or revitalizes neighborhoods

A CIP helps a local government to plan and provide the infrastructure needed to support healthy neighborhoods. Neighborhood groups and associations can play significant roles in the CIP process at the local level.

The 2002–2007 CIP of **Madison Heights, Michigan,** gives special emphasis to neighborhood development projects. Of $38.6 million in total CIP spending, $14.8 million is for neighborhood projects. Most of these projects are infrastructure—neighborhood streets and roads, storm sewers, sanitary sewers, and water lines—and many are financed with funds from a special tax levy approved by the city's voters in 1996.[42]

Maintains or improves bond rating

Local governments finance large capital improvement projects partly or wholly with debt. When the debt is in the form of bonds, certificates of participation, or other publicly sold obligations, the locality issuing the debt usually obtains one or more ratings from the national bond rating agencies to broaden the market for the debt and lower the interest rate and costs for such borrowing.

The rating agencies usually expect a local government that is going to the bond market and seeking ratings to have a CIP. Indeed, *Standard & Poor's Public Finance Criteria* refers to the importance of the CIP in ratings of "tax-backed debt":

> As part of the debt rating process, Standard & Poor's requires a well-documented capital improvement program (CIP). Necessary components of this plan include the outlook for capital needs, the flexibility to modify the program in difficult economic periods, and the ability to finance investment through operating surpluses.[43]

Coordinates planning with other jurisdictions and organizations

By anticipating capital needs before decisions must be made to approve and fund them, a CIP gives officials in a jurisdiction the time to coordinate its capital plans with those of other local governments, public entities, and private organizations in the same community. Coordination is easier, of course, if each organization serving the community has a CIP, but even if some do not, it is still beneficial if only the largest or most important entities do. With the CIPs of those two or three primary organizations in hand, officials of other jurisdictions and organizations serving the community can share information about future projects, avoid overlap, and possibly create joint projects to meet common needs and save money.

Mecklenburg County, North Carolina, has a joint-use task force to coordinate its three-year CIP and ten-year capital needs assessment with the capital plans of other public agencies serving the county, including the city of Charlotte, the separate Mecklenburg County/Charlotte school system, the local housing authority, the Carolinas Medical Center, and the local community college.[44] The task force, which meets monthly, serves as a clearing-house for information on joint-use possibilities and provides a forum for local agencies to plan for shared sites and facilities. Mecklenburg County shares all its CIP requests with the task force. The task force's work has led to the creation of a city–county joint facilities master planning effort, an evaluation of the land acquisition needs for parks and recreational purposes of several participating agencies, and other planning focused on joint-use facilities.

Lays foundation for an adequate public facilities ordinance

In some states, local governments experiencing fast growth are adopting or considering the adoption of an adequate public facilities ordinance. Such an ordinance usually requires that the public facilities and services needed to support development be available "concurrently" with the development.[45] Local officials may use a "concurrency" or "adequate public facilities" ordinance to deny or postpone new development when existing public facilities and services are working at full capacity and cannot serve the proposed new development.

However, to withstand court challenges, a local government's adequate public facilities ordinance must be accompanied by plans to provide public facilities to meet reasonable growth over time. A well-prepared CIP that addresses existing infrastructure and public facility inadequacies and provides for some level of growth enables a local government to show that it is making a good-faith effort to accommodate future increases in population and development.[46]

Currituck County, North Carolina, a fast-growing beach and resort community on the Outer Banks of North Carolina, has an adequate public facilities ordinance and a related CIP. Most of the growth in Currituck County has been residential, stretching the county's capacity to provide the schools and other facilities needed to serve the development. As a result, the county passed an adequate public facilities ordinance.

Developers challenged the ordinance in court, but the county prevailed in the suit.[47] County officials believe that the CIP, which identified school and major county facilities to be built in the future, helped to demonstrate to the court the county's good-faith efforts to put public facilities and services into place to accommodate a reasonable pace of growth over time.[48]

Issues in CIP preparation and approval

When they organize the CIP process and prepare and approve a CIP, officials often face issues of coordination of the CIP process, steps in the CIP process, the CIP calendar, citizen involvement, relation of the CIP to long-term needs assessment and planning, use of asset replacement and rehabilitation schedules in the CIP, and accounting for inflation when estimating CIP project and acquisition costs.

Coordination of the CIP process

A single official usually is responsible for coordinating the CIP preparation process for a local government. This official may work with a staff committee composed of officials of the jurisdiction with a stake in the CIP process or with a citizens' committee or a combined staff-citizens committee that is involved in the process. Such committees may recommend or establish policies for CIP preparation, review and make recommendations about specific requests and the CIP, or advise the CIP coordinator and city or county manager about preparation issues.

If there is to be a CIP in many small towns, the town manager must prepare it because there is no other staff member who can take on this responsibility. Unfortunately, the pressures that most small-town managers face deprive them of the time and inclination to prepare a CIP. Attention to immediate problems leaves little time for multiyear planning.

In some medium-size local governments without a budget officer or staff, the finance director coordinates the CIP process. Not surprisingly, CIPs prepared by local finance directors often have strong financial orientations, with considerable emphasis given to financial planning and debt forecasting and less attention given to long-term capital needs assessment and project planning.[49]

In some local jurisdictions the planning director or a senior planner coordinates the CIP process. Most infrastructure and capital facility needs arise from development, which the planning staff monitors. As a result, planners typically play a key role in the local CIP process and sometimes coordinate the process. Indeed, the planning profession defined the key CIP concepts that we use today,[50] and planners and planning boards prepared the first local government CIPs in the country. In many local governments, planning boards and commissions continue to play the key role in the local CIP process. In Greeley, Colorado, for example, the city manager and an interdepartmental committee screen CIP requests while the planning commission reviews new CIP requests and recommends priorities in terms of the city's comprehensive plan to the city council and manager.[51]

The public works or utilities director, the engineer, or another official who directs or works in a department that has major capital needs is sometimes assigned the responsibility of coordinating the CIP process. The reasoning is that this official has experience in planning for and managing capital assets, understands the importance of the CIP, and will make it a priority. Like the manager, the finance director, and the planning staff, however, directors of line departments often face more immediate duties. In addition, many department directors may lack the perspective to coordinate a jurisdiction-wide CIP process.

In a city or county with a separate budget officer or staff, that officer or staff is often assigned the responsibility for coordination of the CIP process. The budget officer or staff has a jurisdiction-wide perspective and is usually capable of doing the analysis needed for both capital needs assessment and financial forecasting. Because of the CIP's relation to the operating budget, the budget officer also is likely to be willing to make CIP preparation a top priority.

In a medium-size local government where the assistant manager or assistant to the manager has experience in capital planning and budgeting, that assistant may coordinate the CIP process.

A few medium- and small-size local governments without a budget director or staff have jump-started their CIP processes by contracting with consultants who get the process going and coordinate it for the first year or two. For example, Henderson, North Carolina, contracted with a retired city manager with considerable experience in capital budgeting to prepare the city's first CIP.[52]

If a staff committee sets policy for the CIP process, all the above-mentioned officials are likely to serve on that committee or assist in some way. For example, Smyrna, Georgia, has a seven-member CIP staff committee. Five members—the public works director, community development director, budget administrator, city administrator, and parks and recreation director—are permanent; two members serve on an annual rotating basis, one representing public safety and the other representing the library, human relations, and other departments.[53]

Steps in the CIP process

The steps that a local government follows to prepare and approve a CIP generally mimic the steps followed in preparing the operating or annual budget. In medium- and small-size local governments, CIP preparation usually consists of the following steps:

Formulation, review, and approval of goals and policies   The CIP coordinator plays a key role in identifying and recommending goals and policies or changes in them, or by facilitating the process by which this occurs. If there is a CIP committee, this group would be involved and presumably also have a key role. Actual approval of the goals and policies would ordinarily be the responsibility of the city or county manager and the governing board. Before the CIP process or annual budget process gets under way, a growing number of local governing boards hold retreats to review, update, and approve polices and goals to guide capital budgeting. Once goals and policies are approved and the CIP calendar is set, the CIP coordinator prepares and issues request forms and instructions to local government departments and any outside agencies participating in the process. The coordinator may also train officials and others in the use of these forms.

Preparation of CIP requests   Two interesting issues, which are addressed later in this chapter, can arise during the preparation of CIP requests:

- To what extent do the CIP requests by city or county departments and outside agencies participating in the process reflect long-term strategic or master planning?
- Are fixed-asset and infrastructure records used to formulate capital maintenance, rehabilitation, and replacement schedules in the CIP process?

Review of CIP requests and preparation of the recommended CIP   Different officials or groups may be involved in reviewing requests, identifying financing sources, determining financing capacity, and preparing a recommendation for the governing board and community. At a minimum, the CIP coordinator, the city or county manager, and several other key staff officials, such as the finance or planning director, should be involved. If there is a CIP staff committee, it is likely to play a review role and make recommendations on CIP requests to the manager. If a planning commission has a role in the CIP process, as in Denton, Texas, or if there is a citizens' capital budget advisory committee, as in Largo, Florida, such a commission or committee often reviews CIP requests or comments on the manager's recommended CIP. In some local governments, the board or committee actually recommends a CIP for consideration by the governing board and the community.

Typically, however, it is the city or county manager or chief executive officer of a jurisdiction who recommends a CIP to the board and the community. The manager and management team are usually in a good position to balance capital needs and requests with the financial resources available to a local government.

Governing board review and approval of the CIP   As the governing board reviews the CIP, there is likely to be further citizen involvement. At a minimum, this would consist of one or more hearings on the CIP. It could also include review and comments by a citizens' budget committee, CIP advisory committee, and other community organizations and groups.

If the groundwork has been done well, the governing board will approve the CIP. This may also authorize projects and appropriate money for projects and spending included in the first year of the CIP forecast period—the capital budget year. In the following discussion of the CIP calendar and its relation to the calendar for preparation of the operating or annual budget, the CIP process is illustrated with examples from several local governments.

The CIP calendar

The time given to CIP preparation and approval varies with the size of a jurisdiction, the magnitude and kinds of CIP requests, the sources of financing used, and the extent to which citizens and community groups participate in the process. The CIP process might span only a month or two in a small jurisdiction—for example, a city or town with five thousand or fewer people. In many of those jurisdictions, most CIP requests are for recurring equipment and rehabilitation projects, new construction projects occur only occasionally and the financing is predominantly from pay-as-go and local sources, and participation in the process is limited mainly to local officials.

In a medium- to large-size jurisdiction, the CIP process is likely to take much longer—four to eight months or so. Here CIP requests include proposals for large new improvement projects as well as for major recurring equipment and rehabilitation spending. Substantial debt financing and grants from outside agencies may be involved, and community organizations and the public at large are likely to participate in the CIP process.

Local governments coordinate their CIP and operating budget preparation calendars in different ways, reflecting differences among them in law, financial resources, commitment to planning, and a host of other factors. Two representative approaches, illustrated by the experiences of two local governments, are presented here.

Sequential processes   In Largo, Florida, the CIP process is basically undertaken before the operating or annual budget process gets under way.[54] Largo has an October 1 to September 30 fiscal year. CIP preparation begins in December and continues through January. The city's charter requires the manager to submit a recommended CIP to the commission (governing board) by March 1. The manager presented the 2001–2005 CIP to the commission on February 8, several weeks before the March 1 deadline. In February and March, a finance advisory board—a citizens' committee appointed by the commission—reviews the CIP. In April, the commission reviews the recommended CIP and the finance advisory board's comments. The city charter requires the commission to adopt the CIP by May 1. The commission adopted the 2001–2005 CIP on April 18. The annual budget process for Largo starts at the beginning of March when budget request instructions are issued to departments. Requests are due in early April. They go through various reviews in April and May. The manager submits the recommended budget in early June. The commission reviews and holds hearings on the budget during the summer and adopts the budget by mid-September for the new fiscal year beginning on October 1.

Overlapping preparation and simultaneous presentation and approval   In Asheville, North Carolina, the CIP requests are submitted before annual budget requests, and the review of CIP requests by the manager's staff partly precedes and partly overlaps the review of annual budget requests. The manager then combines both sets of requests into the annual budget presentation to the board. The board usually reviews both requests together and enacts the annual budget ordinance and approves the CIP at essentially the same time.[55]

The CIP preparation process starts in early November, and departments submit their CIP requests in mid-December. Departments prepared their annual budget requests in January and submit them in early February. The Asheville city council holds its annual budget retreat in early February to identify budget issues and set goals for the manager's proposed budget. The city manager and staff review the CIP and annual budget requests in February and through March. This review includes meetings with departmental officials on both CIP and the annual budget. The council reviews and holds hearings on both, and adopts in June the annual budget ordinance and capital projects ordinances for first-year CIP spending.

The overlapping of the CIP and annual budget preparation calendars in Asheville is probably more common among local governments than the mainly sequential CIP and operating budget calendars in Largo, Florida. The overlapping calendars offer greater assurance that the same general goals and priorities drive both capital project and operating budget decisions and that the two types of decisions are coordinated. On the other hand, Largo's sequential CIP and operating budget calendars spread out the work of capital planning and operating budget preparation more evenly during the year, allowing officials to decide on major capital projects before having to tackle the year-to-year operating budget issues. Some officials who have used the sequential CIP and operating budget calendars say that this greatly facilitates annual budget preparation.[56]

Citizen involvement

Because the decisions and issues faced in a CIP are often substantial and carry long-term implications, involving citizens can help ensure that the projects selected are valued by the community and that citizens understand the need for issuing debt and levying taxes to finance projects.

State statutes or local charters require officials in some local governments to involve citizens in the CIP process or in making financing decisions stemming from the process. For instance, a city's charter may require the governing board or the city's planning commission to hold one or more public hearings on the recommended CIP, or state statutes may require a voter referendum for authorization of general obligation (GO) bonds to finance CIP projects.

In many jurisdictions where there are no, or only limited, legal requirements for public participation in the CIP process, local officials choose to involve citizens in important ways. Officials may survey citizens to get their suggestions for specific projects and their views about relative priorities among different areas of capital investment or among specific projects. Public hearings, town meetings, community forums, and focus groups may be held for the same purposes. Community groups and neighborhood organizations may be informed about the CIP process and invited to submit requests or to offer their ideas about relative priorities. A newspaper ad may be run that contains an abbreviated request form and invites any citizen or reader to send in project ideas.

The local planning board may play a role in the process, as in Denton, Texas, or a special CIP citizens' advisory committee may advise the governing board about the CIP, as in Largo, Florida. Where such committees are used, the governing board usually appoints the committee members, attempting to ensure that the committee members provide good representation of community interests, organizations, and groups.

The interest and involvement of citizens in the CIP process vary from community to community and over time in the same community, depending on a number of factors. Citizen involvement and its utility are likely to be greater to the extent that one or more of the following conditions holds: the CIP includes major projects, projects address new rather than replacement or rehabilitation needs, citizens will directly use the infrastructure and facilities, and citizens will be asked to vote for bonds or pay higher taxes or new taxes to finance the CIP.

Broadening the CIP process beyond local officials to active participation by community groups, citizen committees, and the public increases the visibility of the process and the risks associated with it. The adverse repercussions resulting from any missteps made in the process are likely to be felt more broadly in the community. Thus, when officials are new to capital programming and not sure what to expect, they may choose to limit participation to city officials. As they become more experienced and confident in their ability to handle the risks associated with capital programming, however, they will be more likely to open the process up and invite the community to participate.

In response to a failed bond referendum in 1997, **Winston-Salem, North Carolina,** made a concerted effort to involve citizens in the CIP process.[57] The city's 2000–2004 CIP identified about $120 million for general public improvement projects. Before officials introduced another bond referendum, they solicited citizens' ideas about which projects to include in a bond referendum and how to prioritize them.

First, officials conducted a telephone survey asking a sample of citizens to rank five general areas of capital needs—transportation, public safety, housing and community development, economic development, and recreation and leisure. Citizens were also asked to rank eight specific CIP projects by priority and to identify any other specific needs that city officials should consider.

The city then held a three-hour public forum, widely advertised in local media, to which all citizens were invited. A total of 170 citizens attended, as did the city council and top staff. After the mayor and the city manager provided an overview of the needs of the city and its financial capacity, the citizens were divided into thirteen small groups. Each group had a city staff member who served as facilitator and a citizen who served as chair and spokesperson. The groups were asked to rank the five functional areas in order of importance and to identify specific project needs within the two top-ranked functional areas. After they finished, the groups reported their recommendations in the forum at large.

Winston-Salem also held focus-group meetings with citizens to learn their ideas about the city's capital needs and priorities. City officials believe that these citizen involvement activities were crucial in winning approval of all $71 million in bonds submitted to the voters in November 2000 to fund the top-priority projects identified by citizens in Winston-Salem's 2000–2004 CIP.[58]

Greensboro, North Carolina, involves citizens in the CIP process in another way. Each year the city planning board sends out forms to community organizations and neighborhood associations inviting them to submit projects to include in the CIP. Many do. City staff review and comment on the requests, and the city planning board and city council hold hearings at which representatives of the organizations are invited to present and comment on the requests.[59]

Greeley, Colorado, has a planning commission composed of citizen members that plays an important role in the CIP process. After all CIP requests have been submitted and the city manager and staff have reviewed them, the planning commission meets with department officials to discuss their requests and priorities. The commission then delivers a report to the city council and city manager recommending project priorities. The manager considers the planning commission's five-year CIP report, available funding, operating budget impact, and other factors when presenting a preliminary budget with the recommended CIP projects to the city council.[60]

Long-term needs assessment and planning

The CIP is a multiyear plan, but it is usually more effective if other long-term planning efforts are under way and the CIP is related to them. Local officials can better anticipate capital needs over a five- or six-year CIP forecast period if they have already thought about needs for future services and conceptualized general plans to meet those needs. Such needs assessment and service planning could span the same period as the CIP, or they could extend farther into the future (for example, ten years). Needs assessment often involves citizens and community leaders who are users of particular services. It may assume the continuation of services at current levels or, what is more likely, build in service enhancements that meet citizens' expectations for expanded, new, or higher-quality services. Needs assessment and service planning often build in service standards, such as acres of parkland per one thousand residents for parks and recreation programs or specific response times for emergency medical service calls.

If long-term needs assessment and service planning have been done, departmental officials can look to the plans when making CIP requests. In some cases, the plans identify particular capital facilities and equipment that are required to meet service objectives and provide improved or expanded service. In other cases, the plans are not so specific, but they generally inform officials about particular CIP needs. These plans also help the manager and governing board judge the relative priorities of capital requests in different service areas and match these priorities to available financing.

The value of a CIP is similarly enhanced if a local government has a long-term master plan or comprehensive plan that identifies trends in the community's employment, income, population, housing, traffic, and land use and attempts to project those trends over a ten- to twenty-year period. A long-term master plan thus enables local officials to anticipate infrastructure and capital facility needs to accommodate those changes. In some jurisdictions, master planning is broadened into a strategic planning process in which officials, community leaders, and citizens agree on long-term goals for the community. Local government officials in communities where there is a master, comprehensive, or strategic plan can refer to it when making CIP requests or prioritizing requests and preparing and approving the CIP.

In **Birmingham, Michigan,** several strategic-planning and goal-setting initiatives shape the city's five-year CIP.[61] The first is "Downtown Birmingham 2016," a plan that includes major streetscape improvements, the development and construction of a civic center, the replacement of streetlights, and other projects; the city is in the process of implementing this plan through the CIP and the annual budget. Second, Birmingham has approved a ten-year sewer improvement program to replace deteriorated sewers. The projects in the sewer improvement plan feed directly into the CIP. Third, to guide city planning, capital programming, and budgeting, city officials have approved strategic and service planning goals such as "Preserve the city's residential character" and "Maintain and promote a vibrant and healthy downtown area."

Hickory, North Carolina, makes multiyear service planning a top priority. Long-range service or "master" plans shape both the annual budget and the city's capital improvement program:

• The landscape master plan prioritizes planting projects throughout the city and is implemented over a ten-year period.

• The parks and recreation master plan prioritizes current and future recreation projects and also extends over ten years.

• The sidewalk and bikes master plan projects sidewalk and bike path improvement projects citywide for the next twenty years.

• The stormwater plan is related to the creation of a metropolitan area stormwater utility.

• The business and industrial development master plan sets guidelines for funding economic development activities and economic incentives to firms.

• The comprehensive downtown development plan identifies sustainable economic renewal projects in the city's downtown area.

• The water and sewer extension plan prioritizes major water and sewer extensions over a five-year period.

• The long-range library plan identifies service expansion goals and facility and equipment enhancements over a ten-year period.[62]

Most of these plans were formulated and approved initially in the mid- to late 1990s in a broad-based process involving community leaders and citizen representatives as well as city officials. The plans address immediate, ongoing, and long-term needs. They are updated annually or periodically and are implemented in the annual budget and the CIP.

Inclusion of asset replacement and rehabilitation schedules in the CIP

Capital assets need to be maintained and repaired, and they must be periodically renewed or rehabilitated to keep them in serviceable condition. Expenditures for ongoing maintenance and repair are current outlays rather than capital outlays. They are properly charged to the operating or annual budget rather than included in the CIP. Expenditures to renew or rehabilitate capital assets that involve structural or mechanical change and that improve the utility of capital assets or extend their useful life are usually classified as capital outlays and are often included in the CIP. In this category are projects for street repaving and reconstruction, water and sewer line renewals, roof replacements, major renovations of buildings, and equipment and vehicle overhauls. Although the useful life of buildings and other facilities is usually twenty years or longer, major renovations and expansions may be necessary after only ten years to meet growing and changing needs.

Eventually, capital equipment needs to be replaced: police patrol cars every two to four years, sanitation vehicles every five to seven years, construction equipment about every ten years, and first-line fire trucks every twenty years. Computer equipment may need to be replaced or upgraded every five years or so.

Without regular maintenance and periodic rehabilitation or renewal and replacement, capital assets fall into disrepair, make service delivery more difficult, drive up other expenditures, and eventually result in lower quality and levels of service. A local government can use a CIP as an effective tool to plan and finance capital replacement and rehabilitation spending. For this to happen, however, a local government must have equipment replacement and facility and infrastructure rehabilitation schedules that tie into the CIP. With such schedules and one or more recurring revenue sources that are earmarked for this purpose, capital replacement and rehabilitation can become a regular routine in the CIP.

Cedarburg, Wisconsin, effectively integrates equipment replacement and infrastructure rehabilitation schedules into its CIP.[63] The city's equipment replacement schedule shows all vehicles and capital equipment by department, and it records or calculates the following information for each: vehicle or equipment type and name; fixed asset number; vehicle identification number if applicable; purchase price; expected useful life; remaining useful life; estimated replacement cost; and annual cost. The annual cost is a charge made each year to departments for the use, maintenance, and replacement of equipment. It accumulates funds to meet replacement needs.

Exhibit 3–12 shows the equipment replacement schedule for emergency government, administration, police, and the senior center in Cedarburg. The city uses this schedule to plan the replacement of public works vehicles and equipment in the CIP.

Exhibit 3–7, presented earlier in the chapter, shows the Cedarburg CIP plan for ongoing street improvements and related special projects. Most of the street projects are modest in size. They are being undertaken pursuant to a regular schedule and are being financed mostly with annual property taxes.

Accounting for inflation and changes in costs and prices

Because a CIP projects capital needs over a multiyear period—usually five or six years—project or acquisition costs are likely to change over the forecast period. The possibility of inflation must be considered in estimating costs for future projects and acquisitions.

For instance, a medium-size city's fire department may need two new fire trucks of the same type and capacity during the CIP forecast period, and both trucks are in the city's CIP. One is included and will be acquired in the upcoming budget year. The second is included in planning year four of the six-year CIP forecast period. Should both trucks be included in the CIP at the current price for a truck of that type or capacity, or should the second

Exhibit 3–12
Equipment replacement schedule, Cedarburg, Wisconsin

CITY OF CEDARBURG
EQUIPMENT REPLACEMENT CHARGES - 2003

Vehicle No.	Year	Make Model	Vehicle Identification Number	Purchase Price	Life Expectancy	Remaining Life	Replacement Cost	Annual Cost
EMERGENCY GOVERNMENT								
1	1989	Ford Ambulance-Como Van	1FDKE30M7KHB44403	25,000	25	11	50,000	2,000
2	1984	GMC Suburban Sierra	1G5GK26M3EF530456	17,000	15	5	34,000	2,267
3	1999	Jeep Cherokee	1J4FF68S7XL612748	22,845	10	6	28,000	2,800
4	1986	GMC Pickup Truck	1GTGK24M8GS530300	16,000	10	0	25,000	2,500
5	1991	GMC Sonoma Pickup Truck	1GTCT19Z2M8541098	15,006	10	0	23,400	2,340
6	1954	FWD Rescue Truck	SN260186	14,000	15	0	0	0
7	1970	KAISER-Jeep 2.5 Ton	04K-21370-0525-14505	2,940	10	0	15,000	1,500
8	1991	Oshkosh-UCBC	4CDB5XE22M2103362	13,500	10	0	15,000	1,500
Total Emergency Government				$126,291			$190,400	$14,907
ADMINISTRATION								
51	1998	GMC Jimmy - Engineering/Recreation	1GKDT13W8W2522097	14,182	7	3	25,000	3,571
53	1993	Ford Taurus, Teal (P)- Building Inspection	1FACP52U3PG255111	14,035	7	0	20,000	2,857
52	1995	GMC Jimmy, 4 door(P) - Engineering	1GKDT13W4S2527937	12,000	7	0	25,000	3,571
50	1997	Crown Victoria	2FALP71WXVX142195	14,000	7	1	20,000	2,857
Total Administration				$54,217			$90,000	$12,857
POLICE DEPARTMENT								
1	1995	Chev. Caprice - Detective/Juvenile	1G1BL52W2SR146003	17,111	6	0	24,000	4,000
2	1998	Oldsmobile 4dr Sedan - Chief	1G3HN52K2W4840041	16,389	6	1	24,000	4,000
3	2002	Chevy-Impala	2G1WF5DE129239461	18,496	8	7	28,000	3,500
4	2000	Chev.Blazer-4Door - Patrol (M)	1GNDT13W6YK214139	28,395	6	3	30,000	5,000
5	2000	Chev.Blazer-4Door - Patrol (M)	1GNDT13W8YK214837	22,398	6	3	23,000	3,833
6	2001	Crown Victoria 4 door - Patrol (M)	2FAFP71W81X146981	23,590	4	2	28,000	7,000
7	1999	Ford Crown Victoria - Sgt.	2FAFP71W7XX184100	24,465	6	2	28,000	4,667
8	2002	Ford Crown Victoria - Patrol (M)	2FAFP71W32X156352	20,223	8	7	28,000	3,500
9	2001	Chevy-Venture - Detective	1GNDX03E81D220508	22,200	10	8	24,000	2,400
Total Police Department				$193,267			$237,000	$37,900
SENIOR CENTER								
59	1999	Dodge Caravan	2B4GP44G9XR250293	$17,322	10	6	$24,000	$4,000 (F)
EQUIPMENT REPLACEMENT SUBTOTAL				$391,097			$541,400	$69,664

truck be included at a higher price, assuming the cost for that type of truck will increase due to inflation, improvements in features, or other factors?

If general inflation is nonexistent or very low—less than 1 or 2 percent per year—and if the price for that type of fire truck has remained stable in recent years, officials have a basis for disregarding possible future inflation and putting each truck into the CIP at the current price. On the other hand, if general inflation is running at more than 2 percent annually, or if the price of that type of fire truck has been increasing and there is no reason to believe that such increases will stop or reverse, they should take inflation into account. In other words, the fire truck in planning year four of the CIP forecast period should be included at a higher price than the one in the upcoming budget year.

Fayetteville, Arkansas, and **Madison Heights, Michigan,** make it their policy to account for inflation in estimating capital project and acquisition costs in their CIPs. Fayetteville's 1999–2003 CIP states that all CIP project requests are initially costed at 1998 dollars.[64] Then, once a determination is made as to what year a project will be initiated and how it will be phased, inflation is taken into account in estimating project and acquisition costs for any year of the CIP forecast period. This is done using a "cost increase multiplier." The 1999–2003 CIP assumes a 6 percent annual inflation rate. Given this, a cost increase multiplier was calculated for each year of the CIP forecast period:

CIP year	Annual cost multiplier @ 6%
2002	1.060
2003	1.124
2004	1.191
2005	1.262
2006	1.338

Application of the multipliers is straightforward. For example, all project and acquisition costs included in year 2005 of the CIP forecast period are increased by 26.2 percent over the prices in effect for these items in 2001, the year in which the 2002–2006 CIP was prepared.

Madison Heights, Michigan, accounts for inflation in its CIP somewhat differently. The city's 2000–2004 CIP adjusts cost estimates for vehicles and equipment by 4 to 7 percent a year during the CIP forecast period. The percentage used for specific vehicles or equipment depends on how cost increases have been running in recent years for those types of vehicles or equipment. The inflation rate assumed for construction projects in the 2000–2004 CIP is 8 percent per year over the CIP period. The higher adjustment for construction reflects the surge in construction costs that occurred in the late 1990s as the demand in this sector outpaced the availability of qualified firms to do the work.[65]

Project and acquisition requests should make clear whether cost estimates include inflation and how the inflation or price increase rate was determined.

Costs for some equipment and for construction may be declining. Officials must then decide whether to include such equipment or projects in future years of the CIP forecast period at current or at lower costs or prices. Officials, assuming that price declines will not continue, generally put such equipment and projects into the CIP at current cost. This assures that sufficient funds will be available. If costs continue to decline, downward adjustments in cost estimates can be made for such assets in the preparation of future-year CIPs.

CIP presentation

The local government manager or administrator and his or her staff usually select and design CIP presentation formats and materials and make the presentation to the governing board and community at large. In some jurisdictions a planning board has this responsibility. In medium- or small-size local units without a manager or administrator or active planning board, the finance director, planning director, or another administrative official may present the CIP to the governing board.

Occasionally a city or county manager and staff prepare a CIP without presenting it to the governing board or otherwise making it public. The CIP remains an administrative document that the manager uses to decide which specific capital projects and acquisitions to recommend to the governing board in any year. These projects and acquisitions are incorporated into the operating budget or a one-year capital budget that the governing board reviews and approves, but the full, multiyear CIP never goes to the board for public consideration, review, and approval.

An unpublicized CIP that is strictly administrative is better than no CIP at all, but it is not recommended. Of course, if the press or interested citizens find out that the manager and staff have prepared a multiyear CIP and are using it to decide which projects to recommend to the board each year, they are unlikely to keep silent about it.

To improve the likelihood that the governing board will use and approve the CIP, local governments can take the following steps when presenting the document.

Coordinate with the operating or annual budget presentation

If state statutes, the local charter, or other legal provisions require the CIP to be presented to the governing board on a different date than the annual budget, the CIP will, of course, be a separate document. In Largo, Florida, the manager presents the recommended CIP in a separate document prior to presentation of the annual budget, and the board reviews and adopts the CIP separately from the annual budget. Following governing board review and adoption of both the CIP and the annual budget, the approved CIP—or at least an abbreviated version of it—is included in the adopted annual budget document.[66]

A separately presented CIP focuses attention on the capital projects and acquisitions being recommended. Governing board review of the CIP is likely to occur separately from the board's review of the annual budget. If the manager presents the CIP to the governing board as part of the annual budget, CIP recommendations and long-term capital planning considerations may be overlooked because the governing board may focus on annual budget issues and setting the tax rate for the upcoming year. For this reason, even when there is no legal requirement, many jurisdictions present the CIP as a separate document apart from the annual budget.[67]

On the other hand, combining the CIP and annual budget into one presentation document can make budget and CIP presentation more straightforward and less complicated. The CIP is more readily seen as a part of the overall program and financial plans of the jurisdiction. This is why many small local governments (for example, Mauldin, South Carolina, and Gainesville, Georgia) favor this approach.[68] It may also be the way to go for a local jurisdiction that is undertaking a CIP for the first time.

Emphasize projects and spending in the first year of the CIP forecast period

Every CIP gives special attention to the capital projects and acquisitions included in the first year of the CIP forecast period. This is the budget year, and the governing board must approve and fund the spending planned for this year. However, some CIP presentations focus more attention on first-year spending than do others. The reasons vary. Sometimes it is primarily a matter of presentation, and planning for needs in the outlying years is not neglected. Emphasis in the CIP on first-year spending may reflect little planning for the out years, however. This denotes a weak CIP process.

The document presenting the CIP for **Cary, North Carolina,** emphasizes projects and acquisitions in the first year of the CIP forecast period. Cary uses a separate document entitled *Capital Improvements Budget* to present its capital budget and CIP. The 2003 issue of this document is 152 pages long; all but 23 pages toward the end of the document address the 2002–2003 capital budget and the projects in it. Although Cary's CIP document emphasizes first-year spending, substantial effort and planning are given in the CIP process to the identification and forecasting of out-year needs, that is, needs over the period 2004–2013. Many projects and substantial spending are planned for those out years.[69]

Address accomplishments, projects implemented, and progress on projects in process

The CIP is a plan to guide future capital spending, but it is based on past spending for capital purposes. Moreover, if the CIP allocates project costs by year based on when expenditures (rather than appropriations) for projects and acquisitions occur, the CIP serves partly to monitor project implementation as well as to plan and make decisions about future spending. Regardless of the basis used for allocating costs by year in the CIP, officials often have questions about progress on projects already approved and being implemented. A CIP should point to past results and accomplishments. This can demonstrate that previous CIPs have resulted in positive outcomes and reinforce expectations that planning in the current CIP will be similarly fruitful.

The 2003–2008 CIP of **Alexandria, Virginia,** has a two-page section entitled "Accomplishments of the Past Year" that lists projects approved and funded in the prior year's CIP and briefly describes for each project progress in planning and design, preparation of contract documents, awarding of contracts, and initial construction.[70]

The village of **Deerfield, Illinois,** introduces its 2000–2004 CIP with a one-page "Summary of Capital Projects Completed" over the years 1997 through 2001.[71]

Show changes from the CIP presented or approved in the prior year

Local governments usually repeat the CIP process and update the CIP annually. The updating can involve dropping some projects planned in last year's CIP; redefining, changing, and adjusting the scope and cost estimates for other projects coming forward from that CIP; and adding new projects. Few CIPs show how the CIP under consideration this year differs from the one approved for the jurisdiction last year. This is unlike the way the annual budget of most local governments carefully compares the proposed budget for the coming year with the approved budget or estimated spending for the current year and with actual spending for one or more past years.

The 2001–2005 CIP for **Maplewood, Minnesota,** is an exception.[72] This CIP is presented in a separate CIP document. The page following the city manager's CIP message is titled, "Highlights of the Capital Improvement Plan," and it starts with a short table that compares CIP spending by function in the 2000–2004 CIP and in the 2001–2005 CIP. (See Exhibit 3–13).

A second, short table in the Maplewood CIP shows the changes in project costs for each comparable year of the 2000–2004 and the 2001–2005 CIPs (see Exhibit 3–14).

Besides the tables in Exhibits 3–13 and 3–14, the "Highlights" section lists the four largest projects in Maplewood's 2001–2005 CIP. Finally, it lists nine large new projects—those appearing the first time in the CIP.

	Function	2000–2004 CIP ($)	2001–2005 CIP ($)	Increase or decrease ($)	Increase or decrease (%)
Exhibit 3-13 Comparison of project spending by function, 2000–2004 and 2001–2005 CIPs, Maplewood, Minnesota	Buildings	2,543,000	2,109,000	(434,000)	17.1
	Equipment	3,512,800	2,022,135	(1,490,665)	(42.4)
	Parks	3,970,000	800,000	(3,170,000)	(79.8)
	Public works	13,225,000	10,545,000	(2,680,000)	(20.3)
	Totals	23,250,800	15,476,135	(7,774,665)	(33.4)

	Year	2000–2004 CIP ($)	2001–2005 CIP ($)	Increase or decrease ($)	Increase or decrease (%)
Exhibit 3-14 Comparison of project spending by year, 2000–2004 and 2001–2005 CIPs, Maplewood, Minnesota	2001	3,254,400	3,286,000	31,600	25.6
	2002	2,536,000	2,991,000	455,000	17.9
	2003	3,505,000	2,431,000	(1,074,000)	(30.6)
	2004	5,610,000	3,350,135	(2,259,865)	(40.3)
	Totals	14,905,400	12,058,135	(2,847,265)	(19.1)

Include a list of existing buildings and facilities

Before they decide to approve funding for projects in the first year of a CIP, members of the local governing board may question how these proposed projects relate to already existing buildings and facilities. The manager may find it useful to include in the CIP document a list of existing buildings and facilities to demonstrate to the governing board and the community that structures and facilities have been evaluated before planning any spending for renovation, replacement, or expansion.

The FY 2002–2008 CIP of **Greensboro, North Carolina,** lists major city facilities that will undergo renovation (see Exhibit 3–15 for one of the pages in the public safety section). For each building, the list provides the locations, the date built or last renovated, an assessment of condition, whether the city plans to renovate or replace the building, and the projected date and cost for renovation or replacement. Statement No. 34 of the Governmental Accounting Standards Board (see Chapter 1) requires recording and reporting of all fixed assets, including infrastructure, and also depreciation of assets used for general government as well as enterprise functions. These requirements are likely to improve local governments' fixed-asset records and facilitate the preparation of a city-owned facilities list for the CIP.[73]

Exhibit 3–15

Sample page from CIP, Greensboro, North Carolina

CITY OF GREENSBORO
CAPITAL IMPROVEMENTS PROGRAM 2002-2008

SERVICE AREA	*DEPARTMENT*	*DIVISION/PROGRAM*	*DISTRICT*
Public Safety	Fire	Stations & Buildings	5

PROJECT TITLE	*ACCOUNT NUMBER*
Fire Station # 10 Replacement	101 - 40 06 - 00

PROJECT DESCRIPTION/JUSTIFICATION

This project will allow the aging and overcrowded Fire Station # 10, located at 4208 High Point Road, to be replaced with a more mission appropriate facility. The current facility is 43 years old and in poor condition. Built in 1958, the facility now houses 2 fire companies, that serves approximately 15,000 residents and the surrounding heavy merchantile, manufacturing and warehousing district. There is no space to provide adequate facilities for female firefighters. The facility is also operating beyond the edge of its perimeter due to the Adams Farm and Grandover development. Service in this area is supplemented through a contract with Pinecroft-Sedgefield Fire Department.

PROJECTED STATUS - JUNE 30, 2002		*PROJECTED DATES:*	*TYPE REQUEST*
TOTAL APPROPRIATION	$2,560,000	BEGINNING 07/05	X CONTINUATION
TOTAL EXPENDITURI	$0	COMPLETION 09/06	REVISION
PROJECTED BALANCE	$2,560,000		NEW

EXPENSES	2002-03	2003-04	2004-05	2005-06	2006-07	2007-08	**TOTAL**
PLANNING/DESIGN	$0	$0	$0	$60,000	$0	$0	$60,000
LAND	$0	$0	$550,000	$0	$0	$0	$550,000
CONSTRUCTION	$0	$0	$0	$1,450,000	$500,000	$0	$1,950,000
EQUIP/FURNISHING:	$0	$0	$0	$0	$0	$0	$0
TOTAL	$0	$0	$550,000	$1,510,000	$500,000	$0	$2,560,000

REVENUES	2002-03	2003-04	2004-05	2005-06	2006- 07	2007- 08	**TOTAL**
GENERAL FUND	$0	$0	$0	$0	$0	$0	$0
ENTERPRISE FUNI	$0	$0	$0	$0	$0	$0	$0
ST. SIDEWALK FUN	$0	$0	$0	$0	$0	$0	$0
STATE REVENU	$0	$0	$0	$0	$0	$0	$0
AUTHORIZED BOND:	$0	$0	$0	$0	$0	$0	$0
UNAUTH. BONDS	$0	$0	$550,000	$1,510,000	$500,000	$0	$2,560,000
UNAUTH. BONDS 2	$0	$0	$0	$0	$0	$0	$0
REVENUE BOND:	$0	$0	$0	$0	$0	$0	$0
GRANTS/OTHEF	$0	$0	$0	$0	$0	$0	$0
TOTAL	$0	$0	$550,000	$1,510,000	$0	$0	$2,060,000

OPERATING	2002-03	2003-04	2004-05	2005-06	2006- 07	2007- 08	**TOTAL**
PERSONNEL	$0	$0	$0	$0	$0	$0	$0
MAINT./OPERATIONS	$0	$0	$0	$0	$0	$0	$0
CAPITAL OUTLAY	$0	$0	$0	$0	$0	$0	$0
(REVENUES)	$0	$0	$0	$0	$0	$0	$0
NET COST	$0	$0	$0	$0	$0	$0	$0

Exhibit 3–16
2002 Sidewalk Replacement project, Oak Park, Michigan

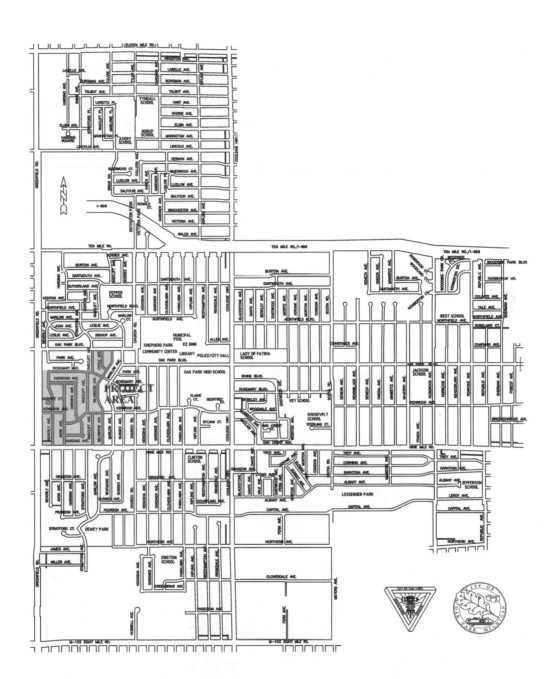

Exhibit 3–17
Community profile, Kansas City, Missouri

COMMUNITY PROFILE

From humble beginnings as a trading post in 1821, Kansas City has become the largest city in a metropolitan area of 1.6 million people. Kansas City is the nation's 36th largest city in population and the sixteenth largest in land area. Located near the geographic and population centers of the nation, it truly is the "Heart of America."

The metro area straddles the Missouri-Kansas state line and includes more than 136 cities and 11 counties. Kansas City, Missouri covers parts of four counties — Jackson, Clay, Platte and Cass — not to mention all or part of 15 school districts.

Kansas City boasts more fountains than any other city except Rome and more boulevards than any except Paris. Its 1,769 acre Swope Park is one of the largest urban park in America. However, Kansas City is perhaps best known for its steaks, barbecue and jazz.

With more than 60 barbecue restaurants and numerous cook-off competitions, it is arguably the nation's barbecue capital. Kansas City became a hotbed of jazz shortly after World War I in the now-famous area around 18th & Vine. Jazz is undergoing a renaissance here, a factor in the creation of the complex that houses the Kansas City Jazz Museum and the American Jazz Museum. The district also houses the Negro Leagues Baseball Museum.

Date of Incorporation	June 3, 1850
Date of Charter	February 24, 1925
Form of Government	Council/Manager
Area of City	317 Square Miles
Submitted Budget Level	$974,915,047
Expenditures per capita	$2,204.76

Household Income

$200,000 or greater	1.6%
$150,000 - 199,999	1.5%
$100,000 - 149,999	5.4%
$75,000 - 99,999	8.8%
$50,000 - 74,999	18.4%
$35,000 - 49,999	17.2%
$25,000 - 34,999	13.8%
$15,000 - 24,999	14.1%
$10,000 - 14,999	6.5%
under $10,000	12.7%

POPULATION

2001 Estimate	442,187
2000 U.S. Census	441,545
1990 U.S. Census	435,187
1980 U.S. Census	448,159
1970 U.S. Census	507,080
1960 U.S. Census	475,539

DWELLING UNITS

Single Family units	148,017
Multifamily units	53,317

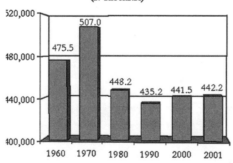

KANSAS CITY POPULATION
(IN THOUSANDS)

Exhibit 3–17
(continued)

Kansas City is hometown to the headquarters of Hallmark Cards, Farmland Industries, Utilicorp, Russell Stover Candies, Yellow Freight, H&R Block, the Nazarene Church, Payless Cashways, Interstate Bakeries, AMC Theaters, American Century and numerous other businesses.

It ranks first in inland foreign trade zone space, underground storage space, greeting card publishing, frozen food storage and distribution, and hard winter wheat marketing. It ranks second in wheat flour production and the size of its rail center. Both General Motors and Ford have major plants here, ranking Kansas City eighth in the nation in automobile assembly.

The city also is a major transportation hub. Approximately 400 flights a day come and go from Kansas City International Airport, where the maximum distance from aircraft to curb is less than 75 feet. Eleven regulated barge lines transport goods through Kansas City on the Missouri River. Kansas City is one of only five cities with three intersecting interstate highways (I-70, I-29 and I-35). The city's rail system carries 300 daily freight arrivals and departures.

For sports fans, Kansas City, Missouri, has seven professional sports teams: the Kansas City Chiefs (football), Kansas City Royals (baseball), the Kansas City Blades (ice hockey), the Kansas City Wizards (outdoor soccer), Kansas City Attack (indoor soccer), the Kansas City Knights (ABA basketball) and the Kansas City Explorers (tennis).

EMPLOYMENT OF RESIDENTS BY INDUSTRY

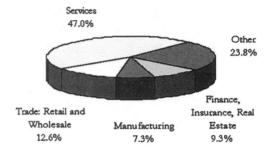

Services
47.0%

Other
23.8%

Trade: Retail and
Wholesale
12.6%

Manufacturing
7.3%

Finance,
Insurance, Real
Estate
9.3%

RACIAL COMPOSITION

White	60.7%
Black	31.2%
Hispanic (of any race)	6.9%
Asian	1.9%
Native American	0.5%
Pacific Islander	0.1%
Other	5.6%

AGE COMPOSITION

65 years and older	11.7%
64-45 years	20.6%
44-25 years	32.5%
24-21 years	5.8%
20-18 years	3.9%
17-5 years	18.2%
5 years and under	7.2%

EDUCATIONAL ATTAINMENT

Graduate or Professional Degree	10.7%
Bachelor's Degree	16.8%
Associate Degree	5.7%
Some College, no degree	22.9%
High School Degree	23.8%
No High School Degree	19.9%

EDUCATION

Number of School Districts	15
Enrollment	
Preprimary	7,293
Elementary or High School	77,939
College	27,746
Total Enrollment	112,978

Include a list of projects under consideration

Financing capacity is rarely sufficient to accommodate all worthy capital requests in the CIP forecast period. Some CIPs list capital projects and acquisitions that fulfill legitimate needs but are not of high enough priority to be included in any of the planning years of the CIP forecast period. They are listed to indicate that they remain under consideration and may be included in the CIP when it is updated in a subsequent year. Such a list should not include CIP requests that are unlikely to be approved and funded in the future.

The 1999–2004 CIP of **Forsyth County, North Carolina,** includes a list of "projects under consideration but not in the plan."[74] These projects would cost a total of $94.4 million. (The total of all projects included in the county's five-year CIP is $143.5 million.) A sheriff training facility, a community college building, a community library, a new animal control building, and several other major projects are listed. The CIP does not rank those projects in order of importance because priorities will undoubtedly shift before they can be added to the CIP.

Include maps and photographs to present project information

Because of the physical nature of infrastructure and capital facilities, a CIP can incorporate maps and photos to show the location, nature, and to some degree magnitude of projects such as streets, sidewalks, parks, libraries, and schools. One or more maps can usefully show which neighborhoods or parts of the city or county will benefit from CIP projects. (It is often politically advantageous to show that all parts of the city or county will benefit at some point during the CIP forecast period.) Modern mapping methods, including geographic information systems, make the inclusion of maps in the CIP feasible for medium-size and even many small local governments. Exhibit 3–16 on page 81 shows a map highlighting the sidewalk replacement and repair projects included in the 1999–2004 CIP of Oak Park, Michigan.

Include a community profile

A community profile is a snapshot of the key demographic, economic, and social statistics of a city or county. To serve this purpose, the profile must be no more than a page or two in length. If the CIP is presented as a separate document, the CIP document can include the same profile used in the operating budget document. Exhibit 3–17 on pages 82 and 83 presents the two-page community profile for Kansas City, Missouri.

Some may consider a community profile superfluous. After all, the primary audience for the CIP is the governing board, and its members are familiar with the facts presented in the profile. However, even the best-informed governing board member may not be able to recall these statistics and may find it helpful to refer to them when reviewing the CIP. The CIP is also addressed to the broader community. The profile can help the press and public put CIP recommendations into context.

Notes

1 Rocky Mount, North Carolina, Capital Improvement Program, 2002–2007, 9.

2 See, for example, Chatham County, 2002–2007 Recommended Capital Improvement Program, "Expenditure Summary," www.co.chatham.nc.us.

3 Town of Hillsborough, FY 2002 Annual Budget and FY 2002–04 Financial Plan, section presenting CIP.

4 City of Campbell, California, Operating and Capital Budget, Fiscal Year 1999–2000, 493. See www.ci.campbell.ca.us for a list of projects for the first year of Campbell's 2001–2007 CIP.

5 City of Raleigh Adopted 2002–2003 Budget and CIP, section presenting the 2002–2003 through 2011–2012 Capital Improvement Program, www.raleigh-nc.org.

6 City of Reno, Nevada, 2000/01 Budget Capital Improvement Plan, 2000–2020, 194–195.

7 Mecklenburg County, North Carolina, Ten-Year Capital Needs Assessment, Fiscal Year 2002–2011, especially 1-3.

8 City of Norman, Oklahoma, Capital Improvements Project Budget, Fiscal Year Ending June 30, 2001; Capital Improvements Projects Plan Fiscal Year Ending 2001–2005, 10.

9 City of Madison Heights, Michigan, Adopted Budget for Fiscal Year 2002–2003, 225, www.ci.madison-heights.mi.us.

10 Capital Improvement Program, Instruction Manual, FY 2002–2006, City of Winston-Salem, North Carolina, 15.

11 Capital Improvement Plan, 2001–2005, City of Maplewood, Minnesota, 1-12, 1-13, and 1-15.

12 2002–2003 Adopted Annual Budget, Forsyth County, North Carolina, section presenting CIP, www.co.forsyth.nc.us.

13 City of Fayetteville, Arkansas, 2002–2006 Capital Improvement Program, vii, www.uark.edu/ALADIN/cityinfo/cityweb.

14 City of Greeley, Colorado, Biennial Budget, January 1, 2001–December 31, 2002, 387–388.

15 City of Largo, Florida, Annual Budget, Fiscal year 2001, CIP-1.

16 Greensboro, North Carolina, Capital Improvement Program, 2001–2007, 180.

17 City of Loveland, Colorado, 2000 Adopted Budget, 18-3.

18 City of Greeley, Colorado, Biennial Budget, January 1, 2001–December 31, 2002, 378.

19 Town of Cary, North Carolina, Capital Improvements Budget, Fiscal Year 2003, 13–20. This document also presents the town's ten-year CIP for 2004–2013.

20 City of Greeley, Colorado, Biennial Budget, January 1, 2001–December 31, 2002, 384–385.

21 Town of Avon, Capital Improvement Program, Fiscal Year 2000–2001, R-10.

22 Alamance County, North Carolina, 2002–2003 Annual Operating Budget and Capital Improvement Plan, 8-4–8-7.

23 City of San Clemente, California, Annual Budget & Capital Improvement Program, Fiscal Year 2000–2001. The CIP is presented on pages 315–385. See pages 23–26 for the section of the budget message summarizing and highlighting 2000–2001 capital projects and the CIP.

24 City of Greeley, Colorado, Biennial Budget, January 1, 2001–December 31, 2002, 377–388.

25 Town of Hillsborough FY 2002 Annual Budget and FY 2002–04 Financial Plan, section presenting the CIP.

26 City of Loveland, Colorado, 2003 Adopted Budget, 19-10, www.ci.loveland.co.us.

27 City of Cedarburg, Wisconsin, 2003 Annual Budget, 135.

28 City of Greeley, Colorado, Biennial Budget, January 1, 2001–December 31, 2002, 389–390.

29 Chatham County, 2003–2008 Capital Improvement Program, www.co.chatham.nc.us. Material on social services building expansion provided by assistant county manager.

30 Capital Improvement Program, Instruction Manual, FY 2002–2006, City of Winston-Salem, North Carolina, Appendix: Capital Project Request Form.

31 The Unified Government of Athens-Clarke County, FY 2000 Annual Operating & Capital Budget, July 1, 1999–June 30, 2000, D-1–D-3.

32 Operating Budget and Capital Improvement Program, Adopted 2001, City of Rockville, Maryland, 341.

33 City of Winston-Salem, 1999–2000 Annual Budget Program and 2000–2004 Capital Plan, 264.

34 Town of Elizabethtown Capital Improvement Plan, March, 1999.

35 This consists of $500,000 for water and $2.3 million for sewer projects. Data provided to author by town manager on April 29, 2003.

36 City of Loveland, Colorado, 2000 Annual Budget, 18-7.

37 City of Campbell, California, Operating and Capital Budget, Fiscal Year 1999–2000, 494–496.

38 Orange County, North Carolina, Manager's Recommended 2000–2010 Capital Investment Plan, iv and 67.

39 This is based on an exchange of messages among e-mail discussion group members, including a Greensboro budget analyst; electronic discussion group sponsored by the North Carolina Local Government Budget Association.

40 City of San Clemente, California, Annual Budget and Capital Improvement Program, Fiscal Year 2000–2001, 315–382.

41 Lenoir County, North Carolina, Fiscal Year 1999–2000 Submitted Budget, 150–153.

42 City of Madison Heights, Michigan, Adopted Budget for Fiscal Year 2002–2003, 226, 234–235, www.ci.madison-heights.mi.us.

43 *Standard & Poor's Public Finance Criteria* (New York: S&P, 1998), 22.

44 Mecklenburg County, North Carolina, Ten-Year Capital Needs Assessment, Fiscal Year 2002–2011, 17; also Mecklenburg County, North Carolina, County Manager's Budget and Work Program, Fiscal year 1999–2000, 112–113.

45 David Brower and Ann Schwab, An Introduction to Law for Planners, Chapter 4. Also see Florida Administrative Code Chapter 9J-5, Concurrency Management System (1985).

46 Two early court cases that address this issue are *National Land and Investment Co. v. Kohn*, 419A Pa. 504, 528; 215 A.3d 597, 602 (1965); and *Golden v. Planning Board of Ramapo*, 285 NE.2d 391 (NY) (1972). Also see Peter Ray, "Adequate Public Facilities Ordinances," Capstone Paper, Master of Public Administration Program, University of North Carolina at Chapel Hill, April 2000.

47 *Tate Terrace Realty Investors, Inc. v. Currituck County*, 127 N.C. Ap. 212 (1997).

48 "Adequate Public Facilities Provisions, Currituck County, North Carolina, April 1998. Presentation handout distributed by Currituck County Finance Officer; confirmed in telephone conversation with this official on April 29, 2002.

49 The 1999–2003 Capital Improvement Plan of Alamance County is financially oriented. It was prepared by the assistant county manager, who also served as county finance officer and is a CPA. He is now county manager.

50 See, for example, National Resources Planning Board, *Long Range Programming of Municipal Public Works* (Washington, D.C.: NRPB, 1941).

51 City of Greeley, Colorado, Biennial Budget, January 1, 2001–December 31, 2002, 385–387.

52 The consultant is a former city manager of Charlotte, North Carolina.

53 City of Smyrna, Georgia, Annual Financial Plan, Fiscal Year 1997, 307.

54 These CIP and annual budget calendars are based on preparation of the fiscal year 2001 budget. Largo, Florida, Annual Budget, Fiscal Year 2001, BG-4, CIP-1.

55 City of Asheville, North Carolina, Adopted Annual Budget, 2002–2003, 15, 135.

56 Comment by a retired assistant manager of Raleigh, who coordinated the city's CIP and annual budget processes for many years.

57 These efforts are described in a special city report, "Building Winston Together." The author of this book was involved in these efforts, advising officials on the content of the telephone survey instrument and organizing and facilitating the public forum.

58 Winston-Salem: Annual Financial Report for the Fiscal Year Ending June 30, 2001, 20. Both the city manager and city budget director expressed this view of the importance of citizen involvement to passage of the bond referenda.

59 Greensboro, North Carolina, Capital Improvement Program 2001–2007, 3, 181–182.

60 City of Greeley, Colorado, Biennial Budget, January 1, 2001–December 31, 2002, 386–387.

61 City of Birmingham, Recommended 2000–2001 Budget, 19, 22–23, and 311.

62 Hickory, North Carolina, Annual Budget, 2001–2002, 23–33; see also City of Hickory, 1997–1998 Annual Budget, 10–11, 17–36, and 197.

63 City of Cedarburg, Wisconsin, 2000 Annual Budget, 137–139.

64 City of Fayetteville, Arkansas, 2002–2006 Capital Improvement Program, x, www.uark.edu/ALADIN/cityinfo/cityweb.

65 City of Madison Heights, Michigan, Annual Budget, 1999–2000, 235.

66 City of Largo, Florida, Annual Budget, Fiscal Year 2001, BG-4, CIP-1.

67 For example, City of Newton, North Carolina, Strategic Financial Plan for Capital Improvement, Fiscal Years 2002–2006.

68 Mauldin, Fiscal Year 1999–2000 Budget, 78–80; and City of Gainesville, Georgia, Annual Budget for the Fiscal Year Ending June 30, 2001, 157–187.

69 Town of Cary, North Carolina, Capital Improvements Budget and Plan, Fiscal Year 2001–2002.

70 City of Alexandria, FY 2003–2008 Capital Improvement Program, 10–12.

71 Annual Budget, Fiscal Year 2001–2002, Village of Deerfield, Illinois, 149.

72 Capital Improvement Plan, 2001–2005, City of Maplewood, Minnesota, 1-4, 1-34.

73 Governmental Accounting Standards Board (GASB), *Statement No. 34: Basic Financial Statements—and Management's Discussion and Analysis—for State and Local Governments* (Norwalk, Conn.: GASB, 1999), paragraphs 18–29.

74 2002–2003 Adopted Annual Budget, Forsyth County, North Carolina, section presenting the CIP, www.co.forsyth.nc.us.

4

Prioritizing capital projects

Because capital requests and needs invariably exceed available financing, they have to be prioritized. Decisions must be made about which requests to approve and fund in the upcoming year's capital budget, which ones to schedule for future approval and funding in the capital improvement program (CIP), which ones to exclude from this year's capital budget and CIP but to consider in a later CIP, and which ones to turn down altogether.

This chapter examines six approaches that local governments use to prioritize CIP and capital budget requests:

- Experience-based judgment
- Departmental or functional priorities
- Broad categories of need
- Urgency-of-need criteria
- Weighted rating of urgency-of-need and related criteria
- Program priorities, goals, and service needs assessment and planning.[1]

Most local governments combine several of these approaches when prioritizing requests for capital projects and acquisitions. The experience-based judgment of local officials is often the most significant factor for setting priorities in capital budgeting. Many local governments use judgment combined with broad ranking categories, specific urgency-of-need criteria, and/or weighted rating systems. In other local governments, board-adopted program and project goals and an assessment of capital needs provide the basis for prioritization.

Although cost-benefit analysis is not one of the six ranking approaches examined in this chapter, all of these approaches consider benefits and costs in ranking projects. The approaches focus more attention on benefits than on costs because the benefits associated with most local capital projects are not quantifiable. Most of the ranking or rating criteria included in these approaches to prioritization identify and assess such nonquantifiable or difficult-to-quantify benefits. Costs—the direct costs of local government capital projects and acquisitions as well as the future operating costs and revenues of a project—are quantifiable. They can be estimated or at least roughly forecast and are also considered in the priority-setting systems examined in the chapter. Several of the systems or approaches include criteria that address intangible and external costs that, like benefits, are difficult to quantify or estimate.

In their CIPs and capital budgets, some local governments compare and rank all capital requests together. Other local governments distinguish among different types or categories of capital requests and rank them into priority separately, often by different criteria or approaches. For example, some jurisdictions rank requests for replacement capital projects separately from requests for new projects. "New requests or projects" may be defined to include new buildings or facilities that meet brand-new needs as well as the rehabilitation of existing facilities to accommodate new needs or uses for which the facilities were not originally designed. Some local governments rank capital requests financed from different funding sources separately (see the Winston-Salem example on page 96).

Experience-based judgment

The ranking of capital project and acquisition requests is sometimes based exclusively or primarily on the judgment of experienced managers, service professionals, budget and finance staff, governing board members, other officials, citizens, and anyone else who may be involved in the decision-making process. This fundamentally intuitive approach to setting priorities in capital budgeting is probably the most common approach used by medium- and small-size local governments.

If officials in the ranking process are in touch with citizens, clients, and service providers and are up-to-date about the problems facing the community, this approach can result in the selection and funding of projects that address a jurisdiction's most pressing infrastructure and capital needs. Especially in medium- and small-size jurisdictions, the judgment of local officials is usually well informed by personal experience, complaints from citizens, notices from federal and state regulatory agencies that certain local facilities are out of compliance with current standards, and media stories about shortcomings in public infrastructure and public views about it.

Nevertheless, experience-based judgment will fall short under certain conditions, four of which are identified below:

- **Many capital requests** If decision makers are faced with just ten, twenty, or even thirty capital requests, they can be sufficiently familiar with all the underlying needs to apply experience-based judgment when prioritizing them. With adequate consultation and deliberation among officials, decision makers can rank the requests without referring to ranking criteria or using an organized approach. However, if decision makers have to rank fifty, one hundred, or two hundred separate capital requests, the challenge becomes much more complicated. Officials involved in the ranking process for a jurisdiction are much less likely to be familiar with all the requests and underlying needs, and some projects that meet urgent needs may be left out while others that could wait may receive approval and funding.

- **Complex capital requests** Some capital project and acquisition requests are technologically complex. Expansion of a wastewater treatment plant is an example. Other requests involve complicated and difficult-to-judge choices—for example, sizing a proposed new thoroughfare to meet projected traffic flows in the future. Without professional advice, reference to specific urgency-of-need criteria, and/or a needs assessment and review of previously established goals, even the most experienced officials may be hard-pressed to prioritize capital requests.

- **Many decision makers** The more people involved in priority setting, the less likely it is that they will agree on requests. The task may be simplified if the decision makers first reach an agreement on decision criteria or program goals to guide priority setting and then follow an organized approach to ranking requests.

- **A need to justify priorities and project selection to others** These "others" can include the agencies that have made the requests for capital projects and acquisitions, other officials who have not been involved in the ranking process, the media, interested citizens, and the community at large. If decision makers have arrived at their priorities intuitively and quickly, relying solely or predominantly on their own familiarity with community needs, they may have trouble explaining priorities when they are questioned or challenged. On the other hand, if they have based their selection of projects on explicit criteria or particular program or project goals, they can readily refer to those criteria or goals as the basis for their choices. An organized and formal approach for planning and choosing among project and acquisition requests is more likely to be viewed as fair than a strictly informal approach.

For all these reasons, and because the financial stakes are often high in capital budgeting, officials in many local governments refer to decision criteria and use organized approaches to prioritize capital project requests. The use of urgency-of-need criteria, program or project goals, ranking or rating systems, or cost-benefit analysis does not make priority setting in capital budgeting "objective." The views of those who select and define the criteria, identify the program and project goals, and participate in the ranking process influence the priorities. Thus, the ranking of projects remains subjective. But objectivity is enhanced to the extent that the criteria, goals, and ranking or rating approach help officials to consider the relevant factors affecting priorities and to select projects and acquisitions that meet the community's most pressing needs.

Departmental or functional priorities

Departmental ranking of capital project or acquisition requests prioritizes the requests in each functional or program area. Departmental officials are directly familiar with the capital needs in their respective areas. This generally puts the director and staff of each department in a very good position to establish priorities among capital requests made by the department. The manager and the governing board more often than not will follow department-recommended priorities.

Departments may be given full discretion to establish the priorities as they see fit, or they may be asked to consider certain criteria. For instance, they may be asked to give a higher priority to requests that address health and safety concerns or legal mandates, or for which outside grant funding is available.

Individual departmental or functional priorities are useful when there are pressing needs in each department or functional area or when, for organizational or political reasons, top officials find it necessary to include in the recommended CIP and capital budget a number of capital requests from each department or function or from most of them. While spreading money among departments or functions may meet legitimate high-priority needs, or be expedient, or both, there are times when the most pressing capital needs are concentrated in a few functional areas. At such times, each department's ranking of its own requests offers only limited help to top officials in determining jurisdiction-wide priorities for the capital budget.

Furthermore, a department's priorities may not reflect the priorities that the manager and other top officials have for the department's capital needs. Departmental directors and staff tend to have a narrower perspective than the jurisdiction-wide view of the manager, governing board members, and top staff. If departmental officials are not aware of jurisdiction-wide priorities affecting their department's needs, or if they choose to ignore these priorities when prioritizing their capital requests, it will fall to top officials, who bring a broader view to bear, to juggle the priorities suggested by individual departments.

Departmental officials may be more willing to identify their top priorities than to rank all of their requests because they do not want to say that some requests are of low priority. They may also be more willing to reveal their priorities in private meetings or briefings with the manager and other decision makers than in public meetings or in public documents.

Broad categories of need

Decision makers can rank capital requests into several broad categories to prioritize the requests of an individual department or to prioritize requests across service areas for the entire jurisdiction. The focus here and in the rest of the chapter is on priority setting for the jurisdiction as a whole.

Priorities might be categorized simply as

- **High**   Projects that are essential and impending, and should be approved and funded in the upcoming budget year or in one of the early planning years of the CIP forecast period.

- **Medium**   Projects that meet an essential or important need but do not have to be funded immediately. These should be included in the CIP but in one of the later planning years.

- **Low**   Projects that benefit the community but not enough to merit inclusion in the CIP in the current year, given other needs and funding limitations.

The low-priority category could be subdivided into projects that will be considered in a CIP (in either the next year or subsequent years) and projects that are turned down in the current year's CIP with no indication that they will be considered in the future.

In experience-based ranking, decision makers often compare one request directly with another, going back and forth among requests and attempting to determine which ones are more important. In contrast, when general ranking categories are used, each particular request is assessed on its own merits and placed in one of the categories according to that assessment; it is not directly compared with other requests. If too many requests fall into the high- or medium-priority categories, the process can be repeated for those categories to winnow the choices. The officials who use this approach to prioritize requests are often asked to consider specific factors—health and safety, legal mandates, and available outside funding—in their deliberations. More will be said about these and other so-called urgency-of-need criteria in the next section.

After the process is finished, decision makers should examine and discuss the resulting rankings to identify the specific factors underlying the assignments made. This analysis is likely to produce further information and insights about the requests and how they meet needs, often producing some changes in the original assignments or rankings.

Ranking capital requests by broad categories of need is a straightforward and simple approach used by many local governments. It relies heavily on the judgment and experience of decision makers. The basic structure enables decision makers to prioritize requests and examine each one on its own merit.

In **Greeley, Colorado,** the following general descriptive categories are used in deciding funding priorities for the city's capital budget and CIP:

- **Priority 1 (imperative, must do)**   Projects that cannot reasonably be postponed without causing harmful or otherwise undesirable consequences

- **Priority 2 (essential, should do)**   Projects that meet clearly demonstrated needs or objectives

- **Priority 3 (important, could do)**   Projects that benefit the community but could be delayed without impairing basic services.[2]

In allocating projects among the categories for its 2001–2002 capital budget and 2001–2005 CIP, Greeley's departments, its planning commission, and the city manager considered many specific factors. Two are embodied in the definitions for priorities 1 and 2: avoiding harmful consequences that would occur if a request is not funded, and meeting clearly identified needs and objectives. Other specific factors that the administrative committee weighed when it assigned requests to particular priorities include mandates, health and safety, and operating budget impact. Decision makers bring these factors into the ranking process as needed or when applicable during deliberations and analysis.

Assigning requests for capital projects and acquisitions to a few, broad, qualitatively defined categories of need and ranking them by this approach has a disadvantage. Some officials may rank a particular project high while others may rank it low. Putting each decision maker's ranking on the table allows the group to discuss the reasons underlying each ranking and paves the way for consensus, but when disagreements cannot be resolved and contradictory rankings persist, the manager or official responsible for recommending priorities must make the final decisions. If a board or committee is establishing priorities, voting may be needed to set priorities for projects on which the board cannot reach consensus.

A numeric or ordinal scale can help resolve differences (see Exhibit 4–1). To use a scale like this, decision makers may be required to consider additional specific ranking criteria or factors in determining whether the benefits resulting from a request are large, modest, insufficient, or negligible and whether the need is pressing. They also may need an estimate of the resources available for capital financing. Ranking categories based on a numeric or ordinal scale simply allows averaging or another numeric summary of the assessments of different decision makers. Otherwise, the nature of the process is similar to that used with the broad ranking categories.

Exhibit 4-1   Scale for rating the need for, or urgency of, capital projects: A prototype

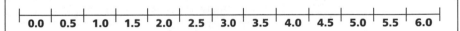

0.0   0.5   1.0   1.5   2.0   2.5   3.0   3.5   4.0   4.5   5.0   5.5   6.0

- **4.0–6.0**   Projects that will yield very large benefits or meet pressing needs. Those projects must be funded.
- **3.0–4.5**   Projects that will yield large benefits and should be funded given current estimates of available funding. If funding is reduced, projects in this category may be postponed or cut.
- **1.5–3.0**   Projects that will yield insufficient benefits to justify funding them with available resources. If resources increase, these projects will be considered for funding.
- **Below 1.5**   Projects that will yield negligible benefits. These projects should not be seriously considered now or in the future.

To rank requests for capital projects and acquisitions, many local governments use specific criteria to rank capital requests instead of or along with the broad categories that have been described.

Urgency-of-need criteria

This section discusses urgency-of-need criteria and how funding affects their application in ranking capital project requests.[3] As shown in the following examples, medium- and small-size local governments use a variety of urgency-of-need ranking criteria:

- **Meets legal mandates** A project that is required by federal or state statute, court order, or regulation, or a project that moves a local government into further compliance with such mandates
- **Removes or reduces hazards** A project that eliminates or reduces obvious hazards or threats to public health and safety
- **Advances the governing board's goals or objectives** A project that addresses the goals or objectives approved by the governing board for the jurisdiction generally or for the CIP specifically
- **Improves efficiency** A project that lowers operating expenses or that increases productivity (for example, the rehabilitation of infrastructure to improve its use or lower its annual maintenance costs)
- **Maintains standard of service** A project that is needed to continue service at current levels or maintain standards for existing citizens and customers; or a project that extends service at current standards to new citizens and customers
- **Supports economic development** A project that directly supports or benefits economic development, job growth, and/or increased local government revenues
- **Improves service** A project that improves service quality or provides for higher standards of service
- **Facilitates new services** A project that makes possible new services or programs
- **Improves quality of life or aesthetic values**
- **Offers convenience** A project that is for the convenience of users or staff.[4]

These criteria are listed in rough order of importance. Projects that help a local government comply with legal mandates or lessen threats to public health and safety usually have the highest priority. Projects that support board-approved goals and objectives, improve efficiency, maintain a standard of service, or support economic development tend to have an intermediate priority. Projects undertaken to improve a service, to support new services, or for convenience are usually accorded a lower priority. Priorities vary from one local government to another and over time for the same local government, depending on conditions. Thus, the priorities implicit in lists of urgency-of-need categories or criteria are general and conditional.

Of course, many if not most capital projects and acquisitions meet more than one of the above urgency-of-need criteria. For example, a request for a new public safety communications system may remove or reduce a hazard to public safety, improve operating efficiency, and represent an improved service. In some local governments, the more urgency-of-need criteria a project meets, the higher it tends to be ranked.[5] Keep in mind that some categories relate to more basic and pressing needs than others. Most local governments that use urgency-of-need criteria use them as general guidelines that point to rather than determine priorities among capital project and acquisition requests.

In evaluating the urgency of need, local governments also look at affordability. What is the overall cost of the project (including its impact on the operating budget)? Can the local government afford the project? Are grants, outside revenues, or other nontax or noncity revenues available to fund it?

The following local governments vary in size, so although they use similar urgency-of-need criteria, the specific number of criteria used and the complexity of the ranking approach vary.

Smyrna, Georgia   The 2003–2008 CIP of Smyrna refers to five urgency-of-need criteria for establishing priorities among capital project and acquisition requests:

- Vital to conduct or continue a mandated or required function
- Needed to conduct or continue a mandated or required function in an efficient manner
- Needed for the cost-efficient operation of an essential function
- Scheduled replacement of necessary resources or obsolete facilities to improve efficiency
- Scheduled for expansion or addition of services.[6]

While Smyrna's CIP does not say that these categories are in order of priority, the definitions for each suggest a decreasing urgency and a lower priority as one moves from the top of the list to the bottom. The first two categories refer to mandated or required functions. Efficiency runs through three of the five categories, suggesting that a capital project or acquisition request that addresses efficiency is more likely to be approved and funded than one that does not. The CIP administrative committee voted to fund projects in all five categories in the 2003 capital budget; projects in all five categories were also scheduled over the planning years of the city's CIP.

Denton, Texas   The 2002–2007 CIP of Denton refers to eight ranking criteria for prioritizing capital project and acquisition requests:

- Public safety, health, and life
- Service demands
- Legal requirements, liability, or mandates

- Quality and reliability of current service level
- Economic growth and development
- Recreational, cultural, and aesthetic values
- Funding ability
- Operating budget impact.[7]

Discussion of priority setting for Denton's CIP makes clear that these ranking criteria are not the only factors that the manager and staff consider in prioritizing capital requests for the CIP. Also taken into consideration are council CIP priorities, which are identified in a workshop held at the outset of the process to prepare the annual budget and CIP, and priorities that emerge from a public hearing held on CIP needs.

Conyers, Georgia   Conyers uses a two-tier approach, distinguishing between primary and secondary ranking criteria:

Primary

- Prevents or eliminates a public hazard
- Eliminates existing capacity deficit
- Is required by city ordinance, other law, or a federal or a state regulation
- Is essential to maintain current service levels affecting public health, safety, or welfare.

Secondary

- Maintains current nonessential service
- Accommodates public facility demands and needs of new development or redevelopment on the basis of projected growth patterns
- Is financially feasible, that is, a funding source is available and verifiable cost estimates are provided

- Meets special need or enhances a facility or a service
- Contributes to the objectives of the city council and administrative staff.[8]

At first, the Conyers process groups CIP requests by type: rolling stock, equipment, construction, and land. Projects of each type are then evaluated in terms of the primary and secondary criteria and are given points reflecting the extent to which a request fulfills each criterion. The assignment of points and weighting are greater for the primary criteria than for the secondary criteria.

Greeley, Colorado   Greeley's 2001–2002 capital budget and 2001 CIP combine general ranking categories, introduced above, and more specific urgency-of-need criteria into a multitiered system to rank capital project and acquisition requests. The general categories and the specific urgency of need criteria that define each category are:

Priority 1 (imperative, must do)

- Corrects a condition dangerous to public health or safety
- Satisfies a legal obligation (law, regulation, court order, or contract)
- Alleviates an emergency service disruption or deficiency
- Prevents irreparable damage to a valuable public facility.

Priority 2 (essential, should do)

Rehabilitates or replaces an obsolete public facility or attachment to the facility

- Stimulates economic growth and private capital investment
- Reduces future operating and maintenance costs
- Leverages available state or federal funds.

Priority 3 (important, could do)

- Provides a new or expanded level of service
- Promotes intergovernmental cooperation
- Reduces energy consumption
- Enhances cultural or natural resources.[9]

Winston-Salem, North Carolina   In Winston-Salem, capital requests financed from different funding sources are ranked separately.[10] The ranking process begins with each department prioritizing its own CIP requests. Citywide ranking begins with the city's budget and planning staffs. Their prioritization of requests is then reviewed by the city manager and assistant city managers before the recommended CIP is presented to the city council. The budget and planning staffs, manager, and assistant managers first consider major funding sources that are available for particular types of projects and then rank projects funded from each major source separately, taking into account departmental priorities, citizens' views as reflected in survey data and public forums, and urgency-of-need criteria. Funding sources and types of projects used in this ranking process are:

- Revenue bonds for water–sewer projects
- Enterprise reserves for stormwater and landfill projects
- Federal and state grant funds for housing and mass transit projects
- Sales tax revenue for housing projects
- Gasoline tax revenue for street resurfacing projects
- General fund reserves for economic development projects and city council–identified projects
- Leasing proceeds for major equipment, computers, and communication systems
- Nonvoted general obligation (GO) bonds for capital maintenance and annexation projects
- Voted GO bonds, capital reserves, and excess investment income from self-insurance and retirement funds for major new general-purpose infrastructure and facilities.

Within each of these funding categories, capital project and acquisition requests are prioritized in accordance with the following urgency-of-need and related criteria:

- Projects needed to ensure the health and safety of city residents and employees
- Projects needed to meet federal or state mandates
- Projects needed to maintain current facilities and service levels
- Projects identified by the city council as needs
- Projects identified by neighborhoods, community organizations, and citizens as needs
- Projects identified by internal planning documents as needs

- Projects that had been included in the planning years of a CIP in a prior year

- Projects that would improve operating efficiency or effectiveness of city services.

The relative importance of each of these criteria varies depending on the purposes and limitations associated with particular funding sources and how well a capital project request fits with these purposes and limitations. Health and safety, mandates, maintenance of current service standards, and operating efficiencies are usually the most important criteria for evaluating and ranking projects financed with enterprise funds, gasoline tax money for street resurfacing, lease proceeds, and nonvoted GO bonds. Needs identified by the council, community, or citizens drive the allocation of voted GO bonds, capital reserves, and excess investment income. Internal planning documents are particularly significant in defining priorities for housing and mass transit programs, which rely heavily on grant money.

Weighted rating of urgency-of-need and related criteria

When local governments rank capital project and acquisition requests using multiple criteria, officials may weight each criterion equally. Usually, however, some criteria refer to situations of greater urgency than others. These criteria then are given greater weight or priority than the others. Weighting becomes more difficult as the number of ranking criteria increases. To address this problem, some local governments assign numeric weights or maximum values to ranking criteria. They evaluate each capital request in terms of each criterion, assigning a score up to the maximum value for that criterion. After a request has been evaluated in terms of all criteria, it has a total score, value, or rating, which is used to determine its rank.

Weighted rating system: A prototype

The rating system presented in Exhibit 4–2 has six criteria, each assigned a maximum score of 6. The weightings, of course, could be varied to reflect local conditions and decision makers' views about the importance of the various criteria. Each project is rated on each criterion, so that the maximum rating a project can receive is 36.

Exhibit 4–2
Multidimensional system for rating capital requests: A prototype

Rating question	Clearly No		Clearly Yes
Is the request legally mandated?	0 — 1 — 2 — 3 — 4 — 5 — 6		
Does the request eliminate or reduce a hazard or a threat to public health or safety?	0 — 1 — 2 — 3 — 4 — 5 — 6		
Does the request fit with or advance the goals and objectives of the governing board?	0 — 1 — 2 — 3 — 4 — 5 — 6		
Does the project support economic development in the community?	0 — 1 — 2 — 3 — 4 — 5 — 6		
Would the consequences be severe if the request were not funded?	0 — 1 — 2 — 3 — 4 — 5 — 6		
Do the benefits balance or exceed the costs?	1/1 2/1 3/1 4/1 5/1 6+/1		
Total score or rating:	0		36

Following are the six criteria that are weighted in Exhibit 4–2.

- **Meets legal mandates** Although it would seem that a legal mandate either exists or does not exist, there are often uncertainties about whether a mandate applies to a local government and about the extent to which a requested project brings the local government into compliance with it. Some mandates are also more compelling than others; this depends on their source—whether they are constitutional, statutory, court ordered, regulatory, contractual, or otherwise required. For these reasons, a scale to assess mandates can be appropriate.

- **Removes or reduces a hazard** The weight given to this criteria can depend on whether the hazard or threat to public health and safety is actual or potential, how serious it is, and to what extent the request for a capital project or acquisition responds to it.

- **Advances the governing board's objectives** Many governing boards have established goals and objectives to guide the jurisdiction's capital budget. This criterion assesses the extent to which requests meet those goals and objectives.

- **Supports economic development** While many, if not most, capital projects support a community's economic development, this criterion evaluates how much or how directly a request contributes to development.

- **Prevents serious problems** Analysis of the consequences that would ensue if a project is not funded can be very useful in separating "must do" projects from those that can be postponed without serious harm to the community.

- **Provides benefits that balance or exceed costs** A project rated highly on the previous criteria has considerable benefits. Nevertheless, this final criterion is added to bring the costs of requests into the assessment and ensure that the range of costs and benefits associated with each request is considered. The scale starts with a 1:1 cost/benefit ratio. A request with costs exceeding benefits presumably would not be considered.

Most rating systems that local governments use in capital budgeting have more than six ranking criteria, and these criteria are seldom weighted equally. Budget, planning, and finance staff usually design the system. The city or county manager approves it before the rating system is used to evaluate projects for inclusion in the CIP. In some local governments, the governing board as well as the city or county manager approves the specific ranking criteria and weights. In others, the governing board approves staff use of the rating system but does not review and approve the criteria and weights that staff use to rank requests and develop the recommended CIP.

Such rating systems are typically used by the manager and staff to rank projects and prepare the recommended CIP. Local governing boards see and use the results of the ratings but seldom rate projects in reviewing and approving the CIP or specific projects included in the CIP. However, in some jurisdictions, governing board members and sometimes other officials fill out a questionnaire with the weighted rating criteria, asking a few questions regarding each criterion or category to help rate each request accordingly. Further explanation of such a questionnaire is provided in the discussion of the weighted rating system in Chatham County, North Carolina, on page 100.

Weighted rating systems in practice

This section examines the weighted rating systems used by four local governments: Charles Sturt, Australia; Chatham County, North Carolina; Reno, Nevada; and Yuma County, Arizona.

The weighted systems in Charles Sturt and Reno are designed specifically for ranking requests for capital projects and acquisitions. Chatham County uses its system to rate capital projects in its CIP process, and also to rate expansion requests in the operating budget. Yuma County uses its system in the county's annual budget process to rank requests for new or expanded services, including capital outlay or equipment, but the system could be adapted for ranking capital requests in a CIP. The Yuma approach is noteworthy because it incorporates annual data from a citizen survey into the process.

One important caution applies to the weighted rating systems in all four jurisdictions: Even though it results in numeric scores, a numerical evaluation of capital project and acquisition requests is still based on decision makers' subjective assessments or judgments. Numerical scoring does not transform assessments and judgments by officials into necessarily objective evaluations.

Charles Sturt, South Australia Charles Sturt, a local municipal council that serves about 100,000 people in the Adelaide metropolitan area, uses four general criteria or categories, each one assigned a weight based on its importance relative to the other criteria.[11] The criteria, with specific questions used to define them, are as follows:

Fit with corporate (city) plan (weight: 40 percent)

- Does the project help the city council meet its vision?
- Is the project consistent with the goals and strategies within the corporate plan?
- Is the project specifically mentioned in the corporate plan or in neighborhood plans?
- Does the project represent a core function of the council?
- Will the project result in "best practices"?
- Does the project improve the quality of service delivery?
- Does the project improve operational efficiency?

Urgency (weight: 25 percent)

- Is there a legal requirement for the project?
- Is there any contractual obligation in relation to the project?
- Is there a prior commitment to the project?
- Does the project relate to a risk issue?
- Does the project present the council with a window of opportunity?
- Is there seed money or grants available for the project?
- What are the implications of not completing the project this year?

Identified need (weight: 20 percent)

- Was the project identified as a result of consultation with the community?
- Do citizen survey data support the project?
- Does the project arise from an agreed-upon maintenance or replacement program?
- Does the project arise from a long-term needs assessment?
- Was the project submitted by a community group?
- How large a cross section of the community will benefit from the project?
- How well will the project meet identified needs and objectives?

Financial issues (weight: 15 percent)

- Is external funding available for the project?
- What will be the impact of the project on future capital and operating budgets?
- Will the project provide future financial benefits to the council?
- Is the cost-benefit analysis for the project positive?

Charles Sturt's combination of criteria or categories, the weighting of these categories, and the specific questions provide a well-defined approach for prioritizing capital project and acquisition requests. Weightings reflect the judgment of local officials about local conditions, needs, and the relative importance of different ranking criteria. Each capital request is evaluated in terms of the four criteria, and a score, from 6 to 1, is assigned to each request for each criterion:

6 points   Excellent or highest priority
5 points   Very good priority
4 points   Good priority
3 points   Adequate priority
2 points   Poor priority
1 point   Definitely unsatisfactory.

A request's score for each criterion is then multiplied by the criterion's weight. As shown below, a hypothetical project has been evaluated on all criteria and has received a score of 4 for fit with corporate plan, 3 for urgency, 4 for identified need, and 5 for financial

issues, with an overall weighted score for this project of 3.90, calculated as follows:

Evaluation criteria	Project score	Weight as percentage	Weighted score
Fit with corporate plan	4	40	1.60
Urgency	3	25	0.75
Identified need	4	20	0.80
Financial issues	5	15	0.75
Total		100	3.90

The most noteworthy components of this approach to evaluating capital projects are the general ranking criteria, the underlying questions for each, and the accompanying weightings. While the scoring embedded in the approach enables officials to assign a single rating or score to each project, as already mentioned, the evaluation of capital project and acquisition requests using numeric scores is still based on decision makers' judgments.

Chatham County, North Carolina   Chatham County first used a weighted rating system in the mid-1990s when the county prepared its first CIP.[12] The assistant manager–budget director and the county manager designed the system. The county commissioners approved the criteria and weightings and they see the results of the ratings.

The original Chatham County project rating system was modified in three significant ways in 2002:

- A criterion addressing the fit of projects with goals and objectives of the county commissioners (maximum of 25 points) was dropped. Because of a budget shortfall, the commissioners directed that the primary goal for the manager and staff in developing the budget and the CIP should be holding down spending. (This left staff without direction from the board about which projects would be consistent with other board goals and objectives.)

- A criterion for functional area ranking (maximum of 5 points) was added, allowing project rankings by the county's functional teams to be incorporated into the countywide ranking process.

- A criterion for timeliness of submission (maximum of 5 points) was removed because all departments were submitting their CIP requests on time.

The revised rating system, which the county manager and staff have used to rank projects in preparing the 2003–2008 CIP, has thirteen urgency-of-need criteria and a total of 132 points (see Exhibit 4–3).

Chatham County's budget steering team consists of the county manager, the assistant manager–budget director, the county finance officer, and a representative from each of the eight functional teams: administration, education/culture, recreation, general government, public safety, human services, natural resources, and law enforcement and courts. Each functional team, composed of representatives from the different departments that make up the functional area, prioritizes the CIP requests of those departments. In doing so, each team is free to devise its own approach for ranking requests. The teams tend to take an informal approach to this task although they consider the same criteria included in the county's overall capital project rating system. As already mentioned, project rankings by the functional teams are a criterion considered by the county budget steering team in assigning project scores using the weighted rating system.

To establish countywide CIP priorities, the county's budget steering team uses the weighted rating system as one tool in reaching decisions about the requests. This process begins with a questionnaire that requesting departments fill out for each project request. Budget

Exhibit 4–3
Criteria and weights for rating capital requests, 2003–2008 CIP, Chatham County, North Carolina

Rating criteria	Definition/ explanation	Maximum points	Percentage weighting
Functional area priority	Priority of project among requests in functional area: 5 for top-ranked project to 0 for any project ranked sixth or below in priority.	5	3.79
Safety	Extent to which project eliminates, prevents, or reduces an immediate hazard to safety.	14	10.61
Mandates	Extent to which project helps county meet existing or new mandates.	13	9.83
Timing/linkages	Extent to which project is timely, a continuation of a project currently under way, related to other high-priority projects, etc.	12	9.09
Economic impact	Extent to which project enhances economic development in county, while it protects the environment, or directly or indirectly adds to the tax base.	11	8.33
Efficiencies	Extent to which project contributes to savings in county operating or capital spending.	10	7.58
Maintaining current level of service	Extent to which project is necessary for county to continue to provide one or more services at current standards.	9	6.82
Improving access	Extent to which project improves citizen access to current services.	8	6.10
Service improvement	Extent to which project improves the quality of existing services.	7	5.30
Service addition	Extent to which project increases the quantity of existing services.	3	2.30
Operating budget impact	Projects that decrease future operating expenses receive a positive score, ranging from 0 to 15. Projects that have no effect on operating expenses receive a score of 0. Projects that increase operating expenses score anywhere from 0 to −15.	0 to 15, 0, or 0 to −15	11.34
Community support and county long-term plans	Extent to which project has broad and/or strong support from the community and is consistent with the county strategic plan or other long-term plans.	10	7.58
Financing	Extent to which project can be financed with non-general fund revenue sources.	15	11.34
Maximum points, all categories		132	100.00

steering team members then use the filled-out questionnaires to evaluate and rate project requests (see Exhibit 4–4). The assistant county manager–budget director adds the individual ratings to produce a summary score for each CIP request. With these ratings in hand, and taking numerous other considerations into account, the team arrives at the recommendations the manager makes concerning priorities for the CIP.

Chatham County's weighted rating system provides a common framework for the budget steering team's evaluation and ranking of capital project and acquisition requests. The budget steering team and the board of county commissioners continue to endorse use of the system to rank projects for inclusion in the recommended county CIP.

Exhibit 4–4

Categories and questionnaire for rating capital requests, 2003–2008 CIP, Chatham County, North Carolina

---

1. Functional area ranking

| What is the functional area priority/ranking for project? | Number ranking _____ of _____ project |

2. Safety

A. Does the project eliminate an immediate safety hazard (an imminent, obviously hazardous situation; not only a remote possibility) for county citizens or employees?   Yes ☐   No ☐

B. Identify and describe the nature of the hazard:

C. Is this project absolutely necessary for eliminating the hazard?   Yes ☐   No ☐

D. Do serious alternatives besides the project exist to correct the safety hazard?   Yes ☐   No ☐

E. If so, explain alternative:

3. Mandate

A. Does the project enable the county to provide a new or existing state or federal mandate (an item imposed on the county by federal or state government)?   Yes ☐   No ☐

B. If so, please cite and describe the mandate:

C. Can the mandate be carried out without the project?   Yes ☐   No ☐

D. If yes, what are the alternatives for fulfilling the mandate?

4. Timing/linkages

A. When does the project need to be completed?   (month/year)

B. Why does the project need to be completed in this time frame?

C. Is this project related to a completed project or previously approved program or related to another priority project(s)?	Yes ☐ No ☐
D. If yes, which project(s) and how is this project related?	
E. When will the project be ready to start and proceed to completion in a timely manner?	Fiscal year _____ Why?
	Estimated time to complete project? _____ (months)
F. Are elements of the project complete?	
i. Land/right-of-way acquisition	Yes ☐ No ☐
ii. Design	Yes ☐ No ☐
G. Are regulatory approvals needed?	Yes ☐ No ☐ Explain:
H. Is the time frame critical due to a special circumstance?	Yes ☐ No ☐ Explain:

5. Economic impact

A. Does the project contribute to the tax base and economic development or generate additional tourism/consumer spending in a way that ensures environmental protection?	Yes ☐ No ☐ How?
B. Estimated private investment:	$
C. Number of new jobs	
D. Annual additional tourism/consumer expenditures:	$
E. Estimated annual property tax revenue from project:	$

6. Efficiencies

A. Will the project save the county future operating costs?	Yes ☐ No ☐
B. If yes, how?	
C. Amount of projected savings on an annual basis:	$
D. Compare project costs with operating savings; will the project eventually pay for itself?	Yes ☐ No ☐
E. If yes, how long will the project take to pay for itself?	_____ (years)
F. Will the project save the county future capital costs?	Yes ☐ No ☐
G. If yes, how will the project save future capital costs?	
H. Amount of projected capital savings:	$

(continued)

Exhibit 4–4
(continued)

7. Maintain current service levels

A. Is the project necessary to maintain current service levels?   Yes ☐   No ☐

B. If yes, why?

C. What are the immediate consequences of rejecting the project?

D. What are the long-term consequences of rejecting the project?

E. Does the project protect investment in existing assets or infrastructure?   Yes ☐   No ☐

F. If yes, how?

8. Improve access

A. Does the project improve access to county services and information?   Yes ☐   No ☐

B. Who will benefit from improved access (such as other departments, certain members of the public, commissioners, the press, etc.)?

C. Describe how they will benefit.

9. Service improvement

A. Does the project improve the quality of service provided?   Yes ☐   No ☐

B. Which of the following services does the project improve?

☐ Public safety
☐ Public health
☐ Quality of life
☐ Internal services
☐ Other (specify)

C. Describe how the project will improve the quality of the identified service.

10. Service additions

A. Does the project increase the quantity of service provided?   Yes ☐   No ☐

B. Which of the following services does the project increase?

☐ Public safety
☐ Public health
☐ Quality of life
☐ Internal services
☐ Other (specify)

C. Describe how the project will increase the quantity of the identified service provided.

11. Operating budget impact

A. Additional operating revenue generated (on an annual basis): $

B. Source of revenue:

C. Additional operating expense (on an annual basis) $

D. Increased/(decreased) operating expenses (subtract A from C):

12. Consistency with long-range plans/community support and impact

A. Does the project help meet the priorities established by the Strategic Plan/Land Use Development Plan/Water Master Plan or other long-range plan adopted by the board of commissioners?   Yes ☐   No ☐

B. If yes, which plan?

C. If yes, identify the priorities:

D. How does the project further these priorities?

E. Can the priorities be reached without the project?   Yes ☐   No ☐

F. Degree of citizen/community support: ☐ High
                                             ☐ Medium
                                             ☐ Low
                                             ☐ Unknown

G. How was support determined?

E. Can the priorities be reached without the project?   Yes ☐   No ☐

H. Extent of service area?   ☐ Countywide
                               ☐ Intercounty/regional
                               ☐ Section(s) of county

I. Does the project serve a special need of a segment of the community?   Yes ☐   No ☐

J. If yes, how?

13. Financing

A. What does the project cost? $

B. Besides county general fund revenues, what funding sources are available to fund this project?

   i. Source:

   ii. Amount: $

C. What is the likelihood that the county will receive revenues from this funding source?

D. Can fees be charged or other revenues (besides taxes) raised to cover the cost of the project?   Yes ☐   No ☐

E. If yes, which fees/revenues?

F. How much in additional revenues will the fee increase generate? $

G. What portion of the project cost can these fees/revenues cover?

Reno, Nevada Reno, Nevada, has a twenty-year CIP that presents projects and funding sources by year for the first five years and then in five-year blocks for the next fifteen years. The city uses a rather sophisticated weighted rating system to rank CIP requests (see Exhibit 4–5).

The thirteen specific criteria shown in Exhibit 4–5 include factors not explicitly mentioned in the ranking approaches examined so far: project life, cost-effectiveness, environmental impact, and percentage of popula-

tion benefiting. Each criterion is subdivided, and each subdivision is scored from 5 to 0, 4 to 0, or 3 to 0. Each criterion is also weighted: 3, 2, or 1. Thus, the criterion "legal mandates" has three times the weight in the rating system as the criterion concerning recreational, cultural, and aesthetic value. The maximum score for a criterion is the product of the highest possible score associated with each of the criterion's subdivisions, and the criterion's weighting. A project's overall rating is the sum of its score on each criterion, to a maximum of 128.

Exhibit 4–5

Rating criteria and weights for rating capital requests, 2000–2020 CIP, Reno, Nevada

Criteria	Criteria subdivisions (score)	Multiplier (weight)	Maximum score
Funding	Ongoing funding from already identified sources (OR)*	3	12
	Existing funding available (4)		
	Potential funds now available (2)		
	Potential funds to be applied for (2)		
	No identified funds available (1)		
Legal mandates	Court decision (OR)*	3	12
	Regulatory requirement (OR)*		
	Pending legal action (4)		
	Potential legal action (3)		
	Normal project liability (0)		
Public health and safety	Existing hazard (severe) (OR)*	3	9
	Existing hazard (minor) (3)		
	Potential hazard (severe) (3)		
	Potential hazard (minor) (1)		
	No health or safety issue (0)		
Preservation of facility	Loss of facility imminent without project (5)	3	15
	Additional damage likely without project (4)		
	Project constitutes normal maintenance (3)		
	Project constitutes normal minor maintenance (1)		
	New facility or none of the above (0)		
Project life	Greater than twenty years/no extraordinary maintenance (5)	2	10
	Greater than twenty years/ extraordinary maintenance (4)		
	Greater than ten years/no extraordinary maintenance (3)		
	Greater than ten years/extraordinary maintenance (2)		
	Less than ten years (0)		

Criteria	Criteria subdivisions (score)	Multiplier (weight)	Maximum score
Conformity to city plans and goals	In the city master plan (5)	2	10
	In neighborhood plans (which plan?) (4)		
	Under consideration for master plan (3)		
	Recommended by board/commission (2)		
	Recommended by citizen action (1)		
Conformity to departmental plans and goals	Critical to accomplishing established goals/plans (5)	3	15
	Desirable to accomplishing established goals/plans (4)		
	Will assist accomplishing established goals/plans (3)		
	Won't hinder accomplishing established goals/plans (2)		
	Necessary for department, but may harm another (1)		
Operating budget impact	Decreases operating/maintenance costs (5)	2	10
	No impact on operating/maintenance costs (3)		
	Increases operating/maintenance costs $5K–$15K (2)		
	Increases operating/maintenance costs $15K–$25K (1)		
	Increases operating/maintenance costs >$25K (0)		
Cost effectiveness	Most cost-effective alternative (5)	2	10
	Cost-effective compared with doing nothing (4)		
	Same as cost of other alternatives (2)		
	Not cost-effective (0)		
Environmental or pollution impact	Enhances environment/reduces pollution (5)	1	5
	Benefits environment/slightly reduces pollution (3)		
	No environmental change/status quo pollution (2)		
	Minor negative environmental impact/slight pollution (1)		
	Diminishes environment/creates pollution (0)		
Percentage of city population benefiting	50 percent or more (5)	2	10
	35–50 percent (4)		
	25–35 percent (3)		
	10–25 percent (2)		
	<10 percent (1)		

(continued)

Exhibit 4–5
(continued)

Criteria	Criteria subdivisions (score)	Multiplier (weight)	Maximum score
Recreational/ cultural/aesthetic value	Major value (5)	1	5
	Moderate value (4)		
	No value (1)		
	Slightly detrimental (0)		
Frequency of use	Seven days a week (5)	1	5
	Five days a week (4)		
	Less than five days a week (2)		
	Once a week or less (1)		

*A project that meets or is in one of the four override (OR) subdivisions is automatically considered to be essential.

Reno's rating system has four override (OR) subdivisions: (1) ongoing funding from already identified sources (under the funding criterion), (2) court decision, and (3) regulatory requirement (both under the legal mandates criterion), and (4) existing hazard (severe), which is under the public health and safety criterion. If one of these subdivisions applies to a project, the project is considered essential, and it is funded and approved.

A capital project's overall score using the rating system in Exhibit 4–5 places it in one of five priority categories (see Exhibit 4–6). Projects that receive 100 points or more, or that fall into one of the four override categories, are considered to be essential; they merit inclusion in the upcoming year's capital budget or in one of the first few years of the CIP forecast period. Requests that receive scores from 80 to 99 points are considered to be desirable and are usually included in the first five years of the forecast period. Projects rated from 60 to 79 are classified as acceptable and are usually placed in one of the three five-year blocks following the first five years of the forecast period. Projects rated from 40 to 59 are deferrable; if they are included in the CIP, they are placed in the distant planning years—years ten through twenty. Projects that are rated 39 or lower are put on hold; and usually they are placed in the last year or two of the twenty-year CIP period.

Exhibit 4–6
General priority categories for ranking capital requests, 2000–2020 CIP, Reno, Nevada

General priority categories	Category definitions	Rating or scoring range
Essential	Projects needed to comply with a court order or legislative mandate, or projects that are critical to the health, safety, and general welfare	100 or more points
Desirable	Projects important to the general welfare of the community, operation, or maintenance of a physical facility; not critical relative to CIP objectives	80–99 points
Acceptable	Projects that provide a public operational improvement; not critical or important in relation to the city's financial capabilities, needs, or other program requirements	60–79 points
Deferrable	Projects that conflict with the master plan or for which there are serious need, cost, justification, or timing questions	40–59 points
Hold	Projects that will not be started until the completion of a study or submission of additional data	0–39 points

Yuma County, Arizona In its annual budget process, Yuma County uses a weighted rating system to rank requests that exceed 2 percent of the prior year's base budget for the general fund and the county's library district, for general fund money for new positions, new programs, and capital projects or equipment (Exhibit 4–7).[15] Although developed and used for the operating budget, the system could readily be adapted by a local government for use in a CIP or capital budget process.

A budget review team, which includes the county manager, the finance director, and a senior management analyst, designed the rating system. The system consists of seven general rating criteria or categories. Some categories are divided into subcategories. The maximum number of points that a request can be given is 105.

In preparing the budget for 2002–2003, the budget review team used the system to score 104 requests, including requests for capital equipment. After they were all scored, the requests were ranked in a table from the highest to the lowest score. Because of the limited funding available, a cutoff was drawn at a score of 43.5. Requests with ratings of 43.5 or higher were included in the manager's recommended budget, and those with ratings below 43.5 were cut. This resulted in the inclusion of 38 of the 104 requests in the county manager's recommended budget for 2002–2003.

Yuma County's rating system incorporates the views of customers or citizens in two rating categories—customer spending preferences and customer confidence in performance (see Exhibit 4–7), which together account for 40 of a total maximum score of 105. Customer spending preferences (20 points) and the subcategory "value for the dollar" (5 points) are assessed with an annual telephone survey of five hundred randomly selected county residents. The survey questions evaluate about eighteen different services provided by the county. For each service, four questions are asked:

• How familiar is the respondent with the service?

• How important does the respondent judge the service to be?

• How good a value is the service relative to its cost?

• Should more, less, or the same amount of money be spent on the service?

Customers' views about service quality (15 points) are assessed with point-of-service questions asked of citizens just after county services are provided to them.

The manager of Yuma County says that the weighted rating system has worked well. The budget team has relied on it heavily to determine top-priority programs and capital projects to include in the manager's recommended annual budget. The system makes explicit the criteria underlying the manager's budget recommendations, and the board of county supervisors has, by and large, accepted these priorities.

One caution is appropriate here: Although citizen surveys are useful for rating services in Yuma County and in many other places, they may be less useful as a tool to prioritize capital project requests because the public does not see many of the facilities and equipment that local government staff use to provide services.

Exhibit 4–7
System for rating agency budget requests (including for capital projects), 2002–2003 Annual Budget, Yuma County, Arizona

Rating categories (maximum points)	Subcategories (maximum score)	Scoring method/ points
Fit with county strategic plan and objectives (20)	Magnitude of impact (8)	No impact (0) to high impact (8)
	Cost (6)	High cost = 0; no cost = 6
	Existing vs. new strategy (6)	Existing strategy = 6; new strategy = 3
Service impact (10)		New/expanded/improved service = 3; maintain existing service = 10; no significant impact = 0
Customer spending preference (20)		Up to 20, based on customer spending level preference and rating of agency service as very important

(continued)

Exhibit 4–7
(continued)

Rating categories (maximum points)	Subcategories (maximum score)	Scoring method/ points
Customer confidence in performance (20)	Value for the dollar (5)	Up to 5, based on percentage of customers who rate the agency's service as good/ excellent value
	Quality (15)	Up to 15, based on percentage of customers who rate the agency's service as good/ excellent quality
Increased productivity (10)	Return on investment (ROI) over three years	From 15% return = 1, to 75% return or more = 10
Federal/state mandates or prior board commitments (15)	Consequences of noncompliance (10)	From none = 0 to high = 10; mandates rated very high will cause project to be included in manager's recommendations
	Cost of compliance (5)	From high cost = 0 to low cost = 5
Agency priority (10)		Agency's top-ranked request = 10; 2nd = 7; 3rd = 4; and 4th = 1

Total possible score = 105

Assessing weighted rating systems

Project rating systems and ranking criteria create a common framework for decision makers to use when they evaluate capital requests. Systems ensure that important factors are not overlooked. Rating systems can be useful when many capital requests must be ranked, and some are complex. They can help decision makers sort out requests near the margin—those that would be funded if more money were available or those that would be cut if available funds were reduced. Finally, rating systems can help officials explain their selection of some projects and rejection of others.

Rating systems and ranking criteria have their limitations, however. Officials may overlook or fail to give sufficient consideration to other factors relevant to a community's capital needs. The use of a rating system, particularly one with many criteria and one that requires decision makers to fill out a questionnaire to rate requests, can take a considerable amount of time. If the system is well designed and addresses a jurisdiction's needs, and if decision makers use the resulting rankings to put together the CIP and capital budget, this is time well spent. But if decision makers largely ignore the rankings produced, the time spent by staff using the system is wasted.

Various factors may lead decision makers to disregard rankings produced by a rating system or to stop using such a system altogether. Priorities may become so clear that a rating system is no longer necessary. The system may omit relevant factors or weigh them inappropriately. It may not be revised often enough to respond to newly emerging needs. Finally, political or community pressures may override nonpolitical criteria to determine capital funding priorities.

This was the case in Wake County, North Carolina. For several years budget staff and the manager used a weighted project rating system to develop CIP priorities that the county manager recommended to the board of county commissioners. The system was based on responses of county commissioners to a questionnaire asking them to rank all county functions across five functional areas. After several years the county budget staff stopped using the rating system because growth pressures had centered Wake County's capital needs on new school construction, and community sentiments and related political pressures had begun to determine the priorities for the county's capital funding, rendering the rating system unnecessary.[16]

In local governments where rating systems are used to establish priorities among capital project and acquisition requests, these systems complement or support rather than displace the judgment and deliberation of experienced local officials.

Program priorities, goals, and service needs assessment and planning

In most of the weighted systems described earlier, the extent to which a project meets program goals is one of the rating factors, but it usually accounts for less than one-quarter of a project's rating.[17] However, capital project and acquisition requests can be ranked solely or mainly on the basis of program priorities, program goals and policies, and/or long-term program or service needs assessment and planning. Some local government officials feel that priority setting in capital budgeting should be based predominantly on these criteria. They reason that with good program priorities, goals, and plans, rating systems are not needed.

The terms "program" and "service" are used interchangeably here and refer to substantive activities by local government such as law enforcement, provision of transportation, maintenance of streets, parks and recreation, and support for schools. The priorities and goals of a program are usually established formally by the local governing board: either annually at the outset of the CIP or operating budget process or more generally from year to year and revised as needed.

Often goals are set as part of a long-term needs assessment and planning process. This process may be part of a jurisdiction-wide strategic or comprehensive planning effort. Some priorities and goals may be quite specific and pertain to the project level. Others may be general, giving officials considerable flexibility each year in choosing among projects in any program or service area. Use of long-term program or service needs assessment and planning to establish program goals frequently involves users of the service and participants from the broader community, as well as local government officials. Service needs assessments and planning can lead to specific recommendations concerning service standards or to quantitative measures to help officials identify capital needs and spending priorities.

Program priorities of the governing board

Officials of a local government may prioritize programs, functions, or areas of service to help them rank and select capital projects. The program or functional priorities of a local government, from highest to lowest, might be, for example, transportation; public safety; environmental health; cultural and recreational facilities and open space; housing and community development; economic development; and general government. The priorities may be formally approved by the governing board or, if not formally approved, at least suggested by the tenor and direction of board members' comments. The manager and staff then rank capital project and acquisition requests and develop the CIP by reference to these priorities.

Formal, board-approved programmatic categories have two disadvantages that limit their use. First, many local board members find it politically risky to explicitly identify some programs, services, or functions as low in priority, especially at the start of the CIP or capital budgeting process. Second, some projects fit into more than one functional category. For instance, a street reconstruction project in a neighborhood could be placed under transportation, housing and community development, or even public safety.

Rather than prioritize all the programs, the governing board might designate only the high-priority programs or service areas. For example, the board might identify two or three program areas for attention in the upcoming CIP and capital budget process and remain silent about the rest. This approach has several benefits. It gives the manager and staff a basis for establishing priorities among capital requests and deciding which ones to include in the recommended CIP. It limits board members' political risks in setting program priorities at the outset of the CIP process. Finally, it preserves the manager's and the board's flexibility in approving some projects in program areas that have not been identified as high priority—because they have not been formally identified as low in priority either. As a result, the manager and board can more convincingly refer to special conditions that justify the approval of projects outside the selected high-priority service areas.

The 2002–2008 CIP of **Buncombe County, North Carolina,** includes a short list of county commissioner–approved priorities:[18]

- Mandated services by the state and federal government, including the health department and social services department
- Public safety, including the sheriff's department and emergency services
- Parks and recreation facilities
- Increased productivity (in) county government.

The four priorities are not rank ordered. They are program priorities that the board of county commissioners approved and that the manager and staff used in developing the county's CIP. The first three priorities refer to departments, services, or functions; these are partly or wholly program categories. Priority 1 also refers to "mandated services," so it includes an urgency-of-need dimension as well as a program dimension.

Priority 4 refers to "increased productivity," which is also an urgency-of-need criterion.

The commissioners originally approved these four priorities in a strategic planning effort involving Buncombe County officials as well as staff of the two public school systems serving Buncombe County residents. The priorities have been used to guide CIP development for the county over the past several years. They are now being revised and updated.[19]

Buncombe County's program priorities favor project requests in the public health, social services, public safety, and parks and recreation areas. However, the broad way in which the priorities are stated has given the manager flexibility in evaluating and ranking requests in the recommended CIP, and it has preserved the commissioners' flexibility in reviewing and ultimately approving the CIP. Projects in other program areas (those that involve mandates, for example, or result in increased productivity) have also been recommended and approved.

Program goals and policies of the governing board

In some local governments, the governing board establishes program goals and policies to guide policymaking and administrative activities, including the preparation of the CIP and capital budget. The goals and policies may be based on general mission or value statements, or they may reflect long-term strategic or comprehensive plans. The governing board typically approves the goals and policies. This usually occurs before or at the start of the annual budget process. If goals and policies are ongoing, as is often the case, the board reviews and updates them in light of recent developments. The goals and policies established or updated by the governing board for the annual or operating budget often also apply to the CIP and the capital budget. In some local governments, the governing board establishes program goals and policies specifically to guide priority setting for the CIP and the capital budget. Goals and policies for the CIP often apply at the project level; the board indicates specific projects it expects the manager and staff to include in the CIP or to recommend in the capital budget.

Rockville, Maryland, uses board-approved program goals and objectives set specifically for its CIP to guide the ranking and selection of project requests in that process.[20]

The goals and objectives for the Rockville CIP emerged from three long-term planning efforts that have been guiding budget and CIP prioritization in Rockville in recent years. These planning efforts have involved citizens and community leaders as well as Rockville officials.

• **Master plan** Rockville's current master plan was originally approved in 1993. It reflects development policies for the entire Washington, D.C., metropolitan area and translates them into a strategy for the development of Rockville. The master plan has been a useful guide for city planning for capital improvements and a framework for the creation of neighborhood plans that tie into the city's CIP.

• **Strategic plan** The city's first strategic plan was produced in 1998. The stated purpose of the strategic plan is to establish targets and guidelines for the capital, personnel, operating service, and facility needs of the city government over the ten-year period from 1999 to 2008.

• **"Imagine" Rockville** This visioning process intended to lay a foundation for the city over the next ten years and beyond. It involved broad citizen participation and resulted in plans, programs, and projects for the community to accomplish.

The 2001–2006 Rockville CIP specifies twenty-three programmatically oriented and governing board–approved objectives that guide the prioritization of project requests within four program areas: (1) recreation and parks, (2) transportation, (3) environment (water, sewer, and stormwater), and (4) general government, technology, and community enhancement (see Exhibit 4–8).[21]

Exhibit 4–8
Governing board–approved goals and objectives, 2001–2006 CIP, Rockville, Maryland

A. **Recreation and parks goal:** Preserve, protect, and enhance the environment within the city's public park system, and promote wholesome and stimulating leisure-time opportunities which foster the enrichment of individual and family experiences.

1. Ensure well-planned, functionally designed and safe parks, open spaces, forest areas, and facilities, which meet the present and future leisure-time needs of all Rockville citizens.
2. Ensure that the city's parks and facilities are designed and consistently maintained at high standards.
3. Foster the protection and enhancement of the city's environment and natural resources.

(continued)

Exhibit 4–8
(continued)

4. Provide accessible special service facilities, including the senior center, the golf course, swim center, nature center, and community recreation centers, which offer opportunities for desirable leisure-time activities.

5. Foster the preservation and enhancement of historical resources located within the public park system.

6. Acquire additional parkland, particularly forested and/or environmentally sensitive parcels adjacent to existing city parks.

7. Beautify the city's neighborhoods, rights-of-way, facility grounds, parks, and business/commercial areas with flowers and quality landscaping.

8. Provide public programs devoted to the furtherance of art intended to beautify the city.

B. **Transportation goal:** Have a balanced transportation system that enhances the convenience, utilization, accessibility of, and interaction among the residential, commercial, educational, recreational, industrial, and governmental sectors within the city and within the metropolitan area.

9. Facilitate the movement of through-traffic around, instead of across, Rockville, and to help eliminate traffic congestion in the center of the city and residential neighborhoods. Most of the road projects proposed are required to alleviate traffic hazards, upgrade streets, or complete the circumferential system as recommended in the master plan.

10. Promote a system of public/private transportation circulation among neighborhoods.

11. Protect residential neighborhoods from through traffic and truck traffic on major roadways.

12. Encourage a citywide pedestrian and bicycle transportation system.

13. Continue full support of Metro Rail and feeder bus systems.

14. Establish a system of mass transportation circulation within downtown Rockville.

15. Develop a parking plan for the city that is compatible with the circulation system for vehicular traffic.

C. **Environment goal:** Achieve an environment that enhances a sense of community that is responsive to diverse cultural, social, and physical needs of the people of the city of Rockville as well as maintain Rockville's image of being a pleasant and desirable city in which to live, work, and play.

16. Provide for and maintain adequate sewage treatment facilities which accommodate existing and planned development in an efficient, economical, and environmentally sound manner.

17. Provide a network of stormwater management facilities designed to minimize adverse effects of development on local and state ecosystems and waterways.

D. **General government, technology, and community enhancement goal:** Provide appropriate facilities for the conduct of the city's business; maintain and improve the city's information and communication systems; and promote infrastructure enhancements that promote the use of the central business district as a focal point of civic, social, business, and government activity served by a full range of supporting cultural and service facilities.

Exhibit 4–8
(continued)

18. Provide pedestrian-oriented circulation and public gathering areas.
19. Provide effective transportation access and adequate parking.
20. Inspire imaginative urban design.
21. Ensure that attractive, readily accessible streetscapes are in place.
22. Promote expansion of the city's economic base.
23. Carry out necessary projects.

Source: Operating Budget and Capital Improvement Program, adopted FY 2001, Rockville, Maryland, 201, 251, 291, and 337.

The length of the list in Exhibit 4–8 and the breadth of program coverage embodied in the goals and objectives give a sense of the far-reaching planning efforts that underlie Rockville's CIP process. In addition to the goals and objectives, the governing board in Rockville approves "Capital Financing and Debt Management Policies" and a "Mayor and Council Policy Agenda." These documents also guide CIP preparation (Chapter 1 addresses board-approved capital financing polices; also see Exhibit 4–9 for a summary of Rockville's policy agenda). The policy agenda establishes five mega-policies for Rockville. While not all of the specific items in the agenda relate directly to the city CIP priorities, others—for example, one relating to a new library for the downtown area and another concerning city information and technology infrastructure—do.

Rockville's CIP goals and objectives provide a framework for officials in ranking projects within each program area when they develop the CIP each year. When combined with the city's policy agenda, the goals and objectives also help officials to establish project priorities across program areas in the CIP. The long-term and ongoing nature of Rockville's planning activities, goals, and objectives as well as the community-wide approach used in developing them give continuity to annual CIP priority setting and a very strong basis for justifying CIP priorities to the community.

Exhibit 4–9
Summary of mayor and council policy agenda, 2001 budget, and 2001–2006 CIP, Rockville, Maryland

Creative growth management   This agenda item calls for a review and update of the city's master plan, resolution of the big-box retail store issue, creation of smart growth transportation solutions, and update of Rockville's pike and neighborhood plans.

Neighborhood revitalization and code enforcement   This targets the revitalization of Rockville's housing stock through home improvement programs, incentives for rehabilitation of older homes, addressing issues of abandoned homes, and tracking the status of properties with recurring code violations.

Town center   This refers to efforts to stimulate the development of the Rockville town center and involves the creation of a town center master plan, a marketing study to analyze commercial and residential market potential, work with the county to build a new regional library in the town center, and work with the county and state to fund parking facilities in the town center.

Technology   This identifies strategies for Rockville to take advantage of emerging technologies by enacting a telecommunications ordinance, creating an information and technology master plan, determine budget implications of rapidly changing technology, and continue to upgrade information and technology infrastructure at city hall, such as GIS, e-commerce, Intranet, mobile commuting, and institutional networks.

Source: Operating Budget and Capital Improvement Program, Adopted FY 2001, Rockville, Maryland, 25.

Long-term service needs assessment and planning

Long-term service needs assessment and planning can be useful to local officials in establishing priorities for capital planning and budgeting. The master planning, strategic plans, and visioning of Rockville, Maryland, show that long-term needs assessment and planning provide a foundation for a local governing board to establish, revise, or update program goals and objectives for the capital budget and the CIP. Even where no program goals or objectives are formally established, long-term service needs assessment and planning can be directly useful to local officials in setting projects into priority for the capital budget and CIP.

Chapter 3 describes the experiences of two local governments with long-term service and capital needs assessment and planning. Birmingham, Michigan, tied a fifteen-year capital needs assessment for the downtown area and a ten-year sewer replacement and improvement plan directly into its capital improvement program. Hickory, North Carolina, developed a set of long-range service plans, or master plans, that shape CIP priorities each year. Birmingham's and Hickory's experiences are similar to those of Rockville, Maryland.

Long-term service needs assessment and planning as practiced in Birmingham, Hickory, and Rockville not only identify capital needs but also prioritize them within specific service or program areas and across those areas. This can happen in several ways. First, if service needs assessment and planning are done well, they document needs. Decision makers are likely to view CIP requests based on such needs assessment as legitimate and are more likely to assign such requests a higher priority than requests from service areas where needs have not been documented. Second, when citizens, community leaders, and local governing officials, including board members, are involved in long-term service needs assessment and planning, capital requests emerging from such a process often have community and political support, giving them an edge over requests coming from other service areas. Third, long-term needs assessment sometimes extends to the formulation and approval of service standards. These standards may link growth in the use of a facility by citizens to the need for a new or expanded facility, or they may indicate when certain infrastructure and facilities need to be rehabilitated or replaced. Such "approved" service or facility standards help establish project and funding priorities for the CIP or a portion of it in any year. Combining such standards with an earmarked funding source can virtually ensure that projects triggered by the standards will go forward and be approved and funded on schedule.

Of course, local officials do not always accept or approve the results of long-term service needs assessment and planning. Some service needs and plans may turn out to be off the mark. New facts may emerge after a plan is done. Special conditions may arise that require officials to change or juggle the priorities that such assessments and plans suggest. Unforeseen capital needs may arise in a particular year that draw funds away from projects identified by service needs assessment, causing those projects to be delayed.

Another problem is that service needs assessment as well as program goals, objectives, and policies in capital budgeting are typically approved by program and service area. This can limit their value to officials in setting priorities across different program or service areas. For example, Hickory's twenty-year-plus master plan for sidewalk improvement and its ten-year plan for library improvement do not suggest whether projects in these areas deserve funds more than do projects in other areas. And there is nothing in Rockville's program goals and objectives alone that suggests that projects in the transportation area should take precedence over projects in other areas. Rockville complements the CIP program goals and objectives with the mayor and council policy agenda to give officials a broader basis for sorting out priorities across the different program areas.

Program priorities, program goals and objectives, and long-term service needs assessment and planning—like multidimensional rating systems—complement rather than replace the judgment that local officials must exercise in ranking requests for capital projects and acquisitions and developing the CIP and capital budget.

Notes

1 On priority setting in budgeting, see Roland Calia, *Priority Setting Models for Public Budgeting* (Chicago: Government Finance Officers Association, 2001).

2 Greeley, Colorado, Biennial Budget, January 1, 2001–December 31, 2002, introduction to 2001–2002 capital budget and 2001-2005 CIP.

3 A. John Vogt, "Capital Planning and Budgeting in Local Governments," *Popular Government* (Fall 1975): 12–24. This article reflects the use of urgency-of-need categories by a few local governments in the mid-1970s. The article was revised and updated in 1996. See A. John Vogt, "Budgeting Capital Outlays," in *Budgeting: Formulation and Execution,* ed. Jack Rabin et al. (Athens, Ga.: Vinson Institute of Government, 1996), 276–291. For documentation as of 1988, see Annie Millar, "Selecting Capital Investment Projects for Local Governments," *Public Budgeting and Finance* (Autumn 1988): 63–77. Local governments today continue to use these as well as other categories for ranking capital needs.

4 This list of urgency-of-need categories is based on one that Durham, North Carolina, used many years ago. It is augmented with criteria added from lists used by other local governments.

5 The town of Carolina Beach, North Carolina, follows this approach.. The author facilitated a retreat for the governing board at which the town planning director presented capital project priorities based on the number of urgency-of-need criteria that different project requests fulfilled.

6 City of Smyrna, Georgia, Annual Financial Plan, Fiscal Year 2003, 249.

7 Annual Program of Service, 2002–2003, City of Denton, Texas, 340–341, www.cityofdenton.com. The Denton Program of Service for 2002-2003 includes the 2002–2007 CIP.

8 City of Conyers, Georgia, Fiscal Year 2002–2003 Operating Budget, 119. This operating budget presents the city's 2002–2007 CIP.

9 Greeley, Colorado, Biennial Budget, January 1, 2001-December 31, 2002, introduction to section presenting the city's 2001–2002 capital budget and the 2001–2005 CIP.

10 This overview of Winston-Salem's approach to ranking capital projects is based on a presentation handout, "City of Winston-Salem Capital Project Priority Setting Process," prepared by the city's budget and evaluation director for the Budgeting and Financial Planning course sponsored by the Institute of Government, University of North Carolina at Chapel Hill, in January 2003.

11 This summary of the Charles Sturt weighted rating system is based on a staff document, "Guidelines for Evaluation Local Government Projects," section 4, www.charlessturt.sa.gov.au/html/city_statistics.html.

12 This overview is based on Chatham County staff budget and CIP preparation forms and instructions, and on phone conversations and e-mail messages between the author and the county's assistant manager–budget director.

13 Reno's weighted rating system is referred to in general terms in the City of Reno, Nevada, 2000/01 Budget, Capital Improvement Plan, 2000–2020, 5. The system is set out in full in a "Capital Improvement Project Checklist" sent to the author by city staff. This information was confirmed in a phone conversation with Gayela Emory, senior management analyst in the Reno budget office.

14 Ibid.

15 This is based on a Yuma County staff document, "Budget Request Priority Setting," and on e-mail messages from the Yuma County manager.

16 This overview is based on a staff document, "Wake County, Setting Priorities for Capital Projects" (December 1989), and on e-mail from the former budget director of Wake County, who now serves as manager of Yuma County, Arizona.

17 The original Chatham County and Reno rating systems assess projects to the extent that they meet county or city goals and objectives. An important criterion in the Charles Sturt rating system is "fit with corporate plan," and departmental or functional priorities are a rating criterion in the current rating systems of Chatham County and Yuma County. However, such programmatic criteria account for less than 20 percent of a project's overall rating in the Chatham County, Reno, and Yuma County rating systems. "Fit with corporate plan" is 40 percent of the rating for Charles Sturt.

18 Annual Budget, Fiscal Year 2001–2002, Buncombe County, North Carolina, 201.

19 This information was provided by the assistant county manager.

20 Operating Budget and Capital Improvement Program, adopted FY 2001, Rockville, Maryland, 182–356.

21 Ibid., p. 26.

5 Capital financing strategy

A local government's capital financing involves major decisions and long-term commitments that require planning as careful and as deliberate as the planning that goes into its capital improvement program (CIP). Without a capital financing strategy, some local governments doggedly refuse to incur debt in order to avoid interest costs; and, in refusing to do so, they fail to meet major capital needs. Others accustomed to borrowing to meet capital needs may fail to develop and use other sources and ignore or underestimate the impact of heavy debt financing on future operating budgets.

A capital financing strategy should:

- Limit the cost of providing capital infrastructure and equipment while meeting the community's needs
- Ensure financial strength and flexibility in the future
- Strengthen the local government's standing with the bond rating agencies, bond buyers, regulators, and the local community.

This chapter presents eight policies that together create a capital financing strategy (see sidebar). All eight policies are important, but the relative emphasis given to each should reflect a local government's financial condition and general economic resources and challenges. An assessment of the jurisdiction's financial and economic condition and its prospects should be part of its capital financing strategy.[1] The assessment can involve financial trend monitoring or a similar systematic study, or it can be informal, intended to increase the working familiarity of officials with the community's conditions and prospects. Explicit, written policies adopted by the governing board provide the strongest and most consistent foundation for capital financing.

Capital financing policies

- Maintain adequate operating fund balances
- Create capital reserves and commit annual revenues to fund them
- Balance pay-as-go and debt financing
- Determine and remain within local debt capacity
- Maintain or improve the jurisdiction's bond ratings
- Plan, sell, and manage debt effectively
- Prepare a multiyear financial forecast to support both the capital and operating budgets
- Adopt governing board policies to guide capital finance practices.

Some of these policies are covered in more depth in subsequent chapters: Chapter 6 addresses pay-as-go sources of capital finance, including capital reserves; Chapter 7, types of debt; Chapter 8, bond ratings; Chapters 9, 10, and 11, planning and selling debt; and Chapter 12, financial forecasting. This chapter introduces the elements of a local government's capital financing strategy. It explains the role of the operating fund balance in capital finance and how to determine debt capacity and balance debt and pay-as-go sources. Adoption of capital financing polices by the jurisdiction's governing board also is discussed.

Operating fund balances

The first essential policy in a local government's capital financing strategy is to maintain adequate balances in the general fund and other operating funds. This provides:

- Working capital for paying bills on time
- A rainy-day fund to meet unanticipated needs
- Resources to take advantage of unexpected opportunities
- Financing to meet cash flow needs during the year
- Money to invest and thereby hold down property taxes.[2]

Operating fund balances or reserves are important in capital budgeting because when they are not available, officials are apt to use accumulated capital funds to meet operating needs and avoid increasing taxes. Even more at risk in such a situation are planned contributions to a capital reserve. Planned contributions are too often cut in the face of pressures to balance the operating budget and hold down taxes or fees. A local government with adequate balances in the general fund or other operating fund is in a much better position to keep capital reserves and contributions to such reserves intact.

There is a second reason why adequate operating fund balances are important in capital budgeting. When a local government sells debt publicly, the bond agencies evaluate its financial position, and they consider operating fund balances a key indicator of financial health. In their view, operating fund balances provide a margin of safety for meeting debt service payments and financing capital needs in the face of unanticipated needs or problems in the operating budget.

Measuring the general fund balance

The general fund is the principal operating fund for most local governments. A conservative definition equates the fund balance to the sum of cash and investments in the fund, less current liabilities and encumbrances.[3] A less conservative definition would add receivables. Only cash and investments that can be made available to support operations should be included in these calculations. All fixed or long-term assets and liabilities are excluded.

The general fund or other operating fund balance is most often measured as a percentage of annually recurring spending from the fund. For example, a local government has a general fund balance of $3 million on June 30: add the fund's cash ($500,000) and investments ($3 million) and subtract its current liabilities ($400,000) and its encumbrances ($100,000). This available **fund balance** may be compared with fund spending for either the year ending on June 30 or the year beginning on July 1. Only recurring spending is used for this calculation. Extraordinary items should be excluded. Spending should include recurring transfers out of the general fund to other funds. If the ending year's spending is used, and it is $20 million, and it does not include any extraordinary items or transfers, available fund balance is 15 percent of that year's spending. If the upcoming year's recurring spending is used, and it is $22 million, available fund balance for the general fund is 13.5 percent of spending.

Alternatively, the fund balance may be compared with annual revenues.

Determining adequacy of the general fund balance

What is an adequate *available* fund balance for the general fund? Is it 5, 10, 15, or 20 percent, or another percentage, of general fund spending (or revenues)? The rating agencies do not recommend a specific fund balance as a percentage of spending.[4] They do recommend that local governments maintain strong financial positions and carry significant fund balances.[5]

In North Carolina, the Local Government Commission, a state agency that oversees local government finance, specifies that the *minimum* available general fund balance on June 30 (the close of the fiscal year) should be equal to 8 percent of general fund spending for the year ending on June 30.[6] General fund spending is adjusted to exclude extraordinary items and include transfers out of the general fund for this measure. Eight percent equates roughly to operating spending for one month.

Many small towns carry general fund balances that are 50 percent or more of general fund spending.[7] While this seems very high, a 50 percent fund balance for a small town may be no more than $100,000, which even a small town could quickly spend in recovering from a major storm or emergency. Moreover, many small towns face challenges in accessing debt markets, rely mainly on pay-as-go capital financing, and use accumulated general fund balances as de facto capital reserves. They build operating fund balances and periodically draw them down to fund capital projects.

In North Carolina, most counties carry general fund balances that range between 15 and 25 percent of general fund spending, and most medium- and large-size cities carry general fund balances between approximately 15 percent and 30 percent of general fund spending.

For a particular local government, the adequacy of its available general fund balances or other operating fund balances (in actual amount and as a percentage of spending) needs to be judged in terms of the conditions that the local government faces.[8] If a local government is budgeted tightly, if actual revenues will match budgeted estimates, and if actual spending will use up all appropriation authority, the government needs a larger general fund balance for operating reserve purposes. Another local government of a similar size and facing similar economic prospects, but that has a budget in which actual revenues will exceed revenue estimates and spending will be within appropriations, can probably get by with a lower general fund balance.

Economic conditions and prospects should be factored into a local decision about carrying fund balance. If the economy falters and, as a result, revenue growth slips or revenues decline and spending for certain mandated programs such as public assistance grows, higher levels of fund balance will help local governments weather these events. On the other hand, when economic growth is strong and revenue collections exceed estimates, a local government can probably draw down its fund balance for specific purposes, including capital projects. Like many very small jurisdictions that regularly use accumulated general and other operating fund balances as capital reserves, medium- and large-size jurisdictions periodically use operating fund balances to finance capital needs.

Measuring the balance of enterprise funds

An **enterprise fund** is a public service budgeted and accounted for apart from the general fund, supported entirely or in significant part with user fees, and operated with business principles. To measure the balance or current financial position of enterprise funds, a local government can use the same definition of available fund balance as is used for measuring the general fund balance—cash plus investments less current liabilities and encumbrances— and the enterprise fund balance can be calculated as a percentage of enterprise fund spending. The **quick ratio** and **net working capital** are other suitable measures of the current financial position of a local government's public enterprise.[9] The quick ratio is the ratio of current assets (cash and cash equivalents or investment plus accounts receivable) to current liabilities. Current assets are usually understood as those that can be converted to cash within a year's time, and current liabilities are those that are payable within a year. Net working capital is current assets less current liabilities.

Commonly accepted guidelines for judging the adequacy of fund balance across different types of enterprises do not exist. Although the general funds of many local governments receive major revenues only quarterly, semi-annually, or even only annually, many enterprise funds receive significant revenues monthly and can get by with lower fund balances. Available operating balances or reserves for local government utility or enterprise funds can probably be kept to one or two months' spending, depending on the utility's size, the challenges it faces, and the availability of special reserves for rate stabilization or emergency purposes.

The ability of a local government to transfer money back and forth between its general fund and major utility or enterprise funds also affects the balances carried by each type of fund. Where such transfers or loans are possible, enterprise or utility fund balances and general fund operating balances can be lower. A general fund with ample cash can cover a utility fund facing temporary cash flow problems, or vice versa. However, where loans and transfers between the enterprise funds and general fund are not possible, each fund type must stand on its own financially. This means that the enterprise funds as well as the general fund must carry significant operating balances.

Measuring the balance of other governmental funds

Other governmental funds might include special revenue funds established by law or local policy for specific services (for example, parks and recreation or library services). Such funds are most often used when particular revenues are legally restricted to fund the services. Operating fund balance for these governmental funds can be measured using the same approach as fund balance for the general fund (cash plus investments less current liabilities and encumbrances). If the available general fund balance is healthy, there is less need to carry significant operating fund balances in these other funds. On the other hand, if the general fund balance is low, having significant fund balances in other, important governmental funds can help a local government meet short-term cash-flow needs and avoid drawing down capital reserves to shore up these funds.

Capital reserves

The second capital financing policy is to create capital reserves and commit annual revenues to fund them. A capital reserve is a savings account. Revenues or other money is raised, set aside in the reserve until needed, and then used to finance capital spending. Capital reserve financing is a pay-as-go or cash-based approach to capital finance. With a capital reserve, capital spending does not occur until after taxes or other revenues are accumulated to pay for the spending. Capital reserves can be combined with earmarked annual revenue to provide an ongoing resource to meet recurring capital needs.

A capital reserve can be a separate accounting fund or a designated portion of the general fund. The advantage of creating a separate fund is that it is more difficult to raid it to cover operating fund shortfalls. If the capital reserve is a separate fund, it can be a revolving fund replenished with specific annual or recurring revenues.

To be effective, a capital reserve must be adequately funded. If a capital reserve fund is established to finance the acquisition of a new elevated platform truck for the fire department four years in the future, officials might, for example, specify that an annual appropriation be made from the general fund to the reserve each year over the coming four years. These appropriations are set at a level that, by the fourth year, the amount accumulated plus the interest earned are sufficient to buy the fire truck.

Officials might fund a capital reserve to finance roof replacements and other renovation projects by dedicating specific annual taxes or revenues to the job. Such taxes or revenues could be a portion of a general tax (a designated number of cents of the city's property tax rate, for example) or a portion or all of a special tax or revenue (50 percent of a hotel and motel room occupancy tax or all of 911 charges on local phone bills, for example). The earmarking may allow the reserved revenue to be spent for any capital projects or equipment, or it may restrict spending to projects in a single functional area or to a specific project or acquisition.

Certain capital reserves may be funded with special assessment or impact fee revenue. Some local governments place special assessment revenues in a reserve or special revenue fund to finance street improvements or water or sewer infrastructure projects that benefit the specific properties assessed. Similarly, impact fees are typically deposited into reserve funds used to finance infrastructure and capital facilities needed to serve growth and development.

Chapter 6 examines capital reserve financing in more depth and considers legal requirements and the purposes for which reserves are established, types of capital spending, and the risk or problem of diversion of reserves. Chapter 6 also discuss how annual revenues, special assessments, and impact fees are earmarked and used for funding capital projects.

Pay-as-go and debt financing

To finance capital projects and acquisitions, local governments need to balance pay-as-go financing sources and debt financing sources. Pay-as-go sources can be created by levying taxes or revenues, accumulating and using reserves, or obtaining grants or contributions to finance capital spending. Government reliance on pay-as-go sources for capital financing is analogous to private sector use of **equity** sources to finance business capital needs. Broadly conceived, equity sources in the private sector include owners' contributions of capital (including stock proceeds), retained earnings from operations, and special charges to operating revenue to finance capital assets.

The other general way that local governments can finance capital projects is **debt** financing. A local government borrows or obtains the use of money belonging to others to finance capital spending and then, while using the financed asset, makes periodic debt service or lease payments over many years to pay back the lender(s) or lessor(s).

Chapters 6 and 7 describe the common types of pay-as-go and debt financing and the reasons for and against using each type. This section considers only the issues involved in achieving an appropriate balance between the two broad categories of capital financing.

Achieving a balance

Most local governments can finance capital needs most effectively by relying on both debt and pay-as-go sources. A jurisdiction that finances all or most of its capital program with pay-as-go sources may delay projects or fail to undertake them altogether, thereby creating infrastructure and public service deficiencies. On the other hand, a local government that relies entirely or predominantly on debt financing for its capital program, even for recurring equipment replacement and ongoing facility rehabilitation, is building up fixed debt service and lease charges in its operating budget. These charges can crowd out other operating budget spending and leave the jurisdiction without adequate flexibility to respond to a budget crisis occasioned by an economic downturn.

How much of a community's capital program should be financed with debt and how much from pay-as-go sources depends very much on the capital projects needed and on the financial condition and prospects of the community. However, the following examples show how the local government can adopt a general policy defining the desirable balance between pay-as-go financing and debt financing.

Fast-growing community If a local government serving a fast-growing community has large operating fund balances and a tradition of allocating a significant portion of annual revenues to recurring capital needs and to capital reserves, it may be able to finance 50 percent or more of its capital program from pay-as-go sources, but it probably will need to issue debt to finance major new facilities. A local government serving a fast-growing community that carries limited operating fund balances and has allocated only small amounts of annual revenue to recurring capital needs or reserves will probably have to fund a much larger share—perhaps 75 or 80 percent—of its capital program with debt. If growth is very rapid, even the first local government might have to finance as much as 75 percent of its capital program with debt and only 25 percent from pay-as-go sources.

Rapid development in a community is likely to expand the tax base and improve the community's ability to service substantial borrowing. However, to preserve flexibility in future operating budgets so that it can respond to economic downturns and budget crises, even a growing community may choose to finance at least 20 percent to a third of its capital program from pay-as-go sources.

Slow-growing community A slow-growing or relatively stable community faces a different set of capital financing challenges when it needs to rehabilitate or replace aging infrastructure, modernize facilities, replace and upgrade equipment, or construct new infrastructure and facilities to meet changes in service demand or to provide new services. This local government may choose to finance as much as two-thirds to three-quarters of its capital program from pay-as-go sources. Spending for equipment replacement and most infrastructure or facility rehabilitation could be scheduled to recur at similar or predictable amounts from year to year, and special taxes or recurring revenues could be earmarked to roughly match this spending. In years when capital spending falls off, the earmarked revenues would accumulate in capital reserves to be used in subsequent years when capital spending is higher than usual. Debt would be issued occasionally (for example, when a large project is needed to accommodate new or redefined services, when a major facility needs to be replaced, or when unanticipated equipment acquisitions are necessary).

Community with a shrinking tax base   In a low-income community that is in decline or facing a shrinking tax base, the local government's main capital financing challenge is to find the money to keep equipment and facilities in repair and up to date and to replace or rehabilitate them as they wear out. The government should allocate at least a small portion of annual revenues to repair and replace small capital equipment, and it should fund capital reserves for major equipment and large rehabilitation projects. Intermediate-term lease financing can also be used for major equipment or projects. When a local government in a low-income community undertakes a major project, its access to debt markets will be facilitated to the extent that it is carrying significant operating fund balances and is using recurring revenues and reserves to meet a portion of replacement needs. Such a local government should also aggressively seek any available grant or subsidized loan financing for its capital needs. Many state loan and grant programs for local governments are intended specifically to help economically stressed communities.

Measuring the balance

The most obvious measure of the balance between pay-as-go financing and debt financing is the ratio of direct capital spending from pay-as-go sources (annual revenues, capital reserves, charges to property, for example) to spending from debt sources (general obligation bonds, other bonds, installment- or lease-purchase debt, among others), for the full term of the CIP forecast period or for any specific year within that period. The disadvantage of this measure is that the ratio of pay-as-go financing to debt financing can swing greatly from one year to the next or from one group of years to another. Early in the life of a major bond issue, spending from debt proceeds dwarfs financing from pay-as-go sources. In later years, the ratio swings strongly in the other direction, as spending from pay-as-go sources outweighs spending from debt sources.

A better measure of the balance between pay-as-go financing and debt financing is the ratio of annual payments for debt service and capital lease obligations to direct spending for capital purposes from annual revenues, capital reserves, and other pay-as-go sources. Annual debt service and lease payments distribute the impact of debt over many years, and they provide a better figure for year-to-year comparisons with spending from pay-as-go sources. This measure provides a good basis for comparing reliance on pay-as-go financing versus debt financing over the full term of a CIP and for any individual years within the CIP forecast period. However, even it can be misleading in years when spending from capital reserve funds is heavy. When contributions into capital reserves are made regularly or at comparable amounts from year to year and spending from the reserves is much greater in some years than others, the ratio can be modified to count contributions into capital reserve funds rather than withdrawals or spending from them to provide a more reliable measure.

Wake County, North Carolina, which is part of the fast-growing Research Triangle area of the state, compares annual payments for debt service for bonds and other debt issued for capital projects with appropriations for direct spending on capital projects from annual revenues, withdrawals from reserves, and other pay-as-go sources. An informal policy was introduced to guide the county's CIP and capital financing practices in the mid-1980s as the county began to issue substantial debt to build schools and other facilities to meet growth: the county used no more than 50 percent funding from debt sources, as measured by annual debt service, and it used at least 50 percent funding from pay-as-go sources. This policy shaped Wake County's capital financing decisions for more than a decade. Revised in 1999, the policy now allows up to 80 percent of total capital funding in a year to be from debt sources and at least 20 percent to be from direct, pay-as-go sources of financing of projects and acquisitions.[10]

Local debt capacity

Determining how much debt for capital financing a local government can afford to issue is a key step in capital planning and finance. Officials can assess the financial resources that will be available to pay debt service and lease obligations in future years—the local government's debt capacity—by looking at its current financial position, its prospects, and key debt ratios.

Multiyear financial forecasting is discussed later in this chapter and in Chapter 12. Judgment and assumptions are involved in estimating revenues that will be available in the future, ongoing services that must be supported from those revenues, the extent to which the jurisdiction will use pay-as-go financing, and the revenues that will be left to pay debt service and lease obligations.

Net debt ratios

To decide how much debt it can afford to issue, a local government must look at bond or debt ratios. Numerous ratios are available for measuring local debt burden, but the most frequently used are:

- Net debt per capita
- Net debt as a percentage of taxable or market valuation
- Annual debt service on net debt as a percentage of general fund revenues or spending. If funds besides the general fund provide significant support to government services or operations, spending from these funds should be included with general fund spending for this ratio.

All these ratios refer to **net debt.** Net debt is debt that is paid from general revenues or taxes (that is, revenues and taxes budgeted and accounted for in the general fund). General obligation bonds are included in net debt, unless the bonds were issued to finance improvements for a self-supporting enterprise and enterprise revenues fully cover debt service on the bonds. Lease-purchase and installment-purchase debt, certificates of participation, and other capital leases are also included in net debt if they finance the acquisition or construction of governmental or general public facilities (for example, many city or county office buildings, schools, law enforcement centers, jails, fire stations, and equipment for these types of facilities or functions). Revenue bonds are excluded from net debt, as are special obligation bonds that are secured and paid entirely from a special revenue or tax fund that is budgeted and accounted for apart from the local government's general fund.

A local government's net debt can be described as the bonds, capital lease obligations, and other debt that is not self-supporting or self-liquidating. It must be paid from general revenues and taxes. If there is any doubt about whether a particular debt or capital lease obligation is self-supporting, it is better to include it rather than exclude it from the calculation of net debt. Calculations of net debt for legal purposes usually include authorized and unissued general obligation debt as well as outstanding GO debt. The calculation of net debt in ratios to evaluate debt burden should also include authorized and unissued general obligation debt and other non-self-supporting debt, assuming the local government will issue the debt sometime in the future. Net debt, of course, does not include debt that has been **refunded** or debt that has been **defeased** with **advance refunding bonds** (addressed later in chapter). Advance refunding bonds that defease non-self-supporting bonds or debt are included in net debt. Net debt may be reduced by reserves that are set aside for the retirement of net debt.

Each of these ratios is discussed in this section (see also the sidebar below on current debt ratios of triple-A-rated local governments).

Current debt ratios

A 2001 study by Standard & Poor's of the forty-one municipalities that the corporation rated triple A at that time revealed the following ratios for net debt per capita, net debt as a percentage of market valuation, and annual debt service on net debt as a percentage of general fund and other governmental fund spending.

Municipal population range (number of units)	Average population	Net debt per capita	Net debt as percentage of market value	Net debt service as percentage of budget
Small: less than 50,000 (12)	25,178	$2,331	1.8%	8.2%
Medium: 50,000-250,000 (22)	116,863	$1,912	2.3%	9.3%
Large: more than 250,000 (7)	575,692	$1,773	3.7%	16.6%
All municipalities (41)	168,365	$2,011	2.4%	10.2%

Source: Karl Jacob and Geoffrey Buswick, "Annual Review of 'AAA' Rated Municipalities," *Standard & Poor's Public Finance,* February 8, 2001.

From the data in the table, the following two observations can be made.

First, per capita debt and debt as a percentage of market valuation seem to be related inversely. The small units that are rated triple A have fewer people relative to market valuation, suggesting that the small units are wealthier than the medium and large jurisdictions among the triple-A-rated jurisdictions. This suggests that to be rated triple A, a small jurisdiction must be relatively well-off economically.

Second, debt service as a percentage of the operating budget increases with the size of the jurisdiction. Operating budget here includes general funds and special revenue funds that support the local jurisdiction's governmental (as opposed to enterprise) programs and activities. Apparently, large jurisdictions issue more debt relative to operating spending and perhaps as a portion of overall capital needs than do the smaller units. Small jurisdictions rely more on pay-as-go capital financing.

Net debt per capita   Net debt per capita for a local government is net debt divided by the permanent resident population of a jurisdiction. This is probably the most widely used measure of debt burden. The advantage of the measure is that reliable population data are available, and net debt per capita in different local governments can be readily compared. The disadvantage of the ratio is that it does not assess debt capacity for a jurisdiction. Capacity depends on a jurisdiction's wealth, tax base, revenues, and other financial factors.

If two cities have roughly the same population but one is wealthy and growing and the other is hard-pressed financially, the capacity of the first city to issue and carry debt is greater than the capacity of the second city. Debt per capita, which could be the same for both cities, says little about each city's capacity to pay debt. Care must be exercised in interpreting net debt per capita figures for some local jurisdictions. For example, a beach community with a small permanent resident population, a very large tax base, and a summer tourist population that swells to ten times the permanent resident population can safely carry a much higher net debt per capita than a local government where the permanent resident population is the same throughout the year.

Despite its disadvantages, net debt per capita is widely used. Officials should refer to this ratio when they assess a local government's debt burden and compare its net debt with similarly situated local jurisdictions.

Net debt as percentage of taxable or market valuation   Net debt as a percentage of taxable or market valuation compares net debt with the primary tax base or with a very important measure of wealth for a community. Property tax revenue is the largest general revenue source for most local governments across the country. For these local governments, comparing net debt with taxable or market valuation relates the debt to the primary resource that the jurisdiction draws on to repay the debt. Net debt as a percentage of taxable or market valuation can be a good measure of debt capacity as well as debt burden. Even where local governments are not authorized to levy the property tax or where the tax is a secondary local revenue resource, net debt as a percentage of property market value can be a useful surrogate measure of debt capacity.

This measure of a local government's debt burden can be misleading, however. Taxable valuation is affected by state and local property valuation policies and practices. For example, in a fast-growing jurisdiction, taxable valuation can diverge significantly from market valuation or from tax valuations in other communities if the fast-growing jurisdiction does not revalue property every year or two. Even when net debt is compared with the market valuation of property, available data on market values in some communities may be out of date or the property included in making the calculation in one community may be different from the property included in another. Nevertheless, data on local market values are becoming more reliable and comparable from jurisdiction to jurisdiction, and net debt as a percentage of taxable or market value can help local officials assess their jurisdiction's debt capacity and debt burden and compare them with those of similar local governments.

Annual debt service on net debt as a percentage of general fund revenues or spending   This ratio measures the portion of the operating budget that is absorbed by debt service on bonds or other debt issued for general or non-self-supporting facilities and improvements. If the percentage of the general fund budget being spent for debt service on net debt is already high and is expected to remain high over the next several years, local officials may need to postpone or reduce a new issue they are considering. On the other hand, if this ratio is currently low, the local government may be in a good position to issue the debt and consider other major debt issues to meet needs in upcoming years.

Although no one standard ratio applies to all local governments, the bond rating agencies usually view debt service on net debt that is between 15 percent and 20 percent of recurring general fund spending or revenues as high.[11] A ratio above 20 percent would be excessive, unless a jurisdiction was experiencing tremendous growth. A ratio below 5 percent would be low and would usually allow for the issuance of significant new debt.

Comparisons of local governments that are based on the ratio of annual debt service on net debt to general fund spending or revenues can be misleading. Some local governments budget and account for certain general governmental services (for example, street maintenance or parks and recreation services) outside the general fund, while others include in the general fund practically all services defined as governmental. Comparisons using general fund spending for the ratio may overstate the relative magnitude of annual debt service for those local governments accounting for significant services in other funds. Any comparison of local governments using the ratio should include spending for all general government services, even if they are budgeted in special revenue funds instead of in the general fund.

Other ratios for assessing net debt Other ratios for assessing net debt capacity and burden relate local government debt to an income measure such as median family income, personal income, or per capita income for a community. Income is typically the best measure of a community's wealth and therefore ultimately of the ability of citizens to pay debt service on net debt and support other local government spending. Moreover, in a community where the local government levies a personal income or payroll tax or receives revenue from this source, a measure of net debt in relation to income directly assesses the debt-carrying capacity of the local government. However, most local governments do not levy or receive income or payroll taxes, and such a ratio is only an indirect measure of debt capacity for them. Income data are not available for many medium- and small-size jurisdictions.

Forecasting debt ratios

When a local government's debt capacity is assessed, it is not enough to calculate current debt ratios. A local government's ability to issue additional debt and make debt service payments in the future depends on future revenues, spending, and debt position. Debt ratios should be projected for the same planning period covered by the capital program and integrated into the financial forecast.

Bond ratings and rating criteria

A local government's capital financing strategy should address ways to maintain or improve its bond rating or ratings. This introduction defines what a bond rating is, comments on its importance to local government debt issuers, and identifies rating factors for different types of local government debt. Chapter 8 examines these topics in depth and also covers the national rating agencies and the rating categories they use, the rating process, the characteristics of top-rated local governments, and how to improve a bond rating.

A bond rating is an opinion of the creditworthiness of a debt issuer with regard to specific debt, a type of debt, or a financing program. A rating evaluates an issuer's strength or weakness on factors that bear on the issuer's ability and willingness to make timely principal and interest payments on the debt. According to Standard & Poor's, one of the three national rating agencies, an issuer's rating for long-term debt is based on three general factors:

- Likelihood of the issuer meeting its financial commitment under the debt contract

- Nature and provisions of the debt contract (the security pledged for the debt and other protections afforded to investors under the contract)

- Protections available to investors under laws that authorize and limit local debt and/or provide for its repayment—such laws include state constitutional, statutory, and regulatory provisions that can extend to state oversight of local debt issuance and repayment as well as federal laws that affect creditors' rights under debt contracts.[12]

A local government that obtains nationally recognized bond ratings to support the sale of debt typically increases the number of investors who are interested in buying or able to buy the debt. This, in turn, can lower the interest rate(s) the issuer pays because more investors compete to buy the debt, more than offsetting the costs of the rating(s). In addition, the independent review that is part of a bond rating can help local officials identify strengths and weaknesses in planning, finance, management, and governance and provide a basis to address and overcome problems. Maintaining a good bond rating says to investors, regulators, and the local community that local officials are doing a good job. Improving a local government's rating sends a message to the same interested parties that local officials are successfully meeting the challenges that their jurisdiction faces, strengthening its condition and prospects, and generally moving the jurisdiction forward.

Ratings of general obligation bonds, which are secured by the full faith and credit or unlimited taxing power of the issuer, usually apply to all GO debt of the issuer. In other words, when a local government issues new general obligation bonds and obtains a rating for the issue, that rating also applies to previously issued and outstanding GO bonds of the issuer. Because the issuer's general credit underlies its ability to repay *all* GO bonds, a GO bond rating is similar to what Standard & Poor's calls an "issuer rating" (rather than an issue rating): the rating applies generally to the issuer, not to specific debt of the issuer.[13]

In contrast, each issue of most local revenue bonds, certificates of participation, and special obligation debt has unique security provisions, indentures, and payment provisions that distinguish that issue from other issues of the same type of debt by the same issuer. This is often true even for different issues of revenue bonds for the same enterprise, secured by the same special revenue sources. Specific security provisions and indentures often vary from issue to issue. As a result, a separate rating is assigned to each of these debt issues.

A debt rating also takes into account credit support, if any, from bond insurance or other forms of financial guarantee for debt. Bond insurance guarantees to investors debt service payments and is now widely used in the debt market by local governments. Bond insurance raises a rating of the issuer to the triple-A rating of the insurance company.

The national rating agencies evaluate all of the different types of debt that local governments sell: GO bonds, revenue bonds, certificates of participation and other capital lease debt, and various kinds of limited or special obligation debt. The rating criteria for each of these types of debt are identified here and discussed fully in Chapter 8.

GO bonds

Ratings of local GO bonds are based on an assessment of the issuer's general creditworthiness. The criteria for rating GO debt fall into four categories:

- **Local and regional economy**   Size, wealth, growth or change, diversity, stability, infrastructure and facilities, and policies related to sustainable growth or progress
- **Local government finances**   Growth or change in revenues and spending, fund balance and reserves, budget practices, accounting and financial reporting, tax and revenue administration, investment practices, and other factors
- **Debt burden**   Net debt per capita and as a percentage of tax or market valuation, annual debt service on net debt in relation to general fund and other governmental fund spending, net debt in relation to personal income, pay-down pace for long-term net debt, and net debt of overlapping and underlying jurisdictions
- **Governance and planning**   Coherence in local governmental structure, ability of local elected officials to work together and reach decisions, management, and multiyear planning.

Revenue bonds

Ratings of local revenue bonds depend above all on the extent to which the utility or enterprise for which the bonds are issued produces revenues or earnings to cover or pay all expenses, especially debt service. Coverage is a key factor used in evaluating revenue bonds. It is the ratio of annual net revenues for the enterprise to annual debt service. Usually maximum annual debt service is used for the ratio. Revenue bond ratings also depend on the competition, if any, that the enterprise faces; the ability of the enterprise to raise rates to meet needs; the extent to which indentures or contractual provisions in the bond contract protect investors; debt levels and financial position of the enterprise; policies concerning transfers of enterprise resources to other funds of the issuer; and management experience.

Capital lease debt

Ratings for certificates of participation and other capital lease debt are based on the essentiality of the asset(s) financed with the lease and pledged to secure the debt. The more essential the asset is, the less likely is the local government lessee to stop making payments on the debt and risk loss of the asset or property. If the capital lease debt finances general public improvements and general revenues are used to make the lease payments, the general creditworthiness of the issuer, based on the GO rating criteria, also will influence the rating. Most capital leases have nonappropriation clauses allowing the governmental lessee to stop making payments on the lease by not appropriating money for such payments. The rating agencies consider the risk of nonappropriation in assigning ratings. Ratings for lease debt are also affected by the pledge of additional collateral beyond the property being leased and the indentures included in the debt contract intended to protect investors' interests.

Limited and special obligation debt

Ratings of the different types of limited or special obligation debt of local governments depend primarily on the certainty, breadth, and risks associated with the taxes or revenues pledged to secure and pay the debt. Chapter 8 discusses rating considerations for special assessment, tax increment, and non-property-tax debt, and certain other types of special obligation debt.

Planning, selling, and managing debt

Planning, selling, and managing debt effectively involves a variety of issues that are identified here and examined fully in Chapters 9, 10, and 11. Following are the issues that a local government's capital financing strategy should address:

- Setting the full term over which a debt issue will be retired
- Scheduling debt service payments
- Choosing debt features
- Deciding whether to issue short-term debt to finance capital assets
- Deciding whether to use taxable debt rather than tax-exempt debt
- Selling the debt in a competitive or negotiated public sale or through a private placement
- Working with market professionals in selling or placing debt
- Managing debt.

Debt term

The full term of a bond or debt issue is the total number of years that the issue (or any portion of it) is outstanding. The term of a debt issue should not exceed the useful life of the capital asset financed with the debt. Useful life provides an outside limit for the full debt term. Changes in service needs and in technology can make a capital asset obsolete well before the end of its estimated useful life; this possibility favors the selection of a shorter debt term. In practice, the municipal debt market often limits the debt repayment term to a period that is shorter than estimated useful life. For example, the term for GO bonds is usually limited to around twenty years, even if the assets financed with the debt have a much longer useful life. Finally, future financing needs should influence the setting of the debt term. Paying off debt on capital assets before they must be replaced frees up debt issuance capacity to finance new capital assets to meet growth.

Schedules for debt service payment

Local government debt issued for capital financing can be repaid in three ways: serially (a portion of the debt issue is repaid annually over the debt term), in a single payment at the end of the term, or with a combination of serial and term repayments.

There are two general models for structuring annual debt service payments: even annual debt service and even annual principal retirement. Under the first, annual debt service, including interest and principal, remains the same over the term of the debt. Payments made in the early years are mostly interest and in the latter years mostly principal. The second model provides for roughly even principal retirement over the term of the debt. Annual debt service declines because annual interest declines, while the annual retirement of principal remains the same. Even annual principal retirement frees up debt capacity in future years and reduces total debt service over the life of the debt issue. A local government that has outstanding debt and is planning to issue new debt usually "blends" debt service on the new debt with existing debt service obligations.

The term of the debt and the repayment schedule affect the issuer's interest rate. The market usually charges lower interest rates for shorter debt terms. Thus, the longer the term of the debt and the longer principal repayment is delayed, the higher the interest rate and total interest paid will be.

Debt features

Planning debt involves making decisions about which features to include with a bond or debt issue. Some features, such as an early call option, give the issuer flexibility in managing debt in the future. A call option allows the issuer to call in or redeem debt before an issue is scheduled to mature. If interest rates drop in the future, a call option gives the local issuer the opportunity to refund still outstanding bonds from the original issue with new, lower-interest-rate bonds. Market practices and conditions shape the availability and use of these features. The most important features are examined in Chapter 9.

Short-term debt

Short-term debt is conventionally defined as having a term of one year or less. To finance capital assets, local governments usually issue intermediate to long-term debt, that is, debt retired over a term ranging anywhere from a few years to twenty or thirty years or so. In certain situations in capital financing, however, some local jurisdictions, even medium-size ones, also use short-term debt.

For example, when federal or state grantor agencies are financing a project, the grantor agency may approve long-term financing for a project but not actually provide the financing until after the project is built. Consequently, the local unit issues bond or grant anticipation notes to pay for the construction of the project. Once the construction is finished, the grantor agency provides the long-term financing, which is used to pay off the short-term bond or grant anticipation notes.

Sometimes local governments issue short-term debt to undertake a project when officials do not wish to lock themselves into prevailing high interest rates. When interest rates fall, they refund the short-term debt with long-term debt. Some local governments issue short-term, variable rate debt to finance capital projects to take advantage of the lower interest rates available for short-term debt. The interest rate on such debt is subject to change, usually weekly, and investors holding the debt can demand full repayment of the debt in any week. If this occurs, the jurisdiction must issue new debt to replace the debt for which investors were repaid. The use of such short-term debt can be a risky strategy for local governments, even large ones, because the issuer is assuming the interest rate risks. It is difficult to predict what interest and debt service costs will be in the future.

Tax-exempt versus taxable debt

Most debt issued by local governments is tax exempt. Investors who buy the debt do not have to pay federal income taxes and, in certain cases, state income taxes on the interest they receive. Consequently, tax-exempt debt can be sold at interest rates lower than other market interest rates. The federal tax code requires that, to avoid federal penalties, local governments spend the proceeds from tax-exempt debt sales within certain defined periods of time. For this reason, some local governments use taxable debt for certain purposes, although these purposes seldom include capital financing (see the discussion of arbitrage on the next page).

The sale of debt

The method chosen for selling debt can save significant amounts of money. A local government can sell debt through a competitive or a negotiated public sales process or in a private placement (see also Chapter 11).

In a public sale, the sales staff of one or more investment banking firms advertises the debt and markets it to investors. A public sale can be competitive or negotiated. State law often requires that general obligation bonds be sold using a formal competitive bid process in which underwriters submit bids to buy the bonds. The bid offering the lowest **net interest cost** (NIC) or lowest **true interest cost** (TIC) is selected. The winning bidder then remarkets the debt to investors. Chapter 10 explains the concepts of net interest cost and true interest cost.

Revenue bonds and most types of limited or special obligation debt are usually sold in a negotiated public sales process. The local issuer first selects an investment banker or underwriter and then works with the underwriter to plan the sale (selecting a repayment term, a debt service repayment schedule, bond features, and more). The local issuer and investment banker negotiate all of these conditions and, most important, the interest rates and prices for which the bonds or debt will be sold. The average interest rate for the issue is calculated using true interest cost.

In a private placement of debt, a local government places the debt with one bank or investor or with a small group of investors rather than marketing the debt through underwriters to the general investing public. Local governments use private placement for debt issues of relatively modest amounts (for example, to acquire equipment or for small construction projects). Because of federal tax laws, private placements of debt are usually not used for financings that exceed $10 million.

Market professionals

When selling debt, a local government, even a large one, typically requires the advice and assistance of market professionals such as a bond counsel, financial adviser, underwriter, consulting engineer for enterprise revenue bonds, rating agencies, bond insurer, a trustee (except for general obligation debt), a registrar and paying agent, and sometimes others. The roles of these professionals are discussed in Chapter 11.

Debt management

The local government that issues debt must devise and follow an investment plan that puts the proceeds to work before they are spent. Its objective is to earn investment income without violating federal arbitrage restrictions. The local government must also decide whether debt that has been outstanding for a number of years should be refunded or advance refunded. It may also be presented with a proposal to swap interest and debt service obligations as a way to manage debt. Arbitrage, refunding, advance refunding, and interest rate swaps are introduced here and explained fully in Chapters 9 and 10.

Arbitrage refers to the profit made by selling securities and investing the proceeds in higher-yielding securities. In the case of local government debt, arbitrage occurs when a local government borrows money by selling its tax-exempt debt at a relatively low interest rate and invests the proceeds in taxable securities that have higher interest rates. Federal arbitrage regulations prohibit or limit arbitrage profits resulting from investment of tax-exempt debt. Any profits made from arbitrage must be rebated to the U.S. treasury, unless the local issuer of the debt qualifies for an exemption. An investment plan for local government debt proceeds should make use of these exemptions and avoid or minimize rebate and arbitrage penalties.[14]

Refunding is possible only for local government debt that has a call or early redemption option. Using the option, the local unit calls in or retires existing debt and replaces it with new debt that carries lower interest rates or fewer restrictions on the issuer than the called-in debt. If lower interest rates trigger the refunding, which is usually the case, the lower interest costs for the refunding debt must more than compensate the issuer for the cost of issuing new debt.

Advance refunding is used when a debt issue does not have a call or early redemption option. It can also be used before the date at which a call option may be exercised. With advance refunding, new debt is issued, put into an escrow account, and invested in certain securities that **defease** the existing debt. Defease means that the refunding debt plus the interest that it earns cover all future debt service on the debt being advance refunded. The interest earned on the securities purchased with the refunding debt may not exceed the interest paid on the existing debt without violating arbitrage regulations of the Internal Revenue Service.[15] The escrowed funds pay all future debt service on the older existing debt, with its higher interest rates. The local issuer is responsible solely for debt service on the new advance refunding debt with its lower interest rates.

A few local governments, mainly larger ones, are using **swap contracts** to manage debt. In such contracts, the local unit transfers payment obligations on its debt to a "counterparty," usually a bank or an investment banking firm. The local jurisdiction then assumes payment obligations on the debt of the counterparty or on debt made available by the counterparty. A swap can allow a local unit that has issued short-term, variable-rate debt to exchange its payment obligation on that debt for payment obligations on long-term, fixed-rate debt. This might occur because of decreases in long-term interest rates since the variable-rate debt was issued, and the local unit wants to lock in the lower, fixed interest rates. Alternatively, a local government might swap its payment obligations on longer-term, fixed-rate debt for payment obligations on short-term, variable-rate debt in order to take advantage of interest rates that are lower on the short-term debt. Swap contracts can be a less-expensive alternative to advance refunding of debt. The duration of a swap contract can match the term of the original debt. A local unit considering an interest rate swap must first determine its legality. If it is legal, the local unit must then consider the risks and be assured that savings in debt payments justify the risks. Swap contracts are usually not appropriate except for sophisticated local government debt issuers.

Multiyear financial forecasting

Preparation of a multiyear financial forecast to support both the capital and operating budgets is an important part of a capital financing strategy. A multiyear forecast projects revenues and other financial resources available to a local government over the forecast period. It also projects expenditures or uses of those revenues and resources—operating spending for salaries and fringe benefits, contractual services, supplies and other operating needs, annual debt service and lease or rental payments, pay-as-go spending for capital projects and acquisitions, contributions to and spending from capital reserves, contributions to or disbursements from operating or other reserves, and any spending for other purposes. Chapter 12 examines multiyear financial forecasting in depth and illustrates its use by local governments. This discussion briefly comments on the importance of forecasting and identifies key issues in designing a multiyear financial forecast.

Multiyear financial forecasting is a useful tool for capital planning and finance because capital improvement programs extend over many years. Major capital projects take years to plan and build. Financing may take years to arrange, and debt service and lease payments for equipment and projects extend many years into the future. When growth pressures are great and capital plans become ambitious, or when a local government faces economic challenges that threaten the capital program and a jurisdiction's overall financial prospects, a multiyear financial forecast becomes a very useful tool.

Financial forecasting can help a local government meet certain requirements of the Governmental Accounting Standards Board's new financial reporting model. The new model requires local governments to depreciate fixed assets or to estimate the amount of money needed annually to maintain infrastructure properly.[16] A multiyear financial forecast can provide the framework for local officials to calculate and present estimated future depreciation or maintenance requirements on fixed assets and infrastructure.

A multiyear financial forecast supports the operating and capital budgets. It can tell officials whether future operating revenues will support both the continuation of current service levels and the start-up of a new program or operating initiative that the governing board is currently considering or is likely to consider in the near future.[17] It supports the capital budget because sooner or later all capital projects and acquisitions are paid from annual or operating revenue. Where pay-as-go sources fund capital spending, operating revenues go directly to pay for capital needs. Where debt or lease obligations are issued to finance capital needs, operating revenues in future years must be raised to support the resulting annual debt service and lease payments.

The design of a multiyear financial forecast involves decisions about the forecast's scope, time period, categories for presenting data, assumptions, methodology, use of indicators that monitor trends, and, finally, process-related issues.

Scope

One decision is whether to create one forecast for the jurisdiction as a whole or many forecasts, one for each major fund of the jurisdiction (for example, the general fund and the water-sewer enterprise fund). A local government that finances all or nearly all of its major programs from the general fund and has only a few other funds for relatively small programs can have one consolidated forecast and fold the smaller funds into the general fund forecast. A combined forecast of two or more major governmental funds, such as the general fund and a separate streets fund, usually works better than having separate forecasts for each fund. If a local government has one or more major enterprise funds in addition to the general fund, separate forecasts for each are usually recommended. The operating and financing issues are sufficiently different in major enterprise funds to justify separate forecasts.

Time period

If a jurisdiction has a CIP, the forecast period usually covers the same number of years as the CIP. The CIP and the financial forecast are closely connected. The CIP drives capital financing, and the financial forecast indicates whether the CIP is affordable. Most CIPs forecast capital needs five or six years into the future. Five or six years is also a practical period for forecasting annual revenues and spending The forecast of some variables, such as annual debt service or lease payment obligations, can be extended farther into the future.

Forecast assumptions

Assumptions have to be made about probable future growth or changes in revenues and spending, and these assumptions are usually shaped by officials' philosophy about the forecast: should it be as realistic as is practical, or should it be conservative and deliberately underestimate revenues or overestimate spending, or should it allow for revenues to be pushed up and spending trimmed from realistic estimates? Conservative assumptions are usually advisable with regard to growth in revenues. Assumptions about spending must address likely changes in costs to maintain existing services at current service levels, possible expansions or reductions in services, and the possible addition of new services or positions during the forecast period. Chapter 12 addresses forecasting philosophy and assumptions in detail.

Forecast methodology

In all jurisdictions, methodology relies heavily on the judgment of experienced officials about any likely changes in revenues and spending over the forecast period. In many jurisdictions, finance and budget officials refer to trend data from past years for key revenues and spending, graph the data, and use regression analysis to create projections for the future. These projections are tempered and modified by officials' knowledge and views about likely developments occurring in the forecast period. In some large jurisdictions, forecasts are based on deterministic or econometric models that relate growth in revenue sources or in spending to specific economic activity.

Process

Finally, designing a financial forecast involves decisions about developing, presenting, and using the forecast. Budget and financial staff typically develop the forecast. A key question here concerns the extent of involvement of program or line department directors in this process. Another important process question concerns whether the forecast is included as part of the annual budget and/or CIP presentation or whether it is presented separately at an earlier time.

Local government officials must decide what the bottom line for the forecast will include. Will the presentation of forecast results show simply the difference between revenues and spending for a year, the effect of that difference on fund balance, the tax rate equivalent of the difference, the effect on debt ratios, another outcome, or some or all of the above?

Governing board policies on capital financing

As discussed in Chapter 1, policies can guide a local government's capital planning, budgeting, and finance. Three sets of policies were identified: policies that require and structure multiyear capital planning, capital financing and debt policies, and policies that prioritize projects. This section focuses on the capital financing and debt policies of the local governing board.

Policies adopted by the governing board specifically for capital finance provide a framework that helps local officials stay within a jurisdiction's financing capacity and select suitable financing sources for specific capital projects and acquisitions. Capital financing policies should be long term and be used to inform year-to-year capital budgeting and financing decisions. Such policies are an essential part of the infrastructure needed for capital planning and finance.

The National Advisory Council on State and Local Budgeting recommends that state and local governments adopt policies for budget planning, preparation, and administration. The council recommends two specific policies concerning capital finance (see the next page). Both concern debt. One calls for policies on debt issuance and management, and the other calls for policies on maximum debt and debt capacity. The council also recommends that governments undertake long-term financial planning and forecasting to evaluate the effects of budget, capital budget, and debt issuance decisions.

The literature on municipal finance also suggests that governments adopt policies to shape capital financing, particularly debt levels and issuance. A debt policy connects operating budget decisions and capital program goals and helps ensure that decisions concerning the use of debt do not exceed a local government's financial resources, notes Michael Zino. He recommends that governments have clear, written statements of debt policy and follow a schedule for updating that policy regularly. The specific policies recommended by Zino, covering planning and pay-as-go financing as well as debt, encompass at least the following:

- Statutory debt limits and restrictions
- Debt capacity
- Capital program goals and commitments
- Projection of future debt and debt service costs
- Use of pay-as-go financing
- Refunding of existing debt when advantageous.[18]

Some of these components of debt policy correspond to particular capital financing strategies discussed in this chapter. They are also consistent with the capital planning and debt policies recommended by the National Advisory Council on State and Local Budgeting. In *Evaluating Financial Condition: A Handbook for Local Government*, the International City/County Management Association recommends specific indicators that can be used to evaluate debt levels and capacity and that can be incorporated into debt and capital financing policies.[19]

The city or county manager and the finance officer are likely to be the persons responsible for developing policies to guide capital financing. Review

Recommendations by the National Advisory Council on State and Local Budgeting

On debt issuance and management

"A government should adopt policies to guide the issuance and management of debt."

The rationale of the National Advisory Council on State and Local Budgeting for this policy states, "Issuing debt commits a government's revenues several years into the future, and may limit the government's flexibility to respond to changing service priorities, revenue inflows, or cost structures. Adherence to a debt policy helps ensure that debt is issued and managed prudently in order to maintain a sound fiscal position and protect credit quality."

On maximum debt and debt capacity (by type of debt)

"A government should adopt a policy on the maximum amount of debt and debt service that should be outstanding at any one time."

The council's rationale for a policy on debt level states: "Policies guiding the amount of debt that may be issued by a government help ensure that outstanding and planned debt levels do not exceed an amount that can be supported by the existing and projected tax and revenue base." Another part of the council's recommendation on maximum debt states: "A government should develop distinct policies for general obligation debt, debt supported by revenues of government enterprises, and other types of debt such as special assessment bonds, tax increment financing bonds, short-term debt, variable rate debt, and leases." This suggests that the council is recommending a separate policy on maximum debt and debt service for each of these different types of debt.

On long-range financial planning

"A government should have a financial planning process that assesses the long-term financial implications of current and proposed policies, programs, and assumptions and that develops appropriate strategies to achieve its goals."

The rationale for this recommended practice states, "Financial planning expands a government's awareness of options, potential problems, and opportunities. The long-term revenue, expenditure, and service implications of continuing or ending existing programs or adding new programs, services, and debt can be identified. The financial planning process helps shape decisions and permits necessary and corrective action to be taken before problems become more severe."

The council endorses two other recommendations on capital planning:

On inventorying capital assets

"A government should identify and conduct an assessment of its capital assets, including the condition of the assets and factors that could affect the need for or ability to maintain the assets in the future."

On developing options for meeting capital needs

"A government should develop specific capital project options for addressing capital needs that are consistent with financial, programmatic, and capital policies and should evaluate alternatives for acquiring the use of capital assets." The recommended budget practice addresses capital planning, priority setting, and evaluation.

Source: National Advisory Council on State and Local Budgeting, *Recommended Budget Practices: A Framework for Improved State and Local Government Budgeting* (Chicago: Government Finance Officers Association), 13, 19, 20, 30, 43.

of polices should not stop there. The policies need to be taken to the governing board for serious consideration. If the board deliberates about the policies before it adopts them and does not rubber stamp its approval, the policies are more likely to be effective and hold up under challenges. Program officials who provide local government services as well as interested citizens should have the opportunity to comment on proposed policies. They will be the ones using the infrastructure, facilities, and equipment planned and financed pursuant to the policies.

Irvine, California, has an extensive set of governing board–approved financial policies intended to ensure the city's fiscal strength and stability and guide the development of the operating and capital budget.[20] The policies are comprehensive and address revenues, the operating budget, capital improvements, debt issuance and management, accounting and reporting, investments, and community development financing. Specific objectives of the policies include strengthening the policymaking role of the city council in addressing financial challenges facing the city and establishing sound principles to guide decisions by the council. Many of these policies address capital financing and cover the same policies or practices that make up the capital financing strategy recommended and discussed in this chapter. The policies related to capital finance are summarized here:

Fund balance   To maintain Irvine's bond rating and meet seasonal cash flow needs and emergencies, the city's budget shall provide anticipated fund balances for the general and enterprise funds. If the fund balance falls below 5 percent of spending at the end of any year, the city shall rebuild the balance within one year. Current-year operating expenses shall be funded with current revenues and not from fund balances. Finally, the governing board specified that carryover funds shall first be allocated to the strategic business plan's rehabilitation plan. Additional carryover funds shall then be allocated as follows: 60 percent to new capital projects, 20 percent to the city council's discretionary fund, and 20 percent to the city's asset management plan.

Maintenance of capital assets   The operating budget shall provide sufficient funds for the regular maintenance and repair of all of Irvine's capital assets. The budget shall not be balanced by deferring these expenditures.

Equipment replacement reserves (internal service funds)   The governing board in Irvine established several policies. First, the city shall maintain two equipment internal service funds: one for rolling stock and the other for other equipment. Equipment costing more than $10,000 and with a useful life of more than one year shall be financed from reserves and revenues of these funds. Second, each fund will be funded by rental rates to the departments that use the equipment. These rates shall include depreciation, maintenance, fuel if applicable, and any applicable financing costs. Third, decisions concerning replacement of equipment shall consider the estimated useful life of the equipment and criteria specified in the financial policies.

Capital financing sources   Within the limitations of state law, Irvine will utilize various funding sources for capital improvements.

Grants and federal funding   The city will aggressively pursue all grant opportunities, but before accepting grants, it will consider matching fund requirements, in-kind services that must be provided, and the length of the grants.

Debt   Following are the debt policies approved by Irvine's governing board:

- All debt issuance shall comply with federal, state, and city charter legal requirements.
- Debt issuance is an acceptable method of capital finance.
- Debt financing shall generally be limited to one-time capital improvement projects.
- The term of any debt shall not exceed the useful life of the asset(s) acquired with the debt.
- Each debt issue will be accompanied by an assessment of the city's capacity to repay the debt. The assessment will address the effects of the debt and the projects that the debt finances on current and future operating budgets. Reliable sources of revenue for debt retirement will be identified.
- The city shall establish a performance reporting system for managing outstanding debt.
- Pursuant to state law, GO debt shall remain within the legal debt limit of 15 percent of the city's taxable valuation. The legal debt limit of the city on June 30,

1999, was about $2.5 billion. The city had only about $3.5 million in outstanding GO debt at that date, far below the legal debt limit. The city also had $7.3 million of certificates of participation and $64.8 million in revenue leases on that date.

- Lease purchases shall be used only when the useful life of the asset leased is equal to or greater than the lease term. If the asset is subject to technologic obsolescence or is likely to need major repair during the lease-purchase term, the asset should be either purchased or placed on a true lease.

Bond rating The city should take a proactive approach to improving the city's bond rating and the marketability of the city's debt.

Long-term financial planning The city shall promote economic development through prudent, long-range financial planning.

The city will project revenues for the current fiscal year and the following five fiscal years, re-evaluating each existing and potential revenue source. Finally, the city shall develop methods for the inventory and projection of current and future development on the city's budget and revenues.

Irvine's policies on capital finance offer specific and rather sophisticated guidelines for capital financing decisions. They make up an excellent capital financing strategy for the city.

Notes

1 A well-developed system for evaluating a jurisdiction's financial condition is presented in *Evaluating Financial Condition: A Handbook for Local Government,* 4th ed. (Washington, D.C.: ICMA, 2003), revised by Karl Nollenberger.

2 The purposes served by fund balance and a discussion of its calculation and use by local governments appear in Lee Carter and A. John Vogt, "Fund Balance in Local Government Budgeting and Finance," *Popular Government* 54, no. 3 (Winter 1989): 27–35. In state government budgeting, rainy-day funds serve the same purposes as local government operating fund balance.

3 A variation of this definition is provided in North Carolina General Statute 159-8 (a), which defines the maximum amount of fund balance that may be budgeted as the sum of cash and investments less liabilities, encumbrances, and deferred revenues arising from cash receipts, since these figures stand on the last day of the fiscal year preceding the budget year. Deferred revenues from cash receipts are revenues collected in advance. They tend to be relatively small amounts. Although they are removed from available fund balance in this formula, they are credited to estimated revenues for the budget year.

4 See "Your General Fund Balance—One Size Does Not Fit All!" Special Comment (New York: Moody's Investors Service, Inc., February 2002).

5 See, for example, Richard P. Larkin, "Impact of Management Practices on Municipal Credit," *Government Finance Review* 17, no. 1 (February 2001): 23–24.

6 This policy is widely accepted and generally followed by local governments in North Carolina. The formal statement of the policy appears in North Carolina Department of State Treasurer, *Policies Manual,* section 18, "Budgeting."

7 Local government fund balance data are available annually from reports of the North Carolina Department of State Treasurer. See, for example, "Average Available Fund Balances of North Carolina Counties and Cities, June 30, 2001," http://ncdst-web2.treasurer.state.nc.us/lgc/units/unitlistjs.htm.

8 "Your General Fund Balance."

9 Net working capital is mentioned in Moody's Investors Service, *Moody's on Revenue Bonds: The Fundamentals of Revenue Bond Credit Analysis* (New York: Moody's Investors Service, Inc., 1994), 18.

10 Wake County's policy balancing debt and pay-as-go financing is discussed in Annual Budget 2001–2002, Wake County, 197–198. The county's budget director, Raymond G. Boutwell, provided information about the county's current and past use of the policy.

11 Standard & Poor's Corporation, *Public Finance Criteria 2000* (New York: S&P, 2000), 21.

12 Ibid., 7.

13 Standard & Poor's defines an "issuer rating" as an opinion on the issuer's overall financial capacity. It does not apply to any specific debt. It takes into account neither the nature and provisions of particular debt contracts nor laws that authorize and limit the issuer's ability to sell and repay debt. See Standard & Poor's, *Public Finance Criteria 2000,* 8–9.

14 Internal Revenue Code, Sections 1.148-0 through 11, 1.149(b)-1, 1.149(d)-1, 1.149(g)-1 1.150-1 and 1.150-2 (1993). A good summary of arbitrage laws and regulations, including rebate requirements, appears in Terrence P. Burke, *Guide to Arbitrage Requirements for Governmental Bond Issues* (Chicago: GFOA, 1992) and *1994 Supplement to the Guide* (Chicago: GFOA, 1994).

15 Ibid., chapter 7, "Refunding and Transferred Proceeds Rules."

16 Governmental Accounting Standards Board, Statement No. 34, "Basic Financial Statements—and Management's Discussion and Analysis—for State and Local Governments" (Norwalk, Conn.: GASB, 1999), paragraphs 21–26.

17 A very good overview of financial forecasting is presented by ICMA in James L. Cavenaugh and Pamela S. Caskie, "Multiyear Budgeting," *IQ Service Report* 31, no. 6 (June 1999): 15.

18 Michael Zino, "The Development of a Planned Debt Policy," in *Budgeting: Formulation and Execution,* ed. Jack Rabin, W. Bartley Hildreth, and Gerald J. Miller (Athens, Ga.: Carl Vinson Institute of Government, University of Georgia, 1996), 323–328.

19 *Evaluating Financial Condition,* 74–97.

20 City of Irvine 2000–2001 Budget, "Financial Policies" section.

6 Pay-as-go capital financing

Pay-as-go sources provide a significant share of the financing for many local government capital improvement programs. Indeed, pay-as-go financing is either the predominant or the only source of capital financing for many small local governments that have difficulty accessing the debt markets and for local governments severely limited in their ability to issue debt for capital purposes by restrictive constitutional and statutory provisions. Pay-as-go financing is the preferred alternative if local officials are reluctant to incur debt and pay the interest costs associated with debt. Many medium- and large-size local governments that issue debt also use pay-as-go financing to balance debt and equity sources and avoid building up excessive debt service charges in future annual budgets.

Pay-as-go financing in the public sector is comparable with equity financing in the private sector. Equity refers generally to the value of assets above and beyond any liability or debt. In business, equity includes the capital contributed by owners and stockholders and the accumulated net earnings of the enterprise. Equity accounts for a major part of business capital financing for many types of businesses.

Two of the most common pay-as-go sources for local governments are:

- Annual taxes and revenues that remain after annual operating expenses are met
- Cash balances or capital reserves accumulated from savings in prior years.

Local government capital financing from annual taxes or revenues in excess of operating expenses is equivalent to business financing from current income. Local use of capital reserves is comparable with business financing from retained earnings or designated reserves. Business financing of capital needs from equity reflects sophisticated and sound investment principles. Likewise, responsible pay-as-go financing of at least a portion of a local government's capital budget can add significantly to the effectiveness of its capital improvement program and capital financing strategy.

Advantages of pay-as-go financing

Pay-as-go financing allows a local government to avoid interest and other debt issuance expenses, expedite inexpensive or recurring capital projects, preserve flexibility in future operating budgets, sidestep bond and debt markets, and improve its financial position.[1]

Avoids interest and other debt issuance expenses Interest expenses over the life of a twenty-year bond issue can add 50 percent or more to cash outlays for the project. For example, if a local government issues $10 million in bonds at a 5 percent annual interest rate for a twenty-year term, with annual principal retirement of $500,000 per year, the interest payments total $4.8 million. More than $3.0 million of the interest is paid during the first ten years of the twenty-year term for the bonds. Public debt issues also involve up-front charges for financial advisory, bond counsel, bond rating, underwriting, trustee, and other services. Some public debt issues have additional expenses for bond insurance, feasibility studies, and debt service reserves. Up-front issuance costs for a $10 million bond issue are likely to exceed $100,000. A local government that uses pay-as-go financing for a project can avoid all of these expenses and charges.

Expedites inexpensive or recurring capital projects   Pay-as-go funding is generally more expedient than debt financing for small capital acquisitions or projects (for example, office equipment and furniture) and for recurring spending (for example, for vehicle or equipment replacement when changes in costs are limited from year to year). Operating fund revenues can usually be made available for modest capital expenditures, and they can be appropriated immediately or very quickly; debt financing takes time to arrange. Moreover, issuing debt financing is a complex process involving outside parties as well as local officials, but using operating revenues usually requires decisions only by local officials and occurs in a routine process suitable for expenditures that occur annually or routinely.

Preserves flexibility in future operating budgets   Partial or full reliance on pay-as-go capital financing gives a local government flexibility in future operating budgets. When a local government issues debt, it is legally obligated to pay the annual debt service until the debt is paid off. And if a local government finances capital assets with long-term leasing arrangements, market requirements, if not state laws, demand that the periodic lease payments be made until the lease is paid off. If a budget shortfall develops for a local government, its officials do not have the option of reducing debt service or capital lease payments to help fund the shortfall. They must look, instead, to other parts of the operating budget for funds. On the other hand, officials can reduce or postpone pay-as-go capital spending to free up money to help balance the operating budget.

An example illustrates this advantage of pay-as-go financing. A small county has a $20 million general fund budget, including $2 million for debt service on bonds. If this county experiences a recession that reduces its revenues to $19.5 million and increases mandated spending (perhaps for public assistance) by $500,000, it faces a $1 million budget gap. The $2 million in debt service cannot be cut to help close that gap; the county must cut spending elsewhere or raise taxes or fees. On the other hand, if the county has been relying predominantly on pay-as-go capital financing and pays debt service of only $500,000 because it uses pay-as-go capital financing for $1.5 million, part of the $1.5 million can be allocated to help close the $1 million budget gap. Of course, reducing or postponing pay-as-go capital financing delays implementation of the capital program, and delay can be avoided or limited if a local government carries operating fund balances large enough to accommodate most unexpected expenses.

Sidesteps bond and debt markets   Officials in small local governments that undertake major capital projects infrequently—for example, once every four or five years—have little experience in planning, issuing, and managing debt.

Banks and underwriters focus their attention on local governments with greater and more regular financing needs. A community that is poor as well as small may not be able to sell debt at reasonable rates in the conventional debt markets and, when borrowing, may have to rely on state grants, subsidized loans, or bond banks if it is to use debt to finance its capital projects. A large local government that has had financial problems and has suffered bond rating downgrades may be able to issue debt only at higher than acceptable interest rates. Many local governments like these find it expedient and inexpensive to turn to pay-as-go financing to meet many of their capital needs.

Improves financial position   Pay-as-go capital financing can help a local government strengthen its financial position and bond ratings. Consider the similar effect of a down payment on a borrower's ability to acquire a house. The more money a borrower contributes for the down payment, the less debt incurred and the less interest paid. The down payment adds to the net worth or financial position of the homeowner. In a similar way, partial pay-as-go financing holds down debt and lowers debt service costs for a local government, strengthening its financial position regardless of the interest rate charged. In addition, the accumulation of reserves and fund balances that typically accompanies pay-as-go capital financing is viewed favorably by the municipal debt markets, helping the local government improve its bond rating and lower interest rate(s) paid on debt issued.

Pay-as-go financing as a political preference

Many medium- and small-size local governments rely on pay-as-go financing for capital programs because their political and social culture discourages debt financing. In relatively well-off suburban or retirement communities, many residents view borrowing as an expensive and even irresponsible method of finance. In communities that are struggling financially and where economic events—for example, layoffs at a local industry—create uncertainty, local leaders may want to avoid building up debt service obligations in future budgets. Still other local governments are led by citizens with business backgrounds. These officials may favor equity financing: using savings from prior years' budgets or charging current revenues to pay for capital needs or, in business terms, funding depreciation on capital assets.

Voters in some communities believe that paying cash for capital assets leads to more responsible spending: they want officials to accumulate money for capital needs from current budgets because this will be an incentive for them to set their priorities more carefully, cull marginal projects, design projects to meet basic needs, and include fewer frills. They know that when borrowed funds are used for capital financing, payments are put off to the future and the result may be more ambitious projects. If officials can afford to incur debt of $10 million for a basic project, they may find it relatively painless to expand the project and borrow $12 million or even $15 million. On the other hand, if the project is financed partly on a pay-as-go basis and officials must raise, for example, $5 million from several annual budgets, perhaps with a tax rate increase, these officials are likely to look more critically at proposals to expand the project's scope or features, add costs, and increase the financing challenge.

Disadvantages of pay-as-go financing

The disadvantages associated with pay-as-go capital financing come into play for local governments that rely exclusively or predominantly on this method of financing and do not balance pay-as-go financing with debt. Many major projects cannot be financed with pay-as-go sources alone. Major projects can exhaust all reserves and rob the operating budget for many years of funds needed for services. In addition, pay-as-go financing sometimes:

Misallocates the costs of major capital facilities that have very long useful lives. During the handful of years when the facilities are built, taxpayers and rate payers pay the full costs for the facilities; during the next ten, twenty, or thirty years when the facilities are being used, taxpayers and rate payers avoid charges for the costs of building them.

Results in opportunity costs when resources that could be used in other ways are used to finance capital projects. For example, interest income is forgone when fund balances and reserves are drawn down to pay for capital projects.

Calls on current taxpayers to pay the full cost of major capital projects. Debt financing typically spreads out a major project's costs over many years and can help officials maintain a stable tax rate.

Substitutes for sound planning. In contrast, the long-term debt service and/or lease payments imposed by debt financing serve as an incentive for local officials to plan for the future. They must determine whether the jurisdiction can afford the future debt service or lease payments given other needs. Pay-as-go financing without planning can cause a local government to overlook debt instruments suitable for financing some of its capital needs.

Sources of pay-as-go financing

Sources of pay-as-go financing are annual revenues, capital reserves, charges to property or development that benefit from local infrastructure and facilities, and federal and state grants and other external sources of financing participation.

Annual budget revenues and fund balances

Some local governments use annual or operating budget revenues and fund balances to renovate and upgrade infrastructure and facilities. Others use these revenues to finance specific kinds of infrastructure such as roads. Some combine multiyear identification and planning of capital needs and the earmarking of one or more recurring revenue sources. Governing-board policies usually set the framework for these creative practices.

This section discusses the general approaches that local governments follow in using annual or operating budget revenues and balances for pay-as-go capital financing and then refers to actual pay-as-go practices by local governments. Local governments can choose from three general approaches: allocation of annual revenues or fund balances for capital purposes as they are available, local earmarking of annual general revenues or special revenues for capital purposes, and state earmarking of revenues for local capital funding.

Intergenerational equity

The economic concept of intergenerational equity underlies arguments against pay-as-go financing and in favor of debt financing for major, long-lived projects. According to this concept, each generation of taxpayers and citizens should bear its fair share of the costs of capital facilities and infrastructure, proportional to use of the infrastructure and facilities. Thus, if a local government builds many large capital facilities in one decade and few in the following decade and if those facilities are used through both decades, intergenerational equity requires the taxpayers and citizens in both decades to bear the costs for the facilities, in proportion to their use in each decade. When pay-as-go financing is used, the taxpayers and citizens in the first decade bear most of the cost of the facilities, while those in the second decade use the facilities without paying their fair share of the costs for them. If debt is used to finance the facilities and debt service payments extend over both decades, taxpayers and citizens in both decades pay the costs for the facilities, roughly proportional to their use of the facilities.

In stable communities, each generation may be willing to raise the money for capital assets and projects that will be used well into the future. The generation before did so, and local leaders and citizens are willing to follow suit, passing on paid-for capital facilities and infrastructure to the next generation. However, in communities where the population is less stable, taxpayers and citizens may be much less willing to levy the taxes and raise the revenues needed to finance major capital projects on a pay-as-go basis. They know that they or their children may move out of the community well before the useful lives of the projects end. In such communities, the principle of intergenerational equity is important, and local officials are more likely to use debt rather than pay-as-go financing.

Allocation of annual revenues or operating fund balances as available   A local government can make significant appropriations in the annual budget of annual revenues for operating capital and for other capital acquisitions and projects. Operating capital items are small equipment, furniture, and other permanent property replacements needed to keep services going, and they are usually funded from capital or permanent property lines in departmental operating budgets. Other capital acquisitions and projects include the replacement or addition of major equipment and renovation, rehabilitation, or new construction projects.

Allocation of annual revenues as available to fund such other capital acquisitions and projects is not a dependable method for financing because outlays for salaries and wages, employee fringe benefits, operating supplies, operating capital items, and the other costs associated with ongoing services have the first claim on operating revenues. Requests for service improvement or expansion, new programs, and major replacement or new capital equipment and projects compete for any remaining revenue or fund balance. Often the result is that insufficient funding is left for major capital equipment or projects.

A local government, however, can designate a generous portion of available operating fund balance to capital spending. When budget estimates are conservative, actual revenue collections exceed estimates, and spending falls below appropriations, significant fund balances may be left at the end of a year. Through an amendment to the current year's budget, some portion of the balance may then be used immediately to purchase major equipment or to help fund capital projects. Alternatively, the fund balances can be appropriated for capital assets or projects in next year's budget, or the balances may be held and accumulated over several years, like a capital reserve, and eventually used for one or more large capital projects.

It is difficult to predict the annual or operating budget revenues or balances that will be available for capital financing. Even if the local government ends many years with significant operating fund balances, this money is easily drawn off to fund service enhancements or to avoid tax increases instead of being spent on capital projects.

The **Germantown, Tennessee,** 2002–2007 capital improvement program (CIP) includes $33.3 million in capital projects and spending to which the city's general fund is contributing $2,941,000 million in cash. This cash contribution comes from the general fund reserve, which comes from operating revenues in excess of oper-

ating expenditures in the general fund. Of the $2,941,000 million in cash, $2,741,000 million covers capital spending in 2002, $50,000 in 2003, and $50,000 in 2004. This pay-as-go funding from annual revenues appears to be provided on an as-available basis. [2]

Local earmarking of annual revenues for capital purposes   Annually recurring revenues that local policy earmarks for capital purposes can be a portion of a general revenue source (for example, a certain number of cents of a city's property tax rate) or a portion of a special tax (for example, 50 percent of a real estate transfer tax), or all of a special tax or revenue source (for example, the full proceeds of a hotel- and motel-room occupancy tax). The earmarking may be broad, allowing the earmarked revenue to be spent for capital projects or equipment across many different functional areas or for any local infrastructure or major capital project. Alternatively, the earmarking may restrict spending to projects in one functional area (for example, schools or street reconstruction). Sometimes the earmarking restricts the revenue to spending on just one specific project—construction of a high school or the reconstruction of a specific road. This kind of earmarking often has a sunset provision so that it comes to an end after the project is finished. When funds are earmarked for a functional area or for a broad range of capital needs, the earmarking usually continues from year to year until the local governing board ends the arrangement. The most common practice is for local governments to earmark annual revenues for capital spending by functional area.

In some cases, funds earmarked for capital purposes may be spent to pay annual debt service on bonds or other debt that is issued for capital projects. Funds spent in this way, however, are not considered pay-as-go financing.

Annual revenues earmarked for capital purposes can be optioned in different ways. The earmarked revenue can be raised in the general fund and spent from that fund for the intended capital purposes. This happens when the earmarked revenue is a portion of a tax that is raised through the general fund budget, or when the revenue finances capital acquisitions and projects that recur at similar amounts annually or are closely linked to ongoing general fund services. For example, the portion of the property tax that is earmarked for annual street resurfacing may be budgeted and spent from the general fund because it is levied in the annual budget ordinance, recurs annually, and is closely linked to street maintenance financed from the general fund.

A second option is for earmarked annual revenue to be raised in the general fund and then transferred to another fund (for example, a capital projects fund) to be spent from there. This option is used when the earmarked revenue is a tax or revenue levied in the annual budget ordinance but is spent for large, long-lived projects or for capital purposes that are not closely linked to services financed from the general fund. Local government illustrations of this option are provided below.

A third option is to raise, budget, and spend the earmarked revenue from a capital projects fund or other special fund established specifically for the capital spending financed from the earmarked revenue. This option is used when the earmarked revenue is not raised through the general fund; when the annual amounts of earmarked revenue are substantial; and when the revenues finance major, long-lived projects or substantial ongoing capital asset replacement or rehabilitation programs. This option is used by many local governments that rely heavily on pay-as-go financing.

The 2002–2007 CIP of **Alexandria, Virginia,** projects a total of $283.8 million in project spending for school and city purposes over this inclusive six-year period. Financing for the projects will come from three sources. The first is planned general fund appropriations, which range from $12 million to $15.2 million per year and total $82.6 million. This represents local earmarking of general fund revenues for capital projects in general in the CIP. The money goes directly for pay-as-go financing of projects rather than for debt service on bonds issued for the projects. General obligation (GO) bonds are the second source. They contribute another $93 million for CIP project spending. Most of the rest of Alexandria's 2002–2007 CIP is funded from the third source—fund balances ($61.4 million of capital project fund balances and $34.2 million of general fund balances). Clearly, general fund annual revenues are a very important source of capital financing for the Alexandria CIP. [3]

Oklahoma City, Oklahoma, earmarked revenues from a special 1 percent sales tax enacted in 1993 for the purpose of revitalizing the city's downtown area. The tax had a sunset provision and ended in 1999. It raised more than $50 million per year and provided the bulk of the funding for major projects in the downtown area in the 1990s and into the current decade. Projects are still being built with proceeds from the tax although it is no longer being collected, and total spending on the projects it financed will exceed $300 million. Although the sales tax authorization allowed for the issuance of debt with repayment from sales tax money, no debt was issued. The city's finance director comments that this is one example of how Oklahoma City is relying on pay-as-go financing and limiting its use of debt to fund capital improvements. [4]

State earmarking of revenues for local capital purposes State earmarking of specific annual revenues for capital purposes is similar to earmarking by local ordinance or policy. In this case, however, only a change in state legislation or regulation can end the earmarking. The earmarked revenue is usually revenue that the state collects and shares with local governments. For example, the state might collect a special gasoline tax and share it on a 50-50 basis with local governments. The state law authorizing the tax may require local governments to spend the local portion only for specific types of capital projects (for example, street improvements). Or the state may authorize local governments to impose a special local tax (for example, an additional 0.5 percent sales tax) but require any local unit levying the tax to apply at least half of the proceeds to certain types of capital projects (for example, school construction or water-sewer system improvements).

When a state levies and shares a tax with local governments or authorizes them to levy a tax but restrict some or all of the tax proceeds to certain capital purposes, the tax revenues may be budgeted and accounted for in one or more special capital project funds or special revenue funds rather than local general funds. State law may require separate funds, or local officials may choose to use a special fund in order to keep decisions about spending of the earmarked revenue separate from the operating budget and to provide better accountability for spending of the earmarked funds.

In some cases, annual revenues earmarked by local act or state law for local capital purposes are spent almost as fast as they are received to fund capital projects each year. When revenues are not accumulated or reserved over many years but go directly to capital spending, the financing is considered annual since funding comes from annual sources instead of from reserves. However, if the annual revenues are commonly reserved or held for years before being spent, especially if the revenues are held in a separate fund, this would be considered reserve financing, which is examined in the next section.

The state of California levies a tax on gasoline purchases under the state's Streets and Highways Code, and a portion of the proceeds from this tax is distributed to cities on the basis of a sharing formula prescribed by law. The cities receiving the funds must spend them for the rehabilitation, improvement, and maintenance of public streets. [5] North Carolina offers another example of state earmarking of a tax for local capital projects, except in this case it is a locally levied tax. When the state authorized counties to enact two additional 0.5 percent sales taxes in the mid-1980s, it required counties to spend approximately half of the proceeds from the tax for direct capital spending or debt service on school projects. All 100 counties in North Carolina have enacted the additional taxes, raising a tremendous amount of financing for school construction and modernization. While some of this money goes to pay debt service on county bonds or debt issued for school purposes, many counties have used much of it for pay-as-go financing for school projects. [6]

Capital reserves

A capital reserve is a savings account. Revenues are raised, set aside in the reserve until needed, and then used to finance capital spending. The timetable for raising revenues for reserve financing is the opposite of that for debt financing. With debt, a capital project is undertaken with borrowed funds, and then revenues are raised in future years to make principal and interest payments on the debt. With capital reserves, revenues are raised before undertaking the project. Thus, reliance on capital reserves is a conservative approach to capital financing.

Types of reserves   Capital reserves can take various forms: they can be separate from the general fund or part of the general fund, and they can be funded by dedication of one-time revenues or by recurring revenues.

- **Separate capital reserve fund**   A separate accounting fund for capital reserves has its own assets, liabilities, fund balance, revenues, and expenditures or other disbursements. Much more than a separate account or designation in the general fund, this kind of capital reserve is an altogether separate fund. It clearly separates the resources being accumulated for capital purposes from operating fund balances. This makes raiding the capital reserve for operating budget purposes more difficult. In some states, the law prohibits local governments from using separate capital reserve fund money for operating purposes. [7]

  A separate capital reserve fund ordinarily needs a designated funding. If a capital reserve fund is established to finance a new fire station needed four years from now, officials must identify revenues or other resources to fund the reserve. They may specify that an annual contribution will be made to the reserve from the annual budget over each of the next four years. These contributions may be set at a level so that, with the interest earned on them, the amount accumulated by the fourth year is sufficient to build the fire station.

The capital reserve fund could be more general (for example, a fund to finance roof replacements and other renovation projects on buildings). Officials could finance the fund by dedicating either a portion of an annually recurring general tax or all of one or more special revenue sources. Then, as these revenues are raised each year, they are deposited into the reserve fund. They are withdrawn and spent as roof replacements become necessary or as other renovation projects are undertaken. A local government can also designate general fund "excesses" to a capital reserve fund.

Hickory, North Carolina, created a general capital reserve fund to provide financing for expensive equipment acquisitions and small capital improvement or renovation projects. Hickory funds it with occasional contributions from the general fund balance. When the general fund balance exceeds 30 percent of general fund spending, the "excess" is transferred to the general capital reserve fund. This fund had a balance of $1.5 million at the end of 2002, and $700,000 was expected to be spent from the fund for equipment and projects in 2003. [8]

- **Part of general fund** A second and less formal capital reserve is a designation of a portion of general fund or other operating fund balances for capital purposes. The designation is not equivalent to budgetary appropriation but is an indication of probable future use for capital purposes. This type of reserve gives officials flexibility in future use of the designated money. Because the designated money remains in the general fund or another operating fund, the presumption is that officials can undo the designation to apply the money to operating needs. The reserve is much more tentative than resources set aside in a separate capital reserve fund—an advantage or disadvantage, depending on one's point of view. Greensboro, North Carolina, is an example of a local government that earmarks a portion of the general fund balance for capital projects and spending to be undertaken in upcoming years. [9]

- **Capital reserve revolving fund** A capital reserve revolving fund is a separate accounting fund with a specific, recurring revenue source or set of sources committed to it on an ongoing basis. Similarly, resources in the reserve are withdrawn annually or fairly regularly and spent for specific types of capital assets or construction.

  One example of such a fund is an equipment replacement fund financed with annual usage or depreciation charges to departments using the equipment. The fund "owns" the equipment or vehicles in question and charges the departments using the equipment or vehicles a periodic rental, lease, or use fee. The using departments of the local government pay the annual or periodic fee from their operating budgets. The money is transferred from the departmental budgets to the equipment/vehicle replacement fund where it is held until it is needed to pay for new equipment and vehicles. While such a fund may be classified for accounting purposes as an internal service fund, it is also a capital reserve since monies are accumulated in it to meet capital needs.

Loveland, Colorado, for example, has a fleet replacement fund that accumulates money from annual or periodic charges to all departments based on the useful lives and estimated replacement costs of the vehicles. [10]

Another example of a capital reserve revolving fund is a special assessment fund for financing ongoing repaving of streets. Residents whose homes face the streets that are repaved pay assessments that go into the assessment fund to fund additional repaving projects. An illustration of such a fund is provided in the upcoming section on special assessments and impact fees.

Laws authorizing capital reserves   Some taxpayers may object if a local government imposes taxes and revenues to accumulate money in anticipation of future capital spending. They may argue that government should not function as a bank, earning interest on money collected, but instead should let taxpayers keep their money until it is needed to fund specific capital projects. Because this view is not uncommon, the local government may need authorization under a state law or local charter to set up capital reserve funds and levy taxes or raise other revenues to fund reserves for future capital purposes. [11]

Revenue-raising and budgeting powers of jurisdictions vary, but governing board action is ordinarily needed to create a reserve and fund it. The enabling statute or local charter might also require board approval for any specific transaction to move money into or out of a capital reserve fund. Alternatively, the law and accepted practices may be broad enough to permit a local governing board to delegate to the manager or finance officer authority to make certain transfers in and out of the reserve.

Purposes of reserves   Local board decisions creating a capital reserve typically specify purposes relating to the capital projects or spending to be funded with the reserve. As with the dedication of annual revenues for capital spending, the purpose of a capital reserve can be project specific, functional, or general.

A capital reserve may be established to fund or help fund a specific project (for example, the construction of a fire station or the acquisition of two refuse collection vehicles). Alternatively, the purpose for a capital reserve can be stated in broader functional terms (for example, the funding of future capital facility and equipment needs for the fire department or funding of collection vehicles and other equipment for the sanitation department). Money goes into this kind of reserve without being earmarked for any particular project or acquisition.

A third approach is the establishment of a capital reserve for general public improvements or equipment acquisition and replacement in the future without specifying a functional or project purpose for the reserve or for money being deposited into the reserve. When a capital reserve has a functional or broadly stated general purpose, specific designations for projects usually occur when the money is withdrawn from the reserve or budgeted for the projects.

Capital reserves can be effective for financing capital projects or acquisitions that are modest in scope and cost or have short- to intermediate-term useful lives, or occur with predictable regularity: equipment acquisitions, annual infrastructure rehabilitation, and the construction or renovation of facilities that are modest in size. These kinds of needs can be foreseen far enough ahead to allow sufficient time to accumulate funds for the spending.

Capital reserves are rarely effective financing devices for major construction projects such as those with large infrastructure and facilities with useful lives of twenty years or longer. The actual useful life of a major capital asset is often a function of the adequacy of annual maintenance, changing technology and needs, growth, and other factors besides aging or deterioration. The need for a major new facility or improvement is seldom foreseen early enough to allow accumulation of sufficient funds in a capital reserve to fully fund the project. However, a capital reserve fund can be used to accumulate the down payment for major construction or to finance specific phases of a project, such as planning and design or the acquisition of land, furniture, or equipment.

Diversion of reserves In some states, the statutes authorizing local governments to establish and fund capital reserve funds prohibit the diversion of these reserves for funding operating expenditures. Without such a legal prohibition, the risk of diversion is significant when a local government faces an operating budget crisis or when officials are trying to avoid a tax increase. Diversion can wreak havoc with the capital improvement plan and budget. However, the flexibility to amend a capital reserve's purpose as priorities change—for example, to use money in a reserve created for future fire station construction to fund sanitation collection vehicles instead—is usually an advantage as long as funds are not diverted entirely away from capital projects and the capital program to fund operating needs.

Capital reserves in practice Many local governments create and fund capital reserves and use them to help finance capital projects and acquisitions in general or certain capital needs in particular, such as fire equipment, right-of-way acquisition, parking improvement, fleet replacement, and water-sewer renewal.

Junction City, Kansas, has two special revenue funds that function as separate capital reserve funds. One is a capital improvement fund that serves as a financing mechanism for the "repair, restoration, and replacement of the city's facilities and fixed assets." It is funded from annual property and motor vehicle tax revenues and from one-time or special resources (for example, proceeds from the sale of assets). The fund received between $200,000 and $1 million in annual revenues or other resources during the late 1990s. Expenditures from the fund in 1999 included $25,000 for sidewalk improvements, $125,000 for downtown parking, $17,500 for renovations to the city's swimming pool, $77,400 for updating the city's computers, and $25,000 for demolition of blighted buildings. Junction City also has a fire equipment replacement fund. It is funded by an annual tax levy by the governing body. Annual revenues to the fund ranged between $100,000 and $200,000 during the late 1990s. [12]

San Clemente, California, uses several revolving reserve funds, including a fleet maintenance replacement reserve, a capital equipment replacement reserve, a water depreciation reserve, a water acreage fee reserve, a sewer depreciation reserve, a sewer connection fee reserve, a golf depreciation reserve, and a golf capital improvement reserve. All of these reserves are separate funds. The water depreciation reserve is used to replace water fund equipment and make major repairs to water system infrastructure. It is funded from depreciation charges to the water fund operating budget, where those charges are treated as normal operating expenses and are computed by dividing the acquisition cost of equipment by its estimated useful life. Depreciation charges and other revenue to the fund were budgeted at $798,250 in 2000 and $738,260 in 2001. Budgeted improvement projects financed from the fund were $960,480 in 2000 and $1,080,000 for 2001. Funds were also budgeted for street improvements related to water system maintenance and for certain other purposes. The excess of spending over depreciation charges and other revenues in each year was covered by drawdowns of fund balance. The water depreciation reserve's fund balance at the end of 1999 was $3,025,550. Projections put fund balance by the end of 2000 at $2,348,064 and by the end of 2001 at

$1,745,260. The excess of spending over depreciation charges and other revenues in each year was covered by drawdowns of fund balance. The reserve balance in the water depreciation fund at the end of 1999 was $3,025,550. Projections put fund balance by the end of 2000 at $2,348,064 and by the end of 2001 at $1,745,260.[13]

Special assessments, impact fees, and other charges to property

Special assessments, impact fees, and other charges to property impose the costs of local infrastructure and capital facilities on that property. Such charges are like user fees in that the properties that benefit from projects pay for them.[14] The charges are a form of private financing insofar as private property contributes to the cost of public infrastructure and facilities. Special assessments and impact fees are the primary charges to property that local governments use in financing infrastructure and capital facilities. This section also discusses exactions, a negotiated in-kind or cash contributions from developers.

Special assessments   Special assessments are charges to benefiting property for specific infrastructure located on-site or near the property paying the assessments. The infrastructure's benefit to the property paying the assessment is typically direct and evident.[15]

Like property taxes, special assessments are levied against property, not persons. Special assessment payment obligations are often placed on property tax bills, and the same collection and foreclosure procedures are often used for both. Unlike property taxes, special assessments are based on benefits accruing to the property paying the assessments. (Property or property taxpayers do not have to benefit proportionately or even at all, in a strict legal sense, from the expenditure of property tax proceeds.)

Special assessments may be charged not only against private property but also against government property and other types of property that most states exempt from local property taxes (for example, educational, church, and nonprofit property). However, federal and state properties are usually exempt from local special assessments.

Special assessments, like user fees, are charged to benefiting property or users. However, while user fees typically finance ongoing services, special assessments finance mainly infrastructure and capital facilities. Like user fees, special assessments, impact fees, and other charges to property are based on the benefits principle of public finance (see sidebar and Table 6–1).

- **History and legal basis**   Local governments have used special assessments for financing capital infrastructure since colonial times.[16] The original legal basis for special assessments was a local government's police powers.[17] For example, local government construction of a sewer line serving specific property and assessment of the benefiting property owners may be justified as an exercise of the police power to maintain public health. Similarly, a local government may replace unsafe sidewalks and assess the bordering property for the cost in order to protect public safety.

  More recently, local taxing power has provided the primary legal basis for special assessments. Just as a local government can create a special district and levy taxes there that are not levied in the rest of the community, it can levy special assessments against some property but not others because the former property derives special benefit from the

Table 6–1

Property taxes, user fees, special assessments, and impact fees

Type of charge	Basis of charge	Connection to benefit	Allowed use of revenue	Public finance principle
Property tax	Levied against property; based on value of property	Benefit and tax not necessarily connected	Any authorized local public purpose	General ability to pay
User fee	Levied against persons; based on use of service	Direct connection between benefit and fee	Expenses of serving user, or any authorized local purpose	Benefits principle
Special assessment	Levied against property; often based on front footage	Direct connection between benefit and fee	Infrastructure directly benefiting property assessed	Benefits principle
Impact fee	Levied against property; often based on residential equivalent unit	Connection between benefit and fee	Infrastructure or facilities that serve needs created by development	Benefits principle

improvements financed with the assessments.[18] The courts have ruled that the basis that a local government uses for determining the benefit accruing to specific property and allocating the costs of improvements to that property must be reasonable or approximate, but it does not have to be exact. For example, front footage has been determined to be a

---

The benefits principle and the ability-to-pay principle

According to the benefits principle of public finance, the beneficiaries or users of a public service or of public infrastructure, rather than general taxpayers, should pay for it. The benefits principle can be applied only when one person's or property's use of a local government service or facility can be separated from another person's or property's use of that service or facility, or when a specific group in a community derives significantly more benefits from a service or facility than the rest of the population.

According to the ability-to-pay principle, the costs of public goods and services, including capital assets, should be distributed among citizens according to their ability to pay. Ability to pay is usually measured in terms of income. At the local level, ability to pay can be measured in terms of the market value of property subject to the property tax. According to the ability-to-pay argument, high-income households or higher-valued property should pay more in taxes and fees than the value of the benefits they receive from public services and facilities, and low-income households or lower-valued property should pay less in taxes and fees than the value they receive from public services and facilities.

reasonable basis for allocating the costs of street improvements to the benefiting property owners.[19] The evolution of law for special assessments has paralleled legal acceptance of special districts and targeted taxes to support special services in those districts.[20]

- **Projects financed with special assessments**   Street construction, resurfacing, curbs and gutters and sidewalks along streets, arterial roads, water collector lines and mains, sewer collector lines and mains, stormwater and erosion control facilities, and beach replenishment are the most common types of local infrastructure for which special assessments are levied. Street lighting, community or neighborhood parks and recreational facilities, and nuisance abatement are also projects for which special assessments are levied. These kinds of infrastructure typically border the property being assessed or are very near to it, and the benefit to the property is typically clear. The projects are often of intermediate size and cost compared with other capital projects of a jurisdiction, allowing projects to be financed at least in part with assessments that are affordable to the property owners paying the assessments. Special assessments may be levied against property abutting a street or against property in a defined area, neighborhood, or assessment district.

- **Allocation of benefits and costs**   During the early part of the twentieth century, most of the costs for infrastructure or projects financed with special assessments were charged to specific benefiting properties. In recent decades, however, there has been greater recognition that infrastructure and projects that serve specific properties benefit the entire community. Consequently, special assessments levied by local governments in certain states for street projects cover only a portion of the costs.[21] Payments for the rest of the street project's costs must come from general taxes or revenues. The more accessible infrastructure is to the general public or to citizens other than the specific benefiting property, the more likely it is that a portion of that project's costs will be paid from general taxes and revenues.[22]

   Once the total proportion of infrastructure costs to be assessed to benefiting properties is determined, the amount to be assessed against each benefiting property must be decided. In theory, the benefit accruing to each individual property is the amount by which a property increases in value because of the capital project, and assessable costs should be allocated among specific properties on the basis of how much each one increases in value. In practice, determining increases in property values owing to new infrastructure is usually challenging and often impossible, and alternative bases are used. Front footage of property along a street or abutting an assessment project is commonly used for street improvement projects and often for assessments for water feeder and sewer collector or lateral lines. Front footage can provide a fair allocation of assessable costs when streets are rectangular. When this is not the case, another basis is used, or several bases are combined to make the allocation.[23] Other bases used to allocate assessable costs among benefiting properties are lot area or acreage, building or improvement square footage, number of residential units, and number and size of water-sewer meters or hookups for water-sewer infrastructure.

Calculating special assessments and impact fees

Local governments usually calculate impact fees in terms of a certain number of dollars per residential unit. Special assessments are calculated most often using front footage. Square footage of improved space, lot size, meter size, and number of plumbing fixtures for water-sewer improvements as well as other measures are also used as bases for determining impact fees and special assessments.

- **Administration** The administrative process for levying and administering special assessments is usually established in some detail by state law.[24] A petition from the property owners to be assessed may be required for some types of assessment projects. For example, before it can levy a special assessment for a street project, a North Carolina city must secure a petition signed by a majority of the property owners to be assessed, requesting the assessment. These property owners also must own more than 50 percent of the front footage of the property to be assessed.

  Total costs for projects to be financed through special assessments are computed and usually charged only after construction is completed. Costs may include construction contracts, engineering and design, legal and financing fees, the value of work performed on the project by local government staff and work crews, and administrative overhead. If the project partly benefits the community at large, costs associated with such a benefit are deducted from total costs, and only the remaining balance is allocated among the benefiting properties in the assessment zone or district. The assessable costs are billed to each benefiting property and become a lien on that property. Property owners pay the full assessment immediately or in installments with interest over a period of years.[25] If special assessments are levied for water feeder lines, sewer collector or lateral lines, or other water-sewer infrastructure, the assessments charged to undeveloped property in the assessment zone may be held in abeyance for a period of years or until the property is developed.

- **Role of special assessments in local capital finance** Because special assessments are usually not levied until after project costs have been incurred and are known and because assessments are usually paid in installments over many years, they are usually not available to provide up-front or pay-as-go financing for the project. How then can they be considered a pay-as-go financing source? If assessment payments from infrastructure and improvement projects done in the past are made available or earmarked to finance assessment projects undertaken in the current year, in a revolving fund system, the payments of prior years' assessment projects become a pay-as-go financing source for today's assessment projects. As will be discussed in the next chapter, some local governments issue special assessment bonds and use assessment payments to secure and pay debt service on the bonds. In this case, special assessments are used not as a pay-as-go financing source but as a special revenue, like enterprise earnings, for securing and paying debt issued to meet infrastructure needs for which the assessments are levied.

  Special assessments typically do not provide large amounts of financing for most local governments—they provided less than 5 percent of local government construction revenue in 1998–1999.[26] The following cases illustrate this limited role of special assessments in capital financing.

Special assessments, however, can provide important niche financing for particular types of local infrastructure such as streets, water-sewer lines, and neighborhood parks. Special assessment revenue can be especially valuable to fast-growing communities that are hard-pressed to provide infrastructure to meet growth.

San Clemente, California, has a street improvement fund for financing rehabilitation of city streets in a "benefit assessment district" created by the city council in 1995.[27] Expenditures of the special assessment revenues and other revenues in the fund are restricted to street improvements that benefit the properties paying the assessments. Special assessment revenue flowing into the fund annually was estimated to be $685,000 each year for 2000 and 2001. The city transferred substantial sums from other funds each year to supplement the assessments, and the street improvement fund supported project spending in 2000 and 2001 that greatly exceeded the annual assessment revenue: $5.7 million in 2000 and a projected $3.3 million for 2001, for about seventy-five projects ranging in cost from around $10,000 to more than $500,000. In San Clemente's 2001–2005 CIP, the street assessments are a minor source of revenue (less than 5 percent of the $12.8 million in 2001 estimated project spending), but they provide the leverage or down payment that draws other money into the fund and enables the city to undertake the rehabilitation projects.

Grafton, Wisconsin, also relies on special assessments to help finance street improvements and certain other projects. Grafton's 2000 adopted budget includes $3.1 million in total revenues for the town's capital improvement fund.[28] Of this total, $447,427, or 15 percent, comes from special assessments. Much of this assessment revenue is from installment payments in 2000 for projects undertaken in past years. Table 6–2 shows the projects proposed for 2000 and for which assessments will be charged, expenditures or costs estimated for 2000, and the amount of project costs to be recovered through special assessments. The assessments were not all paid in 2000 but in installments over future years.

While not a major source of capital financing for Grafton's overall capital budget, special assessments appear to cover much to all of the costs of certain projects. In other words, the special assessments are a useful supplemental source of financing for Grafton's capital budget.

Table 6–2
Use of special assessments, proposed projects for 2000, Grafton, Wisconsin

Project	Cost ($)	Assessment ($)
North Green Bay Road	255,000	32,000
Bobolink Avenue	180,000	90,000
Sidewalk rehabilitation	40,000	40,000
Fifth Avenue	90,000	80,000
Stormwater management	511,000	479,000

Impact fees Impact fees are charges made to builders or developers for public infrastructure or capital facilities that are needed to serve or are associated with new development. The infrastructure or facilities may be on-site or off-site—that is, near or at some distance from the new development. The need for the infrastructure or facilities may be immediate or projected for the future. If existing infrastructure and facilities can serve new development, impact fee revenue may be reserved until the time when new infrastructure and facilities are made necessary by the accumulated impact of growth.

Although impact fees paid by a new development are not necessarily used to finance the specific infrastructure and facilities serving that development, the fees must be spent for the same types of infrastructure and facilities for which they are charged. Because impact fees can finance infrastructure and facilities that are off-site, built in the future, and may not serve the development paying the fees, the benefit of impact fees to the specific development paying the fees is often indirect.

Like special assessments, impact fees are a type of user fee, and they are based on the benefits principle of public finance. Both special assessments and impact fees are charged to property and development that benefit from the infrastructure or, in the case of impact fees, the kinds of infrastructure and facilities for which the fees are charged. Key differences between special assessments and impacts fees are identified below:

Special assessments:	Impact fees:
Finance specific infrastructure that directly serves the property paying the assessments	Often finance types of, rather than the specific, infrastructure and facilities that serve new developments paying the fees
Finance improvements located on-site, near, or in the same district as the property paying the assessments	Often finance infrastructure and facilities that are located off-site or far from the development paying the fees
Finance mostly infrastructure that is intermediate in size and cost, such as local street projects, water feeder and sewer collector lines, neighborhood parks, and stormwater facilities	Often finance large-scale and costly infrastructure and projects: arterial roads, water and sewer mains, water and sewer treatment plants, large parks that serve an entire community, stormwater mains, and major buildings
Seldom can be adapted to finance facilities that serve an entire local government or community	More readily adapted for financing general community facilities, like a law enforcement center, a municipal office building, or expansion of a public works service center
Charged to existing property	Charged only to new development that creates a need for new or expanded infrastructure and facilities
In many if not most local governments are not paid until after the infrastructure is built	Usually paid early in the development approval process—often when a development plan is approved or when building permits are issued—making funds available immediately

Impact fees and exactions

The term "impact fees" is just one of several terms commonly used to describe charges to developers or builders. Facility fees, capital recovery charges, developer fees, and exactions are also used to describe the charges referred to in this book as impact fees. Exactions technically refer to in-kind contributions of land, streets, utility lines, and other facilities or infrastructure that a developer builds or turns over to a local government in connection with a new development. The term is sometimes used, however, to mean impact fees and other fees that a developer pays for infrastructure or public facilities associated with a new development.

- **History and legal basis**   Local impact fees evolved from local special assessments. As discussed earlier, special assessments were initially charged to benefiting property only if the infrastructure financed with the assessments was directly and exclusively attributed to the property. Eventually, assessments were charged for on-site improvements that served the community at large as well as specific property paying the assessments, with the assessed property charged only for the portion of the improvement it used or benefited from. The landmark case in this regard was *Ayers v. Los Angeles* (1949), which established that Los Angeles could require street improvements and right-of-way dedications that provide general benefit as well as benefit to specific development.[29] In the face of growth pressures during the 1960s and 1970s, local governments began either to require dedications of land or to charge fees for infrastructure and facilities that were off-site. Local governments in some states, especially fast-growing ones, gradually expanded the use of these impact fees to financing all types of local infrastructure and facilities, not only the traditional street, water-sewer, and park projects but also schools, public safety facilities, general government projects, and even equipment.

  Developers and builders in some states and local governments challenged the impact fees. Several important cases came out of Florida. While a few of these cases overturned particular impact fees, the cases generally upheld the principle that local governments could charge fees to new development that required new public infrastructure or that caused a local government to have to expand, sooner or later, its infrastructure or facilities.[30] These cases also established that the impact fees could be spent only for the purposes for which they were charged. A local government must establish procedures that guarantee that revenues from such fees will not be drawn off to other purposes.

  In 1987, the U.S. Supreme Court ruled that impact fees must meet a "rational nexus" test. In other words, for a local government to charge impact fees on new development to help finance new public infrastructure or facilities, the new development must create or contribute to the need for new infrastructure or facilities.[31] In 1994, the Supreme Court extended the rational nexus principle when it decided that the impact fee charged to development or property must be roughly proportional to the need for additional infrastructure or facilities created by the new development.

  Because impact fees are potentially controversial, explicit legal authorization is needed before a local government can charge impact fees. Such authorization can take the form of a general state statute authorizing local governments in general or specific local governments to charge impact fees. If a general state statute authorizing impact fees does not exist, one or more local governments in the state may secure specific legislation authorizing them to charge impact fees for certain purposes. Such specific legislation might take the form of amendments to the charters of the local governments.[32] In North Carolina, for example, the courts have ruled that local public utilities and enterprises have the authority to levy capital recovery charges or impact fees to finance future infrastructure even if no state statute specifically authorizes this. The courts in these cases have ruled that the general rate-setting powers of public utilities and enterprises include the power to charge impact fees to finance current or future capital infrastructure facilities needed by the utility or enterprise.[33]

Legal challenges to impact fees have been filed under the equal protection, due process, and taking (without just compensation) clauses of the U.S. and state constitutions.[34] The most frequently brought challenges make one or more of the following three arguments:

- Specific development does not create the need for local public infrastructure or capital facilities.

- Infrastructure or facilities being financed with the impact fees do not benefit the new development.

- The amount of the fees charged to development exceeds the proportionate share of the benefit that new development receives from the infrastructure or facilities.

To answer the first two challenges, a local government should have a capital improvement program that relates new public infrastructure and facilities to development and growth, and it should adopt standards of service for infrastructure and facilities that indicate when their capacity to continue serving existing residents and property are exceeded. To answer the third challenge, a local government should base the fees charged to development on an in-depth analysis, often by a consultant recognized for experience with impact fee systems. Proportionality is determined by estimating the demand that each property that pays impact fees puts on the infrastructure or facilities.[35]

- **Allocation**   The most common basis for allocating impact fees for new development is the single household or residential unit. This is also called the equivalent residential or dwelling unit or the single family detached equivalent.[36] Separate, per-residential-unit charges may be used for single-family and multifamily residences. A per-residential-unit charge may be graduated in terms of the number of rooms, front footage, square footage of improved space, or for water and sewer infrastructure, meter or connection size, or number of fixtures. Separate impact fees charged to commercial and industrial development are sometimes based on residential equivalents. For example, a business consuming water at three times the rate of the average household may be charged an impact fee that is three times the fee charged to a residential unit. Other common bases for impact fees charged to business and industrial development are square footage, meter or connection size for water and sewer infrastructure, and area of impervious surface for stormwater improvements.

  The Government Finance Officers Association surveyed use of local government impact fees in the United States and Canada in 1989. Table 6–3 shows the bases for setting or charging impact fees that were reported, by type of infrastructure.

  Impact fees are usually levied and administered in conjunction with development review and approval. They are often part of efforts to control growth as well as generate revenues to provide the infrastructure to accommodate growth. As already mentioned, the fees are usually levied and paid when development or subdivision plans are approved or when building permits are issued. According to the 1989 GFOA survey, a little over one-half of the impact fees imposed were collected when building permits were issued and one-fifth when subdivision plats were approved. Fewer than one-fifth were paid when the new development was built and certificates of occupancy were issued.[37]

Table 6–3
Bases for setting impact fees by type of infrastructure, 1989 survey

Type of infrastructure or capital facility	Basis for impact fee
Water lines	Connection size, front footage, base plus front footage, square footage of structure(s), lot
Water treatment facility	Connection size, meter size, residential unit, base plus square footage or average consumption, acreage
Sewer lines	Connection size, lateral connection, base plus front footage or consumption, square footage of structure(s)
Sewer treatment facility	Connection size, residential unit, lot or acre, base plus square footage of structure(s) or average consumption
Stormwater/drainage	Impervious service, acreage, residential unit
Streets and roads	Trip, peak-period trip, residential unit, parking space, square footage of structure(s)
Parks	Acreage, lot, residential unit, square footage of structures, bedrooms, new residents or occupants, construction costs
Schools	Residential unit, square footage, valuation
Libraries	Residential unit, square footage
Police and fire	Residential unit, square footage
Administrative and community facilities	Residential unit, square footage

Source: Joni Leith with Matthew Montavon, *Impact Fee Programs: A Survey of Design and Administrative Issues* (Chicago: Government Finance Research Center of the Government Finance Officers Association and David M. Griffith and Associates, 1990), 15–19.

- **Calculation and administration** The calculation of the impact fees owed by specific properties in a new development must follow a defensible procedure. Table 6–4 shows a hypothetical calculation of the impact fees to be paid by commercial and residential development for a new local law enforcement facility. The calculation is a condensed version of the many steps that local governments typically follow to determine impact fees. Outside experts or consultants are often hired to do the calculations.

Actual calculations of impact fees are far more complicated than the relatively simple set of steps shown in Table 6–4. For example, there could very well be a deduction from the cost of the new law enforcement facility chargeable to the new development that depends on the current or predevelopment value of the land and property on which the new development is being built. Law enforcement services are presumably already being provided to this property, and if this land/property is not included in the existing property referred to in the second step in Table 6–4, it probably would need to be deducted in another step from costs chargeable to new development for the law enforcement facility.

If the new law enforcement facility for which the impact fees are calculated in Table 6–4 is not built for several years, any impact fees that are collected to build it must be held in a reserve fund. When the facility

Table 6–4
Summarized calculations of impact fees for law enforcement facility

Step	Amount
1 Determine the cost of the new law enforcement facility necessitated at least in part by new development.	$10,000,000
2 Subtract the portion of the cost that will serve existing property or existing development.	$5,000,000
3 Subtract the portion of the cost that is contributed in-kind by the developer (for example, contribution of land).	$1,000,000
4 Determine the amount of the new law enforcement facility cost chargeable to new development.	$4,000,000
5 Select square footage as the basis for allocating $4 million between residential and commercial property: 75 percent of square footage is residential and 25 percent is commercial.	Cost charged to new residential units: 75 percent of $4 million or $3,000,000; cost charged to new business: 25 percent of $4 million or $1,000,000
6 Select household or residential units as basis for allocating $3 million among residential units in the new development. Number of new residential units: 3,000.	Cost charged per residential unit: $3,000,000 / 3,000 units; $1,000 per residential unit

is built, the fee revenue is withdrawn from the reserve and used to help finance construction. Impact fee revenue may be held in reserve for a limited time, usually five to ten years. If it is not spent within that time, it must be returned to the developer or property owners who paid it. Because of this, impact fees are usually levied for capital improvements or equipment in a functional area rather than for specific projects. In the hypothetical example shown in Table 6–4, the $4 million in impact fee revenue paid for by the new development could be used for any capital spending for expanding law enforcement capital needs in the jurisdiction, including the acquisition of new law enforcement equipment as well as construction of other projects for law enforcement. However, the $4 million could not be used to finance replacement of law enforcement equipment and facilities already in place when the new development is built. Such equipment and facilities serve existing property and development, and impact fees paid by the new development may be used to finance only law enforcement facilities and equipment needed to meet growth in the community.

- **Role of impact fees in local capital finance** Impact fees seldom provide the majority of financing for a local capital program, and they are usually not sufficient to fully fund a major, long-lived project in a timely way. Nonetheless, impact fees are a significant source of financing, and they can contribute much of the financing for particular types of new infrastructure (for example, streets) in a jurisdiction. A survey of local government use of impact fees appears in ICMA's *Municipal Year Book 2003*. The survey found that 25 percent of responding cities and 7 percent of responding counties imposed impact fees. Impact fee use was more widespread among cities (62 percent) and counties (30 percent) in the Pacific Coast states.[38]

A local government's experience with impact fees seems to increase its reliance on them in infrastructure and capital facility financing. The 1989 GFOA survey showed that impact fees accounted for about half of the financing for CIP programs in California.[39] The importance of impact fees in California in the late 1980s is attributed to the many years of experience that local governments in the state had with impact fees by then. Indeed, many California jurisdictions began using impact fees in the 1970s and even before. The 1978 enactment of Proposition 13 that restricted local taxes encouraged their use. Since the 1989 GFOA survey, impact fees have grown in importance for local governments in California and elsewhere.[40]

Some local governments, however, have been slow to use impact fees for capital financing for various reasons: arguments by developers that such fees add too much to the cost of new development, the complexity of impact fee calculations and administration, and, finally, lack of experience charging these fees. As a local government gains experience, impact fees can become a key financing source in its capital improvement program.

Two local governments' experiences using impact fees illustrate their importance. The Loveland, Colorado, example shows the purposes for which impact fees can be levied and their relative importance in capital financing for general public improvements. The Cary, North Carolina, example illustrates the use of impact fees for water-sewer systems and presents information on specific fees and how they are calculated.

Loveland, Colorado, charges impact or "capital expansion" fees for streets, parks and trails, fire and rescue, law enforcement, library, the museum, and general government projects.[41] The city also charges impact fees for its utility or enterprise systems: water, wastewater, stormwater, and power projects. The fees are charged only to new development associated with the growth in the community. Revenue from the fees may be spent only for new infrastructure and for facilities that add to the city's capacity to provide services. Revenue from the fees may not be spent for projects to maintain, rehabilitate, or replace existing infrastructure and facilities.

Loveland's 2001–2005 CIP shows capital expansion fee revenue totaling $39.5 million over the five-year CIP forecast period. Projected revenues collected annually during this period consistently remain near $8.0 million. Projected expenditures of impact fee revenue over the period total $27.4 million: $21.5 million for streets, $2.0 million for parks, $3.8 million for fire and rescue, and $100,000 for general government projects. Impact fee revenues collected in excess of spending will build impact fee fund balances to a projected $26.2 million by the end of 2005.

The relative importance of impact fees in Loveland's overall capital budget is apparent from its 2001 capital spending. Of the $16.4 million in total capital project spending in 2001 for general capital improvements, $5.4 million, or about one-third, comes from the city's capital expansion fees for streets, parks, fire and rescue, and general government projects. Loveland's impact fees are clearly a very important source for financing its general public improvement projects and water-sewer, power, and stormwater enterprise systems.

Cary, North Carolina, a fast-growing community in the Research Triangle area of North Carolina, has a ten-year capital improvement program and a one-year "capital improvement budget."[42] Cary's impact fees on new development are important sources of financing in its 2001–2002 capital improvement budget. Water development fees account for about one-fourth of water-sewer improvements ($6.5 million of $27.1 million), and transportation development fees account for almost one-fifth of street and transportation projects ($6.6 million of $36.2 million). The $6.6 million represents 12 percent of all financing for the town's general public improvements in 2001–2002. Cary's ten-year capital improvement program, extending to 2012, indicates that impact fees will continue to be important in the town's future.[43]

The water and sewer development fees, levied in addition to connection or tap fees, are based for residential property on square feet of finished area. For business and other nonresidential property, they are based on meter size at an equivalent dwelling unit rate of $1,780 for water and $3,770 for sewer. The fees are due when building permits are issued for new construction. Table 6–5 shows Cary's schedule of charges for

water and sewer development fees. The charges are derived from formulas that reflect the new water-sewer capacity generated by residential and nonresidential property and the costs for new water-sewer infrastructure and facilities.

Cary's street and transportation development fees vary by type of property, zone, and (for retail property) by square feet of improved space. Fees are calculated for twenty-seven different types of nonresidential property or uses. Table 6–6 shows transportation fees for nine different types of property and by zone. The fees are calculated using formulas based on the traffic volume generated by different types of property and the costs of street improvements in different zones of the city.

Table 6–5
Water and sewer development fees in 2001–2002, Cary, North Carolina

	Water ($)	Sewer ($)
Residential development fees		
Square feet of finished area		
<1,700	1,773	3,061
1,701–2,400	1,960	3,103
2,401–3,100	2,405	3,770
3,101–3,800	2,720	4,094
>3,800	3,432	4,664
Irrigation	1,159	N/A
Apartment (per unit)	1,551	2,533
Nonresidential development fees		
Meter size[a]		
5/8"	2,405	3,770
1"	5,075	9,425
≥1½"	Calculated by staff	Calculated by staff

Source: Town of Cary, North Carolina, Capital Improvement Budget, Fiscal Year 2001–2002, 11.
[a]Meter size is measured in inches; the measurement refers to the diameter of the pipe coming from the water meter or sewer meter and going to the residence or nonresidential establishment.

Table 6–6
Selected transportation development fees in 2001–2002, by type of property and zone, Cary, North Carolina

Property type	Unit of measure	Central	North	Northwest	Southeast
Single-family detached	Dwelling	$1,458	$2,529	$3,127	$2,702
Multifamily	Dwelling	$895	$1,552	$1,920	$1,659
Hotel/motel	Room	$780	$1,352	$1,673	$1,445
General retail < 50,000 sq. ft.	1,000 sq. ft.	$2,238	$3,881	$4,800	$4,147
General retail >1 million sq. ft.	1,000 sq. ft.	$1,556	$2,698	$3,337	$2,883
Bank	1,000 sq. ft.	$3,231	$5,603	$6,929	$5,987
Restaurant (sit-down)	1,000 sq. ft.	$2,621	$4,545	$5,621	$4,856
Hospital	1,000 sq. ft.	$1,061	$1,840	$2,276	$1,966
Industrial park	1,000 sq. ft.	$1,328	$2,303	$2,849	$2,461

Source: Town of Cary, North Carolina, Capital Improvement Budget, Fiscal Year 2001–2002, 17.

Exactions Many local governments negotiate other charges when developers seek local approval of new development or large-scale improvements to major tracts or parcels of existing property. It is common for local governments to require developers of a new residential subdivision or commercial tract to build streets and install water-sewer lines and facilities within the subdivision or tract, on its borders, and, if needed, leading to it. Local subdivision, zoning, and building regulations often require such infrastructure to be constructed to local specifications and then dedicated to the local government once the development is finished and ready for occupancy. If the development is residential and includes many new homes and apartments, the developer may be required to donate land in the tract for a park, greenways, school, fire station, and public community center. Some local governments require developers of large new subdivisions to build public facilities (like fire stations and recreation centers) as well as streets and utility infrastructure and then dedicate them to the local unit.

Such construction and dedication of public infrastructure and facilities by developers or builders are commonly called **exactions**.[44] Local government exactions of streets, water-sewer infrastructure, and land for parks from developers date back to the early decades of the twentieth century and predate impact fees by many decades. Exactions for local public facilities like fire stations, recreation centers, and other public buildings are relatively recent, coming into existence in the 1980s and 1990s in some parts of the country.

Local governments may allow developers to make cash contributions in place of in-kind contributions or dedications of land or public facilities. If the development is small and streets and water-sewer utilities are already in place, perhaps constructed by the local unit or by another developer, the local government may require the developer to make a contribution to "buy in" to the existing infrastructure. If the local government had built the streets and installed the water-sewer lines, it would keep this money. If another developer had constructed this infrastructure, the local government would collect the buy-in fee from the new developer and reimburse the developer who had done the original construction. Cash in lieu of dedication or in-kind contributions can also be applied to parks or greenways and public facilities.

A developer may prefer to make a cash contribution rather than give up land that can be developed and sold.

Exactions for streets, utilities, and park or recreational land are well accepted and are incorporated into many local subdivision and zoning ordinances. Usually they are not subject to negotiation when developers apply for local approval of development plans. However, exactions of other in-kind or cash contributions from developers often are subject to negotiation between a developer and local officials. If the tract to be developed is attractive and the community is experiencing considerable growth, local officials may be able to secure more in exactions of land and facilities. On the other hand, if the tract is not any more desirable than other parts of the community and if the community is experiencing only modest growth, the developer is likely to be in a better bargaining position to avoid all but the basic or required exactions.

When a local government asks for and negotiates exactions, it must be careful to follow due process procedures and to treat developers fairly and impartially. Many local governments prefer impact fees to exactions because impact fees impose standard fees on all new development and are therefore less subject to charges of arbitrariness than are negotiated exactions. However, a local government may choose to negotiate additional exactions for large or unique developments that impose particularly heavy burdens on local infrastructure and capital facilities.

Evaluation of impact fees and other charges to property Proposals for impact fees on new development and other charges to property often refer to the benefits principle of public finance (see the sidebar on page 155). Critics of impact fees, however, affirm the ability-to-pay principle. Many impact fees and other charges to property are usually calculated in terms of measures—residential units and front footage are two examples—not related to income or wealth. For example, when an impact fee is based solely on the number of residential units, a $1 million house is assessed the same impact fee as a mobile home worth $80,000. If the impact fee is $2,000 per residential unit and the fee is passed on to the home buyer, the person buying the million-dollar home pays just 0.02 percent of that house's value, while the buyer of the mobile home pays 2.5 percent of the mobile home's value. This impact fee most probably also constitutes a much smaller proportion of the income of the person buying the expensive home than of the income of the person buying the inexpensive home. Calculating impact fees more like property taxes (for example, basing them on square footage of improved or heated space) will bring them more into line with the ability-to-pay principle.

Also, impact fees and other charges to property reflect the benefits principle only if the facility financed with the fee is used equally by each household and each household pays the same fee. If a fee finances water-sewer improvements, for example, and one household uses more water than the others, the per household fee is not proportional to actual benefits. If the fee finances the construction of new schools, and four school-age children live in the mobile home and only two live in the $1 million house, the per residential unit fee again does not accurately reflect the benefits received by each household and does not reflect the benefits principle.

In practice, impact fees are advocated and are growing in use not because they favor people at one income level over another or because they reflect the benefits received by different households or properties in a jurisdiction, but because they impose the cost of new infrastructure and facilities on the new property and development instead of on general taxes and revenues. To the extent that new property and development are asked to pay the costs of the new, expanded, or improved infrastructure and facilities they make necessary, the aggregated impact fees and other charges do reflect the benefits principle. However, they are usually adopted because of more practical considerations, most notably the avoidance of tax increases on existing property and citizens to finance infrastructure to serve newcomers and to limit or manage growth.

Grants and other external financing of local projects

Federal and state grants have provided major funding for local government capital projects over the years. Other external sources also occasionally provide capital financing. For example, several local governments may pool their resources to jointly fund a project that serves all of the participating jurisdictions. Several local investors and a local government may build a joint public–private sector project.

This section discusses federal and state grants in local capital financing: their importance, advantages, and disadvantages as well as strategies for better use of grant funding in its CIP. The section then briefly discusses and illustrates interlocal and public–private sector capital projects.

Federal and state grants and aid   While federal grants and aid given directly to local governments have fallen relative to local capital needs and financing from local sources, the total dollar amount of federal grants and aid has actually risen significantly. Direct federal aid to local governments increased from $20.1 billion in 1991–1992 to $31.7 billion in 1998–1999.[45] In 1985–1986, there were 989 federal domestic assistance programs; by 2001–2002, there were 1,454.[46]

Federal dollars also flow through state government and are allocated by state officials, under federal rules, to local governments. State aid to local governments, including both federal money that states pass through to local governments and money that the states raise and share with local governments, grew from $195.9 billion in 1991–1992 to $296.3 billion in 1998–1999.[47] Although much of the direct federal assistance and state aid, including federal pass-through funds to local governments, goes to fund public assistance, public education, and other local services or programs, significant portions of federal and state assistance and aid to local governments finance local infrastructure and capital facilities.

Some federal funds available for local government capital financing are provided in the form of loans, usually at subsidized rates and for longer terms than are available in the municipal debt markets. Much of the money is allocated in the form of grants, that is, as pay-as-go financing that local governments do not have to repay.

Many state governments also have significant grant programs to help local governments finance infrastructure and capital projects. Some of these programs rely entirely on federal grant funds that are given to the states and then reallocated by state officials under federal regulations to local governments. Others provide only state-appropriated money, and still others combine federal and state funds in programs that fund local infrastructure and facilities. For example, in some states, federal grants for capitalizing state waste and drinking water revolving loans not only fund loans to local governments but have led to the creation of complementary state grant programs. State-funded grants are also available in many states to help fund local government facilities and equipment for law enforcement, parks and recreation, emergency communications, and many other local needs.

Some cities rely heavily on federal grants: for example, in Madison Heights, Michigan, federal transportation grants account for 21.4 percent or

Major federal grant programs

Eight of the more significant federal grant programs that make money available for local government infrastructure and capital projects are listed here.

Community Development Block Grant Entitlement Program Administered by the U.S. Department of Housing and Urban Development. Eligible local governments include cities with populations over 50,000 in metropolitan statistical areas and qualified counties with over 200,000 in population. More than 1,000 local governments participated in the program in 2000. The grants are used to finance different types of local infrastructure as well as for other purposes.

Community Development Block Grant Small Cities Program Administered by the U.S. Department of Housing and Urban Development and channeled through the states. Eligible local governments include small cities under 50,000 in population and qualifying counties. The grants may be used to finance local infrastructure and capital facilities.

Urban Parks and Recreation Recovery Program Administered by the U.S. Department of Interior. Grants are available to rehabilitate local government parks and recreational facilities, and cities and counties are eligible. Individual grants as high as $5 million have been given.

Local Law Enforcement Block Grant Program Administered by the U.S. Department of Justice. Grants are available to local government agencies for the acquisition of equipment and new technology as well as for new or innovative local law enforcement programs. Individual grants as high as $25 million have been given.

Public Safety Partnership and Community Policing Grant Program (Cops) Administered by the U.S. Department of Justice. Grants are available to local government law enforcement agencies to acquire equipment and technology as well as hire additional police officers. Individual grants as high as $28 million have been given.

Federal Transit Capital Investment Grant Program Administered by the U.S. Department of Transportation. This program finances urban mass transit capital costs, including the acquisition of equipment and construction of facilities. Local governments with bus or other mass transit systems are eligible. The average grant amount is $7 million.

Capitalization Grants for Wastewater State Revolving Funds Administered by the U.S. Environmental Protection Agency. This program provides state revolving loan financing for the upgrade and renovation of local government wastewater treatment facilities. Many state programs are supplemented by state appropriations and provide grants as well as subsidized loans to local governments for wastewater system improvements. Federal grants to the states have ranged from $10 million to $216 million.

Capitalization Grants for Drinking Water State Revolving Funds Administered by the U.S. Environmental Protection Agency. This program provides state revolving loan financing for improvements to local governments' drinking water treatment facilities. Many programs are supplemented by state appropriations and provide grants as well as subsidized loans to local governments for water system improvements. Federal grants to the states have ranged from about $8 million to $84 million.

$8.3 million of the $38.5 million in total revenue or financing in the city's 2002–2007 CIP. State-shared revenues for major streets provide another 12.2 percent or $4.7 million in financing for the CIP.[48] Federal and state grants do not play as prominent a role in financing CIPs in most local governments as they do in Madison Heights, but the grants are essential for financing capital needs for specific functional areas in many jurisdictions.

- **Advantages and disadvantages of federal and state grants** Federal and state grants and other external sources enable a local government to finance a portion of its capital needs with money provided by others. Best of all, the money does not have to be paid back!

  Small local governments with limited resources often have difficulty gaining access to the municipal debt markets to borrow money at affordable rates. Grant funding enables them to fund needed capital projects. Many states create and fund local government infrastructure improvement programs to try to keep small, rural communities intact and revive them. State loans and grants for infrastructure and capital facilities in such communities in effect transfer the cost of the infrastructure from hard-pressed local property tax bases to statewide income, sales, and other tax revenues that are more responsive to economic growth.

  State grants to large, more prosperous cities and counties can further statewide goals and priorities and help local governments raise adequate funds and limit the debt they issue.

  One disadvantage of federal and state grants is that they are usually targeted to achieve national or state priorities. A local government seeking grant funding for local projects may have to subordinate its own priorities to those implied in the grant programs. Second, local officials and citizens may not operate and properly maintain projects fully or mainly funded from grants because operating budget resources are limited or because local priorities lie elsewhere. Because of this, federal and state regulations may prescribe how local officials operate grant-financed facilities. Although this ensures that sufficient resources are budgeted for operation and maintenance of the facilities, it can deprive other areas of the operating budget of resources or result in tax or rate increases to which citizens object.

- **Strategies for securing and using federal and state grants** A successful strategy for securing and using federal and state grants includes capital improvements planning, "grantsmanship," project scope and priorities, and reserves.

  Capital improvements planning It can take months and sometimes years for local officials to identify grants and other outside funding sources, develop relationships with grantor agencies, and prepare the documents and justifications that must accompany grant applications. A CIP gives officials the time needed to seek out federal and state sources of funding and modify the scope or features of local projects to meet grant requirements. Many grantor agencies expect local governments to have a CIP that shows how a particular project for which a grant is sought fits with the local government's overall capital needs. The CIP can also demonstrate to grantor agencies that the local government is planning for the future and that any grant funding will be well used and complement other local projects.

  Grantsmanship The city or county manager of a jurisdiction or one or two other key local officials (for example, the planning director and community development director) need to become familiar with the major grant opportunities and develop contacts with grantor agencies or others who have such contacts. Local officials should have access to the *Catalog of Federal Domestic Assistance* prepared by the U.S. Office of Management and Budget.[49] Commercially published catalogues of federal domestic assistance are also available. The *Government Assistance Almanac* is a more concise book that provides much of the same information.[50] The *Almanac* identifies all federal domestic assistance programs, summarizes their purposes and eligibility requirements, and provides data about types and amounts of grants. The *Almanac* also offers useful guidance about how to obtain grants.

Contacts with officials in grantor agencies can be developed directly or indirectly, through regional, state, and national associations that represent local governments—such as a regional council of governments or a state league of municipalities. These groups are informed about federal and state grant opportunities and have contacts with key officials in grantor agencies.

Project scope and priorities   A third element of a strategy for obtaining and using grant funding in local capital programs concerns priorities. Local governments must mesh their priorities with the broader priorities that accompany federal and state grants and other external funding sources. When a local government pursues grant funding, local officials need to be flexible in defining the scope and features of the project and in choosing the priorities they assign to projects. Grants to cover one-quarter, one-half, or more of a project's costs are usually worth the changes that must be made in the scope and features of the project to obtain the funding. If a project is low in priority and local officials would not undertake it at all if only local funds were available, seeking grant funding is recommended only if the funding will cover nearly all of the project's costs, the project will yield some benefits for the community, and there are no significant negative consequences to undertaking it.

Reserves   The final element of a strategy for securing and using federal and state grants is to maintain adequate fund balances and create and fund capital reserves. The balances or reserves can provide a ready source of matching funds needed to secure a grant. Most grants cover only a portion of the costs of a project. Fund balance or a capital reserve can be the best, most accessible source for the match.

Grant funding is sometimes not paid to the local grantee until after the project for which the grant is given has been completed. In such cases, a local government has to "front-end" its own money to build the project or acquire the capital asset. If the project is large, the local government might be able to issue grant anticipation notes to provide the up-front financing or bridge financing needed while the project is being completed. If the project is of modest size, the issuance of grant anticipation notes is likely to be impractical. If a local government has adequate operating fund balances and capital reserves, it often can provide the up-front money needed for a modest-size project for which grant funding is provided only after the project is finished.

Interlocal and public–private sector projects   Two or more local governments may join together to build a facility or undertake a project that serves all of the participating jurisdictions. Because of economies of scale, a single facility is more cost-effective than several individual facilities. Interlocal projects are sometimes undertaken for office buildings that house the staffs of local governments serving the same geographic area.

Loveland, Colorado, for example, joined with Larimer County, the county in which Loveland is located, to build a police and courts facility.[51] Construction was completed in 2000. Loveland police headquarters and municipal and county courts share the facility. Loveland's share of the costs was $11 million, far less than it would have cost the city to build a separate facility for its police headquarters and municipal courts.

A jail serving both Burke and Catawba Counties, North Carolina, is a second example of interlocal cooperation to take advantage of economies of scale.[52] In the early 1990s, **Burke County, North Carolina,** spent $6 million to construct a new jail with 176 inmate beds and space for the sheriff's department. Built to meet future as well as current needs, the jail when it opened in 1993 had a capacity about double the county's need

for additional jail places. In 1995, neighboring **Catawba County,** with a growing inmate population, approached Burke County to see if it would allow Catawba County to buy into the new jail and use the excess jail beds. Officials from the two counties negotiated an agreement in which each county would be allotted 50 percent of the jail's capacity and contribute 50 percent of the jail's capital and operating costs. Catawba County has paid Burke County a buy-in fee of $257,000, equal to depreciation on the jail portion of the facility in its first two years of operation. Since then, Catawba County pays 50 percent of the jail's operating costs, including a pro rata share of the annual payments on the debt that Burke County had issued to finance the facility. The Burke County sheriff's department operates the jail, and Catawba County makes the payments to Burke County.

Public–private sector projects can occasionally be a key element in local capital financing strategy; they can enable a local government to provide needed public facilities while the government shares the financing burden with or shifts it to the private sector.

In **Winston-Salem, North Carolina,** the city and a local developer representing multiple local investors partnered to develop two parcels of land near city hall.[53] The city owned the parcels, which were also adjacent to a ten-acre tract that the city, two local universities, and investors were developing as the Piedmont Triad Research Park. The city, which used the parcels as parking lots, had long-term plans to put up an office building for city staff and a parking deck for citizens and staff. The developer was interested in building a hotel and restaurant on a portion of this city land and also an office building for the city to use as a customer service center.

With a special law enacted by the state legislature to provide legal authorization, the city and the developer negotiated the following arrangement:

- The city would convey title for the parcels of land to the developer, and the city would retain perpetual rights to 270 parking spaces in a new parking deck that the developer would build.

- The developer would build a four-level parking deck with 493 spaces and a four-story office building and an adjacent restaurant with a total of 87,000 square feet.

- The developer would construct a hotel with 77 guest rooms and small commercial and meeting areas.

- The city agreed to lease the office building and 100 additional places in the parking deck from the developer under a long-term true lease of twenty-five years, with four ten-year options for renewal.

- The city's risk management program, owned and operated by a nonprofit corporation separate from the city, provided the financing for the developer to add a 17,000 sq. ft. fifth floor to the office building and another parking level with an additional 102 parking spaces that the risk management corporation leases to the city for city staff use.

- At the end of fifteen years, the city has the option to buy the office building at its fair market value, using debt to finance the transaction.

- The city would cover the annual payments on the debt from resources that it had been using to cover lease payments to the developer.

Winston-Salem and the developer signed the contracts for this public–private sector project in December 1998. Construction began in January 1999, and the complex was finished by March 2000. Construction took only fifteen months.

By partnering with the private sector, Winston-Salem avoided using its own reserves or issuing debt for the project. The city has use of valuable new office space over a long term. The city's annual lease payments and costs for the project are covered by rental payments previously made for other leased space, taxes paid by the developer on the complex, and tax revenues from additional new development attracted partly because of the project. For example, the complex has triggered new business devel-

opment in the Piedmont Triad Research Park. The Winston-Salem public–private sector project is complex and not suitable for all but a very few local governments. A local entity considering such a transaction must have considerable financial expertise on its staff or access to and full confidence in outside parties who bring such expertise.

Notes

1 The reasons for pay-as-go capital financing have been put forward in previous works; see, for example, A. John Vogt, "Budgeting for Capital Outlays and Improvements," in *Budgeting: Formulation and Execution,* ed. Jack Rabin, W. Bartley Hildreth, and Gerald J. Miller (Athens, Ga.: Carl Vinson Institute of Government, University of Georgia, 1996), 286–288.

2 CIP document, and telephone conversation with Rosemary A. Zink, finance director, Germantown.

3 Proposed City of Alexandria, Virginia, FY 2002 Budget, 14, and a telephone conversation with Daniel A. Neckel, director of finance, Alexandria.

4 The City of Oklahoma City Annual Budget Fiscal Year 2000–01, 76–77. This information was confirmed during a telephone conversation with Catherine O'Connor, finance director, Oklahoma City.

5 California Streets and Highways Code, sections 2105 through 2107.5. For one city's use of this earmarked state shared tax, see City of Mission Viejo, California, Operating Budget and Capital Improvement Program, 1999–2001, 50. Also see City of Mission Viejo, California, 2001–2003 Budget and Capital Improvement Program, City Manager's Budget Message, 17–18, www.ci.mission-viejo.ca.us.

6 Articles 42 and 43 of Chapter 105 of the North Carolina General Statutes.

7 North Carolina is an example. North Carolina General Statute 159-18 says that money in a capital reserve fund may be spent only for purposes for which bond proceeds may be spent. Local governments in the state may spend bond proceeds only for capital purposes.

8 Hickory, North Carolina, Annual Budget 2001–2002, and Recommended Budget. Information and data provided by telephone and e-mail by Ken Larking,

Hickory's budget and performance manager.

9 City of Greensboro, North Carolina, Annual Financial Report for the Year Ending June 30, 2000, combined balance sheet. About one-fourth, or $11.2 million, of Greensboro's general fund balance (equity and other credits) at June 30, 2000, was designated for capital projects.

10 City of Loveland, Colorado, 2001 Adopted Budget, 19-7.

11 North Carolina General Statute 159-18 authorizes the state's cities and counties to establish and fund capital reserves.

12 City of Junction City, Kansas, 1999 Budget, 145–146.

13 City of San Clemente, California, Annual Budget and Capital Improvement Program, Fiscal Year 1999–2000, table of contents and 265.

14 This view is expressed by Thomas P. Snyder and Michael A. Stegman, *Financing the Public Costs of Growth: Using Development Fees, Exactions, and Special Districts to Finance Infrastructure* (Chapel Hill, N.C.: Department of City and Regional Planning and the School of Business Administration, University of North Carolina, for the U.S. Department of Housing and Urban Development, 1985), 10.

15 Glen W. Fisher, *Financing Local Improvements by Special Assessments* (Chicago: Municipal Finance Officers Association, 1974), 7. Also see Snyder and Stegman, *Financing the Public Costs of Growth,* 35.

16 Ibid.

17 Fisher, *Financing Local Improvements by Special Assessments,* 12–13.

18 Ibid., 14–15.

19 Ibid., 15.

20 Snyder and Stegman, *Financing the Public Costs of Growth,* 37.

21 See North Carolina General Statute 160A-217(a).

22 Fisher, *Financing Local Improvements by Special Assessments*, 30–31.

23 Ibid., 37–44.

24 See, for example, Article 10 of Chapter 160A of the North Carolina General Statutes.

25 In North Carolina, property owners may pay in installments over a period of up to ten years. See North Carolina General Statute 160A-232.

26 U.S. Census Bureau, State and Local Government Finances by Level of Government: 1998–1999, www.census. gov/govs/www/estimate.html.

27 City of San Clemente, California, Annual Budget and Capital Improvement Program, Fiscal year 2000–2001, 242–244.

28 Village of Grafton, Wisconsin, 2000 Annual Program Budget, 170–173.

29 Snyder and Stegman, *Financing the Public Costs of Growth*, 45–46.

30 For example, *Contractors & Builders Association of Pinellas County v. City of Dunedin*, 326 So.2d 314 (Fla. 1976). For an overview of the legal history and commentary on court cases relevant to impact fees, see Duncan Associates in association with Cooper Consulting Company, *Impact Fee Study: Policy Directions Memorandum, Fayetteville, Arkansas,* April 2001, www.uark.edu/ALADDIN/cityinfo/city web/pdfs/fayetteville_policy%20memo 3rev.pdf.

31 *Nollan v. California Coastal Commission* (1987). See also *Impact Fee Study,* 8–9.

32 North Carolina has no general statute authorizing local governments to levy impact fees for general public improvements. About ten cities and counties have secured local acts allowing them to use impact fees to help finance such improvements. See, for example, North Carolina Session Laws–1986, Chapter 936, which authorizes the town of Chapel Hill to levy impact fees for streets and roads, parks and greenways, and certain other projects.

33 North Carolina General Statute 160A-314 authorizes cities to set rates, fees, and charges for public utilities and enterprises. The courts ruled that such rates, fees, and charges may include impact fees. See *South Shell Inv. v. Town of Wrightsville Beach,* 703 F. Supp. 1192 (EDNC 1988), affirmed, 900 F. 2d 255 (4th Cir. 1990).

34 Joni Leithe with Matthew Montavon, *Impact Fee Programs: A Survey of Design and Administrative Issues* (Chicago: Government Finance Research Center of the GFOA, and David M. Griffith & Associates, 1990), 4–6.

35 Ibid., 5. Also see Arthur Nelson, ed., *Development Impact Fees* (Chicago: Planners Press, 1988), 3–4.

36 Leithe and Montavon, *Impact Fee Programs,* 14.

37 Ibid., 26.

38 Larry L. Lawhon, "Development Impact Fee Use by Local Governments," in *The Municipal Year Book 2003* (Washington, D.C.: ICMA, 2003), 27–31.

39 Ibid., 23.

40 According to a study published in 2001, at least twenty-three states have general enabling statutes authorizing local governments or certain types of local governments to levy impact fees. Duncan Associates, *Impact Fee Study,* 7.

41 This information comes from City of Loveland, Colorado, 2001 Annual Budget, section 19 on the city's capital improvement program.

42 Town of Cary Capital Improvement Budget, Fiscal Year 2001–2002, 19–22.

43 Ibid., 119–132.

44 Snyder and Stegman, *Financing the Public Costs of Growth,* 42.

45 U.S. Census Bureau, State and Local Government Finances by Level of Government and by State, 1998–1999, 1991–1992, 1979–1980, www.census. gov/govs/www/estimate.html.

46 J. Robert Dumouchel, *Government Assistance Almanac 2001–2002,* 5th ed. (Washington, D.C.: Foggy Bottom Publications; and Detroit: Omnigraphics, 2001), 4.

47 U.S. Census Bureau, State and Local Government Finances by Level of Government and by State, 1991–1992, www.census.gov/govs/www/ estimate.html.

48 City of Madison Heights, Michigan, Annual Budget, 1999–2000, 237. This information was confirmed by telephone with Herbert V. Herring, finance director, Madison Heights.

49 *Catalog of Federal Domestic Assistance,* prepared by the U.S. Office of Management and Budget and available

from the U.S. Government Printing Office or online at www.cfda.gov/default.htm.

50 Dumouchel, *Government Assistance Almanac 2001–2002.*

51 City of Loveland, Colorado, 2000 Adopted Budget, 18-7.

52 This information was provided by Judy V. Ikerd, budget officer, Catawba County, North Carolina.

53 This information was supplied by Loris Colclough, finance director, Winston-Salem.

7 Types of debt

This chapter examines the different types of bonds or debt that local governments issue to finance capital projects or acquisitions. Such debt is distinguished primarily in terms of pledged security.[1] The security pledged for debt is generally the collateral or guarantee that the issuer or debtor provides to the lenders, investors, or creditors to back its promise to repay the debt with interest. The chapter identifies the following general categories or types of local government debt:

- General obligation (GO) bonds secured by the full faith and credit or unlimited taxing power of the issuing local government
- Revenue bonds or debt secured by specific revenues generated by or associated with a self-supporting local enterprise, service, or activity
- Lease or lease-purchase debt secured by the property financed with the debt and sometimes also by other property or by payments (lease revenues) made by the local government lessee to an on-behalf-of organization established by the local government to serve as the lessor; the security for some lease debt includes both property and lease revenues.
- Special obligation bonds or debt, including limited tax debt, special assessment debt, non-property-tax debt, and moral obligation debt.

This chapter's examination of these different types of local government debt covers not only the security pledged for the debt but also other identifying legal or contractual features; the process of authorizing the debt; the kinds of projects financed with the debt; and the advantages, disadvantages, or uses of each type of debt in a local capital improvement program (CIP).

Security pledged for debt

The most important characteristic of a debt transaction to the lender or investors (hereafter, investors) is the promise of the debtor or issuer to repay the debt with interest. The investors typically require the issuer to pledge some collateral or security as a guarantee of repayment. A local government issuing debt might pledge its power to levy property taxes, specific revenues, or the property being financed with the debt as collateral to secure or guarantee its promise to repay with interest.

If the local government fails to make debt service payments as required under the contract, the pledge or security gives the investors options to enforce such payment or otherwise satisfy the debt. If the local government had pledged unlimited taxing power to secure the debt, the option would be to obtain a court order compelling the locality to levy taxes to make the debt service payments. If the property financed with the debt is pledged as security and if the local jurisdiction fails to make debt service or lease payments, the investors can seize the property to satisfy the debt. For some debt, the issuer may pledge several different assets as security: one or more specific revenue sources as well as the property financed with the debt. The ability of the investors to compel action by the local borrower or seize property to satisfy the debt is called the security for the debt.

If particular revenue is pledged to secure debt, it is often used to fund the debt service payments. For instance, local parking system revenue bonds may be secured by parking system rental revenues, and they also may be repaid from such revenues. There can be a difference, however, between the security pledged to guarantee debt and the revenues actually used to make debt service payments on the debt. For example, some local governments issue GO bonds, secured by a pledge of unlimited taxing power, to finance water-sewer system improvements, but they use water-sewer user revenues to make debt service payments on the bonds. The local governments issue GO bonds because they have lower interest rates and issuance costs than other debt (for example, revenue bonds). Here, in the normal course of events, the pledged security and the source of revenue to pay debt service are different. However, if water-sewer revenues fall short and the local issuer fails to pay debt service on the bonds, the unlimited tax pledge gives the investors the legal right to compel the issuer to levy taxes to pay this so-called water-sewer debt. If this happens, the pledged security and revenue used to satisfy the debt become the same.

Much local government installment- or lease-purchase debt is secured by the property financed with the debt. Often such property does not produce revenue, and general taxes or specific revenues or enterprise earnings are used to fund the periodic lease payments on the debt. If the local government fails to make these payments, the lessors or investors may take legal steps to seize the leased property to satisfy the debt.

In sum, local government debt is classified first and foremost in terms of the security pledged to guarantee the debt. For some debt, security is the same as the revenues used to make debt service payments. For other debt, security and the revenue used for debt service are different. State constitutional provisions and statutes specify and limit the security that local governments can pledge for debt, and interpretations of such provisions and statutes by state courts are crucial in shaping a local government's debt practices.[2] Types of debt, in terms of pledged security, authorized for local governments in one state may be prohibited for local governments in other states. In a single state, some local governments (for example, home-rule cities) may be able to issue certain debt that other local governments in the same state are not authorized to issue.[3]

Federal law, particularly Internal Revenue Code and Internal Revenue Service regulations, also limits or shapes the security that local governments may pledge for certain debt. This is particularly true for local government debt issued to finance private purposes (for example, low- or moderate-income housing).[4]

General obligation bonds

GO bonds account for about one-third of the long-term (more than one year) debt issued by state and local governments.[5]

Security for general obligation bonds

GO bonds are often called full-faith-and-credit bonds or debt. This phrase means that all available revenues and resources of the issuer, including taxes, stand behind the bonds. In most states, a local government's full-faith-and-credit pledge means that the locality's authority to levy the property tax or ad valorem tax secures the debt.[6] To be a true GO bond, this tax-levying authority must be unlimited. In other words, neither state law nor local law may limit the ability of the issuing local government to levy and raise property taxes to make debt service payments on the bonds. If there is a cap or limit on the property tax pledged for this purpose and there is no other unlimited local taxing power, the bonds are really limited rather than GO debt. A state government's GO bonds are typically secured by a full-faith-and-credit pledge,[7] which includes all available revenue sources, especially a state's power to levy income and/or sales taxes.[8]

With full-faith-and-credit GO bonds secured by an unlimited property tax, the investors look first to the property tax as security for the debt. However, if the issuer defaults and there are problems in satisfying the debt from property taxes, the investors may seek payment of the debt from other local revenues. Only revenues earmarked before the issuance of the bonds for other, specific purposes (for example, public assistance) would be unavailable as part of the GO pledge. Earmarking non-property-tax revenue after the issuance of GO bonds does not remove that revenue from the full-faith-and-credit pledge for the bonds.[9]

Caps on GO bonds

Because the full-faith-and-credit pledge for GO bonds is broad, many states have constitutional and/or statutory caps on this type of debt. While these caps limit the amount of GO debt and sometimes other debt that a local government may have outstanding or incur, they do not limit the security pledged, that is, the authority of the issuer to levy taxes to make debt service payments on outstanding GO bonds.

While most states that cap GO debt define this limit as a percentage of property tax valuation, certain states, like Pennsylvania, limit it to a percentage of the local government's annual revenues.[10]

A full-faith-and-credit pledge

In 2001, **Johnston County, North Carolina,** issued $25 million in GO bonds for school construction. The bonds were secured by the following full faith and credit, unlimited property tax pledge:

> The bonds will be general obligations of the County secured by a pledge of the faith and credit of the County, all the locally taxable property within which will be subject to the levy of taxes, without limitation as to rate or amount, to pay the bonds and the interest thereon.

This statement is based on a statute that authorizes local governments in North Carolina to pledge unlimited taxing power to secure GO bonds and debt.

Source: Official statement, "Notice of Sale and Bid Form," County of Johnston, North Carolina, $25,000,000 General Obligation School Bonds, Series 2001, May 15, 2001.

Caution is advised when interpreting the practical significance of a legal cap on debt and when comparing caps from state to state. Although GO debt is almost always subject to a state debt cap, other types of debt included in "net debt" and subject to a cap are not the same in every state. Even within one state, local property tax valuation standards, practices, and cycles vary, making it misleading to compare unused debt capacity in relation to taxable valuation from one jurisdiction to another. If local revenues, rather than tax valuation are used to calculate a debt cap or limit, the definition of what constitutes a revenue for this purpose and, thus, the practical effect of the limit also will vary from one jurisdiction to another.

Authorization of general obligation bonds

In the great majority of states, the authorization of GO bonds or debt requires the approval of a jurisdiction's voters in a bond referendum. In some states, this requirement is stated in a general way that would seem to apply not only to GO debt but also to other types of local debt. Court decisions, however, often limit the requirement for voter approval to GO or tax-secured debt.[11]

Some states grant exceptions to a general requirement for voter approval of GO bonds (for example, when the amount to be authorized and issued is relatively small). North Carolina exempts GO bond issues from the voter approval requirement if the amount of new bonds issued in any year does not exceed two-thirds of the amount of net GO debt that the issuer retired in the prior year. (Net debt retired means total GO debt retired less any new GO debt issued in a year.)[12] Cities in Virginia are authorized to issue full-faith-and-credit GO bonds without voter approval so long as this debt does not exceed 10 percent of the assessed value of taxable property.[13]

The charters for some home-rule cities authorize their local governing boards to issue GO bonds without a voter referendum. For instance, Memphis, Tennessee, may issue GO bonds without a referendum.[14]

Some states permit certain local governments to issue these bonds without voter approval up to a certain amount per year or as a percentage of tax valu-

---

State limit on general obligation debt

Iowa's constitution limits the amount of debt that local governments in the state may incur:

> No county or other political or municipal corporation shall be allowed to become indebted in any manner, or for any purpose, to an amount, in the aggregate, exceeding five per centum per annum on the value of the taxable property within such county or corporation: to be ascertained by the last State and county tax lists, previous to the incurring of such indebtedness.

This 5 percent cap applies to GO bonds and certain other debt such as tax increment bonds that are secured by property or ad valorem tax revenue.

Source: Iowa Constitution, Article XI, Section 3. This provision is discussed in Gelfand, *State and Local Government Debt Financing*, Vol. 2, Chap 9, 11–13. Chapter 9 was updated and reissued in 1996. The *Des Moines, Iowa, Comprehensive Annual Financial Report*, on page 154 shows that GO bonds and tax increment bonds are subject to the 5 percent constitutional debt limit. Des Moines also has revenue bonds for sewer, airport, and certain other purposes that are not subject to the 5 percent limit.

ation. Amounts issued above such limits must be approved in a referendum. For example, Virginia Beach, Virginia, may issue up to $10 million in new GO debt in a year without voter approval. For GO debt issued in excess of that annual limit, voter approval is needed.[15] In Arizona, local governments do not need voter authorization to issue GO bonds up to 6 percent of taxable valuation. They may issue debt equal to between 6 percent and 15 percent of taxable valuation only if a majority of the voters approves the debt.[16]

Voter authorization of local GO bonds usually requires a simple majority of those voting. In some states, however, a supermajority, usually two-thirds or 60 percent of the voters, must be obtained. The courts in most cases have upheld supermajority requirements.[17]

Types of projects financed with general obligation bonds

Local governments issue GO bonds mainly to finance buildings or infrastructure that benefit the general public and are supported by taxes and other general revenues: city halls, county courthouses, and local government office buildings; schools and community college buildings; public safety facilities, such as law enforcement centers, jails, and fire stations; streets and roads; public works facilities; libraries and other cultural facilities; and parks, recreational centers or facilities, greenways, and open space.

Financing with GO bonds is usually reserved for large, visible, long-lived projects or infrastructure for several reasons. First, the authorization of GO bonds usually requires the approval of voters in a referendum, and seeking this approval involves some political risks for local officials. Officials may be willing to take that risk only for major projects that have broad public benefit. Second, while GO bonds issued for riskier projects such as beach renourishment often have terms of ten years or less, most GO bond issues have repayment terms of around twenty years. As explained in Chapter 5, long-term debt like this is not suitable for financing small capital projects or acquisitions with useful lives that are less than twenty years. Third, GO bond issues are typically sold publicly, and the issuance costs are significant. Many of these costs are fixed, regardless of the size of the issue, and when added to the interest costs for the bonds, they can make a GO bond issue for a relatively small amount more expensive than an alternative financing method (for example, privately placed installment-purchase or lease-purchase debt).

Some local governments issue GO bonds to finance major projects for water-sewer systems and other local enterprises because GO bonds have lower interest rates and issuance costs than revenue bonds. Voters usually approve referenda for water-sewer systems and certain other "essential" enterprise projects, and this form of financing allows local officials to retain full operating control of the utilities or enterprises. If they issue revenue bonds to finance enterprise projects, decisions of local officials about utility rates, the issuance of new debt, and certain operations are limited by the bond contract and subject to review by a trustee who represents the bondholders.

Some local governments issue GO bonds for public enterprises (for example, public transit systems) that are not self-supporting. Special taxes or transfers from the general fund must supplement user-fee revenue. Revenue bonds secured by enterprise user fees are not an option because the fee revenue is not sufficient to cover both operating costs and debt service. If the local government is not authorized to issue limited tax or special obligation bonds for the enterprise, GO bond financing may be the only alternative.

Advantages and disadvantages of general obligation bonds

Advantages

- GO bonds typically have lower interest rates than other types of long-term debt.
- Voter approval of GO bonds in a referendum signals the markets that citizens support the project.
- GO bonds do not involve market-imposed restrictions on how a debt-financed project will be managed and used.
- GO bonds do not require the local issuer to maintain reserves for debt service, something the other types of local government debt usually require.
- GO bonds usually cost less to issue than other types of local government debt.

Disadvantages

- Local voters may reject a proposed GO bond issue.
- Because of the requirement for voter approval of most GO bonds, they usually take more time to authorize than other types of local debt.
- Net GO debt that a local government carries is often limited by state law.

Voter approval of the GO bonds, if required, is more likely if the enterprise's services extend to citizens throughout the community.

Local officials must carefully consider the consequences of nonapproval when choosing to finance a project with GO bonds. If a project is mandated, the consequences can be particularly serious. For example, if state regulations make it impossible for a county to continue to use an old jail—in effect, requiring the county to build a new jail—and voters turn down GO bond financing for the project, local officials could have to resort to other nonvoted debt to finance the new jail. Going against the voters' wishes as expressed in the referendum adds risks to the alternative financing, raising the financing's interest costs. Local officials would have done better by forgoing the attempted GO financing and going directly to the alternative financing method.

Interest rates on general obligation bonds

Typical interest rates on GO bonds are usually lower than rates on other types of long-term debt that local governments use to finance capital projects. This is because the full-faith-and-credit pledge or unlimited tax pledge is considered to be superior to the various pledges that underlie other types of debt. Bond rating agencies tend to assign a higher rating to a local government's GO bonds than to the same issuer's revenue bonds, capital lease debt, or special obligation debt.[18] For example, if a jurisdiction's GO bonds are rated AA, its revenue bonds might be rated AA− or A+.

The interest rate spread between GO bonds and revenue bonds, about 0.3 percent, usually widens when market interest rates rise and narrows when rates fall, but a lower interest rate for GO bonds usually prevails in the market. The spread reflects not only the market's higher valuation of the credit quality of GO bonds but also their shorter average term. While many revenue bond issues mature over a thirty-year term, GO bonds are usually issued for terms of twenty years or less. The higher interest rate for revenue bonds reflects the relatively greater risk attached to longer-term debt.

In May 2001, *Bond Buyer's* twenty-year GO bond index was 0.28 percentage points less than its thirty-year revenue bond index.[19] What difference does 0.30 percentage point make in interest paid on long-term bonds over time? If a local government issues $40 million in bonds and retires this debt in even, annual principal amounts of $2 million annually over a twenty-year term, and if each $2 million in bonds maturing annually pays a 5 percent rather than a 5.30 percent interest rate, the savings in total interest paid over the twenty-year period is $1,260,000!

Revenue bonds

Revenue bonds rely on a specific revenue or related specific revenues as security. The pledged revenues also serve as the source for payment of the debt service on the bonds. These revenues are most commonly user fees and other revenues from a self-supporting enterprise system or project.[20]

Local governments began issuing revenue bonds in significant amounts in the 1930s.[21] Today, local governments issue revenue bonds most notably for self-supporting local enterprises or projects. Some authorities refer to bonds secured by special taxes or nonenterprise revenues as revenue bonds,[22] but this book classifies them as special obligation debt (see discussion later in this chapter).

Security for revenue bonds

The typical security pledged for revenue bonds is revenue from fees or charges generated by the project financed with the bonds or from the enterprise system of which the project is a part. Revenue bonds are a limited liability payable only from the pledged revenues. The issuer is not obligated to use general revenues or taxes or any revenues other than those pledged to pay the bonds. Revenue bonds require that the project or enterprise system financed with the bonds be self-supporting or self-liquidating.

Net revenues are typically the specific pledge or security for revenue bonds for enterprises. Net revenues equal total or gross revenue less operating and maintenance expenses. In addition to recurring user fees or consumption charges, gross revenues may include assessments, hookup fees, and other charges. Operating and maintenance (O&M) expenses include salaries and benefits for personnel, contractual services, supply items, and other recurring outlays to operate the enterprise system or project. They do not include debt service and depreciation. With a net revenue pledge, gross revenues are committed first to cover operating and maintenance expenses.

The rationale for giving O&M priority over debt service is that an enterprise or project must first operate to produce revenues to pay debt service on the bonds.[23] The specific revenues pledged to secure revenue bonds also provide the resources to pay debt service on the bonds.[24] Reserves, however, also may be set aside for debt service on most revenue bonds, and they are part of the pledged security. If enterprise operating revenues are insufficient to make debt service payments, the debt service reserve provides resources to make those payments for a time.

Some revenue bonds are secured not only by specific pledged revenue but also by a mortgage on project or enterprise property, a special tax, or even unlimited property tax revenue. When a mortgage on project or enterprise property is added as security, the bonds remain revenue bonds.[25] If a special tax is added as security, the markets generally classify the bonds based on the stronger pledged security. For example, debt that a county issues to build a sports arena may be secured by both admissions and other revenue generated from events held at the arena as well as by a special prepared-food and beverage tax levied by the county. If the tax is the stronger security, the market would treat the debt as special tax more than as revenue bonds. When general or unlimited taxing power is added as security, the market typically treats the bonds as GO bonds rather than as revenue bonds.

Revenue bonds are issued not only by state and general-purpose local governments but also by numerous public or special authorities. Some of these authorities are independent governmental entities that operate utility or other enterprise systems and facilities. They have their own governing boards, substantial administrative autonomy, and revenue sources to support operations and debt service on the revenue bonds that they issue.

Other authorities act on behalf of a state or a general-purpose local government and have little or no real autonomy. Their revenue bonds are usually used to build or acquire facilities and equipment for the sponsoring state and local government entity. The facilities and equipment are then leased to that entity, and lease payments from the state or local government, and often a mortgage on the leased property, secure the bonds issued by the authority. (The authority here acts as an on-behalf-of debt issuer for the state or local government lessee.) Although such bonds are often referred to as revenue bonds or lease-revenue bonds, this book treats them as lease- or installment-purchase debt because the pledged revenues come more often from general sources and are not the earnings of a self-supporting project or enterprise system.

Many special districts with tax-levying authority operate enterprise systems for which they issue revenue bonds to make system improvements. Like most other revenue bonds, special district revenue bonds are secured with user charges and other revenues. The charges and other revenues must be sufficient to cover operating and maintenance expenses as well as debt service on the bonds. If enterprise revenues are not sufficient to do this but the district's ability to levy property taxes to pay debt service is unlimited, the district can issue "double-barrel" bonds secured by both enterprise revenues and unlimited taxes.

Interest rates on revenue bonds

The limited liability pledge for revenue bonds offers less security than the full-faith-and-credit or unlimited tax pledge for GO bonds. This is the main reason why the revenue bonds of most local government issuers have higher interest rates than their GO bonds.[26] Some local governments with exceptionally strong utility systems, however, have obtained very high bond ratings, even triple A, on their revenue bonds and consequently have been able to sell them for interest rates that come very close to their rates on GO debt.[27]

Types of projects financed with revenue bonds

Revenue bonds are suitable for local government projects or enterprises that have identifiable users who pay fees that cover all project or system costs. The issuer must demonstrate to the markets that annual revenues will be sufficient to cover all operating and maintenance expenses, debt service on bonds, and other recurring spending, as well as maintain reserves for contingencies. Usually, the more profitable a project or enterprise, the more feasible is revenue bond financing. A history of profitable or self-sustaining

Net revenue pledge for revenue bonds

The water and sewer revenue bonds issued in 2001 by **Henderson, North Carolina,** includes the following net revenue pledge for revenue bonds:

The 2001 Bonds will be special obligations of the City, solely secured by and payable from the Net Receipts of the Combined Enterprise System, except to the extent payable from proceeds of 2001 Bonds, investment earnings and certain other moneys hereinafter described. The Combined Enterprise System is currently composed of the City's water and wastewater systems (the "Existing Facilities"). The Bond Order authorizes additions or improvements to the Combined Existing Facilities and the Improvements will become a part of the Combined Enterprise System.

Further description of the security for the bonds defines "Net Receipts" as follows:

Generally, "Net Receipts" means Receipts after paying Current Expenses. "Receipts" means all moneys in the Revenue Account representing amounts held for the credit of the Appropriate Operating Funds which represent all payments, proceeds, fees, charges, rents and all other moneys received by or for the account of the City from the ownership and operation by the City of the Combined Enterprise System and all rights to receive the same and the proceeds of such rights, but excluding certain items. "Current Expenses" means the reasonable and necessary current expenses of operation, maintenance and repairs of the Combined Enterprise System as determined in accordance with generally accepted accounting principles, but excluding certain items.

Source: Official Statement, "$15,630,000 City of Henderson, North Carolina, combined Enterprise System Revenue Bonds, Series 2001," 9.

operations is often needed to show that annual revenues will be sufficient to cover all spending or reserve requirements.

Most local government revenue bonds have been issued for utility projects or enterprises—water, sanitary sewer, stormwater, and energy systems. Local governments have also issued revenue bonds for transportation projects like toll roads, parking decks or systems, airports, and marine facilities as well as for hospitals and health care facilities.[28] Revenue bond financing has been less feasible for stadiums and convention centers, recreation projects, mass transportation projects, and solid-waste projects. Local governments have issued some revenue bonds for low- or moderate-income housing and for economic development projects. Most bond issues for these kinds of initiatives, however, have been private-purpose rather than government or public-purpose debt.[29]

Projects or enterprises that provide a basic service used by many people, or that have a monopoly or a strongly competitive position relative to other existing or potential providers of the service, are the best candidates for revenue bond financing.[30] For instance, if a city's water enterprise is the sole provider of water in the jurisdiction and the surrounding area and if the system is large enough to take advantage of economies of scale, the security for revenue bonds would generally be considered to be strong.

Service demand for particular projects or enterprises can change. For example, local providers of solid-waste services, including disposal and collection, once faced little competition from the private sector, and environmental requirements were limited.[31] Today, however, local government landfills and solid-waste collection services can face stiff competition from private firms. Increasing environmental requirements and citizens' resistance to siting local landfills in or near their neighborhoods create further risks for revenue-bond-financed landfill and solid-waste projects.

For financing local enterprises that serve many outside users as well as local citizens, revenue bonds may be viewed as preferable to GO bonds. The rationale is that it is fairer to issue bonds secured by enterprise revenues collected from all enterprise customers, many of whom are outside the jurisdiction, than bonds secured by the taxes levied on only those customers who are taxpayers of the local government. A legal issue can arise in states with laws stipulating that local government enterprises be operated principally for the benefit of the citizens of the local government and only incidentally for outside enterprise customers.[32] In these states, a local government's enterprise services must center on the jurisdiction itself. If services beyond the jurisdiction's borders become so extensive that benefit to the local government's citizens is no longer dominant, then the local government may want to establish a special authority or district to provide the enterprise services.

Local government authorization of revenue bonds

The typical legal steps required for local government authorization of revenue bonds are much simpler than for GO bonds. Because revenue bonds are not secured by the full faith and credit or taxing power of an issuer, authorization usually does not require voter approval.[33] Nor are revenue bonds subject to the state caps that apply to GO debt and certain other types of debt.[34] However, if an issuer secures revenue bonds with a pledge of general taxing power as well as specific revenues, the bonds are subject to voter approval requirements and state debt ceilings in states where such requirements and ceilings exist.[35]

Governing board approval is usually the legal authorization for local revenue bonds secured by a pledge of specific revenues alone. One or more public hearings may also be required, and some states require one or more state oversight agencies to approve local issuance of revenue bonds.

The authorization of revenue bonds is almost always based on one or more feasibility studies that demonstrate the viability of the project, enterprise, or activity to be financed with the bonds. Indeed, the authorization effectively occurs through the feasibility study. Bond rating agencies require a feasibility study before they rate revenue bonds, and prospective investors expect one before they buy the bonds. The feasibility study must be an outside, independent verification that a proposed project, or the enterprise of which it is a part, will produce enough revenues to cover operating and maintenance costs and all other costs, including debt service. The issuer contracts for the study with a consulting engineering or a professional firm with experience in evaluating the types of projects to be financed with the proposed revenue bonds. Although the study covers all aspects of project or enterprise operation and financing, its focus is on the demand for project or enterprise services, future annual revenues and expenses, and the availability of net revenues to cover debt service on existing debt and the proposed new revenue bonds.

Coverage, covenants, and the trustee for revenue bonds

Because the security for revenue bonds is specific to a particular project or enterprise, investors require the issuer to maintain revenues high enough to cover all operating and maintenance costs and debt service on existing rev-

---

Feasibility study for projects financed with revenue bonds

Moody's Investors Service identifies the following components of a "well-structured" feasibility study:

- Project overview: purposes, scope, cost estimates, contingencies, and future financing requirements and sources
- Description of existing facilities or system
- Project construction schedule
- Laws, policies, conditions, and assumptions that affect operations and financing
- Project or enterprise demand, including identification of competing providers
- Historical and anticipated operating trends
- Analysis of historical and anticipated revenues and spending
- Customer base and user trends
- Debt service requirements
- Future rates and charges required to produce sufficient revenues
- Economic, social, and demographic factors that are likely to affect needed increases in future rates
- Revenue and expenditure performance under indentures that may differ from generally accepted accounting principles (GAAP)
- Reconciliation of revenues and expenditures between GAAP and indenture accounting
- How rates and charges are derived under bond contract or ordinance
- Costs at competing facilities or systems
- Methodology and assumptions used in the feasibility study
- Conclusions and recommendations.

Source: Moody's Investors Service, *Moody's on Revenue Bonds: Fundamentals of Revenue Bond Credit Analysis* (New York: Moody's Investors Service, Inc. 1994), 3–4.

---

enue bonds and any new bonds that are issued. To protect their interests, the investors also require the bond contract to include covenants or indentures. These are provisions with the force of law that require the issuer to meet certain standards or to refrain from doing certain things in operating and financing the project or enterprise. A trustee representing the investors monitors the issuer's compliance with the covenants and is given authority under the bond contract to take legal action to compel the issuer to comply.

Coverage Under the conventional definition, coverage requires, for any year revenue bonds are outstanding, that net revenues equal or exceed a specified percentage of debt service on existing revenue bonds and on any new ones. An alternative expression of this coverage definition states that net revenues must equal or exceed a specified percentage of maximum annual debt service on existing and any new revenue bonds. For example, coverage for the Henderson, North Carolina, water-sewer revenue bond highlighted in the sidebar on page 185 calls for net revenues to equal 125 percent or more of annual debt service in any year that the revenue bonds are outstanding.[36]

Coverage helps to assure investors that net revenues will be sufficient to offset overly optimistic assumptions in the feasibility study or unforeseen events that lower expected project or enterprise revenues or increase expected spending. In the past, the coverage ratios required of revenue bonds were often between 150 to 200 percent of debt service.[37] More recently, the ratios required for many types of projects and enterprises have been lower (for example, 125 percent of debt service, or even less for projects or enterprises deemed essential or that have long histories of successful operation. Many water-sewer projects fall in this category). Higher coverage (for example, 130 to 150 percent or more) is expected of projects or enterprises that face significant market competition or risks or that have limited operating histories. Many solid-waste and parking projects fall in this category.

Covenants   The most important covenants for revenue bond issues concern project or enterprise rates, maintenance of a debt service reserve fund, the issuance of additional debt, construction and operating requirements, and flow of funds.[38]

Covenant on rates   A rate covenant requires the issuer to set user rates and charges at levels sufficient to meet or exceed the coverage ratio specified in the bond contract. If net revenues do not meet coverage requirements, the rate covenant usually requires the issuer to hire a consultant to study the project or enterprise and recommend changes in the rates and/or operations. If the issuer fails to adopt the recommendations, the trustee, representing the bondholders, may sue to compel the issuer to do so. For some revenue bond issues, the rate covenant prohibits the local issuer from taking any action that would impair its ability to set rates to meet O&M, debt service, and other costs.[39]

Covenant on a debt service reserve   Most revenue bond issues also have a debt service reserve covenant that requires the issuer to maintain a reserve fund equal to debt service for one year or six months.[40] The debt service reserve, which is used to pay debt service when revenues fall short, gives the issuer time to resolve problems creating the shortfall. If the situation is dire, the reserve protects the investors for one year or six months and gives the trustee representing the investors some time to compel the issuer to resolve the problems or otherwise satisfy the investors' claims against the issuer. The required balance for a debt service reserve is established in terms of debt service on existing revenue bonds and proposed new ones. It may be equal to maximum annual debt service, average annual debt service, some percentage of average annual debt service (for example, 125 percent), or average or maximum semiannual debt service. The trustee representing the bondholders holds or controls the debt service reserve fund. If debt service reserve money is used to make a debt service payment, the covenant requires the reserve to be replenished to the required level when net revenues are sufficient to do so.

A very strong issuer of revenue bonds may be able to substitute a surety bond covering debt service for one year or six months for a debt service reserve fund. The issuer pays a one-time premium for the surety bond.[41]

Covenant on additional bonds   A covenant on additional bonds prohibits the issuer of revenue bonds from selling additional bonds or debt in the future for the project or enterprise unless the issuer meets specified coverage requirements. The requirements usually involve both a historic test and a future-earnings test. The historic test might require net revenues to equal or exceed 125 percent of debt service in the past year, or each of the past several years, before new bonds or debt may be issued. A future-earnings test usually requires a consultant's study to show that net revenues will cover maximum annual debt service (for example) on both existing bonds and any additional bonds that are proposed in the future. The coverage ratios required under the additional-bonds covenant have dropped over the years, from two to three times to one and a half times or less of maximum or annual debt service. The covenant often allows for the issuance of subordinate, long-term debt or various types of short-term debt with lower coverage requirements and fewer restrictions.[42]

Covenants on construction and operations Most construction and operating covenants represent sound business practices that any issuer should follow on its own. Construction covenants help to ensure that spending of bond proceeds and other resources available for construction achieve the intended purpose. They include requirements for payment and performance bonds, certification by a consulting engineer that work is satisfactorily completed before progress payments are made, and approval by the trustee of disbursements for construction. Operating covenants include insurance requirements and promises to maintain the project or enterprise properly and hire competent staff, for example.

Flow of funds Typical revenue bond contracts include covenants that establish certain funds; usually the funds are construction, revenue, O&M, debt service, debt service reserve, repair and replacement, and surplus or reserve funds.[43] There also may be an arbitrage rebate fund and a separate debt service fund for GO bonds if any have been issued and are outstanding for the project or enterprise. Although revenue bond contracts refer to these as separate "funds," they are more properly understood as "accounts" under generally accepted accounting principles. Besides establishing the funds, the revenue bond contract specifies priorities in the flow of funds, that is, the application of project or enterprise revenues or resources to particular purposes.

The construction fund receives bond proceeds and other resources and disburses them as construction progresses. It also pays bond issuance costs and debt service during construction. When construction is finished, this fund is closed, and any remaining balance is transferred to another fund, usually the debt service or debt service reserve fund.

The revenue fund receives all operating revenues or resources and then disburses them to the other funds pursuant to flow-of-funds requirements. The O&M fund has the first priority in drawing resources from the revenue fund. The second priority is the debt service fund for payment of bond principal and interest. The third priority is replenishment of the debt service reserve fund if necessary. The fourth is funding the repair and replacement fund. The final priority is building and maintaining contingency and surplus funds.

The revenue bond contract should clearly prohibit transfers of resources from the project or enterprise to another local government fund if the transfer jeopardizes O&M spending or debt service. If the contract does not include this prohibition, local policies should rule out transfers unless reserve, contingency, and surplus funds for the project or enterprise are first provided for.

The specific covenants included in a revenue bond contract are often negotiable.[44] For example, prospective investors may demand coverage of net revenues to maximum annual debt service of 130 percent and a debt service reserve equal to maximum annual debt service. However, for a project with a strong earnings history, the issuer may be able to negotiate for a lower coverage ratio (for example, 120 percent of average annual debt service) and a waiver of the debt service reserve in favor of a surety bond. The issuer does not negotiate covenants directly with investors but negotiates instead with the underwriters buying and reselling the bonds, the rating agencies, and, if applicable, the bond insurance company. These market professionals are in touch with prospective investors and convey investors' expectations and flexibility regarding covenants to the issuer. Once covenants are agreed to and the revenue bond contract is final, the issuer must abide by them. Once entered into, revenue bond covenants are not changed.[45]

Trustee   A trustee plays a key role in revenue bond financing. The revenue bond contract appoints the trustee, usually a bank or trust company. The trustee represents the interests of investors or bondholders in the financing and while the bonds are outstanding. The trustee usually

- Approves the amount of bonds to be issued
- Receives and disburses bond proceeds
- Monitors construction
- Oversees receipt of the revenues pledged to secure and pay off the bonds, receives funds from the issuer for debt service, and makes debt service payments to the bondholders[46]
- Approves the issuance of additional bonds
- Approves outside consultants or engineers hired by the issuer
- Monitors operations and approves changes in operating and financing policies and practices in accordance with the bond contract
- Enforces bondholders' remedies.[47]

Lease financing of capital assets

Leasing has become an important capital financing tool for many local governments for both equipment acquisitions and major improvement and construction projects. This section describes authoritative sources for classifying leases, types of capital leases, the concepts of nonappropriation and abatement, security for capital leases, the concept of essentiality, marketing of leases, and authorization of leases.

GASB and IRS criteria for classifying leases

Three authoritative sources classify state and local government leases: the Governmental Accounting Standards Board (GASB), the Internal Revenue Service (IRS), and state laws that authorize and limit state and local leasing. GASB and IRS criteria for classifying leases are addressed first.

Accounting classifications: operating leases and capital leases   GASB has adopted private sector rules for governmental leases that distinguish between operating and capital leases.[48] An operating lease gives the lessee the use of the lessor's property for a time but no ownership interest in it; periodic lease payments compensate the lessor for such use.[49] Local governments use oper-

---

Leasing terminology

In this book the term **capital lease** is identical with capital lease as in the criteria set by the Governmental Accounting Standards Board (GASB). It refers to any leasing arrangement that a state or local government uses to finance the acquisition or construction of a capital asset, including buildings, equipment, and infrastructure.

With a **tax-exempt** or **municipal lease,** the interest paid by the jurisdiction is exempt from federal income taxes, as it is on most state and local bonds.

Installment-purchase agreement, lease-purchase agreement, lease-purchase financing, and **revenue lease** are terms found in state laws authorizing local governments to use specific kinds of capital leasing. They also are "terms of art" that public officials often use to refer to capital leasing by state and local governments.

Certificates of participation and **privately placed lease** refer to particular structures or methods for marketing capital leases to investors. Certificates of participation are used to publicly sell large capital-lease financings to interested investors, while private placement is used for smaller lease-financing transactions sold to or placed with one investor or only a few investors.

Regulations of the Internal Revenue Service distinguish leases that effectively transfer ownership of the leased property to the lessee, **conditional sales leases,** from true leases in which the lessee just uses the lessor's property (see discussion of conditional sales leases in section on tax classifications on the next page).

Source: Vogt and Cole, *A Guide to Municipal Leasing,* Chap. 2, "Types of Leases and Identifying Characteristics of Tax Exempt Leases." Although twenty years old, this source's identification and analysis of different types of leases and discussion of lease terminology is still current. A more recent discussion of federal and state laws governing public sector leasing, Gelfand, *State and Local Government Debt Financing,* Vol. 1, Chap. 3, "Leasing as a Financing Device," also identifies, defines, and discusses some of the above terms; although Gelfand was originally published in 1986, chapter 3 was updated and reissued in 2000.

---

ating leases when the need for the property is short term, when technology is changing rapidly and a local government lessee does not wish to acquire property that is likely to be outdated soon, when the lessor insists on retaining ownership of the leased property, and for other reasons. The term or period covered by an operating lease is usually relatively short—a few years, one year, less than a year, month to month, or day to day. If the lease term spans several years, it often can be canceled by either party annually or at more frequent intervals. Many operating leases have purchase options. For the lease to remain an operating lease, the purchase option should be exercisable near estimated fair market value rather than at a bargain price or a nominal amount.

In a capital lease, the lessee assumes the risks and has the benefits of ownership. Under accounting standards, a capital lease is an (effectively) noncancelable contract that meets one or more of the following criteria:

- The lease transfers ownership (legal title) of the leased property to the lessee.
- The lease contains a bargain or nominal purchase option.
- The lease term equals 75 percent or more of the estimated economic life of the leased property.

- The present value of the lease payments (excluding executory costs) equals or exceeds 90 percent of the fair value of the leased property at the inception of the lease.[50]

Whether a lease is noncancelable depends as much on the intent of the lessor and lessee as on specific contractual provisions associated with the lease. A long-term lease may have a nonappropriation clause that legally allows the local government lessee to end the lease contract in any year by not budgeting funds to make the lease payments that year. On its surface, this is a lease that can be canceled annually. On the other hand, if the lessor and lessee both intend that the lease continue to the end of the full term and if the lease otherwise qualifies as a capital lease, it is properly accounted for as a capital lease under generally accepted accounting principles.

If a lease is a capital lease for accounting purposes, the lessee records the leased property as its capital asset. The lessee also has a long-term liability equal to the present value of its remaining payment obligations under the lease.[51]

Tax classifications: conditional sales leases and true leases IRS regulations distinguish between conditional sales and true leases. These types of leases for tax purposes are generally comparable with capital and operating leases for accounting purposes. All or practically all conditional sales leases are also capital leases. Most but not all capital leases are conditional sales leases. Most but not all true leases are also operating leases.

Under IRS regulations, a conditional sales lease is a transaction that meets one or more of the following criteria:

- The lessee acquires legal title to the property at the lease inception or after paying money that may include periodic lease payments and a purchase option.
- Some portions of the periodic lease payments are designated as interest.
- Some portions of the periodic lease payments are specifically made applicable to the buildup of equity in the property for the lessee.
- The periodic lease payments materially exceed the fair market rental value for use of the property.
- Total payments that the lessee makes over a period significantly shorter than the lease property's useful life make up an inordinately large portion of the leased property's original purchase price.
- The lessee may acquire the leased property at a purchase option price that is nominal or significantly less than the fair market value of the property when the option is exercised.[52]

A lease that is not a conditional sales contract is a true lease under IRS regulations. That is, it is an arrangement in which the lessee simply uses the lessor's property for a time and acquires no ownership interest in it.

If a lease is a conditional sales lease for federal tax purposes and the lessee is a state or local government entity, the interest portions of the periodic lease payments are generally exempt from federal income taxes.[53] In other words, the interest on a conditional sales lease is treated the same as interest on state or local government bonds. The tax-exempt nature of state and local government capital leases results in lower interest charges and lease payments for the lessees. If a lease is a true lease under IRS regulations, the lease payments do not formally include any interest. However, since the lessor continues to own the property, the lessor may charge depreciation as an expense against lease income.

Types of capital leases by local governments

As noted earlier, a capital lease transfers title to the leased property to the local government lessee, covers a predominant portion of the property's useful life, has lease payments with a present value equal to all or nearly all of the leased property's value at the lease inception, or contains a bargain or nominal purchase option. If any one of these conditions is met, the leased property is the lessee's asset from the start of the lease term, and the lessee has a long-term liability for the lease payments.

Local governments' capital leases are structured in a variety of ways to comply with accounting standards and to meet IRS guidelines. Three general types of local government capital lease structures are identified here: installment-purchase financings; lease-purchase financings; and long-term, true capital leases (see Table 7–1).

Table 7–1

Local government capital lease structures

Lease feature	Installment-purchase financing	Lease-purchase financing	Long-term, true capital lease
Title	Passes to lessee at lease inception.	Passes to lessee at end of lease term.	Remains with lessor.
Identification of interest	Yes. Each payment often separately shows interest, principal, and outstanding principal balance.	Yes. Each lease payment often separately shows interest, principal, and outstanding principal balance.	No.
Primary basis for setting periodic lease payments	Amount of financing plus interest on outstanding principal balance.	Amount of financing plus interest on outstanding principal balance.	Approximate fair rental or use value of leased property.
Purchase options	Lessee may purchase for an amount equal to outstanding principal balance on any lease payment date. Option price may or may not be related to fair market value of property when option is exercised.	Lessee may purchase for an amount equal to outstanding principal balance on any lease payment date. Option price may or may not be related to fair market value of property when option is exercised. Nominal purchase option at end of lease term.	Any purchase option must be exercised at estimated fair market value of property when option is exercised.
Term	Multiple years—several to 20 years or more. Covers major portion of property's useful life.	Multiple years—several to 20 years or more. Covers major portion of property's useful life.	Multiple years—several to 20 years or more. Covers major portion of property's useful life.

All three are capital leases under generally accepted accounting principles. Installment-purchase and lease-purchase financings are conditional sales leases for federal tax purposes, while long-term, true capital leases, as the name indicates, are true leases for federal tax purposes, even though they are capital leases under accounting standards. The three types are discussed in terms of title, interest, basis of payments, purchase options, and term.

Title   In an installment-purchase financing, title to the leased property passes to the lessee at the inception of the contract, and the lessee gives the lessor a security interest or mortgage in the property (see discussion on page 196 on security for capital leases). In a lease-purchase financing, title to the leased property passes to the lessee at the end of the lease term, after all lease payments have been made and a nominal purchase option price has been paid. In a long-term, true capital lease, title stays with the lessor.

Interest   Installment-purchase and lease-purchase financings are structured to qualify as conditional sales leases under IRS rules. This means that interest is identified in these leases; usually the interest and principal portions of the periodic lease payments are specified separately. The interest rate implied may also be shown. The identification of interest, more than any other feature, points to a state and local government capital lease as tax-exempt—the interest portions of the periodic lease payments qualify for exemption from federal income taxes. In a long-term, true capital lease, neither interest nor an interest rate is specified or cited. If one of them were, the lease would be at risk of being treated as a conditional sales lease by the IRS, with consequent loss of depreciation deductions for the lessor.

Payment basis   In installment-purchase and lease-purchase financing, the periodic lease payments are based on the amount of financing that the lessor provides to the lessee at the inception of the lease arrangement, allowing the lessee to acquire the leased property. This financing is equal to the cash-purchase price or fair market value of the property at the outset of the lease transaction, plus costs incurred to arrange the financing, less any down payment that the lessee may make to acquire the leased property. The periodic lease payments are calculated considering not only the financing amount but also the term and the interest rate charged on outstanding financing or principal balances. In a long-term, true capital lease, the periodic lease payments are supposed to be based on the approximate fair rental or use value of the leased property in each year or period. For any capital lease, but especially for a true capital lease, the periodic lease payments may also include charges for insurance, maintenance, and other items.

If the full cash purchase price or market value of leased property at the inception of a lease is financed in an installment- or lease-purchase transaction, the present value of the lease payments (or the sum of the total principal paid over the term of the lease) would equal that price or value. The present value of lease payments excludes any charges for insurance or maintenance included in the lease payments.

Purchase options   Two purchase options are typically found in lease-purchase financings—one exercisable on each lease payment date at an amount equal to the outstanding principal balance at that time, and the other exercisable at the end of the lease term at a nominal amount (for example, one dollar). Exercise of either of these options transfers title of the leased property to the lessee and ends the financing. Purchase options are often found in long-term, true capital leases, but they must be exercised at or near estimated fair market value. Otherwise, the IRS may challenge the lease's status as a true lease.

In an installment purchase-financing, the lessee has title from the outset of the transaction. However, the lessee often has the option to pay the outstanding principal balance on any lease payment date. If this fully pays off the lease obligation, it removes the lessor's security interest or mortgage in the leased property and is tantamount to a purchase option.

Term   All capital leases have relatively long terms. They may last several years to twenty years or more. The term will depend on the leased property's useful life. Typically, a capital lease covers a significant portion of that useful life. The term also depends on the debt service and lease payment scheduling policies, the capabilities of the lessee and lessor, and the expectations of the lessor for the term or pace of repayment.

State law concepts of nonappropriation and abatement

To a great extent, capital leasing by state and local governments has arisen to avoid voter referenda requirements and limitations on GO debt and other types of debt. Indeed, the use of capital leasing by governmental units in any state depends on the willingness of the legislature and the courts to view such leasing as "falling outside the applicable debt limitations or voter approval requirements."[54]

The difference between a *capital lease* and *indebtedness* under state law centers on the obligation of the lessee to make lease or debt service payments. With GO bonds, revenue bonds, and most other types of bonds, the obligation is unqualified. With most capital leases, the obligation is contingent upon the lessee's making annual or periodic appropriations to fund the lease payments.[55] This makes the lease an annual or operating budget obligation rather than a long-term debt under state law. Alternatively, the annual or periodic lease payment obligations are contingent on the lessor making available the leased property each year. Because the lessor makes the leased property available on a year-to-year basis, the obligation of the governmental lessee to make lease payments occurs annually and again is not long-term debt. If the lessor abates or ceases doing this in any year, the obligation of the lessee to make lease payments ceases.

Nonappropriation   A nonappropriation clause in a lease agreement permits the governmental lessee to cancel a capital lease, without defaulting, in any fiscal or budget year or period by not appropriating the money needed to make the payments due that year. Other terms for such a clause include "annual appropriation," "fiscal funding out," "annually renewable," "automatically renewable," and "year-to-year appropriation."[56] Regardless of name, the legal effect is the same—the capital lease payments are due only one year or fiscal period at a time as the money to make them is appropriated. Thus, in many states, future years' payments under capital leases are contingent obligations and thus are not debt subject to voter referenda requirements and state debt limitations. Lease payments are not legally due until they are appropriated.

Despite the nonappropriation clause, if the lessor and lessee intend the lease to provide long-term capital financing for the lessee, and if the lease meets the appropriate IRS and accounting criteria, it is classified as a conditional sales lease for tax purposes and as a capital lease for accounting and financial reporting purposes. Investors and other municipal debt market participants also view capital leases, with or without the nonappropriation clauses, as long-term obligations or debt of the issuer rather than as current or year-to-year obligations.[57] Investors would view exercise of a nonappropriation clause in a capital lease as an event of default, even if it is not considered a default under state law.

Abatement A nonappropriation clause is not generally used in capital leases in states such as California and Indiana, where the law makes state or local payment obligations under these leases dependent upon the availability of the leased property to the lessee. The leased property is presumed to be available to the governmental lessee only on a year-to-year basis. The lease payments are current obligations rather than long-term debt because they are tied to the yearly availability of the leased property.[58]

Despite abatement, leases that meet the appropriate IRS and accounting criteria are considered to be conditional sales leases or capital lease obligations for these purposes. Moreover, investors and others in the municipal debt markets view capital leases with abatement provisions as long-term debt. They expect the lessor to make available the leased property over the full term of the lease, and they expect the lessee to make all of the periodic lease payments called for in the lease contract.

Security for capital leases

The primary security for most capital leases is the property being financed with the lease. If a city enters into an installment-purchase or lease-purchase

---

Nonappropriation of funds

A typical nonappropriation clause states:

> In the event no funds or insufficient funds are appropriated and budgeted or are otherwise not available in any fiscal period for lease payments due under the lease, then this lease shall terminate on the last day of the fiscal period for which full appropriations were made, without penalty or expense to the lessee of any kind whatsoever.

Many capital leases modify the nonappropriation clause by incorporating language that requires the lessee to exert "best efforts" to seek appropriation of annual funding to make lease payments. For example, some installment-purchase or lease-purchase contracts require the executive or manager of a local government to prepare a recommended budget that requests the appropriation of funds by the legislature or local governing body for lease payments due in a year for the capital lease. In states where allowed, a nonsubstitution clause may be placed in a capital lease to inhibit exercise of the nonappropriation clause. One version of nonsubstitution provides that if the lessee cancels a capital lease through nonappropriation, the lessee may not replace the property that was being leased with other property that performs the same or a similar function.

Sources: Vogt and Cole, *A Guide to Municipal Leasing*, 65–69. Although twenty years old, the illustrations of nonappropriation and nonsubstitution clauses in this book are representative of these clauses as they appear in local government capital lease contracts today. For a more recent discussion of nonappropriation, see Gelfand, *State and Local Government Debt Financing*, Vol. 1, Chap. 3, "Leasing as a Financing Device," 4–11. Although volume 1 was originally published in 1986, chapter 3 was updated and reissued in 2000.

agreement to finance the acquisition of a new fire truck, the security guaranteeing payment to the bank or the lessor is the fire truck itself. If the lessee exercises the nonappropriation clause and stops making lease payments on the truck, the lessor's **security interest** in the truck gives the lessor the right to take possession of the truck and sell or use it. Or if a county finances the construction of a new office building with a capital lease, the security that the county gives the lessor or investors to guarantee the county's future lease payments is likely to be the office building itself. If the county, through nonappropriation, stops making lease payments, the lessor, investors, or trustee acting on behalf of the investors may take legal action to seize the office building and sell or re-lease it to another party, thereby satisfying the county's payment obligations under the original capital lease.

Many capital leases of substantial amounts that finance major projects are divided into shares, called **certificates of participation,** that are marketed in public sales to investors. In these transactions, the governmental lessee often establishes an on-behalf-of nonprofit agency or organization that sells the lease obligations to investors, obtains the proceeds, builds the facilities with the lease financing, and leases the completed facilities to the governmental lessee. The on-behalf-of organization serves as lessor in these capital leases and pledges the governmental lease payments (that is, the lease revenues) as collateral to secure the capital lease. Although these lease payments or revenues serve as collateral, the buildings or facilities financed under the capital lease are still the main or primary collateral. If the governmental lessee stops making lease payments, the investors or the trustee representing the investors can take legal steps to seize the facilities and satisfy the governmental lessee's obligation under the capital lease by selling, re-leasing, or otherwise using the leased property.

If state law permits, the security for a capital lease may be strengthened by adding other property as pledged collateral to the property being financed with the capital lease. For example, **Durham, North Carolina,** used as security not only its baseball stadium but also a water treatment plant to obtain capital lease financing to construct a new baseball stadium for its minor league team, the Durham Bulls.[59]

The security for capital lease financing for equipment can be strengthened by bundling equipment and vehicles in one master leasing arrangement.[60] The alternative is to separately finance individual or small groups of equipment items and vehicles with several capital leases, each secured by the equipment or vehicles financed by that lease.

A local government can finance improvements to several buildings in one capital lease and secure the entire transaction with the pledge of one or more of the valuable or essential buildings as collateral; this improves the security for the other buildings financed through the transaction and lowers interest costs more than financing each of the other buildings under separate capital leases.

A special tax or revenue may be added as pledged collateral to the security for a capital lease and/or levied and earmarked to help make payments on a capital lease. In such cases, the security or resources supporting the lease includes both the building or property financed and the special tax or revenue.[61] For example, room occupancy taxes and a special tax on prepared foods and beverages were levied in Mecklenburg County, North Carolina, to provide money for lease payments on the capital lease that the city of Charlotte issued to finance a new convention center.[62] Although the proceeds from these taxes are not formally pledged as security for the lease, the proceeds are earmarked by the authorizing state legislation, first, to provide funds to make the periodic lease payments and, second, if any proceeds are left, to pay marketing and operating costs for the convention center. The authorization of the taxes and earmarking of the proceeds from them made the capital lease for financing the convention center very attractive to the market and investors.

Contractual provisions or certain features associated with a capital lease can strengthen the security for it. Like a revenue bond, publicly sold capital leases often require a debt service reserve fund, with a minimum balance equal to maximum or average annual lease or debt service payments. The fewer conditions placed on future lease payments, the stronger the security for the lease. Therefore, a capital lease without a nonappropriation clause usually offers more security than does a lease with the clause. Of course, insurance guaranteeing lease or debt service payments to the investors can greatly improve a capital lease's security, as is true for other types of debt for which debt service payments are insured. Chapter 11, Selling Local Government Debt, examines the role of insurance in marketing all types of debt.

Essentiality

The concept of **essentiality** is closely linked to pledged security. Both address investors' questions about whether the governmental lessee will make future lease or debt service payments. While pledged security gives investors recourse if the lessee fails to make such payments, essentiality reduces the chance that the lessee will exercise a nonappropriation clause or stop making payments on some other basis.

Essentiality has to do with the importance of the leased property to the governmental lessee. An assessment of essentiality asks how important a particular asset is to a governmental service and how vital that service is to the community. The more essential the property that a local government finances with a capital lease, the less likely the local lessee will exercise a nonappropriation clause. Rarely will a governmental lessee exercise its right of nonappropriation and walk away from its lease payment obligations if the asset financed with the lease is central to a basic governmental service.[63] Control and/or seizure by the lessor means that the lessee can no longer use the property or can use it only subject to severe restrictions.

Several questions arise in evaluating a project's essentiality. How vital to the community is the project? Could the community get on without it? Could the governmental lessee provide the service supported by the project using an alternative method of service delivery? What would be the impact on the community if the service were not provided? How much citizen and political support does the project or the service have, or does it have a committed client base? How does a general-purpose project that is to be financed with a capital lease fit into the governmental lessee's overall delivery system for public services?[64]

Following are the kinds of capital projects usually evaluated as essential by market professionals and investors:

- Projects mandated by federal or state law or that are needed for a mandated service
- Projects for a basic or core governmental service
- Projects for a service for which there is little or no competition
- Projects for a service that has a history of successful operation and a secure customer base
- Projects where feasibility is proved and for which there is a record of successful completion and operation
- Projects for capital assets that have long, useful lives and the risks of technologic obsolescence are limited.[65]

Services usually considered essential to local governments include law enforcement, fire protection, education, water and sewer, and general government services. The more essential local capital assets are usually found in these service areas.[66]

Because of essentiality, capital leasing has been used much less often for recreation facilities, convention centers, coliseums, and sports arenas. If capital lease financing is involved in projects like these, a pledge of a special tax or revenue, as in the case of the Charlotte convention center, is often added to the security and used to help pay lease payments on the financing.

Essentiality is not the only criterion for identifying projects or types of projects for which capital lease financing is appropriate. Because capital leases are secured by the property financed with the lease, the value of the leased property to the lessor, if the lessee exercises the nonappropriation clause or defaults on the lease, may determine whether capital lease financing is practical. Capital assets such as street improvements, while essential, offer little value to the lessor or investors.[67] Consequently, capital leasing is not often used for this kind of infrastructure.

Structures for marketing capital leases

Decades ago local governments began using capital leases to finance equipment like fire trucks and computers. The equipment vendors served as the lessors, and the leases were simple two-party, lease-purchase or installment-purchase contracts or true leases with purchase options. By the early 1980s, it became clear that a properly structured, installment- or lease-purchase contract provided tax-exempt interest income to the lessor. This prompted banks, other financial companies, and some individuals to become third-party lessors in local government capital leases structured as conditional sales contracts. Local governments continue to use these three-party lease- or installment-purchase contracts today to finance both equipment and real property. The structure for these transactions is described below.

A broadening in local governments' use of capital lease financing began in the late 1980s and has continued. Many local governments now use installment- and lease-purchase debt to finance not only equipment but also large-scale real property acquisitions and construction projects. If an installment- or lease-purchase financing is for $10 million or less, the lease financing is usually privately placed with one bank or investor or with a small group of investors. Financing for more than $10 million is typically divided into certificates of participation, usually $5,000 each, that underwriters buy and resell publicly to individual investors, mutual funds, and others.

Private financing   Capital lease financing placed privately with a single bank or investor is generally structured as a relatively simple, three-party transaction. If the lease is to acquire equipment or real property, the governmental lessee arranges the lease financing with a bank or another investor who serves as lessor. If the lease is an installment-purchase contract with title passing to the governmental lessee at the lease's inception, the lessor pays the equipment vendor or real property owner the full cash price for the property, or provides funds for the lessee to do so. Title passes to the governmental lessee, and the lessee gives the lessor a security interest or mortgage to the property. The equipment vendor or real property owner is then out of the picture, and the lessee makes the periodic installment payments directly to the bank or lessor. A lease-purchase structure works the same way, except that title to the equipment or property passes to the bank or lessor who holds it during the lease term. If the financing is for a construction project, the lessor usually controls or monitors the disbursement of lease proceeds for construction, using the services of a consulting engineer to ensure that construction goes as planned.

If several investors finance a privately placed capital lease, one of them may serve as a general partner and represent all of their interests in dealings with the governmental lessee. Alternatively, the investors may rely on a trustee to handle their interests during construction and while the lease is outstanding. Bond ratings and underwriters would normally not be involved in the lease. Rating agencies are not needed because the lease is placed privately with a bank or other sophisticated investors who are familiar with and are able on their own to evaluate the credit strength of the local issuer. Underwriters are unnecessary because the debt is not marketed to the public. A bond counsel is also often not required because the bank or investors taking the debt are satisfied with the opinion of the local issuer's attorney about the validity of the capital lease and other legal matters.

Certificates of participation   A capital lease that is divided into certificates of participation and sold publicly has a much more complicated structure than one placed privately with a single bank or investor or a small group of investors. Usually a separate, on-behalf-of agency serves as the lessor of the leased property and a trustee also plays a major role.[68]

The on behalf-of-agency is a shell entity established under IRS regulations by the governmental lessee; officials of the governmental lessee serve as its officers.[69] The agency issues the lease certificates and usually serves as a conduit to obtain the financing for the governmental lessee. The agency is needed because there are multiple investors, and bank trustees are unwilling to act in the roles of issuer and lessor because of liability and other concerns. While the on-behalf-of agency remains in existence and technically serves as lessor as long as the lease debt is outstanding, its role effectively ends when the lease certificates are issued and lease proceeds are obtained. At that point, lessor rights, titles, interests, and obligations under the lease are transferred from the agency to the trustee for the lease financing. Responsibilities for acquisition and construction of the lease property are assigned to the governmental lessee, subject to trustee monitoring.

The trustee represents the interests of the investors who hold the certificates of participation. The trustee has the same general role as a trustee in a revenue bond financing. The trustee receives and holds the proceeds from the sale of the certificates of participation or controls these proceeds; approves disbursal of the proceeds for the intended purposes; holds, on behalf of the investors, assignment of title, security interest, or mortgage in the leased property; controls any reserve funds; monitors and enforces all lease indentures; receives the periodic payments from the governmental lessee and distributes them to the investors or oversees such receipt and disbursement; and enforces remedies to protect the investors' interests. The trustee is typically a bank and trust corporation.

In addition to the on-behalf-of agency and the trustee, public sale of certificates of participation in capital leases requires bond counsels, bond ratings, underwriters, and often bond insurance. Chapter 8 discusses ratings of capital leases. Public sales of certificates of participation or other capital lease obligations follow the same general process as sales of revenue bonds. Chapter 11 discusses the sales process for these types of debt.

Authorization of capital leases

Because capital leases are *not* secured by the full-faith-and-credit pledge or unlimited taxing power of the local government lessee, authorization is not subject to voter approval in a referendum, nor to the legal caps that apply to GO debt and certain other debt in many states.[70]

Typically, a resolution of the governing board authorizes an installment- or lease-purchase financing that is privately placed. If the financing is relatively modest in size—less than $1 million or $500,000 depending on the jurisdiction—and is placed with a single bank or investor, the authorization may be based solely on an analysis and recommendation by the local government's manager and staff. The analysis might refer to the need for the property to be leased, identify the revenue source(s) for making the lease payments, and confirm that the jurisdiction can afford the lease payments. If the financing is significant—more than $1 million—and if the jurisdiction has a financial adviser, that person might be asked to do the analysis and prepare a recommendation. One or more public hearings may be required by law or held as a matter of local policy before the governing board approves the financing.[71]

If the capital lease is divided into certificates of participation to be sold publicly, authorization occurs by decision of the governing board, but the documentation is typically much more extensive than with a privately placed capital lease. The documentation is summarized in an **official statement (OS)** prepared by the underwriter selected by the local issuer to sell the certificates of participation; regulations of the Securities and Exchange Commission (SEC) require an OS for public sale of state or local government debt, including certificates of participation of $1 million or more.[72] Chapter 11 lists the requirements for an OS and discusses its contents by type of debt. In large and medium-size local governments, the issuer's own staff often has a major role in the preparation of the official statement. The OS for a certificate of participation issue would explain the need for the project and financing and generally show that the lessee will be able to afford the lease payments.

Because certificate-of-participation financing is more expensive than GO bonds, the OS may need to explain why such financing is preferable to GO bonds. This is especially important when the certificates are clearly an alternative to GO bond issuance. The explanation will vary depending on the project, but for some projects it could have to do with meeting a mandated need.

There is usually little need to explain why a privately placed capital lease of modest amount is preferable to GO bond financing. Many privately placed capital leases are for equipment acquisitions (most with terms of three to seven or eight years), or they are for modest construction or renovation projects (with terms no longer than twelve years or so). Because GO bonds are usually issued for major projects and for terms of fifteen years or more, they are usually not a reasonable alternative to privately placed capital leases. Moreover, because privately placed capital leases have shorter repayment terms and cost less to issue than GO bonds, their costs are very competitive compared with GO bond financing.

Special obligation bonds

Special obligation (SO) bonds or debt are secured by special or limited taxes or other revenues rather than by the full faith and credit or unlimited taxing power of the issuing jurisdiction. State statutes and court decisions determine the availability of particular types of SO bonds to local governments. Because such statutes and decisions authorize a wide variety of revenues to secure SO bonds, there are many different variations of local SO bonds or debt across the country.

Most SO bonds combine some features of GO bonds and revenue bonds. Like GO bonds, SO bonds are used to finance either general-purpose facilities and infrastructure that do not generate revenues of their own, or projects or enterprises that, while generating some of their own revenues, do not generate enough to support revenue bonds. Like revenue bonds, SO bonds are secured by specific revenues. Because of this, SO bonds do not usually require the approval of voters, and in many states they are not subject to the legal caps that apply to GO bonds and debt. Debt service on some SO bonds must be from the specific revenues securing the bonds. On other SO bonds, debt service may be paid from any available or unrestricted revenues or taxes.

In some states, SO bonds are authorized to provide financing for particular types of local government projects (for example, solid-waste projects or public infrastructure needed to support private economic development). These bonds provide niche financing to meet particular kinds of capital needs.

Five types of SO bonds are important sources of capital financing for local jurisdictions in the states that authorize their use. The five types are distinguished by pledged security:

- **Special or limited tax or revenue bonds,** secured by one or more special or limited tax or revenue sources or by a limited, general tax. These special and limited tax or revenue bonds are issued both by general-purpose local governments and by many special districts or authorities.[73]

- **Special assessment bonds or debt,** secured by special assessments against properties that benefit from public improvements financed with the bonds.[74]

- **Tax increment or economic development bonds,** secured by growth in property tax valuation and revenues resulting from private development or redevelopment and sometimes by other revenues in a specific zone.[75]

- **Non-property (ad valorem) tax bonds and non-local-tax bonds;** the former are secured by all available revenues except property taxes levied by the issuing jurisdiction, and the latter are secured by all available revenue except any taxes levied by the issuing unit.[76]

- **Moral obligation bonds,** secured by a pledge to pay that is not legally enforceable.[77]

Each of these types of SO bonds or debt is discussed in terms of the pledged revenue and other security for the debt, the purposes for which they are issued, key legal provisions, and factors that affect their credit quality.

Special or limited tax or revenue bonds

This is debt secured by and usually paid from a special or limited tax or revenue source or from a set of similar taxes or revenues.[78] One example of special tax or revenue debt is highway bonds secured by motor fuel taxes, vehicle registration fees, and other revenue related to motor vehicle use of highways and streets. A second example is bonds secured by and paid from a limited, general sales tax to finance capital projects like schools, mass transit, and street improvements in places where the local government is not permitted to use a property tax. Other special tax bonds are debt secured by a pledge of a franchise tax or special sales taxes such as a prepared-food and beverage tax or a hotel occupancy tax. Franchise taxes, levied as a percentage of the gross receipts of certain businesses, have been used to secure debt for financing public recreational facilities, and prepared-food and beverage taxes and hotel occupancy taxes have been levied to help secure bonds for convention centers and other public facilities.

Security for special or limited tax bonds   As implied in their name, special or limited tax or revenue bonds usually have fixed caps on the rates or fees that may be charged to secure them; these are specified by law. Because the issuer pledges only taxes or revenues available from the capped tax or revenue source—it does not pledge its full faith and credit—to secure the bonds, they are SO instead of GO bonds. If the issuer has the ability to increase rates, up to a limit, for any special tax or revenue used to pay debt service on the bonds, this improves the credit quality of the bonds. Even so, if the issuer is unable to pledge unlimited tax revenue or its full faith and credit to secure the bonds, they remain SO debt.

Because special or limited tax or revenue bonds are payable from specific and fixed revenue sources, the bonds include covenants, similar to those for revenue bonds, to increase their attractiveness to investors. The pledged taxes or revenues for the bonds must produce enough revenue to "cover" debt service by a specified ratio. The calculation of revenues for determining coverage would first deduct O&M costs and any other expenditures that must be paid from the pledged taxes and revenues. A coverage ratio—net revenues to debt service—of 125 percent or more might be required. The more limited the tax or revenue source supporting the bonds and the more vulnerable the source is to changing economic conditions, the higher the coverage ratio that will be required. Special tax or revenue bond contracts usually specify that new bonds secured by the same tax or revenue source may be issued only if certain coverage requirements are maintained. There also is usually a debt service reserve or a surety bond requirement, equal to one year or six months of debt service on the bonds.

Cities, counties, and other general-purpose local governments in many states issue special tax or revenue bonds for specific capital purposes such as street improvements, downtown revitalization, or solid-waste management. Special districts and authorities at the local level also issue special or limited tax or revenue bonds.

Special districts and authorities   A special district or authority is a separate governmental entity established under state law to provide a specific service or set of related services in a specific geographic area. It is used in many states to provide a wide array of local services: utility, drainage and stormwater, soil and water conservation, parks and recreation, hospital and public health, library, fire protection, street, and other services.

The service areas of many special districts and authorities extend over regions that include areas and citizens of several general-purpose local governments. Economies of scale are achieved in having a single special district or authority provide the service throughout the region rather than having each general-purpose local government in the region provide the service to its own citizens. Sometimes, however, the service area for other special districts or authorities is entirely within one general-purpose jurisdiction (for example, the downtown or a neighborhood in a city or part of a county experiencing drainage and flooding problems); citizens in this area want a service that citizens in other parts of the city or county do not want, or they desire a level of service over and above that provided elsewhere in the jurisdiction. And some special districts and authorities have service areas that are coterminous with that of a general-purpose local government. They are established to recognize special needs or to allow a service to be administered and financed separately from the general activities of the local government.

Special districts or authorities serving multiple jurisdictions or broad geographic areas usually have their own governing boards, staffs, and substantial policy-making and administrative autonomy. Many districts that serve a specific area that is within or coterminous with a general-purpose local government are governed by the governing board of the general-purpose local government.[79]

Almost every special district or authority has its own specific tax or revenue source. Special districts usually depend on user fees and related revenue associated with an enterprise or service, and they levy one or more taxes. Many districts also charge user fees and raise other revenues that support their services.

If the user fees and related revenues charged by a special district or authority cover the full cost of the service it provides and can also cover debt service on bonds, the district or authority can issue revenue bonds to finance capital improvements. Because many special authorities do not have taxing power, the bonds or debt that they issue must be revenue bonds or capital lease financing secured by the property financed. Such authorities cannot issue special tax or GO bonds. If the user fee and related revenue stream of the authority is strong, revenue bonds are probably the most practical and economical alternative for financing a major project or improvement.

Many special districts do not charge fees for the services they provide, or they charge fees that cover only a portion of the full cost of the services. To generate the revenue needed to support the services, these districts rely on specific taxes (a limited property tax, a tax on alcoholic-beverage sales, or another special sales tax, for example). When such special districts issue debt to finance capital improvements, the debt is often special tax or revenue debt secured by the limited or special taxes available to the district. State authorizing law or a charter provision usually establishes specific tax rates or sets a ceiling on the tax rates that districts may charge. This limitation makes the tax-secured debt that they issue a special or limited tax rather than GO debt. For example, if a district is authorized to levy a property tax, the tax authority is usually limited to a certain number of cents per $100 or mills per $1,000 of value or is capped in some other way, with no exception for debt service on bonds.

The credit quality of the special or limited tax debt issued by special districts depends on the breadth, growth, and reliability of the tax base generating the taxes and related revenues pledged to secure the bonds or debt. This, in turn, depends on the strength of the local and regional economy, the extent to which the district's tax base grows in response to economic expansion in the district or region, the district's susceptibility to swings in the business cycle, and its ability to annex property and expand its tax base and revenues. Tax, fee, and other revenue must be sufficient to cover O&M expenses and debt service and also meet unforeseen needs.

Few special districts or authorities are able to rely on contributions or transfers from general-purpose governments whose citizens they serve. Most are expected to stand on their own if they intend to sell debt secured by special or limited taxes or revenues.

Special tax or revenue bonds issued by special districts or authorities have the same covenants as such debt issued by general-purpose local governments, but the covenants tend to be more demanding. The narrower revenue and tax sources supporting special districts increase the credit risks associated with their debt. Pooling special district or authority debt and selling shares in the pool to investors can significantly reduce risk because the investor is not exposed to significant loss if only one or two of the special districts in the pool defaults.[80]

If a special district is able to levy an unlimited property tax, it can also issue unlimited tax or GO bonds. Some special districts have issued GO bonds, secured by unlimited property taxes, but then paid debt service on the bonds from user fees charged for the services that they provide.[81] The credit quality of this debt depends on the breadth of the tax base subject to the district's taxing authority. If the tax base spans a relatively small geographic area or pertains only to certain kinds of property, the bonds are rated as special tax debt rather than as GO bonds, and the covenants required for the debt are similar to those for special tax or revenue debt.

Special assessment bonds

Special assessment bonds (or debt) are issued to finance public improvements that benefit adjacent or nearby property. The bonds are secured by assessments against the benefiting property and are levied by the local government that is undertaking the project. See Chapter 6 for a discussion of special assessments.

In some but not all states, local governments may finance a special assessment project by issuing debt secured by assessment revenues. The assessment revenues in any year must be sufficient to cover debt service on the special assessment debt. Investors look for considerable excess coverage to

---

Mello-Roos special districts in California

California's Mello-Roos districts deserve special mention. Mello-Roos districts throughout California have issued substantial amounts of debt needed by many California local governments to finance infrastructure. Since the state's citizens approved Proposition 13 in 1978, California's local governments have been effectively barred from issuing significant amounts of full-faith-and-credit GO bonds. Two-thirds of a local jurisdiction's voters must approve GO bonds.

The 1982 Mello-Roos Community Facilities Act provides a financing alternative to GO bonds for many local governments in California. It allows a local governing board to create a Mello-Roos special district, levy new taxes in the district, and pledge those taxes to secure bonds issued to finance public improvements. Mello-Roos districts give California local governments, particularly in growing communities with large, undeveloped tracts, a flexible tool for financing general facilities and infrastructure. The act allows a district to have any shape or boundary and to finance public improvements beyond as well as within the district. While the creation of a district requires the approval of voters, the way the district is drawn limits the voters to a few landowners or developers interested in having the local entity provide public facilities to accommodate their development plans. Any type of tax may be imposed in a Mello-Roos district, as long as the tax is not levied against property values. The tax is often levied as so much per home or residential unit, front footage, or acre. Taxes in Mello-Roos districts are similar in nature to special assessments or impact fees or taxes.

For more information about Mello-Roos districts, see Standard & Poor's, *Public Finance Criteria*, 58–60.

compensate for possible nonpayment of assessments by particular property owners or to compensate for a more general falloff in assessment collections in an economic downturn. By issuing bonds secured by revenues from a variety of assessment projects rather than just one project, a local government can broaden the security for the bonds, improve their attractiveness to investors, and hold down interest costs. The larger the assessment zone supporting a project or group of projects, the stronger the credit of special assessment bonds or debt. The next chapter discusses the specific factors considered by the bond rating agencies when they evaluate special assessment bonds or debt.

Some local governments set up districts in which special taxes as well as special assessments are levied against property in that district; money collected is used for public improvements that benefit that property. This broadens the security for debt issued to finance improvements in the district.[82]

Tax increment bonds

Tax increment bonds or debt finance public infrastructure and facilities that support private development or redevelopment in a specific **tax increment district** (TID) or zone.[83] Security for the bonds is the expected growth of the property tax base and resulting revenues (the tax increment) in the district after the district is established. The incremental tax base and revenues remain legally earmarked to secure the bonds for the length of time the bonds are outstanding. The tax increment property tax revenues may be spent only for debt service on the bonds or for other purposes benefiting the district as authorized in the bond contract. These other purposes are usually pay-as-go capital project financing or spending for public services in the district as long as such financing and spending do not detract from the resources needed to pay debt service on the tax increment bonds.

Formation of a TID captures growth in the property tax base of the local government establishing the district and issuing bonds. It also often captures growth in the tax base and revenues of any governmental entities that tax property in the TID.[84] In other words, if a city forms a tax increment district, and if the county (within which the city and TID are located) levies taxes on property in this district, the county's tax rate applies only to the property tax base that existed when the TID was formed. New property tax revenues resulting from growth in the tax base after the TID is formed secure the bonds, and use of the revenues will be limited to paying debt service on the bonds and to spending for other purposes within the TID until the bonds are paid off. This can occur even if the overlapping and underlying governments that are taxing property in a TID have no say in its creation and in the issuance of the bonds. After the bonds are paid off, revenues resulting from the growth in the TID property tax base become available to the issuer and to any overlapping and underlying governments that tax property in the TID.

Tax increment bonds are also called **economic development bonds.** They have been used most often to spur redevelopment in central cities and blighted neighborhoods. The rationale is that redeveloped property will produce more revenue than marginal or dilapidated private property. Some local jurisdictions issue tax increment bonds to finance public facilities and infrastructure to support new business and residential development on vacant or previously undeveloped tracts of land. Some of that new development and growth may be up-scale commercial and residential development.[85]

Tax increment bonds can be issued directly by a local government or through a local redevelopment or development agency that serves the local jurisdiction. Even when an agency is used, the markets consider the local government to be, in effect, the issuer.

Specific constitutional and statutory authorization is usually required for a local government to issue tax increment bonds. More than forty states now authorize local governments, or their redevelopment or development agencies, to issue them.[86]

One of the arguments against tax increment bonds is that they limit or dilute the unlimited tax base that secures GO bonds.[87] The courts have not been persuaded by this argument because this dilution occurs only with regard to growth in the tax base after a TID is formed. If tax increment bonds were to dilute or weaken the property tax base and revenues already securing GO bonds when a TID is formed, the courts would be much more likely to strike down, rather than affirm, the authorizing law.

Some tax increment bonds are targeted to finance infrastructure that serves just one development or property owner, or only a few major developments or property owners. For example, a local government may form a TID, issue tax increment bonds, and spend the proceeds to build roads and utility facilities that are used predominantly by a single manufacturing firm. If more than 10 percent of the proceeds of bonds issued by a state or local government benefits a single individual or firm, the bonds are classified under federal tax laws as private activity rather than governmental or public purpose debt.[88] Private activity bonds do not have tax-exempt status. As a result, some tax increment bonds issued by local governments are taxable securities; that is, investors buying the bonds must pay federal income taxes on the interest that they earn on the bonds. To qualify for tax-exempt status, the proceeds from local government tax increment bonds must be spent to finance facilities and infrastructure that benefit the public rather than only one firm or a few firms or property owners.

Another issue in tax increment financing concerns the size of the district. If the TID is only a small geographic area, the small size limits the security for tax increment bonds and also increases the probability that the bonds will be taxable rather than tax exempt. The larger and more diverse the tax base supporting the bonds and generally the larger the TID, the better the credit quality of tax increment bonds. On the other hand, a large TID removes more growth from the general tax base for the local issuer and for any overlapping or underlying local governments that levy tax on property in the district. Because some local governments have overreached in extending TID boundaries, some states limit the local governments that can create TIDs, the purposes for which the districts can be created (development versus redevelopment), the types of growth (real versus personal, residential versus business) in the property tax base that can be pledged to secure the bonds, and the term and duration of the TID.[89]

Several other important issues arise in creating TIDs and issuing tax increment bonds. The creation of a TID usually requires an official finding that development would not occur without the TID. Second, while overlapping and underlying units may not need to approve the TID and issuance of tax increment bonds, their overt or tacit support may be needed to win sufficient political backing for creation of the district. Third, many TIDs are created only after important development commitments are in hand.[90]

If tax increment bonds are issued before private development commitments are in place, the bonds are secured by estimated future property growth. In some cases, estimates of such growth are firm and provide a strong enough security for investors. In other cases, the estimates are not so convincing, and the issuer must offer additional security for the bonds. Additional security may include one or more of the following: bond insurance, water-sewer revenue or other revenue collected by the issuer from within the TID, special or limited taxes in the TID, or a citywide special tax. In some cases, the local issuer provides a backup full-faith-and-credit pledge for tax increment bonds, making them GO debt and considerably improving their attractiveness. Rather than issue tax increment bonds before private development occurs, some issuers require the developer to put in the public infrastructure. With private development in place and future property tax revenue assured, tax increment bonds are then issued to repay the developer for the cost of the public improvements. As an alternative, tax increment bonds can be issued and the proceeds escrowed until the development, including public improvements, is complete. The proceeds are then released to reimburse the developer for the cost of the public improvements.[91]

Because of the risks associated with tax increment bonds, the bonds include the same sort of security provisions that are in revenue bonds, capital leases, and special tax bonds. Some of these provisions are more stringent, however. For example, a high debt service coverage ratio is typically required. One authority says that incremental and any other revenues dedicated to the bonds should be at least 150 percent of annual debt service.[92]

Non-property-tax debt and non-local-tax debt

In some states, local governments have the authority to issue debt secured by all legally available revenue except the local property (ad valorem) tax. Florida was the first state to authorize such debt.[93] Such debt enables local governments to switch the burden of financing improvements from the local property tax base to other taxes or revenues.[94] Still other states authorize local government to issue SO debt secured by any revenues other than taxes levied by the issuer.[95] Because neither unlimited taxing power nor the issuer's full faith and credit are pledged to secure non–ad valorem or non-local-tax debt, such debt does not have to be approved by the voters in a referendum.

In addition to the property tax or all locally levied taxes, other revenues may be practically, if not legally, unavailable to secure these kinds of SO bonds. For example, enterprise revenue is unavailable to the extent that it is already committed to secure revenue bonds and to meet coverage requirements for debt service on the bonds. Revenues or other financial resources that are in trust funds or that are earmarked by federal or state law for specific purposes, such as welfare payments, are also unavailable.

In Florida, the courts have helped define the general nature and the specific covenants that must accompany non–ad valorem tax bonds. The central covenant is a promise by the local issuer to raise and budget annually from "all legally available non–ad valorem revenues" sufficient amounts to cover debt service on the bonds secured by the covenant. To prevent the use of ad valorem tax revenue for the payment of debt service on non-property-tax bonds, the courts in Florida have limited the amount of such debt that a local government may issue based on the non–ad valorem tax revenue available.[96]

A more restrictive security for this type of debt is a pledge of all available revenue *except taxes levied by the issuer.* North Carolina's cities and counties use this pledge for their SO debt. Cities in the state levy only the property tax and a few other minor taxes. If not otherwise restricted or already pledged to secure other debt, a North Carolina city may include any one or more of the following revenues in this pledge: utility or enterprise revenue, alcoholic beverage control profits, solid-waste tipping fees and other solid-waste revenue, revenue from the local sales tax (counties rather than cities levy this tax and share the proceeds with cities), all state-enacted taxes that are shared with cities, and certain other local revenues. Except for the local sales tax, which they levy, North Carolina's counties may pledge the same sources to secure SO bonds.[97]

Although a North Carolina city or county may not secure SO debt with any of the taxes that it levies, it may use its property or any other tax revenue to help make debt service payments on the debt. This again brings to mind the difference that can exist between the security for debt and the sources of revenue used to repay debt.[98]

Local use of non–ad valorem tax bonds has grown in recent years in states such as Florida, where tourism is important.[99] The rationale is that many local public facilities in these states serve tourists and other visitors as well as local citizens. Therefore, to finance these facilities, it is more appropriate to issue bonds secured by a variety of revenue sources that visitors as well local residents pay, rather than GO bonds secured by property taxes that only local residents pay.

When a local government issues non–ad valorem or non-local-tax bonds, it may have to identify one or more specific revenue sources to pay debt service on the bonds. If the sources are substantial and reliable, this improves the bonds' credit quality. Indeed, the rating agencies recommend that issuers identify several different specific revenue sources to repay such debt.[100] One authority suggests that this can be viewed as changing the nature of the bonds from non–ad valorem tax or non-local-tax debt to special revenue debt.[101]

Non–ad valorem tax and non-local-tax bonds typically include the same security provisions as revenue bonds, capital leases, and other forms of SO debt:

- A debt service reserve fund or a surety bond equal to one year or six months of debt service
- Pledged revenues exceeding debt service by a specified ratio before additional bonds of the same type can be issued (an additional bonds test)
- A trustee to approve payments for construction and monitor the issuer's compliance with bond covenants.

Moral obligation debt

Moral obligation debt differs from other state and local debt in that the pledge or security imposes no legal requirement to make debt service payments. The pledge is a promise of the issuer to ask for the appropriation of revenues to make debt service payments in the future.[102] Moral obligation debt came into use in the 1960s, and, like capital leasing and most other types of SO debt, it was created to sidestep voter approval requirements for GO bonds.

A moral obligation pledge is often a backup pledge for bonds that are secured first by a specific revenue source or asset. If specific program or project revenues are insufficient to cover debt service on the bonds, bondholders will look to the moral obligation pledge of the state or local issuer and expect the issuer to find other revenues to pay the debt service.

State governments have issued most moral obligation debt, using the moral obligation pledge to strengthen the security for special tax or revenue bonds issued by state agencies for specific purposes. For example, some state housing agencies and state bond banks for local governments issue special revenue bonds to which the states also give their moral obligation pledge.[103] Some cities and counties have issued moral obligation debt in recent years for local housing, downtown redevelopment, and certain other projects.

Market assessment of the credit quality of a moral obligation pledge depends on how clearly the issuer of the pledge specifies the promise to provide revenue to cover debt service payments on the debt. Chapter 8 addresses factors that the rating agencies consider in evaluating such debt.

Conclusion

Local governments issue different types of debt to meet their capital financing needs. GO bonds secured by the full faith and unlimited taxing power of the issuer continue to be widely used for general-purpose infrastructure such as street and road improvements; facilities that are used directly by the public, such as parks and recreational complexes; projects associated with new initiatives, such as a new local library; and other projects that have broad public or community support and that are likely to be approved by the voters in a referendum. Because they offer the highest security to investors, GO bonds typically have interest rates and issuance costs lower than other types of local government debt.

Revenue bonds are secured by the earnings and other revenues of a self-supporting enterprise or service. Because revenue bonds are not secured by unlimited taxing power, they are not subject to voter approval in a referendum in most states. Local governments issue revenue bonds to finance the infrastructure and facilities for self-supporting utilities (such as water-sewer systems) and for other services organized as enterprises (such as airports, parking facilities, and solid-waste collection and disposal).

Capital leasing has become a very important capital financing source for local governments in many states. Like bonds, local capital lease debt is generally tax exempt; that is, the interest portions of the periodic lease payments are exempt from federal income taxes. Typical leases are secured by the property financed. To avoid state referenda requirements for debt, the issuer's payment obligations under typical capital leases are subject to annual appropriation or abatement. Local governments often use capital leases to finance mandated facilities and projects such as jails that may not be popular with voters, essential facilities and infrastructure for which the issuer is unlikely to exercise nonappropriation or abatement, utility or other projects that serve a specific clientele rather than the whole community and for which user fees are not adequate to support revenue bonds, and other kinds of projects.

Local governments and special authorities or districts in many states issue various kinds of special or limited tax or revenue bonds. The security for such bonds may be a limited or special tax or other revenue source, special assessments or charges against benefiting property, growth in property tax valuation, revenue sources other than the local property tax or ad valorem and/or any locally levied taxes, or a moral obligation to repay the debt. Local governments use these types of debt to impose the cost of bonds on specific, benefiting property or users of capital facilities, to provide infrastructure to spur development or redevelopment, and to avoid seeking voter approval of GO bonds to meet certain local capital needs such as solid-waste projects. Moral obligation pledges are often used to strengthen a special tax or revenue pledge through a general promise of repayment by the issuer. In some states, one or more of these types of debt are used because GO bonds are not available.

Notes

1 This discussion of different types of debt, and particularly the discussion of the security for debt, draws on two major sources. The first is M. David Gelfand, ed., *State and Local Government Debt Financing* (Eagan, Minn.: West Group, Vol. 1, 1986; Vol. 2, 1986; and Vol. 3, 1990). Cumulative supplements are issued annually to update the book's treatment of specific topics or issues. Most of the chapters in the three volumes have been updated and replaced by new chapters issued from 1995 through 2001. The second source is David M. Lawrence, *Financing Capital Projects in North Carolina*, 2nd ed. (Chapel Hill, N.C.: Institute of Government at the University of North Carolina at Chapel Hill, 1994).

2 Gelfand, *State and Local Government Debt Financing*, Vol. 1, Chap. 1, "Authority of State and Local Governments to Issue Debt: Sources and Limitation," and Vol. 3, Chap. 11, "State Laws Regarding Issuance of Bonds and Notes." Both chapters were updated and reissued in 1999.

3 Generally, a home-rule city or local government is one to which state law grants substantial powers of self-government, for example, the power of the city council to authorize and issue GO bonds without a voter referendum. In Virginia, cities have broader authority to issue GO debt than counties. See Benjamin B. Canada, "Finance Criteria and Options for Virginia Localities after a School Bond Defeat" (master's thesis, University of North Carolina at Chapel Hill, April 3, 2000).

4 Gelfand, *State and Local Government Debt Financing*, Vol. 1, Chap. 5, "Federal Tax Exemption: History and Overview," and Vol. 1, Chap. 6, "Private Activity Bonds." Chapter 5 was updated and reissued in 2002; Chapter 6 was updated and reissued in 1998.

5 See "A Decade of Municipal Finance," *The Bond Buyer*, May 8, 2001, and the U.S. Census Bureau, *Statistical Abstract of the United States 2000* (Washington, D.C.: U.S. Government Printing Office, December 2000), 313.

6 Gelfand, *State and Local Government Debt Financing*, Vol. 1, Chap. 2, "Traditional Bonds and Notes," 3–4. Chapter 2 was updated and reissued in 1998.

7 Ibid., 4–5.

8 Lawrence, *Financing Capital Projects in North Carolina*, 5–6.

9 Ibid. and Gelfand, *State and Local Government Debt Financing*, Vol. 1, Chap. 2, "Traditional Bonds and Notes," 3–4.

10 Gelfand, *State and Local Government Debt Financing*, Vol. 2, Chap. 9, "Debt Ceilings and Other Restrictions on Debt Financing: Compliance, Avoidance, and Evasion," 12–13. Chapter 9 was updated and reissued in 2002.

11 Ibid., Vol. 3, Chap. 11, "State Laws Regarding the Issuance of Bonds and Notes," 62–65. In many states, voters must also approve the issuance of revenue bonds. Chapter 11 was updated and reissued in 1999.

12 See the North Carolina Constitution, Article V, Section 4(2).

13 See the Virginia Constitution, Article VII, Section 10. This limitation does not apply to debt issued for self-supporting public enterprises or to revenue anticipation notes maturing in one year or less. More full-faith-and-credit GO debt than the amount allowed by the 10 percent limit may be issued if the voters approve the additional debt in a referendum. See City of Portsmouth, Virginia Adopted Operating Budget, Fiscal Year July 1, 1998, through June 30, 1999, with estimates for July 1, 1999, to June 30, 2000, p. 39. Debt authorizations and limitations in Virginia vary according to the type of local

government (for example, county or city). See Canada, "Finance Criteria and Options for Virginia Localities after a School Bond Defeat."

14 Sheila Lee, debt administrator, finance department, Memphis, Tennessee; telephone conversation with author, March 2003; orig. in A. John Vogt and Lisa Cole, *A Guide to Municipal Leasing* (Chicago: GFOA, 1983).

15 Virginia Beach City Charter, Section 6.05:1.

16 Gelfand, *State and Local Government Debt Financing,* Vol. 3, Chap. 11, p. 68.

17 Ibid., Vol. 3, Chap. 11, 75–76.

18 Standard & Poor's, *Public Finance Criteria* (New York: S&P, 2000), 95–99. A local government's lease debt is usually assigned a rating one full category below the issuer's GO debt. Revenue bonds are also usually rated below GO bonds. The spread can be less than one full rating category, depending on the credit and earnings history of the revenue bonds. The revenue bonds for very strong enterprises can be rated nearly as high as the issuer's GO bonds.

19 *The Bond Buyer,* May 3, 2001, p. 41.

20 Robert L. Ehlers, *Ehlers on Public Finance: Building Better Communities* (Rochester, Minn.: Lone Oak Press, 1998), 371; and Standard & Poor's, *Public Finance Criteria,* 106.

21 Moody's Investors Service, *Moody's on Revenue Bonds: The Fundamentals of Revenue Bond Credit Analysis* (New York: Moody's Investors Service, Inc., 1994), 1.

22 Standard & Poor's, *Public Finance Criteria,* 106 and 154. Gelfand separates special tax bonds from revenue bonds and defines revenue bonds as those secured by and paid from the revenues of a self-supporting enterprise system or project. See Gelfand, *State and Local Government Debt Financing,* Vol. 1, Chap. 2, 7–8 and 15–17.

23 Moody's Investors Service, *Moody's on Revenue Bonds,* 5.

24 Gelfand, *State and Local Government Debt Financing,* Vol. 1, Chap. 2, 15–16.

25 Moody's Investors Service, *Moody's on Revenue Bonds,* 9–10.

26 Ibid., 1–2.

27 Winston-Salem, North Carolina, sold revenue bonds for its strong water-sewer system on April 15, 2001. The bonds

were rated AAA by Standard & Poor's, Aa2 by Moody's, and AA by Fitch. The interest rates for the different maturities ranged from 3.75 percent to 5.25 percent. The city has a triple-A GO bond rating from all three rating agencies. See Official Statement, prepared by Salomon Smith Barney, "$105,400,000 City of Winston-Salem, North Carolina, Water and Sewer System Revenue and Revenue Refunding Bonds, Series 2001," cover page.

28 Revenue bond purposes or types of projects are discussed in Moody's Investors Service, *Moody's on Revenue Bonds,* 3, 10–15; and in Standard & Poor's, *Public Finance Criteria,* Chap. 3, "Revenue Bonds."

29 For an analysis of laws regulating private activity bonds issued by state and local governments, see Gelfand, *State and Local Government Debt Financing,* Vol. 1, Chap. 6. The interest on certain private activity bonds or debt, such as interest on state housing finance agency debt, small-issue industrial revenue bonds, and qualifying 501(c)(3) hospitals and certain other organizations, is tax-exempt subject to state and project dollar or volume caps on private activity bonds, as provided by federal law.

30 Moody's Investors Service, *Moody's on Revenue Bonds,* 2–3; and Standard & Poor's, *Public Finance Criteria,* 106. Moody's classified revenue bond projects in terms of essentiality and demand; this classification, although useful, is outdated. Since 1994, when the classification was done, conditions for some enterprise services have become more competitive. These changed conditions would affect the classification scheme if it were updated.

31 Moody's Investors Service, *Moody's on Revenue Bonds,* 12; and Standard & Poor's, *Public Finance Criteria,* 129–134.

32 For example, North Carolina General Statute 159-96. See Lawrence, *Financing Capital Projects in North Carolina,* 47–48, for a discussion.

33 Gelfand, *State and Local Government Debt Financing,* Vol. 1, Chap. 2, p. 15, states that revenue bonds are not generally subject to voter approval and state debt ceilings. However, in Vol. 3, Chap. 11,

63–65, Gelfand says that most states require an election to authorize local government revenue bonds.

34 Ibid., Vol. 1, Chap. 2, 15.

35 Ibid., Vol. 1, Chap. 2, 16.

36 Official Statement for "$15,630,000 City of Henderson, North Carolina, Combined Enterprise System Revenue Bonds, Series 2001," 10.

37 Moody's Investors Service, *Moody's on Revenue Bonds*, 8.

38 See Lawrence, *Financing Capital Projects in North Carolina*, 12–14, for information on covenants.

39 Gelfand, *State and Local Government Debt Financing*, Vol. 1, Chap. 2, 18.

40 Ibid., 17–20.

41 Moody's Investors Service, *Moody's on Revenue Bonds*, 8. Staff of the North Carolina Local Government Commission, which approves and sells North Carolina local government debt, in March 2003 confirmed that debt service reserve requirements have been waived for strong issuers of revenue bonds in the state.

42 Moody's Investors Service, *Moody's on Revenue Bonds*, 9.

43 Ibid., 50–52. Lawrence identifies the different funds that are associated with revenue bond issues and discusses the priorities that exist in the flow of resources among them. Lawrence, *Financing Capital Projects in North Carolina*, 50–52.

44 Staff member of the North Carolina Local Government Commission, which approves and sells all revenue bonds issued by the state's localities, conversation with author, March 2003.

45 Gelfand, *State and Local Government Debt Financing*, Vol. 1, Chap. 2, 19.

46 In some revenue bond issues, the trustee actually receives operating receipts, pays O&M expenses and bondholders, and then transmits the balance of receipts for the period to the issuer. In most issues, the trustee monitors the collection and disbursement of operating revenues to ensure that flow-of-funds requirements are met.

47 A fuller description of the role of the trustee in revenue bond and SO bond financing is provided in Lawrence, *Financing Capital Projects in North Carolina*, 48–50.

48 These rules appear in "Accounting for Leases," *Statement of the Financial Accounting Standards Board, No. 13* (Stamford, Conn.: FASB, 1976). Also see National Council on Governmental Accounting, Statement No. 5, "Accounting and Financial Reporting for Lease Agreements of State and Local Governments," which appears in Governmental Accounting Standards Board, *Governmental Accounting and Financial Reporting Standards-Statement 34 Edition* (Norwalk, Conn.: GASB, June 30, 2001), 100–104. paragraphs 18–21.

49 For an overview of operating leases and capital leases, see Vogt and Cole, *A Guide to Municipal Leasing*, 16–17. Although this book was published in 1983, its coverage of different types of leases in Chap. 2, "Types of Leases and Identifying Characteristics of Tax-exempt Leases," is still current.

50 Donald E. Kieso and Jerry J. Weygand, *Intermediate Accounting*, 4th ed. (New York: John Wiley & Sons, 1983), 979 ff.

51 Vogt and Cole, *A Guide to Municipal Leasing*, 16–17.

52 Ibid., 12–16. IRS Revenue Ruling 55-540 and these criteria that the ruling puts forward are still in effect and guiding administrative decisions by the IRS in ruling on particular lease transactions. See, for example, IRS CCA 200237020, September 13, 2002. A recent discussion of the criteria for distinguishing between conditional sales and true leases appears in Gelfand, *State and Local Government Debt Financing*, Vol. 1, Chap. 3, 15–22.

53 Vogt and Cole, *A Guide to Municipal Leasing*, 27–29. If lease obligation is for a private rather than a governmental purpose, interest may not be exempt. Such interest also could be subject to the alternative minimum tax.

54 Gelfand, *State and Local Government Debt Financing*, Vol. 1, Chap. 2, 20.

55 Moody's Investors Service, *Moody's on Leasing: The Fundamentals of Credit Analysis for Lease Revenue Bonds and Certificates of Participation* (New York: Moody's Investors Service, Inc., 1995), 1–2.

56 Ibid.

57 Ibid., 3 and 8–16.

58 Ibid., 3–4.

59 Janice Burke, executive secretary, North Carolina Local Government Commission, conversation with author, March 2003. The commission approves and sells North Carolina local government debt.

60 Moody's Investors Service, *Moody's on Leasing*, 13.

61 Standard & Poor's, *Public Finance Criteria*, 100–101.

62 The levy of these taxes in Mecklenburg County was authorized by the North Carolina General Assembly; see *Session Laws of North Carolina, 1989 General Assembly, Extra Session 1990*, 63–70.

63 Moody's Investors Service, *Moody's on Leasing*, 10 and 12.

64 These questions are adaptations of questions appearing in Standard & Poor's, *Public Finance Criteria*, 96.

65 This list of projects is based on criteria that Moody's considers in gauging essentiality. See Moody's Investors Service, *Moody's on Leasing*, 12–13.

66 See Standard & Poor's, *Public Finance Criteria*, 96.

67 Moody's Investors Service, *Moody's on Leasing*, 13.

68 Lawrence, *Financing Capital Projects in North Carolina*, 62–63.

69 Revenue Ruling 63-20, 1963-1 C.B. 24. Although 40 years old, this ruling continues to be the basis for state and local governments to establish on-behalf-of, nonprofit organizations as conduits for the issuance of debt. An example of IRS application of 63-20 to local government debt financing is provided by an IRS Private Letter Ruling issued on January 6, 1995; see Priv. Ltr. Rul. 95-01-002 Jan. 6, 1995. For an explanation of the application of Revenue Ruling 63-20 to local government capital leasing, see Vogt and Cole, *A Guide to Municipal Leasing*, 52–54 and 223.

70 In North Carolina, capital leases need not be approved by the voters, but they are subject to the net debt limit (8 percent of taxable valuation) that applies to GO debt and other general-purpose debt.

71 North Carolina General Statute 160A-20 requires that a local government hold a public hearing for any capital lease financing involving real property.

72 This requirement is found in SEC Rule 15c2-12 (effective January, 1990). The rule established disclosure requirements for underwriters who buy and sell municipal securities. The rule requires the preparation and distribution of an official statement in connection with sales of municipal securities of $1 million or more. See Gelfand, *State and Local Government Debt Financing*, Vol. 2, Chap. 8, especially 44–45.

73 Gelfand, *State and Local Government Debt Financing*, Vol. 1, Chap. 2, 7, refers to such bonds as special tax bonds. Standard & Poor's actually classifies many bonds secured by special taxes or revenues as revenue bonds. See Standard & Poor's, *Public Finance Criteria*, Chap. 3, "Revenue Bonds."

74 Gelfand, *State and Local Government Debt Financing*, Vol. 1, Chap. 2, 11–13. For a more detailed discussion of special assessment bonds, see Ehlers, *Ehlers on Public Finance*, Chap. 26; Also see Standard & Poor's, *Public Finance Criteria*, 45–46.

75 An overview of tax increment debt is provided in Gelfand, *State and Local Government Debt Financing*, Vol. 1, Chap. 2, 8–10, 52–57.

76 For other discussions of bonds secured by all available revenue except ad valorem taxes, see Standard & Poor's, *Public Finance Criteria*, 35; and Gelfand, *State and Local Government Debt Financing*, Vol. 1, Chap. 2, 10–11. SO bonds secured by all legally available revenue except locally levied taxes are described in Lawrence, *Financing Capital Projects in North Carolina*, 16–19.

77 See Standard & Poor's, *Public Finance Criteria*, 103–105, for another discussion of moral obligation bonds.

78 This discussion draws on Gelfand, *State and Local Government Debt Financing*, Vol. 1, Chap. 2, 7–8; and Standard & Poor's, *Public Finance Criteria*, 30–42.

79 For many fire districts in North Carolina, for example, the county commissioners serve as the governing boards of the districts, set the tax rates for them, and contract with volunteer fire departments to serve the districts.

80 Standard & Poor's, *Public Finance Criteria*, 51.

81 For example, the Raleigh-Durham Airport Authority is also a special tax district. GO bonds issued by the district

are secured by unlimited property taxing authority in both Durham and Wake counties, North Carolina. Issuance of the bonds had to be approved not only by the airport authority but also by the boards of commissioners of both counties. Debt service on the bonds has been paid exclusively from airport user fees. No property taxes have had to be levied for this debt service.

82 Ehlers, *Ehlers on Public Finance*, 253.

83 See Craig Johnson, "Tax Increment Debt Finance: An Analysis of the Mainstreaming of a Fringe Sector," *Public Budgeting and Finance* 19, no. 1 (Spring 1999), 26–46, for a report on the use of tax increment bonds in the early and mid-1990s and an analysis of their credit quality.

84 Ibid., 263.

85 Sonya Smith, "The Texas Tax Increment Financing Act: In Houston, Blight Is in the Eye of the Beholder" (master's thesis, University of North Carolina at Chapel Hill, April 3, 2000), 3.

86 Smith, "The Texas Tax Increment Financing Act," 1.

87 *Leonard v. City of Spokane*, 127 Wash 2d 194, 897 P2d 358 (1995).

88 Gelfand, *State and Local Government Debt Financing*, Vol. 1, Chap. 2, 9.

89 Ehlers, *Ehlers on Public Finance*, 261, 267.

90 See Ibid., Chap. 27 for an in-depth discussion of these issues.

91 Ibid., 264.

92 Ibid., 267.

93 Gelfand, *State and Local Government Debt Financing*, Vol. 1, Chap. 2, 10.

94 Standard & Poor's *Public Finance Criteria*, 35.

95 Lawrence, *Financing Capital Projects in North Carolina*, 16–17.

96 Gelfand, *State and Local Government Debt Financing*, Vol. 1, Chap. 2, 10.

97 Lawrence, *Financing Capital Projects in North Carolina*, 16–17.

98 Ibid.

99 Standard & Poor's, *Public Finance Criteria*, 35–36.

100 Ibid.

101 Lawrence, *Financing Capital Projects in North Carolina*, 18.

102 The discussion here on moral obligation debt draws on Standard & Poor's, *Public Finance Criteria*, 103–105.

103 State municipal bond banks lend money to smaller local governments that have difficulty borrowing from the municipal bond market at reasonable interest rates.

8 Bond ratings

A bond rating is a current opinion on the creditworthiness of an issuer with regard to particular debt, a type of debt, or a financing program of the issuer.[1] A rating assesses the willingness and ability of the issuer "to make timely payments of amounts due" over the term of the debt.[2] Local governments obtain nationally recognized bond ratings to make their bonds and debt more attractive to investors. Bond ratings broaden the market for local government debt, and this increases the number of investors who are interested in buying a local issuer's debt. The more investors who compete to buy the debt, the lower the interest rates the issuer must pay, more than off-setting the costs of the ratings. In addition, the independent review necessary for a bond rating can identify problems in finance, management, and governance, providing valuable information that can help local officials remedy those problems. This chapter:

- Provides an overview of bond ratings and the bond rating process
- Identifies rating agencies' criteria for evaluating different types of local government debt (general obligation [GO] bonds, revenue bonds, capital leases including certificates of participation, and several types of special obligation [SO] debt)
- Identifies important characteristics of local governments with top-rated GO debt and considers what local government officials can do to maintain or improve their jurisdiction's bond ratings.

Overview

This section defines what a bond rating is, explains the importance of bond ratings, identifies the national bond rating agencies and the rating categories that they use, provides an overview of the rating process, and briefly comments on rating costs.

What is a bond rating?

A bond rating evaluates a debt issuer's strength or weakness on factors that bear on the issuer's ability and willingness to make principal and interest payments on the debt when due and to comply with other obligations that the issuer assumes under the debt contract. A rating addresses not only the probability that the issuer will make debt service payments but also the legal protection afforded to investors by laws, regulations, and the debt contract. Such protection or security varies by type of debt and also depends on state and federal laws and regulations. According to Standard & Poor's Corporation, a national rating agency, an issuer's rating for long-term debt is based on three general factors:

- **Likelihood of payment**   This refers to the ability and willingness of the issuer to meet its financial commitment under the debt contract.

- **Nature and provisions of the debt contract**   This refers to the security pledged for the debt and other protections afforded to investors under the contract.

- **Protections available to investors**   Laws authorize and limit debt and require or provide for its repayment. Such laws include state constitutional, statutory, and regulatory provisions, as well as state oversight and regulatory practices affecting local debt issuance. They also include federal laws, such as laws on bankruptcy, that affect creditors' rights under debt contracts.[3]

A bond rating is not a recommendation to investors to purchase or hold particular debt. Ratings do not comment on market prices or on the suitability of debt for particular investment portfolios. Neither do they provide any indications of directions or trends in market interest rates, which affect investors' decisions to purchase debt and other fixed income securities.

While a bond rating evaluates the creditworthiness of an issuer, the rating itself applies to particular debt or to a debt program. For example, ratings of local government revenue bonds, capital leases, and SO debt are typically specific to a particular debt issue. Each issue of these types of debt has its own security, indenture provisions, and payment provisions that make the issue unique and result in a unique rating. This is true even when several different issues of, for example, revenue bonds are issued for the same enterprise or are secured by the same special revenue sources. Even here, specific security provisions and indentures can vary from one bond issue to the next. For example, the **parity** (priority of payment of different debt securities generally and in the event of default or bankruptcy) among different revenue bond issues for the same project or enterprise can vary from issue to issue. However, if all security and indenture provisions for different revenue bonds of the same project or enterprise are the same, and if the debt issues have the same parity or standing, all of these bond issues would have the same rating or, in a sense, be rated together or as one class of debt.

GO bonds that are issued by a local government and secured by the full-faith-and-credit pledge or unlimited taxing power of the issuer are also rated as a single class of debt. When a local government obtains a rating for a new issue of GO bonds, that rating is typically the same as the rating for all previous and outstanding GO debt of the issuer. Any changes in the rating of a new issue are applied to outstanding GO debt. Because an issuer's general credit underlies its ability to repay GO bonds and because a GO bond rating usually applies across the board to all of the issuer's GO debt, a GO bond rating has some similarities to what Standard & Poor's calls an "issuer" (rather than an issue) rating. An issuer rating applies generally to the issuer rather than to any specific debt of the issuer.[4]

A debt rating also takes into account credit support from bond insurance or other forms of financial guarantee for debt. Bond insurance guarantees to investors timely debt service payments, and it is now widely used in the municipal debt market. It raises a "stand-alone" rating of the issuer for debt to the triple-A rating of the insurance company. The effect of bond insurance on credit ratings is discussed later in this chapter. Chapter 11 on selling debt examines bond insurance in depth.

While the preponderance of local government debt issued for capital financing purposes is long term (maturing in more than one year), local jurisdictions occasionally issue short-term debt to meet their capital financing needs. Some local governments have issued variable-rate demand bonds to finance certain capital projects. Although such bonds have a term extending over many years, the interest rate(s) for them can vary frequently, often weekly, and investors may "put" or sell the debt back to the issuer each week or period when rates may reset. Ratings of variable-rate demand bonds consider liquidity support for the debt as well as the ability of the issuer to repay the debt when it is due. Two ratings are assigned to such debt, one assessing the long-term creditworthiness of the issuer and the second evaluating the strength of the liquidity support for the put or demand feature of the debt.[5] Local governments also issue other short-term debt, such as bond or grant anticipation notes, for capital financing purposes. Like variable-rate demand bonds, the rating agencies evaluate and rate such notes differently from long-term debt.[6] The sidebar on the next page presents and explains the rating categories for short-term debt that are used in local government capital financing programs.

The importance of bond ratings

Four considerations make bond ratings important to local governments issuing debt. First, a national rating broadens the market for a local government's debt by increasing the number of investors who are able to buy or invest in it, thus creating competition among investors that can lower the interest rates the issuer pays. Many mutual funds, beneficial trusts for individual investors, and insurance companies that buy state and local debt are unable to invest in particular municipal securities unless they are rated, and many other investors, most notably individuals, who buy municipal debt are interested only in rated issues. For this reason, market professionals advise a local government selling debt to obtain at least one and preferably two national ratings for the debt.[7]

Second, investors in municipal debt often trade the debt while it is outstanding, and national ratings can make the debt more marketable and hold down the yields and raise or support the prices at which the debt trades. (Chapter 10 addresses debt interest rates, yields, and prices.)

Third, the independent and comprehensive assessment involved in a bond rating identifies good planning and financial management practices and provides an incentive for officials to continue such practices or to put them into effect. A good bond rating often signals to taxpayers and the community, as well as to investors, that the jurisdiction's officials are good stewards of the taxes and other revenue they are raising and spending and are planning to meet present and future needs. An upgrade in a local government's bond rating suggests to the same interested parties—taxpayers, the community, and investors—that its planning and financial practices or prospects are improving. On the other hand, a rating downgrade often signifies that the local government has planning or management weaknesses or that the balance between political considerations and fiscal discipline and necessities has tilted too far toward the former. In the latter situation, a rating downgrade can catch the attention of local officials and cause them to overcome differences and begin the planning needed to meet current and future challenges.

Finally, bond insurance to guarantee future principal and interest payments is available only for rated debt.

Short-term debt

Several types of short-term debt are used by local governments in capital financing. Both large and small local governments occasionally use bond anticipation or grant notes for projects where long-term debt or grant financing is not available until after a project is built. A growing number of large and medium-size cities and counties are using variable-rate demand bonds or notes for capital projects. This allows them to take advantage of the lower interest rates generally available for short-term debt but not for long-term debt.

The table shows the rating categories used by the three national rating agencies for short-term debt.

Credit quality	Fitch	Moody's	S&P
Exceptionally strong credit quality	F-1+	(Not rated)	SP-1+, A-1+
Strong credit quality	F-1	MIG-1, P-1, VMIG-1	SP-1, A-1
Satisfactory or good credit quality	F-2	MIG-2, P-2, VMIG-2	SP-2, A-2
Adequate or fair credit quality	F-3	MIG-3, P-3, VMIG-3	SP-3, A-3
Speculative	B	SG, NP, NR; no other	B
High default risk	C	designations used	C
In default	D	for speculative or default obligations	D

Sources: Standard & Poor's Corporation, *Public Finance Criteria, 2000* (New York: S&P, 2000), 7 and 85–95, Moody's Investors Service, *Guide to Moody's Ratings, Rating Process, and Rating practices,* 3rd ed. (New York: Moody's Investors Service, Inc., 1997), 28; "Fitch Ratings—Public Finance Rating Definition," www.fitchratings.com.

Standard & Poor's and Moody's include more than one rating designation in certain categories. Standard & Poor's SP designations are for fixed-rate, short-term debt such as bond or grant anticipation notes; S&P rates such debt only if it is investment grade. S&P's letter grades (A, B, C, D) are for commercial paper and variable-rate demand obligations. Only a few very large local governments issue commercial paper, and such paper typically finances short-term cash flow, not capital needs. Some local governments use variable-rate demand obligations for capital financing. The A designations are for investment grade obligations, and the B, C, and D categories are for speculative or defaulted obligations.

In Moody's system, Moody's investment grade (MIG) is for short-term, fixed-rate debt; prime (P) for commercial paper; variable-rate Moody's investment grade (VMIG) for variable-rate demand obligations; SG for speculative fixed-rate obligations, NP for commercial paper that is not prime, and NR for variable-rate demand obligations that are not rated.

Using the S&P rating categories as an example, a local government issuing variable-rate demand bonds would receive two ratings: one for the risks associated with annual debt retirement over the full term of the bonds (for example, twenty years) and the other related to the weekly or other short-term put feature, giving investors the right to demand payment for the bonds at any time that interest rates may vary or reset (for example, weekly). The rating for the put feature evaluates liquidity support for the debt in the case put should occur. The dual ratings might be A+ for the long-term credit risk and A-1 for the put feature of the bonds or debt. An S&P rating for bond anticipation notes maturing in one year and with strong credit features might receive a SP-1 rating.

Rating agencies and categories

Local government debt is rated by three national bond rating agencies: Standard & Poor's Corporation (S&P), a division of McGraw Hill Companies; Moody's Investors Service (Moody's); and Fitch IBCA (Fitch). S&P and Moody's have been rating local government debt for many, many decades. Although Fitch was founded in the early part of the twentieth century, it was not active in the municipal debt market until after 1989. Since then, Fitch's role in rating municipal debt has grown greatly. In 1994, it rated 24 percent of the dollar amount of new municipal debt issued that year. Fitch rated 70 percent of the municipal debt issued in 2002.[8] All three agencies provide independent credit ratings and financial information and have strong research capabilities. All three are headquartered in New York. S&P and Moody's have regional offices in different parts of the country. Rating analysts of all three agencies specialize in rating the debt of particular regions or states, travel extensively throughout their assigned regions and states, and are very familiar with the issuers that they rate. Rating agencies also have analysts who specialize in certain types of debt (for example, leases, refunding bonds, and hospital debt).[9]

Bond rating agencies, for the most part, evaluate and rate publicly sold debt. This is debt that is advertised and marketed through investment bankers or brokers and their sales representatives to investors who may be interested in buying the debt. The investors include mutual funds, banks, insurance companies, and individuals. Ratings of publicly sold local debt are requested and paid for by the issuer. Occasionally, the bond rating agencies also rate local government debt that is privately placed with an individual investor or a small number of investors. In private placements, investors often trigger the rating, requiring the issuer to obtain one or more ratings to gauge the risks involved in the debt. Depending on the relative bargaining positions of the issuer and investors, either may pay for the rating.

The national rating agencies use alpha or letter categories to rate long-term debt (maturity of more than one year). The sidebar on the next page shows the rating categories of each agency and the modifiers of + or − or 1, 2, 3 to indicate relative quality within certain categories. Credit quality for particular categories or groups of categories also is described.

The four highest general categories (AAA, AA, A, and BBB for S&P and Fitch; and Aaa, Aa, A, Baa for Moody's) are investment grade or bank eligible ratings. Any local government issuing debt or having outstanding debt should have investment grade ratings. Banks and some other financial institutions (for example, many municipal mutual funds) are either prohibited from investing in debt that does not have an investment grade rating or those investments are severely limited. Debt rated BB, Ba, or below is speculative and often referred to as junk bonds. Although some mutual funds (junk bond funds) invest large portions of their portfolios in speculative debt, most funds and other investors avoid such debt. Debt rated D by S&P or in one of the D categories by Fitch is in default. Debt rated Caa, Ca, or C by Moody's may be and often is in default.

Most local governments in the municipal debt markets have investment grade ratings. For example, only 0.32 percent of the GO bond ratings and 1.0 percent of the revenue bond ratings of Moody's in 2003 were below investment grade. In 1994, the comparable statistics for GO bonds were 0.8 percent and for revenue bonds 1.7 percent.[10] Most local governments that are not able to achieve investment grade ratings for their debt are small jurisdictions. They often sell debt through state bond banks or other credit guarantee programs

Credit quality	Fitch	Moody's	S&P
Highest grade, maximum safety	AAA	Aaa	AAA
High grade	AA+	Aa1	AA+
	AA	Aa2	AA
	AA−	Aa3	AA−
Upper medium grade	A+	A1	A+
	A	A2	A
	A−	A3	A−
Lower medium grade	BBB+	Baa1	BBB+
	BBB	Baa2	BBB
	BBB−	Baa3	BBB−
Non-investment grade or speculative	BB+	Ba1	BB+
	BB	Ba2	BB
	BB−	Ba3	BB−
Highly speculative	B+	B1	B+
	B	B2	B
	B−	B3	B−
S&P and Fitch: Extremely weak and high potential for default; Moody's: Caa debt may be in default, Ca is often in default; C has little prospect of attaining investment standing	CCC+	Caa	CCC+
	CCC		CCC
	CCC−		CCC−
	CC	Ca	CC
	C	C	C
In default	DDD	—	D
	DD		—
	D		—

Sources: Standard & Poor's Corporation, *Public Finance Criteria, 2000* (New York: S&P, 2000), 7; Moody's Investors Service, *Guide to Moody's Ratings, Rating Process, and Rating Practices,* 3rd ed. (New York: Moody's Investors Service, Inc., 1997), 29. Also see Moody's Investors Service, Public Finance Department, "On Municipal Issues," January 13, 1997. For the Fitch categories, see "Fitch Ratings—Public Finance Rating Definition," www.fitchratings.com, and Philip Angelides, California State Treasurer, "Fitch—Definitions of Bond Ratings," www.treasurer.ca.gov/ratings/fitch. The designations of credit quality are modified versions of the designations used by Tax-Free Bond Headlines, "Long-Term Bond Ratings," www.bondsonline.com.

to raise their debt to investment grade status. Alternatively, they may use federal or state programs established to finance the infrastructure of local governments that have trouble accessing the municipal debt markets.

Within the investment grade categories, AAA or Aaa ratings are given to debt that is sometimes referred to as "gilt edged." Triple-A ratings are assigned only in cases of exceptionally strong capacity to meet principal and interest payments. Adverse conditions are unlikely to affect their capacity to make such payments. In 1998, twenty-one counties and a total of thirty cities, towns, and townships in the nation were rated triple-A by S&P.[11] Despite the economic challenges of recent years, the number of S&P triple-A-rated counties and municipalities nearly doubled from 1998 to early 2003. In early 2003, S&P rated thirty-seven counties and fifty-eight cities, towns, and townships triple-A.[12] The sidebar on pages 223–225 lists these triple-A jurisdictions.

Standard & Poor's Triple-A Ratings, February 27, 2003

Municipalities (cities, towns, and townships) rated AAA by S&P

Arizona	Scottsdale
California	Mountain View
	Palo Alto
	Santa Monica
Connecticut	Avon
	Fairfield
	Greenwich
	Norwalk
	Ridgefield
	Stamford
	West Hartford
Florida	Boca Raton
	Coral Gables
Georgia	Roswell
Illinois	Hinsdale
	Naperville
	Northbrook
Indiana	Indianapolis
Kansas	Overland Park
Massachusetts	Cambridge
	Needham
	Sudbury
	Wellesley
	Weston
	Dover
Michigan	Birmingham
	Bloomfield Hills
	Troy
Minnesota	Bloomington
	Edina
	Minneapolis
	Rochester
	St. Paul
Missouri	Town & Country
Nebraska	Lincoln
	Omaha
New Jersey	Bernards Township
	Millburn Township
	Princeton Township
	Ridgewood Village
	Summit
New York	Bedford Town

(continued)

Municipalities (cities, towns, and townships) rated AAA by S&P

North Carolina	Cary
	Charlotte
	Durham
	Greensboro
	Raleigh
	Winston-Salem
Ohio	Columbus
	Westlake
Pennsylvania	Lower Merion Township
Tennessee	Germantown
Texas	Dallas
	Irving
	Plano
Virginia	Alexandria
	Charlottesville
Washington	Seattle

Counties rated AAA by S&P

Delaware	New Castle
Florida	Palm Beach
Georgia	Cobb
	Gwinnett
Illinois	Du Page
	Lake
Kansas	Johnson
Maryland	Baltimore
	Howard
	Montgomery
Michigan	Kent
	Oakland
Minnesota	Hennepin
	Olmsted
	Ramsey
Missouri	St. Louis
New Jersey	Middlesex
	Monmouth
	Morris
	Somerset
New York	Westchester
North Carolina	Durham
	Forsyth
	Guilford
	Mecklenburg
	Wake
Ohio	Franklin
South Carolina	Greenville

Counties rated AAA by S&P

Texas	Collin
	Dallas
	Tarant
	Travis
Utah	Salt Lake
Virginia	Arlington
	Chesterfield
	Fairfax
	Henrico

Sources: Standard & Poor's Rating Group, " 'AAA' Listing" (February, 27, 2003), sent to the author by Geoffrey Buswick, analyst, Standard & Poor's, Boston.

Debt rated in the AA or Aa categories is high-quality. Such obligations differ from triple-A obligations only in small degrees. A-rated debt indicates strong capacity to pay principal and interest, although it is more vulnerable to adverse conditions than double-A or triple-A debt. Debt in the BBB or Baa categories is associated with adequate capacity for payment, but adverse economic changes or events could weaken this capacity.[13] The preponderance of local government bonds and debt rated by the national rating agencies is in the categories from AA/Aa2 to BBB-/Baa3. In early 2003, 93.8 percent of Moody's GO ratings and 94.94 of its revenue bond ratings were in these categories.[14]

A bond rating evaluates credit risk for debt over its full term. The rating incorporates expectations about future conditions or events as they are known when the rating is given. Actual conditions and events may turn out differently. The bond rating agencies use terms like CreditWatch or RatingAlert to signal unforeseen changes in the future. S&P places debt on CreditWatch when conditions have changed or are expected to depart shortly from the expectations embodied in the original rating. It then conducts a review, normally completed within ninety days, that often does result in a rating change. A listing on CreditWatch is not always followed by a rating change, and ratings for some debt are reviewed and changed without ever appearing on CreditWatch. S&P uses "rating outlook" to provide a long-term assessment for most debt that it rates. The outlook designations are positive, stable, or negative. "Positive" means that a rating may be raised, "stable" that the rating is likely to remain the same, and "negative" that the rating may be lowered. A fourth outlook category, "developing," is used when the future is so unclear that a rating could be raised or lowered.[15] Fitch provides a RatingAlert designation to indicate to investors that there is a reasonable probability for a rating change. RatingAlerts may be positive, indicating a possible upgrade; negative, suggesting a possible downgrade; or evolving, meaning that a rating could go up or down.[16]

Bond ratings from the national agencies tend to track one another, but differences in perspective and varying weightings of criteria by the agencies can result in somewhat different ratings for the same debt. For example, in January of 2001, the GO debt of Greensboro, North Carolina, was rated Aa1 by Moody's and AAA by S&P (next level higher). Fitch has not rated Greensboro's debt.[17] Coral Springs, Florida, provides another example of differences between rating agencies on GO debt. While Fitch and Moody's rates Coral Springs's GO debt triple-A, S&P rates it AA+.[18]

In some parts of the country, local government debt may be rated by state-level or regional organizations. The North Carolina Municipal Council rates city and county debt issuers in that state (using numerical ratings on a 100-point scale); the South Carolina Municipal Council reports on but does not rate local debt issuers in South Carolina. Each council is a private organization composed of bankers, securities dealers, bond attorneys, and certain other participants in the municipal debt markets in those states. The same staff, located in Raleigh, serves both councils. While national bond ratings apply to debt being issued or outstanding, North Carolina Municipal Council ratings apply to the issuer. These ratings or reports are initiated by council staff. Each local government issuing new GO debt or other publicly sold general-purpose debt is rated. Any local government with outstanding GO or general-purpose debt is rated at least once every three years, whether or not it has issued any new debt. Membership dues and assessments to underwriters and other council members rather than charges to issuers cover the expenses and rating or reporting for both councils.

Rating process

The national rating agencies follow a well-defined rating process.[19] To secure a rating from a national agency for new debt, a local government must request it. Generally, three to four weeks are required from request to agency release of the rating. Another week or two is usually needed if an agency is rating a local issuer for the first time or if the rating analyst needs to visit the local issuer. A shorter rating time is possible for frequent—every year or two—issuers of debt that the rating agency has rated many times before.

The rating agencies usually need the following kinds information to rate local government debt:

- Prior three years of annual financial reports and audits, including a description of accounting practices
- Current budget and current capital improvement program
- Official statements for recent debt and financings
- Description of project to be financed with the proposed debt
- Nature of the security for the debt
- Sources and uses of funds for the project
- Cash flow statement for the project
- Engineering and feasibility report if applicable
- Land use map and applicable zoning regulations
- Statements of long-term and short-term debt and lease obligations, maturity dates, and debt service payments, as applicable
- Statement concerning remaining borrowing capacity, tax rate, levy, and general revenue capacities
- Legal authority for debt issuance, including documentation of charter, constitution, and laws concerning debt issuance, if rating agency does not already have these
- Issuer's investment policies

- Names of the bond counsel, financial adviser, underwriter(s), engineer if applicable, and other professionals who are working with the issuer on the proposed debt.

The agency needs other information as well, much of which is probably already in the rating agency's files if it has rated the local government's debt before. If the agency is rating the issuer for the first time, the issuing local government will have to provide information about the type of local government that the issuer is, its powers and relationship with the state and other governmental entities, the election or selection of principal officials, the ways in which decisions and policies are made, services provided, relevant property tax and revenue data not in the financial reports or budgets, any short-term borrowing by the issuer to cover operating expenses or deficits or for other purposes in the past three to five years, identification of federal or state laws or regulations that could affect the issuer's ability to repay debt, information about the issuer's employee pension systems, risk management practices, and insurance carried by the issuer.

To rate revenue bonds, the rating agencies need the feasibility study and related information about the project or enterprise to be financed with the debt (see the sidebar on page 235). Once a rating is requested and necessary documents are available, the rating agency analysts review information in the agency's files about the issuer and new material submitted about the planned debt and the issuer.

A meeting of the analysts with key officials is often required for an issuer that has not been previously rated by the agency and may be useful for experienced issuers as well. The meeting usually takes place in New York, but it can be held in the agency's regional office closest to the issuer or at the issuer's location. The rating agencies recommend that only representatives of the issuer who can make a constructive contribution to the meeting attend. Several representatives of the rating agency usually attend. Local officials should prepare carefully for the meeting by checking with the rating analysts about the subjects they want the officials to cover and preparing an agenda and supporting materials or a booklet that addresses those subjects.[20] The meeting gives local officials the opportunity to make a case for maintaining a good rating (obtaining an improved rating) and for the rating agency's analysts to resolve questions they have about the debt and the issuer.

The rating analysts will probably make a site visit when it is a new issuer or when there have been significant changes since the last time the agency rated the issuer's debt.

The rating analysts formulate a rating profile and present it to the agency's rating committee for that type of debt. The committee renders a rating decision, which is then communicated to the issuer's authorized representative. The issuer may appeal the rating, but this is done infrequently. A rating agency usually considers an appeal only when the issuer submits new information that was not previously available during the rating process. If there is no appeal or after the appeal review is complete, the agency formally notifies the issuer of the rating and publishes or releases the rating to the markets.

After a rating is assigned and the debt is issued, the issuer must maintain its rating. To maintain a rating, the issuer must send to the agencies that rated the debt the annual financial reports, budgets, capital improvement programs (CIPs), and other positive or negative information and documents that bear on its financial condition and prospects. If a rating agency does not receive such information regularly, it is likely to suspend or withdraw its rating for the debt. If there is any material change in a local government's financial condition, the rating agency may place its debt on a credit watch, review the rating, and possibly change it. Ongoing or gradual changes that could result in eventual rating changes are indicated by positive or negative credit outlooks that are communicated by the agencies to the markets.

Cost of rating

The cost of a bond rating is based on the size of a debt issue, its complexity, the frequency with which a local government or another issuer sells debt, and the time and expenses involved in rating the debt. S&P's fees for rating new local government debt in 2000 ranged widely from $2,500 to $65,000. Its fees for rating or rerating re-funding debt are at the low end of this range.[21] A national rating for a GO bond issue of several million dollars typically costs at least $5,000. National ratings for bonds of $10 million to $100 million cost from $10,000 to $25,000, depending on the complexity of the issue, how recently the issuer has been rated, and other factors.[22] Chapter 11 on selling local government debt presents data on actual rating costs for local government issues of GO bonds, revenue bonds, and capital leases.

Rating criteria by type of local government debt

The national bond rating agencies evaluate all of the different types of debt that local governments issue: GO bonds, revenue bonds, certificates of participation and other capital lease debt, and various kinds of SO debt. This section examines rating criteria for each type.

General obligation bonds

Ratings of GO bonds that are secured by the full-faith-and-credit pledge or unlimited taxing power of the local government issuer are based on an assessment of the issuer's general creditworthiness in four general areas: economic base, financial condition and practices, debt factors, and governance and planning.

Economic base   The local or regional economy is a critical factor in determining the creditworthiness of any local government. The ability of a local government to raise revenue, provide services, and repay debt ultimately depends on the health of its economy. In a GO bond rating, a community's economic base is evaluated in terms of the following factors:

- **Population**   Size, growth, and other demographic features are considered.
- **Wealth**   Relevant measures of wealth—and changes in wealth over time, which is of interest to rating agencies—are per capita personal income and median family income. Comparisons between a specific local government issuing debt and the state or the nation are often made using these measures. If such income statistics are not available for the local jurisdiction issuing the debt, they are often available for the county or the standard metropolitan statistical area in which the jurisdiction exists.
- **Local tax base**   The tax base and changes in it can be measured by such indicators as property tax valuation, the value of building permits issued, and retail sales.
- **Economic diversity**   The distribution of the labor force by economic sector reflects a jurisdiction's economic diversity. Concentration of

employment in one or two major manufacturers or businesses is a disadvantage for bond rating purposes, particularly if the manufacturers or businesses can be adversely affected by economic downturns.

- **Economic stability**   A relevant measure is the local or regional unemployment rate. Significant increases in the unemployment rate during recessions indicate economic volatility rather than stability, and they affect a bond rating adversely.
- **Local infrastructure**   Infrastructure to support development (such as transportation systems, utilities, schools, housing, health care facilities, and cultural and recreational amenities) is an important part of a jurisdiction's economic base and is increasingly important to bond ratings.
- **Local and regional policies**   A jurisdiction's creditworthiness also is influenced by local and regional policies to support sustainable development and growth.

Financial condition and practices   A local government's financial condition depends on its current, past, and prospective situation with regard to revenues, expenditures, and fund balances or operating reserves. Growth or changes in revenues and spending directly affect a local government's ability to repay debt. Fund balances provide reserves for a jurisdiction to weather adverse events and give assurance to investors that resources exist to meet obligations even in difficult budget periods. Responsible financial practices by a local government underlie its good financial condition and are an indication that debt service payments will be made when due. Relevant financial practices include budgeting, accounting and financial reporting, tax and revenue administration, and cash management and investments. In rating a local government's GO debt, rating agencies evaluate the jurisdiction's financial condition and practices in terms of the following factors:

- **Growth or change in major general revenue sources** such as the property tax, local sales tax, intergovernmental revenue, and general fund user fees in relation to local population growth and general fund expenditure growth.
- **Growth or change in permanent or full-time equivalent positions** for general government activities.
- **Spending per capita** for salaries, wages, and fringe benefits for general government services compared with spending by jurisdictions of similar size and situation.
- **General fund balances** and other operating fund balances, which are key factors in bond rating, enable a local government to meet cash flow needs, fund unanticipated spending occasioned by emergencies or unforeseen opportunities, and avoid short-term borrowing for operating purposes. Fund balances are usually measured in relation to recurring spending. Although rating agencies do not recommend a particular level of fund balance in relation to spending, they look for medium- and small-size local governments that are issuing debt to have an available general fund balance equal to 10 percent or more of general fund spending.
- **Budgeting practices** such as adoption of the operating budget by or before the start of the fiscal year or period, revenue collections that meet or exceed revenue estimates, and expenditures within appropriations. If a local government fails to budget in fiscally disciplined ways, its bond rating and ability to issue debt will suffer.

- **Accounting and financial reporting practices** in compliance with generally accepted accounting principles, annual independent audits, and good internal control procedures characterize creditworthy debt issues. An issuer cannot expect to receive investment-grade bond ratings without having acceptable accounting and financial reporting.
- **Tax and revenue administration** is important because for local governments levying the property tax, the rating agencies consider the percentage of the property tax levy that is collected by the end of the fiscal year for which it was levied.[23] The amount and change in accounts receivable and uncollectible accounts for key tax or revenue sources are other relevant measures here.
- **Investment practices** such as the presence of governing-board-approved policies to guide local investment practices, compliance with laws and local policies, priority given to safety and liquidity over yield in investment policies, and limits on the term of the investments of idle operating funds are relevant measures.

Debt factors A local government's outstanding debt, its authorized but unissued debt, and even the debt of other local governments that tax the same citizens or property are among the factors that affect its ability to finance future capital projects. If a local government has substantial GO or other general debt, if it is making large annual debt service and lease payments from general revenues that will continue at current levels for many years, and if balancing the operating budget in upcoming years will take significant tax or fee increases or cuts in spending, the local unit's ability to issue new debt without risk to its bond ratings may be slim. On the other hand, if a local government has only modest amounts of GO debt or other general-purpose debt, has annual debt service payments that will decline in upcoming years, has revenue growth that matches or exceeds expected spending growth in future years, and otherwise is in good financial condition, in all likelihood it can issue new debt without risk to its bond ratings. Indeed, if this jurisdiction is experiencing rapid growth, the rating agencies will probably view new debt issuance in a very positive light, realizing that it is needed to provide infrastructure to meet growth.

The measures rating agencies use to assess the general debt position of a local government relate to the non-self-supporting debt, or **net debt,** of the jurisdiction. Net debt includes GO debt and any other debt issued to finance general public improvements and for which debt service is paid from general revenue sources. In the case of GO bonds, net debt includes authorized and unissued as well as outstanding GO debt. The measures are:

- **Net debt per capita** This ratio, discussed in Chapter 5, is a rough measure of debt burden. Data for this measure are readily available, and one local government can easily compare its net debt position with that of another jurisdiction. Such comparisons, however, can be misleading. For example, for a resort community with a large tax base but a relatively small permanent population this measure can overstate debt burden in relation to both need and capacity.
- **Net debt as a percentage of tax valuation or market valuation** Also discussed in Chapter 5, net debt as a percentage of tax valuation can be a very useful measure if the property tax is an important general revenue source and tax valuation is up to date. Comparisons of jurisdictions using net debt as a percentage of market valuation are useful if the valuation data are up to date in all jurisdictions being compared.

- **Net debt as a percentage of personal family income**   This is a useful but indirect measure of debt-carrying capacity for most local governments. It is directly relevant to any local government with a local income tax. For medium- and small-size cities and towns, data often are not available.

- **Annual debt service on net debt as a percentage of general fund spending or revenues**   For most local governments, the rating agencies consider debt service to be high when it is between 15 and 20 percent of general fund spending or revenues.[24] When debt service takes from 15 to 20 percent of a local government's operating budget, this can crowd other spending needs and create some flexibilities in the operating budget. A problem in using this measure can arise because local governments include different types of revenues and spending in the general fund. If a local government uses special funds as well as the general fund to finance general government, revenues or spending of the special funds should be included in the calculation. In applying this measure, extraordinary revenue or spending items should not be included in the calculation of annual revenues or spending.

- **Pay-down pace for net long-term debt**   The rating agencies like to see local debt issuers retire about half of a long-term GO debt issue by the half-way point in the overall debt's term. In other words, if a city issues $10 million in GO bonds to be repaid over a twenty-year term, $5 million or half the debt would be retired by the tenth year. As Chapter 9 points out, debt retirement for new debt must be "blended" with debt service on existing debt. This often means that debt retirement on new debt may not meet the norm suggested here. The rating agencies allow for this so long as the pay-down pace for all net debt, existing as well as proposed new debt, approximates the norm.

- **Net debt of overlapping and underlying local governments**   Several different local governments may serve the same residents and taxpayers in a local area, and if one local government issues GO debt or other net debt and levies taxes to pay it off, other local governments' ability to issue debt and levy taxes can be hindered. The rating agencies consider the net debt of overlapping or underlying jurisdictions when they assign a rating to the GO debt of a local government. Thus, if a city is issuing new GO debt, the agencies will consider how the net debt position of the county affects city residents who are county as well as city taxpayers.

Governance and planning   Rating agencies' evaluation of governance and planning necessarily relies on more intangible criteria than the criteria for assessing a local government's economic base, financial condition and practices, and debt burden. Nonetheless, these factors are becoming more important in debt ratings. "The management or administrative structure of a government will move a rating up or down probably more significantly and swiftly than any other element of a credit review," noted an S&P report in 2000.[25] Good governance systems and sound planning and management practices improve capital planning and fiscal decision making. When rating GO bonds, agencies look at the following factors in this area:

- **A coherent structure of governance**   This is indicated by clear assignment of responsibility to different officials, good decision-making or policy-making processes, and administrative systems that allow for the effective and efficient implementation of policies. Local governance structures are usually established under state statutes or local charters.

- **A cooperative governing board** Members who work together, arrive at a consensus, exercise fiscal discipline, plan for the future, and provide responsible leadership reflect well on local governance.
- **Professional management and staff** The rating agencies like the council-manager form of government, especially in medium- and small-size jurisdictions.
- **Multiyear planning processes in place** Examples include capital improvement plans, multiyear financial forecasting, long-term service and facility needs assessment, and strategic or comprehensive planning. The involvement of the broader community in planning is seen as a plus.

Revenue bonds

The ratings for revenue bonds depend first and foremost on the adequacy of the specific revenue stream pledged to secure them and to make periodic principal and interest payments. Local government revenue bonds are most commonly issued to finance capital needs for self-supporting projects or enterprises, and the ratings for these bonds are usually based on the following factors: the coverage that project or enterprise net revenues provide for debt service, the service area or market of the project or enterprise, revenue-raising flexibility, protections provided to investors by indentures in the debt contract, transfer policies and practices, management capabilities, and debt levels for the project or enterprise.

Coverage for the revenue bond–financed project or enterprise Coverage is the key ratio used to measure the extent to which a project or enterprise generates annual revenues sufficient to meet O&M expenses and debt service. Coverage is calculated by dividing enterprise net revenue (gross revenue and income less O&M expenses) by annual debt service. Depreciation and interest are excluded from operating expenses in calculation of net revenue.[26] Debt service on proposed and existing revenue debt for the project or enterprise is counted, and maximum annual debt service is usually used for the calculation.

The bond rating agencies require positive coverage, that is, something above 1 times debt service. In past years, the ratios required for most revenue bonds ranged from 1.5 to 2 times debt service. The ratios required for most revenue bonds today are lower, around 1.25 times debt service, or even lower for very strong projects and enterprises. If debt service on a revenue bond issue is insured, which occurs for many such issues, the insurer usually requires a coverage ratio of 1.25 times debt service or higher. Higher ratios, 1.30 to 2.00 times debt service, often prevail in practice, even though they are not required for many projects and enterprises. Such high coverage ratios are required for weaker projects.[27] Higher coverage ratios are required for projects or enterprises that have limited customer bases or less than stellar operating and financial histories or that face significant competition from other providers of the service. When a project or enterprise faces one or more of these situations, its ability to achieve high coverage is an indication that the project or enterprise can operate successfully, compete, and generate revenues sufficient to cover all costs, including debt service. For revenue bonds for these types of enterprises, the greater the coverage ratio is, the higher the credit quality of the bonds.

For revenue bond issues for projects or enterprises with a strong customer base, a record of strong operating and financial results, and limited competition, revenue flows to the project or enterprise are typically secure.

Coverage in these situations, while it must be positive, often influences the rating less than do the other factors discussed in this section. Local water-sewer utilities tend to be in more of a monopoly position than local parking or transportation systems; consequently, the rating agencies require higher coverage for parking or transportation revenue bonds than for water-sewer revenue bonds, and they typically rate the former lower than the latter.

The calculation of coverage for some strong projects or enterprises may include project or enterprise retained earnings or fund balance in the calculation of coverage. In other words, some portion of retained earnings or fund balance is added to net revenues and the sum is divided by debt service to calculate the coverage ratio. Here, two coverage ratios are often used: one including retained earnings or fund balance and one without. For example, a 1.10 coverage ratio is required if retained earnings or fund balance is not considered in the calculation, and a higher 1.25 ratio is needed with the inclusion of fund balance or retained earnings.[28]

Service area or market served by the project or enterprise   Whether the issuer is in a monopoly position or faces competition in the service area is not the only relevant factor in the rating of revenue bonds. The geographic size of the service area, the number of customers served by the project or enterprise, and demand for the service or the number of potential customers also affect the rating. Economies of scale are generally associated with projects and enterprises financed with revenue bonds, and a rating is strengthened to the extent that the service area and customer base are enlarged. Diversity in the customer base is also preferable. If one customer or only a few customers use a significant portion (for example, 20 percent or more) of a project or enterprise's services, and if these customers are in one economic sector (for example, textile manufacturing), this hurts the credit quality and can lower the ratings of revenue bonds for the project or enterprise. The extent to which the volume or usage of the project's or enterprise's services can be affected by downturns in the economic cycle also affects ratings.

Revenue-raising flexibility   Because revenue bonds are secured and paid from specific revenues, usually dedicated fees paid by users, the ability of the issuer to raise or otherwise adjust fees and charges to customers enters into a revenue bond rating. If an issuer has very broad legal latitude to raise or change fees, and the record shows that the issuer has done this to cover increasing costs, fund capital needs, or meet market opportunities and challenges, this can strengthen revenue bond ratings. On the other hand, if laws and regulations impose strict limits on rate setting, or if the governing board and community have not adjusted rates and fees when needed, lower ratings for revenue bonds may result.

Investor protections in the revenue bond contract   As explained in Chapter 7, revenue bond contracts usually include indentures to protect investors' interests and enhance the credit quality of the bonds. These indentures may require the issuer to fund and maintain a debt service reserve equal to maximum annual debt service, set rates sufficient to meet minimum coverage (for example, 1.25 times debt service), follow a prescribed flow-of-funds hierarchy that applies annual revenues first to O&M outlays and debt service before other spending, avoid issuing additional parity bonds or debt for the project or enterprise unless a specific coverage ratio is met or exceeded, and limit the securities in which project or enterprise resources can be invested.

Many revenue bonds cannot receive an investment grade rating unless the bond contract includes the types of indentures just outlined. In the case of weak revenue bond issues, the common indentures can be strengthened with additional contract provisions that further protect investors. For example, it is not unusual for the issuer to give investors a mortgage on project or enterprise property to strengthen the security for a revenue bond and improve its ratings. Conversely, for revenue bonds for especially strong projects or enterprises, the conventional indentures are sometimes waived or weakened without harming the credit quality or lowering the ratings for the bonds. For example, a debt service reserve requirement may be waived in favor of a surety bond provided by the issuer for a year of debt service payments.

Transfer policies and practices Since the early 1990s, the rating agencies have given more weight to policies and practices governing transfers between a project or enterprise and the issuer's general fund or another fund. This is particularly true for revenue bonds issued for local electric and natural gas enterprises. In the past, many local governments operated such enterprises at what might be termed a profit and transferred large amounts of money annually from the enterprise fund to the issuer's general fund to lower taxes or subsidize general government services. This practice became a problem for many of these enterprises as their costs rose relative to surrounding investor-owned energy utilities and as they faced more competition from these utilities and alternative energy sources. Large transfers deprived many local electric utilities and other utilities of the resources they needed to improve their facilities to remain competitive. As a result, the rating agencies now look at the transfer policies and practices of local enterprise systems in rating revenue bond issues for these systems. The worst transfer policy can be no policy at all.[29]

A transfer policy should:

- Balance the needs of the project or enterprise making the transfer and the needs of the fund receiving it
- Avoid overreliance of the general fund or any other fund on transfers from the project or enterprise
- Result in predictability of cash or resource flows between the project or enterprise and the general fund
- Respond to competitive pressures
- Allow for lowering or adjusting the transfer in response to adverse events
- Avoid political challenges from project or enterprise customers or other persons or entities affected by the transfers specifically or project or enterprise services generally.[30]

Management capabilities The rating agencies assess the ability of the management of a project or enterprise to implement policies successfully and to be proactive in meeting future challenges. Management here refers not only to managers for the specific project or enterprise but also to the local government that owns and operates the system. Planning, capital improvement programming, and financial forecasting for five to ten years are expected for utilities and some other enterprise projects, and their existence and quality can have a significant effect on the ratings for revenue bonds.

Debt levels and financial condition and prospects To rate revenue bonds, like GO bonds, the rating agencies use a variety of financial measures to assess the debt position and the financial condition of the project or enterprise. The coverage ratio is one key measure. Another is the debt ratio, which relates debt for the project or enterprise, less any reserves or sinking funds available to repay the debt and interest on it, to net fixed assets plus net working capital. Net fixed assets are fixed assets at historical cost less depreciation. Net working capital is net current assets (current assets less current liabilities). The median debt ratio varies by type of enterprise system, depending on the assets and facilities used. For example, in the early 1990s, the median ratio was 44.7 percent for airports and 28 percent for water-sewer systems.[31] The rating agencies evaluate the debt level for a given project or enterprise in relation to the norms prevailing for that type of project or enterprise. They also look at many other measures such as the operating ratio (O&M expenses divided by operating revenue) to assess a project's or enterprise's condition.

Capital leases, including certificates of participation

Capital leases, including certificates of participation, are usually secured by the property or asset financed with the lease obligation. Common rating factors for local government capital leases include the general creditworthiness

---

Information required for rating revenue bonds

Rating agencies require the issuer of revenue bonds to supply numerous documents about the project or enterprise to be financed, including

- All relevant legal documents
- The bond resolution or trust indentures
- Five years of audited financial statements
- The budget for the current year
- Engineering report or feasibility study
- Rate study
- Capital improvement program for the project or enterprise
- List of largest customers and customers by class
- Sales or revenues in total and by class
- Average and peak system demands
- Five years of historic rates and of projected rates
- Comparison of rates with those of other providers in the locality or area
- Three years of key performance or operating statistics for the project or enterprise
- Population and income trends in the service area
- Composition of employment by sector and unemployment in the service area

A local government's financial adviser and/or the engineer doing the feasibility study for a revenue bond–financed project or enterprise gathers the necessary documents or oversees this process. If a local government has issued revenue bonds in recent years, the rating agencies are likely to already have many of the documents they need, and the primary task becomes updating the information.

Standard & Poor's, Municipal Finance Criteria, 2000, 110.

Revenue bond ratings, Henderson, North Carolina

In April 2001, **Henderson, North Carolina,** issued $15,630,000 in revenue bonds to improve its water-sewer system and to refund installment-purchase debt that had been issued for the system. These were the first revenue bonds ever issued by Henderson. The stand-alone—uninsured—ratings for the bonds were A from S&P, A2 from Moody's, and A+ from Fitch. With insurance factored in, the bonds were rated triple-A by all three agencies.

Henderson does not have any outstanding GO bonds and it does not have current GO bond ratings. The city's last payments on GO bonds occurred in December 1999, at which time the city's GO bonds were rated A by S&P and A3 by Moody's—Moody's rating is equivalent to S&P's and below Moody's uninsured ratings on the 2001 revenue bonds. Because of significant commercial and other growth in recent years, Henderson's financial position has improved, and if it were to issue GO bonds today, its ratings most probably be equal to or above the uninsured ratings on the 2001 revenue bonds.

The generally lesser credit quality of revenue bonds compared with GO bonds is evident in the Henderson bonds. The average interest rate(s) that Henderson obtained on the 2001 revenue bonds can be compared with two market indices—one for A-rated and the other for AA-rated GO bonds maturing in 2011—published on May 1, 2001, by *Bond Buyer.* The midpoint of the repayment term for the Henderson revenue bonds is in 2011.

Henderson revenue bonds, average interest rate:
    True interest cost basis: 4.88 percent
    Net interest cost basis: 4.80 percent

GO index, 2011 maturity (published by *Bond Buyer* on May 1, 2001):
    A-rated GO bonds: 4.76 percent
    AA-rated GO bonds: 4.63 percent

Chapter 10 defines the concepts of true interest cost and net interest cost in calculating average interest rates. In simple terms, the true interest cost calculation considers the time value of money while the net interest cost basis does not.

Although the Henderson revenue bonds were rated A (S&P) and A2 (Moody's)—these are equivalent categories—the average interest rates for these bonds, on both a true interest cost basis and a net interest cost basis, were higher the *Bond Buyer* indices for GO bonds maturing in 2011.

Sources: "Official Statement, $15,630,000 City of Henderson, North Carolina Combined Enterprise System Revenue Bonds, Series 2001," and *The Bond Buyer,* May 1, 2001, 44.

---

of the issuer and the following four factors, briefly addressed here and explained more fully in Chapter 7: the essentiality of the asset financed with the lease and pledged as security for the financing, the risk of nonappropriation, pledges of collateral as security in addition to the asset financed with the lease, and specific indentures or other protections given to investors in the lease contract.

General creditworthiness of the issuer Many if not most capital leases finance general-purpose projects or projects that produce revenues insufficient to cover all project or facility costs. Money for the lease payments, therefore, comes partly or wholly from taxes or general revenues. When this is the case, ratings of the capital lease depend on an assessment of the same factors that are considered in a GO bond rating (economic base and strength of the issuer, financial condition and practices, net debt burden, and governance and planning) as well as the following factors.

Essentiality of the asset   The more essential the asset financed with the lease and pledged to secure the lessee's payments, the less likely the issuer will be to exercise any nonappropriation clause associated with the lease and walk away from the debt. Facilities like jails, schools, and water-sewer facilities are usually considered to be essential. They are needed to provide mandatory or core government services. If the issuer is generally creditworthy, capital lease financing for these types of facilities is feasible, and the rating agencies are likely to assign respectable ratings to the financing. On the other hand, local park and recreational projects are generally considered to be much less essential, and their financing will be given lower ratings.

Risk of nonappropriation of funds   In most states, certificates of participation, other lease-purchase or installment-purchase contracts, and other capital leases have a nonappropriation clause. As explained in Chapter 7, such a clause gives the governmental lessee the right, in a strict legal sense, to cancel its debt obligation in any year by choosing not to appropriate the funds to make the lease or installment payments in that year. The non-appropriation clause enables local governments to issue certificates of participation or another type of long-term capital leasing arrangement without pledging future taxing power for lease payment obligations and securing voter approval of the debt in a referendum. Although a local government can legally exercise the nonappropriation clause in a capital lease, this rarely happens.

The rating agencies address specific questions when they evaluate the risk of nonappropriation and, conversely, the issuer's willingness to continue making periodic payments for capital lease debt.[32] For instance, do the lessee's governing board and other top officials view lease obligations as debt that must be paid? Any suggestion that officials would consider exercising the local government's contractual right of nonappropriation or abatement in a capital lease, even though technically not a default, would be viewed very negatively by the rating agencies. Other questions concern the strength of the local government lessee's commitment to the project to be financed with the lease. Did the local governing board approve the project and the lease financing unanimously, or was there a split vote? Is there organized opposition in the community to the project? Have voters turned down the project in a recent GO bond referendum? What is the likelihood that significant opposition to the project will develop after it is up and running?

Additional collateral pledged to secure a capital lease   The rating for a capital lease can sometimes be improved if the issuer pledges collateral in addition to the asset being financed. Durham, North Carolina, added one of its water treatment plants as security for the certificates of participation issued in 1992 to finance a new baseball stadium (see Chapter 7). Likewise, financing for a master leasing arrangement that bundles equipment and vehicles is likely to receive a higher rating than financing for individual pieces of equipment with several capital leases.[33]

A special revenue or tax can be pledged as additional security for capital lease debt.[34] As noted in Chapter 7, occupancy and prepared-food and beverage taxes were levied in Mecklenburg County, North Carolina, to provide revenue to cover lease payments for certificates of participation that the city of Charlotte issued to finance a new convention center.

Lease features that protect investors' interests   Contractual provisions that strengthen security are often a part of capital leases and are considered by the rating agencies in assigning ratings to such debt. Many capital lease arrangements include a required lease payment or debt service reserve fund. Such a reserve may equal maximum or average annual payments, including principal and interest, on the lease obligation.

The term for repayment of a capital lease can be adjusted to strengthen its rating and improve its attractiveness to underwriters and investors. For example, a local government may be considering the issuance of certificates of participation for a city hall renovation and expansion project. Although the repayment term for the certificates could extend to as many as twenty years, higher ratings might be obtained by shortening the repayment term to fifteen years or less.

The municipal debt markets expect the local government lessee to provide certain types of insurance: property insurance for the leased property, title insurance, and possibly rental interruption insurance to continue lease payments for a recovery period when the property is damaged and unavailable to the lessee. Of course, insurance guaranteeing lease or debt service payments to the investors greatly improves a capital lease's security, typically raising it to triple-A status.

Special obligation debt

Special obligation debt is secured by special or limited taxes or other revenue sources. The ratings for debt, like revenue bonds, are determined by the certainty, breadth, and risks associated with the limited or special taxes or revenues pledged to secure and pay off the bonds or debt. Discussed here are bond rating criteria for four types of SO debt: non-property-tax (or non–ad valorem tax) debt, non-local-tax debt, special assessment debt, and tax increment debt. Non-property-tax debt and non-local-tax debt are considered together. Chapter 7 identified the security for and major features of each of these types of SO debt.

Non-property-tax debt and non-local-tax debt   Non-property-tax debt issued by a local government is secured by all legally available revenue except the property tax or ad valorem tax. Non-local-tax debt that a local jurisdiction issues is secured by all legally available revenues except any taxes that the issuer levies. S&P considers a non-property-tax pledge that encompasses a variety of substantial local revenues to be second only to a full-faith-and-credit pledge or unlimited tax pledge for local government debt.[35] The credit quality of non-local-tax debt is usually not as strong as non-property-tax debt because no taxes levied by the local issuer may be pledged as security for the non-local tax debt. In other words, if an issuer of non-local-tax debt levies both property and sales taxes, neither may be pledged to secure the debt. If such debt were non-property-tax debt, the issuer could pledge the sales tax as well as any other non-property-tax revenues to secure the debt.

Capital leases and general obligation bonds, Brunswick County, North Carolina

In 2001, **Brunswick County, North Carolina,** a rapidly growing coastal county with a large seasonal tourist population, issued GO bonds and certificates of participation, both to be paid from the county's general revenues. The GO bonds were for school projects and were secured by the county's full-faith-and-credit pledge and unlimited property taxes. The certificates of participation were issued to finance courthouse and county office renovations and expansions and were secured by these facilities.

	GO bonds, May 2000	Certificates of participation, July 2000
Rating	A+ (S&P), A1 (Moody's)	A- (S&P), A2 (Moody's), A (Fitch)*
Interest rate	5.7270% (net interest cost basis)	5.47% (net interest cost basis), 5.57% (true interest cost basis)

Note: Both these debt obligations have repayment terms going out to 2020 and have similar average maturities.

*These are stand-alone ratings; with insurance, the certificates of participation received triple-A ratings.

Standard & Poor's rated the certificates of participation two notches below the rating that it assigned to the county's GO bonds, issued just two months prior to the certificates. Moody's rated the certificates one notch below the rating it gave the GO bonds. The county's creditworthiness did not change in the two-month interval between the issuance of these two debt obligations by the county. The lower ratings for the certificates are based on the lesser credit quality of such debt compared with GO bonds.

The higher average interest rate for the GO bonds (5.7270 percent, net interest cost basis) compared with the interest rate for the certificates of participation (5.47 percent net interest cost and 5.57 percent true interest cost basis) seems to contradict the point that capital leases have higher credit risk and higher interest rates than GO bonds. However, interest rates moved a sharply upward between May and July of 2000; *Bond Buyer* indices for municipal, long-term debt show a spike of almost 0.4 percent—40 basis points—over this period.

If these 40 basis points are added to the average interest rates for the certificates of participation, they become 5.87 percent on a net interest cost basis and 5.97 percent on a true interest cost basis, both considerably higher than the 5.7270 percent on the GO bonds. These higher adjusted rates for the certificates of participation reflect their greater credit risk compared with the same county's GO bonds.

Chapter 10 defines the concepts of net interest and true interest cost rates.

Sources: "Official Statement: $16,000,000 Certificates of Participation, 2000, County of Brunswick, North Carolina," and information provided staff of the Local Government Commission, North Carolina Department of State Treasurer. The commission approves and sells nearly all North Carolina local government debt.

Specific non-property-tax or non-local-tax revenues are identified in the debt contract to pay debt service in many non-property-tax or non-local-tax debt issues. In these cases, the ratings assess the revenues specifically identified or pledged to pay debt service on the debt as well as the revenues that are generally available to secure the debt. When evaluating this type of debt, rating agencies evaluate both the specific revenues identified to pay debt service and the same factors that are used to evaluate GO debt—strength of the local economy, financial position and procedures of the issuer, debt burden, and the issuer's planning and management capabilities.[36]

Special assessment debt   Special assessment debt is typically secured by assessments against property that benefits from public improvements (like street paving, curbs and gutters, utility lines, and other infrastructure) financed with the special assessment debt. If a local government wants to issue special assessment debt and levy special assessments, it must first form a special assessment district. The debt is issued, the improvements are made, and the benefiting property is assessed. It is typical for property owners to pay the assessments in installments with interest over many years, and their payments cover debt service on the special assessment debt. The bond rating agencies consider the following factors when evaluating special assessment debt:

- District size and wealth
- Marketability of the assessed property
- High ratio of property value to assessment lien
- Essentiality of improvement projects
- Basis for assessment (fair and equitable, unlikely to be controversial)
- Legal protections in the authorizing statute or assessment debt contract of investors' interests (for example, continuation of the assessment lien when assessed property changes hands)
- A lien on the assessed property that has parity with local property tax levies
- Collection of assessments (billing of special assessments on the property tax bill, use of incentives that encourage timely payment and penalize late payment, and adequate sanctions to enforce payment)
- Sufficiency of cash flow when adverse events occur; S&P expects an excess cash flow to cover the risk of nonpayment of special assessments by one or more of the largest property owners in the district
- Ability of the assessing jurisdiction to increase assessment if necessary
- A debt service reserve (usually necessary)
- A debt service schedule in which combined principal and interest payments are either the same or decline from year to year (see Chapter 9).[37]

Some local governments set up one district that combines special assessment and taxing authority. These local governments then levy taxes as well as special assessments against property owners for public improvements in the district. This broadens the security for special assessment debt issued to finance improvements in the district. Such debt may be more like special or limited tax debt than special assessment debt.[38]

Tax increment bonds   The security for tax increment debt is the growth in the property tax base and revenues in a defined district. The new tax base and revenues result from private development that is triggered by or associated with public improvements in the district that are financed with the tax increment debt. Debt service on the debt is paid from the incremental property tax revenue and sometimes from other revenues raised in the district that are pledged to the debt.

Following are factors, and related questions, that are relevant in the ratings of tax increment debt:

- **District analysis**   What is the size, wealth, income, and population of the tax increment district (TID)? Generally, a district must be more than 150 acres to be sufficiently diverse.[39] The wealth and general credit characteristics of the local jurisdiction creating the district are also relevant.

- **Tax increment analysis**   What is the history of property tax base growth in the district? What growth in the district's property tax base is projected? How likely are taxpayers in the district to appeal their property tax valuations or assessments? To what extent is the current tax base and projected future tax base concentrated in a few owners? A shopping mall or a single condominium complex may comprise most of the incremental tax base in a district. Having only one (or a few) major taxpayers tends to lessen credit quality.

- **Type of property in district**   Does a district's incremental tax base include considerable personal property (for example, manufacturing equipment or computer equipment)? If so, what is the probability of that property eventually being taken from the district?

- **Development powers**   What authority does the issuer have to acquire, hold, and develop property? If this authority is substantial, the district has important tools to further economic development and tax base growth in the district.

- **Security**   Is there a funded debt service reserve, an additional bonds requirement, and other security provisions in the contract for the tax increment debt? What has been coverage on debt service on tax increment debt in the district in the past and what is coverage likely to be in the future? It is typical for S&P to expect a minimum coverage of 1.25 times maximum annual debt service to justify the issuance of additional bonds supported by tax increment revenue from the district.[40]

- **State laws**   Have changes in state law defined away portions of the tax base in the tax increment district?

- **Collection of property taxes**   What percentage of the incremental property taxes levied is collected? How large are delinquent incremental tax collections? What is the history of debt service coverage for tax increment debt issued for the TID?

- **Application of extra collection**   If tax increment growth is greater than expected, can it be applied to accelerate the retirement of outstanding tax increment debt?[41]

Ten ways to improve a local government's bond ratings

Standard & Poor's recommends ten ways to improve a local government's GO bond rating.[42] These policies and actions address financial position, planning and management, debt management, and economic vitality. Although the recommendations have implications mainly for GO ratings, many can help a local government improve its ratings for revenue bonds and for capital lease or SO debt.

Establish rainy day and budget stabilization reserves

Having a rainy day fund, reserves, or fund balances gives a local government flexibility to meet unforeseen needs. The size of the reserve(s) can be geared to cash flow requirements, the volatility of revenue sources, and legal requirements if any. A formal policy is recommended that sets the size of the reserve, specifies the conditions under which the reserves may be drawn down, and identifies ways to rebuild them.

Review economic and revenue trends to identify potential budget problems

Periodic monitoring of economic and financial trends is especially important for local governments that depend primarily on revenue sources such as income and sales taxes that are sensitive to changes in the economic cycle. An annual review is usually sufficient. Some local governments begin the annual budget process with such a review.

Prioritize spending and establish contingency plans for budget shortfalls

Spending needs always exceed available resources, even in the best of times. When there are budget shortfalls, usually only the top priorities can be funded. Chapter 4 identifies different approaches that local governments use for setting priorities among capital projects.

Develop a formal capital improvement program and a debt affordability model

Most local governments face numerous capital spending needs. A CIP helps to set those needs into priority and plan for their implementation. A debt affordability model helps a local government avoid excessive debt and balance pay-as-go and debt sources. Local governments that issue top-rated debt all have CIPs. A growing number have developed debt affordability models that use ratios like net debt per capita and net debt as a percentage of tax valuation. Chapter 3 examines CIPs, and Chapter 5 addresses debt affordability. Chapter 9, which covers debt planning, is also relevant to this recommendation.

Incorporate pay-as-go financing in capital plans and operating budgets

Significant use of pay-as-go sources in capital financing holds down annual debt service costs and preserves flexibility in future operating budgets. Chapter 6 addresses pay-as-go capital financing.

Anticipate the impact of capital and operating budgets in a multiyear financial forecast

Capital projects, debt financing of such projects, and many annual budget decisions affect budgets far into the future. A multiyear forecast helps local officials spot these impacts and plan accordingly. Chapter 12 addresses financial forecasting by local governments.

Establish benchmarks and priorities

Benchmarks and priorities provide direction and help local governments stay on course. Strategic planning requires the identification of performance measures that local officials can use to determine the extent to which policies and limitations are met.

Establish and maintain effective management systems

The implementation of policies and effective and efficient service delivery depend on good management and up-to-date management systems. The use of information technology and other technology is a key part of successful management.

Consider the affordability of actions and plans before they become a part of the budget

Too often local officials create new programs and consider their costs only in the upcoming budget. Careful and long-term cost accounting should be a part of the analysis that takes place when budget decisions are reviewed.

Have a well-defined and coordinated economic development strategy

Economic growth, the foundation for progress in a community, is furthered by an economic development strategy that addresses long-term employment needs. Deciding how many resources to devote to economic development and the types and amount of incentives to offer businesses is a key part of the strategy.

In 2002, S&P published a revised list of policies and actions that a local government can take to improve its bond rating. The list reflects the serious budget challenges that most governments across the nation faced during the recession early in the decade. It is significant that the title for the revised list is "Top 10 Ways to Improve *or Maintain* a Municipal Credit Rating." Many local governments have been hard-pressed since 2000 to maintain their ratings in the face of economic woes and budget shortfalls. The revised list is much the same as the 2000 list, with the following exceptions:

- Added a separate recommendation for local units to develop a debt affordability model; in 2000, this was included with the recommendation that local units have a formal CIP

- Added a new recommendation that local governments undertake long-term planning for liabilities, including pension obligations and contingent liabilities, and comprehensively assess the risks to future budgets arising from these liabilities

- Eliminated the separate recommendation that local governments establish benchmarks and priorities to provide direction for the jurisdiction; this remains as a component of the recommendation that local jurisdictions develop and use effective management systems.[43]

Characteristics of top-rated local issuers of GO debt

Standard & Poor's reviews triple-A-rated municipalities (cities, towns, and townships) and identifies and analyzes characteristics that underlie their triple-A ratings. In the review conducted in 2001, forty-one municipalities had triple-A GO bond ratings from S&P. In the review, population, income, employment, market valuation of taxable property, debt service, spending, and fund balance data for the forty-one jurisdictions were used as well as the following key ratios: market property valuation per capita, per capita effective-buying income, market tax valuation per capita, net debt per capita, net debt as a percentage of market tax valuation, debt service on net debt as a percentage of market tax valuation, total and unreserved general fund balance as a percentage of general fund spending, and the percentage of total debt that the municipality retires in ten years.

The S&P analysis found that neither size nor geographic location mattered much to achieving a triple-A rating. The triple-A-rated municipalities in 2001 ranged in size from Dallas, Texas, with 1,083,500 people, to Bloomfield Hills, Michigan, with 4,363 people; and the jurisdictions could be found in every part of the United States. However, all forty-one municipalities with the prized triple-A rating for their GO bonds do have the following characteristics:

Vibrant and diversified economy   A triple-A municipality can have its own economic base or it can be part of a region with a dynamic economy. Most of the triple-A municipalities have wealth levels above the national average, and all have strong employment growth and relatively low unemployment rates. A significant number have major research universities that have spun off technology and bio-medical businesses that contribute to high employment levels even in economic downturns. The larger cities (more than 250,000 population) have an average per capita market tax valuation of $50,000, while the average for smaller municipalities (less than 50,000 population) is $150,000—a significant difference.

Strong financial position and management   The municipalities rated triple-A have growing tax bases that generate new revenues to meet growth, and they have been able to accumulate significant fund balances. The average available general fund balance as a percentage of the general fund budget for the forty-one jurisdictions was 25 percent. This gives these local governments flexibility to respond to emergencies and meet unanticipated needs.

Modest to low debt levels   The triple-A municipalities carry affordable debt as evident in key debt ratios. Average net debt per capita was $2,000. Six of the smallest municipalities had more than $3,000 of net debt per capita. Median debt per capita for all forty-one jurisdictions was $1,700. The average net debt as a percentage of market valuation was a modest 2.4 percent. All the municipalities have rapid pay-down schedules for their debt: they plan to pay off 70 percent of the net debt in ten years. Debt service on net debt was 9.1 percent on average of general fund and other general government spending.

Strong and proactive governance and management   The triple-A municipalities have governing boards and management teams that can work together and plan for the future, follow conservative and disciplined budgeting practices, and manage through bad as well as good times.

Source: Karl Jacob and Geoffrey Buswick, "Annual Review of AAA Rated Municipalities," *Standard and Poor's Public Finance*, February 8, 2001.

Notes

1 Standard & Poor's Corporation, *Public Finance Criteria 2000* (New York: S&P, 2000), 6. This chapter draws heavily on this publication as well as its predecessor, Standard & Poor's, *Public Finance Criteria, 1998*. See also Moody's Investors Service, *Guide to Moody's Ratings, Rating Process, and Rating Practices*, 3rd ed. (New York: Moody's Investors Service, Inc. 1997); and Fitch IBCA, "Local Government General Obligation Rating Guidelines," *Tax Supported Special Report—Public Finance* (New York: Fitch IBCA, May 2000). The Moody's publication is six years old, but Rebecca Blackmon-Joyner, a bond analyst for Moody's in New York, advised that it has not been revised and still correctly characterizes ratings of municipal debt by Moody's Investors Service. Similarly, the Standard and Poor's and Fitch publications accurately describe current rating criteria and processes used by these rating agencies.

2 Moody's Investors Service, *Guide to Moody's Ratings*, 4. An excellent analysis of the historical record of defaults on municipal debt since the late 1970s is provided by David Litvack and Frank Rizzo, "Municipal Default Risk," *Fitch IBCA Public Finance* (September 1999).

3 Standard & Poor's, *Public Finance Criteria 2000*, 6–7.

4 Standard & Poor's defines an "issuer rating" as an opinion on the issuer's overall financial capacity. The term does not apply to any specific debt; it does not take into account the nature and provisions of particular debt contracts; and it does not consider laws that authorize and limit the issuer's ability to sell and repay debt. See Standard & Poor's, *Public Finance Criteria 2000*, 8–9.

5 Ibid., 10.

6 Ibid.

7 This recommendation is made by staff of the Local Government Commission, North Carolina Department of State Treasurer. The commission approves and sells nearly all North Carolina state and local government debt.

8 David Becker, senior director and manager of ratings, USA Southeast Region, Fitch IBCA, conversation with author, April 2003.

9 Moody's Investors Service, *Guide to Municipal Ratings*, 5–6.

10 Rebecca Blackmon-Joyner, analyst, Moody's Investors Service, New York, conversation with author, April 2003. The percentages refer to the number of GO and revenue bond issues rather than the dollar amount of GO and revenue bonds. Certain revenue bonds for universities, hospitals, and charter schools are excluded from the calculations. The 1994 data are from Moody's Investors Service, *Moody's on Revenue Bonds: The Fundamentals of Revenue Bond Credit Analysis* (New York: Moody's Investors Service, Inc., 1994), 1–2. Moody's Investors Service has not revised this book; although it is almost 10 years old, Blackmon-Joyner advised that it is generally current in 2003.

11 These data were provided in a presentation handout by Standard & Poor's staff at the joint spring conference of the North Carolina Government Finance Officers Association and the North Carolina Association of County Finance Officers, 1999.

12 "Standard & Poor's Ratings Group, 'AAA' Listings" (February 27, 2003); provided to the author by Geoffrey Buswick, analyst, Standard & Poor's, Boston.

13 These descriptive phrases of credit quality for the investment grade categories are paraphrased from Standard & Poor's, *Public Finance Criteria, 2000*, 7; and from Philip Angelides, California State Treasurer, "Fitch—Definitions of Bond Ratings," www.treasurer.ca.gov/ratings/fitch.

14 Data provided by Rebecca Blackmon-Joyner of Moody's; Moody's published comparable statistics in 1994. See also Moody's Investors Service, *Moody's on Revenue Bonds*, 1–2.

15 Standard & Poor's, *Public Finance Criteria 2000*, 10.

16 "Public Finance Rating Definitions," provided by Rebecca Hall, Fitch rating analyst, New York.

17 Local Government Commission, North Carolina Department of State Treasurer, "North Carolina Bond Ratings, Units Whose Highest Rating is Between AAA and A," January 31, 2001. Data provided by Rebecca Hall indicates that Greensboro debt is still not rated by Fitch.

18 Ellen Liston, assistant city manager, Coral Springs, Florida, provided information about Coral Springs GO bond ratings.

19 This discussion of the rating process is based on Standard & Poor's, *Public Finance Criteria 2000*, 12–18; and on Moody's Investors Service, *Guide to Moody's Ratings*, 9–12.

20 See Charles K. Coe, "A Guide to Improving a Local Government's Bond Rating," *Popular Government* (Winter 1994): 30–36.

21 Standard & Poor's, *Public Finance Criteria 2000*, 12.

22 Staff of the Local Government Commission, North Carolina Department of State Treasurer, April 2003. The commission approves and sells nearly all debt issued by local governments in the state.

23 In North Carolina, the norm for this is 95 percent or above. See David M. Lawrence and A. John Vogt, "Capital Budgeting and Debt," in *County Government in North Carolina*, ed. A. Fleming Bell and Warren Jake Wicker (Chapel Hill, N.C.: Institute of Government, University of North Carolina, 1998), 340.

24 Standard & Poor's, *Public Finance Criteria 2000*, 25.

25 Robin Prunty, Richard J. Marino, and Steven J. Murphy, "Top 10 Ways to Improve a G.O. Rating: Best Management Practices Make a Difference," *Standard & Poor's Public Finance*, June 1, 2000, 1.

26 Moody's Investors Service, *Moody's on Revenue Bonds*, 5, 18.

27 Ibid., 8.

28 Ibid. Information about this variation in the calculation of coverage was also provided by staff of the Local Government Commission, North Carolina Department of State Treasurer.

29 Standard & Poor's, *Public Finance Criteria, 2000*, 109.

30 Ibid., 108.

31 Moody's Investors Service, *Moody's on Revenue Bonds*, 6, 17–18.

32 Standard & Poor's, *Public Finance Criteria, 2000*, 96.

33 Moody's Investors Service, *Moody's on Leasing: The Fundamentals of Credit Analysis for Lease Revenue Bonds and Certificates of Participation* (New York: Moody's Investors Service, Inc., 1995), 13. Rebecca Blackmon-Joyner, a Moody's analyst, advised in 2003 that the publication is generally current.

34 Standard & Poor's, *Public Finance Criteria, 2000*, 100.

35 Ibid., 35.

36 Ibid.

37 Ibid., 45–46.

38 Ehlers, *Ehlers on Public Finance*, 253.

39 Standard & Poor's, *Public Finance Criteria, 2000*, 53.

40 Ibid., 57.

41 Ibid., 56–57.

42 Prunty, Marino, and Murphy, "Top Ten Ways to Improve a G.O. Rating."

43 Robin Prunty and Karl Jacob, "Top 10 Ways to Improve or Maintain a Municipal Credit Rating," *Standard & Poor's Public Finance*, February 2002.

9 Planning and structuring debt

To plan and structure debt, local governments set debt retirement terms and annual debt service schedules. They also decide whether to include early redemption options and other features in the debt they issue. Effective debt planning enables a local government borrower to address capital needs in a cost-efficient way, comply with legal debt limits and requirements, meet the expectations of markets and investors, and hold down interest rates and issuance costs.

Local governments issue predominantly long-term debt to finance capital projects and acquisitions. Long-term debt is defined as debt that will be retired after more than one year.[1] Some local governments also issue short-term debt to finance capital projects or for certain capital financing purposes. This chapter presents debt scheduling models, discusses the principles involved in structuring different types of debt, and uses bond issues of specific local governments to illustrate several repayment structures. The chapter covers the following specific topics:

- Debt retirement terms
- Debt maturity and debt retirement schedules
- Models of debt service and actual practices
- Delayed principal retirement and capitalization of interest
- Years' average maturity for long-term debt
- Use of taxes or other revenue for annual debt service
- Early redemption options and advance refunding
- Short-term debt
- Capital appreciation bonds.

Debt retirement terms

The full period over which a bond or debt issue is outstanding is the debt retirement term. The overall retirement term for long-term bonds or debt issued to finance a capital asset should be shorter than the estimated useful life of the asset for several reasons. First, investors are unwilling to accept a retirement term beyond an asset's useful life because they know that the issuer's motivation to make payments on the debt is less after the issuer stops using the asset. Moreover, it is to the advantage of the issuer to have fully retired the debt before new debt must be arranged to replace the asset or to finance major capital renovations to it. For example, a city constructing a new office building with an estimated useful life of thirty years might issue bonds with a twenty-year term to finance the project. City officials could reasonably expect to have to make significant capital renovations to the office building sometime after twenty years—renovations for which new debt might have to be issued.

A second factor that an issuing jurisdiction and its financial advisers consider when they set a debt retirement term is the capacity of the issuing jurisdiction to carry debt (that is, to make annual debt service or lease payments on the debt while the debt is outstanding). If this capacity is strong—either because revenue growth relative to spending needs will be strong in the future or because of little existing debt—the issuer is in a position to shorten debt retirement terms. For example, the city erecting the above-mentioned office building might use a fifteen-year retirement term for the bonds. If debt carrying capacity is limited, because revenue growth will be modest compared with needs in the future or because outstanding debt is already substantial, the retirement on new debt probably needs to be at or near the outside term that the market allows. If general obligation (GO) bonds will be used to finance the city office building, a retirement term of about twenty years could be the most appropriate.

The issuer must also consider its capital needs in future years. If a local government expects to face major capital financing needs in the next, say, five to fifteen years, it might wisely keep retirement terms on debt issued today considerably shorter than the useful lives of at least some of the assets financed with the debt. For example, the issuer might finance an elevated platform truck—costing $600,000 and estimated to be used in a first-line capacity for twenty years—with a seven-year installment-purchase agreement. Although seven years is less than half the fire truck's estimated useful life, this term frees up debt capacity to help the issuer to meet some of its future capital needs after seven years. If the local jurisdiction's capital improvement program (CIP) and related plans for longer-term facilities suggest that capital financing needs will be modest in the future, the issuer is in a position to extend repayment terms on debt issued today: the retirement term on the fire truck might be extended to ten years or more.

Finally, the debt markets impose limits on retirement terms for bonds or debt. For example, investors are usually unwilling to provide GO bond financing for a term much beyond twenty years, even if the estimated useful life of the capital asset financed with the bonds extends well beyond that period. Investors perceive twenty years to be a reasonable time horizon for tax-backed or general debt—enough time for the issuer to spread out debt service payments to affordable annual amounts. Occasionally when investor demand for GO bonds is strong, a highly rated issuer is able to sell GO bonds to finance a long-lived facility with a retirement term extending to twenty-two or even twenty-five years.[2]

Special or limited obligation bond issues that are secured by substantial revenue sources and that finance facilities with long, useful lives can be issued for overall terms extending up to 20 years and sometimes more. Special obligation (SO) bonds that are secured with and paid from revenues that are less substantial or that finance capital facilities such as landfills that have intermediate useful lives typically have overall terms that span fifteen years or less.

Revenue bond retirement terms are usually based on both the useful life of the asset financed with the bonds and the flow of net revenues pledged to secure and pay debt service on the bonds. These terms can be longer than for other types of debt. Some revenue bond issues have retirement terms of twenty years or less. For example, the Henderson, North Carolina, revenue bond issue discussed later in this chapter is being repaid over twenty years.

However, some have retirement terms that extend to twenty-five or thirty years or more. For example, in 2001 Winston-Salem, North Carolina, issued $105.4 million in water-sewer revenue bonds that are being retired over a term of twenty-eight years.[3] Such long-term revenue bond financing is possible because the facilities financed with the bonds have very long useful lives. Very long-term financing is sometimes necessary because the revenue-generating capacity of the project or enterprise financed with the bonds takes many years to develop. Moreover, debt service on the bonds must come from project or enterprise revenues—another reason to stretch out the financing period.

Debt maturity and retirement schedules

Different types of debt maturity and retirement schedules are used for repaying long-term debt. Such schedules can be made up of serial, term, or combined serial-term maturities.

Four maturity schedules are illustrated in Table 9–1, which shows a hypothetical, $10 million bond issue with a full term of ten years.

A typical serial maturity schedule for long-term debt provides for debt retirement in annual installments.[4] In other words, the debt is divided into amounts of principal, and each is retired in a different year over the full term of the debt issue. The amount of any maturity and principal retirement for a year are the same for serial bonds. All maturities may be equal in amount; that is, the same principal is retired each year over the full term of the bond issue (see column 2 of Table 9–1). Alternatively, maturity amounts and principal

Table 9–1

Maturity schedules for a hypothetical, $10 million, ten-year bond issue (principal only)

End of year	Serial maturity		Single-term maturity (bullet principal)	Combined serial-term maturity or principal
	Even principal	Varying principal		
1	$1,000,000	$500,000		$500,000
2	1,000,000	700,000		700,000
3	1,000,000	800,000		800,000
4	1,000,000	1,000,000		1,000,000
5	1,000,000	1,200,000		1,200,000
6	1,000,000	1,300,000		1,300,000
7	1,000,000	1,300,000		1,300,000
8	1,000,000	1,200,000		
9	1,000,000	1,100,000		
10	1,000,000	900,000	10,000,000	3,200,000
Total	$10,000,000	$10,000,000	$10,000,000	$10,000,000

Note: Retirement of principal coincides with the maturity schedule (the maturity and principal retirement schedules are identical) for both of the serial maturities shown above and the single-term maturity. For the combined serial-term maturity, however, principal retirement coincides with the maturity schedule for only the serial maturities; principal retirement for the $3,200,000 term maturity (Year 10 in column 5) would normally occur each year in Years 8, 9, and 10 through sinking-fund contributions and mandatory call of the bonds.

retirement may vary from one year or maturity to another (see column 3 of Table 9–1).

Local issues of GO bonds typically consist entirely of serial maturities, and many have varying principal schedules in order to coordinate debt retirement on new bonds with annual debt service payment on existing debt. For example, the lower amounts shown in Years 1, 2, and 3 of the varying principal schedule in Table 9–1 might accommodate gradually declining yet significant payments on existing debt in those years. As the payments on existing debt decline, principal retirement on the new debt increases to a peak of $1,300,000 in Years 6 and 7.

A single-term maturity schedule can provide for retirement of an entire debt or bond issue with a single bullet payment made at the end of the debt's full term, as shown in column 4 of Table 9–1. There is just one principal payment and maturity date for the debt. Since 1930, local governments have rarely used term debt alone.[5] Very occasionally, a large local government has used term bonds to finance a strong enterprise, with resources for repayment specifically identified and set aside annually to cover the single bullet payment.

Serial and term maturities can be combined in one bond issue. Term bonds today usually refer to a portion of a long-term debt issue that represents several years of principal if these bonds had been issued as serial debt. Often several term bonds are combined serial-term maturity schedule, and each term bond consists of two or more annual principal amounts if the bonds were serial debt. Serial bonds make up the rest of the combined serial-term maturity schedule. Typical serial bonds are retired in the first half or two-thirds of the overall debt term, and typical term bonds are placed and retired in the second half of the overall debt term. Combined serial-term maturity schedules are used to help sell the bonds. Some investors, including individuals, are interested in buying the earlier serial maturities, while other investors, especially insurance companies and certain mutual funds, are interested in the later, longer-term maturities.

In a combined serial-term schedule, some years in the span of the bonds do not show a maturity amount due (see column 5 of Table 9–1). The issuer is required during those years to make contributions to a **sinking fund.** The contribution is equal to a portion of the term bonds and is principal retirement for the issuer just as if that portion of the term bonds were serial bonds. A mandatory call feature usually accompanies the sinking fund, and it requires the payment of the contribution into the sinking fund by the issuer in any year to be paid to the investors. Such payment to the investors is principal retirement on the bonds.

A combined serial-term maturity schedule is the most common debt retirement structure used today for revenue bonds, certificates of participation and other capital leases, and many types of SO bonds. More will be said about combined serial-term maturity schedules later in the chapter.

Models of debt service and actual practices

Annual debt service consists of principal repayment of the bonds making up a year's maturity and interest on the total amount of the bond issue outstanding that year. For example, if all maturities of the $10 million bond issue in Table 9–1 have a 5 percent annual interest rate[6] and if $1 million of principal is retired each year, debt service in year 1 is $1,500,000, comprising $1 million in principal and $500,000 in interest ($10,000,000 × 0.05 [5 percent]). Debt service in Year 2 is $1,450,000, comprising $1,000,000 in principal and $450,000 in interest ($9,000,000 × 0.05).

The principal on local government long-term debt is usually paid annually, and the interest is paid semiannually. Debt service payments on the $10 million, 5 percent bonds would include the following specific payments during the first two years:

- At twelve months, $250,000 in interest and $1 million of principal
- At eighteen months, $225,000 in interest
- At twenty-four months, $225,000 in interest and $1 million of principal.[7]

Annual debt service may occasionally include other financing charges such as agent fees. Additional charges are usually small relative to principal and interest.

Two models of debt service offer a starting point for many local governments that are structuring their annual debt service payments: even annual principal with declining debt service (see Table 9–2) and even annual debt service (see Table 9–3).[8] In the example in Table 9–2, annual debt service declines as the interest payments decline from year to year. Interest declines because the total principal outstanding falls. In the second model, even annual debt service, the principal portion of annual debt service grows by the same amount that the interest portion declines each year. Even annual debt service is like the payment structure for the typical home mortgage.

Tables 9–2 and 9–3 use the $10 million, ten-year bond issue from Table 9–1 and assume a 5 percent annual interest rate. In actual bond issues, as discussed in Chapter 10, interest rates usually vary for different maturities in a bond issue.

The model of even annual principal retirement with declining debt service represents a conservative approach to debt repayment.[9] It pays down bonds and frees up debt service capacity more quickly than the even annual debt service model.[10] It also results in lower interest payments overall. With even principal retirement, interest on the $10 million bond issue is $200,470 less than with the even annual debt service. On the other hand, even principal retirement requires the issuer to make larger debt service payments in the earlier years of the term, when revenues are likely to be less and debt

Table 9–2
Even annual principal with declining debt service model for a hypothetical, $10 million, ten-year, 5 percent bond issue

End of year	Annual principal	Annual interest	Annual debt service (principal plus interest)	Debt outstanding at end of year
1	$1,000,000	$500,000	$1,500,000	$9,000,000
2	1,000,000	450,000	1,450,000	8,000,000
3	1,000,000	400,000	1,400,000	7,000,000
4	1,000,000	350,000	1,350,000	6,000,000
5	1,000,000	300,000	1,300,000	5,000,000
6	1,000,000	250,000	1,250,000	4,000,000
7	1,000,000	200,000	1,200,000	3,000,000
8	1,000,000	150,000	1,150,000	2,000,000
9	1,000,000	100,000	1,100,000	1,000,000
10	1,000,000	50,000	1,050,000	0
Totals	$10,000,000	$2,750,000	$12,750,000	

Table 9–3

Even annual debt service model for a hypothetical, $10 million, ten-year, 5 percent bond issue

End of year	Annual principal	Annual interest	Annual debt service (principal plus interest)	Debt outstanding at end of year
1	$795,047	$500,000	$1,295,047	$9,204,953
2	834,797	460,250	1,295,047	8,370,156
3	876,537	418,510	1,295,047	7,493,619
4	920,364	374,683	1,295,047	6,573,255
5	966,383	328,664	1,295,047	5,606,872
6	1,014,702	280,345	1,295,047	4,592,170
7	1,065,437	229,610	1,295,047	3,526,733
8	1,118,710	176,337	1,295,047	2,408,023
9	1,174,645	120,402	1,295,047	1,233,378
10	1,233,378	61,669	1,295,047	0
Totals	$10,000,000	$2,950,470	$12,950,470	

service payments on previously existing debt are likely to be more. With even annual debt service, new debt service capacity over the ten-year term of the $10 million bond issue must come entirely from revenue growth or a decrease in other spending. No new capacity is made available by declining debt service over the ten-year term.

In practice, local governments' debt service payment schedules usually diverge from both of the models shown in Tables 9–2 and 9–3. Debt planning may start with one or the other model, but officials make modifications as they blend debt service on new bonds with annual debt service on previously existing debt. For example, officials may start with the even annual principal model but then modify it by lowering principal retirement in the first few years to limit cash flow requirements during construction of the project financed with the bonds. Alternatively, they may start with even annual debt service payments and then reduce or increase the payments in particular years in light of annual payment obligations on existing debt in those years.

Debt service on GO bonds, capital leases, and other debt that is paid from general revenues is often structured initially according to the model of even annual principal with declining debt service. This model is later modified to fit overall, future revenue and spending flows, including debt service on existing debt.

For debt service on revenue bonds paid from enterprise earnings, local government officials may use the level debt service model because it helps them maintain a stable rate structure for the enterprise from year to year. Alternatively, for debt planning for revenue bonds for some enterprises or for special tax bonds, officials could use a model that provides for gradually increasing annual debt service. Annual revenue for these enterprises, projects, or services takes time to build, requiring the issuers of debt to keep principal retirement and annual debt service low in the early years of the bond retirement schedule and then increase principal retirement and debt service as annual revenues grow.

Delayed principal retirement and capitalization of interest

While principal retirement on most local long-term bond issues begins one year after the debt is issued, some serial bond issues or combined serial-term bond issues defer the start of principal retirement until approximately two to five years after issuance. Annual interest is paid during those years but not principal. State laws vary in the authority they give local governments to defer principal retirement on bonds or debt. Usually payment of principal is deferred to hold down debt service payments during construction, to recognize limited revenue flow during the first few years of a revenue bond issue, or for other reasons.

Capitalized interest is interest on debt that the issuer adds to project costs and may pay from bond proceeds or other revenues available for the project. If interest on debt during construction is not paid from project revenues, it becomes part of annual debt service and is paid from annual revenues. The law in some states as well as generally accepted accounting principles allow interest and other financing costs during a project's construction to be charged to the project and paid from bond proceeds or other project resources rather than operating revenue.[11] Although they have the authority to do so, many local governments do not capitalize interest payments during construction; instead they charge interest payments to ongoing debt service in the operating budget. Capitalization of interest is most likely to occur for revenue bond projects.

When capitalization of interest occurs, it does not reduce debt service during construction but instead shifts the source of payment for the interest portion of such debt service. Increased debt often has to be issued to cover additional project costs when interest during construction is capitalized. This, in turn, increases the overall cost of debt service.

Years' average maturity

Years' average maturity is a measure of how long, on average, a bond or debt issue that is retired in annual or other periodic installments over many years is outstanding. Two bond issues, each outstanding for the same overall term, may have different average maturities, depending on the debt retirement schedule for each. If debt retirement on the first issue is front loaded (much of the debt is retired in the first half of the full term) and debt retirement on the second issue is back loaded (more of the debt is repaid in the second half of the full term), the years' average maturity for the first issue will be less than for the second.

Interest rates vary with the average maturity of debt. Generally, the longer that debt is outstanding, the greater the risk associated with it and the higher the interest rates usually incurred for the debt. Thus, if two debt issues of equal credit quality have varying maturity schedules and different years' average maturities, the issue with the shorter average maturity would ordinarily have a lower average interest rate.

The calculation of years' average maturity is not complicated. First, total bond years for a bond or debt issue is calculated by multiplying the princi-

Table 9–4
Years' average maturity for two hypothetical, $60,000, three-year debt issues with different retirement schedules

Year	Maturity or principal amount*	Number of years principal is outstanding	Bond years
Bond issue no. 1: Heavy up-front principal retirement			
1	$30,000	1	$30,000
2	20,000	2	40,000
3	10,000	3	30,000
Totals	60,000		100,000

Years' average maturity:
total bond years/total principal = $100,000/$60,000 = 1.67 years

Year	Maturity or principal amount*	Number of years principal is outstanding	Bond years
Bond issue no. 2: Delayed principal retirement			
1	$10,000	1	$10,000
2	20,000	2	40,000
3	30,000	3	90,000
Totals	60,000		140,000

Years' average maturity:
total bond years/total principal = $140,000/$60,000 = 2.33 years

*Maturity and principal are one and the same or equal here.

pal amount of each maturity in the issue by the number of years that maturity is outstanding (columns 2 and 3 on Table 9–4) and summing each maturity's bond years (column 4 total). Second, the total bond years for the issue is divided by the dollar amount of the bond issue. The result is years' average maturity for the bond issue.

Table 9–4 shows years' average maturity for two hypothetical debt issues of $60,000 for a three-year term. The issues, however, have very different debt retirement schedules: the first has heavy up-front retirement of principal, and the second has delayed principal retirement.

The years' average maturity for bond issue no. 1 is much shorter (1.67) years than for bond issue no. 2 (2.33 years). Retirement of principal for issue no. 1 is concentrated in the first two years, while principal retirement for issue no. 2 is concentrated in the second and third years.

Table 9–5 shows bond years and years' average maturity for the debt repayment schedules of the $10 million, ten-year bond issues in Tables 9–2 and 9–3. The years' average maturity for the gradually increasing principal retirement schedule (column 5) is longer because principal repayment is concentrated more in the latter years of the ten-year term. If market interest rates are higher for long-term debt than for short-term debt of the same credit quality, the second bond issue will probably have a higher average interest rate than the first.

Use of taxes or other revenue for annual debt service

Annual debt service on local government debt is typically paid from annual revenues raised in the operating budget. Debt service on debt used to

Table 9–5
Years' average maturity for two hypothetical, $10 million, ten-year bond issues, one with even annual principal retirement and another with gradually increasing principal retirement

End of year	Bond issue with even annual principal retirement			Bond issue with gradually increasing principal retirement		
	Principal retirement	Number of years maturity or principal is outstanding*	Bond years for maturity and issue	Principal retirement	Number of years principal or maturity is outstanding*	Bond years for maturity and issue
1	$1,000,000	1	$1,000,000	$795,047	1	$795,047
2	1,000,000	2	2,000,000	834,797	2	1,669,594
3	1,000,000	3	3,000,000	876,537	3	2,629,611
4	1,000,000	4	4,000,000	920,364	4	3,681,456
5	1,000,000	5	5,000,000	966,383	5	4,831,915
6	1,000,000	6	6,000,000	1,014,702	6	6,088,212
7	1,000,000	7	7,000,000	1,065,437	7	7,458,059
8	1,000,000	8	8,000,000	1,118,710	8	8,949,680
9	1,000,000	9	9,000,000	1,174,645	9	10,571,805
10	1,000,000	10	10,000,000	1,233,378	10	12,333,780
Totals	$10,000,000		$55,000,000	$10,000,000		$59,009,159

Years' average maturity:
$55,000,000/$10,000,000 = 5.5 years

Years' average maturity:
$59,009,159/$10,000,000 = 5.9 years

Note: Maturity and principal are identical for both bond issues.

finance projects for self-supporting enterprises is usually covered by enterprise user fees and related revenues. If the bonds or debt finance general public improvements, general taxes and revenues pay annual debt service. Special taxes and revenues are earmarked to pay debt service on SO bonds issued to finance specific or general public improvements.

Some local governments relate annual debt service on bonds issued for general public improvements to the tax rate needed to pay annual debt service on the bonds. In some jurisdictions, a specific tax rate is authorized and legally earmarked by state law or local charter to cover debt service on bonds.[12] Other local governments, because of their governing board policies, earmark a portion of the tax levy, or a certain number of cents of the property tax rate, or a portion of other general revenues to pay debt service on bonds to finance general public improvements.[13] Such legal or policy-based earmarking sets aside a portion of general taxes or revenues for annual debt service and thereby helps to provide the resources needed to meet capital needs. Alternatively, a local government may simply identify how many mills (1/10 of a cent) per $1,000 of taxable value or how many cents per $100 of taxable value of the tax rate is going to fund annual debt service on such bonds. This sort of identification reveals the contribution that general taxes and revenues are making to the capital program and, conversely, the burden that debt issuance for general public improvements is placing on taxpayers.

Table 9–6 presents annual debt service for the $10 million, ten-year, 5 percent bond issue first presented in Table 9–2. It assumes even annual principal retirement and declining debt service. It also presents a hypothetical property tax valuation for each year that debt service is paid, starting with $3 billion in Year 1 and increasing by 4 percent per year, reflecting economic

Table 9–6
Tax rate needed to cover annual debt service (principal and interest) on a hypothetical, $10 million, ten-year, 5 percent bond issue and tax revenue available for debt service on new bonds

End of year	Annual debt service	Property tax valuation	Tax rate needed for debt service (cents/$100)	Tax revenue yielded by 5 cents per $100 tax rate	Tax revenue available for debt service on new bonds
1	$1,500,000	$3,000,000,000	5.000 cents	$1,500,000	$0
2	1,450,000	3,120,000,000	4.647 cents	1,560,000	110,000
3	1,400,000	3,244,800,000	4.315 cents	1,622,400	222,400
4	1,350,000	3,374,592,000	4.001 cents	1,687,296	337,296
5	1,300,000	3,509,575,680	3.704 cents	1,754,788	454,788
6	1,250,000	3,649,958,707	3.425 cents	1,824,979	574,979
7	1,200,000	3,795,957,055	3.163 cents	1,897,979	697,979
8	1,150,000	3,947,795,338	2.913 cents	1,973,898	823,898
9	1,100,000	4,105,707,151	2.679 cents	2,052,854	952,854
10	1,050,000	4,269,935,437	2.459 cents	2,134,968	1,084,968

Note: Tax revenue figures in the table assume that 100 percent of the property tax levy is collected. This collection rate would be unusual, however, because good tax collection percentages range from 95 percent to more than 99 percent. In an actual situation, the collection percentage for property taxes would have to be built into the calculations.

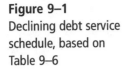

Figure 9–1
Declining debt service
schedule, based on
Table 9–6

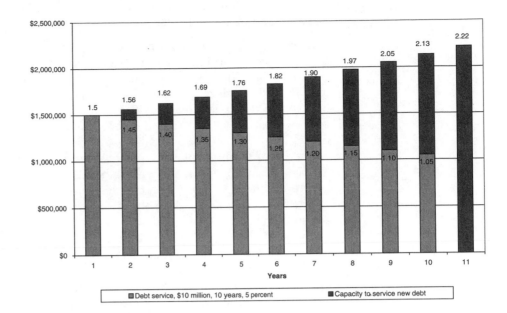

development and tax base growth. The table shows the tax rate needed to cover debt service on the bonds each year. A tax rate of 5 cents is required in Year 1. This amount declines annually to 2.459 cents in Year 10. Column 6 of Table 9–6 shows the amount of revenue available to cover debt service on new bonds if the 5-cent tax rate is maintained beyond Year 1.

Figure 9–1 clearly shows the advantage of this declining debt service schedule and earmarking taxes or revenues for covering annual debt service on bonds. The combined effect of declining debt service and earmarked taxes reduces the tax rate needed to pay debt service on the $10 million bond issue from 5 cents per $100 in Year 1 to less than 2.5 cents in Year 10. As a matter of policy, officials for this jurisdiction could earmark the 5 cent tax rate for debt service. As a result, the tax revenue available to cover debt service on new bonds would grow from $110,000 in Year 2 to $1,084,968 in Year 10. The latter amount would be enough to cover debt service for a new $7 million bond issue, assuming a ten-year term, 5 percent interest rates, and even retirement of principal. After Year 10, the original $10 million bond issue would be paid off, and, if no new debt had been issued, more than $2,134,968 would be available to cover debt service on new debt issued in Year 11.

All of this points to the value of earmarking a portion of annual taxes or revenues to cover debt service to finance a capital improvement program. The earmarking, along with a reasonably paced pay down of existing debt, ensures that some revenues will be available to meet capital needs in the future. Annually recurring revenues earmarked for a capital improvement program may be used to cover not only debt service on bonds but also pay-as-go capital financing.

Early redemption options and advance refunding

Local governments may pay off debt before it is scheduled to mature by the exercise of a call feature if it is included in the bond contract. Local governments may also advance refund debt. Either of these options usually involves the issuance of refunding bonds or debt that is used to pay off or **defease** the existing debt.

Early redemption options

The **early redemption** feature in a bond contract gives the issuer of long-term bonds the option to call in (**call**) and pay off the bonds before their maturity dates. For example, the issuer of the bonds shown in Table 9–3 may have the option to redeem the bonds scheduled to mature in Years 6, 7, 8, 9, and 10 before their maturity dates arrive. The issuer might call in and pay off any or all of the bonds scheduled to mature in Years 9 and 10 in Year 7, for example.

Early redemption options typically have a call protection period in which the issuer may not call in and redeem bonds otherwise subject to redemption before maturity. In many bond issues, this call protection period extends over roughly the first half of the debt repayment term. In the case of the $10 million bond issue in Table 9–3, the call protection period might extend from Years 1 through 5. The call protection period has two effects. First, it prevents the issuer from redeeming any of the bonds in Years 1 through 5 before their scheduled maturity dates. These bonds are not subject to early redemption at all. Second, the bonds scheduled to mature in Years 6 through 10 that are subject to early redemption may not be called in and paid off any time during the call protection period (that is, before Year 5 has elapsed). The issuer may call in any of the bonds scheduled to mature in Years 6 through 10 in Year 6 or afterwards.

Early redemption or call features are commonly used in local governments' long-term bond or debt issues. The most common reasons for an issuer to redeem outstanding bonds before maturity is to take advantage of lower interest rates. If interest rates fall after the issuer sells a bond issue, the issuer calls in some or all of the original bonds and refunds them with the proceeds of new bonds issued at the new, lower interest rates. Other issuers use the early redemption option to call in revenue bonds or SO bonds that have restrictive indentures to replace them with refunding bonds with indentures that are less restrictive. Some issuers redeem bonds before maturity because extra money becomes available to them to do so. The money, perhaps, is restricted and may not be used for other purposes, or the issuer decides that early redemption is the best use of the money, saving future interest costs and perhaps having other advantages.

The early redemption option typically has a price. The price is the **call premium.** This premium, when charged, is usually in the range of 0.5 percent to 2 percent of the principal amount of the bonds redeemed before maturity. The percentage often varies depending on how long before maturity that bonds are called. For the $10 million issue in Table 9–3, the following call premium schedule might apply:

- Bonds scheduled to mature at end of Years 6, 7, 8, 9, or 10 redeemed during Year 6: 1.5 percent

- Bonds scheduled to mature at end of Years 7, 8, 9, and 10 redeemed during Year 7: 1.0 percent

- Bonds scheduled to mature at end of Years 8, 9, and 10 redeemed during Year 8: 0.5 percent

- Bonds scheduled to mature at end of Years 9 and 10 redeemed during Year 9: redeemed at par.

Early redemption options are available for the GO bond issue of Johnston County, North Carolina, and the revenue bond issue of Henderson, North Carolina, described later in this chapter.

Advance refunding

An issuer can advance refund bonds even if they are not subject to early call or redemption. Advance refunding occurs frequently when interest rates are falling or have fallen significantly. It allows the issuer to replace outstanding debt that has high interest rates with new debt that has lower rates.

Local governments did a lot of advance refunding during the mid- and late 1990s that extended even into the first years of the twenty-first century. Market interest rates were generally falling during these years. Rather than wait for call protection periods on their bonds or debt to end, local governments advance refunded outstanding debt or bonds and replaced them with debt paying significantly lower interest rates. In advance refunding, the issuer sells refunding bonds at low interest rates and puts the proceeds into an escrow account controlled by an outside party, a bank or trust company, where they are invested in certain securities authorized by IRS regulations. The refunding bond proceeds plus the interest earned on them are matched with debt service on the issuer's existing, higher-interest-rate debt. This defeases the existing debt, which means the issuer is no longer effectively responsible for paying debt service on it. The debt service is paid from the escrow account with the advance refunding bonds. The issuer then becomes responsible for paying debt service on the advance refunding bonds, which is lower than that on the defeased debt.

Johnston County, North Carolina; Henderson County, North Carolina; Brunswick County, North Carolina; Dallas, Texas, and Buncombe County, North Carolina; and Richmond County, North Carolina, show how local governments can plan and structure their debt. Principal retirement and debt service schedules for GO bonds, revenue bonds, capital leases, and two types of SO bonds are described in the following examples. The description of Richmond County shows the debt retirement and debt service schedules for refunding bonds, and it presents an analysis of debt service savings resulting from the refunding.

Johnston County, North Carolina, is located on the edge of Research Triangle Park, a high-tech growth area near the cities of Raleigh, Durham, and Chapel Hill. Growth in the triangle during the past decade has propelled rapid development in the surrounding local jurisdictions, including Johnston County. To keep up with the growth, the county has issued large amounts of GO debt and other debt to build new schools and other public facilities. Table 9–7 shows annual principal, interest, and debt service payments for the county's previously existing GO bonds and for the $25 million in new GO bonds sold in May 2001.

Of Johnston County's $78,950,000 in existing GO debt, all but $1,050,000 was issued for school purposes. Most of it resulted from two school bond sales: $30.5 million in 1997–1998, and $35 million in 1999–2000. The $25 million bond issue in 2001 was the third increment of a major school construction and improvement program. When the county issued the $25 million in new GO bonds, it had $23 million in authorized but unissued

GO bonds for school and community college financing. The county planned to issue them within a few years.[14]

Johnston County has used the conventional twenty-year term or approximate twenty-year term for its GO bonds. Existing GO bonds will be repaid over a nineteen-year period, from 2001 to 2019. The $25 million in new GO bonds will be outstanding for twenty years from issuance. They will be retired with nineteen principal payments. Interest is being paid semiannually over the full term of the bond issue.

The debt payment schedules for Johnston County's existing and new GO bonds closely approximate the even annual principal and declining debt model shown in Table 9–2. The schedules free up debt capacity to support new debt, enabling the county to meet growth expected in future years. For the existing debt, principal retirement is the same—$4,225,000—in all but two years. Debt service gradually declines from a peak of $8,211,975 in 2002 to $4,236,000 in 2019. For the $25 million in new GO bonds, principal retirement is almost even each year:

Table 9–7
Debt service (principal retirement and interest) schedules for GO bonds, previously existing and 2001 bond issue, Johnston County, North Carolina

Fiscal year	Previously existing GO bonds			$25 million in 2001 GO bonds			Total GO debt service
	Annual principal	Interest	Debt service	Principal	Interest	Debt service	
2001	$3,125,000	$4,141,700	$7,266,700				$7,266,700
2002	4,225,000	3,986,975	8,211,975		1,195,000	1,195,000	9,406,975
2003	4,225,000	3,771,750	7,996,750	1,300,000	1,195,000	2,495,000	10,491,750
2004	4,225,000	3,556,525	7,781,525	1,300,000	1,136,500	2,436,500	10,218,025
2005	4,225,000	3,341,300	7,566,300	1,400,000	1,078,000	2,478,000	10,044,300
2006	4,225,000	3,124,475	7,349,475	1,400,000	1,015,000	2,415,000	9,764,475
2007	4,225,000	2,907,650	7,132,650	1,400,000	952,000	2,352,000	9,484,650
2008	4,225,000	2,690,825	6,915,825	1,400,000	889,000	2,289,000	9,204,825
2009	4,225,000	2,474,000	6,699,000	1,000,000	826,000	1,826,000	8,525,000
2010	4,225,000	2,255,650	6,480,650	1,300,000	781,000	2,081,000	8,561,650
2011	4,225,000	2,035,700	6,260,700	500,000	722,500	1,222,500	7,483,200
2012	4,225,000	1,811,950	6,036,950	1,400,000	700,000	2,100,000	8,136,950
2013	4,225,000	1,587,200	5,812,200	1,400,000	630,000	2,030,000	7,842,200
2014	4,225,000	1,362,450	5,587,450	1,400,000	560,000	1,960,000	7,547,450
2015	4,225,000	1,137,700	5,362,700	1,400,000	490,000	1,890,000	7,252,700
2016	4,225,000	912,950	5,137,950	1,400,000	420,000	1,820,000	6,957,950
2017	4,225,000	688,200	4,913,200	1,400,000	350,000	1,750,000	6,663,200
2018	4,225,000	463,450	4,688,450	1,400,000	280,000	1,680,000	6,368,450
2019	4,000,000	236,000	4,236,000	1,400,000	210,000	1,610,000	5,846,000
2020				1,400,000	140,000	1,540,000	1,540,000
2021				1,400,000	70,000	1,470,000	1,470,000
Totals	$78,950,000	$42,486,450	$121,436,450	$25,000,000	$13,640,000	$38,640,000	$160,076,450

Source: For existing bonds, Official Statement, April 27, 2001, prepared by the Local Government Commission of North Carolina, "County of Johnston, North Carolina, $25,000,000 General Obligation School Bonds, Series 2001, dated June 1, 2001," 18. The debt service schedule for the $25 million in new GO bonds was provided by the finance officer of Johnston County.

$1.4 million annually for fourteen years, $1.3 million for three years, $1 million in 2009, and $500,000 in 2011. (Besides GO bonds, Johnston County has $39.3 million in installment-purchase debt that is paid from general fund revenues.[15] The payment obligations on the installment-purchase debt extend to 2022, and they generally decline from year to year although they spike from $2.1 million in 2010 to $3.3 million in 2011 and then drop to less than $1.5 in subsequent years.) Principal retirement for the new GO bonds was lowered to $500,000 in 2011 to even out the sum of GO and installment debt service or lease payments in that year.

Johnston County did not begin to repay principal on the $25 million in new GO bonds until June 1, 2003, two years after issuance. This represents a one-year deferral of principal retirement, arranged because debt service on the existing GO bonds increases from $7,266,700 in 2001 to $8,211,975 in 2002, declining gradually thereafter. Postponing principal retirement on the new bonds makes debt service requirements in 2001 and 2002 more manageable and gives the county a year

to realize more revenue growth to help finance these requirements.

The years' average maturity for the $25 million in new GO bonds is 11.16 years. This is calculated by dividing total bond years of $279,000,000, calculated in Table 10–6, by $25 million. This is close to the middle of the overall repayment term for the issue, which is consistent with an even principal retirement schedule.

Johnston County's GO bonds mature from 2002–2003 through 2020–2021. Bonds maturing after June 1, 2012, are subject to early redemption, but redemption may not be exercised earlier than June 1, 2011. The early redemption or call premium for these bonds ranges between 0.5 percent and 2 percent of the amount redeemed, with 0.5 percent charged for each twelve months that bonds are redeemed prior to maturity, up to a maximum premium of 2 percent.

Henderson County, North Carolina, issued $15,630,000 in water-sewer revenue bonds in 2001. Table 9–8 presents the maturity schedule and Table 9–9

Table 9–8
Maturity schedule for $15,630,000 in water-sewer revenue bonds, Henderson, North Carolina

Fiscal year	Principal or maturity	Type of maturity
2002	$75,000	Serial
2003	230,000	Serial
2004	580,000	Serial
2005	600,000	Serial
2006	625,000	Serial
2007	645,000	Serial
2008	670,000	Serial
2009	705,000	Serial
2010	730,000	Serial
2011	765,000	Serial
2012	790,000	Serial
2014	1,700,000	Term
2016	1,880,000	Term
2018	2,090,000	Term
2019	1,125,000	Serial
2021	2,420,000	Term
Totals	$15,630,000	

Source: Official Statement, April 5, 2001, prepared by Salomon Smith Barney and BB&T Capital Markets in cooperation with the Local Government Commission of North Carolina, "$15,630,000, City of Henderson, North Carolina, Combined Enterprise System Revenue Bonds, Series 2001, dated April 1, 2001," cover page.

Table 9–9
Principal retirement, interest payment, and debt service schedule for $15,630,000 in water-sewer revenue bonds, Henderson, North Carolina

Fiscal year	Principal retirement	Interest	Debt service
2002	$75,000	$794,016	$869,016
2003	230,000	730,500	960,500
2004	580,000	722,680	1,302,680
2005	600,000	701,800	1,301,800
2006	625,000	677,800	1,302,800
2007	645,000	654,363	1,299,363
2008	670,000	628,563	1,298,563
2009	705,000	601,763	1,306,763
2010	730,000	572,858	1,302,858
2011	765,000	542,198	1,307,198
2012	790,000	509,685	1,299,685
2013	825,000	474,925	1,299,925
2014	875,000	431,613	1,306,613
2015	915,000	385,675	1,300,675
2016	965,000	337,638	1,302,638
2017	1,020,000	286,975	1,306,975
2018	1,070,000	233,425	1,303,425
2019	1,125,000	177,250	1,302,250
2020	1,180,000	121,000	1,301,000
2021	1,240,000	62,000	1,302,000
Totals	$15,630,000	$9,646,723	$25,276,723

Source: Official Statement, April 15, 2001, prepared by Salomon Smith Barney and BB&T Capital Markets in cooperation with the Local Government Commission of North Carolina, "$15,630,000 City of Henderson, North Carolina, Combined Enterprise System Revenue Bonds, Series 2001, dated April 1, 2001," 15.

the principal retirement, interest payment, and debt service schedules for those bonds. The bond proceeds provide the lion's share of a $16,906,000 project. The other project revenues are a $1,130,000 state grant and $146,000 from miscellaneous sources. The project has two general purposes: refinance existing installment-purchase debt for the water-sewer system ($7,055,000) and make improvements to the system ($7,677,643). The balance of project revenues are for a debt service reserve ($1,307,200), capitalized interest ($441,200), issuance costs ($389,944), and accrued interest ($34,611). Chapter 7 explains the use of debt service reserves in revenue bond financing, capital leases, and SO debt. An earlier part of this chapter explained capitalized interest. Chapter 11 on selling debt covers debt issuance costs and accrued interest.

Table 9–8 shows that the Henderson revenue bonds combine both serial and term maturities, which is typical of revenue bond issues. Serial bonds make up $7,540,000 and term bonds $8,090,000 of the issue amount. The first eleven maturities, 2002 through 2012, and the bonds to be repaid in 2019 are also serial bonds. The rest of the issue consists of four term maturities, due to be paid in 2014, 2016, 2018, and 2021. Each of these term maturities encompasses two years of principal.

In the years when no bonds are scheduled to mature, Henderson makes a contribution into a sinking fund. For example, even though no bonds are shown to mature in 2013 (see Table 9–8), the city makes a principal payment of $825,000 and a debt service payment of $1,299,925, including principal, to the sinking fund, which, as explained below, goes to the investors that year (see Table 9–9).

Henderson's revenue bonds that mature on or after May 1, 2012, are subject to early redemption at the option of the city. Portions of the term maturities for 2014, 2016, 2018, and 2021 are subject to mandatory sinking fund redemption in 2013, 2014, 2015, 2016, 2017, 2018, 2020, and 2021. These portions are equal to the principal amounts shown in Table 9–9 for these years. The city's contributions to the sinking fund in each year equal debt service—including both principal and interest— for the year. The revenue bond trustee uses the city's debt service payment or contributions to redeem the portion of term bonds with accrued interest due pursuant to the debt service schedule and under the mandatory call feature.[16] Interest rates and pricing on the term bonds are based on the term maturity date. This gives investors an interest rate higher than if the bonds were serial maturities.[17]

Henderson's revenue bonds are outstanding over a full term of twenty-one years from issuance, and principal retirement and annual debt service occur in twenty installments. These features of debt structure for Henderson's revenue bonds are like the corresponding features for Johnston County's GO bonds. Johnston County's bonds have even principal and declining annual debt service, but Henderson's revenue bonds have increasing principal payments and, except in the first two years, fairly equal annual debt service. The even annual debt service structure helps Henderson maintain stable water-sewer rates and, as already mentioned, is a structure for revenue bonds.

The city may exercise the early redemption option only after May 1, 2011. A redemption premium of 1 percent of the principal amount of the bonds redeemed is charged if the redemption option is exercised between May 1, 2011, and April 30, 2012; and a redemption premium of 0.5 percent is charged if the option is exercised between May 1, 2012, and April 30, 2013. If the option is exercised after May 1, 2013, the bonds are redeemed at par.

The consultant's feasibility study for Henderson's revenue bonds indicates that the city will be able to maintain coverage (annual net revenues to annual debt service) well in excess of the 1.25 percent coverage ratio requirement (for parity debt) in the revenue bond's rate covenant. Using realistic assumptions, the projected coverage will be 3.33 in 2002, 3.15 in 2003, 2.51 in 2004, 2.59 in 2005, and 2.53 in 2006.[18] These high coverage ratios in the first several years of the revenue bond's term suggest that the city's water-sewer system

will produce much more than enough net revenue to pay annual debt service. By 2004 when annual debt service on the bonds rises close to its annual maximum, projected coverage is double the legally required ratio of 1.25 percent. If repayment of Henderson's revenue bonds had been structured like Johnston County's GO bonds, with even annual principal and declining debt service, projected coverage on the revenue bonds would have dropped much closer to the contractually required minimum.

The years' average maturity for Henderson's revenue bonds is 12.51 years. This is calculated by dividing bond years for the issue, $195,450,000, by the amount of the issue, $15,630,000. The longer average maturity for these bonds, compared with the 11.15 years' average maturity for the GO bonds in Johnston County, reflects the more gradual principal-retirement schedule for the revenue bonds.

Principal retirement and debt service structures for capital leases combine features of GO bonds and revenue bonds. Like GO bonds, most capital leases issued to finance general public improvements are paid off in twenty years or less. Like revenue bonds, leases that are publicly sold include both serial and term maturities, have debt service reserves, and have sinking fund and mandatory call requirements for the term bonds in the issue.

Brunswick County, North Carolina, in 2000 issued $16 million in certificates of participation (COPs) to make improvements to the county's courthouse and office facilities.[19] COPs are publicly sold capital lease obligations. Chapter 7 presents capital leases generally and COPs in particular.

The Brunswick County certificates of participation have an overall retirement and debt service term of twenty years (2001–2020). See Table 9–10, which shows the principal retirement and debt service schedule for the certificates. The certificates consist of $10,480,000 in serial maturities and $5,520,000 in term maturities. The serial maturities are retired in annual installments concentrated in the first half of the retirement term. The serial maturity years are 2001 through 2012, 2015, and 2016. The term bonds consist of two maturities: 2014 and 2020. The principal retirement schedule gradually increases over the term: $400,000 per year in 2001 and 2002, $600,000 annually in 2003 and 2004, $800,000 annually from 2005 to 2010, and $920,000 per year from 2011 to 2020. Annual debt service gradually rises from $1,174,253 in 2001 to a peak of $1,544,640 in

Table 9–10

Debt service schedule for $16,000,000 in certificates of participation, Brunswick County, North Carolina

Fiscal year	Principal retirement	Interest	Debt principal and interest
2001	$400,000	$774,253	$1,174,253
2002	400,000	824,640	1,224,640
2003	600,000	804,640	1,404,640
2004	600,000	774,640	1,374,640
2005	800,000	744,640	1,544,640
2006	800,000	704,640	1,504,640
2007	800,000	664,640	1,464,640
2008	800,000	624,640	1,424,640
2009	800,000	584,640	1,384,640
2010	800,000	538,640	1,338,640
2011	920,000	498,640	1,418,640
2012	920,000	451,720	1,371,720
2013	920,000	403,880	1,323,880
2014	920,000	355,580	1,275,580
2015	920,000	307,280	1,227,280
2016	920,000	257,600	1,177,600
2017	920,000	202,400	1,122,400
2018	920,000	151,800	1,071,800
2019	920,000	101,200	1,021,200
2020	920,000	50,600	970,600
Totals	$16,000,000	$9,820,713	$25,820,713

Source: Official Statement, prepared by Wachovia Securities and J. C. Bradford & Co., in cooperation with the Local Government Commission of North Carolina, "$16,000,000 Certificates of Participation, Series 2000, Evidencing Proportionate Undivided Interest in Right to Receive Certain Revenues, Pursuant to an Installment Purchase Contract with the County of Brunswick, North Carolina, July 1, 2000," 14.

2005. It then declines gradually thereafter. For the first five years, this debt service payment structure is like one for revenue bonds. After that, it looks more like a GO bond payment structure. More will be said about this Brunswick County capital lease in subsequent chapters.

The fact that many SO bonds have retirement terms of fifteen years or less reflects investor unwillingness to accept a longer term given the limited revenue stream pledged for such SO bonds as well as the fact that many SO bonds finance facilities with intermediate lives rather than long, useful lives. In 2000, **Dallas, Texas,** issued $7.6 million in tax increment bonds that will be retired over a twelve-year term, from 2001 to 2012 (see Table 9–11). That same year, to finance landfill improvements, **Buncombe County, North Carolina,** issued $5.1 million

in SO bonds secured by nonlocal taxes and paid from tipping fees and certain other special revenues. The bonds have a fifteen-year repayment term, extending from 2001 through 2015 (see Table 9–12 on page 266).

Debt retirement for many SO bonds, like revenue bonds, gradually increases in most years of the debt term. For example, annual debt retirement for Dallas's $7.6 million in tax increment bonds rises gradually from $585,000 in 2001 to a peak of $820,000 in 2009. It then drops to around $500,000 in each of the next three years. Debt retirement for the $5.1 million Buncombe County bonds increases consistently from $215,000 in 2001 to $475,000 in 2015. Debt service on Dallas's tax increment bonds is about $940,000 per year until 2010, when it drops to near $530,000 for that year and annu-

Table 9–11
Debt service schedule for tax increment bonds, previously existing and $7.6 million 2000 bond issues, Dallas, Texas

Fiscal year	Subtotal for previously existing bonds	Bonds issued in 2000		Subtotal debt for service	Total for previously existing bonds and 2000 bonds
		Principal	Interest		
2001	$474,650	$585,000	352,388	937,388	$1,412,038
2002	469,810	570,000	370,374	940,374	1,410,184
2003	469,410	605,000	337,599	942,599	1,412,009
2004	468,170	640,000	302,811	942,811	1,410,981
2005	466,090	675,000	266,011	941,011	1,407,101
2006	466,370	715,000	227,199	942,199	1,408,569
2007	465,792	750,000	186,086	936,086	1,401,878
2008	469,342	785,000	150,461	935,461	1,404,803
2009	471,953	820,000	112,781	932,781	1,404,734
2010	468,428	465,000	72,806	537,806	1,006,234
2011	473,785	480,000	50,137	530,137	1,003,922
2012	472,500	510,000	26,138	536,138	1,008,638
Totals	5,636,300	7,600,000	2,454,791	10,054,791	15,691,091

Source: Official Statement, prepared by city staff and consultants, "$7,600,000 City of Dallas, Texas, Tax Increment Financing Reinvestment Zone Number Two, Tax Increment Bonds, Series 2000, Dated October 1, 2000," 32.

ally thereafter. Annual debt service on the SO bonds in Buncombe County is near $500,000 per year, except in 2001 when it is $412,000.

For both Dallas and Buncombe County, the 2000 bonds are in addition to bonds that each jurisdiction issued in prior years for the same purposes and secured with the same revenues. Remaining principal and interest (debt service) on the previously existing Dallas tax increment bonds are near $470,000 per year from 2001 through 2012. Total annual debt service on these and the 2000 bonds is a little over $1,400,000 per year from 2001 through 2009 and at about $1 million annually for the next three years. The 2000 Buncombe County SO bonds are for landfill improvements, and they supplement other SO bonds issued for the landfill in 1996. Debt service on the 1996 bonds was $871,115 in 2000 and $868,465 in 2001 and then dropped to around $780,000 per year from 2002 through 2011. Debt service on both the 1996 and 2000 bonds is about $1,280,0000 per year from 2001 through 2011.

Richmond County, North Carolina, refunded $8,378,500 in GO debt in 2003. This debt consisted of five different debt issues: four had been sold to the Farmers Home Administration (FmHA), a federal agency that provided low-interest and long-term financing in the 1970s, 1980s, and into the 1990s to small- and medium-size local governments for water-sewer and other public improvements. Richmond County sold debt to the FmHA in 1976, 1979, 1984, and 1992. Only portions of these issues were still outstanding in 2003. The 1992 issue included maturities extending to 2032. The fifth Richmond County debt issue that was refunded in 2003 was GO bonds sold in the municipal bond market in 1993. This issue had maturities extending to 2015, and interest rates on different maturities were between 5.0 percent and 5.5 percent.

Richmond County contracted with the investment banking firm of Ferris, Baker Watts, Inc., to analyze the savings that the county might realize by refunding the five GO debt issues totaling $8,378,500. While the county had issued all this debt at what were then very

Table 9–12
Debt service schedule for special obligation bonds, 1996 and $5.1 million 2000 bond issues, solid waste improvements, Buncombe County, North Carolina

Fiscal year	1996 bonds, subtotal for principal and interest	2000 bonds Principal	2000 bonds Interest	Subtotal for debt service	Total for 1996 and 2000 bonds
2000	$871,115				$871,115
2001	868,455	215,000	197,040	412,040	1,280,495
2002	783,845	250,000	251,970	501,970	1,285,815
2003	781,520	260,000	239,470	499,470	1,280,990
2004	782,760	275,000	226,470	501,470	1,284,230
2005	782,280	285,000	212,720	497,720	1,280,000
2006	785,030	300,000	198,470	498,470	1,283,500
2007	780,705	315,000	183,470	498,470	1,279,175
2008	784,505	335,000	167,720	502,720	1,287,225
2009	781,850	350,000	150,970	500,970	1,281,820
2010	779,940	375,000	133,120	508,120	1,288,060
2011	781,440	385,000	113,995	498,995	1,280,435
2012		405,000	93,975	498,975	498,975
2013		425,000	72,713	497,713	497,713
2014		450,000	50,187	500,187	500,187
2015		475,000	25,888	500,888	500,888
Totals	9,563,445	5,100,000	2,318,178	7,418,178	16,981,623

Source: Official Statement, prepared by Wachovia Securities, Inc., in cooperation with the Local Government Commission of North Carolina, "$5,100,000 County of Buncombe, North Carolina, Solid Waste System Special Obligation Bonds, Series 2000, dated June 1, 2000," title page, 16.

competitive interest rates, market rates had dropped since the debt had been issued, raising the question of refunding. The analysis performed by Ferris, Baker Watts, Inc., showed that Richmond County would realize substantial savings by refunding the $8,378,500.

The result of refunding analysis is shown in Table 9–13. The refunding debt extends from 2003 through 2021, eleven years less than the final maturity of the refunded debt. The average, annual debt service savings for years 2004 through 2020 is $23,159, and the average annual savings for the life of the refunding issue is $117,835. Total savings come to $3,417,201.44.

Because savings from refunding debt typically extend many years into the future, an analysis of refunding savings must calculate the present value of the savings. Money has a time value; and the farther out in years that refunding savings occur, the less valuable

they are. A present valued calculation of refunding savings considers not only annual savings in debt service (principal and interest on the refunded debt less principal and interest on the refunding debt), but also issuance costs for the refunding debt, call premiums for early redemption of the refunded debt, and any other up-front costs associated with the refunding. The present value of the savings from refunding debt must be positive. Otherwise, a debtor loses money by refunding. To approve refunding debt for a local government in North Carolina, that state's Local Government Commission requires the net present value of refunding savings to be at least 3 percent of the amount of the debt being refunded.

Ferris, Baker Watts, Inc., calculated the net present value of Richmond County's savings in refunding the $8,378,500 in GO bonds. This calculation considered the

Table 9–13
Analysis of Refunding Savings, GO Bonds, Richmond County, North Carolina

| Date | Debt service | | Annual savings[a] | Discount factors for calculating present value[b] | Present value of annual debt service savings |
	2003 refunding debt	Refunded debt five issues 1976–1992			
6/01/2004	$810,679.70	$834,352.50	$23,672.80	0.9750185	$24,686.76
6/01/2005	806,168.76	827,632.50	21,463.74	0.9479099	21,624.59
6/01/2006	794,068.76	818,715.00	24,646.24	0.9215551	23,913.68
6/01/2007	786,968.76	809,527.50	22,558.74	0.8959331	21,334.97
6/01/2008	774,768.76	797,192.50	22,423.74	0.8710234	20,582.46
6/01/2009	757,568.76	783,332.50	25,763.74	0.8468062	22,797.96
6/01/2010	745,468.76	769,997.50	24,528.74	0.8232624	21,107.33
6/01/2011	706,856.26	728,137.50	21,281.24	0.8003732	17,890.94
6/01/2012	617,356.26	641,147.50	23,791.24	0.7781203	19,322.01
6/01/2013	604,731.26	628,327.50	23,596.24	0.7564862	18,603.31
6/01/2014	591,475.00	616,627.50	25,152.50	0.7354536	19,200.90
6/01/2015	452,587.50	474,970.00	22,382.50	0.7150057	15,783.03
6/01/2016	426,187.50	449,347.50	23,160.00	0.6951263	15,797.18
6/01/2017	420,237.50	444,342.50	24,105.00	0.6757997	16,049.13
6/01/2018	418,212.50	438,875.00	20,662.50	0.6570104	13,397.25
6/01/2019	400,862.50	420,940.00	20,077.50	0.6387435	12,707.10
6/01/2020	323,206.26	347,637.50	24,431.24	0.6209844	15,113.20
6/01/2021	67,356.26	345,740.00	278,383.74	0.6037192	168,055.50
6/01/2022	—	333,820.00	333,820.00	0.5869339	195,930.28
6/01/2023	—	299,900.00	299,900.00	0.5706153	171,127.54
6/01/2024	—	275,080.00	275,080.00	0.5547505	152,600.76
6/01/2025	—	264,960.00	264,960.00	0.5393267	142,900.00
6/01/2026	—	254,840.00	254,840.00	0.5243318	133,620.71
6/01/2027	—	244,720.00	244,720.00	0.5097537	124,746.93
6/01/2028	—	234,600.00	234,600.00	0.4955810	116,263.30
6/01/2029	—	224,480.00	224,480.00	0.4818023	108,154.99
6/01/2030	—	214,360.00	214,360.00	0.4684067	100,407.67
6/01/2031	—	204,240.00	204,240.00	0.4553836	93,007.54
6/01/2032	—	194,120.00	194,120.00	0.4427225	85,941.30
Total	$10,504,761.06	$13,921,962.50	$3,417,201.44	—	$1,912,668.32

Source: Ferris, Baker Watts, Inc., Richmond, Va., June 1, 2003 (analysis done earlier).
a Debt service refunded less refunding debt.
b Discounting done with an average discount rate of 2.8396603. This is the effective interest rate for the refunding debt; it considers issuance costs, all premiums, and other costs of the transaction as well as annual savings in debt service.

savings in annual debt service of $3,417,201.44, issuance costs for the refunding debt, call premiums for the 1992 refunded debt, and all other costs associated with the transaction. The net present value came to $1,912,668.31 (see the final column of Table 9–13). The average interest rate on the refunding debt, considering all costs associated with the transaction, was 2.84 per-cent, much less than 5–5.5 percent interest or coupon rates on the refunded debt. The 2.84 percent rate was the average discount rate used to calculated the net present value of $1,912,668.32. This present value is 22.83 percent of the amount of debt refunded. Clearly, Richmond County saved substantial money by refunding the $8,378,500 in debt in 2003.[20]

Short-term debt

Long-term, fixed-rate debt matches capital projects or assets that have long useful lives with long-term financing. Long-term, fixed-rate debt also transfers to investors the risks associated with changing market interest rates. The disadvantage of long-term, fixed-rate debt is that generally it has higher interest rates than short-term debt because of the greater risks for investors.

To lower the interest rates for their capital financing, some local governments—mostly large ones—have begun to issue short-term debt. These jurisdictions usually have top bond ratings and staff who can devote the necessary time to debt planning and management. They also finance only a small to modest portion of their capital programs with such short-term debt.

Variable-rate debt

Variable-rate demand notes, bonds, and COPs are the main short-term debt instruments used for ongoing capital financing. The interest rates on such short-term debt are subject to frequent change—usually weekly or sometimes monthly. On any date that the rates may change (or reset), whether they change or not, investors holding the debt may put it back to the issuer. In other words, the investors can turn in the debt to the issuer and demand to be repaid, which the issuer must then do or else default. Because the debt may be put back to the issuer weekly or monthly, the markets treat the debt as short term. As a result, the interest rates charged on variable-rate debt are usually lower than those charged on the long-term, fixed-rate bonds or debt that local governments typically issue for capital financing purposes.

An issuer of variable-rate demand debt must be in a position to refund the debt or any part of it when investors put it back and demand to be repaid. As a result, such debt must have a remarketing agent whose job is to refund or resell any variable-rate demand debt that investors put back to the issuer. Investors putting bonds back to the issuer expect to be repaid immediately. Because of this and because refunding may take several days, variable-rate demand debt must be supported by a **credit facility** or **letter of credit** (LOC) from a bank or financial institution. The credit facility or LOC provides bridge financing while the remarketing agent is refunding the put bonds or debt. Initiation and annual renewal fees are associated with remarketing and credit-facility services for variable-rate debt. Typical initial fees for each are less than 0.5 percent of the principal amount of the debt and are paid from debt proceeds. The annual fee for remarketing ranges from 0.125 percent to 0.25 percent of the outstanding principal amount of the variable-rate demand debt in any year. The annual fee for the credit facility or LOC varies depending on the creditworthiness of the issuer; it can be as low as 0.125 percent and as high as 1 percent of principal.[21]

The overall repayment term for variable-rate demand debt is set in relation to the particular project or asset that is financed with the debt. Variable-rate demand GO bonds and variable-rate demand COPs can have terms extending to around twenty years. Variable-rate demand revenue bonds can have terms of thirty years or so. Interest on this debt is usually paid monthly. Principal retirement on most local government variable-rate demand debt is repaid in annual installments. Payments usually go into a sinking fund and then to the investors pursuant to mandatory call requirements. Principal on some variable-rate demand debt is paid quarterly or monthly, again pursuant to sinking fund and mandatory call requirements; these more frequent payments of principal usually arise because of stipulations imposed by bond insurance.[22]

If $10 million, ten-year, variable-rate demand GO bonds, with interest subject to change weekly, are issued, they might be retired in equal annual installments of $1 million each. Even though the bonds have a fixed repayment term and are retired in annual installments like conventional serial bonds, the market treats them as short-term weekly debt because the bonds may be put in any week.

Some local governments combine fixed-rate and variable-rate demand bonds in a single bond or debt issue. Such a structure for bonds with a twenty-year repayment term might include fixed-rate bonds over the first five years of the issue and variable-rate demand notes for the remaining fifteen years. This structure allows the issuer to lock in low interest rates commonly associated with early maturities in a bond issue and also have low rates on the later maturities because variable-rate demand bonds or notes that may be put weekly, for example, make up the later maturities.

The lower interest rates of variable-rate demand debt can lower debt service costs for the issuer. Nevertheless, the risks associated with such debt make it suitable only for large and sophisticated local governments.[23] One risk is that after issuance of the debt, short-term interest rates may rise above what the issuer could have obtained for long-term, fixed-rate debt. While such inversions of normal short-term and long-term rates are unusual, they are seen occasionally when liquidity shortages occur in financial markets.

Interest rate swap contracts have been used by some local governments that had previously issued variable-rate demand bonds. Such swaps enable the issuer to exchange obligations: it takes its obligation to make payments on variable-rate debt and exchanges it for a different obligation to make payments on long-term, fixed-interest-rate debt. The swap contracts are made available by investment bankers and banks, and the contracts are between the bank and the local government. A local government with variable-rate debt would consider such a swap if short-term rates rise above long-term fixed rates, or if long-term rates decline and the issuer is willing to commit to long-term fixed interest payments at the new lower levels.

A local government must determine whether it has the legal authority to enter into interest rate swaps before considering this option. If such authority exists and the issuer has short-term variable-rate debt, the availability and use of interest rate swaps can help a sophisticated issuer manage the interest rate risk associated with the variable-rate debt.

Other risks exist for variable-rate debt. If the issuer's credit suffers, the issuer could lose its LOC and not be able to find a replacement LOC. It would then have to refund the variable-rate demand debt with long-term fixed-rate debt, perhaps at higher rates than it would have paid had it initially issued fixed-rate debt. Although the issuer may save interest costs by using variable-rate demand debt, the issuance costs and annual remarketing and LOC fees may absorb most of the savings, especially for an issuer with less than a top rating. Variable-rate demand debt is especially risky for medium- and small-size local governments with limited staff time for debt planning and management. These jurisdictions take on the interest rate risks associated with changing market conditions without having the resources needed to monitor and react to such changes.

Bond and grant anticipation notes

Bond anticipation notes and grant anticipation notes are other types of short-term debt used by local governments to finance capital projects. They can provide temporary financing for a project until permanent financing is authorized or becomes available. Bond anticipation notes, as the name indicates, are issued in anticipation of permanent bond or debt issuance. Grant anticipation notes precede and are paid off from grant revenue. Both types of notes usually have fixed terms that range from one or two months to several years, depending on how soon permanent financing can be arranged. Bond and grant anticipation notes can usually be rolled or extended if there is good reason (for example, if note financing is being used for construction that is taking longer than planned).

Bond and grant anticipation notes are used when certain federal or state grantor agencies are involved in financing a local government project. The grantor agency may approve a project and commit to provide long-term financing but not extend the financing until after the project is built. The financing may be a loan, a grant, or a combination of loan and grant funds.

If the financing consists partly or wholly of a loan, it is likely to be for a longer term and a lower rate than what is available in the conventional debt market. With the loan and/or grant commitment in hand, the local jurisdiction issues bond or grant anticipation notes to pay for the design and construction of the project. Once the construction is finished and the grantor agency specifically approves the finished project, permanent financing is obtained. If the financing consists partly or wholly of grant revenue, it is used to pay off the grant anticipation notes. If the permanent financing is bonds or a loan, the bonds are issued or the loan is secured and used to pay off the bond anticipation notes.

Sometimes local governments issue bond anticipation notes or other short-term debt temporarily because market interest rates are unusually high, and the local issuer does not wish to commit to the currently high interest rates on long-term debt. The expectation is that market rates will come down in a relatively short time—within a year or two. Therefore, the local government issues bond anticipation notes, planning to refund the notes with permanent, long-term, fixed-interest-rate debt within a year or two. The advantage of this strategy is that the issuer avoids committing to the high interest rates for a long period of time. If the issuer's expectation that interest rates soon will fall proves correct, the issuer can sell long-term debt at the lower rates and save a substantial amount in interest expenses. On the other hand, if interest rates do not fall, the local government might have to issue permanent, long-term debt at the still-high interest rates. Moreover, the local government will have incurred the costs of two debt sales—for the bond anticipation notes as well as for the permanent bonds— without recouping any costs of such issuance from lower, long-term interest rates. Of course, the local government could roll or reissue the short-term debt or convert it into a variable-rate demand bond. When long-term interest rates finally fall, it might then issue permanent, fixed-rate debt at the lower long-term rates.

Capital appreciation bonds

Capital appreciation bonds (CABs) are issued at a discount from par or face value, and they appreciate, or accrete, over the term of the bonds to par value. The appreciation represents interest on the bonds. CABs do not otherwise pay annual or other periodic interest.

CABs are similar to U.S. savings bonds. The federal government issues them at a discount from par and pays the investors par value at maturity. Although no interest per se is paid, investors earn the equivalent of interest in the form of the discount. CABs are sometimes called zero coupon bonds or securities because they do not have interest coupons on which periodic interest is paid.[24]

Table 9–14 shows the accreting value by year for a $10 million, ten-year bond issue at a 5 percent discount rate. The discounted or present value of the bonds at issuance is $6,139,000. This amount is what the issuer receives from the investors when it sells the bonds. After ten years, the issuer has to pay par value (that is, $10 million). The $3,861,000 difference between the discounted value and par value represents the interest on the bonds.

Only a few local governments have issued capital appreciation bonds for capital financing or for any other purposes, and most local government issuers have been large in size. Special circumstances—for example, the presence of investors interested in buying the bonds—usually prompt the use of CABs by local governments.

CABs have several disadvantages. Effective annual interest rates on them are usually a 0.25 to 0.50 percent higher than on serial bonds.[25] Because interest accrues but is not paid until the end of the bond issue's term, the debt owed actually grows year to year from the original issuance amount, as shown in Table 9–14.

Table 9–14

Accreting value of a hypothetical $10 million, 10-year, 5 percent capital appreciation bond issue

End of year	Annual accreted value
Discount value at issuance	$6,139,000
Accreted value at end of Year 1	6,446,000
Accreted value at end of Year 2	6,768,000
Accreted value at end of Year 3	7,107,000
Accreted value at end of Year 4	7,462,000
Accreted value at end of Year 5	7,835,000
Accreted value at end of Year 6	8,227,000
Accreted value at end of Year 7	8,638,000
Accreted value at end of Year 8	9,070,000
Accreted value at end of Year 9	9,524,000
Accreted value at end of Year 10	10,000,000

Note: The accreted values in this table were calculated with discounted single-payment, present-worth factors taken from a 5 percent interest rate table.

Conclusion

Debt issued today to finance capital projects is retired over many years extending into the future, and payments on such debt commit significant portions of the local issuer's annual revenues or operating budget for many years. Effective planning and structuring of debt service payments enables a local government to remain within its debt-carrying capacity as well as meet market demands or expectations and thereby sell debt quickly and at interest rates and costs that are as low as possible. This chapter explains the basic concepts associated with debt planning, presents the dominant debt retirement and debt service models for structuring long-term debt, illustrates debt retirement and debt service structures, and explains the role that certain types of short-term debt can play in local government capital financing programs.

Notes

1 *The Bond Buyer* defines long-term debt as debt that is outstanding for thirteen months or longer. Short-term debt is retired in twelve months or less.

2 Charlotte, North Carolina, which has a triple-A GO bond rating from all three national rating agencies, has been able to sell GO bonds with maturities extending to 20 years. These bonds were authorized and sold as part of a well-planned capital financing strategy.

3 Official Statement, prepared by Salomon Smith Barney, "$105,400,000 City of Winston-Salem, North Carolina Water and Sewer System Revenue and Revenue Refunding Bonds, Series 2001," 12.

4 A few bond issues consist of semiannual serial maturities; in other words, principal is repaid every six months instead of annually.

5 Before 1930, local governments issued much debt with single bullet terms. When annual revenues fell during the Great Depression, many of these issuers defaulted because they were unable to pay the single bullet maturities as they came due. Sinking funds accompanied many of these term bonds, but the monies in them were often insufficient when the bonds matured. See Robert L. Ehlers, *Ehlers on Public Finance: Building Better Communities* (Rochester, Minn.: Lone Oak Press, 1998), 45.

6 In actual bond issues, the interest rates for bonds retired in different years often vary. Rates are generally higher for the later maturities, reflecting the normal yield curve and the greater risks associated with bonds to be retired in the more distant future. In many bond issues,

underwriters' expenses and compensations are covered through higher interest rates and discounted bond prices on early maturities. Subsequent chapters address these issues.

7 The payment of interest every six months rather than annually actually results in an effective annual interest rate that is somewhat higher than 5 percent. This is discussed in Chapter 10.

8 James C. Joseph, *Debt Issuance and Management: A Guide for Small Governments* (Chicago: Government Finance Officers Association, 1994), 65–67.

9 Ehlers, *Ehlers on Public Finance*, 45.

10 Ibid.

11 See, for example, *General Statutes of North Carolina,* chapter 159-48(h)(4).

12 Portions of county-levied local sales taxes in North Carolina are earmarked by state law to pay for the construction of local school buildings and facilities or for debt service on bonds or other debt issued to finance local school buildings and facilities. Many of the state's counties have issued bonds and debt to build schools and used such earmarked local sales tax revenue to pay debt service on the bonds and debt. See *General Statutes of North Carolina,* chapter 105-463 through 105-504.

13 The village of Deerfield, Illinois, maintains an "even debt service levy" to pay debt service on bonds or debt for general public improvements. See Annual Budget, Fiscal Year 2001–2002, Village of Deerfield, Illinois, 17.

14 Official Statement, April 27, 2001, prepared by the Local Government Commission of North Carolina, "County

of Johnston, North Carolina, $25,000,000 General Obligation School Bonds, Series 2001, Dated June 1, 2001," 17.

15 Ibid., 20.

16 Official Statement, prepared by Salomon Smith Barney and BB&T Capital Markets in cooperation with the Local Government Commission of North Carolina, "$15,630,000 City of Henderson, North Carolina, Combined Enterprise System Revenue Bonds, Series 2001, Dated April 1, 2001," 4–5.

17 Ehlers, *Ehlers on Public Finance*, 46.

18 Official Statement, "$15,630,000 City of Henderson, North Carolina Revenue Bonds," B-20 to B-33, especially B-29.

19 Official Statement, prepared by Wachovia Securities, Inc., and J. C. Bradford & Co., in cooperation with the Local Government Commission of North Carolina, "$16,000,000 Certificates of Participation, Series 2000, Evidencing Proportionate Undivided Interest in Right to Receive Certain Revenues, Pursuant to an Installment Purchase Contract with the County of Brunswick County, North Carolina, July 1, 2000."

20 Table 9–13 and information about Richmond County, North Carolina's 2003 refunding were provided by Alison W. Peeler and Blair D. Bennett of Ferris, Baker Watts, Inc.

21 Ehlers, *Ehlers on Public Finance*, 306; staff of the North Carolina Local Government Commission in March 2003 agreed with these percentages.

22 Staff of the Local Government Commission of North Carolina, March 2003.

23 Ehlers, *Ehlers on Public Finance*, 304.

24 Securities that pay periodic interest are sometimes called coupon securities. The term "coupon" dates from when bonds were issued exclusively in certificated form. Bond certificates used to have attached interest coupons that investors clipped and presented for the payment of periodic interest. Municipal bonds are now issued in electronic, registered form, and coupons are no longer used. Nonetheless, the term coupon is still used to refer to the periodic interest paid on a bond.

25 Ehlers, *Ehlers on Public Finance*, 304.

10 Interest rates, yields, and pricing for local government debt

Interest is a defining characteristic of debt. From the debtor's standpoint, interest is the cost for the use of another's money. For the creditor, lender, or investor, it is the return or income received for lending money.

Calculations of interest rates, yields, and prices for local government debt can be complicated, but it is important for local officials to know the concepts involved and the basics of the calculations. A good understanding of the principles involved will help officials plan and limit interest and issuance costs when jurisdictions sell debt. This chapter discusses:

- The concepts of interest, interest rate, and yield in relation to local government debt
- The exemption of the interest paid on most state and local government debt from the federal income tax and, in some states, state income taxes
- Interest rate, re-offer yield, and pricing structures for long-term debt, with examples of three debt issues by local governments
- Two methods used in the municipal debt markets to calculate the average interest rate for a long-term debt issue: net interest cost (NIC) and true interest cost (TIC). A third method, effective interest cost (EIC) is also discussed briefly.

Interest rates and yield

Interest is generally the dollar amount charged at the end of a period of time for money owed or borrowed (the principal) during the period. The **interest rate** is the ratio of interest to principal. Interest may be paid or earned annually or more frequently—quarterly, monthly, weekly, or daily. When interest is earned, it is either paid immediately or added to principal. If it is added to principal (compounded), interest in the following year or period is charged on the original principal plus the accrued and unpaid interest. Even when interest is compounded more frequently than annually, it is quoted on an annual or annual-equivalent basis.

Yield usually refers to the lender's or investor's annual or periodic return from making a loan or investment. It is equivalent to the effective annual interest rate that the debtor pays on a loan. Yield or the effective annual interest rate often is different from the interest rate used to compute the debtor's interest payment for a period and the quoted interest rate.

The calculation of yield considers annual or periodic interest, the price actually paid by the investor to buy debt or to make a loan (proceeds actually received by the debtor), the principal or par value of the debt, the frequency with which interest is paid or compounded, and the yield that the investor earns when interest payments are reinvested. The calculation of yield also considers the time value of money.[1] That is, the calculation values interest and other payments made at one point during a debt's term differently from payments made at other points.

The relationship and differences between interest rate and yield or an effective annual interest rate are affected by the price that investors pay for debt as well as how often interest is paid or compounded.

Price paid   If a local government issues $1 million of one-year debt at a quoted 5 percent annual interest rate, payable at the end of the year, and the investors give the issuer $1 million—the face or par value—in debt proceeds, the interest rate paid by the issuer and the yield earned by the investors are the same—5 percent ($50,000/$1,000,000).

If investors pay a premium of $10,000 on top of the $1 million face value for the debt, the interest rate for the issuer and the yield to the investors differ. The issuer pays interest at 5 percent on the debt's principal or face value (0.05 × $1,000,000 = $50,000) but does not have to pay interest on the premium (nor does the issuer have to repay the premium). Meanwhile, the investors receive $50,000 in interest payments but must subtract the price of the premium, bringing net earnings on an investment of $1,010,000 to $40,000. The investors' yield drops below 5 percent to 3.96 percent, calculated by dividing net earnings, $40,000, by the amount actually invested, $1,010,000. Because the issuer can also subtract the $10,000 premium from the $50,000 it pays in interest on an effective sum of $1,010,000, the *effective* annual interest rate for the issuer is the same as the investor's yield.

If investors discount the debt and pay the issuer only $990,000 in debt proceeds, the issuer's interest payment is still computed at 5 percent of the principal or par value. Despite receiving only $990,000, the issuer must pay interest on the full $1 million and will have to repay that amount rather than $990,000. The yield to the investors increases to 6.06 percent, calculated by dividing the sum of $50,000 interest, plus the $10,000 discount that is part of the $1 million principal repaid at maturity, by the amount that the investors actually provide, $990,000. Again, the effective annual interest rate paid by the issuer is actually the same as the investors' yield. The issuer receives only $990,000 but pays $60,000 in effective interest ($50,000 interest and the $10,000 discount included in the $1 million of principal that must be paid at maturity).

If the term of the debt or loan extends over multiple years, the total premium or discount for the purpose of calculating yield is amortized or allocated over the number of years that the debt is outstanding.[2]

Compounding   The frequency with which interest is paid or compounded can affect the relationship between the interest rate and the yield of a debt or a loan. For example, suppose an issuer borrows $1 million at a 5 percent annual interest rate for one year, receives the full $1 million par value in proceeds, and makes two interest payments of $25,000 each during the year. The 5 percent annual interest rate is simply divided by half and applied to the debt's par value to compute the semiannual interest. While the interest rate used to compute the payment is 5 percent annually, the annual yield that the investors earn on the debt exceeds 5 percent if the investors reinvest over the second six-month period of the debt the interest they receive at six months. Assuming they do so at a 5 percent annual rate, the investors receive the amounts of interest shown in Table 10–1.

The investors receive $50,625 in interest by the end of the year, $50,000 earned on the original debt and $625 on the $25,000 of interest paid at six

Table 10–1
Compounding of interest

Month	Interest on loan	Interest on interest	Total interest
6 months	$25,000	—	$25,000
12 months	25,000	625	25,625
Totals	50,000	625	50,625

months. The $625 equals 2.5 percent (half of 5 percent) of $25,000. The semi-annual payments of interest enable investors to earn a 5.0625 percent annual yield ($50,625/$1,000,000) for the $1 million that they put up at the start of the year. If interest had been paid or compounded annually, the investors' annual yield would have been only 5 percent ($50,000/$1,000,000). More frequent payment or compounding of interest within a year increases the annual yield earned by investors over the stated interest rate or the rate used to compute the issuer's periodic interest payments. While the stated or computational interest rate in this case remains 5 percent, the effective annual interest rate for the issuer and the investors equals the investors' annual yield.

The interest on variable-rate demand bonds or notes is usually paid monthly. If a local government sells variable-rate demand bonds at a quoted annual interest rate of 5 percent but pays the interest monthly, the 5 percent converts to an annual equivalent yield (effective annual interest rate) of 5.255 percent for the investors if the investors are able to reinvest the monthly interest payments at a 5 percent annual rate compounded monthly.[3] Here again, an interest rate quoted on an annual basis but compounded more frequently, monthly in this case, results in a yield to the investors and an effective annual interest rate that is higher than 5 percent.

Tax-exempt nature of state and local debt

Most debt that state and local governments issue for capital financing and other purposes is **tax exempt.** The interest paid on the debt is generally not subject to federal income taxes.[4]

For example, an investor who buys $10,000 in tax-exempt local government bonds paying 5 percent annual interest will receive $500 in interest income each year and does not pay any federal income tax on the interest income. If the investor's federal marginal tax bracket is, for example, 30 percent, the savings in federal income tax is $150 ($500 × 0.30) per year. The equivalent taxable income for the tax-exempt interest income is $714 ($500/0.70), and the corresponding taxable equivalent return would be 7.14 percent ($714/$10,000). A tax equivalent rate of return for tax-exempt municipal debt is the rate that an investor would have to earn on a taxable security to produce after-tax income that is equal to the tax-exempt interest income on municipal debt.

Many states with an income tax exempt interest income earned by state residents on bonds or debt issued by the state or its local governments. North Carolina is an example of this.[5] If the above-mentioned investor is a North Carolina resident buying bonds issued by a North Carolina local government, the $500 in annual interest income is exempt from state income tax as well as from federal income tax. If the investor is in the state's 7 percent marginal tax bracket,[6] the tax equivalent income on the $10,000 in bonds, after both the federal (30 percent) and the state (7 percent) exemptions are summed and then subtracted from 1.00, is $794 ($500/0.63); and the tax equivalent return or yield is 7.94 percent ($794/$10,000).

Figure 10–1 shows three types of state and local government debt—tax-exempt, taxable, and alternative minimum tax debt—issued for the years 1992 through 2002. Although the proportion of tax-exempt debt dropped from 91 percent to 81 percent of total long-term debt issuance over the nine-year period, tax-exempt debt continued to dominate. Indeed, the tax-exempt nature of most state and local government debt continues to define the municipal debt market. Market professionals, investors, issuers, and others often refer to the municipal debt market as the tax-exempt market, using "tax-exempt" synonymously for all state and local debt or municipal debt.

Important changes in federal tax laws that occurred in the 1980s imposed limitations on the ability of state and local governments to issue tax-exempt debt and account for much of the increase in taxable and alternative minimum tax debt shown in Figure 10–1. One of these changes occurred in 1986 when Congress imposed the alternative minimum tax on interest income derived from most private-activity debt as well as on a portion of interest income from all municipal debt earned by corporations subject to the federal corporate income tax. A second change occurred in 1988, but it related to laws passed by Congress in prior years that restricted state and local tax-exempt debt. In *South Carolina v. Baker* (1988), the U.S. Supreme Court ruled that Congress may impose restrictions on state and local government tax-exempt debt.[7] (Until 1988, many believed that the U.S. Constitution affirmed the tax-exempt status of state and local debt in its prohibition against the U.S. government taxing any state government or any state government instrumentality or subdivision.) The 1988 decision affirmed that Congress has the authority to preserve, curtail, limit, or eliminate the ability of state and local governments to issue debt that is exempt from federal income taxes or to otherwise restrict such tax-exempt debt. Although Congress has not imposed across-the-board taxes on the interest of state and local debt, it has capped and restricted tax-exempt debt issued for so-called private purposes and has imposed other restrictions on state and local tax-exempt borrowing.[8]

Some state and local governments during the 1990s increased their use of taxable debt for certain purposes in order to avoid federal arbitrage restrictions and rebate requirements on tax-exempt debt.[9] For example, some large local governments funded self-insurance programs by issuing taxable debt.[10] The proceeds of the taxable debt provide ongoing reserves that can be

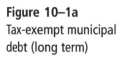

Figure 10–1a

Tax-exempt municipal debt (long term)

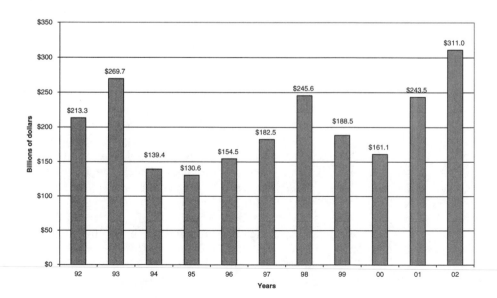

Figure 10–1b
Taxable municipal debt
(long term)

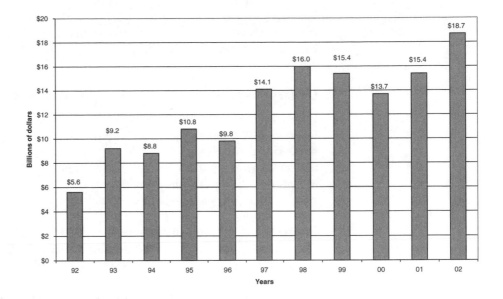

Figure 10–1c
Alternative minimum tax
municipal debt (long term)

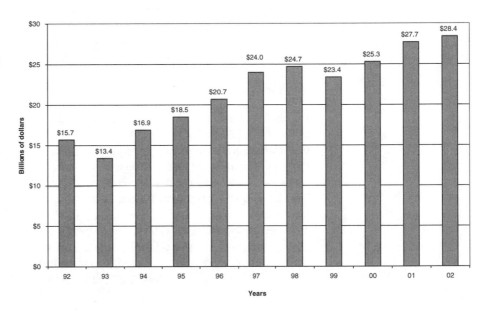

invested to produce income for the programs that do not have to be rebated to the federal government. If tax-exempt debt were issued to fund such reserves, profits earned by investing the proceeds in taxable securities (income earned on investments less the interest paid on the proceeds) would have to be rebated to the U.S. Treasury under the arbitrage rebate requirements, and the tax-exempt proceeds would be subject generally to federal arbitrage restrictions.

Interest rate, re-offer yield, and pricing structures for long-term debt

This section discusses the relationships that exist among bond or debt interest rates, re-offer yields, and prices in long-term local government debt issues and then illustrates these relationships by reference to three local debt issues. All three examples were used in Chapter 9 to illustrate bond retirement and debt service schedules. The illustrations are extended here to show how interest rates, yields, and prices for debt are structured.

Underwriter bids on interest rates, yields, and pricing

When buying and selling long-term debt, underwriters identify a specific interest rate, re-offer price, and re-offer yield for each year or maturity that make up the debt issue. As explained earlier in this chapter, the interest rate is the rate at which the issuer pays interest, and it is different from the yield that investors receive when they buy the bonds from underwriters at a premium—a price above par value—or at a discount price below par.

Interest rates When underwriters bid on a local government debt issue, they specify an interest rate for each maturity or year in the issue. Although the underwriters can specify the same rate for all years or maturities, this seldom happens. Usually higher interest rates are bid for the later maturities and lower rates for the earlier ones, reflecting the greater risk for longer-term debt. Thus, when underwriters buy a local government's bond issue—for example, the $10 million, ten-year bond issue shown in Tables 9–1 and 9–2—they are not likely to charge 5 percent per year for all maturities. Instead they might specify a 4.7 percent interest rate for Years 1, 2, and 3; a 5 percent rate for Years 4, 5, and 6; a 5.2 percent rate for Years 7, 8, and 9; and a 5.3 percent rate for Year 10.

Prices and re-offer yields Underwriters' bids for bonds also specify the prices that they will charge the investors who buy the bonds and the **re-offer yields** that are implied by these prices. Prices and re-offer yields also often vary by maturity or year in the bond issue.

Bond prices can be at **par** (equal to the principal amount or face value of the bonds), at a **premium** (a price above par value), or at a **discount** (below par value). Premium and discount prices for bonds result from shifting supply and demand for debt, underwriters' perceptions about supply and demand, changes in interest rates while sales of debt are in process, compensation of the underwriters, and pricing to make bonds more attractive to investors. (See Chapter 11 for information about selling debt.)

Coupons

The interest that an issuer pays on debt is often called **coupon interest**, and the interest rate is called the **coupon rate**. Bonds once were sold in certificate form, and a coupon was attached to the certificate for each semiannual interest payment. To receive an interest payment, the investor had to detach the coupon and present it for payment. Today nearly all publicly sold state and local government bonds and debt are registered securities and are issued in "book entry" or electronic form. This means that a bond registrar maintains ownership records, and neither bond certificates nor interest coupons are used. Periodic interest payments are made to the registered owners of the bonds on each interest payment date. Nonetheless, the interest that local governments and other debt issuers pay on debt is still referred to as coupon interest, and the rate at which such interest is paid is referred to as the coupon rate.

Bond prices are quoted using 100 to represent par value. For example, if a price of 100 is quoted for $1 million in bonds, the bonds sell at par value, that is, for $1 million, which is also the principal amount that the issuer will repay at maturity. If a price of 101 is quoted for the same bonds, investors pay 1,010,000 for them ($1 million × 1.01), which consists of $1 million in par value or principal plus a premium of $10,000. The issuer will repay only the $1 million when the bonds mature. If a price of 99 is quoted for the bonds, investors pay $990,000 ($1 million × 0.99); $990,000 equals the par value less a $10,000 discount. Receiving only $990,000 in bond proceeds at issuance, the issuer will repay the $1 million in par value or principal at maturity. Underwriters receive proceeds from the prices paid by investors to buy the bonds and then turn over to the issuer the proceeds, less the underwriters' commissions on competitively sold debt.

Re-offer yields, like interest rates, are quoted as percentages. They are the yield at which underwriters resell bonds to investors after buying them from the issuer. If underwriters sell bonds at par, the re-offer yield that investors who buy the bonds earn is the same as the interest rate that the issuer pays. Thus, if $1 million in bonds paying a 5 percent annual interest rate are sold at par, the investors earn a 5 percent yield. If underwriters sell bonds at a premium, the re-offer yield that investors buying the bonds earn is less than the interest rate that the issuer pays. And if the bonds are sold to investors at a discount, the re-offer yield is higher than the interest rate that the issuer pays.

Bond prices and yields for fixed-income securities, including municipal bonds or debt, are related inversely. As the price or value of a bond or bond maturity rises, its yield falls. Conversely, a drop in the price or value of a bond means a rise in a bond's yield.

The calculation of re-offer yield for any maturity is complicated. Generally it involves taking the annual interest received by the investor, less the value of a premium or plus the value of any discount, and dividing the result by the amount that the investor pays to buy the bonds (see sidebar on the next page). All of this is factored by the time value of money (that is, when the investor receives interest payments over the period the bonds are outstanding).[11]

Pricing structure   The discussion thus far has focused on bonds for a single year or a single maturity. As already pointed out, different years or maturities in a bond issue often have different interest rates. The prices and re-offer yields in a bond issue also often vary by maturity. Indeed, there usually is more variation in bond prices and re-offer yields than in interest rates among the years or maturities of a bond issue. This can occur because of bond bid requirements that limit the number of different interest rates but do not limit yields or prices that underwriters may specify for the maturities or years of a bond issue.

The usual structure for interest rates and re-offer yields for the different maturities in a bond issue is upward sloping: interest rates and re-offer yields for the later maturities are generally higher than those for the earlier maturities. This ascending structure from the present to the future for rates and yields reflects increasing risk as an investment is extended farther into the future. The ascending rate and yield structure usually prevails and is commonly referred to as a **normal yield curve.**

Occasionally, the demand for bonds in one or several maturities in a bond issue is higher or lower than normal, causing the yields for these maturities to differ from the prevailing yield curve for those maturities and that type of debt. For example, if the demand for bonds in a particular maturity is unusu-

---

Calculating re-offer yield using amortization

A rough approximation of re-offer yield can be calculated by including the amortized premium or discount in the formula without considering the time value of money. **Amortization** refers to allocating or crediting to multiple years an amount of money received or paid in one year. For example, if bonds with a $1 million face value, a 5 percent annual interest rate, and a maturity of five years are purchased for a price of 101 or $1,010,000, the premium is $10,000. Amortization allocates the premium over the five years that the bonds are outstanding (that is, at $2,000 per year). With the above formula, the $2,000 amortized amount would be deducted from the annual interest of $50,000 ($1,000,000 $\times$ 0.05) and divided by the amount invested ($1,010,000) to arrive at an approximation of the investor's yield—in this case, 4.75 percent [($50,000 − $2,000) / $1,010,000].

If these bonds were purchased at a price of 99 or for $990,000, there would be a $10,000 discount that would be amortized over the five-year period. In this case, the approximation of yield to maturity would be 5.25 percent [($50,000 + $2,000) / $990,000].

These are approximations of re-offer yield because the calculations do not take into account the time value of money. They are shown here to illustrate how a premium or a discount is factored into the determination of yield.

A somewhat different, alternative, approach and formula for calculating the approximate value of a bond is presented and illustrated on page 45 of Lipkin, Feinstein, and Derrick, *Accountant's Handbook of Formulas and Tables*.

---

ally high, underwriters may sell those bonds at a price above that prevailing in the market for that maturity and type of debt, and, correspondingly, at a yield below the yield curve for that maturity and debt. Conversely, if demand for the maturity is low, underwriters may sell bonds in the maturity at a price below that prevailing in the market, and, correspondingly, at a yield above the yield curve for that maturity and type of debt.

The underwriters of competitively sold bonds cover their costs and receive compensation by raising the interest rate (they can also raise the price, thereby lowering the yield) on one or several maturities in a bond issue, usually the early maturities. This causes the interest rates and/or the re-offer yields for these maturities to differ from the rates and yields that would otherwise be expected, given the prevailing yield curve for that issue or type of debt.

Aberrant yield curves

Market conditions sometimes bring aberrations in the normal yield curve, causing a flat yield curve or an inverted yield curve. A flat yield curve—short-term and long-term yields are the same—can occur when interest rates are shifting (for example, when the economy is moving into or coming out of a recession). An inverted yield curve—yields on short-term maturities are higher than on long-term maturities—can signal a liquidity crisis in the economy; corporations and financial institutions have trouble securing the day-to-day money they need to function and are willing to pay higher interest for short-term cash.

Interest rates, yield, and pricing structure in practice

The debt issues of Johnston County, Henderson, and Brunswick County, North Carolina, introduced in Chapter 9, are used to illustrate interest rate, yield, and pricing structures for GO bonds, revenue bonds, and certificates of participation.

GO bonds The debt retirement and debt service schedules for the Johnston County, North Carolina, GO bonds were shown in Table 9–7. Here Table 10–2 shows the principal retirement schedule for these bonds plus the interest rates, re-offer yields, prices, the dollar amounts paid by investors to buy the bonds, and the dollar premiums or discounts.

The GO bonds of **Johnston County, North Carolina,** were sold in a competitive auction. The winning underwriters for the Johnston County bonds bid only two interest rates— 4.5 percent for the first nine years in the issue and 5.0 percent for each year thereafter. When the interest rate for any maturity is multiplied by the bond principal in the maturity, the result is the interest that Johnston County will pay on that maturity in any year that the maturity is outstanding.

Bid specifications for local government GO bonds often limit the number of separate interest rates that underwriters may include in a bid regardless of the number of years or maturities in the issue. For example, North Carolina limits the number of separate interest rates that may be bid for GO bonds to six or fewer.[12] Most bids on long-term GO bonds include more than the two interest rates bid for the Johnston County bonds. The bid specifications for GO bonds also often require that the interest rate bid for any year's bonds be the same as or higher than the rate bid for the preceding year's bonds.[13] This requirement reflects the normal yield curve generally prevailing in the market. It also prevents substantial discounting of bonds in early maturities and helps to ensure that the average interest rate for an issue calculated with the net interest cost (NIC) method is close to the average interest rate calculated with the true interest cost (TIC) method. Although the TIC method produces a more accurate calculation of the average interest rate for a bond issue, the types of limitations on interest rate bids noted here enable NIC to be an acceptable method for calculating average interest cost and selecting the winning underwriter(s) on GO bond sales. Both methods are discussed in greater detail later in the chapter.

The re-offer yields for Johnston County's GO bonds consistently increase from year to year, producing a consistently upward-sloping yield curve. The earlier maturities were sold at a premium, indicating considerable demand by investors. Just one maturity, 2011, was sold at par. The last six maturities were sold at discounts.

Several interrelated factors underlie this discounting. First, the interest rate of 5 percent for the later maturities does not fully reflect the risk that the market assigned to them. Consequently, investors were willing to buy them only at discounted prices, which raised the yield to more accurately reflect the risks. Second, many of the investors buying these later maturities were probably mutual funds, insurance companies, or other financial institutions able to negotiate discount prices with the underwriters. Third, underwriters know that many investors like to buy later-maturity bonds at discount prices to give themselves some protection against higher interest rates in future markets; therefore, the underwriters set a face value price they knew would be discounted.

The pricing of the maturities in Johnston County's GO bonds mirrors in an inverse way the re-offer yields. This demonstrates the axiom that price and yield for fixed-income securities are related inversely.

Finally, Table 10–2 (page 284) shows that investors paid a total of $25,180,641 to buy the $25 million Johnston County bonds. Their payments included a premium of $180,641. The underwriters kept $157,514 of this premium to cover their costs and compensation. Johnston County received $23,127 of the premium. This premium was a factor in the county's selection of the winning bidder.

Revenue bonds The maturity schedule for the $15,630,000 in revenue bonds for Henderson, North Carolina, was shown in Table 9–8. Table 10–3 shows whether each maturity is serial or term as well as the interest rates, re-offer yields, prices, the dollar amounts paid by investors to buy the bonds, and premiums or discounts by maturity or year in the revenue bond issue.

Table 10–2

Principal retirement, interest rates, re-offer yields, and pricing for $25 million in general obligation bonds, June 1, 2001, Johnston County, North Carolina

Fiscal year	Principal retirement	Interest rate	Re-offer yield	Bond price	Amounts paid for bonds	Premium (or discount)
2003	$1,300,000	4.5	3.30	102.291	$1,329,783	$29,783
2004	1,300,000	4.5	3.55	102.671	1,334,723	34,723
2005	1,400,000	4.5	3.74	102.791	1,439,074	39,074
2006	1,400,000	4.5	3.89	102.741	1,438,374	38,374
2007	1,400,000	4.5	4.05	102.371	1,433,194	33,194
2008	1,400,000	4.5	4.13	102.225	1,431,150	31,150
2009	1,000,000	4.5	4.28	101.474	1,014,740	14,740
2010	1,300,000	4.5	4.40	100.735	1,309,555	9,555
2011	500,000	4.5	4.50	100.000	500,000	0
2012	1,400,000	5.0	4.64	103.071	1,442,994	42,994
2013	1,400,000	5.0	4.75	102.265	1,431,710	31,710
2014	1,400,000	5.0	4.83	101.625	1,422,750	22,750
2015	1,400,000	5.0	4.93	100.700	1,409,800	9,800
2016	1,400,000	5.0	5.02	99.790	1,397,060	(2,940)
2017	1,400,000	5.0	5.10	98.914	1,384,796	(15,204)
2018	1,400,000	5.0	5.17	98.092	1,373,288	(26,712)
2019	1,400,000	5.0	5.20	97.680	1,367,520	(32,480)
2020	1,400,000	5.0	5.22	97.368	1,363,152	(36,848)
2021	1,400,000	5.0	5.25	96.927	1,356,978	(43,022)
Totals	$25,000,000				$25,180,641	$180,641

Source: Official Statement, April 27, 2001, prepared by the Local Government Commission of North Carolina, "County of Johnston, North Carolina, $25,000,000 General Obligation School Bonds, Series 2001, Dated June 1, 2001"; and "First Union National Bank's Reoffering Sale, Johnston County $25,000,000 General Obligation School Bonds, Series 2001," Parity electronic bid program, Thompson Financial Municipals Group, Inc. Furnished to the author by staff of the Local Government Commission.

Henderson, unlike Johnston County, established interest rates and re-offer yields in a negotiated sales process coordinated by the underwriters and involving city officials, the city's financial adviser, and investors.

The negotiated sale of revenue bonds by **Henderson, North Carolina,** resulted in eleven separate interest rates ranging from a low of 3.25 percent for 2002 to 5.25 percent for three maturities—2014, 2016, and 2018. There is no limit on the number of interest rates that underwriters may specify for revenue bonds in North Carolina. The interest rate structure for the issue is generally but not completely ascending. The 3.75 percent rate for 2006 is less than the 4 percent rate for the 2005 maturity, and the 5.25 percent rate for 2014, 2016, and

2018 is higher than the 5 percent rate for the 2019 serial maturity and 2021 term maturity.

The re-offer yields ascend consistently over the term of the issue, from 3.25 percent in 2002 to 5.15 percent in 2021. The underwriters sold all but two—2005 and 2007—of the early maturities and midmaturities at par or at a discount. None of the discounted maturities, except the 2021 term bonds, sold for prices less than 99. Three of the term maturities—2014, 2016, and 2018— sold at significant premiums, ostensibly indicating

Table 10-3
Principal retirement schedule, interest rates, re-offer yields, and pricing for $15,630,000 in revenue bonds, April 1, 2001, Henderson, North Carolina

Fiscal year	Principal repayment	Type of maturity	Interest rate	Re-offer yield	Bond price	Amount paid for bonds	Premium (or discount)
2002	$75,000	Serial	3.25	3.25	100	$75,000	$0
2003	230,000	Serial	3.40	3.45	99.901	229,772	–228
2004	580,000	Serial	3.66	3.60	100	580,000	0
2005	600,000	Serial	4.00	3.72	101.039	606,234	6,234
2006	625,000	Serial	3.75	3.83	99.635	622,719	–2,281
2007	645,000	Serial	4.00	3.97	100.158	646,019	1,019
2008	670,000	Serial	4.00	4.10	99.392	665,926	–4,074
2009	705,000	Serial	4.10	4.20	99.322	700,220	–4,780
2010	730,000	Serial	4.20	4.30	99.256	724,569	–5,431
2011	765,000	Serial	4.25	4.37	99.031	757,587	–7,413
2012	790,000	Serial	4.40	4.50	99.136	783,174	–6,826
2014	1,700,000	Term	5.25	4.70	104.986	1,784,762	84,762
2016	1,880,000	Term	5.25	4.88	103.336	1,942,717	62,717
2018	2,090,000	Term	5.25	5.02	102.056	2,132,970	42,970
2019	1,125,000	Serial	5.00	5.08	99.06	1,114,425	–10,575
2021	2,420,000	Term	5.00	5.15	98.136	2,374,891	–45,109
Totals	$15,630,000					$15,740,986	$110,986

Source: Official Statement, April 5, 2001, prepared by Salomon Smith Barney and BB&T Capital Markets in cooperation with the Local Government Commission of North Carolina, "$15,630,000 City of Henderson, North Carolina, Combined Enterprise System Revenue Bonds, Series 2001, Dated April 1, 2001." The Official Statement provides interest rates and prices for the serial bonds, and interest rates, prices, and re-offer yields for the term bonds. Re-offer yields for the serial bonds were provided by commission staff.

considerable demand for these bonds. The generally ascending interest rate and yield structures, the closeness of prices to par for most maturities, and the net premium bid for Henderson's revenue bonds suggest efficient pricing and a successful sale.

The final column of Table 10–3 shows that investors paid a net premium of $110,986 to buy Henderson's revenue bonds. The proceeds turned over or credited to the city from the sale totaled $15,740,986, including the issue's principal amount or par value and the full premium. Henderson paid all issuance costs, including the underwriters' fees, from the bond proceeds as well as other revenues available for the bond-financed project.

Certificates of participation (capital lease) As noted in Chapter 9, Brunswick County, North Carolina, issued $16 million in certificates of participation (capital lease) to renovate and expand the county's courthouse and office facilities. Table 10–4 shows the principal retirement schedule, interest rates, re-offer yields, prices, amounts paid by investors to buy the debt, and premiums or discounts by maturity or year. As with Henderson's revenue bonds, the interest rates, yields, and prices for the certificates of participation were established in a negotiated sales process involving the underwriters, local county officials, and investors.

The negotiated sale of the **Brunswick County, North Carolina,** certificates of participation resulted in nine separate interest rates ranging from 5 percent for each of the first eight maturities to 6 percent for the serial bonds maturing in 2016. As with revenue bonds, North Carolina imposes no limits on the number of interest rates that underwriters may specify in pricing structures for local government certificates of participation or other capital leases.

The interest rate structure for these certificates of participation is flat at 5 percent for the first eight years, spikes to 5.75 percent for 2009, drops back to 5 percent for 2010, and then slopes upward to 5.4 percent in 2015. The last two maturities—the 2016 serial and the 2020 term certificates—have rates of 6 percent and 5.5 percent, respectively. The re-offer yields for Brunswick County's certificates of participation ascend consistently from 4.5 percent in 2001 to 5.75 percent for the final maturity, the 2020 term certificates.

Investors paid a substantial premium for the 2009 certificates. Market participants would say that these certificates—with a 5.75 percent interest rate, a re-offer yield of 5.05 percent, and a 104.954 price—have a story. The investors who bought the bonds had special needs that this pricing structure fulfilled. Whatever the story, the county is paying a significantly higher interest rate on this maturity than on any of the nearby maturities or years and much higher than the yield that the investors are earning on the maturity. Still, the re-offer yield for the 2009 certificates is in line with those for nearby maturities.

The prices for all of the early maturities, 2001 through 2007, are at a premium. The only bonds sold at par are the 2008 maturity. The prices for all of the maturities from 2010 onward, except for 2016, are discounted. The price for the 2020 term certificates is discounted substantially to 97.053. The 2016 serial maturity was sold at a substantial premium price—103.632, which reflects the high interest rate paid by the county for the certificates in this maturity. This maturity could have a "story." Perhaps the investors who bought it wished to acquire discounted debt for their portfolio(s).

While the re-offer yields for the Brunswick County certificates of participation are smoothly upward sloping and normal, prices for the certificates depart significantly from the normal pattern, much more than do prices for the Johnston County GO bonds and the Henderson revenue bonds. This "customization" of the issue was probably needed to market the certificates to investors—many of which were large, sophisticated financial organizations—yet hold down interest rates for the county. Certificates of participation are newer and generally not as well accepted in the debt markets as GO and revenue bonds. In other words, certificates of participation are usually viewed as riskier investments. As a result, selling certificates of participation often calls for more departures from a normal pricing structure than selling either GO or revenue bonds.

The Brunswick County certificates of participation were sold at an overall net discount. The county received $15,933,822 in proceeds from the sale, $66,178 less than the par value or principal amount of the certificates. From the proceeds, the county paid issuance costs, including $109,080 in underwriters' fees.

Table 10-4
Principal retirement schedule, interest rates, re-offer yields, and pricing for $16,000,0000 in certificates of participation, July 1, 2000, Brunswick County, North Carolina

Fiscal year	Principal retirement	Type of maturity	Interest rate	Re-offer yield	Bond price	Amount paid for bonds	Premium (or discount)
2001	$400,000	Serial	5.00	4.50	100.423	$401,692	$1,692
2002	400,000	Serial	5.00	4.70	100.529	402,116	2,116
2003	600,000	Serial	5.00	4.75	100.661	603,966	3,966
2004	600,000	Serial	5.00	4.80	100.695	604,170	4,170
2005	800,000	Serial	5.00	4.85	100.639	805,112	5,112
2006	800,000	Serial	5.00	4.90	100.500	804,000	4,000
2007	800,000	Serial	5.00	4.95	100.283	802,264	2,264
2008	800,000	Serial	5.00	5.00	100.000	800,000	0
2009	800,000	Serial	5.75	5.05	104.954	839,632	39,632
2010	800,000	Serial	5.00	5.10	99.225	793,800	(6,200)
2011	920,000	Serial	5.10	5.20	99.170	912,364	(7,636)
2012	920,000	Serial	5.20	5.25	99.556	915,915	(4,085)
2014	1,840,000	Term	5.25	5.40	98.541	1,813,154	(26,846)
2015	920,000	Serial	5.40	5.50	98.986	910,671	(9,329)
2016	920,000	Serial	6.00	5.55	103.632	953,414	33,414
2020	3,680,000	Term	5.50	5.75	97.053	3,571,550	(108,450)
Totals	$16,000,000					$15,933,822	($66,178)

Source: Official Statement, prepared by Wachovia Securities and J. C. Bradford & Co. in cooperation with the Local Government Commission of North Carolina, "$16,000,000 Certificates of Participation, Series 2000. Evidencing Proportionate Undivided Interest in Right to Receive Certain Revenues, Pursuant to an Installment Purchase Contract with the County of Brunswick, North Carolina, July 1, 2000." The Official Statement provided interest rates and re-offer yields. The Local Government Commission staff provided prices.

Average interest rates for long-term debt

Because principal retirement on long-term debt issues typically occurs annually, either through serial bonds or yearly mandatory call and sinking fund contributions for term bonds, and because multiple interest rates are used for long-term debt, determination of the average interest rate for a bond or debt issue requires some calculation. The municipal debt markets rely on two primary methods. One is based on **net interest cost** (NIC) and the other on **true interest cost** (TIC). In the past, NIC was the predominant method that issuers used to compare underwriters' bids to buy bonds in competitive sales. The advantage of NIC is its ease of calculation. The disadvantage is that this method fails to take into account the time value of money. That is, it does not adjust principal retirement and interest payments on the basis of when over the term of a bond issue the payments occur. Such adjustment is accomplished using interest rate formulas that take into account the time value of money.

TIC is becoming the dominant method for comparing underwriters' interest rate and price bids in municipal bond sales. It is used for practically all sales of revenue bonds and certificates of participation and other publicly sold capital leases, for many sales of limited or SO debt, and for a growing proportion of GO bonds. The advantage of TIC is that its calculation considers the time value of money—it factors principal retirement and interest payments on the basis of when they will be made. As the name suggests, it produces a more accurate, or "true," measure of the average interest rate than does NIC. Although the calculation of TIC is complicated, computer programs for doing this are common.

Net interest cost is still used in GO bond sales and certain other bond sales because combined with bid restrictions (for example, requiring an ascending interest rate structure over the term of the bond issue) it produces results that are very close to the TIC. Most important, in this case, the ranking among bids and the selection of the winning underwriter is the same whether NIC or TIC is used. An issuer that imposes bid restrictions on interest rate and pricing structures and uses NIC must be sure that these restrictions do not interfere with the sale of the bonds and thereby result in higher interest rate costs and lower prices.

A third method, effective interest cost (EIC), is available to compute the average interest rate for long-term debt. It is used in advance refundings and by some issuers for other types of debt for evaluating interest costs and rates.

Net interest cost

This method of calculating average interest rates for long-term debt is called net interest cost because it includes discounts and premiums in the calculation. A discount is added to interest because even though the issuer's proceeds at issuance are reduced by the amount of the discount, the issuer, in making principal payments, will repay par value, including the discount. The discount is considered to be an additional financing charge that is added to interest payments. A premium is subtracted from interest costs because even though it increases the issuer's proceeds at issuance, the issuer, in making principal payments, will repay only the par value of the bonds. The premium, therefore, is considered to reduce financing costs or interest to the issuer.

NIC is calculated in three steps:

- First, all interest payments that the issuer pays over the term of a bond issue are summed.

Effective interest cost

Some market participants have begun to use a third method, effective interest cost (EIC), for calculating the average interest rate for a bond or debt issue. Like the true interest cost, EIC considers the time value of money and adjusts principal and interest payments on the basis of when they will be made.

EIC equates net debt proceeds with payments of future principal, interest, and any other payments related to the debt that will be made in the future. Net debt proceeds are the par or principal value of debt plus accrued interest and premium paid at issuance; less the issuance discount, underwriters' commission and costs, any insurance and letters-of-credit premiums, and other issuance costs that can include fees for financial advisory services; bond counsel; issuer's counsel; underwriters' counsel; rating charges; trustee, registration, and paying agent fees; initial letter-of-credit fees for variable-rate debt; and other costs. Except for underwriters' commissions in competitive sales, neither the net interest cost nor true interest cost includes issuance costs. Nor do net interest cost or true interest cost consider ongoing or future payments (for example, letter-of-credit renewal and remarketing fees for variable-rate debt), except debt principal and interest payments.

In the calculation of the EIC, the bond proceeds that the issuer receives are reduced by whatever costs the issuer incurs or pays to plan and sell the bonds. If annual costs—for example, a yearly fee for a credit facility to support bonds that may be put—are incurred and are added to annual principal retirement and interest payments, EIC is calculated using these cash flows over the term of the bond issue. EIC produces the most accurate result for evaluating underwriters' bids and identifying the bid offering the lowest average interest rate on a bond issue. Some participants in the markets calculate EIC, but they do so mainly for information purposes. EIC, being newer, is seldom used as the basis for selecting the underwriter offering the lowest average interest rate in municipal bond sales.

- Second, to calculate the net interest, any discount below par for the issue is added to this total, or any premium above par for the issue is subtracted. (Discount and premium here refer to the overall discount or premium for the bond issue, which is the sum of discounts and premiums for individual maturities in the issue.)
- Third, the net interest is divided by total bond years or by the product of years' average maturity multiplied by the par value or principal amount of the bond issue. (Chapter 9 explains how bond years and years' average maturity for a bond issue are calculated.)

The formula for a NIC-based calculation of the average interest rate for a bond issue is

$$\frac{(\text{Total interest} + \text{Any issuance discount} - \text{Any issuance premium})}{\text{Total bond years}}$$

or

$$\frac{(\text{Total interest} + \text{Any issuance discount} - \text{Any issuance premium})}{\text{Years' average maturity} \times \text{Total principal amount}}$$

Table 10–5 shows the calculation of a NIC-based average interest rate for the same two hypothetical bond issues presented in Table 9–4. Both bond issues are for $60,000 and have a three-year retirement term. Bond issue no. 1 provides for rapid or front-loaded repayment of principal—$30,000 at the end of Year 1, $20,000 at the end of Year 2, and $10,000 at the end of Year 3. Total bond years for this issue is $100,000, and the issue's average maturity is 1.67 years (see Table 9–4). Bond issue no. 2 provides for much slower repayment of principal: $10,000 at the end of Year 1, $20,000 at the end of Year 2, and $30,000 at the end of Year 3. Total bond years for issue no. 2 is $140,000, and its years' average maturity is 2.33 (see Table 9–4). Both bond issues have the same ascending interest rate structure: 5 percent for Year 1, 6 percent for Year 2, and 7 percent for Year 3. Neither issue has a discount or a premium.

Table 10–5 reveals that the total interest paid on bond issue no. 1 is $6,000 and on bond issue no. 2 is $9,200. Substantially more interest is paid on issue no. 2 because much more principal is outstanding for a longer period of time, as indicated by its greater total bond years and years' average maturity (see Table 9–4). The interest rate structures for both issues are the same, but the difference in retirement schedules produces a 5.99 percent average interest rate for issue no. 1 and a 6.58 percent average interest rate for issue no. 2.

Based on data provided in Table 9–7, Table 10–6 shows the total for bond years ($279,000,000) and total interest ($13,640,000) for the $25 million in GO bonds issued by Johnston County, North Carolina.

The Johnston County bonds brought a premium of $180,641 (see Table 10–2). The underwriters kept $157,514 to cover underwriting costs and

Table 10–5
NIC-based average interest rates for two hypothetical $60,000, three-year debt issues with different retirement schedules

Year	Maturity or principal amount	Interest rate by maturity	Annual interest for each maturity	Number of years that interest is paid	Total interest paid by maturity
	**Bond issue no. 1: Heavy up-front principal retirement and ascending interest rate structure**				
1	$30,000	5	$1,500	1	$1,500
2	20,000	6	1,200	2	2,400
3	10,000	7	700	3	2,100
Totals	$60,000				$6,000

Net interest cost (NIC) rate: Total interest cost/(years' average maturity × total principal) = $6,000/(1.67 × $60,000) = 5.99 percent

Year	Maturity or principal amount	Interest rate by maturity	Annual interest for each maturity	Number of years that interest is paid	Total interest paid by maturity
	**Bond issue no. 2: Delayed principal retirement and ascending interest rate structure**				
1	$10,000	5	$500	1	$500
2	20,000	6	1,200	2	2,400
3	30,000	7	2,100	3	6,300
Totals	$60,000				$9,200

Net interest cost (NIC) rate: Total interest cost/(years' average maturity × total principal) = $9,200/(2.33 × $60,000) = 6.58 percent

Table 10–6
Bond years and interest paid on $25 million in GO bonds, Johnston County, North Carolina

Fiscal year	Principal retirement	Years maturity is outstanding	Bond years	Interest rate	Interest per year per maturity	Total interest per maturity
2001						
2002						
2003	$1,300,000	2	$2,600,000	4.5	$58,500	$117,000
2004	1,300,000	3	3,900,000	4.5	58,500	175,500
2005	1,400,000	4	5,600,000	4.5	63,000	252,000
2006	1,400,000	5	7,000,000	4.5	63,000	315,000
2007	1,400,000	6	8,400,000	4.5	63,000	378,000
2008	1,400,000	7	9,800,000	4.5	63,000	441,000
2009	1,000,000	8	8,000,000	4.5	45,000	360,000
2010	1,300,000	9	11,700,000	4.5	58,500	526,500
2011	500,000	10	5,000,000	4.5	22,500	225,000
2012	1,400,000	11	15,400,000	5.0	70,000	770,000
2013	1,400,000	12	16,800,000	5.0	70,000	840,000
2014	1,400,000	13	18,200,000	5.0	70,000	910,000
2015	1,400,000	14	19,600,000	5.0	70,000	980,000
2016	1,400,000	15	21,000,000	5.0	70,000	1,050,000
2017	1,400,000	16	22,400,000	5.0	70,000	1,120,000
2018	1,400,000	17	23,800,000	5.0	70,000	1,190,000
2019	1,400,000	18	25,200,000	5.0	70,000	1,260,000
2020	1,400,000	19	26,600,000	5.0	70,000	1,330,000
2021	1,400,000	20	28,000,000	5.0	70,000	1,400,000
Totals	$25,000,000		$279,000,000			$13,640,000

Source: Maturity principal schedule, Table 9–7; interest rates, Table 10–2.
Note: Bond years are calculated by multiplying a year's maturity by the number of years outstanding. Interest paid per year is calculated by multiplying the interest rate for a maturity by the principal amount of the maturity. Total interest per maturity is the number of years that the maturity is outstanding multiplied by interest per year.

fees, and Johnston County received $23,127 of the premium. A modified version of the formulas presented earlier in this section can be used to calculate the NIC-based average interest rate for the Johnston County bonds. The numerator in the following equation shows total interest paid less the net premium ($13,640,000 − $23,127) turned over to the county. The denominator shows total bond years (the product of the principal amount of the issue [$25 million] and years' average maturity [11.16 years; see Chapter 9 for a description of Johnston County's GO debt]).

$$\frac{\$13,616,873}{\$279,000,000} = 0.04880600 \text{ or } 4.880600\%$$

The NIC-based formula was used to compare bids from underwriters to buy the Johnston County bonds. First Union National Bank (now merged with Wachovia National Bank) won the bid with the 4.8806 percent rate, the lowest of eight NIC-based bids. Competition for the bonds was keen, with all the bids falling within a very narrow range, from 4.8806 percent to 4.949642 percent. Fewer than 7 basis points (7/100ths of 1 percent) separated the bids.

True interest cost

The TIC-based average interest rate takes into account the time value of money.[14] Money declines in value the farther into the future it is received or paid; this is because of the risk and the uncertainty that is associated with the future. Thus, $1 one year from now is worth less than $1 today, and $1 two years from now is worth less than $1 received one year from now. Conversely, $1 today is worth more than $1 one year from now and much more than $1 ten or twenty years from now.

The financial community uses interest and discount formulas and rates to account for the time value of money. Indeed, the reason interest is charged on debt arises from the time value of money. Interest compensates the investor for forgoing consumption or another use of money today.

A TIC-based calculation for a bond issue values differently the debt service payments that the issuer makes at different times. For example, a debt service payment of $500,000 made at the end of Year 1 of a bond issue with a twenty-year debt term is valued much more than a $500,000 debt service payment made in Year 15. Conversely, the $500,000 paid in Year 15 is valued much less than $500,000 in Year 1 or in any year preceding Year 15. In fact, the decline of the value of the money over time can mean that a higher payment (for example, $1 million) made later in a bond issue's term is worth less than a lower payment (for example, $800,000) made much earlier in the term.

According to the Municipal Securities Rulemaking Board, which regulates municipal securities dealers, TIC "is the (interest) rate compounded semiannually, necessary to discount the amounts payable on the respective principal and interest payment dates to the purchase price received for the new issue."[15] A TIC-based average interest rate is the **internal rate of return** for a bond or debt issue. It is the rate that discounts all principal and interest payments in future years for a bond issue back to the amount of bond proceeds (par value, par value less a discount, or par value plus a premium) that the issuer receives in selling the debt.

For example, if $10 million in bonds is issued today and will be repaid with ten equal annual debt service payments of $1.3 million each over the next ten years, TIC is the rate that discounts or equates all of the future payments, totaling $13 million, to $10 million. TIC brings the $1.3 million per year for ten years to its value today, which is $10 million. It does so by discounting or depreciating the payments. The discounting is greater for payments made in the later years than in the earlier years of the ten-year term. In other words, the $1.3 million paid in Year 9 is discounted much more than the $1.3 million paid in Year 3. The TIC-based average interest rate for the $10 million bond issue is about 5.1 percent.

Calculation of a TIC-based average interest rate is complicated. Even in the simplest of cases, like the one above with uniform annual debt service payments,[16] it requires the analyst to refer to tables of interest rates. Sophisticated computer programs, usually in several iterative calculations, are used to find the TIC for actual bond issues. Tables 10–7 and 10–8 show the TIC-based average interest rates for the two hypothetical bond issues presented in Table 10–5. Both issues are for $60,000 and have three-year terms. Both have an ascending interest rate structure—5 percent for Year 1, 6 percent for Year 2, and 7 percent for Year 3. Issue no. 1 provides for faster retirement of principal, and issue no. 2 for slower retirement of principal.

Table 10–7 shows that a rate of 6 percent discounts the future debt service payments for issue no. 1, totaling $66,000, to $59,985. This discounting goes

Table 10–7
TIC-based average interest rate for hypothetical $60,000, three-year debt issue with front-loaded retirement of principal (bond issue no. 1)

Principal and interest payments by year	Year 1	Year 2	Year 3	Total debt service
Interest Yr. 1 maturity @ 5%	$1,500			
Interest Yr. 2 maturity @ 6%	1,200			
Interest Yr. 3 maturity @ 7%	700			
Principal Yr. 1 maturity	30,000			
Total debt service Year 1	$33,400			
Interest Yr. 2 maturity @ 6%		$1,200		
Interest Yr. 3 maturity @ 7%		700		
Principal Yr. 2 maturity		20,000		
Total debt service Year 2		$21,900		
Interest Yr. 3 maturity @ 7%			$700	
Principal Yr. 3 maturity			10,000	
Total debt service Yr. 3			$10,700	

True interest cost: The interest rate that, when applied to debt service payments of $33,400 at end of Year 1, $21,900 at end of Year 2, and $10,700 at end of Year 3 (total $66,000), discounts these payments to total principal amount of bond issue (value today)—$60,000.

	Year 1	Year 2	Year 3	
Amount to be discounted	$33,400	$21,900	$10,700	$66,000
Discounted at 6%	31,510	19,491	8,984	59,985

Note: See the maturity or principal amounts and the annual interest amounts in the top part of Table 10–5.

Table 10–8

TIC-based average interest rate for a hypothetical $60,000 three-year debt issue with back-loaded retirement of principal (bond issue no. 2)

Principal and interest payments by year	Year 1	Year 2	Year 3	Total debt service
Interest Yr. 1 maturity @ 5%	$500			
Interest Yr. 2 maturity @ 6%	1,200			
Interest Yr. 3 maturity @ 7%	2,100			
Principal Yr. 1 maturity	10,000			
Total debt service Year 1	*$13,800*			
Interest Yr. 2 maturity @ 6%		$1,200		
Interest Yr. 3 maturity @ 7%		2,100		
Principal Yr. 2 maturity		20,000		
Total debt service Year 2		*$23,300*		
Interest Yr. 3 maturity @ 7%			$2,100	
Principal Yr. 3 maturity			30,000	
Total debt service Yr. 3			*$32,100*	

True interest cost: The interest rate that, when applied to debt service payments of $13,800 at end of Year 1, $23,300 at end of Year 2, and $32,100 at end of Year 3 (total $69,200), discounts these payments to total principal—$60,000.

	Year 1	Year 2	Year 3	
Amount to be discounted	$13,800	$23,300	$32,100	$69,200
Discounted at 6%	13,091	20,737	26,951	60,707
Discounted at 6.5%	12,957	20,541	26,572	60,070

Note: See the maturity or principal amounts and the annual interest amounts in the bottom part of Table 10–5.

slightly too far. However, from it we can conclude that the TIC-based average interest rate for issue no. 1 is just a little less than 6 percent, perhaps 5.95 percent. Further iteration would pin down the TIC-based rate exactly. TIC is very close to NIC (5.99 percent) for issue no. 1, in significant part because of the ascending interest rate structure for the issue.

In issue no. 2, with slower principal retirement, a discount rate of 6 percent reduces the future debt service payments, totaling $69,200, to $60,707. The $60,707 is not close enough to the $60,000 principal amount or present value for the issue. A second iteration at 6.5 percent discounts the future payments to $60,070, very close to the target of $60,000. We can conclude from this that the true interest cost for bond issue no. 2 is slightly above 6.5 percent, most probably between this rate and 6.55 percent. This is close to the NIC rate of 6.58 percent for issue no. 2, again in significant part attributable to the ascending interest rate structure for the issue.

If a bond issue has an ascending interest rate structure, reflecting the normal yield curve, its NIC-based average interest rate will generally be close to the TIC-based rate. On the other hand, if many early maturities of a bond issue have higher interest rates than later maturities, NIC is likely to be significantly less than TIC for the issue. In this situation, while total interest paid by the issuer may not change, more interest is paid earlier in the issue's term. NIC does not consider the time value of money—when interest and principal payments are made—and therefore it is not affected by such discounting of early maturities and shifting of interest payments to the early maturities of a bond issue. On the other hand, TIC is increased when interest is shifted toward the early maturities. In this case, TIC values the interest payments on the early maturities, with higher interest rates, more than the interest payments on the later maturities, with lower interest rates. Thus, when a bond issue includes a significant number of early maturities with higher interest rates than those for its later maturities, TIC is likely to be significantly higher than NIC.

The TIC-based average interest rate for Henderson's revenue bonds is 4.88 percent. The NIC rate for this issue is 4.88 percent (computed here for information only), the same as the TIC. The effective interest cost, or EIC rate, which is a TIC-based calculation but also deducts issuance costs from the issuer's bond proceeds (see sidebar on page 289), is 5.06 percent. EIC is higher than TIC because more discounting of the future debt service payments is needed to equate them to bond proceeds less the issuance costs. The calculation of the TIC does not consider the effect of issuance costs that the issuer must pay from bond proceeds.

The TIC-based average interest rate for Brunswick County's $16 million certificates of participation is 5.569 percent. The NIC-based rate is 5.472 percent. The difference, a little less than one-tenth of 1 percent, is significant. The interest rate structure for these certificates of participation is not consistently ascending. For example, the 2009 issue has a 5.75 percent interest rate, which is higher than the rates for all subsequent maturities except the rate for 2016. As a result, TIC is higher than NIC.

The EIC rate for Brunswick County's certificates is 5.689 percent. Again, its calculation deducts issuance costs paid from the issuer's bond proceeds and equates this value to the present value of future debt service payments on the certificates.

The TIC, NIC, and EIC rates for Brunswick County's certificates are all higher than the corresponding rates for Henderson's revenue bonds. The certificates were issued in the spring of 2000, when interest rates were higher than a year later when Henderson's revenue bonds were issued. Brunswick County's certificates of participation, secured by mortgages on the county property, are of somewhat lesser credit quality than Henderson's revenue bonds because they are secured by revenues from a well-established water-sewer utility. Both these considerations help explain the higher interest costs for the certificates of participation.

Conclusion

This chapter has examined the key concepts of interest, yield, and bond price; pricing structures that underwriters use in buying long-term debt; and the net and true interest cost methods for calculating the average interest rate for a bond issue. Local officials do not need to know the mathematics of computing interest, yield, bond price, and average interest rate for a debt issue, but they should be familiar with these basic concepts and how they affect the cost of debt. Such familiarity will enable officials to understand more fully the options for structuring and selling debt that financial advisers and underwriters put before them.

Notes

1 A distinction is made between **current yield** and **yield to maturity.** Current yield on debt is calculated by dividing annual interest by the amount paid (market price) by the lender or investors for the debt. The amount paid equals loan or debt proceeds to the issuer or debtor. Yield to maturity is the rate at which future payments on debt must be discounted to sum to the debt's current market price. The yield to maturity considers both future interest payments and the investor's capital gain or loss on a debt or security. See Marcia L. Stigum, *The Money Market,* 3rd ed. (Homewood, Ill.: Dow Jones–Irwin, 1990), 777–778, 1211–1212, 1235.

2 Lawrence Lipkin, Irwin K. Feinstein, and Lucile Derrick, *Accountant's Handbook of Formulas and Tables,* 3rd ed. (Englewood Cliffs, N.J.: Prentice Hall, 1988), 145.

3 This yield of 5.255 percent, assuming monthly compounding at 5 percent (the quoted rate) is calculated by multiplying the single payment compound amount present worth factor for 5/12ths of 1 percent, which is 1.0511, by 5 percent. Ibid., 298. The single payment compound amount present worth factor calculated the value today of a single amount to be received in the future, given a specified interest rate—5/12ths of 1 percent in this case.

4 M. David Gelfand, ed., *Federal Tax Exemption: History and Overview,* vol. 1 of *State and Local Government Debt Financing* (Wilmette, Ill.: Callaghan, 1986), 3. Most of the chapters of this publication were updated and replaced between 1995 and 2001. From 1913 to 1968, every federal tax statute had a general exemption from income taxes of the interest paid for all state and local government debt. Since 1968, the exemption has continued, but it has been restricted in significant ways by changes in federal tax laws and Internal Revenue Service regulations.

5 Article 4 of Chapter 105 of the General Statutes of North Carolina imposes the state's income tax and grants exemptions.

6 Section 105-134.2 of the General Statutes of North Carolina establishes the state's individual income tax rates. Married individuals filing a joint return pay a

7 percent rate on taxable income from $21,250 to $100,000.

7 The full case is reproduced in Gerald J. Miller, ed., *Handbook of Debt Management* (New York: M. Dekker, 1996), 1–12.

8 Gelfand, *State and Local Government Debt Financing,* vol. 1, chapter 5 (1997), 5–7. Also see the Anthony Commission on Public Finance, in *Handbook of Debt Management,* 18 and 28–30. The Anthony Commission was created by Representative Beryl F. Anthony (D-Ark.) to (1) consider the effects of federal tax and other laws on the ability of state and local governments to carry out their responsibilities through tax-exempt financing, and (2) recommend changes in federal law consistent with financial prudence and the rights and interest of the federal, state, and local governments. The commission submitted its report to Representative Anthony in October 1989. The report provides an excellent summary, history, and analysis of federal tax laws and their effect on state and local government tax-exempt financing.

9 Arbitrage restrictions are found in Section 148 of the Internal Revenue Code. Federal arbitrage restrictions and rebate requirements are summarized in Terence P. Burke, *Guide to Arbitrage Requirements for Government Bond Issues* and *1994 Supplement to Guide to Arbitrage Requirements for Governmental Bond Issues* (Chicago: GFOA, 1992 and 1994).

10 Both Winston-Salem and Durham, North Carolina, have issued taxable debt to fund self-insurance reserves.

11 Lipkin, Feinstein, and Derrick, *Accountant's Handbook of Formulas and Tables,* 145–146.

12 See, for example, the Local Government Commission of North Carolina, North Carolina Department of State Treasurer, "Notice of Sale and Bid Form, County of Johnston, North Carolina, $25,000,000 General Obligation School Bonds, Series 2001," 3.

13 Ibid.

14 For a summary of the mathematics of calculating true interest cost, see Amy V. Puelz, "Municipal Bond Issue Structuring," in *Handbook of Debt Management,* chapter 21, especially 409–413.

15 The Municipal Securities Rulemaking Board was created in 1975 by amendments to the Securities Exchange Act of 1934. See Robert L. Ehlers, *Ehlers on Public Finance: Building Better Communities* (Rochester, Minn.: Lone Oak Press, 1998), 163, 367.

16 The interest rate formula for doing this is called the uniform series present worth factor. It discounts a series of equal amounts in the future to their value today. See A. John Vogt and Lisa A. Cole, "Interest Factors for Compounding and Discounting," appendix 1 of *A Guide to Municipal Leasing* (Chicago: GFOA, 1983), 181, which presents six interest rate formulas for compounding or discounting; the examples of the formulas use a 5 percent interest rate. One of these is the uniform series present worth factor.

11 Selling local government debt

Debt issued for capital projects typically requires a long-term commitment of revenue for the issuer and entails risks that extend over many years for the lenders or investors. Well-defined sales procedures have evolved to help make sure that sales of debt meet both the issuer's and the lenders' or investors' needs. A local government selling debt can save issuance expenses and hold down interest costs on the debt by following procedures suitable to the debt being sold. This chapter examines the following topics concerning the sale of local government debt:

- General approaches: competitive public sale, negotiated public sale, and private placement
- Roles of market professionals
- Documents used in the public sale of debt: the official statement and the notice of sale
- Investors who buy local debt
- Costs of selling debt publicly in competitive and negotiated sales
- Arbitrage.

General approaches to selling local government debt

Local government debt may be sold publicly or placed privately.[1] In a public sale, the issuer sells the debt to an underwriter or underwriting group who then resell it to investors.[2] Public sales are generally used for large projects when more than $10 million in debt is issued. They are also used for many smaller projects of less than $10 million. The debt is marketed to potential investors using a notice of sale and a preliminary official statement. Often ads are placed in financial media.

A public sale of debt may be competitive or negotiated. In a competitive sale, different underwriters bid against each other to buy the debt. The issuer sells the debt to the underwriter offering the lowest average interest rate.

In a negotiated public sale, the issuer selects the underwriter to sell the debt, perhaps using a request for proposal (RFP) process. The underwriter and issuer then negotiate the debt's interest rates, prices, and terms, and the underwriter buys the debt and resells it to investors.

Many debt market professionals—bond attorneys, underwriters, rating agencies, depositories, and paying agents—are involved in almost all public sales. Financial advisers, bond insurers, trustees, and other market professionals play an important roles in many sales. Public sales of debt typically involve significant issuance costs.

In private placements of local debt, the issuer places the debt directly with a single investor or a small number of investors. Private placements are often used for modest capital projects and acquisitions that range anywhere from tens of thousands of dollars to millions of dollars depending on the size of the project and the capital financing strategy that the issuer uses. Some private placements occur for large projects for which the financing is customized to meet specific project needs or investor interests. In these transactions, the issuer often works with a placement agent who helps place the debt with investors. Some private placements are strictly negotiated transactions between the issuer and the investors. Others are competitive: different banks or investors bid to provide the financing. Bond attorneys, underwriters, rating agencies, bond insurers, and other market professionals are often unnecessary in private placements. Issuers often rely on a financial adviser to help arrange a relatively large private placement. Issuance or sales costs for private placements are generally much less than for public sales of debt.

Of the long-term debt issued by state and local governments from 1992 through 2002, competitive public sales accounted for about 22 percent; negotiated public sales, about 76 percent; and private placement about 2 percent or less (see Figure 11–1a). Most general obligation (GO) bonds are sold competitively, while most revenue bonds, capital lease debt, and special obligation (SO) bonds were sold in negotiated public sales. GO bonds accounted for about a third of state and local long-term debt issuance during the 1990s and the first years of this decade.[3] The increase in competitive sales from a little less than 20 percent in 1992 and 1993 to 24.4 percent of the total by 2000 and then the decrease to nearly 20 percent by 2002 probably reflects the fluctuations in debt refunding that took place over these years. Debt refunding, as a percentage of total debt, was greater in the early 1990s and in the first few years of the twenty-first century than in the late part of the 1990s.[4] Refunding debt is more likely to be sold in a negotiated process than original issue debt. Laws in many

Figure 11-1a
Sales approaches for long-term state and local debt, percentage

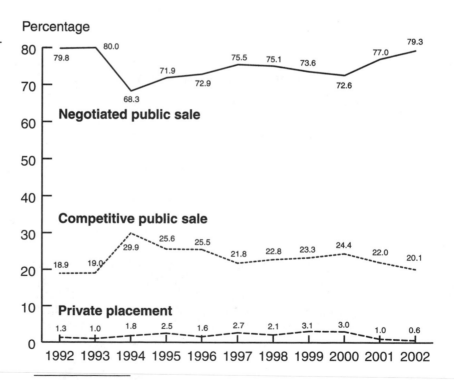

Figure 11-1b
Sales approaches for long-term state and local debt, in billions of dollars

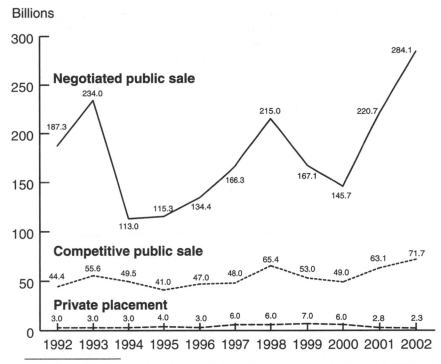

Billions

Source: "A Decade of Municipal Bond Finance," *The Bond Buyer,* May 8, 2001, 38; March 7, 2003, 42.

states allow refunding debt to be sold in negotiated sales even when the debt being refunded was sold competitively.[5]

The private placement amounts shown in Figure 11–1b are those reported to *The Bond Buyer* and do not include all private placements of state and local government debt, especially small transactions. Even if small transactions were included, private placement would probably account for less than 10 percent of total state and local government long-term debt.

Competitive public sale

In a competitive public sale of local government debt, the local issuer, working with bond counsel and often a financial adviser, determines the type of debt to issue, the security to pledge, the amount of the issue, the maturity schedule, and other features of the debt.

This team prepares documents for the sale (most important, the preliminary official statement and notice of sale), obtains bond ratings; secures insurance if advantageous; arranges for bond registration, printing, and other services; sets a date, time, and place for underwriters to submit their bids; and advertises the bonds.

If underwriters' bids are submitted in hard copy, they are sealed. A growing number of issuers are now taking electronic bids. The issuer selects the underwriter or underwriting group offering the lowest average interest rate and highest price for the bonds. In the past, the winning bidder in most competitive sales was selected on the basis of net interest cost. Today probably the majority of competitive sales are being determined on the basis of true interest cost and the rest use net interest cost (see Chapter 10).

The winning underwriters then resell the bonds to investors. Underwriters often notify important customers of a debt issue's availability before bidding to buy the debt. They obtain information about the yields that the customers are looking for and line up potential buyers before the sale. This facilitates resale of the debt and limits the underwriters' risk. Underwriters are often able to resell debt on the day they buy it or in the next day or two.

To cover their costs and compensation, underwriters must resell debt for an overall price higher than they paid to the issuer. This, in turn, means that the investors who buy some of the maturities receive a lower yield than the interest rate that the issuer pays on those maturities in the debt issue. Underwriters lose money if they fail to resell debt for more than they paid for it. This happens occasionally even to the most experienced underwriters. One cause can be a sudden upward movement of market interest rates, causing bond prices to deteriorate and forcing the underwriters to sell the debt for less than they paid. Losses can also happen if underwriters underestimate what investors are willing to accept in yields, bid prices for the debt that are too high, and then have to sell the debt at lower prices.

Negotiated public sale

In a negotiated public sale of local government debt, the issuer selects an underwriter or underwriting group to plan and sell the debt. To select the underwriter, the issuer often asks different underwriters to submit proposals that include their professional qualifications, experience in marketing the type of local government debt proposed, the services that would be provided, how the underwriter would handle the sale, and the issuance costs that would be involved. The issuer should select an underwriter on the basis of the underwriter's ability to render effective professional assistance and sell the debt at competitive interest rates and reasonable issuance costs. Many local governments rely on a financial adviser to help determine what services to look for from the underwriter, prepare an RFP, and specify the criteria used in selecting an underwriter.

The selected underwriter works with the issuer to plan, size, structure, and price the debt issue. The underwriter prepares (or takes the lead in preparing) the preliminary official statement and the final official statements, obtains ratings and bond insurance if advantageous, and advertises the debt issue. A day or so before the sale day, the underwriter sets initial interest rates, prices, and re-offer yields and test markets or premarkets the debt through its sale forces. If the sale is undersubscribed, the underwriter and issuer may lower prices and increase re-offer yields and interest rates for the debt. On the other hand, if demand for the debt is higher than expected, the underwriter and issuer may be able to increase prices and lower re-offer yields and interest rates. When the initial prices, re-offer yields, and interest rates match market demand, they are maintained and used to sell the debt. This process is called final pricing.

The underwriter then sells the bonds at the final prices. Often many bonds in an issue have been effectively presold in initial marketing; then the underwriter's purchase and sale of the debt is almost simultaneous. In some cases, final pricing fails to move the debt quickly, and the underwriter takes a day or two to complete the sale. In this case, the underwriter may need to discount some of the bonds and sell them at higher re-offer yields than planned.

In negotiated sales, the underwriter charges a fee that is paid or deducted from the issuer's debt proceeds. This fee is called the spread, and it is divided into the following four components:

• **Management fee** The management fee compensates the underwriter for working with the issuer to plan and structure the debt and for coordinating the sales process. If several underwriting firms are involved, this fee, or most of it, goes to the lead underwriter.

- **Takedown**   Takedown is compensation for marketing the bonds. It is paid to the underwriting sales force and must be high enough to motivate it to spend time selling the debt. If the issuer presses the underwriter to reduce takedown, the underwriter may choose to place most or all of the debt with a few large institutional investors that demand high yields.[6]

- **Expenses**   This component of the underwriter's fee varies little from sale to sale.

- **Underwriting risk**   If the issuer is strong and the issue includes standard features, this part of the fee may be waived. The more unusual a sale and the more challenges the underwriter expects, the more likely a fee will be charged for underwriting risk, and the higher the fee is likely to be. In markets where interest rates are subject to upward movement, underwriters are apt to include a charge for underwriting risk.[7]

Competitive and negotiated sales

Investment bankers generally prefer negotiated over competitive public sales of debt because in a negotiated sale, the underwriter plans and manages the entire transaction and can design the debt to most effectively meet market demands. This enables the underwriter to presell all or most of the debt and secure low interest rates for the issuer. Underwriters also say that negotiated sales avoid the need for the issuer to have a financial adviser and that the underwriters in negotiated sales often provide a secondary market after original issuance.

At least three criticisms are made about negotiated public sales of debt. First, the underwriter faces a conflict of interest in negotiated sales, attempting to meet the needs of both the issuer and the investors. The issuer wants low interest rates, and the investors want high yields. While the underwriter acts as a broker between these interests, issuers in some negotiated sales wonder whether their interests are being sacrificed to those of the investors.

Second, when underwriters contribute to the political campaigns of elected officials who select underwriters to sell debt, both parties are open to "pay to play" accusations. Is the underwriter selected because of campaign contributions or because of ability to sell proposed debt at competitive rates? During the early 1990s, the Municipal Securities Rule Making Board adopted rules prohibiting municipal bond dealers from engaging in negotiated debt transactions with state and local government issuers within two years of making any contribution to any official of the issuer.

Third, some say the spread and costs of negotiated transactions generally exceed those of competitive sales. This criticism is examined in the section of this chapter that begins on page 325.

Local debt issuers are often advised to use a competitive sale for debt that is standard and that is likely to be well received by investors in the market. Negotiated sales are recommended for debt issues that have unique features, that the market may not automatically accept, or that may raise questions about credit quality.

Sources: Robert L. Ehlers, *Ehlers on Public Finance: Building Better Communities* (Rochester, Minn.: Lone Oak Press, 1998), Chapter 15, "Negotiated v. Competitive Sales." See also James C. Joseph, *Debt Issuance and Management: A Guide for Small Governments* (Chicago: Government Finance Officers Association 1994), Chapter 6, "Selecting the Method of Sale."

Private placement of debt

In a private placement of local debt, the issuer obtains a loan from, or places the debt directly with, a single investor or a small number of investors.[8] Disclosure requirements are less rigorous than for public sales of debt. For example, the issuer does not have to prepare an official statement.[9] Bond ratings are usually not needed. Investors are typically commercial banks, other financial institutions, or wealthy individuals who are familiar with the issuer and able to judge the credit quality of the debt on their own. The investors usually acquire the debt with the intention of holding it in their portfolios. Unlike underwriters, they are not acquiring the debt to resell it. The investors' motivations in buying the debt and lending or providing the financing may be limited to earning a reasonable interest rate. In some cases, investors have a greater stake in the project. The debt may finance public infrastructure that supports private development in which the investors have a financial stake. In other cases, investors are motivated by a sense of civic responsibility. They earn investment income, but they acquire the debt primarily because it finances infrastructure important to the jurisdiction's development.

Many private placements finance equipment acquisitions or small improvement projects costing a few million dollars or less. The repayment terms usually range from a few years to ten years or so. Federal tax laws give a tax advantage to commercial banks when they buy debt from a local issuer that sells or places less than $10 million of tax-exempt debt in a year's time. Therefore, many local governments issue privately placed debt in amounts up to $10 million. Commercial banks are interested in buying this privately placed debt because they earn tax-exempt interest on it and still deduct their own interest and other financing costs to raise the money to buy the debt.[10]

While $10 million is a dividing line to which local governments refer in deciding whether to sell debt publicly or place it privately, the line is not always the deciding factor.[11] Many debt offerings of less than $10 million are sold publicly, and some much larger debt issues are placed privately. Public sales of relatively small amounts can occur when the issuer is able to obtain interest rates low enough to more than offset the higher issuance costs of a public sale. Private placements of large debt issues can occur when the transaction is complex (for example, involving unusual security) or when the investors and the issuer are able to negotiate interest rates, costs, and features that are advantageous and reasonable to all parties.

Market Professionals

The following professionals can be involved in selling local government debt:

- Bond counsel or attorney
- Financial adviser
- Underwriter
- Consulting engineer
- Rating agency
- Bond insurer or other financial guarantor
- Trustee
- Registrar, transfer agent, and paying agent
- Printer

Private placement of debt: Two cautions

Two cautions are offered about local governments' reliance on private placement of debt. First, if the placement takes place without any competition among lenders or investors, the issuer may incur higher costs (both interest and issuance costs) than if a public sale of debt were used.* Typical investors in privately placed debt transactions are banks, financial institutions, or wealthy investors who know the markets and are able to negotiate favorable yields. A private placement without competition also can open officials to charges that they are not getting the lowest rates on the debt or, worse, that they are giving "special deals" to the investors.

Local officials can protect the local issuer's interests and their own reputations by using competition in a private placement of debt. If the financing is fairly standard, the issuer can issue a request for bids to banks or others that might provide the financing. In many parts of the country, banks and leasing firms are accustomed to providing such financing through competitive bid processes. The issuer is likely to receive multiple bids, and it can then select the one offering the lowest average interest rate, providing it is from a reputable and experienced bank or firm.

Second, privately placed debt is usually much less liquid and marketable than publicly sold debt. This means that the investors who buy privately placed debt could very well face difficulties if they wish to sell it to other investors before maturity. They may have to discount the debt below its par or face value. While investors who buy privately placed debt usually do so to hold it to maturity in their portfolios, they may nonetheless demand an interest rate premium to cover the risks arising from the limited liquidity and marketability of the debt.

---

*James C. Joseph, *Debt Issuance and Management: A Guide for Small Governments* (Chicago: GFOA, 1994), 60.

Bond counsel or attorney

The bond counsel or attorney certifies that the issuer has the legal authority to issue the debt and that the debt is a valid obligation of the issuer. Without these certifications, investors will not buy the debt.[12] Bond counsel also certifies whether the interest on the debt is exempt from federal and, if applicable, state income taxes. Without these certifications, investors are unlikely to buy the debt. If the debt's tax-exempt status is uncertified, the debt is treated as taxable debt with higher interest rates.

When a bond counsel renders an opinion about the validity and taxability of debt, the opinion should be based on a conclusion that it would be unreasonable for a court to render a contrary judgment. In other words, the bond counsel testifies to what a court would consider to be settled law as applied to particular debt. If the bond counsel is unable to do this, he or she should not issue an opinion on the debt.[13]

The bond counsel's opinion addresses the municipal debt markets at large as well as the issuer. The opinion appears in the official statement prepared to market debt, usually near the top of the cover page. If debt is issued in certificated form, the opinion also goes on each bond certificate.

The bond counsel's opinion also comments on the security pledged for repayment. If the debt is in the form of GO bonds, the opinion makes clear that the debt is a full faith and credit obligation for which the issuer may levy taxes without restriction. If the debt is secured by enterprise revenues or by a mortgage or security interest on the financed property, the opinion makes clear that the debt is a special obligation rather than a general obligation of the issuer, and it specifies the particular security pledged for the debt. A local government can expect additional advice from the bond counsel about what types of debt are legal for the issuer, the security for and legal limits that apply to each type of debt, procedures needed to issue legally valid debt, and what the law says about how debt should be sold.[14]

Attorneys acting as bond counsels must be independent of the issuer. Although the issuer's own attorney may know as much as the bond counsel about the issuer's authority to issue debt and specific procedural requirements for doing so, that official represents the issuer's interests and therefore, in the market's view, is unable to render an objective or independent opinion on the legal validity of the issuer's debt. An independent bond counsel must do this. The bond counsel must also have standing in the market. In other words, the bond counsel must have a reputation for being knowledgeable about municipal debt. Such experience and knowledge have become more important in recent decades as the federal tax and securities laws applicable to state and local government debt have expanded.

The bond counsel should be hired at the very beginning of the debt authorization and issuance process. In GO bond issues, the bond counsel often prepares all documents or oversees their preparation and also supervises the steps toward authorizing and issuing the debt. Alternatively, for some GO bonds and most other types of debt, the bond counsel presents a checklist of documents, document provisions, and steps that the issuer must take to create a valid debt. Then the issuer's own attorney and other officials oversee completion of the steps and certify the work done, and the bond counsel renders the opinion based on the facts certified to by the issuer.

Thirty years ago, bond counsels' work for state and local governments across the nation was done by a handful of large New York law firms. In recent decades, many more law firms and attorneys have entered the municipal bond field. Some of these firms operate out of New York, but many more are regional or even local firms that have developed the expertise and standing to render legal opinions that investors rely on in purchasing state and local debt.

Nationally recognized municipal bond counsels are listed in *The Bond Buyer's Municipal Marketplace,* also called the "Red Book." Selection of one of these firms or attorneys can be very helpful in marketing debt.[15] When there is pressure to select as bond counsel a local or regional law firm that lacks standing in the municipal debt markets, co-counsel arrangements can be worked out: the less-well-known firm performs some bond counsel tasks and a nationally recognized firm reviews the work and signs off on it. A co-counsel arrangement is more expensive than having just one bond counsel.

The bond counsel is often selected competitively through an RFP process. Firms responding should provide examples of successful sales of the type of debt being sold and list attorneys in the firm who will work on the sale and their experience with municipal debt. Payment of the bond counsel can be on an hourly basis, with enumeration of different attorneys working on the sale and an estimate of the total fee, or it can be a flat dollar amount. The former is usually used for debt issues with special features and the latter for GO bonds and other standard debt sales.[16]

A local unit's own attorney usually plays a limited but significant role, certifying that needed authorizations have been adopted by the local governing board and that no litigation challenges the debt. For debt other than

GO bonds, the unit's attorney also certifies that covenants for the proposed debt will not violate any other contracts the issuer already has in place and that there are no liens against revenues or assets to be pledged as security for the debt. The local attorney is in a better position than the bond counsel to know these things.[17]

A third attorney, the underwriters' counsel, is involved in public sales of revenue bonds, capital leases, and many types of SO debt. The primary role of the underwriters' counsel is to make sure that underwriters and the issuer comply with disclosure requirements of the Securities and Exchange Commission (SEC) for sales of debt and other securities.[18] The underwriters' counsel has a key role in preparing or overseeing the preparation of the official statement (see page 317). The issuer pays for the underwriters' counsel.

If a debt financing is especially complex or unusual, a special tax counsel may be involved to render a second opinion on the tax-exempt status of the debt. A few revenue bond, capital lease, and SO debt issues also involve a trustee's counsel. These special legal services are unusual and, because the issuer typically pays for them, the issuer should be sure to question whether they are necessary.

Financial adviser

Most local governments that do not regularly plan and sell debt do not have staff with the knowledge and experience needed to plan and structure debt and negotiate the issuance process. They often turn to outside consultants, generally called financial advisers. Even large local governments that sell debt every year or two and have staff who specialize in debt planning use financial advisers for special types of debt.[19]

A financial adviser serves several general purposes. Most important, the adviser helps the issuer obtain financing at competitive and affordable rates. Second, the adviser helps to size and structure a financing. Third, the financial adviser represents the issuer's interests in its dealings with the bond counsel, underwriters, rating agencies, insurers, regulators, and other debt market professionals. These professionals have interests besides the issuer's at stake in the sale of debt, and the financial adviser gives the issuer expertise that puts the issuer on a more level playing field with other participants.

The financial adviser, who should be hired at the very beginning of debt planning, can help the issuer

- Determine whether or not to incur debt for specific purposes
- Understand the amount of debt it can afford to carry and identify sources of revenue for paying debt
- Develop RFPs to select other professionals needed to sell debt, and help in the selection process
- Comply with legal requirements by working with the bond counsel and the issuer's attorney during the authorization and issuance process
- Prepare a calendar for any debt sale
- Become informed about debt retirement structures and features
- Prepare for the bond rating process
- Check the accuracy of bids in competitive sales
- Give advice, in negotiated sales, about pricing that the underwriters obtain, and monitor the sales process
- Decide whether to accept bids or offers to purchase debt

- Prepare a postsale analysis comparing the results of the sale and the prices obtained with similar debt issues in the market at the same time.[20]

A financial adviser must know municipal debt finance and be accessible to local officials. Because the financial adviser must be fully committed to the issuer's interests and no others', the adviser should be someone local officials trust completely and can talk to with ease.

Local governments increasingly use an RFP process to select a financial adviser. A firm's response to the RFP should identify the individual(s) in the firm who will work with the local jurisdiction, list the experience of these staff with the specific types of financing the jurisdiction does, identify other local government clients of the firm, and summarize what the firm understands about the jurisdiction's financial condition and prospects in relation to its capital needs. Personal interviews must be part of the selection process.

In the past, financial advisers were hired to work on a specific debt sale, and they were compensated on a fee per $1,000 of debt sold (for example, $1 per $1,000). There are two disadvantages to this approach. First, it provides an incentive for the adviser to increase the amount of debt the jurisdiction issues.[21] Second, it does not necessarily reward the financial adviser for planning. Increasingly, local governments are employing financial advisers not only to help with specific financing but also to advise them more broadly about financing options in relation to capital needs. When financial advisers exercise this broader role, they should be paid on an hourly basis or with a set fee or retainer for a specified period of time.[22]

Many underwriters claim that, in negotiated sales of debt, they can serve as a financial adviser as well as sell debt on behalf of the local issuer. Their first-hand, day-to-day contact with the market puts them in an excellent position to advise a local issuer when to sell debt, how much to sell, and how to structure the debt. This arrangement, however, reflects a narrow view of the financial adviser's role because it focuses on marketing specific debt. Indeed, underwriters are deal oriented. Many have staff with strong capital planning experience, and they promise to help local governments plan to meet capital needs and evaluate financing options as well as sell debt. Some do. But underwriters make their money from the sale of debt, and their interests go in this direction.

A financial adviser should be "issuer oriented." Local governments need financial advisers who evaluate potential debt sales in relation to financing alternatives and the capacity of the issuer to carry the debt in the future.[23] In negotiated sales, the financial adviser can provide an independent assessment of the underwriter's recommendations and relate a particular financing structure to the issuer's overall needs and financial capacity.

Of course, an underwriter cannot serve as a financial adviser in a competitive sale of debt where the underwriter bids to buy the debt. Issuers are more likely to use an independent financial adviser in a competitive sale of public debt than in a negotiated sale. In some states, a state agency serves as the financial adviser to local governments selling debt. The agency helps local officials evaluate financing options, determine debt carrying capacity, size and structure debt, and actually sell it.

Underwriter

As already explained, the underwriter or underwriting group buys debt from the issuer and resells it to investors. Underwriters are financial intermediaries who bring together the issuer, on the one hand, and the investors and lenders, on the other. They do so not as brokers (who merely bring together the two sides in the transaction) but as principals. Underwriters, as the term implies, buy the debt, own or hold it for a time—a very, very short time if they are successful—and then resell it to investors. They have their own money or capital at stake. If they sell the debt for more than they paid for it, they make money; if they sell it for less, they lose money.

Underwriters in the municipal debt market include:

- Municipal securities divisions of the largest securities firms
- Securities or municipal securities departments of large commercial banks
- Investment banking firms that specialize in municipal securities and that operate nationally
- Many medium- and small-size investment banking firms that specialize in municipal securities and that operate regionally or in a single state
- Securities subsidiaries of conglomerate corporations
- Medium- and small-size commercial banks.

The Bond Buyer lists lead underwriters for upcoming, negotiated, state and local government bond sales of $5 million or more.[24]

Consulting engineer

Typical revenue bonds and SO debt secured and paid from special and limited revenues require feasibility studies done by a consulting engineer or another professional experienced with the kind of project(s) financed with the bonds or debt. The feasibility study provides expert and independent verification that is important to all concerned—the issuer, bond counsel, financial adviser, underwriters, rating agencies, insurers, and ultimately the investors. The study needs to demonstrate that the special revenues will be sufficient to cover service on the debt and any operating and maintenance costs or other expenses that must be supported from the special revenues. The study usually focuses on historic and prospective net revenue in relation to debt service on existing and proposed new debt; it must show that net revenues will cover annual debt service by some margin (for example, 125 percent).

Without a positive assessment of feasibility, the proposed debt cannot be issued because investors will not buy it. The feasibility study or a summary is usually reproduced in the preliminary official statement offering the bonds for sale and in the official statement that is finally released.

Rating agency

A bond or debt rating evaluates the capacity and willingness of the issuer to repay specific debt with interest when due, and it evaluates the protection afforded to investors by the legal provisions that govern specific debt obligations.[25] Ratings are vital in selling local government debt. Ratings generate substantial information about an issuer and provide an outside assessment of the credit quality of its debt. Generally, ratings say to investors that the rated debt is safe and will be, or is likely to be, repaid or, conversely, that serious questions exist concerning the issuer's ability and resolve to repay the debt. Few investors today are willing to buy unrated debt. The investment policies of mutual funds and other institutional investors require that they buy only debt of state and local governments that is rated.

Chapter 8 identified the criteria of bond rating agencies for rating different types of local government debt, discussed the bond-rating process, identified and defined rating categories, and examined the central role that ratings have played in developing the municipal debt market in general and in facilitating the sale of specific local government debt issues.

Bond insurer or other financial guarantor

Bond insurance guarantees a debt issuer's periodic debt service payments of principal and interest. If the issuer fails to make a payment to investors, the insurer is obligated to make the payment. For a similar purpose, banks and occasionally other guarantors provide letters of credit and other forms of liquidity support for the variable-rate demand debt that some local governments issue for capital financing purposes (see Chapter 9). Figure 11–2 shows the amount and percentages of state and local government long-term debt that are insured and the amount and percentages backed by letters of credit for groups of years from 1992 to 2002.

Figure 11–2b shows that 44.0 percent of long-term debt issued by state and local governments from 1992 through 2002 was insured. Only 36.2 percent of such debt issued in the 1992–1994 period was insured. Clearly, the use of bond insurance grew during the 1990s and into the first few years of this decade. Letters of credit backed an average of 5.2 percent of state and local long-term debt issued during the 1992–2000 period.

Bond insurance   Less than twenty-five years ago the insurance of debt service on state and local government long-term bond or debt issues was

Figure 11-2a
Insured, letter-of-credit, and uninsured state and local long-term debt, in billions of dollars

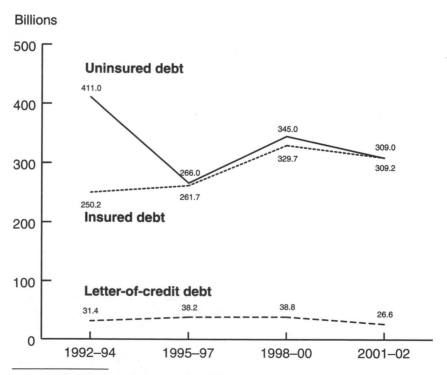

Source: Calculated from 1992–2002 data provided in "A Decade of Municipal Bond Finance," *The Bond Buyer,* May 8, 2001, 38; March 7, 2003, 42.

Note: Uninsured debt refers to debt that is neither insured nor backed by a letter of credit. It includes very small amounts of debt involving insured mortgages, surety bonds, and certificates of deposit.

Figure 11-2b
Insured, letter-of-credit, and uninsured state and local long-term debt, percentage

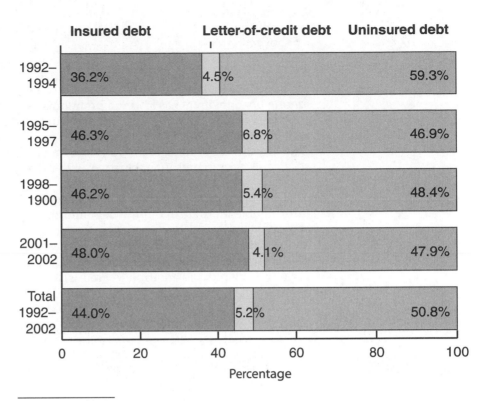

Source: Calculated from data in Figure 11-2a.

Note: Uninsured debt refers to debt that is neither insured nor backed by a letter of credit. It includes very small amounts of debt involving insured mortgages, surety bonds, and certificates of deposit.

unusual. In 1980, only 4 percent of such debt was insured.[26] Insurance began to become significant in the municipal debt markets in the 1980s as state and local issuers sold more revenue bonds, certificates of participation, and different types of special obligation debt. The novelty of some debt types then created questions of credit quality for many potential investors. Insurance guaranteeing debt service payments on the debt provided the assurance investors needed to invest in the new types of debt. In addition, the Tax Reform Act of 1986 limited the advantages of investing in tax-exempt debt for banks and certain other financial institutions. As banks reduced their purchases, individual investors began buying more state and local debt, either directly or through mutual funds, and, in doing so, they sought reduction in the risks through bond insurance.[27]

During the 1990s, the growing experience with bond insurance and the entry of some additional insurance companies into the municipal debt market brought municipal bond insurance premiums down. State and local governments found it economically advantageous to purchase bond insurance for additional types of debt, including GO bonds. Today bond insurers are key players in the municipal debt markets. Many investors, such as mutual funds, expect bond insurance to be used for certain types of state and local debt.

The four largest bond insurers are Ambac Assurance Corporation, MBIA Insurance Corporation, Financial Securities Assurance (FSA), and Financial Guaranty Insurance Company (FGIC).[28] These and other municipal bond insurers have triple-A credit ratings from the national bond rating agencies. Local debt issues for which bond insurance is purchased typically have stand-alone ratings of A+ or A1 or below. By insuring the debt, the issuer raises the debt's rating to the insurer's triple-A status. This makes the debt more attractive to investors and lowers interest rates and costs. Bond insurance is usually not worth the cost for issues with stand-alone ratings of double-A or above.

A local government purchases insurance for debt that it issues by paying a premium at issuance. The premium is a percentage of total debt service—principal and interest—to be paid over the full term of the debt. Competition among bond insurers has lowered premiums as a percentage of debt service over the years. In the mid-1990s, the premiums ranged from around 0.40 percent to 0.80 percent of total debt service on most insured bonds. Some strong debt issues have been insured at a premium of only 0.10 percent of total debt service. The premiums for debt issues with more risk or unusual features can exceed 1 percent of total debt service.[29]

To obtain bond insurance, a local government issuer submits the same information and data about the debt and the issuer that go into the official statement and other documents that go to the rating agencies. The issuer, its financial adviser, or underwriter might request bids from several insurers. Each insurer interested in insuring the debt gives a premium quote. Assuming all bidders are triple-A credits, the issuer chooses the insurer that provides the lowest premium. The lowest premium is based on a comparison of the up-front premium cost and savings in interest over the term of the debt issue, when the time value of money is considered. This is a four-step process:

- Calculate debt service on the debt at the interest rate the issuer expects to pay without insurance
- Calculate debt service on the debt at the interest rate the issuer expects to pay with insurance
- Subtract the insured debt service from the uninsured debt service by year
- Calculate the present value of the difference between the insured and uninsured debt service.

Application of these steps is illustrated with the hypothetical $10 million, ten-year bond issue shown initially in Table 9–1. Assume the uninsured issue has an interest rate of 5 percent and even annual debt service. Assume the insured rate is 4.8 percent. Under these assumptions, even annual debt service at 5 percent is $1,295,052. At 4.8 percent, it is $1,280,000. The difference is $15,052 per year, and the total difference over the life of the bonds is $150,520 (see Table 11–1).

Because the annual debt service associated with either interest rate in Table 11–1 is the same each year of the ten-year period, the calculation of the present value of the difference between the debt service streams uses a single uniform series present worth factor. Using a 5 percent discount factor produces a present value of $116,227 ($15,052 × 7.7217) for the $150,520. At 4.5 percent discount rate, the present value is $119,102 ($15,052 × 7.9127). If the one-time premium that the issuer pays for bond insurance is 0.7 percent of total debt service, or $89,600 ($12,800,000 × 0.007), the bond insurance is worth the cost. The present value of the debt service savings is $116,227 at 5 percent and $119,102 at 4.5 percent. Both of these amounts exceed the premium of $89,600. In an actual bond issue, debt service is seldom the same from year to year, and the calculation of the present value of annual debt service savings is more complicated.

Rather than go through such calculations, a local government issuer can qualify for bond insurance in advance of the bond sale. In competitive sales of debt, the issuer discloses this fact and the amount of the premium, requires bidders to pay the premium if submitting an insured bid, and asks for bids either with or without insurance.[30] In negotiated sales, a pre-qualified issuer

Table 11–1

Even annual debt service for a hypothetical $10 million ten-year bond issue at two different interest rates: 5 percent uninsured and 4.8 percent insured

End of year	Annual debt service at 5% without insurance	Annual debt service at 4.8% with insurance	Difference between insured and uninsured debt service
1	$1,295,052	$1,280,000	$15,052
2	1,295,052	1,280,000	15,052
3	1,295,052	1,280,000	15,052
4	1,295,052	1,280,000	15,052
5	1,295,052	1,280,000	15,052
6	1,295,052	1,280,000	15,052
7	1,295,052	1,280,000	15,052
8	1,295,052	1,280,000	15,052
9	1,295,052	1,280,000	15,052
10	1,295,052	1,280,000	15,052
Totals	$12,950,520	$12,800,000	$150,520

tells the underwriter that the debt qualified for insurance, and the underwriter takes the insurance into account when buying and reselling the debt. Alternatively (and this is more likely to occur), the underwriter obtains the insurance. In either case, the issuer pays the insurance premium, which is deducted from bond proceeds.

Bond insurance is cost-effective for the large amount of local government debt with stand-alone ratings in the single-A or triple-B categories. The savings in interest costs resulting from raising these issues to triple-A ratings is often worth the cost of the bond insurance. Bond insurance is seldom worth the cost of raising stand-alone double-A-rated debt to triple-A status, and the premium for insurance for debt with stand-alone ratings below triple-B is usually too high. Of course, if a local issuer can place low-rated debt with a state loan program or a bond bank, the issuer can often obtain a favorable interest rate and lower interest costs without obtaining bond insurance.

Letters of credit Commercial banks issue **letters of credit (LOCs)** or provide other forms of liquidity for variable-rate demand debt that some local governments issue to finance certain capital needs.[31] As discussed in Chapter 9, the interest rate for variable-rate demand debt can change weekly, and investors may put or sell the debt back to the issuer on any date when the interest rate may reset. If the investors exercise their put option and sell the debt back, the issuer must then refinance it. A letter of credit or a similar liquidity facility gives the issuer money to buy back the put debt, and it gives the issuer time to refinance or refund the debt in an orderly fashion and at a reasonable interest rate.

The initial cost of an LOC ranges from 0.35 percent to 0.5 percent of the principal amount of the debt.[32] Letters of credit also have annual renewal fees that range from 0.2 percent to 1 percent of outstanding principal. Remarketing fees for refunding variable-rate put debt are separate. The initial underwriting or remarketing fee can range from 0.375 percent to 1 percent of principal. Renewal remarketing fees range from 0.125 percent to 0.25 percent of principal.[33]

Trustee

The trustee, typically a trust company or a bank and trust company, plays an important role in financing revenue bonds, publicly sold capital leases, and special obligation debt.[34] The trustee represents the interests of the investors who buy and then hold the debt from the time the debt is sold, while the debt proceeds are being spent, and until the debt is completely repaid. The trustee monitors the issuer's compliance with the indentures in the debt contract. If the issuer fails to comply with one or more indentures, the trustee is authorized to take legal action on behalf of the investors. For example, if the issuer does not set utility rates high enough to meet coverage requirements under the indentures for revenue bonds issued to finance the utility system, the trustee can take other legal steps to compel the issuer to raise rates to meet coverage. This rarely happens, but when it does, the trustee is in a strong legal position to force the issuer to meet its contractual obligations.

No trustee is needed for typical GO bonds. Because of the strong security underlying GO bonds, they do not include indentures that limit the operating and financial practices of the issuer and necessitate a trustee. The more limited security for revenue bonds, capital leases, and SO bonds causes investors to demand the inclusion of indentures in the debt contract, and a trustee is needed to monitor and enforce the indentures.

The specific duties of a trustee include:

- **Authenticate the debt**   By signing the bonds or debt to be issued, the trustee approves the amount of debt. This assures investors that no more debt is issued than is authorized or needed. Without the trustee's signature, the debt may not be issued. Trustee authentication simply approves debt issuance. It is not to be confused with bond counsel certification of the validity and tax-exempt nature of the debt.

- **Take possession of the debt proceeds and disburse them upon requisition of the issuer to meet construction or other project or acquisition payments**   Alternatively, the issuer may receive and hold the proceeds, but the trustee must approve their disbursement. Trustee approval of disbursements from debt proceeds ensures that they are expended only for the authorized purposes. Disbursal of proceeds is usually based on contractor or vendor invoices and certification of the consulting engineer overseeing construction or implementation. The trustee often approves the hiring of contractors and the consulting engineers working on the project.

- **Oversee the issuer's collection and receipt of pledged revenue, make payments of periodic debt service, and approve or make other spending or disbursements**   This enables the trustee to monitor the issuer's compliance with flow-of-funds requirements in the debt contract. (See Chapter 7 for a discussion of flow-of-funds covenants.) If the issuer's credit is marginal, the trustee may hold revenues collected from the issuer's customers or the pledged revenue sources and release funds to the issuer to cover operating and maintenance costs and other purposes.

- **Approve the issuance of any additional debt for the project or enterprise**   Most revenue bonds and many other special debt financings restrict the issuer's ability to incur additional debt. This protects the holders of the debt whose interests the trustee is protecting. Before approving the issuance of additional debt, the trustee must certify that the issuer has complied with any additional bonds tests included in the debt contract for the original debt (see Chapter 7).

- **Monitor and enforce other debt indentures**   For example, revenue bonds require the issuer to maintain rates at high-enough levels so that net revenues cover debt service by a specified margin (see the discussion of revenue bonds in Chapter 7). Revenue bonds, capital leases, and SO debt usually require the issuer to carry insurance on the debt-financed property and maintain debt service and other reserves. The trustee makes sure that the issuer complies with these and other requirements.

- **Receive and review periodic inspection reports or financial reports submitted by the issuer.**[35]

Registrar, transfer agent, and paying agent

The preponderance of local government debt sold publicly is now sold in **book entry** form rather than certificated form. Book entry means that the bonds and debt are entries on the records or books of the Depository Trust Company (DTC) or, in the case of some local debt, on the books of a bank and trust company serving as registrar. (The DTC is a New York corporation owned by securities firms, banks, and other financial companies and institutions. It was established specifically to serve as a national depository for publicly sold and traded securities in the United States.) With book entry securities, an investor does not receive the securities themselves. Instead, the investor gets a confirmation notice or receipt from the underwriter, financial institution, or broker that sold the debt to the investor. The receipt indicates that the investor owns a certain amount, at face value, of the debt, of a specific maturity and interest rate, and with a specific CUSIP (Committee on Uniform Security Identification Procedures) number.

The CUSIP number is a unique number that identifies a security for computerized book-entry registration and other purposes. CUSIP numbers are printed on any certificated security. For securities issued in book-entry form, the numbers appear on the global certificates held by the registrar, typically the DTC. An issuer's financial adviser or bond counsel usually arranges for the assignment of CUSIP numbers to new debt. The CUSIP Service Bureau, a division of Standard & Poor's/McGraw Hill, assigns the numbers.[36]

The DTC's book-entry registration system requires that a single, "global" certificate be printed for each maturity of a debt issue. For example, if bonds in the amount of $10 million are issued and will be repaid in ten equal annual principal installments of $1 million each, the issuer prints ten global certificates of $1 million each and turns them over to the DTC. The DTC holds these certificates and is responsible for maintaining ownership records. The DTC's own records show which of its constituent members—securities dealers, banks, and other financial institutions—own or have a claim to how much of each maturity and the overall debt issue. These records do not show or register all "beneficial" or individual owners unless they are DTC constituent members. The records of the securities firms, banks, and financial institutions selling the debt to investors register individual investors or owners of the debt.

Publicly sold state and local debt is typically issued in denominations of $5,000.[37] If a particular investor owns $25,000 of the third-year $1 million maturity of the above-mentioned $10 million bond issue, the DTC's records include these five bonds among those that it holds for the account of the broker or firm that sold the investor the bonds, and that broker's or firm's records show that that investor owns those particular bonds. If the investor sells the bonds, the bonds are transferred on the DTC's records from the account for the broker representing the seller or original investor to the account of the broker or firm representing the buyer or new investor. The new investor is registered as owner of the bonds on the records of the new investor's broker.

Computerized book entry and registration of debt reduce printing costs to the issuer, which has to print far fewer debt certificates. In the example cited, the issuer prints only ten global certificates of $1 million each. In the past, the issuer would have had to print two thousand separate certificates ($10,000,000/$5,000 per individual bond). Securities brokers do not have to physically transfer certificates when outstanding debt or bonds are traded. All in all, this depository and registration system is much less expensive and cumbersome for everyone involved: issuers, dealers and brokers, the depository, and investors.

Until the early 1980s, state and local government debt was issued mostly in bearer form instead of in registered form. Bearer form means that the debt was represented by certificates, and there was no registry of who owned the certificates. Whoever had physical possession of the certificates or was their bearer was presumed to be the owner. The debt certificates had coupons for each interest payment, and when an interest payment was due, the bearer of a bond clipped and presented the coupon at a bank to receive payment. That bank was reimbursed by the issuer's paying agent, also typically a bank. When the debt matured, the bearer presented it to a bank for repayment of the principal or face amount. Again, the bank was reimbursed by the issuer's paying agent. Investors kept their municipal debt certificates in safety deposit boxes or other safe places. Needless to say, the system was open to theft of certificates, investment of gains from criminal activities in municipal debt, and other abuses. To prevent such abuses, federal tax laws were changed by the Tax Equity and Fiscal Responsibility Act of 1982, which required all state and local securities with a maturity greater than one year to be issued in registered form.[38] Registered form means that central records have to be maintained showing who specifically owns the debt. If certificates are not issued to investors based on the records, the registration system is book entry.

The DTC now serves as paying agent as well as depository and central transfer agent for most state and local government debt issued and sold publicly. The issuer, the trustee representing investor interests, or another paying agent sends or wires all required interest and principal payments to the DTC. The DTC uses the money to credit the accounts of its constituent members—brokers, banks, and firms—representing the investors or "beneficiaries" who actually own the debt. These brokers, banks, and firms then credit the accounts of the investors, who are their customers, for the payment.

A local government may issue certificated debt rather than book entry debt or use a bank and trust company rather than the DTC as registrar and paying agent if major investors insist on it or if the debt has special features that make registration through the DTC difficult or impossible. For example, there may a relatively small number of investors, all of whom are local, and one may be a bank that is interested in serving as registrar and paying agent.

Finally, a few local governments have acted as their own registrars and paying agents for debt they have issued. This is the case for some jurisdictions issuing so-called mini-bonds—bonds with a denomination of $100 or so—to local investors.[39]

Printer

A printer is involved in any public sale of local debt and sometimes in private placements. Bond or debt certificates are printed. Relatively few certificates—one per maturity—are needed when debt is issued in book entry form through the DTC. On the few occasions when book entry issuance does not take place for public sales, many more certificates must be printed. The bond counsel often takes responsibility for selecting the printer because the counsel's opinion goes on the certificates. If the bond counsel does not do this, the issuer, working with its financial adviser, selects the printer. The printer is often selected competitively through a request for proposals. The printer chosen should be a firm with experience in printing securities generally and municipal debt in particular.

Public sales of local government or other debt of $1 million or more also typically require the preparation and distribution of a preliminary official statement (POS) and an official statement (OS), both of which are described in the next section.[40] The print vendor must be able to print accurate documents and provide quick turnaround when changes are made. Competitive selection of the printer for the POS and OS is recommended.

Documents used in selling local government debt

Two kinds of standard documents are used in public sales of local government debt:

- **Preliminary official statement and official statement**   Although they are referred to separately, the POS and OS are different versions or drafts of the same document. The POS and OS are needed for nearly all offerings (public sales) of municipal debt.[41]

- **Notice of sale and the bid form used in competitive sales of debt**   An abbreviated notice of sale is used for some negotiated sales.

Individual underwriters use their own forms to summarize key features of the debt for sale and to confirm sales. The purposes, content, audiences, and general steps involving the POS, OS, notice of sale, and bid forms are discussed below.

Preliminary official statement and official statement

Securities and Exchange Commission regulations impose significant disclosure requirements on underwriters, brokers, and dealers that sell municipal securities.[42] One requirement is the preparation, publication, and distribution of a **preliminary official statement (POS)** and a final **official statement (OS)** in public sales of state or local government debt. These documents present information about the debt for sale; the security for the debt; the issuer; and relevant legal, financial, and other information bearing on the issuer's ability to repay the debt. An OS is not necessary when the debt sold is $1 million or less or usually when the debt is placed privately.

The POS and OS are different versions of the same document. Prepared before the sale, the POS is used by the underwriters to market the debt to potential investors. It is also distributed to the bond rating agencies, the insurer if applicable, and other interested market participants and observers.

The OS includes the same information presented in the POS, plus data about the results of the sale (for example, the interest rates and prices at which different maturities were sold). The OS is distributed after the sale to the bond-rating agencies, the insurer if applicable, investors or customers of the underwriters who buy large amounts of municipal debt, and others. Underwriters are required to distribute the OS to any investor requesting one and to certain municipal security depositories.[43]

In competitive sales, the POS and OS are typically one and the same document or have the same content although the POS is accompanied by the notice of sale and bid form, and the OS is accompanied by a cover sheet presenting the sale results. In negotiated sales, the sale may result in changes in security or other provisions, and in these cases the OS not only presents sale results but also includes information that is not found in the POS.

SEC regulations prohibit the omission of any material fact from the POS and OS. A **material fact** is any information, good or bad, that could be significant in influencing investors to buy or not buy the debt.[44] The underwriters and the issuer must exercise due diligence in preparing the POS and OS, making sure that these documents tell a complete story about the debt and the issuer and that the information and facts presented are accurate so that investors can rely on them.[45] As a result, the POS and OS are lengthy—each running 100 printed, single-spaced pages or more—and present a wealth of information about the debt and the issuer.

A growing number of state and local government debt issuers are placing their official statements and preliminary official statements on their Web sites. Investors and regulatory agencies have been receptive to the use of governmental Web sites for this purpose, and the GFOA has developed a recommended practice encouraging this. Although the OS and the POS must continue to be available in printed form, within a few years electronic distribution of these documents could become the standard method for disclosing information for debt sales to investors.[46]

A comparison of the official statements for a GO bond sale (see page 319) and a revenue bond sale (page 320) shows that the GO bond OS focuses on the general economic, social, and financial position of the issuer, while the revenue bond OS includes not only issuer information but also considerable data about the specific revenues securing the bonds and the enterprise system that will produce those revenues. Like the revenue bond OS, the special obligation bond OS addresses in depth the particular security and sources of revenue pledged to pay the debt. The OS for a capital lease usually covers the same issuer information as that for a GO bond issue, and it also presents considerable information about the particular property offered as security for the capital lease obligation.

The official statements for state and local government that are used today are based on disclosure guidelines that were developed by the GFOA of the United States and Canada. These guidelines were published in full form in 1991 but had evolved over a period of many years in response to disclosure failures and shortcomings in relation to the debt payment moratorium for New York City in the mid-1970s and the default of $2.25 billion in debt of the State of Washington Public Power System in 1983. The GFOA's guidelines recommend information and format for official statements for state and local government GO, revenue, and certain other types of debt.[47]

Officials of the issuer attest to the material completeness and accuracy of the facts presented in the POS and OS. If those facts are in error, the issuer (its officials, advisers, and underwriters) can be held liable for losses that investors incur as a result of having incorrect or incomplete information.[48] Although state and local issuers are generally exempt from the disclosure requirements in federal securities laws and regulations, the underwriters, brokers, and dealers in municipal securities are subject to

Official statement for a GO bond sale

The following types of information appear in an official statement for a general obligation bond sale. This list is based on the official statement for the 2001 sale of 25 million in GO bonds by **Johnston County, North Carolina.**

1. Introduction: issuer, nature of bonds, and notice of sale and bid information if the local government does not issue a separate notice of sale and bid form
2. Bonds offered
    a. Amount, purposes, date, maturities, etc.
    b. Registration and book entry
    c. Authorization
    d. Security
    e. Early redemption
3. Issuer
    a. Location
    b. Demographics
    c. Economy: wealth, economic sectors, employment
    d. Government and services: government structure, education, transportation, human services, utilities, medical facilities, recreation, and so forth
4. Debt information
    a. Legal debt limits
    b. Outstanding GO debt
    c. GO debt ratios
    d. GO debt service and maturity schedules
    e. GO bonds authorized but unissued
    f. GO bonds for underlying or overlapping units of government
    g. Other long-term debt and obligations
5. Tax information
    a. Tax assessment, rate(s), and revenues by major source
    b. Tax collections
    c. Largest taxpayers
6. Budget commentary for recent year(s)
7. Pension plans
8. Contingent liabilities
9. Continuing disclosure
10. Bond counsel approval of legal proceedings
11. Bond counsel opinion on exemption from taxes
12. Certification of the material accuracy of the OS by key officials (such as the mayor, manager, and financial officer) of the local government
13. Attachments that may be relevant (for example, provisions from the state constitution or statutes authorizing or limiting the debt being offered; historical data about the issuer's taxes, revenues, spending, and financial condition; and insurance information if applicable).

Preliminary and final official statement for a revenue bond sale

The POS and OS for a revenue bond issue present the following categories of information and data. These categories are based on the OS used by **Henderson, North Carolina,** when it sold $15,630,000 in revenue bonds in 2001.

- Cover page or introduction summarizing the bonds: amount, purposes, security, maturities, interest rates, prices or yields, bond counsel's opinion, bond ratings, insurance if applicable, underwriters and other professionals involved in the financing, and other information
- Bonds: authorization, security, redemption, registration, and book entry
- Security and sources of payment: special obligation, pledge of net receipts, rate covenant, parity indebtedness, reserve funds, construction and operating funds, existing indebtedness, additional indebtedness, and bond insurance if applicable
- The project or purposes for which bond proceeds will be spent
- Sources and uses of bond proceeds
- Debt service requirements for the bond issue and existing debt supported from pledged revenues
- Enterprise system or project for which the bonds are being sold
- The issuer: general, local government structure, population, income and wealth, economy, employment retail sales, construction activity, major services, tax information, debt information, financial information, contingent liabilities
- Legal matters: litigation, bond counsel's opinion, tax treatment
- Continuing disclosures
- Bond rating
- Underwriters and financial adviser
- Financial feasibility report for the enterprise or project
- City financial statements
- Relevant legal documents
- Other information.

these laws and regulations. Moreover, state and local issuers are directly subject to the securities laws prohibiting fraudulent or misleading dealings in securities.[49]

Finally, SEC regulations require that while the debt is outstanding a state or local government that has sold debt make continuing disclosures about the debt and the financial and economic situation of the issuer. These disclosures are intended to keep investors, underwriters, rating agencies, insurers, and others with an interest in the issuer's debt informed of events that directly or indirectly affect the debt. The disclosures must be made annually, and they can be included in the issuer's annual financial report. Issuers must also disclose the occurrence of material events in a timely way. SEC regulations provide an exclusive list of such events; they are serious occurrences, such as a lowering of an issuer's bond rating or nonpayment of debt.[50] The disclosures should be sent to all interested parties and to one of the national repositories established for holding information that state and local governments continually disclose on their securities.[51]

Eleven events that need to be disclosed

The SEC has identified eleven specific events that state and local government issuers of debt promise to disclose—should any of the events occur—while the debt is outstanding. Although SEC regulations require disclosure only if such an event is material, a local issuer should assume that any such event is material. The issuer must disclose these events in a timely manner after they occur and in a way prescribed by SEC regulations. The requirement for disclosure of these events is over and above annual continuing disclosure requirements. The eleven events are:

1. Principal and interest payment delinquencies
2. Nonpayment-related defaults; these refer to failures of the issuer to perform duties, other than payment of debt, required under the debt contract
3. Unscheduled draws on debt service reserves reflecting financial difficulties
4. Unscheduled draws on credit enhancements reflecting financial difficulties
5. Substitution of credit or liquidity providers, or their failure to perform
6. Adverse tax opinions or events affecting the tax-exempt status of the debt
7. Modifications to rights of debt holders, which could result from actions of the local governing board or changes in state laws affecting local debt
8. Calls of bonds or debt before maturity
9. Defeasances, because this could be fraud committed by an official of the issuer
10. Release, substitution, or sale of property securing repayment of the debt
11. Bond rating changes.

For a comprehensive discussion of SEC disclosure requirements for sales of state and local debt, see Robert Dean Pope, *Making Good Disclosure* (Chicago: GFOA, 2001); chapter 10, "Living with Continuing Disclosure" discusses disclosure requirements that continue after the sale of debt.

Notice of sale

A **notice of sale** advertises debt that is for competitive sale. The notice is usually one or several pages in length and presents key facts about the debt and the issuer that would be of interest to underwriters that might bid to buy the debt. It includes a standard bid form that all underwriters must use if they want to bid on the debt. The issuer and its financial adviser prepare the notice and send it to prospective underwriters. If debt is sold in a negotiated process, the underwriter may develop an abbreviated notice of sale to advertise the debt and to send, along with the preliminary official statement, to prospective investors. Such an abbreviated notice of sale is often placed in a financial or trade news publication such as *The Bond Buyer*.

The notice of sale for debt that is competitively sold customarily includes the following information:

When and where underwriters should submit bids for the debt   The date, time, and place should be specified. Issuers often try to avoid Mondays (underwriters are still evaluating the financial implications of weekend news) and Fridays (there is not time for their sales forces to sell the bonds quickly). Weeks when there is a national holiday, dates when a large issuer like the U.S. Treasury is selling considerable debt, and dates when important economic statistics are released also are avoided if possible.

Issuers have traditionally submitted bids on sealed hard copy delivered by mail or overnight express service. A growing number of local issuers are now taking electronic bids using financial companies that provide this service.[52]

Description of debt   The notice specifies the amount, purposes, security pledged, maturity dates and schedules, early redemption options, and other key features of the debt. The date on which interest begins to accrue (usually the first or fifteenth day of the month) also usually is specified.

Form of bonds and payment of debt proceeds   Form of bonds refers to registration and book-entry issuance of the debt, already discussed. The date for payment of the debt proceeds is called the closing or settlement date. It is the date on which the issuer turns over the debt securities to the underwriter, and the underwriter pays the debt proceeds to the issuer. Payment of the proceeds typically occurs in **federal funds,** the deposits that commercial banks and other financial institutions maintain at U.S. Federal Reserve banks. Federal funds are used to meet reserve requirements for banks and financial institutions under federal law and for borrowing payments among banks.

Assignment of CUSIP numbers   This indicates that the CUSIP Service Bureau will assign CUSIP numbers to the debt.

Bond attorney's opinion   The law firm serving as bond counsel is identified, and the issuer makes a statement that the sale is contingent upon a legal opinion affirming that the debt is a valid authorized debt of the issuer and, if applicable, that interest paid on the debt is exempt from income taxes.

Official statement   The notice of sale discloses how underwriters and others can obtain the OS for the debt.

Commitment to provide continuing disclosure   The issuer commits to provide continuing disclosure of material information and data about the debt and the issuer as long as the debt is outstanding.

Insurance and other credit enhancements   It is important for the notice of sale to indicate whether the issuer has qualified for insurance and whether a bidding underwriter has the option to submit a bid for which the issuer's debt service payments are insured. If the issuer has qualified for insurance, the underwriter pays for the premium and takes this as well as the insured debt service payments into account when bidding interest rates and prices for the debt.

Good faith deposit   A notice of sale usually asks bidders for a good faith deposit, usually equal to 1 percent or 2 percent of the face value of the debt. The deposit is typically made in the form of a certified check or cashier's check that is held until the winning bidder is selected. A surety guarantee by a bank may substitute for the deposit. Deposits of unsuccessful bidders are returned to them a day or two after the bid date. The winning bidder's deposit is deducted from the debt proceeds turned over to the issuer or returned to the underwriter at closing or settlement.

Bid instructions   Bid instructions limit the prices and interest rates that underwriters can bid. The instructions can include some or all of the follow-

---

The bid form

The bid form for competitively sold debt typically requires a bidder to submit the following information:

- Name of senior managers of underwriters participating in the bid
- The interest rate(s) that the issuer will pay on each maturity of the debt
- The average interest rate and basis of calculation (NIC or TIC)
- The price at which the underwriter is offering the principal amount of each maturity of the debt to the public: at par, at a premium above par, or at a discount below par; this may be in a related document certifying issue price
- The amount in bond proceeds (at par, par plus a premium, or par less a discount) that the underwriter will turn over to the issuer at settlement
- The amount of the good faith deposit that accompanies the bid, unless this is waived
- Certification that the underwriter is making a good faith offering of the debt to the public and, if applicable, that the underwriter already has commitments from investors to buy a specific percentage of the debt issue overall or of each maturity.

---

ing: whether a discount bid is allowed or whether the bid has to be at least for par value; whether the same interest rate must be bid for all debt of a particular maturity; how many separate interest rates may be bid for different maturities; whether interest rates are fixed or variable; whether interest rates must be ascending over the term of the debt or can vary up or down from the preceding maturity; and other bid matters.

Requirement to use a specified bid form   A bid form accompanies the notice of sale and underwriters are required to use it. (See sidebar above.)

Basis for selection of the winning bidder   The basis of award can be net interest cost (NIC) or true interest cost (TIC), as explained in Chapter 10.

Financial adviser and other professionals assisting the issuer   These persons or their firms are listed. In the case of a revenue bond issue, for example, the consulting engineer is listed.

The investors

The investors who buy and hold state and local government debt purchase the debt from underwriters in public sales or take it directly from the issuers in private placements. Knowing who the likely investors are can help an issuer respond to underwriters' recommendations about the amount of debt to issue, its term, the retirement structure, and pricing. Different investors look for different types of debt, maturities, and debt features. An issuer that knows the preferences of potential investors can tailor the debt to their needs and thereby lower the interest costs.

Table 11–2 shows how much state and local government debt in 1981, 1990, and 2000 was held by different types of investors: individuals, mutual funds, insurance companies, banks and savings and loan institutions, nonfinancial corporations, and others. The category for individuals

Table 11–2
Holders of state and local government debt in 1981, 1990, and 2000

Holder	Amounts (in billions)			Percentages		
	1981	**1990**	**2000**	**1981**	**1990**	**2000**
Individuals	$160.9	$655.3	$629.6	36.3	55.3	40.2
Mutual funds	9.5	210.7	548.5	2.1	17.8	35.0
Insurance companies	91.1	149.2	220.6	20.5	12.6	14.1
Banks and savings and loans	157.6	120.4	117.2	35.5	10.2	7.4
Nonfinancial corporations	10.6	24.7	34.6	2.4	2.1	2.2
Other holders	14.0	24.2	17.3	3.2	2.0	1.1
Totals	$443.7	$1,184.5	$1,567.8	100.0	100.0	100.0

Sources: For 1990 and 2000, *The Bond Buyer,* April 6, 2001, 34. For 1981, data were faxed to the author on May 14, 2001, by *The Bond Buyer.* Data include not only public purpose debt of state and local governments but also state and local private purpose debt for households and nonfinancial corporate businesses.

includes both individual households and personal trusts. The trusts are managed by trust companies for the benefit of individuals. Mutual funds include both money market funds and other mutual funds. The insurance companies are mainly property and casualty and life insurers. Banks and savings and loans include commercial banks and various types of savings institutions. Nonfinancial corporations include manufacturing and other nonfinancial firms. The other holders are state and local governments, their retirement systems, investment brokers and dealers, and a few other types of investors.

The share of state and local government debt held by mutual funds increased dramatically, from only 2.1 percent in 1981 to 35 percent in 2000. The central role of mutual funds in the municipal debt market mirrors the key place they now occupy in many other financial markets in the country. Today money market mutual funds buy much of the short-term and variable rate debt that state and local governments issue. Other mutual funds buy just maturities at specific places on the yield curve—for example, only intermediate-term debt (five to twelve years or so in maturity) or only long-term debt (more than fifteen years in maturity). Other funds buy municipal debt all along the yield curve.

Individuals continue to be the dominant investors, accounting for 40.2 percent of state and local government debt in 2000, a decline from 55.3 percent in 1990 but up from 36.3 percent in 1981. Individuals concentrate their purchases in the nearer term maturities—years one through ten or so.

Insurance companies continue to be important investors in state and local debt, owning 14.1 percent of such holdings in 2000. Property insurers are the major investors here; for example, in 2000 they bought $199.5 billion of the $220.6 billion insurance company total.[53] Insurers buy many of the later serial maturities, those beyond ten years, and the term bonds found in the latter part of the maturity schedule of many issues of revenue bonds, certificates of participation, and SO debt. Insurers' cash flow needs are based on actuarial analyses that extend far into the future, and later serial and term maturities meet these needs. The insurers also invest large amounts at any one time, which accounts for their interest in term bonds.

Commercial banks and savings and loan institutions have lost importance as investors in the municipal debt market over the past two decades. Their holdings have declined in dollar amounts as well as percentage terms. Changes in federal tax laws have greatly reduced the incentives that banks once had for investing in the tax-exempt debt of state and local governments. Moreover, bank growth and mergers over the past twenty years have changed many banks from state and local financial institutions to national and international institutions and broadened their focus from making loans to local firms and investing in state and local securities to attracting national and international investments.

Of course, national statistics on the holders of state and local government debt do not necessarily tell a particular state or local issuer who will invest in its debt. Small and medium-size local governments often sell or place their debt with regional, state, or local investors rather than in the national marketplace. A local government issuer should find out from its underwriters the types of investors that are buying its debt and, specifically, the largest purchasers. This puts the issuer in a better position to work with its financial adviser and underwriters to design debt that meets market demand and sells at low interest rates.

Costs of selling local government debt

Significant up-front costs are typically involved in selling debt. Nearly all public sales of local government debt include fees for bond counsel services, underwriting, ratings, registration and paying agent services, printing, advertising, and other expenses. Many public sales also include payments to attorneys other than the issuer's bond counsel, fees for financial advisory services, and insurance or other credit enhancement premiums. Issuance of revenue bonds, certificates of participation, and many types of SO debt also requires reserves that are funded with debt proceeds or, for some issuers, surety bonds in place of the reserves.

This final section of the chapter illustrates debt issuance costs by examining local government debt issues in North Carolina from July 2000 through May 2001 (see Table 11–3). Examples from Henderson and Brunswick County, North Carolina, illustrate specific costs and the broad array of uses of debt proceeds that are part of most revenue bond, capital lease, and SO debt issues. In GO bond sales, up-front payments are usually limited to issuance costs.

Table 11–3 shows issuance costs per $1,000 of debt for eighteen local government debt issues in North Carolina. These per $1,000 figures were computed from debt issue cost data reported by local governments to the Local Government Commission of North Carolina. The eighteen issues were selected to show costs of selling different types and amounts of debt. Costs are listed for eight GO, three revenue, and seven certificate of participation (capital lease) debt issues. The issues range in amount from $3.4 million to $101.5 million and were issued by fifteen different local governments. Two GO bond issues for Mecklenburg County are shown because they are of different amounts, and one is variable rate debt. Three Charlotte debt sales are included: two revenue bond issues of different sizes and one certificate of participation issue.

All of the GO bond sales shown in Table 11–3, except Mecklenburg County's $50 million issue, were competitively sold. The Mecklenburg County issue consists of variable-rate debt that was sold in a negotiated process. All of the revenue bond and certificate of participation issues were sold in negotiated sales.

Of the eighteen bond or debt issues, fifteen raised money for new projects, two (the Raleigh and Cumberland County certificates of participation)

Table 11–3
Issuance costs per $1,000 of debt for selected GO bonds, revenue bonds, and certificate of participation debt issued by local governments in North Carolina, July 2000–May 2001

Issuer	Bonds issued ($ millions)	Costs per $1,000 of debt					
		Bond counsel and other attorney fees	Bond rating fees	Under-writing fees	Financial adviser fees	Other fees and expenses	Total issuance costs
GO bonds							
Wilmington	$3.4	$3.86	$2.50	$3.58	$0.00	$2.69	$12.63
Caswell Co.	4.5	3.44	2.67	9.73	1.77	1.77	19.37
Stanley Co.	16.0	0.78	1.29	8.57	0.00	0.28	10.92
Burlington	23.0	0.91	1.06	5.07	0.00	0.37	7.40
Johnston Co.	25.0	0.98	1.04	6.30	0.00	0.43	8.75
Mecklenburg Co.	50.0	1.40	0.96	1.42	0.00	0.04	3.82
Guilford Co.	90.0	0.72	0.68	4.74	0.00	0.15	6.29
Mecklenburg Co.	100.0	0.65	0.52	0.96	0.00	0.10	2.23
Average		$1.59	$1.34	$5.05	$0.22	$0.73	$8.93
Revenue bonds							
Henderson	$15.6	$6.12	$2.30	$8.95	$2.24	$2.82	$22.43
Charlotte	34.7	4.12	0.71	9.25	0.00	0.17	14.25
Charlotte	101.5	0.60	0.76	5.62	0.37	0.25	7.60
Average		$3.61	$1.25	$7.94	$0.87	$1.08	$14.75
Certificates of participation							
Raleigh	$10.5	$6.52	$3.45	$5.76	$0.00	$1.98	$17.72
Brunswick Co.	16.0	2.30	2.33	12.62	0.00	1.57	18.82
Henderson Co.	16.3	6.33	1.95	15.49	0.00	1.43	25.20
Wilkes Co.	24.6	2.81	1.80	11.61	0.00	0.65	16.88
Pitt Co.	28.1	1.64	1.12	15.39	0.00	0.92	19.07
Charlotte	38.3	6.13	0.61	6.64	0.98	0.63	14.99
Cumberland Co.	50.8	3.61	0.62	11.80	0.00	1.56	17.59
Average		$4.19	$1.70	$11.33	$0.14	$1.25	$18.61

Source: Underlying issuance cost data come from the North Carolina Local Government Commission, Department of State Treasurer. The columns labeled "Bond counsel and other attorney fees" and "Other fees and expenses" consolidate several specific categories. These issuance cost data do not include costs for feasibility, architectural, and engineering studies for the projects financed with the debt. Although such costs are reported to the Local Government Commission, they are excluded here because they are not a cost of debt issuance although they are a project expense.

were refunding issues, and one—the city of Henderson revenue bonds—involved both new project spending and refunding.

The costs shown in Table 11–3 are for bond counsel and other legal services; bond ratings; underwriting; financial advisory services; and other expenses that include fees of the North Carolina Local Government Commission, which approves and sells local debt, and printing, registration, trustee, and certain other charges. The fees and charges are usually paid or deducted from the issuer's debt proceeds. The underwriting fees for the competitive GO bond sales are not specific underwriting charges but are the difference between the sum of the re-offer prices realized by the underwriters from the sale of the bonds and the proceeds from the sale turned over to the issuer. The underwriting fees shown for the revenue bonds and capital leases are the specific fees that the underwriters charged and that were paid from the issuer's proceeds. Where bond insurance is used, the premium is included with the underwriting fees. In competitive sales, the underwriter pays the premiums. In negotiated sales, the underwriter arranges the insurance and charges the premium to the issuer, who pays either the underwriter or the insurer directly.

The costs of feasibility, architectural, and engineering studies done in relation to the debt issues shown in Table 11–3 are not shown in the table. In North Carolina, such costs are reported to the North Carolina Local Government Commission and are grouped under a category for architectural and engineering fees. While such fees are a project expense, they are not a cost of issuance. Financial consulting services are included in the category of financial advisory fees.

The debt issuance costs per $1,000 of debt in Table 11–3 are not strictly representative; they are only a portion of the total debt issued by local governments in North Carolina during an eleven-month period. Nevertheless, the data suggest what local governments might expect to pay in issuance costs when they sell different types and amounts of debt.

Issuance costs for different types of debt

Issuance costs per $1,000 of debt are much less for the GO bonds ($8.93 on average per $1,000 of debt) than for either the revenue bonds ($14.75 on average per $1,000) or the certificates of participation ($18.61 on average per $1,000). This finding confirms the lower issuance costs for GO bonds compared with other types of local government debt.

An important reason for the difference is the higher legal fees for the revenue bonds and certificates of participation. The indenture provisions and the need for an underwriters' counsel create more legal work and costs for these types of debt compared with GO bonds. Underwriting fees per $1,000 of debt for the GO bonds are also considerably lower than for the revenue bonds and certificates of participation. Bond rating costs per $1,000 are about the same for the GO and revenue bonds, while they are somewhat higher for the certificates of participation.

The effect of debt size on issuance costs

Economies of scale are apparent in the issuance costs per $1,000 for the GO bonds. Issuance costs per $1,000 for the two smallest GO issues—Wilmington ($3.4 million) and Caswell County ($4.5 million)—were considerably higher than for the other GO bond issues. The Wilmington issue consisted of nonvoted debt for sidewalk and small building improvements. Caswell County is a rural jurisdiction with only 23,501 people. The high issuance costs for these jurisdictions can be attributed to fixed charges for attorney's fees, rating fees, underwriting fees, and other fees and expenses that were spread over a relatively small amount of debt. Caswell County also used an outside financial adviser (see page 329).

The low issuance costs ($3.82 and $2.23 per $1,000) for Mecklenburg County's GO bond issues are partly due to the large size of these issues ($50 million and $100 million). They probably also reflect the excellent credit rating of the county (triple-A) and the ability of underwriters to sell the county's debt quickly.

Economies of scale are also indicated for the revenue bond and in a more limited way for certificate of participation issues shown in Table 11–3. Total issuance cost per $1,000 for the Henderson revenue bonds ($22.43) is much higher than for the Charlotte revenue bond issues. Charlotte's $101.5 million revenue bond issue has a much lower issuance cost ($7.59 per $1,000) than its $34.7 million issue ($14.25 per $1,000). The three smaller certificate of participation debt issues (Raleigh, Brunswick County, and Henderson County) have higher total issuance costs ($17.72, $18.82, and $25.20 per $1,000) than the larger Charlotte certificates of participation issues ($14.99 per $1,000). However, the issuance costs for the Wilkes County issue ($16.88 per $1,000) and higher costs for the larger Cumberland County certificates ($17.59 per $1,000) suggest that factors other than issue size and economies of scale—factors such as the legal complexity of the financing and security for the debt—are important determinants of issuance costs per $1,000 for certificates of participation.

Bond counsel and other attorney fees

Attorney fees accounted for less than one-fifth, on average, of total issuance costs for the GO bonds and over one-fourth of costs for the revenue bonds and certificates of participation. An issuer's bond counsel fee is the universal cost in this category: all of the issuers had bond counsels who rendered opinions on the authenticity and tax status of the debt.

The revenue bond and certificate of participation issues also included fees paid by the issuer for the underwriters' counsel. This counsel reviews the debt to make sure it meets SEC regulations and to protect the underwriters' interests. The underwriters' counsel fee is grouped with bond counsel and other legal fees to show total legal costs for an issue, even though the underwriter selects this counsel.

Many of the debt issues, including the GO bonds and the other types of debt, included fees paid to the issuer's own attorney to certify that required steps were taken in authorizing the debt and to prepare legal documents under the direction of the bond counsel and underwriters' counsel for the sale. If the local issuer's attorney is on retainer or is a staff attorney, the issuer incurs no special charges for this attorney's work. Of course, if the bond counsel handles everything, all charges are included in the bond counsel's fee.

Bond rating fees

Bond rating fees contributed about 15 percent on average of total issuance costs for the GO bonds and are somewhat less than 10 percent on average of such costs for the revenue bonds and certificates of participation. Standard & Poor's fees ranged from $2,500 to $65,000 for most issues in 2000. Ratings for refunding bonds were generally near the bottom of the range. The minimum charge for a national bond rating for new debt in 2002 was around $5,000, which is for a GO bond issue of no more than several million dollars. National ratings for bonds of $10 million to $100 million cost from $10,000 to $25,000, depending on the complexity of the issue, how recently in the past the issuer had been rated, and other factors.[54]

The number of ratings secured for a debt issue determines rating costs. At least two national ratings are secured for most debt issues of $10 million or more. Many investors require at least two ratings. The Henderson, North Carolina, revenue bonds, used for illustrative purposes in previous chapters, had three ratings, each costing $12,000 (Table 11–4 on page 331). The Brunswick County certificates of participation, also referred to in prior chapters, had three ratings. They cost $9,000, $13,250, and $15,000, for a total cost of $37,250 (Table 11–5 on page 332).

Underwriting fees

Underwriting fees accounted for about 50 to 60 percent, on average, of total issuance costs for all three types of debt: the GO bonds, revenue bonds, and certificates of participation. Underwriting fees (Table 11–3) were significantly less on average for the GO bonds ($5.05 per $1,000) than for the revenue bonds ($7.94 per $1,000) and certificates of participation ($11.33 per $1,000) for these North Carolina debt sales. The superior security pledged for GO bonds compared with revenue bonds and certificates of participation probably contributed to the lower underwriting fees for the GO bonds. The competitive sales process for GO bonds also may contribute to the lower underwriting fees for them, confirming what other studies have suggested: underwriting fees for competitively sold debt are lower than for debt sold in negotiated processes.[55]

The creditworthiness of the issuer can affect underwriting costs. Underwriters are able to resell highly rated debt more quickly; therefore they charge less for selling it. As previously mentioned, the low underwriting fees for Mecklenburg County's GO debt are due in part to the county's triple-A ratings. The county is the only triple-A issuer of GO bonds in Table 11–3.

The highest underwriting fees per $1,000 of debt for GO bonds are for the Caswell County, Stanley County, Johnston County, and Burlington issues of GO bonds. Caswell is the smallest and most infrequent GO issuer listed in the table. Stanley County is also relatively small in size and an infrequent debt issuer. Both the Caswell County and Stanley County GO bonds are insured, and the underwriters included the insurance premiums in the underwriting fees. The insurance premium for the Stanley County bonds was $44,300 or $2.77 per $1,000, leaving a net underwriting fee of $92,871 or $5.80 per $1,000. The Burlington and Johnston County GO bonds are also insured. The insurance premium for Burlington was $59,000 or $2.57 per $1,000, leaving a net underwriting fee of $57,610 or $2.50 per $1,000. The premium for the Johnston County bonds was $63,500 or $2.54 per $1,000, leaving a net underwriting fee of $94,000 or $3.76 per $1,000.

The Henderson revenue bonds and most of the certificate of participation debt issues were also insured. The insurance premiums for these types of debt are provided in Table 11–4 on page 331 for the Henderson revenue bonds and Table 11–5 on page 332 for the Brunswick County certificates of participation.

Finally, underwriting fees, especially for negotiated issues, depend partly on how well debt planning and pricing respond to market conditions. If debt is structured and priced effectively to meet investor interests, it will sell quickly and underwriting fees should be less. If pricing is somewhat out of line with investor expectations, more time will be needed for the underwriters to sell the debt, probably increasing underwriting costs and fees. Differences in planning and pricing debt relative to investor needs probably underlie some of the variations in underwriting fees for the revenue bond, certificate of participation, and GO bond issues shown in Table 11–3.

Financial advisory fees

Only four issues in Table 11–3 involved financial advisers: Caswell County's GO bonds, Henderson's revenue bonds, and two Charlotte debt issues. The

Caswell County bonds were for school construction. The county's officials had very limited experience with debt issuance and contracted with a financial advisory firm to help secure bond ratings. Even though the North Carolina Local Government Commission provides this and other financial advisory services for local GO bond sales in the state, Caswell County officials felt they needed additional outside assistance. The city of Henderson employed a financial adviser to help officials there sift among alternative financing options and plan and structure the $15.6 million revenue bond issue, the first revenue bonds Henderson had ever issued. Charlotte's $101.5 million revenue bond issue was for the city's water-sewer system, and the $38.3 million issue of certificates of participation was for land and facilities related to the city's convention center complex. Charlotte uses an independent financial adviser to work with officials and the underwriters on most water-sewer revenue bond financings and also certificates of participation issued for real property. The city also employs another consultant who does financial modeling for the city's water-sewer system.

Other fees and expenses

Other fees are explained in the source line for Table 11–3. Fees for refunding studies are included in "Other fees and expenses" for the Raleigh and Cumberland County certificates of participation. Title insurance is included for the certificate of participation transactions and is important because the leased property serves as security for the financing. Title insurance covers the investors' risk should the governmental lessee not have clear title to the property being leased or to the land on which that property sits.

Other uses of debt proceeds

Issuance costs, such as those identified in Table 11–3, are typically paid from debt proceeds. Some, however, such as underwriting fees and insurance premiums for GO bonds and other debt that is competitively sold are deducted from the amount that investors pay for the debt before the underwriter credits debt proceeds to the issuer.

Other charges are made against the proceeds turned over or credited to the issuer. Revenue bond, capital lease, and SO debt issues usually involve, in addition to issuance costs, other up-front payments or uses for the issuer's debt proceeds. Like debt issuance costs, these payments or uses reduce the amount of money available for a debt issue's primary purpose.

Debt proceeds can be used to reimburse the issuer for the costs of feasibility studies, for debt service reserves and sometimes other reserves, and for capitalized interest, if charged to the proceeds, during project construction or implementation. Debt proceeds can also be used to pay bond insurance premiums (if not already included in the underwriting fee or with issuance costs) and to cover other miscellaneous expenses of the issuer.

In 2001, **Henderson, North Carolina,** issued $15,630,000 in revenue bonds. This amount entailed issuance costs of $350,543 ($22.43 per $1,000) for attorneys' fees, ratings fees, underwriting, insurance, advisers, and other issuance expenses. The specific amounts that Henderson paid for these services and for a feasibility study for the project are shown in Table 11–4.

In addition, Henderson had to fund a debt service reserve of $1,307,197 from the revenue bond proceeds.[56] Such reserves are usually set equal to maximum or average annual debt service (see Chapter 7). For the Henderson bonds, capitalized interest estimated at $441,202 during project construction was also charged to revenue bond proceeds.[57] The sum of the debt service

Table 11–4
Issuance and other up-front costs for $15,630,000 in revenue bonds, Henderson, North Carolina

Category of cost	Specific item or charge	Cost for category	Cost per $1,000
Attorneys' fees		$95,600	$6.12
Bond counsel	60,000		
City attorney	10,000		
Underwriter's counsel	25,600		
Bond rating agency fees		$36,000	$2.30
Fitch	12,000		
Moody's	12,000		
S & P	12,000		
Underwriting fee*		$90,654	$5.80
Bond insurance premium*		$49,289	$3.15
Financial adviser fee		$35,000	$2.24
Other issuance costs		$44,000	$2.82
Local government commission fee	6,500		
Printing and mailing	8,000		
Trustee's fee	3,500		
Other fees and expenses	26,000		
Feasibility study		$65,000	$4.16
Total costs		$415,543	$26.59**

Sources: Staff of the Local Government Commission of North Carolina and the city of Henderson finance officer. The commission requires each local debt issuer to fill out and submit a form that captures issuance costs for bonds or notes that the commission sells. All of the above costs except the $26,000 in "Other fees and expenses" were reported to the commission. Figures on Table 11–3 include all of the above costs except the feasibility study. The statement for sources and uses of funds shown in the official statement for the revenue bonds lists issuance costs of $389,943. See Salomon Smith Barney, "$15,630,000 City of Henderson, North Carolina, Combined Enterprise System Revenue Bonds, Series 2001," 14. The official statement did not include the underwriters' counsel fee of $25,600.
*These two items are combined in "Underwriting fees" in Table 11–3.
**Without the feasibility study, the cost per $1,000 would be $22.43, the same as the total issuance costs per $1,000 in Table 11–3.

reserve and capitalized interest for Henderson's revenue bonds was $1,748,399. The city had to issue revenue bonds to cover not only construction and refunding, the primary purposes of the bonds, but also the issuance costs listed in Table 11–4, the debt service reserve, and the capitalized interest.

Issuance costs for the attorneys' fees, ratings, underwriting, insurance, and other fees and expenses related to the $16 million **Brunswick County, North Carolina,** certificates of participation came to $301,156 ($18.82 per $1,000). Table 11–5 itemizes specific amounts paid for these bond issuance costs.

Another deduction from the principal amount of Brunswick County's certificates of participation is $66,178 for the net discount that the underwriters gave to investors in selling the certificates. While the discount is a deduction from the debt's face or par value instead of from proceeds, the "Estimated Sources and Uses of Funds" statement in the official statement calculated the underwriters' discount and deducted it from the funds available for project construction.[58] The certificates of participation did not involve any feasibility study or special consultants' reports. The issuance costs and net discount deduction for the certificates of participation total $367,334, detailed as shown in Table 11–5.

Table 11–5
Issuance and other
up-front costs for
$16 million in certificates
of participation, Brunswick
County, North Carolina

Category of cost	Specific item or charge	Cost for category	Cost per $1,000
Attorneys' fees		$36,827	$2.30
Bond counsel	21,827		
Underwriter's counsel	15,000		
Bond rating fees		$37,250	$2.33
Fitch	15,000		
Moody's	13,250		
S & P	9,000		
Underwriting fee*		$109,080	$6.81
Bond insurance premium*		$92,955	$5.81
Other expenses		$25,044	$1.57
Local government commission fee	2,500		
Printing and advertising	6,907		
Title insurance	10,550		
Other fees	5,087		
Underwriters' discount		$66,178	$4.14
Total costs		$367,334	$22.96**

Source: Staff of the North Carolina Local Government Commission and the Brunswick County finance officer. The total costs of $367,334 is $14,949 more than the issuance costs of $352,385 shown in the sources and uses of funds in the official statement, page 10. The above costs are the final figures. The sources and uses of fund statement contained estimates.
*These two items are combined in "Underwriting fees" in Table 11–3.
**Without the underwriters discount, the cost per $1,000 would be $18.82, the same as the total issuance costs per $1,000 in Table 11–3.

Unlike the revenue bonds issued by Henderson, the Brunswick County certificates of participation did not have a debt service reserve or capitalized interest to be funded from debt proceeds. The deed of trust given for the debt and the bond insurance provided sufficient security for the investors. Unlike these certificates of participation, many capital leases require debt service reserve funds.

Arbitrage

A state or local government issuer of tax-exempt debt, in investing proceeds from the sale of debt, must take care to avoid violating federal arbitrage regulations. Such regulations must be followed to preserve the tax-exempt status of the interest paid to investors on the debt. Arbitrage occurs when a governmental or other tax-exempt entity borrows money by selling its tax-exempt debt at a relatively low interest rate and invests the proceeds in taxable securities that carry higher yields or interest rates. Federal arbitrage restrictions, which became effective in 1969, and arbitrage rebate requirements, which are based on regulations developed pursuant to the Tax Reform Act of 1986, generally prohibit arbitrage profits on tax-exempt debt—profit made by investing the proceeds of tax-exempt debt in higher-yielding taxable securities. Under certain conditions, however, the earning of such arbitrage profits does not violate federal law. Even though arbitrage profits may be earned on the proceeds of certain tax-exempt debt, federal arbitrage rebate requirements provide that such profits be rebated to the U.S. Treasury unless the issuer of the debt qualifies for one of several exemptions. These exemptions, which are listed quickly here, are complicated. An issuer should consult an arbitrage expert when attempting to take advantage of one or more of these exemptions:

- **Tax-exempt exemption** The issuer invests the proceeds from the tax-exempt debt in other tax-exempt debt

- **Small-issuer exemption** The issuer has general taxing power and issues no more than $5 million of tax exempt debt in a calendar year

- **Six-month exemption** The issuer spends the gross proceeds from the tax-exempt debt, except for the lesser of $100,000 or 5 percent of the issue, within six months of issuance

- **Eighteen-month exemption** The issuer spends 15 percent of the gross proceeds from the tax-exempt debt within six months, 60 percent within twelve months, and all gross proceeds less retainage not in excess of 5 percent of the issue within eighteen months of issuance

- **Construction, or two-year, exemption** This divides the tax-exempt proceeds into two categories and requires spending of the portion of all the proceeds identified for construction within a maximum period of two years of issuance. Within that two-year period, certain percentages of the proceeds must be spent by certain dates after issuance.

Besides the exemptions listed here, there are additional, less important exemptions to arbitrage rebate requirements. Clearly, federal arbitrage regulations are complex. Moreover, they have been modified frequently over the years. Therefore, any issuer of tax-exempt debt must seek advice from bond counsel or other competent professionals who work with the regulations regularly.

Conclusion

Selling local government debt is a complicated and expensive process that is regulated by state laws and by federal tax and securities laws. This chapter has provided an overview of the major approaches that local governments use in selling debt, examined the roles of key market professionals, discussed the types of documents used in public sales of debt, identified the investors that buy and hold state and local debt, and examined issuance costs.

Notes

1 For another overview of the process used to sell or place local government debt, see James C. Joseph, "Selecting the Method of Sale," chapter 6 of *Debt Issuance and Management: A Guide for Small Governments* (Chicago: GFOA, 1994).

2 A bank may buy tax-exempt debt and deduct its interest costs for doing so if the issuer does not sell more than $10 million of debt in a calendar year. Such debt is called bank qualified debt. Ibid., 131.

3 "A Decade of Municipal Bond Finance," *The Bond Buyer,* May 8, 2001, 38; and "A

Decade of Municipal Bond Finance," *The Bond Buyer,* March 7, 2003, 42.

4 Ibid.

5 See, for example, North Carolina General Statute 159–123 (b).

6 Robert L. Ehlers, *Ehlers on Public Finance: Building Better Communities* (Rochester, Minn.: Lone Oak Press, 1998), 79.

7 Joseph, *Debt Issuance and Management,* 59–60.

8 See Joseph, *Debt Issuance and Management,* 60–61, for a good overview of private placement.

9 David M. Lawrence, *Financing Capital Projects in North Carolina* (Chapel Hill, N.C.: Institute of Government, University of North Carolina, 1994), 143–144.

10 See Joseph, *Debt Issuance and Management,* 131. Banks may deduct their financing costs for tax-exempt debt only if the debt is issued for a public purpose and the issuer does not sell or place more than $10 million of debt in the calendar year. This is an exception to the general Internal Revenue Service rule of Section 265(b)(1) for bank purchases.

11 Joseph, *Debt Issuance and Management,* 60–61.

12 Lawrence, *Financing Capital Projects in North Carolina,* 33–37; and Ehlers, *Ehlers on Public Finance,* 143–145.

13 Lawrence, *Financing Capital Projects in North Carolina,* 34.

14 Joseph, *Debt Issuance and Management,* 42.

15 Ibid.

16 Ibid., 43.

17 Lawrence, *Financing Capital Projects in North Carolina,* 37.

18 Ehlers, *Ehlers on Public Finance,* 93.

19 For an excellent overview and analysis of the role of the financial adviser, see Ehlers, *Ehlers on Public Finance,* 75–89. Also see Joseph, *Debt Issuance and Management,* 38–41.

20 Joseph, *Debt Issuance and Management,* 39.

21 Ehlers, *Ehlers on Public Finance,* 81–82.

22 Joseph, *Debt Issuance and Management,* 41.

23 Ehlers, *Ehlers on Public Finance,* 75–76.

24 See, for example, *The Bond Buyer,* March 7, 2003, 10. The lead underwriters or managers listed for negotiated sales tentatively scheduled for Friday, March 7, and for the week of March 10 are Bank of America; J. P. Morgan; William B. Hough; A. G. Edwards; Merrill Lynch; RBC Dain Rauscher; Morgan Keegan; George K. Baum; Lehman Brothers; Salomon, Smith, Barney; Morgan Stanley; UBS PaineWebber; Wachovia Bank; Newman and Associates; Seasongood & Mayer; Seattle Northwest; Legg Mason; Dougherty; SAMCO Capital Markets; Goldman Sachs; Bear Stearns; US Bancorp Jaffray; Fifth Third Securities; and Estrada Hinojosa. This list includes many of the most widely known names among U.S. financial institutions. *Bond Buyer's* Web site is www.tm3.com. Subscription to the Web site can be made by calling 1-800-367-8215.

25 *Municipal Finance Criteria, 2000* (New York: S&P, 2000), 6.

26 Jonathan B. Justice and Stewart Simon, "Municipal Bond Insurance: Trends and Prospects," *Public Budgeting and Finance* (Winter 2002), 115.

27 Ibid., 116.

28 Ibid., 124. These companies are listed again and again as insurers for competitive and negotiated sales of bonds and notes in the *Bond Buyer;* see, for example, March 7, 2003, 7–11.

29 Ehlers, *Ehlers on Public Finance,* 194. Chapter 20 of this book provides an excellent overview of bond insurance. Also see Joseph, *Debt Issuance and Management,* 98.

30 Joseph, *Debt Issuance and Management,* 100.

31 Ehlers, "Variable Rate Demand Notes," chapter 31 of *Ehlers on Public Finance.*

32 Ibid., 306.

33 Ibid.

34 For other overviews of the role of the trustee in debt financing, see Joseph, *Debt Issuance and Management,* 47–48; and Lawrence, *Financing Capital Projects in North Carolina,* 48–50. Lawrence lists and briefly examines the trustee's duties.

35 Ibid.

36 Joseph, *Debt Issuance and Management,* 79; and Ehlers, *Ehlers on Public Finance,* 360.

37 The denomination size for much privately placed debt is $100,000. See Lawrence, *Financing Capital Projects in North Carolina,* 130.

38 Joseph, *Debt Issuance and Management,* 46.

39 Ibid.

40 Lawrence, *Financing Capital Projects in North Carolina,* 144.

41 Although offerings or public sales of less than $1 million do not need a POS or an OS under SEC rules, nearly all public sales of state and local debt are for $1 million or more. See M. David Gelfand, ed., "Application of Securities Laws and Disclosure Standards," chapter 8 of vol. 2 of *State & Local Government Debt Financing* (Eagan, Minn.: West Group, 1986 and 1997) for in-depth treatment of SEC and related disclosure requirements and guidelines for municipal debt.

42 SEC Rule 15c2-12, effective January 1, 1990. For full discussions of this SEC rule, see Ibid., especially 44–151, and Joseph, *Debt Issuance and Management,* 82.

43 Municipal Securities Information Library and the regional depository for municipal security information. See Joseph, *Debt Issuance and Management*, 88.

44 Gelfand, *State & Local Government Debt Financing*, vol. 2, 190–192 and 199–200.

45 Ibid., 238–241.

46 Frank Hoadley, capital finance director, Wisconsin Department of Administration, "Using Your Web Site for Market Disclosure" (presentation at annual conference of GFOA, New York, May 19, 2003).

47 GFOA, *Disclosure Guidelines for State and Local Government Securities* (Chicago: GFOA, 1991); also see Gelfand, *State and Local Government Debt Financing*, vol. 2, 327–336.

48 Under SEC Rule 15c2-12 and other SEC regulations, local officials can be held liable for fraud for publishing misleading information on debt sales. See Joseph, *Debt Issuance and Management*, 82.

49 Lawrence, *Financing Capital Projects in North Carolina*, 144.

50 Gelfand, *State & Local Government Debt Financing*, vol. 2, 178–184.

51 SEC Interpretive Release 33-7049; 34-33741, March 9, 1994. See Joseph, *Debt Issuance and Management*, 87–88.

52 For example, BIDCOM/PARITY of Thomson Financial Municipals Group. See Thomson Municipal Market Monitor or www.tm3.com/Parity/main.

53 "Holders of Municipal Debt: 1991–2000," *The Bond Buyer*, April 6, 2001, 34.

54 Standard & Poor's, *Public Finance Criteria 2000*, 12; and from staff to the Local Government Commission of North Carolina.

55 Ehlers, *Ehlers on Public Finance*, 153.

56 See Salomon Smith Barney, "$15,630,000 City of Henderson, North Carolina, Combined Enterprise System Revenue Bonds, Series 2001," 14. The statement on page 14 concerning estimated sources and uses of funds shows a $1,307,197 contribution to the Parity Indebtedness Reserve Fund. This contribution and other uses of funds are financed from the debt proceeds and some other sources of revenue available to the project.

57 Ibid. Capitalized interest is not always added to revenue or other bond issuance costs because it is included in periodic debt service and paid from recurring annual revenues rather than from debt proceeds.

58 Wachovia Securities, Inc., and J. C. Bradford & Co., "$16,000,000 Certificates of Participation, Series 2000, Evidencing Proportional Undivided Interests in Rights to Receive Certain Revenues Pursuant to an Installment Purchase Contract with the County of Brunswick, North Carolina." This is the official statement for this debt. The discussion of estimated sources and uses of funds appears on page 10 of the OS.

12 Multiyear financial forecasting

A multiyear financial forecast projects revenues and other financial resources available to a local government each year over the stated forecast period. It also projects expenditures or uses of those revenues and resources by year over the forecast period—operating spending for salaries and fringe benefits, contractual services, supplies and other operating needs; annual debt service and lease or rental payments; pay-as-go spending for capital projects and acquisitions; contributions to operating or capital reserves; and other spending or uses of revenues or resources depending on the purposes and type of forecast. A jurisdiction has a choice about the type of forecast to use:

- A multiyear financial forecast may be drawn up for a jurisdiction as a whole. In this type of forecast, a single aggregate forecast is presented for revenues and spending for all funds and for both the operating budget and the CIP or capital budget. Although only a single aggregate forecast is presented, it is likely to be prepared fund by fund or part by part.

- A jurisdiction can forecast only the operating budget. In this case, the impact of a CIP or capital projects on operating revenues and spending is included in the forecast, but this forecast does not include or show revenues and spending for capital projects. A separate forecast that shows capital project revenues and spending may be prepared and used to support both the operating budget forecast and the CIP. As with the single, aggregate forecast, an operating budget forecast is often compiled from separate forecasts of the component funds or parts—the operating funds of the jurisdiction.

- A jurisdiction can prepare and present a separate operating budget forecast for each major operating fund of the jurisdiction; this would include the impact of capital projects on each such fund.

- A jurisdiction can draw up a multiyear financial forecast for only the general fund. This method is used when the general fund includes most or nearly all significant operating revenues and spending for the jurisdiction, and other funds serve mainly to support the general fund. Capital project impacts on the general fund would be included in this forecast.

If a local government has a capital improvement program, the period covered by the multiyear financial forecast usually covers the same number of years as the CIP. To be effective, a forecast needs to be comprehensive, covering all revenues or resources and spending or uses for the jurisdiction or the forecast fund(s). The forecast often also shows the implications of revenues and spending on fund balances, tax levies or rates, key debt ratios, and other bottom-line variables.

Forecasting requires the informed judgment of local officials, observation and analysis of revenue and spending in past years, estimates of local economic growth or changes, and assumptions about the effect of those changes on specific revenues and spending. National, regional, and local economic statistics are sometimes tracked and trends analyzed to help officials project future revenues and spending.

Many of the better-managed local governments across the nation have multiyear financial forecasts. A 2002 telephone survey of the forty municipalities rated triple-A by Standard & Poor's in February 2001 found that 21, or 52 percent, forecast their budgets over a future of three years or more. Fifteen of these municipalities did not have multiyear forecasts, and four municipalities did not respond to the survey.[1]

A major challenge to forecasting in many local governments is getting local elected officials to commit to the multiyear forecasting process and make effective use of the results. In some local governments, interest in forecasting is confined to one or two finance or budget staff members. While including a forecast in the annual budget document may help the jurisdiction win recognition for a distinguished budget presentation,[2] if neither the manager nor the governing board uses it in any significant way in developing and approving the budget or the CIP, it has little value. To be effective, a multiyear forecast should be part of the decision-making process, influencing the decisions of top management and staff as they develop the recommended budget and CIP and board members as they deliberate over the issues and financial commitments included in the annual budget and CIP.

This chapter:

- Discusses the purposes of multiyear financial forecasting
- Examines decisions about the type, time period, scope, detail, format, and philosophy of multiyear forecasts as well as forecasting methods
- Examines issues in forecasting revenues
- Examines issues in forecasting expenditures
- Discusses financial and economic trend monitoring
- Details how to prepare the forecast
- Presents two local governments' multiyear financial forecast systems to illustrate the issues involved in developing and using such a forecast.

Purposes of multiyear financial forecasting

A multiyear financial forecast gives officials the opportunity to see the budget implications of current decisions for future years. A financial forecast is a kind of radar screen that can help local officials see opportunities or problems that are looming, and it gives them time to develop appropriate responses.[3]

Annual budget decisions and financial operations have implications that extend long beyond the current budget year. Like any business or organization, a local government is more likely to succeed to the extent its planning extends beyond the upcoming budget year and addresses the opportunities, challenges, and limits that are likely to occur in the foreseeable future. A multiyear financial forecast can be a very useful and even a necessary tool as officials integrate their objectives and seek solutions to future problems in current budgets.

A multiyear financial forecast supports both the operating and capital budgets. For the annual or operating budget, a forecast can indicate to officials whether future annual revenues will support the continuation of cur-

---

The purpose of financial forecasting

The **Hillsborough, North Carolina,** three-year financial plan for 2000–2002 states the purpose of multiyear financial forecasting clearly: "not to predict future revenues and expenditures down to the penny, but rather to anticipate and rationally plan for expected changes or problems."

Source: Town of Hillsborough, FY 2002 Annual Budget & FY 2002–04 Financial Plan, 23.

---

rent services and the start-up of new programs that the governing board is considering. For the capital plan and budget, a multiyear forecast can reveal whether future annual revenues and resources will support debt service, lease payment obligations, and pay-as-go capital financing on top of ongoing operating expenditures in future years. A multiyear financial forecast puts local officials in a better position to choose programs that can be sustained over time.

Major capital projects take years to plan and build, financing takes months and sometimes years to arrange, and debt service and lease payments extend many years into the future. Faced with a modest set of capital needs, some local officials have a good feel, based on their experience, for whether the local government's capital plan can be supported in the future. They are able to operate effectively without a formal multiyear financial forecast. However, when growth pressures mount and capital plans become ambitious, or when a local government faces economic challenges that threaten its financial prospects, a formal multiyear financial forecast can become a very useful if not necessary item for the budget tool kit.

Financial forecasting can help a local government meet certain requirements of the new financial reporting model of the Governmental Accounting Standards Board (GASB). With Statement 34, the new model requires local governments to depreciate fixed assets and infrastructure or to estimate the amount of money needed annually to properly maintain infrastructure.[4] A multiyear financial forecast can provide the framework for local officials to calculate, plan for, and present annual depreciation and/or maintenance requirements for capital assets and infrastructure in future years.

Decisions in multiyear financial forecasting

Local officials must decide whether to forecast finances for the entire jurisdiction—both operating and capital project revenues and spending—for the operating budget or whether to forecast only for one or more major funds. They must also decide on what time period to cover; what the scope, level of detail, and format should be; and what forecasting methods to use. This section discusses the issues local governments consider in making these decisions.

Type of forecast

Most local government financial forecasts seek to project the impact of operating budget and capital project decisions on future operating revenues and spending. Therefore the discussion here assumes that the forecast is for operating revenues and spending for the general fund only, for the general

Multiyear budgeting

Multiyear budgeting differs from multiyear forecasting. Multiyear financial forecasts generally extend for three years or more into the future, and they estimate—without specifically commiting funds—future annual revenues and spending over the forecast period.

Multiyear budgets, however, are typically biennial—extending two years into the future—and they generally involve commitments to raise revenues and incur spending at specified levels each year as well as estimate such revenues and spending over the two-year period.

Despite their differences, multiyear financial forecasts have some of the same advantages as multiyear budgets:

- Because of frequent elections and the need to respond to the immediate concerns of citizens, local officials may take a short-term perspective in weighing policies and decisions. A multiyear financial forecast can help elected officials and top staff to consider the long-term implications of the decisions they make today or this year.

- Departmental directors and staff in local government are often hard-pressed to keep up with day-to-day service responsibilities. Attending to immediate duties and work leaves little time for planning to improve services or meet future needs. The combination of a capital improvement program and a multiyear financial forecast creates an institutional framework and motivations for departmental and program managers to think about and plan for the future.

- Goal setting is an important first step for effective service delivery and for well-led and managed local governments. Goal setting is more effective and realistic to the extent that it is accompanied by multiyear financial forecasting that shows the financial implications and limits the scope of goals and objectives.

- When a federal or a state agency awards a grant to a local government, it is often for a multiyear period. Just as a multiyear financial forecast can help local officials in capital planning and finance, it can help them decide whether grant funding should be pursued for certain programs, plan for the spending of grant revenue, and decide whether and how to replace grant revenue when the grant period ends.

Source: The nature and reasons for multiyear budgeting are discussed in James L. Cavenaugh and Pamela S. Caskie, "Multiyear Budgeting," *IQ Service Report* 31, no. 6 (June 1999): 4–6. Another overview of multiyear budgeting is provided by Barry Blom and Salomon Guajardo, "Multi-Year Budgeting: A Primer for Finance Officers," *Government Finance Review* (February 2000): 39–43.

fund and separately for one or more other important operating funds, or for the entire operating budget.

A local government that finances all major programs from its general fund and has only a few other funds for relatively small programs can prepare one forecast. In this case, the smaller funds can be folded into the general fund and forecast together with revenues and spending in that fund. If revenues and spending for the secondary funds are small or immaterial, they could be ignored and the forecast prepared only for the general fund. Some local governments with several important operating funds, including the general fund, forecast just general fund revenues and spending because all or practically all significant budget and capital budget decisions that officials must make are related to general fund taxes, revenues, and spending. Well-established policies and/or principles are in place that shape revenue raising, spending, and capital budget decisions for the other operating funds. Although a multiyear forecast is needed to help officials make decisions for the general fund, officials feel that such a forecast for the other funds would contribute only marginally.

Many local governments have two or more major funds (for example, a general fund and a water-sewer enterprise fund; or a general fund, a road maintenance and repair fund, and a social services fund) each with major revenues and spending. Many local governments with major enterprise funds develop and present a separate forecast for each one as well as for the general fund. The revenue sources and dynamics driving revenues and spending for utilities and enterprises usually differ from the revenues and dynamics for the general fund. The unique revenue sources for each fund and the relative independence of these funds from the general fund should play an important role in determining whether the local government uses separate forecasts or a single, consolidated forecast. For example, if the road maintenance and social services funds draw heavily on the same revenue sources as the general fund (local property and sales taxes), one forecast is most probably better for all three funds. On the other hand, if the road maintenance and social services funds each have their own special revenues, separate forecasts for them could be preferable. No forecast may be needed for these other funds, however, if they have their own special revenues and the local government has little discretion in how revenues are spent because state regulations determine such spending and no multiyear issues are present.

A single, consolidated forecast for the entire operating budget creates one set of revenue and spending projections. Although important revenue sources and spending categories from different funds can be separately projected, they are combined together here as components of one overall operating budget presentation, and a single or combined financial or fund balance position is likely to be shown for the operating budget as well as for each major fund making up that budget.

Time period

A multiyear financial forecast often covers the same future planning period as a local government's CIP. A local government with a ten-year CIP should forecast revenues and spending ten years into the future. CIP plans drive capital financing decisions and create debt service and lease payment obligations in the budgets of future years. The financial forecast shows whether the CIP is affordable, that is, whether future annual budgets will generate enough revenue to cover both operating and related needs and payment obligations on capital projects in future years.

If the CIP forecasts capital projects and spending for five or six years, for example, the financial forecast should extend at least that far into the future. Often there is value in forecasting certain revenues or spending farther into the future. For instance, annual debt service on outstanding long-term debt and payment obligations on capital leases is known (or for variable rate debt, can be estimated) far into the future—ten, fifteen, and twenty or more years. A financial forecast should show known payments over their full repayment terms, even when the forecast for most revenues and spending goes out only five or six years. Similarly, the forecast for utility needs, revenues, and spending may usefully extend ten years or more. Planning over such long periods is both useful and possible for utilities because of the capital-intensive nature of utilities and the very long useful lives of utility systems' major capital assets.

Scope

To be useful, a multiyear financial forecast should be comprehensive. If the forecast is for the entire operating budget, it must project all operating revenues and other relevant financial resources available to the jurisdiction and all expenditures or uses of those revenues and resources over the forecast period. If the forecast is for only one fund, it must project all revenues and other relevant financial resources for that fund and all spending or uses of resources from that fund over the forecast period.

A multiyear financial forecast typically includes all annually recurring revenues. For a general fund, these would be

- Property taxes levied annually
- Local sales tax revenues
- Income or payroll taxes, if any
- Other local taxes
- Recurring state-shared or intergovernmental revenues
- Investment income
- User-fee revenue not budgeted in a utility or enterprise fund
- Recurring transfers from reserves, fund balance, or other funds
- Other recurring revenue.

For a utility or enterprise fund, operating or recurring revenues include consumption or use charges and other revenues that recur more or less regularly and support ongoing spending. A multiyear financial forecast also projects all annual or recurring spending for

- Salaries, wages, and fringe benefits
- Contractual services
- Supplies and other operating needs
- Annual or periodic debt service and lease or rental payments
- Spending to replace or acquire capital assets that recurs annually or fairly regularly.

Besides annually recurring revenues, spending, and transfers, a forecast can include special or one-time revenues, spending, and transfers that support operating needs or spending of the forecast entity. Examples are grants received to support programs or operations or one-time or nonrecurring payments related to special program needs that will occur during the forecast period. Nonrecurring or one-time revenue and related spending should be included in the forecast if their receipt during the forecast period is certain or probable and if they finance regular or ongoing programs of the local government. If the receipt of nonrecurring revenues is uncertain or only a possibility, the receipt and spending of the revenues can and probably should be excluded from the forecast.

Because most local government forecasts focus on operating revenues and spending during the forecast period, receipts and spending associated with capital projects that are budgeted in separate project or special revenue funds are excluded from the forecast. Of course, transfers between these projects or special funds and the general fund or fund for which the forecast is being done are included in the operating forecast. As already mentioned, a separate forecast of revenues or resources and spending for capital projects can be made, and it can be very useful. Such a forecast shows the cash flows associated with the implementation of the CIP. One of the local governments described later in this chapter has a forecast for its capital projects funds as well as a forecast of operating revenues and spending. Finally, a typical multiyear forecast shows the impact of revenue and spending flows on fund balances and can portray the implications on the property tax rate and utility system rates.

Level of detail

Although a financial forecast does not have to be very detailed, a certain amount of disaggregation is required. Revenues are broken down at least into major sources, and each major source is projected separately. Typical projections include at least the five to six major sources on which a local government or a major fund relies. For many local governments, the major sources—property tax, local sales tax, revenue from utilities, state-shared revenue, and fees and charges for services—often make up three-quarters or more of total revenues. A more detailed breakdown and forecast of revenues is often necessary or advisable. Regardless of revenue concentration, the financial forecasts of many local governments break revenues down into as many as twenty, thirty, or more specific sources and project each source separately. This level of detail can sometimes, but not always, produce a more accurate revenue forecast. It does add to the work involved.

The most common approach to forecasting spending is to break expenditures down by function or department (for example, public safety, streets, environmental services, public education, social services and health, recreation and culture, and general government). Within each function or department, separate projections can be made by major line-item category: salaries and fringe benefits, contractual services, supplies and operating expenses, departmental capital equipment, and other items; or by many more specific line items, for example, permanent salaries, part-time salaries, each major fringe benefit, and so forth. The projections for the line-item classes or specific line items in a department or function are then aggregated to produce a departmental or functional forecast.

Alternatively, spending for specific line-item or account categories across all departments or functions can be forecast. In other words, total spending by the jurisdiction or the fund is projected for permanent salaries and wages, part-time salaries and wages, other important salary and fringe-benefit lines such as overtime, specific lines for major contractual services, supply items, and different types of capital spending. As few as five broad line-item categories or as many as twenty to thirty or more specific line items or accounts may be separately forecast. This centralized approach to forecasting does not show spending by function or department. An advantage of this is that department and program managers cannot use the forecast as a floor from which to build their annual budget requests. A disadvantage is that the forecasting categories are less meaningful and useful to department staff and most elected officials than forecasts broken down by function or department. The finance staff, the city or county manager, and perhaps the governing board are the beneficiaries and users of the forecast.

Forecast format

Exhibit 12–1 shows a prototype format used by local governments for multi-year financial forecasting. The six-year forecast period includes the upcoming budget year and five planning years. Actual revenues and spending for the past year and estimates for the current year enable local officials to see how the forecast builds on the preceding years. Some local governments include actual data for more than just one year in the past. Although presenting data for several past years can indicate trends in revenues and spending, this adds many numbers to the format and may detract attention from projections for the forecast period. If officials wish to show more than three past years of data, a separate table may be preferable to combining the past years with the forecast years into a single table. Alternatively, data for the past years can be shown in a set of line graphs, also perhaps with projections for the forecast years, on separate pages.

Exhibit 12–1 presents ten separate revenue sources, usually a sufficient number for forecasts of medium- and small-size jurisdictions. Property taxes and the sales tax are listed first and second, reflecting their importance to many local governments. Two specific state-shared revenues, the franchise and gasoline taxes, are listed separately. Intergovernmental revenues that contribute more than 5 percent of general fund revenues should be listed separately, especially if they are earmarked for a specific program (for example, the use of gasoline tax money for street maintenance). Other state-shared and/or intergovernmental revenue can usually be consolidated into one overall category. Charges for services are increasingly important as a general fund revenue source. If charges for a particular service (for example, parks and recreation) make up more than 5 percent of general fund revenues or contribute more than half the support for that service, a local government can justify showing those charges separately in the forecast. If a specific transfer from reserves or another other fund (for example, from the electric fund) is significant—more than 5 percent of revenues—this transfer should be separately identified in the forecast. If each individual transfer from other funds and reserves is small, they can be merged in a general category for transfers from reserves/other funds. Other revenues and resources is a catchall category for miscellaneous revenues and sources.

The functional or departmental categories under annual expenditures in Exhibit 12–1 are typical of city or municipal government in many parts of the country. The first category, general government, consolidates spending (overhead services) for the governing board, manager's office, and central staff. Each of the functions—police, fire, streets, solid waste, parks and recreation, library and cultural—describes a direct service to citizens and should be separately identified in the forecast if spending for that function is significant. The category of nondepartmental spending could include nondepartmental capital equipment, insurance, contributions to outside agencies, and other items. If it is reasonable to show spending classified here in functional or departmental spending categories, this category can be dropped. If a specific transfer out of the general fund to reserves or another fund is significant—more than 5 percent of spending—this transfer should be shown separately. Otherwise transfers out of the general fund can be combined and shown as one category in the forecast. Other spending and uses of resources is a catchall for any spending that cannot be put into another category.

Exhibit 12–1 also presents a set of bottom lines for the forecasting format. "Revenues over (under) spending" is the difference between total revenues/resources and total expenditures/uses. "Fund balance start of year" comes

Exhibit 12–1 Prototype multiyear financial forecast, city general fund

	Past year actuals	Current year estimates	Budget Year 1	Year 2	Year 3	Year 4	Year 5	Year 6	Totals
Annual revenues/ resources									
Property taxes									
Local sales tax									
State-shared revenues									
Franchise tax									
Gasoline tax									
Other									
Charges for services									
Solid waste									
Parks and recreation									
Other									
Transfers from reserves/ other funds									
Other revenue and resources									
Total revenues/resources									
Annual expenditures/uses									
General government									
Police									
Fire									
Streets									
Solid waste									
Parks and recreation									
Library and cultural									
Debt service									
Nondepartmental									
Transfers to reserves, other funds									
Other spending/uses of resources									
Total expenditures/uses									
Revenues over (under) spending									
Fund balance start of year									
Fund balance end of year									
Ending balance as percentage of spending									
Possible tax rate impact									

Planning year estimates spans Year 2–Year 6.

forward from fund balance at the end of the preceding year. "Fund balance end of year" is the sum of fund balance at the start of the year plus the amount by which revenues exceed spending (or less the amount by which spending exceeds revenues). If fund balance available at the end of one year is or must be budgeted as a resource to help fund the next year's budget, then a category for "appropriated fund balance" should be included in the forecast format under annual revenues/resources. To keep the format straightforward, Figure 12–1 reflects the assumption that no available fund balance is appropriated as a revenue source into the subsequent year's budget.

"Ending balance as percentage of spending" shows the relative size of the fund balance from year to year. Elected officials and top management are likely to focus on this statistic as well as the final one, "possible tax rate impact." Tax rate impact equates a year's projected surplus or deficit to the number of cents per $100 or mills per $1,000 on the property tax levy. For the first two columns, "past year actuals" and "current year estimates," the actual tax rate would be shown. If raising or lowering the tax rate is not an option, for political or other reasons, to balance annual revenues with spending, the tax rate implications of any deficit or surplus are not likely to be a part of the forecast's bottom line.

A forecast may show revenues and spending to be balanced each year by appropriations to or from fund balance each year or presuming changes in specific revenue or spending categories. Such fund balance appropriations or changes to revenues and spending are made "above the line," and not to the categories that make up the bottom line. There can be disadvantages to this. It can hide structural imbalances between revenues and spending, and it assumes actions or decisions by policymakers that have not yet been made.

Forecasting philosophy

Local officials can strive for the most accurate or realistic forecast that is practical, they can be conservative and underestimate revenues and/or overestimate spending, or they can push up revenue estimates and trim spending estimates from expected amounts to accommodate more programs and spending in future years. The third scenario is not recommended. It sooner or later puts a local government into a financial hole, eviscerates its ability to carry through with the plans embodied in the CIP and the annual budget, and will eventually require local officials to start over again with more realistic assumptions.

The revenue and spending amounts put into a realistic forecast are those that local officials, based on analysis, expect the local government to receive or spend during the forecast period. The advantage of this approach is that it reveals the best judgment of experienced staff not swayed by political considerations. Their projections will usually be close enough to keep the jurisdiction out of financial trouble during the forecasting period. However, even informed judgments about the future can be significantly off the mark, leading a local government into financial trouble. Local governments with an adequate or ample fund balance can afford to rely on a realistic forecast. The realistic forecast enables officials to plan for and use all future resources that are expected to be available during the forecast period. Fund balances or reserves can be used to cover revenue shortfalls or spending that is higher than expected. However, if fund balances are not ample or adequate, a conservative philosophy in forecasting is the better alternative.

A conservative forecast underestimates revenues or overestimates spending. The underestimate or overestimate can be as much as 5 percent or so of

The bottom line

To be useful, a multiyear financial forecast has to have a bottom line—a few key statistics on which the governing board and top management can focus. Such statistics literally appear at the bottom of the revenue and spending forecast.

The bottom line may be no more than the overall surplus or deficit resulting from revenues and spending for a year. Many local forecasts also include the effect of the surplus or deficit on fund balance. If the forecast is done just for the general fund, this statistic is general fund balance. If it is for several major funds of the jurisdiction, it is the consolidated fund balance of the funds included in the forecast. Both beginning and ending fund balances for the year may be shown. Besides presenting the dollar amount of the ending fund balance, the bottom-line statistics can include ending fund balance as a percentage of spending or revenues for the year. This casts the fund balance resulting from financial operations for a year in relative terms, so that it can be compared in a meaningful way to the ending fund balances for other years, to the fund balance of other jurisdictions, or to some external standard for fund balance.

The tax rate impact of each year's surplus or deficit also may be given for forecasts of the general fund. If the forecast is for a local utility or enterprise fund, the bottom line may show how much the utility rates would have to be raised to cover a deficit, or how much they could be lowered because of a surplus. Alternatively, the bottom line may show a new overall tax or utility rate given an annual surplus or deficit.

Although showing the tax and/or utility rate effects of annual revenues and spending in a multiyear forecast makes the probable or possible impact of current planning understandable to the governing board and the community, it has a disadvantage. It hints or presumes that any annual surplus will be used to reduce taxes or rates, and that any annual deficit will be covered by increasing taxes or rates. The press and community may think, based on the forecast, that local officials intend to lower or raise taxes in the future, not realizing that other courses of action are available to local officials as they plan for the future and sift options. Nevertheless, a significant number of local financial forecasts show the tax rate and/or utility rate impacts of annual revenue and spending estimates in multiyear financial forecasts. If a local government will not or is not likely to close the gap between revenues and spending by adjusting the tax rate, showing the tax rate implications of the forecast can result in misunderstanding.

the amounts that officials expect to collect or spend. The relative size of the underestimate or overestimate often depends on the size of the jurisdiction, with many smaller units using more conservative assumptions and medium- and larger-size local governments less conservative assumptions. In some cases, a conservative forecast is made only for revenues or for one or two of a local entity's most important revenue sources, with best or realistic estimates made for spending and the other revenue sources.[5]

A conservative forecast provides a margin for error. If revenue collections are lower or spending higher than the amounts expected, actual revenues and spending may remain within the conservative forecast parameters, allowing local officials to still meet goals and plans. If more revenues are collected or spending is less than the forecast amounts—as usually happens with a conservative forecast—programs, projects, or spending can be added the next year or several years later. Although this delays programs and projects, a local government is in a position to go forward with them on a safe fiscal footing.

Forecasting methods

An effective methodology for multiyear financial forecasting depends as much on the general knowledge and experience of the local government officials doing the forecasting as on the particular method they use. Nonetheless, the method can make the difference between a forecast that is useful and one that is misleading and not helpful.

One of the classics in the literature on multiyear financial forecasting identifies four approaches or methods for forecasting: judgment-based forecasting, trend analysis, deterministic forecasting, and econometric modeling.[6]

Judgment-based forecasting   While the judgment of experienced officials is necessarily a part of each of the other approaches or methods, judgment-based forecasting can be said to be the methodology used for multiyear forecasting in many medium- and small-size local governments. Past years' data are reviewed and some trend analysis is done for major revenues and spending categories, but this is limited; there is also little reference in the forecast to underlying economic trends or events. Judgment works as long as the officials responsible for the forecast are well informed about revenue and spending trends and events and understand intuitively how changes in the local economy and environment are likely to affect future revenues and spending.

Trend analysis   A forecast that relies on local officials' judgments is often complemented by trend analysis. Historic data for past years—perhaps ten years or more—are collected on important revenue sources such as the property tax, the local sales tax, and state-shared revenues and on categories of spending such as departmental or functional categories or line items like permanent salaries and wages that cut across departments or functions. Spending for particular purposes or items that has been growing rapidly, such as for Medicaid or employee health insurance costs, may be singled out and tracked separately. With spreadsheet computer programs, the data are plotted on graphs; and trend lines, calculated using regression or related formulas, are drawn though the data points on each graph. Graphs show how a particular revenue source or spending category has grown or changed. The forecasters can then make assumptions or judgments about whether revenues and spending will continue along established trends or diverge from them.[7]

Deterministic forecasting   A third method used in multiyear financial forecasting is called "deterministic." It relates the growth or change in a particular revenue source or spending category to growth or change in another statistic related to economic, financial, or other performance. In other words, growth or change in a specific revenue or spending category is determined by growth or change in another variable. The specific revenue or spending is the dependent variable, and the other statistic is the independent variable. Historic data for both variables demonstrate the relationship between them.

Deterministic forecasting is more often used by state governments and large local governments for forecasting certain revenues than by medium- and small-size jurisdictions. For example, state personal income tax revenue might be related to the growth in personal income, and corporate income tax revenue might be related to U. S. corporate profits before taxes and industrial products indices.[8] At the local level, county sales tax revenue projections might be related to expected changes in the gross retail sales expected in the county over the forecast period; this is a forecast based on an analysis of the relationship between these variables in the past. Projections of real estate transfer tax revenue might be related to forecast real property sales, again based on a demonstrated relationship for these variables.

Econometric modeling Econometric modeling relates a government entity's revenues and spending to an array of demographic, economic, and social variables in a complex computer program. Future values of these variables are predicted; and the variables, through the mathematical relationships specified in the computer program, determine the forecasting entity's revenues and spending. Practically all state governments use econometric modeling to estimate revenues for their upcoming annual or biennial budgets. These models make use of national economic forecasts provided by national forecasting services. While some large local governments use econometric modeling for multiyear financial forecasting, only rarely do medium- or small-size units rely on this technique.

Issues in forecasting revenues

For sound multiyear financial forecasts, local government officials must understand the responsiveness of major revenue sources to economic growth or change, document the sources of revenue, and sometimes seek outside expertise.

Several questions in the sidebar on pages 350 and 351 refer to the responsiveness of revenues to economic growth or change. Multiyear financial forecasting for a local government depends on judgments or assumptions about how specific local revenues will grow or change with the economy in the future. Those assumptions are typically based on observations of historic data relating local revenues to economic performance. **Elasticity** is the concept that economists use to describe the responsiveness of revenues (or spending) to economic growth or change.[9]

Economists sometimes use coefficients to measure the elasticity of particular revenues.[10] An elasticity coefficient relates an increase in revenue to a specific measure of economic growth or change, such as gross domestic product, per capita income, or median household income. For example, if median household income increases by 3 percent one year, and local sales tax collections rise by 3.2 percent that year, the sales tax may be said to have an elasticity growth coefficient of 1.07 (3.2 percent / 3.0 percent) for the year. State and local sales tax revenue growth generally keeps pace with economic growth.[11] The sales tax has an elasticity growth coefficient at or around 1.0 in relation to general economic growth. If there is a recession with a decline in economic activity and personal income for several quarters, sales tax revenue is likely to decline more or less proportionately or at least level off from what such revenue was in prior years. Many local governments experienced declines in sales tax revenues in 2001 and 2002 as a result of the recession spanning those years.[12]

The local property tax is less responsive than the sales tax to overall economic growth or change.[13] The property tax generally grows at a slower pace than the economy. For example, when the economy is growing at an annual rate of 3 percent as measured by median household income, property tax revenue in most communities will grow at a lower rate, perhaps by 2 percent. The elasticity growth coefficient in this case is 0.67 (2 percent / 3 percent), less than the 1.07 in the preceding example. Of course, in very fast-growing communities where substantial private development is occurring, property tax revenue growth may match or exceed general economic expansion as measured by increases in median family income. And in communities facing eco-

Questions for revenue forecasting

What are our major revenues? Dependable revenue forecasting demands an in-depth understanding of a government's primary revenue sources. A handful of revenue sources accounts for upwards of three-quarters or more of total revenues for most local governments. Most time in revenue forecasting should be spent on analyzing the major sources. Having good projections for these sources is vital. Shortcomings or errors in forecasts of less important sources will not seriously harm overall forecast accuracy and usefulness, as long as forecasts of the major sources are on or close to target.

How variable are these revenues? A revenue forecaster needs to understand how much and how quickly each of the major sources reacts to growth, to a downturn, or to other changes in the local economy. In **Prince William County, Virginia,** for example, the sales tax closely tracks the economy, while the real property tax usually reacts much less to economic fluctuations.

What factors drive the behavior of each revenue source and to what extent? The forecaster must look behind the historic data on revenue collections to find out what underlying demographic or economic factors are causing revenues to grow or change. For example, to what extent is growth in local property tax revenue attributable to new residential construction, new commercial or industrial construction, increases in property values, growth in personal property subject to taxation, or changes in tax administration? If growth is due primarily to new residential construction, is this caused by population growth, or is the new construction being used by residents who already live in the community? If the latter, might property values level off or fall as excess housing stock is worked off in the community? These are the kinds of questions that a forecaster needs to ask about each of the major sources that make up local revenues. While graphs and statistical correlations of data can help officials spot key causative factors, analysis and judgment in interpreting the graphs are just as important to forecasting.

How does the economy affect local revenues? National, state, and regional economic performance affects growth or change in the local economy and in local government revenues. The preparation of a multiyear revenue forecast should refer to statistics on key aspects of economic performance such as employment, personal income, inflation, housing starts, vehicle sales, interest rates, and manufacturing activity. A local economy often diverges from the national economy—outperforms, underperforms, lags, or runs ahead of the national economy. A local revenue forecaster should maintain or obtain statistics on the regional economy as well as national economic statis-

nomic challenges, the property tax base and property tax revenue may actually shrink while the regional and national economies expand.

In the recent recession, the property tax's inelasticity (coefficient less than 1.0) was a significant advantage for many local governments. Although the recession caused household income, consumer spending, and sales tax revenue to fall, property tax values held up and property tax collections through the recession years matched property tax revenues in the year prior to the recession without increases in the property tax rate. In a few communities otherwise affected adversely by the recession, property tax revenues even grew somewhat because of increasing property values and some new construction.

Questions for revenue forecasting *(continued)*

tics. If statistics for the local region do not exist or are difficult to come by, the revenue forecaster needs to develop a good feel for the local economy—how it diverges from that of the nation and how it is likely to change over the forecast period.

What are the underlying assumptions for projecting revenues?   Assumptions underlie any revenue forecast. They are informed by economic performance, demographic change, and policy or political choices, and how these are likely to affect revenues during the forecast period. Documentation and explicit or transparent presentation of assumptions help local elected officials understand and accept the forecast.

What is the most appropriate forecasting method?   The forecasting method used should depend on the nature of the revenue source, availability of data and predictability or stability of revenues over time. Both qualitative and quantitative methods have a place in revenue forecasting.

How can we best communicate the forecast to stakeholders?   The presentation of the forecast is important in determining whether or to what extent elected officials use it in making decisions and how well the forecast is understood and accepted in the community. Local revenue forecasts draw the attention of elected officials, the press, and other interested parties such as rating agencies and state regulators. How the forecast is structured, the bottom line, the assumptions used, the timing of the forecast presentation, whether it is included in the annual budget or presented separately, and other questions concerning presentation are very important in determining the value of any financial forecast.

Why is it important to monitor revenue projections?   The events and experiences of the past several years make clear that economic conditions can change rapidly. The destruction of the World Trade Center in 2001 created a whole new risk category called "event risk." Multiyear revenue forecasts must be modified in light of events that were unanticipated when the forecasts were made. The multiyear financial forecast should be updated yearly when annual revenue and spending estimates are prepared for the annual budget. Review of forecasts every six months or even every quarter in light of actual revenue collection and spending is recommended.

Source: Based on Laura Morrison, "Improving Revenue Projections: 10 Questions—And Answers," *Government Finance Review* 18, no. 3 (June 2002): 16–19. The author is revenue forecasting manager of Prince William County, Virginia.

The personal income tax, if structured progressively to include personal exemptions and allow for deductions, is an elastic revenue source, more than the sales tax. If median family income increases at 3 percent per year, personal income tax revenue may rise by 4 percent or more annually. This puts the growth coefficient at 1.33 (4 percent / 3 percent), indicating considerable elasticity or responsiveness.

Because recessions occur intermittently and their severity, length, and causes vary, their impact on specific local revenues can be difficult to judge. As a rule, sales and personal income tax revenues are affected more than the property tax by economic contraction. During a short, mild recession, consumer spending is likely to hold up, and sales tax revenue may continue to grow, albeit more slowly. However, if the recession is more serious and lasts for longer than two quarters or so, consumer spending is likely to fall, causing sales tax revenue to decline from one year to the next in the recession. Personal income tax revenue is more likely to decrease from one year to the next when the economy contracts and unemployment increases. The drop in personal income tax revenue is likely to be greater than the drop in sales tax revenue. The property tax is more resistant to a recession. In many communities, property tax revenue continues to grow, providing stability for the local budget throughout a recession, even one lasting several years.

Local revenue sources besides sales, property, and personal income taxes are responsive to the local economy. For example, officials must carefully consider how water-sewer and other local utility demand and income are affected by economic growth or contraction. When a community is growing rapidly, the water-sewer system may be hard-pressed to meet demand. In a recession, major manufacturers and other large users of water-sewer services may curtail operations or close, causing a significant falloff in water-sewage usage and revenues. Because a large portion of water-sewer costs are fixed, or inelastic, water-sewer spending usually does not drop correspondingly when demand for services contracts. Some other local revenues, like real estate transfer fees and hotel and motel room occupancy taxes, tend to be very responsive to changes in the local economy.

Of course, the economy is not the only driver of local revenues. The decisions of local officials about tax rates and user fees, state legislation or local actions that expand or shrink the tax base, the effectiveness of assessment and collection, and success in pursuing grant or other intergovernmental revenue can have a great impact on local revenues.

Effective revenue forecasting depends on good documentation. Prince William County, Virginia, and Wake County, North Carolina, are examples of two local governments that prepare a revenue handbook or manual with a page or two devoted to each revenue source. The documentation includes a brief description of the nature of the tax or revenue, the tax or revenue base, the tax rate, who pays the tax, the legal basis, collections over the past several years—graphed if possible—the change or growth in the tax base over the same period, and sometimes other information or data.[14]

Finally, some local government officials have found it useful to ask economists from nearby universities or banks to advise them on local economic performance and its effects on revenues.[15] Other local governments have convened local business leaders and other community members to seek their advice on the local economy. Their advice, which is likely to reflect what is going on with their businesses, can be very useful as officials attempt to gauge how the local economy is changing in relation to national or statewide economic changes.[16]

Issues in forecasting expenditures

Multiyear forecasts of spending usually assume the continuation of current services. The overriding question is the cost of extending services at the current levels and quality through the forecast period.[17] This involves making assumptions about salary and wage adjustments that will be granted, increases in the local government's costs for employee benefits (such as health insurance or contributions to employee retirement systems), price increases for supply items and contractual service, and other cost increases or adjustments that are likely to occur in the forecast years. Typical forecasts for these spending categories or items reflect their changes in recent years.

Annual debt service payments on existing debt and lease obligations are included in the forecast. Additionally, payments on any new debt or leases that are already authorized and scheduled for issuance during the forecast period should be included, as should estimated lease payments or pay-as-go funding for replacement equipment and capital assets during the forecast period.

If a local government is making transfers into capital reserve funds, or transfers for operating or other purposes to other funds, it would ordinarily assume that the transfers will continue at recent levels, adjusted, of course, to account for anticipated events that will or are likely to change the transfer amounts. The forecast should include these transfers.

Spending increases for service expansion or improvements that are mandated by federal or state laws or regulations and are scheduled to take effect during the forecast period are typically included in the forecast. Similarly, commitments made by the local governing board that take effect during the forecast period are normally built into forecast spending amounts. For example, the completion of construction during the forecast period of a recreation center that had previously been approved by the board and that requires new staff to operate will increase annual spending that should be included in the forecast.

Long-term goals for particular services, even if they have been approved by the governing board, are not likely to be included unless specific costs for reaching those goals have been calculated and the board has approved spending the amounts needed to implement them. Similarly, department service plans that call for service expansion or the creation of new programs in coming years are not ordinarily incorporated in the expenditure forecast unless the board has clearly indicated that it will approve specific spending for the plans some time during the forecast period.

Spending for some programs (for example, welfare and law enforcement) may be inversely related to economic growth. If the economy contracts, raising unemployment and worsening social problems, then spending for these programs, even if it is discretionary, often increases. However, spending for such programs does not necessarily drop in periods of economic growth. Other factors may actually prompt increased spending for these and other programs in good economic times. While much local spending is not nearly as responsive to economic change as are local revenues (making the use of elasticity coefficients meaningless if not impossible), local officials can often relate certain kinds of major spending (for example, Medicaid where this is partly a local responsibility) to economic growth or change.

Local budget or finance staff typically prepare the multiyear financial forecast. Revenue forecasting is often a centralized process, involving limited consultation with department directors. On the other hand, expenditure forecasting can involve significant consultation with department directors and staff about spending in their areas over the forecast period. Department directors and staff are more likely to be committed to the forecasting process if they are involved. However, with their involvement, the forecasting process is likely to take more time, and there may be more pressure to increase spending estimates. Another related concern is the extent to which the spending forecasts become floors, ceilings, or targets for departments when they prepare the annual budget requests.

Financial and economic trend monitoring

Financial trend monitoring identifies key financial, economic, and demographic factors that affect a local government's financial health. It pulls together, tracks, and graphs historic data on these factors. The financial data pertain to local revenues, spending, fund balance or cash position, assets, and liabilities, and the data come from the local government's own financial reports, budgets, and records. The economic, demographic, and other data are usually obtained from outside sources. Most are now available on the Internet. Data are collected for the past five to ten years, and new data are added every year. Graphs summarizing the data and trend lines calculated from the data are presented to top management, the local governing board, and other users when they make decisions (for example, in the annual budget process) that bear on the financial condition of the local government.

The purposes of financial trend monitoring are to present a picture of the local government's financial strengths and weaknesses and help officials understand the factors that contribute to these strengths and weaknesses. Financial trend monitoring also gives local officials a historic basis for making decisions about the future, introduces a multiyear perspective into the annual budget process, helps with multiyear financial forecasting, and assists officials in anticipating and addressing problems as they emerge.[18]

Financial trend monitoring is part of many local governments' financial forecasting systems. Some medium- and small-size local governments focus mainly on their own revenues and spending; they might refer to some key economic and related data, but they do not track the external data themselves and do not include the data as a separate component of the forecasting system. In large local governments, the forecasting system is more likely to include economic data from outside sources. Indeed, the data typically serve other purposes such as strategic or comprehensive planning as well as financial forecasting. See the sidebar on the next page for a list of the data tracked by Forsyth County, North Carolina, as part of its multiyear financial forecast.

Preparing the forecast

Financial forecasting demands significant financial expertise or experience. Therefore, the local government finance officer or the budget director—who is very familiar with the local government's different revenue sources and spending patterns over time—is the logical person to perform this important task. If a junior staff member is assigned the task of preparing the forecast, that person needs to consult the finance officer or budget director about reasonable assumptions for the forecast period and the most appropriate methods to use.

If the forecast is to be presented to the governing board or used by the manager or budget director in preparing the local government's annual budget or CIP, the manager or the budget director have to be involved in the forecasting. The manager or budget director should approve the forecasting format, the bottom lines on which the governing board is likely to focus, the assumptions used, and the forecast revenue and expenditure figures themselves.

Department directors and program staff may be involved in forecasting expenditures, as noted earlier. However, some local forecasts focus on broad spending categories. They use aggregate growth factors for those categories and build in only departmental spending increases that the governing board has approved. In this case, departmental involvement is likely to be limited. In other local governments, the staff member doing the forecasts meets with department directors to get a sense of future spending requests by the departments or to ask for spending projections for departmental programs and major line items or accounts over the forecast period.

Outside parties with economic or local business expertise can be consulted during preparation of the multiyear financial forecast. For example,

---

Economic and financial data for local forecasting

Forsyth County, North Carolina, maintains the following financial and economic statistics to aid in financial forecasting:

- U.S. gross domestic product
- North Carolina nonfarm employment
- North Carolina unemployment rate
- North Carolina real personal income
- Forsyth County total employment
- Forsyth County rate of unemployment
- Forsyth County annual average employment
- Forsyth County employment by sector
- Forsyth County manufacturing employment
- Forsyth County retail/wholesale trade employment
- Forsyth County services employment
- Forsyth County finance/insurance/real estate employment
- Forsyth County per capita income
- Forsyth County per capita income compared with the four other largest North Carolina counties
- Forsyth County retail sales
- Forsyth County sales tax collections
- Forsyth County share of sales tax collection in the region consisting of Forsyth County and five nearby counties
- Forsyth County building permits.

---

university professors or local business leaders may be asked for their perspectives on the local economy and how the economy will affect city or county revenues. Officials from other local governments that serve the same citizens or geographic area may be consulted as well.

Presenting the forecast to the board and the public

A typical multiyear financial forecast becomes a public document, and its presentation to the local governing board and to the community is important. It is usually presented to the governing board. An initial or draft forecast is often presented at a board meeting or retreat, at the start of the annual budget preparation process. Presentation of a more formal or final version of the forecast usually occurs when the manager recommends the annual budget or CIP to the board. The forecast is usually included in the recommended annual budget or CIP. A few local governments include the forecast in a separate document. Regardless of when or how presented, a preliminary forecast usually has been prepared at the outset of budget preparations and has been used by the manager in developing the budget. The multiyear financial forecast is available to the manager and staff to guide budget development and then to the governing board as it considers important budget issues and the manager's recommendations on those issues.

ICMA's Financial Trend Monitoring System

A comprehensive model for financial trend monitoring by local governments is presented in ICMA's *Evaluating Financial Condition: A Handbook for Local Government*. Known as the Financial Trend Monitoring System, this model identifies six general financial factors relevant to a local government's financial condition: revenues, expenditures, operating position (fund balance and/or cash position), debt structure, unfunded liabilities, and condition of capital plant. The model suggests indicators or measures to evaluate strength or weakness for each factor. The specific indicators for revenues, for example, are revenues per capita; the percentage of total revenues that is restricted for spending for certain purposes, that is intergovernmental, that is elastic, that is one-time, and that comes from taxes; the percentage of property tax revenue that is uncollected by the end of the fiscal year; the percentage of service costs paid by user charges; and revenue shortfalls and surpluses. Other specific indicators are used to measure strength or weakness for the other financial factors.

The Financial Trend Monitoring System identifies five general environmental factors that affect a local government's financial health: community needs and resources, intergovernmental constraints, natural disasters or emergencies, political culture, and external economic conditions. Some of the specific measures suggested for tracking community needs and resources include population, personal income per capita, percentage of households below the poverty line, percentage of unemployment, and business activity. While data may be hard to obtain for many environmental factors, the ICMA trend monitoring model emphasizes their importance in determining a local government's financial health and suggests strategies local officials can pursue to manage their jurisdiction's financial condition in times of economic adversity.

Source: *Evaluating Financial Condition: A Handbook for Local Government*, 4th ed. (Washington, D.C.: ICMA, 2003).

The multiyear forecast supports both the CIP and the annual budget. In some cases, the multiyear financial forecast is presented as a part of the annual budget document that the manager presents to the governing board. Where this happens, the CIP is also usually presented as a section of the annual budget document. In other cases, where a separate CIP document is prepared, the multiyear financial forecast is included in the CIP document when it is presented to the board. In a few cases, the multiyear financial forecast is presented as an altogether separate document. No matter how or where presentation occurs, the forecast serves both the annual budget and the CIP.

Content of forecast presentation

Generally, some supplementary schedules should accompany the forecast summary form to show how important parts of the forecast were derived and give the board and other users confidence that substantial work and analysis underlay the overall numbers. Still, the manager must be careful not to overwhelm and confuse the board and the public with numerous schedules, technical calculations, and details. Usually, a handful of supplementary schedules is sufficient. The types of schedules that can be useful are shown in the sidebar on the next page.

Supplementary schedules

A significant number of supplementary schedules back up and provide detail for the 2003–2008 multiyear forecast of revenue and spending amounts in **Forsyth County, North Carolina:**

- Significant revenue issues for 2003
- Significant budget requests for 2003
- 2003 budget and underlying assumptions
- Budgets for the five years beyond 2003
- Additional expenditure needs beyond 2003: personal services, purchased services, materials and supplies, and contributions to outside agencies
- Debt and debt service schedule for forecast period and beyond
- Fund balance activity and outcomes: budget year and future years
- Capital improvement program
- Annual requirements created by the capital improvement program
- Capital projects not included in the capital improvement program but that have merit and are likely to be considered in the future
- County property tax base and rates and sales tax collections in Forsyth County compared with other metropolitan North Carolina counties
- Previous projections compared with actual revenues and spending. This schedule gives county officials a picture of the accuracy of past year multiyear financial forecasts.

The important assumptions underlying the multiyear financial forecast should be listed and briefly explained. Major assumptions for a local government forecast would concern the rate of growth assumed for major revenue sources (the property tax and local sales tax, for example); continuation, increase, decrease, or end of state-shared revenues and grants; salary and wage increases for employees; continued, increased, or reduced spending for major mandated programs and important contributions to outside agencies; how amounts for recurring or replacement capital outlay are handled; the basis for including debt service and lease payments; reasons for any new programs or positions included during the forecast years; and other assumptions about important revenue or spending issues. The major assumptions for a forecast can usually be listed and explained in a few pages.

The forecast presented to the board should also highlight major issues or decisions about revenues and spending that the board will have to make during the forecast period. Special emphasis needs to be given to issues or decisions that face the board immediately, that is, in deciding on the upcoming year's budget. For small local governments, major decisions would be those that involve hundreds of thousands of dollars; for medium-size local governments, decisions involving millions of dollars; and for large local governments, decisions involving several million dollars.

Governing board role

Board approval of a multiyear financial forecast can give the forecast legitimacy, cause those who prepare it to take the process more seriously, and give the board incentive to use the forecast results in budget and financial decision making. An interesting question concerns whether the board approves the assumptions that the manager and staff use to prepare the forecast. One disadvantage of this is that conditions may shift during the preparation process, necessitating board amendment of those assumptions. Another is that it can deprive those preparing the forecast of the flexibility they need. Board consideration of assumptions can also inject politics into the process, make the process less professional, and cause the result to lose credibility. The manager and the staff preparing the forecast can obtain board views informally concerning key assumptions and, if they mesh with professional criteria, consider or incorporate these views in the forecasting process.

The information or items in the forecast that are most likely to draw the attention of the governing board are the bottom-line items: the projected surplus or deficit, fund balance, and tax or utility rate implications for any year. In devising the forecast format, especially what goes in the bottom line, the manager or staff preparing the forecast should confer with the board or board members. For example, do they want to see just the annual surplus or deficit, or do they also want to see fund balance or tax rate implications or adjustments needed to reach a balanced budget? The politics of financial forecasting can open local governing boards to criticism. If the forecast shows a deficit or surplus each year, the press or political opponents may charge that the board is laying plans that will spend or tax too much. Showing how deficits or surpluses might be made up with tax rate or fund balance adjustments may not spare the board this kind of criticism. The important message to present with the forecast is that the local government is prudently looking ahead, estimating future revenues and expenditures so that officials can respond to emerging issues and problems in a timely way and with well-planned solutions.

Examples of local multiyear financial forecasts

Scottsdale, Arizona

Multiyear financial forecasting is a very important part of budget development and capital planning in Scottsdale, Arizona.[19] Scottsdale is located in the Phoenix metropolitan area. Like that entire area, Scottsdale has grown rapidly over the past decade, increasing from a population of 130,069 in 1990 to 202,705 by 2000. Scottsdale's economy has grown commensurately. Even in 2001–2002, a year of recession, 17 new firms moved to Scottsdale and 1,716 jobs were created, helping the city maintain a relatively low 3.8 percent unemployment rate. Tourism is the single largest economic activity.

Scottsdale's multiyear financial forecast is part of the city's strategic planning and budget process.[20] The forecast is intended to guide policy choices and budget decisions by pointing to the city's capacity to fund expenditure requirements and choices in the future. The forecast covers a five-year period including the adopted budget for the upcoming year and four additional years. The city's operating budget and its capital project revenues and spending are forecast separately. Exhibit 12–2 shows the operating budget forecast for 2003–2007 and Exhibit 12–3 shows the forecast for the capital budget for the same five-year period.

Operating budget forecast The 2003–2007 operating budget forecast includes the general fund and all other major operating funds of the city: debt

text continues on page 361

Exhibit 12–2 Operating budget forecast, 2003–2007, Scottsdale, Arizona

	Adopted 2002/03	Forecast 2003/04	Forecast 2004/05	Forecast 2005/06	Forecast 2006/07
Source of Funds:					
Beginning Balance	**94,487,607**	**97,387,364**	**103,856,551**	**105,571,053**	**108,710,463**
Revenues					
Taxes - Local					
Privilege Tax	84,047,534	87,829,673	92,396,816	97,478,641	102,839,966
Privilege Tax - Transportation	16,388,147	17,125,614	18,016,146	19,007,034	20,052,420
Privilege Tax - Preservation	16,640,659	17,522,614	18,433,790	19,447,648	20,517,269
Property Tax	39,158,698	46,322,683	52,109,669	56,581,494	63,192,354
Transient Occupancy Tax	7,600,000	7,980,000	8,379,000	8,797,950	9,237,848
Light & Power Franchise	5,640,622	5,922,653	6,218,785	6,529,725	6,856,211
Cable TV	2,114,113	2,219,818	2,330,809	2,424,041	2,521,003
Salt River Project Lieu Tax	202,864	202,864	202,864	202,864	202,864
Fire Insurance Premium	210,000	220,500	227,115	233,928	240,946
Taxes - From Other Agencies					
State Shared Sales Tax	15,793,835	16,092,500	16,575,275	17,072,533	17,584,709
State Revenue Sharing	21,048,652	21,000,000	21,500,000	22,000,000	22,500,000
Transportation					
Highway User Tax	13,118,064	13,500,000	14,000,000	14,500,000	15,250,000
Auto In-Lieu Tax	6,700,000	7,000,000	7,350,000	7,700,000	8,100,000
Local Trans Assistance Fund	1,146,323	1,157,786	1,169,364	1,181,058	1,192,868
Transit Funding - HB 2565	—	—	—	—	—
Internal Service Charges					
Fleet Management	10,470,441	11,037,431	11,601,998	11,990,966	12,394,075
Self Insurance	4,249,164	4,450,000	4,650,000	5,100,000	5,150,000
Licenses, Permits & Fees					
Development Permits & Fees	15,500,000	15,500,000	15,500,000	15,500,000	15,500,000
Business Licenses & Fees	1,705,250	1,773,460	1,862,133	1,955,240	2,053,002
Recreation Fees	2,129,765	2,236,253	2,348,066	2,465,469	2,588,743
WestWorld	1,300,000	1,385,000	1,446,900	1,533,714	1,625,737
Fines & Forfeitures					
Court Fines	3,464,909	3,603,505	3,783,680	3,972,864	4,171508
Parking Fines	137,000	137,000	137,000	137,000	137,000
Photo Radar	1,150,000	1,150,000	1,150,000	1,150,000	1,150,000
Library Fines	445,659	454,573	463,664	472,937	482,396
Interest Earnings/Property Rental					
Interest Earnings	7,239,858	6,236,597	6,014,677	5,788,441	6,133,900
Property Rental	3,386,842	3,511,116	3,640,360	3,791,576	3,949,597

(continued)

Exhibit 12–2 *(continued)*

	Adopted 2002/03	Forecast 2003/04	Forecast 2004/05	Forecast 2005/06	Forecast 2006/07
Utilities & Enterprises					
Water Charges	65,852,136	71,259,083	76,285,914	79,683,911	82,996,000
Sewer Charges	27,162,211	28,181,171	29,182,684	30,191,970	31,185,328
Refuse/Recycling	16,115,445	16,460,786	16,808,152	17,157,595	17,709,429
Aviation Fees/Charges	2,386,019	2,664,099	2,938,899	3,013,868	3,107,570
Other Revenue					
Improvement District Assessments	2,562,210	2,903,813	2,803,074	1,139,233	1,099,355
Miscellaneous	6,183,542	6,280,162	6,294,597	6,454,233	6,605,577
Special Revenue	2,354,791	3,061,405	3,164,877	3,271,914	3,299,197
Less Internal Service Funds Offset	(14,569,605)	(15,337,431)	(16,101,998)	(16,940,966)	(17,394,075)
Subtotal	***389,035,148***	***411,024,728***	***432,884,312***	***450,986,884***	***474,232,798***
Transfers In					
From Capital Improvement Program	4,958,281	4,969,869	4,953,294	4,953,606	4,903,838
From Operating Budget Savings	3,000,000	3,000,000	3,000,000	3,000,000	3,000,000
Subtotal	***7,956,281***	***7,969,869***	***7,953,294***	***7,953,606***	***7,903,838***
Total Revenues & Transfers In	**396,993,429**	**418,994,597**	**440,837,606**	**458,940,490**	**482,136,636**
Use of Funds:					
Program Expenditures					
Enhance/Protect Community/ Neighborhoods	119,190,430	124,580,466	131814,576	144,905,051	153,856,009
Preserve Character & Environment	20,408,600	21229,648	22,141,628	23,094,721	24,090,849
Movement of People & Goods	26,961,039	27,987,755	29,136,418	30,329,142	31608,687
Long Term Economic Prosperity	7794,343	7,275,424	7,521,722	7,776,811	8,041,025
Balance Infrastructure & Resources	46,147,061	47,901,643	49,907,151	51,898,129	53,817,483
Accessible and Responsive Government	12,298,796	13,159,961	13,386,071	14,388,530	14,631,106
Ensure Fiscal Responsibility	34,097,691	35,446,384	36,851,825	38,316,533	39,843,139
Less Internal Service Fund Offset	(14,569,605)	(15,337,431)	(16,101,998)	(16,940,966)	(17,394,075)
Total	***252,328,355***	***262,243,849***	***274,657,393***	***293,767,950***	***308,494,223***

Exhibit 12–2 *(continued)*

	Adopted 2002/03	Forecast 2003/04	Forecast 2004/05	Forecast 2005/06	Forecast 2006/07
Debt Service					
General Obligation Bonds	29,530,688	35,006,238	39,581,641	44,707,872	43,572,947
General Obligation Bonds-Preserve	9,110,961	9,802,947	12,936,159	12,224,122	12,179,134
Revenue Bonds	9,623,971	9,623,792	9,648,293	9,663,195	9,637,698
Preserve Authority Bonds	6,881,422	6,863,722	6,860,785	6,840,372	6,838,047
MPC Bonds	14,616,000	14,495,904	16,917,751	13,285,364	16,870,397
Special Assessment Bonds	2,562,210	2,903,813	2,803,074	1,139,233	1,099,355
Contractual Debt	4,830,370	8,223,340	6,298,699	6,370,320	5,828,637
Subtotal	*77,155,622*	*84,919,756*	*95,046,402*	*94,230,478*	*96,026,215*
Total Operating Plan	**329,483,977**	**347,163,605**	**369,703,795**	**387,998,428**	**404,520,438**
Transfers Out to Capital Program					
From General Fund	12,880,324	12,301,467	14,726,400	14,241,200	12,785,500
From Highway User Fund	73,184	73,477	74,812	73,039	73,675
From Special Projects Fund	235,500	257,500	—	—	79,800
From Transportation Tax Fund	16,888,147	17,625,614	18,516,146	19,507,034	20,652,420
From Aviation Fund	611,600	222,600	970,700	764,200	10,600
From Water/Sewer Funds	33,453,940	33,738,547	33,073,952	33,161,778	39,814,742
From Solid Waste Fund	18,400	468,500	2,018,900	18,300	18,500
From Internal Service Funds	448,600	674,100	38,400	37,100	37,600
Subtotal	64,609,695	65,361,805	69,419,309	67,802,650	73,472,837
Total Expenditures/ Transfers Out	**394,093,672**	**412,525,411**	**439,123,104**	**455,801,079**	**477,993,275**
Ending Fund Balance					
General Fund	30,842,972	34,015,203	35,959,876	37,216,340	37,752,717
Special Revenue Funds	14,930,137	15,306,798	14,098,701	14,659,389	16,193,410
Debt Service Fund	7,155,509	7,155,509	7,155,509	7,155,509	7,155,509
Enterprise Funds	23,424,592	27,280,079	28,851,319	32,686,905	36,367,493
Internal Service Funds	21,034,155	20,098,962	19,505,649	16,992,320	15,384,696
Total Ending Fund Balance	**$97,387,364**	**$103,856,551**	**$105,571,053**	**$108,710,463**	**$112,853,824**

service, transportation, water-sewer, aviation, solid waste, internal services for fleet maintenance and self-insurance, and several other funds. For each year during the planning period, the forecast shows the beginning combined fund balance for all funds, annual revenues, transfers into the operating funds, program expenditures, debt service, transfers out of the operating funds, and the year's ending balance by type of fund.

Revenue projections are based on economic and demographic information compiled by the city, the chamber of commerce, and other sources. Revenues are estimated with conservative assumptions and are based on historic data for major sources going back many years. While the past years' data are graphed, the forecast of revenues in future years is based mainly on the judgment and experience of the city's chief financial officer and the staff. The transfers-in are modest amounts. They come from two sources: capital funds and savings generated in the operating budget. The transfers from the capital funds are allocated to the water-sewer operating fund to be spent for capital-related purposes there. Operating fund savings are appropriations from the prior year's ending balances of the operating funds. These ending fund balances are forecast to grow from $97.4 million in 2003 to $112.9 million by 2007, despite the appropriation of $3 million of these balances annually over the period.

Scottsdale's revenue forecast shows thirty-four different revenue sources organized into nine general categories. The most important of these revenue categories are local taxes, taxes from other agencies, transportation taxes and fees, and utility and enterprises revenue.

- **Local taxes** include privilege, property, and certain other taxes. This general category accounts for 43 percent of the city's total annual taxes, revenues, and transfers in 2003 and will account for 46 percent by 2007. The privilege tax is a local sales tax, levied at a 1.4 percent rate. Of this, 1 percent goes into the general fund, 0.2 percent is earmarked for transportation, and 0.2 percent goes toward land preservation. The property tax, also an unrestricted revenue, is expected to grow from about 10 percent of total revenue and transfers in 2003 to 13 percent in 2007.

- **Taxes from other agencies** include state sales tax revenue and other state-shared revenue. These revenues accounted for 9 percent of total revenue in 2003. Because only modest growth is projected for them, they drop to 8 percent of total revenues and transfers-in by 2007.

- **Transportation taxes and fees** include highway user or gasoline and auto in-lieu tax revenues. This auto in-lieu tax is a state vehicle licensing tax; 22 percent of the revenue that the state collects from this tax is distributed to cities. These revenues are budgeted in a separate special revenue fund and are restricted for street and transportation spending. They make up about 5 percent of total revenue throughout the forecast period.

- **Utilities and enterprises revenue** includes fees and charges for water, sewer, solid waste, and aviation. Fees to customers and other charges for these systems are set at levels to cover operating and maintenance costs and debt service, to maintain adequate reserves, and to make contributions to pay-as-go capital financing. Scottsdale's utility and enterprise fees and charges are the second largest revenue category, contributing about 28 percent of total annual revenues and transfers-in over the forecast period.

Scottsdale's expenditure forecast, excluding transfers out, is organized into two general categories: program expenditures and debt service. Program spending accounts for about three-quarters and debt service a quarter of operating expenditures each year. The program expenditures include increases to maintain current services, changes in employee compensation, the effects of expected population growth, changes in the consumer price index, and new operating expenses due to the completion of capital projects. They also include certain mandated or council-approved changes in current service levels, the leveraging of technology, and alternative methods of service delivery such as greater use of volunteers in some programs. The forecast of program spending also considers recommendations from the city's interdepartment technology board and technology review team, its interdepartment construction review team, information from citizen surveys, and long-term program priorities suggested by citizen advisory boards. Like the multiyear financial forecast, the citizen surveys and advisory boards are parts of Scottsdale's strategic planning and budgeting process.

The program expenditures in Exhibit 12–2 are organized into seven broad missions or functional categories, each of which involves multiple departments and programs. (For example, there are sixteen different programs within the city's financial services department, and a separate forecast is done for each of these programs.) Following are the missions or functional categories used to present the forecast and the departments:

- **Enhance and protect the community and neighborhoods:** police, fire protection, courts and justice, parks and recreation, community services and neighborhood programs, library, and arts and culture

- **Preserve character of community and environment:** planning and development, mountain and land preservation, and water conservation

- **Move people and goods:** traffic management, enforcement, and engineering; street and right-of-way maintenance

- **Promote long-term economic prosperity:** aviation and economic development

- **Balance infrastructure and resources:** facilities maintenance, water and waste water operations, capital project management, and technology infrastructure

- **Advance accessible and responsive government:** council, manager and administrative staff, clerk and public information, human resources program, and liability management

- **Ensure fiscal responsibility:** financial services, budgeting and accounting, fleet management, and asset management.

Scottsdale's annual debt service during the forecast period includes principal repayment and interest on various types of debt: GO bonds related to city facilities, GO bonds for land preservation purposes, revenue bonds for the city's utilities and enterprises, special authority bonds related to land preservation, Municipal Properties Corporation (MPC) debt,[21] special assessment bonds, and contractual debt. The debt is secured by city excise tax revenue. The 2003–2007 forecast includes annual debt issued before 2003 and proposed new debt that will be issued during the forecast period.

The 2003–2007 operating budget forecast projects annual revenues and transfers-in to exceed program spending and debt service by substantial amounts each year during the five-year forecast period, ranging from about $67.5 million for the adopted budget in 2003 ($397.0 million in total revenues and transfers-in less $329.5 million for the "total operating plan" consisting of program expenditures and debt service) to $77.6 million in 2007 ($482.1 million less $404.5 million). The forecast transfers $340.7 million of these revenues to the capital program, ranging from $64.6 million in 2003 to $73.5 million by 2007 (see subtotals by year under "Transfers Out to Capital Program" of Exhibit 12–2). This provides substantial pay-as-go financing of capital projects and helps the city maintain a balance between pay-as-go and debt financing in its capital program. The general fund, transportation tax fund, and water-sewer funds generated most of this operating budget money for capital purposes, with the general fund slated to contribute $66.9 million, the transportation tax fund $93.2 million, and the water-sewer fund $173.3 million (these are the sums of the annual transfers from 2003 through 2007 for each of these funds under "Transfers Out to Capital Program" in Exhibit 12–2). Another, much smaller, portion—$18.4 million ($112.9 million in "Total Ending Fund Balance" for 2007 less the "Beginning Balance" of $94.5 million for 2003, in Exhibit 12–2)—of the excess operating revenues is allocated to operating fund balances. This helps the city maintain fund balances at a consistent percentage of spending each year during the forecast period.[22]

Capital budget forecast   Exhibit 12–3 shows Scottsdale's 2003–2007 financial forecast for the city's sources and uses of funds for capital projects. The sources for capital financing consist of beginning fund balances or carryover, revenues from bonds and other contractual debt, pay-as-go sources generated from within the city's capital funds, transfers-in from the operating budget, and carry over of unexpended balances from prior years. The debt that Scottsdale issues for capital purposes is identified on page 363 in the discussion on annual debt service. The forecast projects that Scottsdale will issue $491,483,000 in new debt from 2003 through 2007; this is the sum of all the bonds/contracts amounts in Exhibit 12–3—the amounts for general obligation, general obligation-preserve, municipal properties corporation, and municipal properties corporation-arsenic for years 2003 through 2007. The pay-as-go sources include water-sewer development fees, extra capacity development fee, grants, other contributions, interest earnings, and miscellaneous. The total of these sources is $186,456,300. Transfers from the operating budget, which are also a pay-as-go source, account total $340,666,296 (the sum of the annual Transfers-In subtotals in Exhibit 12–3). These combined pay-as-go sources (transfers-in plus the pay-as-go sources themselves) account for 52 percent of the total new resources during the forecast period. This suggests that Scottsdale maintains an even balance between debt and pay-as-go financing for its capital improvement program. The carryover of unexpended money from prior years is for projects in process. They have been approved and funding has been committed to them. Carryover is very substantial in 2003 (about $315 million) but is projected to decline to $100 million by 2007. The expenditure or uses of capital project financing resources are shown by the same mission or broad functional categories used in the operating budget forecast.

The process   Scottsdale's Department of Financial Services is responsible for preparing the city's multiyear financial forecasts. The city's chief financial officer, who heads this department, is directly involved in decisions about the forecast. The city's budget director, who heads the budget division within the financial services department, also plays a key role in these decisions and is immediately responsible for the forecast. Other staff from the budget division are involved, and department directors and program managers are consulted about specific revenues that their departments collect and about spending plans and issues that loom in the forecast period.

The city manager of Scottsdale takes an active role in the financial forecasting process. She approves the format that is used for organizing and presenting the forecast; makes key decisions on budget or financing options, assumptions, and choices that are part of the forecast; reviews the draft prepared by the financial services department; and presents the recommended financial forecast to the city council and to a citizens' budget review com-

Exhibit 12–3 Financial forecast for capital projects, 2003–2007, Scottsdale, Arizona

	Adopted 2002/03	Forecast 2003/04	Forecast 2004/05	Forecast 2005/06	Forecast 2006/07
Source of Funds:					
Beginning Fund Balance	**231,103,141**	**240,813,836**	**192,150,141**	**196,903,051**	**138,758,001**
Revenues					
Bonds/Contracts					
General Obligation	60,400,000	58,500,000	59,000,000	60,700,000	49,500,000
General Obligation-Preserve	15,000,000	—	50,400,000	—	—
Municipal Properties Corporation	17,115,000	5,300,000	—	2,000,000	7,135,000
Municipal Properties Corporation-Arsenic	—	34,915,000	40,745,700	—	30,772,300
Pay-As-Go					
Water/Sewer Development Fees	17,211,600	17,827,300	18,588,400	19,438,100	20,412,000
Extra Capacity Development Fee	11,000,000	—	—	—	—
Grants	6,044,900	5,673,000	2,943,200	8,596,000	—
Other Contributions	9,580,700	4,241,100	1,000,000	1,000,000	1,000,000
Interest Earnings	12,026,700	8,675,000	7,825,000	6,785,000	5,400,000
Miscellaneous	570,100	389,500	77,600	75,100	76,000
Subtotal	**148,949,000**	**135,520,900**	**180,579,900**	**98,594,200**	**114,295,300**
Transfers In					
From General Fund	12,880,324	12,301,467	14,726,400	14,241,200	12,785,500
From Highway User Fund	73,184	73,477	74,812	73,039	73,675
From Special Projects Fund	235,500	257,500	—	—	79,800
From Transportation Privilege Tax Fund	16,888,147	17,625,614	18,516,146	19,507,034	20,652,420
From Aviation Fund	611,600	222,600	970,700	764,200	10,600
From Water/Sewer Funds	33,453,940	33,738,547	33,073,952	33,161,778	39,814,742
From Solid Waste	18,400	468,500	2,018,900	18,300	18,500
From Internal Service Funds	448,600	674,100	38,400	37,100	37,600
Subtotal	*64,609,695*	*65,361,805*	*69,419,309*	*67,802,650*	*73,472,837*
Carryover of Prior Year Unexpended	315,013,700	300,000,000	250,000,000	175,000,000	100,000,000
Total Revenues & Transfers In	**528,572,395**	**500,882,705**	**499,999,209**	**341,396,850**	**287,768,137**
Use of Funds:					
Program Expenditures					
Enhance & Protect Community/ Neighborhoods	96,796,300	96,730,400	56,823,200	34,188,100	9,562,000

(continued)

Exhibit 12–3 *continued*

	Adopted 2002/03	Forecast 2003/04	Forecast 2004/05	Forecast 2005/06	Forecast 2006/07
Preserve Character & Environment	131,198,500	18,925,100	26,451,700	23,889,900	11,932,900
Movement of People/Goods	115,775,900	47,534,200	60,820,100	59,739,400	31,344,500
Long Term Economic Prosperity	23,214,200	1,227,400	3,779,700	2,503,800	750,000
Balance Infrastructure and Resources	139,062,400	62,046,700	39,690,200	21,725,800	62,719,000
Accessible & Responsive Government	367,700	—	—	—	—
Ensure Fiscal Responsibility	7,488,400	3,099,000	2,728,100	2,541,300	3,595,000
Subtotal	*513,903,400*	*229,562,800*	*190,293,000*	*144,588,300*	*119,903,400*
Prior Year Unexpended*	—	315,013,700	300,000,000	250,000,000	175,000,000
Total Capital Improvement Plan	**513,903,400**	**544,576,500**	**490,293,000**	**394,588,300**	**294,903,400**
Transfers Out					
To Water/Sewer Operating Funds	4,958,300	4,969,900	4,953,300	4,953,600	4,903,800
Subtotal	*4,958300*	*4,969,900*	*4,953,300*	*4,953,600*	*4,903,800*
Total Expenditures & Transfers	**518,861,700**	**549,546,400**	**495,246,300**	**399,541,900**	**299,807,200**
Ending Fund Balance	**$240,813,836**	**$192,150,141**	**$196,903,051**	**$138,758,001**	**$126,718,939**

*Prior year unexpended amounts for 2002/03 are estimated and included by program
2003/04–2006/07 unexpended amounts are estimated, but the amount is not known by program

mittee consisting of fourteen members appointed by the city council. The council offers its views and advice on the forecast. Council members usually ask questions about the forecast based on their own concerns and those of the citizens' budget review committee. The city council formally approves only the first or budget year of the forecast. Revenues and spending for the other four years are considered to be tentative.

Scottsdale's multiyear financial forecast is part of its strategic and balanced approach to budgeting and capital planning and financing. The forecast itself and the approach it reveals are important factors underlying the city's triple-A bond ratings from all three national rating agencies. Like most governments across the country, Scottsdale is facing significant budget shortfalls brought on by the recession and slow and uneven recovery from it, 9/11 and war on terrorism, the war with Iraq, and related events. In 2003, the city experienced a third year of declining revenues for the privilege tax, its most important revenue source. As a result, the projection of overall revenues for 2003, based on actual collections in the first half of the year, was reduced by $8 million from the $389 million shown in the operating budget forecast in Exhibit 12–2. The city is responding to this shortfall by reducing planned transfers to the capital projects funds and slowing the implementation schedule for projects in that fund. The approach embodied in the multiyear financial forecast, which includes substantial pay-as-go capital financing, gives the city the flexibility to meet the operating budget challenges it faces. The forecast is proving to be a valuable planning tool in these difficult budget times as it was in the preceding years when revenue growth was strong.

Coral Springs, Florida

Multiyear financial forecasting is a key tool in the strategic and business planning process of Coral Springs, Florida.[23] Coral Springs is located in the Fort Lauderdale–Broward County metropolitan area of south Florida, about twenty miles northwest of Fort Lauderdale. It has been one of the fastest growing cities in Florida and the nation. Its population increased from 93,586 in 1995, to 117,549 in 2000, and to an estimated 125,227 in 2003. Just forty years old, Coral Springs is a planned community of residential, commercial, and light industrial development. Single-family and multifamily housing accounts for about 80 percent of the city's taxable valuation.

Coral Springs prepares a multiyear financial forecast for its general fund. Strategic and business planning focuses on the general fund because it is in the general fund that the city commission (governing board) faces the most difficult choices as it strives to meet the city's needs and balance the budget. Coral Springs's other major operating funds are the water-sewer enterprise fund and the fire fund. Charges to customers cover all expenses of the water-sewer fund; and non–ad valorem assessments to property, based on square footage for businesses and per residential unit for housing, cover fire fund expenses. Fees and assessments support these funds and the commission's commitment to self-supporting operations has made budget choices for these funds relatively straightforward. Other funds are maintained for health and liability insurance, the arts, equipment replacement, pensions, and debt service; these funds support the general, water-sewer, and fire funds. Decisions affecting revenues and spending are made in the business planning and budget process for the general fund and are taken into account in the multiyear forecast for the general fund.

The business planning framework   Coral Springs's strategic and business planning process, of which the multiyear financial forecast is a part, provides a framework for all budget and capital budget decisions that the city commission makes. Following commission elections every two years, the city undertakes a strategic planning process. An environmental scan, involving citizen surveys and focus groups, and revision of the city's multiyear financial forecast are the first steps in this process. These steps occur in March. Summaries of the environmental scan and the financial forecast are presented to the city commission in April. The financial forecast focuses on the gap between projected revenues and spending each year during the forecast period and usually shows a revenue shortfall for the later years. The commission discusses strategic issues and then approves a set of strategic priorities and key intended outcomes. The strategic priorities approved for 2003 and 2004 are customer-involved government; neighborhood and environmental vitality; financial health and economic development; family, youth, and community values; excellence in education; and respect for ethnic and religious diversity. Every other year, the strategic plan is updated.

Coral Springs's business plan implements the strategic priorities established in the strategic plan. The business plan is prepared each spring. The plan starts with an analysis and overview of the local economy and describes citizen or customer expectations and emerging issues as identified in the strategic plan. The main body of the business plan is organized around the strategic priorities, and it identifies intended outcomes, ongoing activities, and new initiatives with associated operating and capital costs for each initiative. The number of new initiatives ranges from three to eleven per strategic priority.

The financial strategy is a key part of the business plan. The strategy includes the financial forecast, and it identifies actions to balance the budget for the upcoming year and reduce the shortfall of revenues in later years of the financial forecast. For instance, the 2003 business plan includes a new non–ad valorem assessment for solid waste services to balance the 2003 budget. Debt refinancing implemented in the business plans of prior years entails ongoing savings that also help balance the 2003 budget and reduce the projected shortfall in revenues in 2004 through 2008.[24] All city departments are involved in the business-planning process. Significant decisions for the upcoming budget are approved by the city commission when it approves the business plan in midsummer.

The city manager's proposed annual budget is based on the decisions that the commission has made in the business plan. The proposed budget, which includes recommendations about capital projects from the CIP, goes to the commission in August. The commission holds two budget hearings in September and then adopts the annual budget on or shortly before October 1. Because of the business-planning process, the preparation and adoption of the annual budget usually occur relatively quickly.

The forecast Coral Springs's general fund multiyear financial forecast displays eight years of revenue and spending (see Exhibit 12–4). The first year, 2001, shows actual revenues and expenditures for the most recent completed year, 2001. The other seven years include the year preceding the budget year (fiscal year 2002), which is in process when the forecast is prepared; the upcoming budget year (fiscal year 2003); and five "planning" years (fiscal years 2004 through 2008) beyond the budget year. The forecast shows revenues by nine general sources and spending by twenty different departments or categories. The forecast shows the annual dollar amount for each source or category and the percentage increase assumed to occur that year over the immediate prior year. For example, ad valorem taxes for 2003 are $22,535,240, which is a 9.6 percent increase over the ad valorem taxes of $20,552,111 in 2002. Revenues are projected by more specific sources within each of the nine major revenue sources, and spending is projected by line items within each department or category.

About seventy-five specific revenue sources are separately projected for Coral Springs's general fund. The major sources are the property tax, intergovernmental revenue, utility franchise fees and taxes, charges for service, and licenses and permits.

The largest revenue is the ad valorem tax, accounting for 31.6 percent of total revenues in 2003 and 33.4 percent by 2008. Ad valorem tax revenue grew at or near double-digit rates in the late 1990s and into the first years of this decade, reflecting substantial new development and population growth. The city by 2003 was built-out, with little vacant land available for new construction. This is the reason for the slower 4.5 percent growth rate for ad valorem taxes projected in 2004 and 2005, much lower than the 7.6 percent and

Exhibit 12–4
General fund financial forecast, 2003–2008, Coral Springs, Florida

	Fiscal Year 2001	Fiscal Year 2002	% D	Fiscal Year 2003	% D	Fiscal Year 2004	% D	Fiscal Year 2005	% D	Fiscal Year 2006	% D	Fiscal Year 2007	% D	Fiscal Year 2008	% D
Revenues															
Ad Valorem Taxes	$19,093,051	$20,552,111	7.6%	$22,535,240	9.6%	$23,549,326	4.5%	$24,609,045	4.5%	$25,593,407	4.0%	$26,617,144	4.0%	$27,548,744	3.5%
Utility Franchise Fees	7,240,685	6,938,592	-4.2%	7,643,700	10.2%	7,847,804	2.7%	8,025,938	2.3%	8,219,062	2.4%	8,476,882	3.1%	8,742,831	3.1%
Utility Service Taxes	7,783,889	8,519,470	9.5%	8,333,000	-2.2%	8,477,665	1.7%	8,601,168	1.5%	8,727,262	1.5%	8,926,698	2.3%	9,203,087	3.1%
Intergovernmental Revenues	18,799,661	17,976,201	-4.4%	17,961,472	-0.1%	18,013,323	0.3%	18,336,057	1.8%	18,662,856	1.8%	19,115,975	2.4%	19,637,125	2.7%
Licenses & Permits	4,038,590	2,905,580	-28.1%	2,949,050	1.5%	2,822,254	-4.3%	2,814,640	-0.3%	2,857,123	1.5%	2,951,836	3.3%	2,998,699	1.6%
Charges for Services	5,575,278	5,719,180	2.6%	7,832,041	36.9%	8,146,743	4.0%	8,474,191	4.0%	8,814,903	4.0%	9,185,965	4.2%	9,572,802	4.2%
Fines & Forfeitures	1,425,696	1,159,111	-18.7%	1,246,427	7.5%	1,282,527	2.9%	1,319,734	2.9%	1,358,082	2.9%	1,397,611	2.9%	1,438,356	2.9%
Miscellaneous	3,431,606	2,616,249	-23.8%	2,778,000	6.2%	2,833,000	2.0%	3,040,155	7.3%	3,099,557	2.0%	3,261,304	5.2%	3,325,498	2.0%
Interfund Transfers	98,785	518,558	424.9%	84,500	-83.7%	628,480	643.8%	688,880	9.6%	657,332	-4.6%	186,895	-71.6%	90,617	-51.5%
Total Revenues	$67,487,242	$66,905,052	-0.9%	$71,363,430	6.7%	$73,601,123	3.1%	$75,909,808	3.1%	$77,989,585	2.7%	$80,120,310	2.7%	$82,557,760	3.0%
Expenditures															
City Commission	$199,908	$225,534	12.8%	$233,334	3.5%	$242,823	4.1%	$252,845	4.1%	$263,441	4.2%	$274,656	4.3%	$286,537	4.3%
City Manager's Office	$1,632,991	1,807,003	10.7%	1,921,324	6.3%	1,997,610	4.0%	2,077,382	4.0%	2,160,835	4.0%	2,248,174	4.0%	2,339,622	4.1%
Human Resources	$1,042,166	1,119,556	7.4%	1,238,267	10.6%	1,291,090	4.3%	1,346,511	4.3%	1,404,683	4.3%	1,465,773	4.3%	1,529,957	4.4%
Financial Services	$2,121,941	2,325,182	9.6%	2,636,077	13.4%	2,753,641	4.5%	2,877,276	4.5%	3,007,360	4.5%	3,144,301	4.6%	3,288,536	4.6%
Information Services	$1,469,284	1,620,755	10.3%	1,740,843	7.4%	1,813,030	4.1%	1,888,700	4.2%	1,968,057	4.2%	2,051,320	4.2%	2,138,727	4.3%
City Attorney's Office	$1,102,459	1,082,531	-1.8%	977,137	-9.7%	1,012,241	3.6%	1,048,836	3.6%	1,087,005	3.6%	1,126,832	3.7%	1,168,410	3.7%
Charter School	$395,578	331,267	-16.3%	331,267	0.0%	340,211	2.7%	349,397	2.7%	358,831	2.7%	368,519	2.7%	378,469	2.7%
Police Department	$22,955,912	24,954,509	8.7%	27,487,778	10.2%	28,703,647	4.4%	29,980,957	4.4%	31,323,421	4.5%	32,735,024	4.5%	34,220,044	4.5%
Emergency Medical Services	$3,678,954	4,247,490	15.5%	4,792,683	12.8%	5,010,448	4.5%	5,239,746	4.6%	5,481,317	4.6%	5,735,957	4.6%	6,004,525	4.7%
Development Services	$4,186,673	4,573,868	9.2%	4,606,083	0.7%	4,566,083	-0.9%	4,537,185	-0.6%	4,520,097	-0.4%	4,690,583	3.8%	4,874,462	3.9%
Public Works	$3,776,348	3,971,345	5.2%	4,248,176	7.0%	4,412,989	3.9%	4,585,467	3.9%	4,766,060	3.9%	4,955,252	4.0%	5,153,562	4.0%
Economic Development	$75,000	75,000	0.0%	50,000	-33.3%	50,000	0.0%	50,000	0.0%	50,000	0.0%	50,000	0.0%	50,000	0.0%
Parks & Recreation	$6,643,738	7,076,944	6.5%	8,009,052	13.2%	8,317,951	3.9%	8,641,181	3.9%	8,979,587	3.9%	9,334,075	3.9%	9,705,621	4.0%
Aquatics	$1,492,218	1,510,643	1.2%	1,866,579	23.6%	1,941,143	4.0%	2,019,237	4.0%	2,101,072	4.1%	2,186,869	4.1%	2,276,870	4.1%
Sportsplex	$798,206	820,288	2.8%	1,080,463	31.7%	1,119,236	3.6%	1,159,607	3.6%	1,201,659	3.6%	1,245,477	3.6%	1,291,154	3.7%
Non-Departmental	$4,233,247	3,003,108	-29.1%	2,724,134	-9.3%	3,231,640	18.6%	3,236,604	0.2%	3,386,437	4.6%	3,536,363	4.4%	3,693,433	4.4%
Interfund Transfers	$983,527	908,554	-7.6%	1,057,277	16.4%	1,075,768	1.7%	1,094,999	1.8%	1,114,999	1.8%	1,135,799	1.9%	1,157,431	1.9%
Capital Financing	$1,828,967	3,527,505	92.9%	4,259,705	20.8%	5,101,922	19.8%	5,345,954	4.8%	5,483,338	2.6%	5,122,780	-6.6%	5,127,280	0.1%
Bond Debt Service	$3,619,131	3,013,970	-16.7%	1,471,901	-51.2%	1,524,220	3.6%	1,519,600	-0.3%	1,181,402	-22.3%	1,181,402	0.0%	1,181,402	0.0%
Miscellaneous	$0	710,000	n/a	631,350	-11.1%	1,974,765	212.8%	2,306,062	16.8%	2,724,209	18.1%	2,929,534	7.5%	2,747,316	-6.2%
Total Expenditures	$62,236,248	$66,905,052	7.5%	$71,363,430	6.7%	$76,480,457	7.2%	$79,557,546	4.0%	$82,563,809	3.8%	$85,518,691	3.6%	$88,613,357	3.6%
Surplus/(Deficit)	$5,250,994	$0	n/a	$0	n/a	($2,879,334)	n/a	($3,647,737)	n/a	($4,574,224)	25.4%	($5,398,380)	18.0%	($6,055,597)	12.2%

9.6 percent growth rates in 2002 and 2003, respectively. Most of the growth in ad valorem tax revenue over the forecast period is expected to come from increasing property values.

The category of intergovernmental revenues is the second most important general fund revenue category, contributing 25.2 percent of total revenues in 2003 and 23.8 percent in 2008. This source consists mainly of revenues from the state: a communications service tax, a half-cent sales tax, a local option gas tax, and state-shared revenues. The low growth rates or negative growth rates projected for intergovernmental revenue reflect state cuts in some of these revenues in 2002 and 2003, the recession and the projected slow economic recovery in the early years of the forecast period, and conservative assumptions about growth in the later forecast years.

Other important revenue sources for Coral Springs are utility franchise fees and utility service taxes, charges for services, and licenses and permits. Utility franchise fees are paid by electric and solid waste companies for the right to operate in the city. The franchise service tax is levied on gross receipts of the electric utilities and on the city's water system. After the 10.2 percent increase in 2003, the annual projected growth rates for franchise fees vary slightly, from 2.3 percent to 3.1 percent. Revenue from utility service taxes jumped by 9.5 percent in 2002 and declined by 2.2 percent in 2003; after 2003 this category is expected to grow at a modest rate of between 1.5 and 3.1 percent annually. This abrupt change is due to build-out, which has dramatically slowed population growth, and to the slowdown in the economy.

Charges for services accounted for 8.5 percent of revenues in 2002. Parks, recreation, and other fees were hiked in 2003, accounting for the 36.9 percent increase in this source in 2003. Growth in this category is projected to occur at about 4 percent per year. By 2008, charges for services contribute 11.6 percent of general fund revenues. Licenses and permits are predominantly building permits and development fees. They declined by 28.1 percent in 2002 because of the recession. Negative or very little growth is projected over the next several years, reflecting the build-out of Coral Springs. Only modest annual growth is forecast for 2006, 2007, and 2008.

These major revenue sources and most other general fund revenues are projected with the use of conservative assumptions. All major revenue sources are graphed, and trends based on data from past years are calculated, shown for past years, and projected forward into the future. The projections also consider and incorporate actual or probable events that are likely to affect revenues during the forecast period and the judgment of experienced staff. Revenue trends for the major sources are presented in the city's annual budget document.[25] The projection of revenues, as well as spending, is also based on a financial trend monitoring system that separately tracks and graphs twenty-five different financial and economic indicators. This system was originally developed by ICMA and is used to monitor Coral Springs's financial and economic health.

The forecast in Exhibit 12–4 shows expenditures by department. Within each department, expenditures are separately projected by line-item categories, the most important being regular salaries, other salaries, FICA, pension, health insurance, workers' compensation, operating expenses, and operating capital.

- Regular and other salaries, FICA, and pension costs are assumed to grow by 4.3 percent annually, which is based on past annual growth rates for salaries. Though employee incentive pay increases may range as high as 7 percent, long-term salary costs are controlled by an annual

4.25 percent cap in the amount of salary increase that may be added to the employee's base salary.

- Health insurance is assumed to increase by 10 percent and workers' compensation by 7 percent annually. These large annual growth rates reflect recent increases in health insurance and workers' compensation premiums.

- Operating expenses are projected to grow by 2.7 percent per year and operating capital, which includes office equipment, furniture, and similar items, by 3 percent annually from 2003 through 2008. These rates are based on changes in price indices for the supplies, contractual services, and smaller capital equipment that the city purchases.

Besides departmental spending, Exhibit 12–4 shows nondepartmental spending, transfers out of the general fund, capital financing, bonded debt service, and miscellaneous spending.

- Nondepartmental spending includes property and general liability insurance, contingency spending, and a variety of small unallocable expenditure items (for example, unemployment insurance premiums, bank charges, and an internal auditor's salary). A separate schedule details all of these items. Based on announced or likely increases in rates, significant increases are projected for some of these items during the first few years of the forecast period. Thereafter, the increases are less than 5 percent annually.

- Transfers out of the general fund go to the fire fund to cover assessments for fire protection for city facilities and to the city center fund to cover maintenance on the buildings.

- Capital financing and bonded debt service are annual payments on loans that the city has incurred or bonds it has issued for its capital program. Payment amounts in future years are fixed or can be estimated with close accuracy.

- Miscellaneous spending is a "plug" figure used in the forecast to include growth or change in spending that is likely to occur, as indicated by recent events or emerging trends, but that is difficult to estimate precisely and to allocate to specific departments or lines. For example, some increases in city spending related to homeland security are anticipated during the forecast period, but the specific purposes of that spending and specifically how much it will be was unknown when the 2003–2008 forecast was prepared. Thus, the miscellaneous line includes some unallocated future spending for homeland security.

The methodology that Coral Springs uses to forecast expenditures combines general assumptions about changes in particular expenditure lines and knowledge of specific program changes that will occur during the forecast period. The assumptions include increased compensation for city employees and likely price changes for a variety of line items. Mandated or likely growth in service loads (for example, the need to add police officers because of population increases) are included. Also included is spending based on equipment replacement needs as shown in the city's ten-year fleet replacement plan, and the operating budget impact of CIP projects during the forecast period. Department directors and staff are closely involved in the forecasting. Care is exercised in reviewing departmental expenditure forecasts to make sure that they do not become self-fulfilling prophecies. Assumptions are reviewed and existing service definitions and levels are challenged as part of the periodic strategic and business planning process described above.

The bottom line for Coral Springs's multiyear financial forecast is the balance or gap between projected revenues and spending for any year. Exhibit 12–4 shows that actual revenue collections exceeded actual spending by approximately $5.3 million in 2001, a result of conservative assumptions built into the forecast in prior years. Revenues and spending are balanced for 2002 and 2003 because the figures for these years are budgeted amounts and must be in balance. Expenditures exceed revenues in each of the following five years, growing from a shortfall of about $2.9 million in 2004 to about $6.1 million in 2008. These shortfalls are viewed as likely if no actions are taken.

Once shortfalls are identified, revenues and spending are analyzed to find areas where changes can be made to reduce the projected annual deficits. Officials look for long-term solutions rather than quick fixes. They identify policies or actions to bring future annual deficits within manageable limits over a period of years. As the forecast is repeated each year, the deficit for coming years is reduced. By the time the business plan is prepared for any given year, the deficit has been eliminated, and a balanced budget can be prepared for that year. Experience has shown that in most years a revenue shortfall of $2 million or less in the first year of the forecast can be resolved through revenue collections that exceed estimates and modest adjustments in planned spending. When the deficit for a year reaches $4 million or more, specific actions must be taken to balance revenues and spending both in the short term and over the entire five-year forecast. These actions can include significant expenditure reductions, service changes, fee increases, debt refinancing, and, as a last resort, an increase in the ad valorem tax.

In the past, the multiyear financial forecast for Coral Springs showed the tax rate implications of the forecast, that is, the increase in the ad valorem millage rate needed to eliminate the revenue shortfall and balance the forecast budget for any year. If this policy were still followed, the 2003–2008 forecast would show an increase in the millage rate each year from 2004 through 2008. For example, the millage rate would have to rise 0.4896 cents per $1,000 from the $3.8715 to $4.3611 per $1,000 of taxable valuation in 2004. By 2008, the rate would have to reach $4.6759. The Coral Springs commission last raised the millage rate in 1993. Because the commissioners look to changes in programs, reductions in expenditures, increases in fees, and other actions before they consider a tax increase, the multiyear forecast no longer shows the tax rate or millage implications of a shortfall in revenues.

The process The department of financial services prepares the city's multiyear financial forecast. Primary responsibility for this falls to the four staff members in the budget division. A financial analyst and the controller, who are in other divisions of the department, also play key roles in preparing the forecast. The city manager, who is an economist by training, and an assistant city manager, who served as a budget director for several local governments, also participate, but their involvement in most years is minor. When economic conditions change or when the city is facing serious challenges, the manager and assistant manager take more direct roles, reviewing and making decisions about significant assumptions and options.

Coral Springs's multiyear financial forecast is at the core of decision making by the city commission, manager, and staff. The forecast establishes the limits and framework for budgeting and capital planning and finance for the city. The strategic and business planning process, of which the forecast is a part, is an important reason why Coral Springs was awarded a triple-A bond rating by two of the national bond rating agencies in 2002.[26]

Conclusion

A multiyear financial forecast is a key part of any local capital financial strategy. A multiyear financial forecast shows the impact in the future of budget and capital project decisions made today and reveals whether a jurisdiction will have the resources to pay for those decisions over the long haul. By pointing to financial trends, a forecast can enable officials to identify emerging issues or problems and give them the time to plan for and address those problems. The multiyear financial forecasts of Scottsdale and Coral Springs play important roles in enabling these jurisdictions to meet the challenges of the future and retain their triple-A bond ratings.

Notes

1 Survey by Mark Bondo, School of Government, University of North Carolina at Chapel Hill, as part of a study of local government multiyear forecasting conducted by the author, David Ammons, and Mr. Bondo. The municipalities rated triple-A by Standard & Poor's are listed in "Annual Review of 'AAA' Rated Municipalities" (Boston: S&P, February 2001).

2 The Distinguished Budget Presentation Awards program, sponsored by the GFOA of the United States and Canada, evaluates budget documents in terms of policy, financial, operational, and other criteria. Winning the award does not necessarily mean that a local government has a sound budget process or that its financial condition is strong.

3 Reference to multiyear forecasting as radar appears in the introduction to the three-year forecast of Hillsborough, North Carolina. See Town of Hillsborough, FY 2002 Annual Budget & FY 2002–04 Financial Plan, 23.

4 "Statement No. 34: Basic Financial Statements—and Management's Discussion and Analysis—for State and Local Government" (Norwalk, Conn.: GASB, 1999), paragraphs 21–26.

5 A study of "conservatism" in state revenue estimation and forecasting appears in Robert Rodgers and Joyce Philip, "The Effect of Underforecasting on the Accuracy of Revenue Forecasting by State Governments," *Public Administration Review* (January–February, 1996), 48–56.

6 Roy Bahl and Larry Schroeder, "The Role of Multiyear Forecasting in the Annual Budget Process for Local Governments," *Public Budgeting and Finance* (Spring 1984): 3–13. This article was later reprinted in

Jeffrey I. Chapman, *Local Government Financial Planning* (Washington, D.C.: ICMA, 1987), 117–128. A later reference to the same approaches or methods that Bahl and Schroeder identify is found in James J. L. Stegmaier and Martha J. Reiss, "The Revenue Forum: An Effective Low-Cost, Low-Tech Approach to Revenue Forecasting," *Government Finance Review* 10, no. 2 (Spring 1994): 13–16. A relatively recent treatment of forecasting methods in local government is provided by Carmen Cirincione, Gustavo A. Gurrieri, and Bart Van De Sande, "Municipal Government Revenue Forecasting: Issues of Method and Data," *Public Budgeting and Finance* (Spring 1999), 26–46. A very useful overview on methodology in financial forecasting is offered by Laura Morrison, "Improving Revenue Projections: 10 Questions—And Answers," *Government Finance Review* 18, no. 3 (June 2002): 16–19. The questions posed and comments provided in this work are summarized in the discussion of issues in revenue forecasting below.

7 One of the clearest overviews of trend analysis is provided in Charles D. Liner, "Projecting Local Government Revenues," in *Budgeting: Formulation and Execution,* ed. Jack Rabin, W. Bartley Hildredth, and Gerald J. Miller (Athens, Ga.: Carl Vinson Institute of Government, 1996), 183–191.

8 William J. Shkurti, "A User's Guide to State Revenue Forecasting," *Public Budgeting and Finance* (Spring 1990): 84.

9 The discussion below focuses on the responsiveness or elasticity of three major local taxes: the sales tax, the property tax, and the personal income tax. For a comprehensive examination of these and

other local government tax and revenue sources, see Robert L. Bland, *A Revenue Guide for Local Government* (Washington, D.C.: ICMA, 1989).

10 For an example that is many decades old but still useful, see Eugene P. McLoon, Gabriella C. Lupo, and Selma Mushkin, *Long-Range Revenue Estimation* (Washington, D.C.: State and Local Finances Project of the George Washington University, 1967), Chapter 12, "Property Tax Projections."

11 Morrison, "Improving Revenue Projections," 17–18. Morrison compares the responsiveness to economic growth or change of three different revenue sources—the sales tax, the real property tax, and the personal property tax—for Prince William County, Virginia. For a more theoretical discussion of elasticity of the property tax, see McLoon et al., *Long Range Revenue Estimation,* 92–93.

12 This occurred for many North Carolina counties. See A. John Vogt, "North Carolina County Finance: Spending Challenges and Revenue Options" (paper prepared for the governor of North Carolina, December 2002). It examined revenue and spending growth for North Carolina's county governments over the most recent decade and presented different spending scenarios and revenue options for the future. On average, sales tax revenue for North Carolina's counties grew less than property tax revenue over the ten years. Overall sales tax revenue per capita for all 100 counties actually declined from 2001 to 2002. Data on North Carolina county sales tax and other revenues are available on the Internet at www.treasurer.state.nc.us.

13 Ibid. North Carolina property tax revenue grew from $417 to $456 per capita from 2001 to 2002, a difficult economic year, if not a recessionary year, in the state. While part of this growth was due to tax rate increases, another part is attributable to growing property tax values and new construction that occurred despite the difficult economy. Also see Morrison, "Improving Revenue Projections," 17.

14 Morrison, "Improving Revenue Projections," 17.

15 The Forsyth County, North Carolina, board of commissioners holds a retreat each year to kick off its consideration of the annual budget. In several recent years, an economist has made a presentation on the economy. One year, the economist came from a major bank with headquarters in Winston-Salem, the Forsyth County seat. Another year, an economist from a nearby major university made this presentation.

16 Stegmaier and Reiss, "The Revenue Forum: An Effective Low-Cost, Low-Tech Approach to Revenue Forecasting."

17 Bahl and Schroeder, "The Role of Multiyear Forecasting in the Annual Budget Process for Local Governments," 5–7.

18 These purposes are identified and discussed in *Evaluating Financial Condition: A Handbook for Local Government,* 4th ed. (Washington, D.C.: ICMA, 2003).

19 This information about Scottsdale's multiyear financial forecast is based on the city's budget document, City of Scottsdale, Arizona, Fiscal Year 2002/03 Budget, 95–98, and on phone conversations with Art Rullo, the city's budget director. The forecast is accessible on the Internet at www.Scottsdaleaz.gov.

20 Scottsdale's strategic planning process is described in Craig Clifford, "Linking Strategic Planning and Budgeting in Scottsdale, Arizona," *Government Finance Review* (August 1998): 9–14.

21 Municipal Properties Corporation is a city-affiliated nonprofit entity that issues special or limited obligation debt to finance city facilities.

22 City of Scottsdale, Arizona, Fiscal Year 2002/03 Budget, 95.

23 This overview is based on City of Coral Springs, Florida, Business Plan, Fiscal Year 2003; City of Coral Springs, Florida, Budget, Fiscal Year 2003, especially pages 113–150 on long-range planning; the city's 2003–2008 capital improvement program; and a meeting and phone conversations with Ellen G. Liston, the assistant city manager of Coral Springs. Both the annual budget and CIP are accessible on the Internet at www.ci.coral-springs.fl.us.

24 City of Coral Springs, Florida, Business Plan, Fiscal Year 2003, 31–34.

25 City of Coral Springs, Florida, Budget, Fiscal Year 2003, 134–135. Accessible on the Internet at www.ci.coral-springs.fl.us.

26 Moody's and Fitch awarded Coral Springs a triple-A rating. Standard & Poor's rated Coral Springs AA+.

Glossary

Abatement A legal concept that underlies local government capital leasing in California and certain other states. Under the concept, a long-term capital lease is a year-to-year transaction. The local government lessee is obligated to make annual lease payment only as the lessor makes available the leased property. This prevents the lease "obligations" from being classified as long-term debt subject to state debt limits and voter approval requirements. *See also* nonappropriation

Accrued interest Interest earned but not yet paid. In debt sales, interest begins to accrue on the "dated date" for the debt. This date often precedes the closing date by days or weeks. In buying the debt, the underwriters must pay the issuer the accrued interest for the period from the dated date to the closing date, as well as the debt proceeds. The issuer will apply this accrued interest to the first interest payment to investors.

Ad valorem tax Tax levied on the value of property. Also generally called a property tax. General obligation bonds issued by most local governments are secured by unlimited property tax–levying authority. *See also* general obligation bond

Adequate public facilities ordinance An ordinance that some local governments use to manage development. The ordinance requires that public facilities needed to serve new development be in place, in process, or at least planned before the development is approved.

Advance refunding Process in which an issuer sells debt to refund existing debt during the period in which call or early redemption is prohibited, that is, before the call option may be exercised. Proceeds from the advance refunding bonds are controlled by a third party, deposited in an escrow account, invested in safe securities, and used to pay debt service on the existing debt as it is due. This defeases the existing debt. Because of this defeasance, the issuer is responsible only for debt service on the advance refunding bonds. *See also* call; defease; refunding

Advance refunding bond Bond or debt issued to refund existing debt in advance of the date or time when the existing debt is subject to call or early redemption by the issuer. *See also* advance refunding

Alternative minimum tax Federal income tax determined by recalculating taxable income to include income that is otherwise not a part of taxable income. The interest earned on so-called private-purpose debt issued by state and local governments is subject to the alternative minimum tax.

Amortization Allocation of a capital investment or cost over a period of years or time corresponding to the investment's term or useful life, or allocation of debt over the debt's term.

Annual budget   *See* operating budget

Appropriation   Authority to spend; this authority is provided in a budget ordinance or resolution. In the annual or operating budget, the authority lasts for only one year or another specific period and ends at the end of that year or period. An appropriation in a project ordinance normally provides spending authority that lasts for the length of time it takes to complete the project. *See also* budget; capital project ordinance

Arbitrage penalty   Penalty that an issuer of tax-exempt debt must pay to the federal government or that it incurs for violating IRS arbitrage regulations and rebate requirements. Such penalties can extend to the loss of tax-exempt status for the debt. *See also* tax-exempt debt

Arbitrage profit   For local governments issuing tax-exempt debt, the difference between the interest that the issuer pays on the tax-exempt debt and the interest income that the issuer earns by investing proceeds from the tax-exempt issue in higher-yielding securities. *See also* tax-exempt debt

Arbitrage rebate   Payment to the federal government of arbitrage profits, except for such profits that the issuer may keep because the profits qualify for one of the exemptions from arbitrage rebate requirements. *See also* arbitrage profit

Average interest rate   The average interest rate for a long-term debt issue. Each maturity on a long-term debt issue has its own interest rate, and there are usually multiple interest rates for any such issue. The average interest rate can be calculated with several methods: net interest cost (NIC), true interest cost (TIC), or effective interest cost (EIC). *See also* effective interest cost; net interest cost; true interest cost

Basis point   One-hundredth of 1 percent (one basis point is .01 of 1 percent).

Bearer bond   Bond for which registration or ownership records are not maintained. Holder or "bearer" of bond is presumed to be the owner. State and local governments have not been able to sell bearer bonds since 1983. All publicly sold state and local government debt must be registered. *See also* registered bond

Benefit-cost analysis   an approach to evaluating capital projects that compares project benefits with costs. The approach generally attempts to identify all benefits and costs: indirect or external as well as direct, and intangible as well as monetary. If benefits and costs occur over many years and are entirely or predominantly monetary, present value analysis can be used to calculate the present value of benefits and/or costs. *See also* present value

Benefit district debt   Debt issued to finance public improvements in a district; the improvements benefit property or citizens in that district. The debt is repaid by special taxes or assessments charged to property, taxpayers, or citizens in that district. *See also* special assessment debt; special obligation debt; tax increment debt

Bond   A written promise to repay debt on a specific date in the future, along with payment of a specified amount of interest at predetermined intervals while the debt is outstanding. "Certificate," "warrant," and "note" are other names that refer to what is defined here as a bond.

"Bond" usually refers to long-term debt, that is, debt outstanding for thirteen months or longer; "note" commonly refers to short-term debt, which matures in a period of twelve months or less.

Bond anticipation note (BAN)   Debt issued temporarily until long-term bonds or debt can be issued. BANs are used sometimes because long-term debt cannot be issued until a project is finished and the exact amount of long-term debt to issue is known.

Bond certificate   The form in which bonds or other debt were once issued—"certificated." Engraved certificates representing the bonds were distributed to investors. Today, nearly all local government bonds and debt sold publicly is issued in "book entry" form. Even today, however, so-called global certificates of $100,000 or more are issued and held by the registrar, usually the Depository Trust Company. *See also* book entry; Depository Trust Company

Bond counsel   Attorney who reviews legal documents and procedures used in authorizing and issuing debt and opines that the debt has been authorized and issued legally and that interest to be paid on it is exempt from taxation. The bond counsel often prepares legal documents and serves as an adviser through the authorization and sales process. The bond counsel's opinion is vital in marketing debt.

Bond insurance   A guarantee provided by a triple-A-rated insurance company of future principal and interest payments on debt. The issuer pays for the insurance with a single premium paid when issuing the debt; the premium is a percentage of total debt service on the debt. Almost half of state and local government long-term debt is now insured.

Bond order   Act of a jurisdiction's governing body authorizing the issuance of debt. For general obligation bonds and certain other types of debt in many local jurisdictions, the bond order must also be approved by the voters in a bond referendum. *See also* bond referendum

Bond rating   Assessment of the credit quality of particular debt. A bond rating evaluates the willingness and ability of the issuer to repay the debt with periodic interest when due and to meet other obligations under the bond contract. *See also* rating agency

Bond referendum   The authorization of other debt by the voters in a referendum. In most states, local government general obligation bonds must be approved by the voters in a referendum.

Bond registrar   Entity that maintains the ownership records for bonds or debt. Today, the Depository Trust Company of New York, a corporation owned by major banks and financial institutions, serves as the registrar for most local government debt sold publicly. A bank and trust company can also serve as the registrar for local government debt. *See also* Depository Trust Company

Bond resolution   *See* bond order

Book entry   A form in which debt is issued. Book entry generally means that the debt exists on the computerized records of the registrar. Such records record the owners of the debt, or of the dealers or financial institutions whose customers own the debt. In the latter case, the records of the dealers and financial institutions record the specific owners.

Budget   A plan for spending revenues and to provide services, achieve objectives, buy items, and/or carry out projects. Budgets generally balance or should balance revenues and spending. The legally enacted budgets make revenues available for spending and/or provide authority to spend. The legal budget may also levy taxes and raise other revenues. Most budgets are for a fixed term—usually one year. Some budgets have project lives, providing spending authority for the length of time it takes to complete a project. *See also* operating budget

Call   Right of the issuer to require the owners of debt to sell the debt back to the issuer. Many local government long-term debt issues include call options. Generally, the options take effect only after the debt has been outstanding for several years. This gives investors protection from call for that time. The issuer is able to call in the debt any time after that call protection period ends. The most common reason for an issuer to call in debt is to refund it with new debt at lower interest rates. *See also* refunding debt

Call option   *See* call

Call premium   The price that an issuer pays to investors to call in or redeem debt before maturity. The call premium is expressed as a percentage of the called debt's par value.

Capital appreciation bond   Bond or debt sold at a significant discount from par value and that pays no interest. As the bonds move toward maturity, they appreciate in value; at maturity, investors receive the full par value of the bonds. The appreciation that occurs between issuance and maturity constitutes interest.

Capital asset   Property that has an initial useful life longer than one year and that is of significant value. The useful life of most capital assets extends well beyond one year. "Significant value" is defined by an organization's capitalization policy. For most local governments today, it ranges between $500 and $5,000. Capital assets include land, infrastructure, buildings, renovations to buildings that increase their value, equipment, vehicles, and other tangible and intangible assets that have useful lives longer than one year. Also called a fixed asset. *See also* infrastructure

Capital budget   A budget that identifies and balances revenues or other financial resources and spending for the acquisition or construction of major capital projects or assets. The recommended capital budget often originates from the first year of a multiyear capital improvement program. It may be presented in the operating budget document or in a separate document for the capital budget. Legal appropriation of money for capital projects may occur in the annual or operating budget ordinance or in one or more capital project ordinances or resolutions. *See also* capital asset; operating budget

Capital budgeting   The process and methods used in preparing and enacting the capital budget. Capital budgeting typically involves the raising and spending of large sums of money and results in the acquisition or construction of long-lived and expensive capital assets. It includes multiyear capital improvement programming and financial forecasting; the translation of capital and financial plans and financial forecasts into capital budgets; capital financing sources and strategies;

and capital project authorization, appropriation, and implementation. *See also* capital asset; capital budget

Capital expenditure   An outlay that results in or contributes to the acquisition or construction of a capital asset. *See also* capital asset

Capital financing   Money that is raised and spent to build or acquire a capital asset. Capital financing can include the proceeds of different types of debt: general obligation bonds, revenue bonds, certificates of participation or capital lease debt, and some forms of special or limited obligation bonds. Capital financing can also include annually levied taxes or revenues, capital reserves, impact fees and other charges to property, grants, and other sources that are allocated and spent to help build and acquire capital assets. Capital financing raised through the issuance of debt must be repaid. *See also* bond; capital reserve; certificate of participation; debt; general obligation bond; grant; impact fee; pay-as-go capital financing; revenue bond

Capital improvement program (CIP)   A multiyear forecast of major capital building, infrastructure, and equipment needs. The forecast period is most often five or six years, although some CIPs cover shorter or longer periods. The CIP not only identifies future capital needs but also the capital appropriations or estimated spending required to make those needs a reality, sources of capital financing, and their impact on future operating budgets. The CIP is essentially a plan with its first year often becoming the capital budget for the year. *See also* capital budget

Capital lease   Lease classification of the Governmental Accounting Standards Board (GASB); in this book, also designates a lease that is used for capital financing purposes. Under GASB rules, a capital lease is one that meets one of four conditions: (1) it transfers ownership of the leased property to the lessee; (2) the lease contains a bargain or nominal purchase option; (3) the lease covers 75 percent or more of the estimated economic or useful life of the leased property; and (4) the present value of the lease payments equals or exceeds 90 percent of the fair value of the leased property at the lease's inception. Local government installment or lease purchase financings and certificates of participation are capital leases. *See also* certificate of participation; Governmental Accounting Standards Board; installment-purchase agreement.

Capital needs assessment   The identification of capital facility, infrastructure, and equipment needs over a long-term future planning period. The planning period for capital needs assessment often extends 10, 15, or even 20 years into the future. Citizens and community groups as well as officials are often involved. Capital needs assessment may take place as part of a long-term comprehensive plan process or strategic planning. Specific financing for capital needs is usually not identified in a capital needs assessment process. *See also* capital improvement program

Capital project ordinance   A budget that estimates revenues and authorizes spending for a capital project. A capital project ordinance typically has a project rather than a fiscal-year life; that is, spending authority does not lapse at the end of a fiscal period or year but is available for the length of time necessary to complete the project. *See also* capital budget

Capital projects fund   A fund established to account for financial resources to acquire or construct large capital facilities or assets, other than those accounted for in enterprise or trust funds.

Capital recovery charges   *See* impact fee

Capital reserve   Money raised and set aside to finance future capital improvements or acquisitions. Capital reserves are essentially savings accounts. They can take various forms: a designation or reserving of general or other operating fund balances, a separate capital reserve fund, an equipment replacement or infrastructure rehabilitation revolving fund, etc. *See also* equipment replacement revolving fund

Capitalization of interest   Payment of interest on debt from the debt proceeds. Under generally accepted accounting principles, the capitalization of interest is allowed during project construction.

Catalog of Federal Domestic Assistance   A list with brief descriptions of federal grants; the catalog is available on the Internet at www.cfda.gov/ and is published by the Office of Management and Budget.

Certificate of participation (COP)   Shares in a debt obligation created by a capital lease (installment- or lease-purchase contract) that are sold to or placed with investors. COPs are typically used for capital leases for large projects where the financing exceeds $10 million. The certificates are secured by the property financed with the debt and are actually sold by an on-behalf-of entity that acts for the state and local government in issuing the debt. That entity serves as the lessor, and the governmental unit acts as the lessee in the transaction. *See also* capital lease; installment-purchase agreement; private placement

Closing date   Date on which the issuer delivers debt securities to the underwriter and on which the underwriter hands over debt proceeds to the issuer. This date is often different from the date on which interest begins to accrue on the debt. *See also* dated date

Collateral   *See* security pledged for debt

Competitive public sale of debt   Sale in which an issuer sends out and/or publishes a notice of sale for the debt and seeks competitive bids from underwriters, selects the underwriter offering the lowest average interest rate (highest price), and sells the debt to that underwriter. The underwriter then resells the debt to investors. *See also* negotiated public sale of debt; private placement; public sale of debt

Compound   Earn or accrue. The interest on long-term municipal debt is earned and paid semiannually. *See also* interest; interest rate

Conditional sales lease   A lease classification of the Internal Revenue Service. Under IRS Rule 55-540, a conditional sales lease is one that meets one or more of six criteria. Some are the same as the criteria of GASB to identify a capital lease. One IRS criterion not used by GASB provides that if some portion of the periodic lease payments identify interest, the transaction is likely to be considered a conditional sales lease. Local government installment or lease purchase financings and certificates of participation are conditional sales leases. *See also* capital lease; certificate of participation; installment-purchase agreement; lease-purchase financing

Consulting engineer   An independent and expert consultant who is needed for projects financed with revenue bonds. The consulting engineer determines whether the project or enterprise for which the project is being built will produce enough net revenue to cover debt service on the new bonds as well as any existing debt of the project or enterprise. *See also* coverage; revenue bond

Coupon   *See* coupon interest

Coupon interest   Interest on bonds or debt. In the past, when bonds were issued in certificated form, coupons were attached to the certificates, one for each interest payment date. When an interest payment date arrived, the investor clipped the coupon for that date and presented it for payment. Today municipal bonds are issued in book-entry or electronic form, and there are no coupons. Nonetheless, the interest due on bonds or debt is still commonly called coupon interest.

Coupon interest rate   The specified annual interest rate payable on bonds or debt. *See also* coupon interest; interest; interest rate

Coupon rate   *See* coupon interest rate

Covenant   *See* indenture

Coverage   The ratio of net revenues or earnings (for an enterprise or project) to annual debt service on revenue and other debt issued to finance capital facilities for the enterprise or project. To issue revenue bonds, a local government must demonstrate through an engineering feasibility study that annual net revenues will be sufficient to cover debt service.

Credit   In capital finance, the ability to incur and repay debt. A local government's general credit depends on the strength of the local and regional economy, the local unit's financial strength, financial management, debt burden, and governance and planning. *See also* bond rating

Credit facility   Accompanies local government issuance of variable rate debt. Investors in such debt generally have the option to put (sell) the debt back to the issuer on any date that the interest rate on the debt may reset or vary. The issuer must have quick access to money (i.e., a credit facility) to be able to repurchase any debt that investors put back to the issuer. A credit facility usually takes the form of a bank letter of credit in which the bank guarantees to pay any debt put back to the issuer. The issuer pays an initial fee and an annual renewal fee for the letter of credit. If the issuer draws funds under the letter of credit, it must repay these funds to the bank. The issuer does so by employing a remarketing agent to resell the put debt to other investors. *See also* put option; variable-rate demand debt

Current yield   The ratio, expressed as a percentage, of the interest on a bond or debt to the purchase price of the bond or debt. *See also* coupon interest; interest; interest rate

CUSIP number   Unique identifying number for a security issued in book entry form. CUSIP numbers are assigned by the Committee on Uniform Securities Identification Procedures, which is a subsidiary of Standard & Poor's Corporation, McGraw Hill, New York. An issuer's financial adviser or bond counsel will typically arrange for the assignment of a CUSIP number. *See also* book entry

Dated date   Date on which interest begins to accrue on debt. *See also* closing date

Debt   Money or other property lent or borrowed and that must be repaid or returned. Debt may be outstanding for a short term (one year or less) or for a long term (one year or more). The debtor is charged interest while debt is outstanding. The interest on most debt that local governments issue for capital financing purposes is paid each year while the debt is outstanding. The interest on some other debt accrues each year or periodically within the year but is not paid until the end of the debt's term. The accrued interest in one period is added to the debt's principal, and interest in the next period is charged on the principal plus any accrued plus unpaid interest. *See also* debt financing; interest; term

Debt capacity   The capacity of a local government or a particular local utility or enterprise to pay principal and interest on debt as well as meet other needs and commitments. General or "net" debt capacity for a local government is evaluated with a variety of debt ratios: net debt per capita, net debt as a percentage of taxable valuation, net debt as a percentage of personal income, and annual debt service on net debt as a percentage of general fund and related expenditures. The debt capacity of a utility or enterprise is evaluated in terms of coverage as well as other factors. *See also* coverage; net debt

Debt certificate   *See* bond certificate

Debt financing   Money obtained by incurring debt and used to build or acquire capital assets or for other purposes. Debt financing for local government capital projects comes mainly from the issuance of long-term bonds or other debt. Debt financing is one of two general approaches to capital financing; the other approach is pay-as-go capital financing. While most local government debt financing is for capital purposes, some local units issue debt to finance cash flow needs or deficits in their operating budgets. *See also* debt; pay-as-go capital financing

Debt issuance   The process of selling debt. Local governments issue debt in public sales or private placement. In a public sale, the local issuer sells its debt to bond or debt underwriters who then resell the debt to the investing public. In a private placement, the issuer places the debt directly with the ultimate investor, usually a bank or other financial institution, which holds the debt in its portfolio. Private placements are typically used for sales of small or modest amounts of debt—less than $10 million—while public sales are typically used to market large debt issues for major projects or financing. *See also* private placement; public sale of debt

Debt limit or cap   A constitutional or statutory limit that many states impose on local government general obligation bonds and sometimes certain other types of debt. The limit is most often expressed as a percentage of the assessed value of taxable property in a jurisdiction. Revenue bonds are typically exempt from such debt limits. In many but not all states, certificates of participation and special or limited obligation debt are also exempt.

Debt retirement   Repayment of debt.

Debt service   Annual or periodic principal and interest payments on debt. Debt service can sometimes include certain other fees, for example, for paying agent services or credit support.

Debt service reserve   A fund that is required for many revenue bond, certificate of participation, and special or limited obligation debt issues. The requirement normally calls for the issuer to maintain an amount in the reserve equal to maximum or average annual debt service on the debt. *See also* surety bond

Debt structure   The retirement or repayment schedule for debt.

Defease   Satisfy an issuer's obligation to pay debt service. Advance refunding defeases existing debt when proceeds from the refunding debt are placed into an escrow account controlled by a third party and are used to pay debt service on the existing debt. *See also* advance refunding

Defeased debt   Outstanding debt for which the issuer's or debtor's obligation to repay has been satisfied. *See also* defease

Deferred maintenance   Maintenance of capital facilities and infrastructure that occurs later than when maintenance should occur. When maintenance is deferred, capital facilities and infrastructure often deteriorate. When maintenance finally occurs, it costs more than it would have cost if it had been done when initially needed. Because of its cost and because deferred maintenance can restore a capital asset's value or utility, it may be called "capital maintenance" and classified as a capital expenditure.

Delayed principal retirement   Postponement for several years of principal retirement on long-term, serial debt. Postponement occurs to blend debt service on the new debt with debt service on existing debt, to put off principal payments until construction is finished, or to provide time for a project financed with revenue bonds to generate new user fees to begin to pay principal on the debt.

Denomination   The amount of a bond or debt instrument. Most state and local government bonds and debt are issued in denominations of $5,000 or multiples thereof.

Depository Trust Company (DTC)   A New York corporation owned by banks, securities firms, and other financial institutions and established for the purpose of serving as a national repository for publicly sold securities in the United States. The DTC serves as the depository and registrar for most local government debt issues.

Deterministic estimation or forecasting   A method of estimating or forecasting a revenue source or spending item by relating the revenues or spending to another variable. For example, sales tax revenue may be estimated and forecast by relating it to changes in disposable personal income. Such income is estimated or forecast, which in turn determines sales tax revenue for the forecast period. Informed judgment tempers or should temper deterministic forecasting.

Discount   An amount below a debt's par value. Underwriters may pay a discounted price for debt, with the price paid equal to par less the discount. *See also* par value; premium; yield

Discount rate   Interest rate used to convert future cash flows to their present value. *See also* present value

Early redemption   Repayment of debt prior to the due date or maturity date of the debt. Many local government long-term debt issues include a redemption feature that allows the issuer to "call in" and repay outstanding debt before maturity. An early-redemption feature can be optional or mandatory. Optional redemption gives the issuer the choice of whether to call in debt prior to maturity. Mandatory redemption, which is used in revenue and special obligation bond issues, requires the issuer to call in or redeem certain term bonds in years prior to their maturity date. *See also* call; call premium; refunding debt

Econometric model   A model that combines a variety of economic and other variables to estimate or forecast revenues and spending. Econometric models are used by state governments and large local governments as tools in budgeting and multiyear financial forecasting.

Economic development bond   Another name for tax increment bond or debt. *See also* tax increment debt

Effective interest cost (EIC)   Method of calculating the average interest rate for a long-term debt issue. The EIC rate discounts all future debt service payments on debt (principal, interest, and other related expenses) to net debt proceeds. *See also* net debt proceeds; net interest cost; true interest cost

Elasticity   In economics, growth or change in a tax or revenue source or expenditure category in relation to growth or change in the economy. Growth or change in the economy is usually measured by a key economic statistic, for example, personal income or gross product. Elasticity coefficients are sometimes used in multiyear forecasts of revenues and spending. Such a coefficient is a ratio with the numerator being increase or change in a revenue source or category and the denominator increase or change in a measure of general economic activity.

Encumbrance   A reservation of budget authority for a particular purpose. An encumbrance typically occurs when a purchase order or contract is approved. An encumbrance assures that the contracting public entity will have sufficient remaining budget authority to meet payment obligations when due.

Enterprise   A government service to the public that is supported primarily by fees rather than taxes, accounted for in a separate enterprise fund, and operated according to business principles.

Enterprise fund   A separate fund that accounts for a government-owned enterprise. Local governments use enterprise funds for water-sewer, electric and gas, solid waste, stormwater, airport, parking, and other services. *See also* enterprise

Enterprise fund infrastructure   Utility or other enterprise capital assets that are long-lived, usually stationary, and that are financed with enterprise system charges and fees or with bonds or debt repaid from enterprise charges and fees. Enterprise infrastructure includes water and sewer lines and systems, electric and gas lines and facilities; drainage systems when organized as a public enterprise; and roads, bridges, and tunnels that are part of a toll-supported or user fee–supported system.

Equipment replacement revolving fund   A fund used for the purchase of equipment and vehicles as existing equipment and vehicles become unusable and are replaced. The fund may be financed by annual appropriations from the general fund or by rental, usage, or depreciation charges to departments using the equipment and vehicles. While this is an internal service fund for accounting purposes, it also serves as a capital reserve.

Equity   Generally, the difference between assets and liabilities. Equity for a business results from financial resources that owners, including stockholders, contribute and from business retained earnings. In government, pay-as-go capital financing is comparable with equity financing of capital projects for a business. Pay-as-go financing includes current revenues contributed annually by taxpayers (owners' financial contributions) and used for capital projects, and money from capital reserves, which are revenues in excess of spending in prior years (revenues retained from those years).

Essentiality   A term that refers to how vital a particular capital asset is in providing a service and how central or vital the service is to the community. If the asset and the service are essential, a local government is less likely to default or stop making payments on debt issued to finance the asset. Water-sewer, education, and public safety and the capital facilities or assets used for them are generally considered to be essential. Essentiality is especially important in evaluating the credit of certificates of participation and other debt secured by the asset financed with the debt.

Even annual debt service   A debt retirement schedule in which annual debt service (principal and interest) remains the same during the term of the debt. The interest portion of debt service decreases and principal portion increases over the term of the debt. *See also* even annual principal

Even annual principal   A debt retirement schedule in which the principal repaid annually is the same over the term of the debt. This results in declining annual debt service. As debt outstanding declines, the interest and debt service paid annually decrease. *See also* even annual debt service

Exaction   Contribution of money or other property by a developer that a local government uses to provide infrastructure, amenities, or service to a development being built by the developer. Exactions arise out of the development review and approval process. They are typically negotiated on the basis of general guidelines and agreed to on the basis of the specific impact that a development will have on local infrastructure and services. Exactions are sometimes an alternative to impact fees. In other cases, exactions supplement impact fees and help a local government provide infrastructure or services that are unique or special to a development.

Expenditure   A decrease in net financial assets in the general fund or another governmental fund. Under the modified accrual basis of accounting, a local government incurs an expenditure when a good or service is provided to it, creating a liability for payment or generating immediate payment.

Face value   *See* par value

Facility fee   *See* impact fee

Federal funds   Money that banks are required to deposit with the Federal Reserve. Such deposits serve as reserves for the U.S. banking system. Member banks lend and borrow the excess reserves among one another at the prevailing federal funds rate. Federal funds are immediately available to settle transactions, including bond sales.

Financial adviser   A consultant who advises an issuer about capital financing options, the amount and type of debt to issue, debt structure, and other matters related to capital budgeting and finance. In negotiated sales of debt, the underwriter provides financial advisory as well as underwriting services. Some firms providing financial advisory services do not underwrite debt. *See also* underwriter

Financial forecast   A projection over a multiyear period of annual revenues and spending. The forecast normally covers the same future period as the capital improvement program. A multiyear financial forecast supports both the operating and capital budgets.

Fiscal year   A designated twelve-month period for budgeting and record-keeping purposes. Many local governments' fiscal years begin on July 1 and end on June 30; others begin on October 1 and end on September 30, which corresponds to the federal government's fiscal year; and still others follow the calendar year, beginning January 1 and ending December 31.

Fixed asset   *See* capital asset

Fixed interest rate   Interest rate on debt that remains the same for the length of time the debt is outstanding.

Fund   A fiscal entity with a self-balancing set of accounts that includes cash and other assets, related liabilities, revenues, expenditures or expenses, and residual equities or fund balances. Governmental accounting information is organized and reported by fund to show the resources involved in carrying out specific functions.

Fund balance   The difference between a governmental fund's assets and liabilities. Portions of the fund balance may be reserved or designated, for example, for encumbrances. For the general funds, fund balance available at the end of one year for next year's budget can be calculated by adding cash and investments or cash equivalents and subtracting liabilities, encumbrances, and any of the following year's revenues that have been collected in advance.

General fund   The main operating fund of most local governments. The general fund typically accounts for governmental functions supported by general taxes and revenues, such as police and fire protection, and financial resources that legal requirements do not require to be accounted for in another fund.

General obligation (GO) bond   Bond secured by a governmental issuer's pledge of unlimited taxing power. GO bonds are also known as full-faith-and-credit debt because of the unconditional pledge to repay the debt with all possible revenue-raising capabilities. In many states, the authorization of GO bonds requires the approval of voters in a referendum. *See also* revenue bond

General purpose infrastructure   Infrastructure such as streets, roads, bridges, tunnels, greenways, parks, and other long-lived property that serves the general public and is financed with general taxes or revenues, either directly or with bonds that are repaid from general taxes and revenues.

Generally accepted accounting principles (GAAP)   Rules, conventions, and procedures that serve as norms for accounting and the fair presentation of financial statements. GAAP for state and local governments are established by the Governmental Accounting Standards Board (GASB). At the federal level, accounting standards are established by the Federal Accounting Standards Advisory Board.

Governmental Accounting Standards Board (GASB)   The body that sets accounting and financial reporting standards for state and local governments.

Grant   Gift of money from one government to another organization. The federal government and state governments give grants to local governments to help finance local capital projects. Unlike bonds or debt, grants do not have to be repaid. Also known as grant-in-aid.

Impact fee   Charge to new development for public improvements that serve that development or that type of development. Unlike special assessments, impact fees may be charged to finance infrastructure or facilities that are located at some distance from the new development paying the fees. They are usually levied when development is approved and often in advance of when the public improvements for which they are levied are built. Impact fees for residential development are often a specified dollar amount per residential unit. Impact fees for commercial and industrial development are often per square foot of improved space. Other terms for impact fees are "capital recovery charges" and "facility fees." *See also* special assessment

Indenture   Provision in a bond or debt contract. Indentures require the debt issuer to meet certain standards or do certain things. Failure by the issuer to comply with indentures are or can be events of default. Common indentures for revenue bonds require the issuer to set rates high enough so that net revenues cover debt service, maintain a debt service reserve, and properly maintain enterprise facilities. *See also* coverage

Infrastructure   Facilities that are available for public use, stationary, and generally have useful lives going out many decades. Local infrastructure includes streets, roads, sidewalks, bridges, tunnels, stormwater and drainage systems, dams, water supply and sanitary sewer systems, and street lighting.

Installment-purchase agreement   Type of capital lease in which the property acquired with the financing secures or collateralizes the lease. Title to the property passes to the lessee at the inception of the transaction, and the lessor or lender holds a security interest or mortgage in the property to secure the lessee's payments. If the lessee fails to make payments, the lessor may take legal steps to seize the leased property. *See also* capital lease; certificate of participation; lease-purchase financing; security interest

Installment-purchase financing   *See* installment-purchase agreement

Intangible asset   An asset that does not exist in physical form or that has a value that is based on only or predominantly nonphysical properties. Intangible assets include licenses, patents, and certain computer software. In the past, governments did not include intangible property among capital or fixed assets. Today a growing number of local governments include certain intangible property among capital or fixed assets. *See also* capital asset

Interest   The price or dollar amount charged at the end of a year or period of time for money owed or borrowed during the year or period. The interest charged on most debt that local governments issue for capital financing purposes is paid each year, usually semiannually. The interest on some debt—for example, debt issued or sold on a discount basis—is not paid until the end of the debt's term. Interest charged and earned in a year or period is added to the principal amount of the debt, and interest in the next year or period is charged on the principal amount of the debt and any earned but unpaid interest. *See also* debt; interest rate; principal; term

Interest rate   Ratio of interest to the principal amount of a loan or debt. Interest may be earned or compounded and paid annually or more frequently—semiannually, quarterly, monthly, or daily. Interest is typically quoted on an annual or annual equivalent basis.

Interfund transfer   The transfer of money from one fund to another. Interfund transfers usually must be approved by the governing body.

Internal rate of return   An interest rate that equates an initial investment or loan to future cash flows that result from that investment or loan. Calculation of an internal rate of return considers the time value of money and uses one or more interest rate formulas. The calculation of a true interest cost (TIC) interest rate for a bond issue is an internal rate of return calculation. *See also* true interest cost

Internal services fund   A fund that may be used to account for any activity that provides goods or services to other departments or funds within the same government. An internal services fund charges fees to the departments using its services, usually on a cost-reimbursement basis. Some local governments use internal services funds to finance equipment replacement. *See also* equipment replacement revolving fund

Investment grade rating   A rating that qualifies debt or another security as nonspeculative. Banks, many mutual funds, and other financial institutions may buy only investment-grade debt. The investment grade ratings of the national rating agencies are BBB- or Baa3 and above. *See also* bond rating; rating agency

Issuance costs for debt   The up-front costs that a debt issuer incurs in selling or placing debt. Issuance costs for publicly sold debt include fees for the bond attorney, bond ratings, underwriting, printing, and paying agent. Additional issuance costs are incurred for certain types of debt; for example, fees for financial advisory services, feasibility studies, underwriters' counsel, trustee, title insurance, liquidity support, and other items. Debt issuance costs are customarily paid from debt proceeds.

Lease-purchase agreement   *See* lease-purchase financing

Lease-purchase financing A capital lease in which title to the leased property remains with the lessor during the lease term or until the lessee exercises a purchase option to transfer title to the lessee. At the end of the lease term, the lessee pays a nominal purchase option to obtain title. *See also* capital lease; installment-purchase agreement

Letter of credit (LOC) Commitment issued by a bank or financial institution to provide a short-term loan under specific conditions. A local government issuing variable-rate demand debt must obtain a letter of credit to provide liquidity support for the debt. Variable-rate debt has a put option, giving investors the right to sell the debt back to the issuer on any date that the interest rates for the debt can vary or reset. The LOC gives the issuer bridge financing while new, permanent financing to refund the put debt is arranged. *See also* variable-rate demand debt

Limited obligation debt Debt that is secured by a limited tax or revenue source. *See also* special obligation debt

Long-term debt Debt that that has an overall term of thirteen months or longer. The *Bond Buyer* distinguishes between bonds, with terms of thirteen months or longer, and notes, with terms of twelve months or less. Bonds include not only bonds but other long-term debt securities, for example, certificates of participation. *See also* short-term debt

Mandate A federal requirement imposed on state and local governments or a state requirement imposed on local governments. Mandates are often imposed without compensation from the higher level of government. They have resulted in significant capital spending and debt issuance by local governments.

Mandatory call Feature of a bond or debt issue that requires the issuer to redeem certain bonds in the issue on specified dates prior to the dates these bonds are scheduled to mature. Mandatory call is required for term maturities or bonds included in many revenue bond, certificate of participation, and special obligation bond issues. The mandatory call feature typically requires the issuer to place money into a sinking fund to fund the redemption of bonds subject to mandatory call before maturity. *See also* call; maturity; sinking fund; term bond

Material fact Fact or information that is significant to a decision. For the sale of bonds, a material fact is information that is significant to investors as they decide whether or not to buy the bonds. If a material fact is omitted from an official statement used in selling the bonds or if a material fact in the statement is in error, the underwriters and others involved in the sale, including officials of the issuer, under Securities and Exchange Commission regulations could be held liable for investor losses and damages. If fraud is alleged, those responsible could be prosecuted criminally.

Maturity Amount of serial bond principal that is scheduled to be retired in a particular year or amount of term bond principal that is subject to mandatory call in a particular year. Issues of long-term debt are made up of multiple maturities. *See also* mandatory call; serial bond; term bond

Maturity date Date on which specific bonds or debt is scheduled to be retired.

Moral obligation debt   Debt that is partly secured by a moral but not a legal pledge of a governmental entity. The primary or initial security for the debt is typically a special revenue source, such as rental payments on subsidized housing. The issuer's additional moral obligation pledge says that it promises, but is not legally obligated, to use other available revenue to pay the debt if the legally pledged revenue proves to be insufficient. *See also* special obligation debt

Municipal debt   In general, this is all debt that state and local governments and their on-behalf-of issuers incur. The preponderance of state and local debt is tax exempt; sometimes municipal debt refers only to such tax-exempt debt. *See also* tax-exempt debt

Municipal lease   Generally, a capital lease in which a state or local government finances the construction or acquisition of a capital asset. Like municipal debt, nearly all municipal leases are tax exempt, and municipal lease usually refers to the same thing as tax-exempt lease. *See also* capital lease; municipal debt; tax-exempt lease

Municipal Securities Rulemaking Board (MSRB)   The MSRB is an independent 15-member board created by the Securities and Exchange Act of 1975 to provide regulatory oversight of dealers, banks, and brokers in municipal or state and local government securities.

Negotiated public sale of debt   A sale of debt in which the issuer first selects an underwriter or underwriting group to handle the sale. The underwriter and the issuer negotiate and agree on debt structure and pricing. The underwriter advertises and markets the debt to potential investors, buys the debt from the issuer, and resells it to investors. *See also* competitive public sale of debt; private placement; public sale of debt

Net debt   Debt that is paid from generally available taxes and revenues. Net debt is usually defined as gross or total debt less (1) money on hand and pledged to pay debt, (2) revenue bonds or debt, and (3) general obligation or other debt paid from the earnings or revenues of a self-supporting enterprise or activity. Net debt also refers to debt subject to state constitutional or statutory debt limits.

Net debt proceeds   The principal amount of the debt, plus accrued interest and any original issue premium, less any original issue discount, and less all issuance costs, including the underwriter's spread, insurance, attorneys' and rating agency fees.

Net interest cost (NIC)   Total interest to be paid on a debt issue less any discount or plus any premium that investors pay in buying the debt. A NIC-based average interest rate is calculated by dividing net interest by the product of the principal amount of the debt issue and its years' average maturity. This calculation of average interest rate fails to take into account when interest and debt service payments are made (the time value of money). The calculation is still used today for general obligation bonds because it is relatively simple to compute and, with limitations on bids, normally produces the same result as the true interest cost (TIC) method. *See also* true interest cost; years' average maturity

Net working capital   The difference between current assets and current liabilities. *See also* quick ratio

Non–ad valorem tax debt   Debt that is secured by available taxes or revenues other than the issuer's ad valorem tax or property tax. The taxes or revenues pledged to secure and pay the debt are limited; therefore the debt is special or limited and is not general obligation debt. *See also* special obligation debt

Nonappropriation   A provision in most installment- or lease-purchase financing or a certificate of participation issue that allows a governmental lessee to cease making periodic lease payments by choosing not to appropriate or budget money to make those payments. The nonappropriation provision keeps future payment obligations of the governmental lessee from being classified as subject to legal debt limits and voter approval requirements under state law. *See also* abatement; capital lease; certificate of participation; installment-purchase agreement; lease-purchase financing

Non–local tax debt   Debt that is secured by available revenues other than taxes levied by the issuer. The revenues pledged to secure and pay the debt are limited; therefore the debt is special or limited and is not general obligation debt. *See also* non–ad valorem tax debt; special obligation debt

Non–property tax debt   *See* non–ad valorem tax debt

Normal yield curve   A yield curve relates yields or interest rates on debt to the maturity, term, or period of time over which the debt is outstanding. Generally, as the term or maturity period for debt lengthens, the yields expected by investors on the debt increase. This reflects the greater risk associated with longer-term compared with shorter-term investments. The normal yield curve reflects this pattern and is upward sloping. In some markets, the yield curve for debt becomes flat (the yields demanded for longer- and for shorter-term debt are roughly the same) or the yield curve inverts (shorter-term debt has higher interest rates and yields than longer-term debt).

Notice of sale   A document that advertises debt for sale competitively. The notice is a document several pages in length that provides key information about the debt and the issuer that would be of interest to underwriters that may bid to buy the debt. In negotiated sales of debt, the underwriter often develops an abbreviated notice of sale.

Obligation   A contractual commitment to pay or perform another duty; often used to refer to debt or bonds. Some obligations are conditional, for example, requiring payment or performance only if the other party (or parties) to the contract fulfill their obligations.

Official statement (OS)   Disclosure document used in debt sales to provide information about the debt and the issuer to investors. Before the sale, the OS is called the preliminary official statement (POS) and provides information that investors need to evaluate the debt. After the sale, the POS is updated with information about the results of the sale and is reissued as the official statement. *See also* preliminary official statement

On-behalf-of issuer   An organization that a state or a local government establishes to issue capital lease, lease revenue, or certain other types of debt for the purpose of building or acquiring facilities to be used by that state or local government. Many state and local governments use such on-behalf-of debt-issuing organizations. Although such an organization is legally separate in important ways from the jurisdiction that establishes it, its officers are typically officials of the jurisdiction, and its purpose is to obtain debt financing for the jurisdiction. *See also* special authority

Operating budget   A budget that identifies revenues and spending for ongoing services and activities. Most operating budgets are prepared and enacted annually and are called annual budgets. Some are prepared for biennial periods. The revenues and spending are or should be balanced for the year or operating period. The recommended operating budget is typically prepared by the manager or chief executive officer and presented in an operating or annual budget document. That document may also contain the recommended capital budget for the year. The legally enacted operating budget is approved by the governing board in an annual budget ordinance or resolution. *See also* capital budget

Operating capital   Equipment, vehicles, and other capital assets that are budgeted and accounted for in the operating budget rather than in the capital budget. Such assets are relatively modest in cost, and spending for them recurs annually or fairly regularly. They are readily financed from recurring revenues in the operating budget.

Operating lease   A lease that is not a capital lease under rules of the Governmental Accounting Standards Board. In an operating lease, the lessee makes periodic payments to obtain use of but not ownership of the lessor's property. *See also* capital lease

Overlapping local government   A local government that levies taxes on and/or raises revenues from some of the same citizens as another underlying local government. For example, a county is an overlapping government for any city in the county if the county levies taxes on city residents. An assessment of the city's debt capacity must consider not only city debt and finances but also county debt and finances. *See also* underlying local government

Par value   The principal amount of debt. This is the amount borrowed that must be repaid at maturity. *See also* maturity; principal

Parity bonds or debt   Bonds or debt that have equal claim on revenues pledged to pay debt service. A local government with outstanding revenue bonds is often prohibited by the bond contract from issuing additional bonds of equal, or parity, standing secured by the same revenues, unless certain additional bonds tests are met. One common test is that net revenues from the revenue bond–financed activity exceed maximum annual debt service on the existing bonds or on the existing and the proposed new bonds by a specified ratio, for example, 1.25:1.

Pay-as-go capital financing   Paying for capital projects and acquisitions from sources other than debt. Pay-as-go sources include current taxes and revenues, taxes and revenues raised in prior years and held as capital reserves, current or prior years' charges to property such as special assessments and impact fees, and grant revenues from the federal, state, or other governments. Also known as pay-as-you-go capital financing.

Pay-down of debt   Schedule for the retirement of the principal amount of outstanding bonds or debt.

Paying agent   Trust company, bank, or financial institution that receives money for periodic debt service from the issuer or trustee for the debt issue and then, on the interest payment and maturity due dates, distributes the money among the owners or holders of the debt. The paying agent also serves as the registrar for debt, maintaining records of who owns the debt. The Depository Trust Company of New York serves as the paying agent as well as registrar for much local government debt. *See also* book entry; Depository Trust Company

Pledged security   *See* security pledged for debt

Preliminary official statement (POS)   Disclosure document used in public sales of debt to describe the debt, the pledged security, indentures or covenants, maturity schedule and dates, the issuer, the issuer's financial condition and operations, economic and social factors that are relevant to the debt offering, risks, and other material information that investors need to evaluate the debt. The POS is issued before the sale of debt and is used to market the debt. After the sale, the POS is updated with information about the results of the sale and is reissued as the official statement. *See also* official statement

Premium   An amount over a debt's par value. Underwriters may pay a premium price for particular debt, with the price including par plus a premium. *See also* discount; par value; yield

Present value   The value today of money to be received or paid in the future. Present value is calculated with interest rate formulas. The calculations are used often in capital finance to, for example, determine the average interest rate with the true interest cost method. *See also* true interest cost

Pricing debt   The process that underwriters use to establish the interest rates that the issuer will pay on debt; par, premium, or discount prices that investors are asked to pay in buying the debt; and the yields that investors will earn given the prices they pay for the debt. Pricing occurs as underwriters buy debt from the issuer and resell it to investors.

Principal   The par value of debt and the amount that must be repaid at maturity.

Private placement   A method of borrowing money and incurring debt. In a private placement, the issuer places the debt with a single lender or investor or with a small number (defined under rules of the U. S. Securities and Exchange Commission) of sophisticated investors. Local governments that issue less than $10 million in debt in a calendar year often place the debt privately with a bank or financial institution. Such debt is called "bank-qualified," meaning that banks can deduct their costs in buying the debt. Private placement of large amounts of debt occasionally occurs. Issuance costs for private placements of debt are generally much lower than for public sales of debt.

Private-purpose debt   Debt issued by state and local governments or their on-behalf-of issuers for essentially private purposes. State and local governments issue private purpose debt to finance capital facilities for private, nonprofit hospitals, schools, and institutions of higher education; housing for low- and moderate-income persons; small business and industrial facilities; and other purposes. Private-purpose state and local government debt may or may not be tax exempt, depending on the objectives of current federal tax policy. Much private-purpose debt is subject to federally imposed state caps on such debt. Private-purpose debt is also subject to the alternative minimum tax.

Project ordinance   *See* capital project ordinance

Public sale of debt   A sale in which an underwriter or underwriting group buys the debt from the issuer, advertises it to potential investors, and resells the debt to investors. Public sales may be either competitive or negotiated, and they are distinguished from private placements of debt. *See also* competitive public sale of debt; negotiated public sale of debt; private placement

Purchase option   Contractual right of the lessee in a leasing arrangement to acquire title or clear ownership of the leased property. In an installment- or lease-purchase financing, the governmental lessee often has an option to purchase the leased property on any lease payment date by paying the unpaid principal balance on the lease. At the end of the term, the lessee acquires title or clear ownership by exercising a nominal purchase option (often just $1). True leases also often have purchase options; they must or should be exercised at or near fair market value.

Put option   The right of holders of debt to sell it back to the issuer. A put option is found in the variable-rate demand debt that some local governments issue. A put option can be exercised on any date that the interest rate may reset. *See also* variable-rate demand debt

Quick ratio   The ratio of current assets (consisting of cash, cash equivalents or investments, and accounts receivable) to current liabilities. This ratio is used as a measure of the capacity of a public enterprise to meet cash flow needs and current or short-term payment obligations (generally those due within one year's time). The quick ratio can affect an analysis of the feasibility or credit strength of a revenue bond issue.

Rating agency   An agency that evaluates and rates debt. Three national agencies rate local government debt in the United States: Standard & Poor's Corporation, Moody's Investors Service, and Fitch/IBCA. They rate local government bonds or debt at the request of the issuer, and the issuer pays for the ratings. There are also some regional and state rating agencies, for example, the North Carolina Municipal Council.

Refunded bond or debt   Debt that has been replaced by the issuance of new debt, called refunding debt. *See also* refunding; refunding debt

Refunding   Process of replacing previously issued bonds or debt with new debt. This is done to lower interest costs, escape limiting bond indentures on the prior debt, or better match future debt service and revenues.

Refunding bond   *See* refunding debt

Refunding debt   Debt issued to refund or defease previously existing debt.

Registered bond   Bond for which ownership records are maintained by the registrar/paying agent for a bond issue. Distinguished from bearer bonds, for which the holder of the bond is presumed to be the owner. *See also* bearer bond; paying agent

Registrar *See* paying agent

Re-offer yield Yield that underwriter offers investors when the underwriter is selling debt that has been purchased from issuers. When the underwriter buys a local government debt issue, the underwriter establishes the interest rate that the issuer will have to pay and the prices that the investors pay to buy the debt. The prices can and often do vary from maturity to maturity. The prices may be at par, at a premium, or at a discount from the face value of a maturity. This pricing creates re-offer yields for investors that often are different from the interest rates paid by the issuer. *See also* yield

Revenue bond Bond secured by and repaid from specific and limited revenues. The pledged revenues are most often net revenues or earnings from a self-supporting utility or enterprise. (This is the meaning given to revenue bonds in this book.) Other revenue bonds secured by and repaid from revenues are derived from special or limited taxes. *See also* general obligation bond

Revenue lease A lease, issued by the on-behalf-of entity, between a government and its on-behalf-of debt issuer that secures debt, which is usually in the form of certificates of participation or revenue-lease bonds. The debt finances the construction or acquisition of assets for use by the government unit. In the revenue lease, the government unit promises to make annual lease payments to the on-behalf-of issuer; the on-behalf-of issuer pledges to secure and pay debt service on the certificates of participation or the revenue-lease bonds. *See also* certificate of participation; revenue-lease bond

Revenue-lease bond Bond or debt secured by lease revenues paid by a state or local government lessee to an on-behalf-of entity that issued the debt in order to acquire capital assets for use by the government unit. The debt is also likely to be secured by the capital asset(s) financed with the revenue-lease bonds. *See* revenue lease

Rule 15c2-12 A Securities and Exchange Commission rule that requires underwriters of municipal debt to obtain and review disclosure documents before committing to purchase the debt.

Sale/leaseback An arrangement in which an owner of property sells it to another party and executes an agreement to lease the property back from the buyer.

Secondary market Dealers, brokers, and investors who buy, sell, or arrange purchases and sales of debt or other securities that were previously issued and are still outstanding. This market is distinguished from the primary or original issue market.

Security interest Legal right that a lender or lessor has in property for which the lender or lessor extends credit to a debtor or lessee to acquire and use. In installment- or lease-purchase financing or other capital leases, the lessor often transfers title of the leased property to the lessee at the inception of the lease agreement. The lessor obtains a security interest in the property. If the lessee stops making lease payments, the security interest gives the lessor the right to take legal steps to seize the property and satisfy the lessee's payment obligations. If the leased property is land or other real property, the security interest is in the form of a mortgage.

Security pledged for debt   The collateral for debt and/or the legal actions that investors or lenders can take to enforce debt or lease payment and recoup the unpaid financing with interest that they had provided. The security pledged for most local government general obligation debt is the unlimited power to levy property taxes. If the issuer defaults, the investors can secure a court order compelling the issuer to levy property taxes to pay the debt. *See also* certificate of participation; general obligation bond; installment-purchase agreement; revenue bond

Serial bond   Bond in a long-term bond or debt issue; matures annually. *See also* term bond

Serial bond issue   Bond or debt issue with a retirement schedule that consists entirely of annual maturities. *See also* maturity; serial bond

Service standard   As applied to capital budgeting, a performance or service capacity of infrastructure, a capital facility, or equipment. When the infrastructure, facility, or equipment is no longer able to perform up to standard or handle that capacity, then rehabilitation, upgrade, or expansion is needed or new infrastructure or capital assets must be provided.

Short-term debt   Debt issue that matures in twelve months or less. Most short-term debt securities are called notes; for example, bond anticipation notes, tax anticipation notes. *See also* long-term debt

Significant value   The specific dollar amount in a local government's capitalization policy that qualifies an asset that lasts for more than one year as a capital asset. If spending to acquire or build such an asset equals or exceeds that amount, the asset is classified as capital. If such spending is below the capitalization amount, the spending is "expensed" and the asset is classified as a supply or current item. *See also* capital asset

Sinking fund   A fund that accumulates money for future debt service payments. Sinking funds are used with term bonds. The issuer is required to make annual or periodic contributions to a sinking fund to accumulate money for the eventual retirement of the term bonds.

Special assessment   Charges to property for public improvements that benefit that property. The assessed property is typically located near or adjacent to the public improvements. An assessment or benefit district or zone is established, and property within the district is assessed for the improvements. The assessments are typically based on the assessed property's front footage or another acceptable basis. Revenues from special assessments are usually collected after the improvements are built. In many states, special assessments secure special assessment debt. *See also* benefit district debt; special assessment debt

Special assessment debt   Debt that is secured by and paid from special assessments. *See also* special assessment

Special authority   Special authority is sometimes like a special district because it provides a specific service; it usually does not have taxing power and services are supported entirely with user fees or other non-tax revenues. The debt that a special authority issues is usually revenue bonds or some form of special or limited obligation bonds or debt. Other special authorities are on-behalf-of or conduit organizations that issue capital lease or special or limited debt for the state and local governments that establish the authorities. *See also* special district

Special district   A district formed to provide a specific service. The district may serve a broad area that includes several general purpose local governments, a specific area within a single general purpose local government, or it may have borders coterminous with a general purpose local government. If the district serves a broad area, it is likely to have its own governing board. If it serves an area within a general purpose local government or has borders that are coterminous with a general purpose local government, that jurisdiction's governing board often, but not always, serves as the governing board for the district. Most special districts are authorized to levy taxes as well as charge fees for service. Many special districts issue debt to finance capital projects. Such debt is usually special or limited tax debt. If the district provides a service fully supported by user fees, the debt may be revenue bonds. Some districts with unlimited taxing power issue general obligation bonds. *See also* special authority

Special obligation bond   *See* special obligation debt

Special obligation debt   An umbrella term that refers to special or limited tax, non–property tax or non–local tax, special assessment, tax increment, and moral obligation debt. Special obligation debt is secured by limited or special taxes or revenues rather than the full faith and credit and unlimited taxing power of the issuer. Some authorities use the term special obligation debt to designate only non–property tax or non–local tax debt.

Special revenue fund   A fund used to account for the proceeds of special revenue sources (other than for capital projects) that are legally restricted to expenditures for a specific purpose. *See also* capital projects fund

Surety bond   Guaranty provided by an insurance or bonding company that is used in place of a debt service reserve for revenue bonds and certain other types of debt. The surety bond would provide money for the payment of debt service for a year should the issuer be unable to pay it. *See also* debt service reserve

Swap contract   A contract in which a debtor swaps its obligations to make payments on its debt for an obligation to make payments on debt of the counterparty involved in the swap, usually a bank or financial institution. In anticipation of rising interest rates in the future, a local government may swap out of its obligation to make payments on variable- or floating-rate debt and into an obligation to make payments on fixed-rate debt. If interest rates are falling, however, a local entity might swap payment obligations on its fixed rate debt for payment obligations on variable- or floating-rate debt. *See also* fixed interest rate; variable interest rate; variable-rate demand debt

Take-down   A component of the underwriter's spread or fee. Take-down is the sales commission for selling debt. *See also* underwriter's spread

Taxable debt   In the municipal debt markets, debt issued by state and local governments on which the interest earned by investors is subject to federal (and, if applicable, state) income taxes. While the preponderance of state and local government debt is tax exempt, some is taxable. *See also* tax-exempt debt

Taxable equivalent yield Yield that an investor in a certain tax bracket would have to earn on a taxable security to equal the yield on a tax-exempt security. *See also* tax-exempt debt

Tax-exempt debt Debt on which the periodic interest paid is exempt from federal (and, if applicable, state) income taxes. The preponderance of state and local government debt is tax exempt. Tax-exempt debt carries lower interest rates than taxable debt of comparable credit quality. *See also* municipal debt

Tax-exempt lease A capital lease in which the lessee is a state or local government and the periodic lease payments include interest that is exempt from federal (and, if applicable, state) income taxes. For income tax purposes, a tax-exempt lease is the same as tax-exempt debt. *See also* municipal lease; tax-exempt debt

Tax increment debt Debt that is secured by growth in the property tax bases and resulting property tax revenues in a tax increment district. The debt is typically issued to finance public infrastructure needed to support private economic development. All but a few states authorize local governments to issue tax increment debt. Such debt is a form of special or limited obligation debt. *See also* special obligation debt

Tax increment district A defined geographic area in which revenue resulting from growth in the tax base, after formation of the district, is pledged and used to pay off tax increment debt issued to finance improvements to support development in the district.

Term For a bond or debt issue, overall period or total number of years that the bond or debt issue or any part of it is outstanding. For particular bonds or debt, the term is the number of years from issuance to the maturity date for those bonds or debt. *See also* maturity

Term bond Long-term bond or debt that matures on a single date in the future. The issuer is normally required to accumulate money in a sinking fund to retire the bonds when they mature. In the first few decades of the twentieth century, many local governments issued term bonds with a single maturity date for all bonds in the issue. Today most local governments issue serial bonds, with a portion of each issue retired annually over the full term of the issue. However, term bonds make up a portion of the latter maturities of revenue bonds, certificates of participation, and other issues. These modern term bonds combine two to several annual maturities of the bond issue but require that the issuer call in the bonds in each maturity annually as if they were serial bonds. *See also* serial bond

Time value of money Because of the risk associated with the future, money today is worth more than the same amount of money in the future, and money in the near-term future is worth more than the same amount in the far-term future. Interest rates and interest-rate formulas are used in capital finance to account for the time value of money and to convert cash flows occurring over time to a comparable basis of value.

Transfer policy Policy of a local government relating to transfers of revenues or financial resources from one fund to another, especially from a utility or enterprise fund to the general fund or vice versa. The bond rating agencies expect local governments to have and follow transfer policies that protect the financial interests of the affected funds.

Trend analysis   Plotting, graphing, and analyzing economic, financial, and other data over a period of many years. Trend analysis is used by some local governments as a tool in budgeting and multiyear financial forecasting.

True interest cost (TIC)   A method of calculating the average interest rate for long-term debt. The TIC-based rate for debt is the rate, with semi-annual compounding, that equates future principal and interest payments with the purchase price of the debt. Unlike NIC, TIC considers the time value of money. TIC is becoming the standard method used in municipal debt markets to calculate the average interest rate on long-term debt. *See also* effective interest cost; net interest cost

True lease   A lease classification of the Internal Revenue Service. In a true lease, the lessee uses but does not obtain title to or an ownership interest in the leased property. *See also* capital lease; conditional sales lease; operating lease

Trustee   A trustee is required for revenue bonds, certificates of participation, and many types of special or limited obligation debt. The trustee is typically a bank and/or trust company. The trustee represents the interests of the investors or bondholders. The trustee approves the sale of bonds, holds and disburses bond or debt proceeds during construction, receives money for debt service payments and passes it on to the paying agent, approves rate setting for revenue bonds, and oversees the issuer's compliance with bond covenants.

Underlying local government   A local government that levies taxes or raises revenue from citizens who also pay taxes and/or fees to an overlapping local government. For example, a city is an underlying local government for a county if the city levies taxes on county taxpayers who live in the city. An assessment of the debt capacity of the county must consider not only county debt and finances but also underlying city debt and finances. *See also* overlapping local government

Underwriter   An investment banker, securities dealer, bank, or another party that buys debt from the issuer and resells it to investors. Underwriters also function as financial advisers in negotiated sales of debt. *See also* financial adviser; negotiated public sale of debt

Underwriter counsel   Attorney who represents the interests of the underwriter in negotiated bond sales. The primary function of this counsel is to make sure that publications and disclosures by the underwriter and the issuer in a debt sale are accurate and meet Securities and Exchange Commission disclosure requirements. *See also* negotiated public sale of debt

Underwriter's spread   Compensation paid to the underwriter for purchasing and selling securities. Underwriter's spread consist of take-down, a management fee, underwriter's risk, and expenses. *See also* take-down

User fees   Fees paid by those who use public services. User fees cover all or most of the costs of local government utility services and many other public enterprises. They secure and pay revenue bonds and other debt issued to finance utility or enterprise capital infrastructure and facilities. User fees also support a portion of the costs of many governmental or general fund services and sometimes are pledged as security for certain special or limited obligation debt.

Variable interest rate   Interest rate on debt that can change while the debt is outstanding. The rate may be subject to change once every several years, yearly, monthly, weekly, or daily. The debt's interest rate is typically pegged to a market index rate; if that rate has changed by more than a specified margin since the most recent reset date, the interest rate charged on the variable-rate debt changes proportionately. *See* variable-rate demand debt

Variable-rate demand debt   Debt with a variable interest rate that investors can sell or put back to the issuer on any date that the debt's interest rate may change. The interest rate on much variable-rate demand debt issued by local governments may reset weekly. *See also* put option

Years' average maturity   A measure of the average number of years that long-term debt is outstanding. Years' average maturity is calculated by computing total bond years and dividing this by the total principal amount of the issue. Bond years is calculated by multiplying the dollar amount of each maturity by the number of years the maturity is outstanding and summing bond years for each maturity to get total bond years. *See also* maturity

Yield   Annual return, expressed as a percentage, that a lender earns by making a loan or an investor earns by purchasing an investment security. The calculation of an investor's yield on debt considers the periodic interest paid on the debt, the frequency with which interest is paid, and the price actually paid by the investors to buy the debt. The yield to an investor on debt can and often does differ from the interest rate paid by an issuer because in buying the security the investor pays more (a premium price) or less (a discounted price) than the par value of the security. *See also* discount; interest rate; par value; premium

Yield curve   The pattern of interest rates or yields on debt or other securities over time. Normally, yields or interest rates rise as maturities extend farther into the future. This occurs because risk increases the more investments extend into the future. This pattern of ascending yields or rates over time is called the normal yield curve. The pattern does not hold all the time. Changing or unusual market conditions can create flat or inverted yield curves.

Yield to maturity   Yield or annual percentage rate that discounts all future cash flows resulting from an investment to the actual price paid by the investor to buy the investment. Yield to maturity assumes that interest earned or received by the investor over the term of the investment is reinvested at the current yield to maturity. *See also* yield

Selected bibliography

Publications that address capital budgeting and finance in local government flow from four major sources: the International City/County Management Association (ICMA); the Government Finance Officers Association of the U.S. and Canada (GFOA); the Association for Budgeting and Financial Management of the American Society for Public Administration; and participants in the municipal debt markets, most notably the three national bond rating agencies—Fitch Ratings, Moody's Investors Service, and Standard & Poor's Corporation. The Bond Market Association and individual bond underwriters have also made important contributions to the literature on local capital budgeting and finance. ICMA, GFOA, and the bond rating agencies have all published books, monographs, and research reports on the overall topics of capital budgeting and finance and also on many specific issues of capital budgeting and finance. The two journals that have contributed most to our knowledge about capital budgeting and finance are *Government Finance Review,* published by the GFOA, and *Public Budgeting & Finance,* published by Public Financial Publications, Inc., an affiliate of the Association for Budgeting and Financial Management. The former publishes short, pithy articles written mostly by public finance professionals, and the latter features the results of empirical and in-depth studies of public sector financial policies and practices. Each of these journals appears numerous times below.

The bibliography here is organized into three sections. The first is Capital budgeting, CIPs, and priority setting. Most of these items come from the ICMA, GFOA, and scholars or teachers of budgeting in university-based public administration programs. The second group in the bibliography addresses capital finance, debt, bond ratings, and planning and selling debt. This literature has been contributed by the bond rating agencies, other professionals and organizations involved in the state and local debt markets, the GFOA, and the journal, *Public Budgeting & Finance.* The third part of the bibliography lists publications that address the topic of financial forecasting. These are mostly articles from ICMA, GFOA, and *Public Budgeting & Finance.* These three sections of the bibliography correspond to the organization and sequence of presentation in the book.

Capital budgeting, CIPs, and priority setting

Ammons, David N. *Tools for Decision-Making: A Practical Guide for Local Government.* Washington, D.C.: CQ Press, 2002. See especially Chapter 13, "The Time Value of Money: Opportunity Costs, Discounting, Compounding, Future Value, and Present Value"; and Chapter 22, "Making Choices Systematically—From Audit Targets to Capital Projects."

Bailey, Stephen D. "Management of Facility Design and Construction." *MIS Report* (ICMA) 20, no. 6 (June 1988).

Bland, Robert L., and Irene S. Rubin. "Planning and Budgeting for Capital Improvements." In *Budgeting: A Guide for Local Government*, edited by Robert L. Bland and Irene S. Rubin, 167–196. Washington, D.C.: ICMA, 1997.

Calia, Roland. *Priority-Setting Models for Public Budgeting.* Chicago: GFOA, 2001.

Forrester, John P. "Municipal Capital Budgeting: An Examination." *Public Budgeting & Finance* 13, no. 2 (Summer 1993): 85–103.

Koven, Steven G., and Thomas S. Lyons. *Economic Development: Strategies for State and Local Practice.* Washington, D.C.: ICMA, 2003.

Matzer, John, Jr., ed. *Capital Projects: New Strategies for Planning, Management, and Finance.* Washington, D.C.: ICMA, 1989.

Michel, R. Gregory. *Decision Tools for Budgetary Analysis.* Chicago: GFOA, 2001.

National Advisory Council on State and Local Budgeting. *Recommended Budget Practices: A Framework for Improved State and Local Government Budgeting.* Chicago: GFOA, 1998. Presents principles and recommended practices on capital budgeting, debt planning, and management.

Rosenberg, Philip, and Sally Rood. "Planning for Capital Improvements." *MIS Report* (ICMA) 16, no. 8 (August 1984).

Tigue, Patricia. *Capital Improvement Programming: A Guide for Smaller Governments.* Chicago: GFOA, 1996.

Vogt, A. John. "Budgeting Capital Outlays and Expenditures." In *Budgeting: Formulation and Execution,* edited by Jack W. Rabin, W. Bartley Hildreth, and Gerald J. Miller, 276–291. Athens, Ga.: Carl Vinson Institute of Government, University of Georgia, 1996.

Vogt, A. John. *Capital Improvement Programming: A Handbook for Local Government Officials.* Chapel Hill, N.C.: Institute of Government, 1977.

Capital finance, debt, bond ratings, and planning and selling debt

"Accounting and Financial Reporting for Lease Agreements of State and Local Governments," Statement no. 5, National Council on Governmental Accounting, on pages 100–104 of *Governmental Accounting and Financial Reporting Standards—Statement 34 Edition.* Norwalk, Conn.: GASB, June 30, 2001.

"Basic Financial Statements—and Management's Discussion and Analysis—for State and Local Governments," Statement No. 34. Stamford, Conn.: GASB, 1999.

Bond Buyer. Published daily by Thomson Corporation, New York.

Burke, Terence P. *1994 Supplement to the Guide to Arbitrage Requirements for Governmental Bond Issues.* Chicago: GFOA, 1994.

Burke, Terence P. *Guide to Arbitrage Requirements for Governmental Bond Issues.* Chicago: GFOA, 1992.

Carter, Lee, and A. John Vogt. "Fund Balance in Local Government Budgeting and Finance." *Popular Government* 54, no. 3 (Winter 1989): 27–35.

Ehlers, Robert L. *Ehlers on Public Finance: Building Better Communities.* Rochester, Minn.: Lone Oak Press, 1998.

Fisher, Glen W. *Financing Local Improvements by Special Assessments.* Chicago: Municipal Finance Officers Association, 1974.

Gamkhar, Shama, and Mona Koerner. "Capital Financing of Schools: A Comparison of Lease Purchase Revenue Bonds and General Obligation Bonds." *Public Budgeting & Finance* 22, no. 2 (Summer 2002): 21–39.

Gauthier, Steven J. *Governmental Accounting, Auditing, and Financial Reporting.* Chicago: GFOA, 2001.

Gelfand, M. David, ed. *State & Local Government Debt Financing.* Eagan, Minn.: West Group, various years. This is a three-volume work; volumes 1 and 2 were published originally in 1986 and volume 3 in 1990 by Callaghan & Company. Annual cumulative supplements have been issued since then to update each chapter. Since 1997, the West Group has published both the book and the annual supplements; and the editor, the West Group, and the contributing authors have updated and reissued all but three of the book's 13 chapters.

Guide to Moody's Ratings, Rating Process, and Rating Practices. New York: Moody's Investors Service, 1997.

Heppenstall, J. C. Talbot, Jr., and Roger G. Hayes. "The Path to Bond Market Efficiency: How Increased Retail Distribution Can Lower Borrowing Costs." *Government Finance Review* 19, no. 3 (June 2003): 25–28.

Jacob, Karl, and Geoffrey Buswick. "Annual Review of 'AAA' Rated Municipalities." *Standard & Poor's Public Finance*, February 8, 2001.

Johnson, Craig. "Tax Increment Debt Finance: An Analysis of the Mainstreaming of a Fringe Sector." *Public Budgeting & Finance* 19, no. 1 (Spring 1999): 26–46.

Joseph, James C. *Debt Issuance and Management: A Guide for Smaller Governments.* Chicago: GFOA, 1994.

Justice, Jonathon B., and Stewart Simon. "Municipal Bond Insurance: Trends and Prospects." *Public Budgeting & Finance* 22, no. 4 (Winter 2002): 114–137.

Kelly, Margaret C., and Matthew Zioper. "Strategies for Passing a Bond Referendum." *Government Finance Review* 17, no. 3 (June 2001): 27–30.

Kleine, Robert, Philip Kloha, and Carol S. Weissert. "Monitoring Local Government Fiscal Health: Michigan's New 10-Point Scale of Fiscal Distress." *Government Finance Review* 19, no. 3 (June 2003): 18–23.

Lawhon, Larry L. "Development Impact Fee Use by Local Governments." Chapter A3 in *The Municipal Year Book 2003.* Washington, D.C.: ICMA, 2003.

Lawrence, David M. *Financing Capital Projects in North Carolina,* 2nd ed. Chapel Hill, N.C.: Institute of Government, University of North Carolina, 1994.

Leithe, Joni L., with Matthew Montavon. *Impact Fee Programs: A Survey of Design and Administrative Issues.* Washington, D.C.: Government Finance Research Center, GFOA; and David M. Griffith & Associates, 1990.

Litvack, David, and Frank Rizzo. "Municipal Default Risk." *Fitch IBCA Public Finance Special Report,* September 15, 1999.

McManus, Karl Pfeil. "Guidelines for Effective Uses of Swaps in Asset-Liability Management." *Government Finance Review* 19, no. 3 (June 2003): 34–39. Also published in *Fitch Ratings Public Finance,* February 6, 2003.

Miller, Gerald I., ed. *Handbook of Debt Management.* New York: Marcel Dekker, 1996.

Miranda, Rowan A., and Ronald D. Picur, *Benchmarking and Measuring Debt Capacity.* Chicago: GFOA, 2000.

Moody's on Leases. New York: Moody's Investors Service, 1995.

Moody's on Revenue Bonds. New York: Moody's Investors Service, 1994.

Pagano, Michael A. "Municipal Capital Spending during the 'Boom'." *Public Budgeting & Finance* 22, no. 2 (Summer 2002): 1–20.

Petersen, John E. *Creative Capital Financing for State and Local Governments.* Chicago: GFOA, 1983.

Pope, Robert Dean. *Making Good Disclosures: The Roles and Responsibilities of State and Local Officials under Federal Securities Laws.* Washington, D.C.: GFOA, 2001.

Prunty, Robin, and Karl Jacob. "Top 10 Ways to Improve or Maintain a Municipal Credit Rating." *Standard & Poor's Public Finance,* February 4, 2002.

Prunty, Robin, Richard J. Marino, and Steven J. Murphy. "Top 10 Ways to Improve a G.O. Rating: Best Management Practices Make a Difference." *Standard & Poor's Public Finance,* June 1, 2000.

Public Finance Criteria 2000. New York: Standard & Poor's Corporation, 2000.

Raftelis, George A. *Comprehensive Guide to Water and Wastewater Finance and Pricing,* 2nd ed. Boca Raton, Fla.: Lewis Publishers, 1993.

Rizzo, Frank, et al. "The 12 Habits of Highly Successful Finance Officers: Management's and Disclosure's Impact on Municipal Credit Ratings." *Fitch Ratings Public Finance,* November 21, 2002.

Robbins, Mark D. "Do State Bond Banks Have Cost Advantages for Municipal Bond Issuance?" *Public Budgeting & Finance* 23, no. 3 (Fall 2003): 92–108.

Snyder, Thomas P., and Michael A. Stegman. *Financing the Public Costs of Growth: Using Development Fees, Exactions, and Special Districts to Finance Infrastructure.* Chapel Hill, N.C.: Department of City and Regional Planning and the School of Business Administration, University of North Carolina, for the U.S. Department of Housing and Urban Development, 1985.

Snyder, Thomas. *Paying for Growth: Using Development Fees to Finance Infrastructure.* Washington, D.C.: Urban Land Institute, 1986.

Temel, Judy Wesalo. *The Fundamentals of Municipal Bonds*, 5th ed. New York: Wiley, 2001.

Tigue, Patricia. *A Guide for Selecting Financial Advisors and Underwriters: Writing RFPs and Evaluating Proposals.* Chicago: GFOA, 1997.

Tigue, Patricia. *A Guide to Preparing a Debt Policy.* Chicago: GFOA, 1996.

Vogt, A. John, and Lisa A. Cole, eds. *A Guide to Municipal Leasing.* Chicago: GFOA, 1983.

"Your General Fund Balance—One Size Does Not Fit All!" *Special Comment.* New York: Moody's Investors Service, February 2002.

Zino, Michael. "The Development of a Planned Debt Policy." In *Budgeting: Formulation and Execution,* edited by Rabin et al., 323–328.

Zobler, Neil, and Katy Hatcher. "Financing Energy Efficiency Projects." *Government Finance Review* 19, no. 1 (February 2003): 14–18.

Financial forecasting

Bahl, Roy, and Larry Schroeder. "The Role of Multiyear Forecasting in the Annual Budget Process for Local Governments." *Public Budgeting & Finance* (Spring 1984): 3–13. This article was later reprinted on pages 117–128 in Jeffrey I. Chapman, *Local Government Financial Planning.* Washington, D.C: ICMA, 1987.

Cavenaugh, James L., and Pamela S. Caskie. "Multiyear Budgeting." *IQ Service Report* (ICMA) 31, no. 6 (June 1999).

Chapman, Jeffrey I., ed. *Long-Term Financial Planning: Creative Strategies for Local Government.* Washington, D.C.: ICMA, 1987.

Cirincione, Carmen, Gustavo A. Gurrieri, and Bart Van De Sande. "Municipal Government Revenue Forecasting: Issues of Method and Data." *Public Budgeting & Finance* 19, no. 1 (Spring 1999): 26–46.

Forrester, John P. "Multi-Year Forecasting and Municipal Budgeting." *Public Budgeting & Finance* 11, no. 2 (June 1991): 47–61.

Frank, Howard A. *Budgetary Forecasting in Local Government.* Westport, Conn.: Quorum Books, 1993.

Liner, Charles D. "Projecting Local Government Revenues." In *Budgeting: Formulation and Execution,* edited by Rabin et al., 183–191.

McLoon, Eugene P., Gabriella C. Lupo, and Selma Mushkin. *Long-Range Revenue Estimation.* Washington, D.C.: State and Local Finances Project, George Washington University, 1967.

Morrison, Laura E. "Improving Revenue Projections: 10 Questions—And Answers." *Government Finance Review* 18, no. 3 (June 2002): 16–19.

Nollenberger, Karl F., ed. *Evaluating Financial Condition: A Handbook for Local Government,* 4th ed. Washington, D.C.: ICMA, 2003.

Rodgers, Robert, and Joyce Philip. "The Effect of Underforecasting on the Accuracy of Revenue Forecasting by State Governments." *Public Administration Review* 56, no. 1 (January-February 1996): 48–56.

Schroeder, Larry. "Forecasting Local Revenues and Expenditures." In *Management Policies in Local Government Finance*, 4th ed., edited by Richard Aronson and Eli Schwartz, 169–200. Washington, D.C.: ICMA, 1996.

Stegmaier, James J. L., and Martha J. Reiss. "The Revenue Forum: An Effective Low-cost, Low-tech Approach to Revenue Forecasting." *Government Finance Review* 10, no. 2 (Spring 1994): 13–16.

List of jurisdictions

Jurisdiction	Population (based on 2000 U.S. census, rounded to nearest 500)
Alamance County, North Carolina	131,000
Alexandria, Virginia	128,500
Asheville, North Carolina	69,000
Athens-Clarke County, Georgia	100,000
Avon, Connecticut	16,000
Birmingham, Michigan	19,500
Brunswick County, North Carolina	73,000
Buncombe County, North Carolina	206,500
Burke County, North Carolina	89,000
Burlington, North Carolina	45,000
Campbell, California	38,000
Cary, North Carolina	94,500
Caswell County, North Carolina	23,500
Catawba County, North Carolina	141,500
Cedar Falls, Iowa	36,000
Cedarburg, Wisconsin	11,000
Chandler, Arizona	176,500
Charles Sturt, South Australia	100,000
Charlotte, North Carolina	541,000
Chatham County, North Carolina	49,500
Conyers, Georgia	10,500
Coral Springs, Florida	118,000
Cumberland County, North Carolina	303,000
Currituck County, North Carolina	18,000
Dallas, Texas	1,188,500
Deerfield, Illinois	18,500
Denton, Texas	80,500
Durham, North Carolina	187,000
Elizabethtown, North Carolina	3,500
Evanston, Illinois	74,000
Fayetteville, Arkansas	58,000
Forsyth County, North Carolina	306,000
Gainesville, Georgia	25,500
Germantown, Tennessee	37,500

Glendale, Arizona	219,000
Grafton, Wisconsin	10,500
Grants Pass, Oregon	23,000
Greeley, Colorado	77,000
Greensboro, North Carolina	224,000
Guilford County, North Carolina	421,000
Henderson, North Carolina	16,000
Hickory, North Carolina	37,000
Hillsborough, North Carolina	5,500
Irvine, California	143,000
Johnston County, North Carolina	122,000
Junction City, Kansas	19,000
Kansas City, Missouri	441,500
Largo, Florida	69,500
Lenoir County, North Carolina	59,500
Loveland, Colorado	51,000
Madison Heights, Michigan	31,000
Maplewood, Minnesota	35,000
Mauldin, South Carolina	15,000
Mecklenburg County, North Carolina	695,500
Memphis, Tennessee	650,000
Norman, Oklahoma	95,500
Oak Park, Michigan	30,000
Oklahoma City, Oklahoma	506,000
Orange County, North Carolina	118,500
Prince William County, Virginia	281,000
Raleigh, North Carolina	276,000
Reno, Nevada	180,500
Richmond County, North Carolina	46,500
Rockville, Maryland	47,000
San Clemente, California	50,000
Sawmills, North Carolina	5,000
Scottsdale, Arizona	203,000
Sedgwick County, Kansas	453,000
Smyrna, Georgia	41,000
Stanley, North Carolina	3,000
Sunnyvale, California	132,000
Virginia Beach, Virginia	425,500
Wake County, North Carolina	628,000
Wilkes County, North Carolina	65,500
Wilmington, North Carolina	76,000
Winston-Salem, North Carolina	186,000
Yuma County, Arizona	160,000

About the author

A. John Vogt, Ph.D., is a professor of public finance and government at the University of North Carolina at Chapel Hill. Dr. Vogt directed the university's municipal and county administration courses (offered through the Institute of Government) from 1991 through 1995 and the North Carolina Local Government Performance Measurement Project from 1995 until 1999. He teaches budgeting and finance as part of the Institute of Government's course series for North Carolina local government officials and in a variety of national programs. Before his service at the university, Dr. Vogt was budget operations coordinator for the Wisconsin State Budget Office. He is also an adviser to the GFOA committee on economic development and capital planning. His publications include *Capital Improvement Programming: A Handbook for Local Government Officials* (published by the Institute of Government) and *A Guide to Municipal Leasing* (published by the Municipal Finance Officers Association), for which he received the Research and Publications Award from the GFOA. Dr. Vogt is the recipient of the 2003 S. Kenneth Howard Career Achievement Award, given by the Association for Budgeting and Financial Management of the American Society for Public Administration.